Confidentiality

Third Edition

R. G. Toulson M.A., LL.B.
A Lord Justice of Appeal and Master of the Bench of the Inner Temple

C. M. Phipps M.A.
A Barrister of the Middle Temple

SWEET & MAXWELL

THOMSON REUTERS

First Edition   1996
Second Edition   2006

Published in 2012 by Sweet & Maxwell, 100 Avenue Road, London NW3 3PF part of
Thomson Reuters (Professional) UK Limited (Registered in England & Wales, Company No
1679046.
Registered Office and address for service: Aldgate House, 33 Aldgate High Street, London
EC3N 1DL)

For further information on our products and services, visit *www.sweetandmaxwell.co.uk*

Typeset by Letterpart Ltd, Reigate, Surrey

Printed and bound in Great Britain by CPI Group (UK) Ltd, Croydon, CR0 4YY.

No natural forests were destroyed to make this product; only farmed timber was used and
re-planted.

A CIP catalogue record of this book is available for the British Library.

ISBN: 978-0-414-02834-0

Thomson Reuters and the Thomson Reuters logo are trademarks of Thomson Reuters.

Sweet & Maxwell ® is a registered trademark of Thomson Reuters (Professional) UK
Limited.

Crown copyright material is reproduced with the permission of the Controller of HMSO and
the Queen's Printer for Scotland.

Preface to the First Edition

Nearly 150 years ago, on October 20, 1848, the Prince Consort applied, *ex parte*, for an injunction against Mr William Strange, a printer and publisher carrying on business at 21 Paternoster Row, to restrain him from exhibiting or reproducing a collection of etchings made by Queen Victoria and the Prince for private use. The matter eventually came before the Lord Chancellor, Lord Cottenham, who began his judgment[1] with the statement that the importance which had been attached to the case arose entirely from the exalted station of the plaintiff and not from the facts, which fell so clearly within the established principles as to present no difficulty. He went on to declare that "a breach of trust, confidence or contract would of itself entitle the plaintiff to an injunction", and with those words he ushered in a jurisdiction broader than had ever previously been recognised.

Development of the jurisdiction was slow over the next hundred years. In 1948 *Saltman's* case[2] gave it a new injection of life. In the last half-century it has grown much faster. It is no accident that this period of growth has coincided with a time of unprecedented change in methods of information storage and copying, communication and surveillance, which have brought with them the computer hacker, the electronic eavesdropper and the peeping Tom with a telephoto lens.

Unlike patent and copyright law, which are governed by statute (and are outside the scope of this book), the law of confidentiality is almost entirely judge-made. In 1981, the Law Commission proposed the abolition of the action for breach of confidence and its replacement by a new statutory tort, but the proposal was not adopted.

Much water has flowed under the bridge since the Law Commission's recommendations. The absence of a statutory framework has allowed flexibility in the development of the law. But it has to be recognised that such development has not always been coherent or consistent, and that it has left fundamental issues unresolved. The jurisprudential foundation and essential ingredients of the law of confidentiality still involve matters of debate. On them depend questions who may sue whom and what remedies are available. There are also major uncertainties regarding defences, including bona fide purchase, change of position and "public interest".

Roscoe Pound,[3] writing more than half a century ago, distinguished between textbooks containing doctrinal writing and those which were a mere key to the cases, he observed that there was a great need for doctrinal writing in modern times as in the formative period of the law, because whereas in its formative

---

[1] (1849) 1 Mac. & G. 25 at 40.

[2] (1948) 65 R.P.C. 203.

[3] Dean of Harvard Law School, 1916 to 1936.

period the courts had little to go on and much to bring about, in modern times judges have too much to go on to permit working over the vast mass of available material:

> "The labours of counsel, with the aid of the modern apparatus of digests and cyclopaedias, put before them an enormous mass of authoritative matter in which they must find starting points for reasoning or analogies or rules."[4]

The law of confidentiality is in many ways still in its formative period, despite a large mass of material.

The objects of this book are to examine the historical origins of the action for breach of confidence and its development through the more important cases; to attempt an analysis of the present state of the law, its foundations and principles (although to try to rationalise all the authorities would be an impossible task); and to discuss particular areas of difficulty and possible answers. We also consider certain relationships involving duties of confidence and confidentiality in the legal process.

Confidentiality is a fascinating and absorbing, as well as an important, branch of the law. The cases are varied and full of interest, and it would be an ideal subject for law students. Unfortunately it is not widely taught at universities. Perhaps if it were taught more, some of the present doctrinal confusion would have been dispelled.

R.G.T.

C.M.P.
April 1, 1996

---

[4] Roscoe Pound, *The Formative Era of American Law* (1938, p.165).

Preface to the Third Edition

Popular journalism and the internet have led to many headline-catching cases in the six years since the second edition, mostly concerning the lives of celebrities. Some have involved relationships clearly importing an obligation of confidentiality; some have involved simple intrusions of privacy; and some have allegedly involved both. It is easy for the concepts to become tangled, although the distinction between contractual or equitable duties of confidentiality and rights of privacy protected by Art.8 of the European Convention, which fall more naturally within the law of tort, is now generally recognised. However, their scope particularly in relation to privacy is still at a developmental stage.

In this edition we have sought to clarify the contours of these two different forms of action for breach of confidentiality, the available remedies and defences.

In the preface to the first edition we commented on the need for doctrinal writing on this fascinating and important branch of the law and regretted that it was not widely taught at universities. It is an excellent thing that there is now more doctrinal writing on the subject, although we still wish that it were more widely taught.

The law is stated at October 1, 2012.

R.G.T.

C.M.P.

TABLE OF CONTENTS

PAGE

Preface to the First Edition..v
Preface to the Third Edition vii
Table of Cases xvii
Table of Statutes xxxvii
Table of Statutory Instruments..xli
Table of Civil Procedure Rules..xliii

PARA

1. Historical Introduction
Early Origins..1–001
  Prince Albert v Strange 1–019
  The century after *Prince Albert v Strange*...........................1–025
  Saltman 1–046
  Saltman to the Human Rights Act 1998 1–051
    Public sector confidentiality 1–052
    Covert and intrusive ways of obtaining information.......................1–053
    Human Rights Act and personal privacy.............................1–055

2. Foundations
Different species of action..2–001
  Relationships giving rise to a duty of confidentiality...........................2–018
  Information obtained by dishonest or discreditable means 2–019
  Information obtained by accident..2–020
  Article 8 cases 2–021
  Conflicting views on information as property 2–025
  Conflicting views on damages 2–062
  Equitable compensation...2–078
  New Zealand, Canada and Australia......................................2–085
  Conclusion 2–099

3. Essential Features of Confidentiality
General Principles..3–001
  Contract..3–002
  Circumstances Importing an Obligation of Confidentiality
    Information imparted in the course of a relationship or venture
      which a reasonable person would regard as involving a duty
      of confidentiality...3–008

CONTENTS

Information received for a limited purpose in the exercise of a
   legal power or furtherance of a legal duty 3–012
Information obtained by improper or surreptitious means 3–030
The principle in Ashburton v Pape 3–031
   Obtaining confidential information through trespass 3–035
Extension of *Ashburton v Pape* to mistake...3–045
Information received directly or indirectly from another person
   under a duty of confidentiality
   Information properly disclosed 3–052
   Information improperly disclosed..3–053
   Innocent recipient with subsequent knowledge of improper
      disclosure 3–054
   "Bona fide purchase" and change of position 3–056
Notice of confidentiality..3–065
   Direct relationship between confider and confidant.......................3–066
   Third party recipient 3–068
   Accidental recipient 3–076
   Improper or surreptitious receipt 3–077
Confidential nature of the information 3–078
   Confidentiality and reasonableness...3–082
   Necessity of identification of information claimed to be
      confidential 3–086
   Trivial or useless information...3–089
   Falsity of information 3–093
   Intention to publish 3–099
   Public domain..3–108
   Hilton v Barker Booth & Eastwood 3–134
   Public record 3–137
   Conclusion on public record...3–153
Misuse..3–154
   Misuse and negligence..3–158
   Misuse and detriment..3–162
Qualifications to a duty of confidentiality 3–168
   Express or implied consent..3–169
   Disclosure required by law 3–170
   Duty to the public 3–172
   Disclosure required in the interests of the confidant 3–173
   Who may sue?...3–182

4. Duration of Confidentiality
General principle..4–001
Loss of secrecy..4–002
Terrapin and the springboard theory 4–004
The *Mustad* and *Terrapin* debate..4–006
Spycatcher..4–012
Injunction to prevent profit from past misconduct?...............................4–020
Conclusions on springboard..4–024
Passage of time and change of circumstances 4–028

CONTENTS

Continuing contractual obligations..4–035
Effect of a repudiatory breach of contract 4–036

5. Public Sector Confidentiality 5–001

6. Public Interest..6–001
The defence of iniquity..6–003
The contractual analysis..6–010
Serious harm to the public..6–015
Spycatcher 6–020
Application of the limiting principle 6–024
Article 10 6–048
New Zealand 6–060
Australia 6–061
Conclusions on public interest...6–070
Clean hands...6–076

7. Confidentiality and Privacy 7–001
Historical background: case law...7–004
Historical background: proposals for reform 7–012
Human Rights Act 1998 7–017
The concept of private life in Article 8..................................7–029
Respect for private life and justifiability of interference........7–033
Serious interference and the ordinary incidents of social
    living...7–034
Justification for interference 7–045
    Disclosure by or to someone with a personal interest in the
        disclosure being made..7–047
    Public interest..7–049
    Public domain..7–057
    The ultimate balancing exercise 7–062
    Privacy and commercialism 7–065
    Privacy and companies..7–073

8. Data Protection and Freedom of Information
The DPA and the FOIA: Introduction
    Data Protection 8–001
        Freedom of information 8–004
    The Information Commissioner 8–007
    The DPA 8–010
        Processing..8–011
        Data 8–012
        Personal data 8–015
        Sensitive personal data...8–017
        The data protection principles.......................................8–018
        Data subject rights...8–020
        Exemptions 8–021
        Public interest...8–024

Offences..8–026
The FOIA...8–027
The DPA and the FOIA in confidentiality cases...................8–032

9. Remedies
Injunction 9–001
The problem of the unidentified defendant.........................9–007
Superinjunctions and anonymity...9–010
Destruction or delivery up...9–013
Account of profits..9–018
Constructive trust..9–022
Damages...9–037
Declaration...9–053
Search order...9–054
Action for discovery..9–058
Delay..9–060

10. Confidentiality and Foreign Law 10–001
Cases where English courts are asked to order production of
confidential documents outside the jurisdiction 10–004
Cases where foreign courts have ordered production of confidential
documents within the United Kingdom 10–011
Assistance by English courts or regulatory authorities to foreign
courts or regulatory authorities 10–018

11. Medical Advisers..11–001
Anonymisation 11–008
Diagnosis, advice and treatment 11–011
Clinical audit and regulation..11–018
Advancement of medicine 11–021
Protection of others..11–023
Self-protection..11–031
Management and record keeping..11–033
Disclosure required by law 11–037
Children...11–038
Persons lacking capacity to consent to disclosure.............11–046
Disclosure to a relative 11–048
The dead..11–051

12. Bankers
The general principle 12–001
Compulsion by law...12–013
Duty to the public 12–014
Interest of the bank 12–020
Consent...12–022

CONTENTS

13. Broadcasting and Journalism 13–001
    Freedom to publish 13–002
    Relationship between Article 10 and rights of confidentiality 13–004
    Article 10 and its application to different kinds of
        information 13–006
    Statutory restriction on grant of injunctions and relevance of privacy
        codes 13–010
        "Privacy"
        "Clandestine devices and subterfuge"
        "The public interest" 13–012
    Disclosure of sources..13–014
        "Disclosure"
        "Necessary" 13–021
        "The interests of justice"..13–023
    The nature of the source and the information revealed 13–027

14. Employees and Employers
    Contract..14–001
    Implied obligation during employment...14–005
    Implied obligation after termination...14–008
    Customer lists..14–018
    Use of confidential information after termination for purposes other
        than use of the ex-employee's skills 14–024
    Express terms 14–027
    Termination as a result of repudiatory breach.......................................14–031
    Employer's obligation..14–032

15. Teachers, Clergy, Counsellors and Mediators
    Teachers..15–001
    Clergy 15–007
    Counsellors...15–011
    Mediators..15–013

16. Lawyers 16–001
    Continuing duty after termination of retainer 16–005
        Limits of the principle in *Bolkiah v KPMG*.....................................16–011
    Legal professional privilege..16–012
    Crime or fraud...16–015
    Use of information in defence of the lawyer's own interests.................16–029
    Disclosure required by law 16–042
    Children..16–044

17. General Principle and Exceptions
    The general principle 17–001
    Exceptions..17–005
    Statutory and regulatory exceptions 17–006
    Common law exceptions..17–007

"Without Prejudice" Communications and Communications to
    Mediators and Conciliators
    "Without prejudice" communications 17–008
Statements to mediators and conciliators 17–016
Legal professional privilege and public interest immunity....................17–019

18. Legal Professional Privilege and Confidence
Origins and basis of legal professional confidence............................18–001
    The scope and depth of the protection afforded by
        privilege..18–004
    Loss of privilege..18–012
    Calcraft v Guest..18–015
    Is *Calcraft v Guest* right? 18–018
    Ashburton v Pape 18–027
    Comparison of *Calcraft* and *Ashburton*................................18–031
    Discretion..18–034
    Waiver of privilege...18–048
Conclusions 18–066

19. Public Interest Immunity
Origins and basis..19–001
Confidentiality and public interest immunity...19–004
Class and contents claims..19–007
Effect of the Human Rights Act 1998..19–012
Reasons for immunity...19–015
Documents whose disclosure would be prejudicial to national
    security or foreign relations 19–017
Documents whose disclosure would expose the inner workings of
    government to ill-informed and captious criticism and increase
    the difficulties of the decision-making process 19–024
Documents whose disclosure would discourage the free flow of
    information communicated for official purposes.............................19–033
    The armed forces...19–035
    Child care records..19–038
    Official medical records 19–040
    The police 19–043
    Financial regulator...19–050
Informants 19–052
Extension of the immunity of informants 19–057
Documents whose disclosure would be oppressive 19–060
The compulsion principle as a head of public interest
    immunity...19–062
Disclosure for an authorised purpose 19–070
The nature of the protection afforded by immunity...............................19–072
Raising the objection 19–082
Waiver 19–087

20. Methods of Partial Protection
Restrictions on the manner in which confidential information is
    disclosed or further disseminated...20–001
Controls on the form of disclosure...20–002
Restrictions operating during and after hearings 20–006
    The general rule...20–007
        An exception: the court's parental jurisdiction..............................20–008
        Hearings in private...20–010
        Anonymity orders and other restrictions on publication...............20–014
        Access to court records...20–018
        Exclusion of confidential material from judgments.......................20–019
Restrictions on the collateral use of information provided for the
    purposes of litigation 20–020
Third parties 20–039
The scope of CPR 31.22...20–049
CPR 31.22 and the effect of public hearings 20–054
Permission to use disclosed information for other purposes 20–056

21. Children
Children's rights of confidence...21–001
Waiver 21–002
The courts' jurisdiction 21–005
    The best interests of the child as "a primary
        consideration"...21–013
    The best interests of the child as "the paramount
        consideration"...21–016
Family Court Proceedings 21–017
    Exclusion of the public...21–018
Restrictions on the disclosure of information or documents relating
    to proceedings..21–021
    The Children and Young Persons Act 1933.......................................21–022
    The Children Act 1989 21–023
    The Administration of Justice Act 1960 21–024
The Family Procedure Rules 2010 21–026
Restricting disclosure to the parties themselves.....................................21–032

22. Arbitrations
The duty of confidence 22–001
    The interface between arbitration and litigation 22–016
Conclusions 22–021
Qualifications/exceptions...22–026
    Order/leave of the court 22–027
    Disclosure in a party's own interests 22–028
    Disclosure in the interests of justice/public interest..........................22–033
    Others involved in arbitrations...22–035

Index 447

TABLE OF CASES

A (A Child) v Cambridge University Hospital NHS Foundation Trust [2011] EWHC 454 (QB);
    [2011] EM.L.R. 18 20–017
A v B Bank (Bank of England Intervening) [1993] Q.B. 311; [1992] 3 W.L.R. 705 10–017,
    10–022, 10–023
A v B plc [2002] EWCA Civ 337; [2003] Q.B. 195 . . . . . . .1–059, 2–016, 7–021, 7–026, 13–013
A v C (Note) [1981] Q.B. 956 12–013
A v Hayden (No. 2) (1984) 156 C.L.R. 532 . . . . .6–032, 6–065, 19–092
A v Ward [2010] EWHC 16 (Fam); [2010] 1 F.L.R. 1497 20–016
A v XB [2004] EWHC 447 QB 17–002
Aas v Benham [1891] 2 Ch. 244 2–035
Abernethy v Hutchinson (1824) 3 L.J. Ch. 209 . . . . .1–016, 1–020, 1–022, 1–032, 3–001,
    3–053
Ackroyds (London) Ltd v Islington Plastics Ltd [1962] R.P.C. 97 . . . . .3–108, 3–138
Addis v Gramophone Co Ltd [1909] A.C. 488 9–044
ADT v United Kingdom [2000] E.C.H.R. 402; (2000) 31 E.H.R.R. 303 7–032
AF Noonan (Architectural Practice) Ltd v Bournemouth and Boscombe Athletic Community
    Football Club Ltd [2007] EWCA Civ 848; [2007] 1 W.L.R. 2614 20–013
AG Australia Holdings Ltd v Burton [2002] N.S.W.S.C. 170 . . . . .3–058, 6–069, 9–017
Air Canada v British Columbia 59 D.L.R. (4th) 161; B.C.L.R. (2d) 145; [1989] 4 W.W.R.
    97 9–026
Air Canada v Secretary of State for Trade [1983] 2 A.C. 394 . . . . .19–003, 19–024, 19–028
AJ Bekhor & Co Ltd v Bilton [1981] Q.B. 923 12–013
Alfred Crompton Amusement Machines Ltd v Customs & Excise Commissioners (No. 2) [1974]
    A.C. 405 . . . . .3–022, 6–074, 19–004, 19–076
Ali Shipping Corp v Shipyard Trogir [1999] 1 W.L.R. 314 . . . . .22–012, 22–031, 22–034
All Party Parliamentary Group on Extraordinary Rendition v Information Commissioner [2011]
    UKUT 153 8–016
Al-Rawi v Security Service [2011] UKSC 34; [2012] 1 A.C. 531 .19–082, 19–085, 19–090, 20–002
Amaryllis Ltd v HM Treasury [2009] EWHC 1666 (TCC) 19–008, 19–082
Ambrosiadou v Coward [2011] EWCA Civ 409; [2011] E.M.L.R. 21; [2011] 2 F.L.R. 617; [2011]
    Fam. Law 690 . . . . .7–038, 20–013
American Cyanamid v Ethicon [1975] A.C. 396 . . . . .9–003, 10–012
AMM v HXW [2010] EWHC 2457 (QB) 7–048
Amway Corp v Eurway International Ltd [1974] R.P.C. 82 3–086
Amwell View School Governor v Dogherty, Employment Appeal Tribunal September 15,
    2006 . . . . .18–065, 19–033
An Informer v A Chief Constable [2012] EWCA Civ 197 3–161
Anderson v Bank of British Columbia (1876) 2 Ch. D 644 18–003
Anderson v Hamilton (1816) 19–072
Andrew v Raeburn (1874) 9 Ch.App.522 20–013
Ankin v London and North Eastern Railway Co [1930] 1 K.B. 527 19–034
Ansell Rubber Co Pty Ltd v Allied Rubber Industries Pty Ltd [1972] R.P.C. 811 3–072
Anthony v Anthony (1919) 35 T.L.R. 559 19–035
Anton Piller KG v Manufacturing Processes Ltd [1976] Ch. 55 9–054
Anufrijera v Southwark LBC [2003] EWCA Civ 1406; [2004] Q.B. 1124 9–049
APIS v Slovakia (2000) 29 E.H.R.R. CD 105 20–007
Aquaculture Corp v New Zealand Green Mussel Co Ltd [1990] 3 N.Z.L.R. 299 . . . .2–085, 9–050,
    9–052
Argyll v Argyll [1967] Ch.302 .1–049, 3–038, 3–089, 4–036, 5–003,
    5–004, 7–008
Armonas v Lithuania [2008] E.C.H.R. 1526; [2009] E.M.L.R. 7 9–048
Arrows Ltd (No. 4) [1995] 2 A.C. 75 . . . . .3–019, 3–021, 19–071
Artedomous v Del Casale [2006] N.S.W.S.C. 146 . . . . . . .3–115, 14–008, 14–015, 14–024, 14–029
ASG v GSA [2009] EWCA Civ 1574 . . . . .7–048, 9–003

TABLE OF CASES

Ashburton v Pape [1913] 2 Ch. 469 . . . . 1–040, 3–001, 3–031, 3–045, 18–026,
18–027, 18–031, 18–032, 18–033,
18–034, 18–036, 18–040, 18–043,
18–044, 18–047, 18–048, 18–050,
18–054, 18–059, 18–063, 18–065
Ashley v Chief Constable of Sussex Police [2007] 1 W.L.R. 398 19–048
Ashworth Hospital Authority v MGN Ltd [2002] UKHL 29; [2002] 1 W.L.R. 2033 HL; [2001] 1
W.L.R. 515 CA 11–003, 11–033, 13–017, 13–027, 13–029
Assistant Deputy Coroner for Inner West London v Channel 4 Television Corp [2007] EWHC 2513
(QB); [2008] 1 W.L.R. 945 13–020
Associated Electric and Gas Insurance Services Ltd v European Reinsurance Co of Zurich [2003]
UKPC 11; [2003] 1 W.L.R. 1041 . . . . .22–013, 22–015, 22–021, 22–025
Associated Newspapers Ltd v Prince of Wales. *See* Prince of Wales v Associated
Newspapers 22–013, 22–015, 22–021, 22–025
AT Poeton (Gloucester Plating) Ltd v Horton [2001] F.S.R. 169 . . . . .14–015, 14–028
Atari Incorporated v Philips Electronics and Associated Industries Ltd [1988] F.S.R.
416 20–002
Atlantic Computers plc, Re [1998] B.C.C. 200 . . . . .19–061, 19–066, 19–067, 19–068
Atos Consulting Ltd v Avis Plc [2007] EWHC 323 (TCC); [2008] Bus. L.R. D20 17–003
Attorney General for the United Kingdom v Heinemann Publishers Australia Pty Ltd (1987) 147
C.L.R. 39 6–065
Attorney General for the United Kingdom v Wellington Newspapers Ltd [1988] 1 N.Z.L.R.
129 6–060
Attorney General v Barker [1990] 3 All E.R. 257 . . . . .3–003, 4–035, 6–046
Attorney General v Blake [1998] Ch. 439; affirmed [2001] 1 A.C. 268 . . . . .1–052, 3–004, 3–151,
4–019, 4–035,
5–012, 6–055, 9–019, 9–021, 9–036,
14–003, 14–004, 14–028
Attorney General v Clough [1963] 1 Q.B. 773 . . . . .3–171, 13–016
Attorney General v Guardian Newspapers Ltd (No. 2); Attorney General v Observer Ltd; Attorney
General v Times Newspapers Ltd ("Spycatcher") [1988] 3 All E.R. 545; [1990] 1 A.C.
109 . . . . .1–052, 2–004, 2–006, 2–007, 2–026,
2–046, 2–069, 2–074, 2–076, 2–083,
3–001, 3–044, 3–048, 3–053, 3–059,
3–065, 3–090, 3–102, 3–109, 3–113,
3–114, 3–115, 3–127, 3–128, 3–146,
3–163, 3–166, 3–167, 4–012, 4–015,
4–016, 4–022, 5–006, 5–007, 5–008,
5–011, 6–001, 6–020, 6–040, 6–042,
6–049, 6–052, 6–056, 6–057, 6–060,
6–063, 6–065, 6–066, 6–077, 7–008,
7–022, 9–009, 9–018, 9–030, 9–035,
9–038, 14–003, 18–060, 19–025
Attorney General v Jonathan Cape Ltd [1976] 1 Q.B. 752 . . . 1–049, 1–052, 4–016, 4–028, 5–003,
5–004, 6–001, 6–057, 19–018
Attorney General v Lundin (1982) 75 Cr.App.R. 90 13–016
Attorney General v Maurice (1986) 161 C.L.R. 475 . . . . .18–069, 18–070
Attorney General v MGN Ltd [2002] EWHC 3201 3–007
Attorney General v Mulholland and Foster [1963] 2 Q.B. 477 . . . . .3–171, 13–016, 15–008
Attorney General v Newspaper Publishing plc [1988] Ch. 333; [1987] 3 W.L.R. 942 9–009
Attorney General v Observer Ltd, Transcript No. 696 of 1986 CA (Civil Division) 3–059
Attorney General v Observer Ltd. *See* Attorney General v Guardian Newspapers Ltd (No.
2) 3–059
Attorney General v Punch Ltd [2002] UKHL 50; [2003] 1 A.C. 1046 . . . . .3–087, 9–005
Attorney General v Times Newspapers Ltd. *See* Attorney General v Guardian Newspapers Ltd (No.
2) 3–087, 9–005
Australian Broadcasting Corp v Lenah Game Meats Pty Ltd [2001] HCA 63; (2001) 208 C.L.R.
199 . . . . .1–053, 2–094, 3–077, 7–023, 7–026,
7–074, 7–075
Australian Football League v The Age Company Ltd [2006] VSC 308 . . . . .3–124, 6–069
Axel Springer AG v Germany [2012] E.M.L.R. 15; (2012) 55 E.H.R.R. 6; 32 B.H.R.C.
493 . . . . .7–052, 13–006, 13–009, 20–014

TABLE OF CASES

Aziz v Aziz [2007] EWCA Civ 712; [2008] 2 All E.R. 501 . . . . 20–014, 20–016
B v A County Council [2006] EWCA Civ 1388 3–160
B v Auckland District Law Society [2003] UKPC 736; [2003] 2 A.C. 736 . . . . . . 18–005, 18–008,
                     18–012, 18–024, 18–046,
                           18–069
B v H Bauer Publishing Ltd, June 14, 2001 QBD 3–074
Badische Anilin und Soda Fabrik v Levinstein [1883] 24 Ch.D. 156 20–013
Balabel v Air India [1988] Ch. 317 18–004
Balfour v Foreign and Commonwealth Office [1994] 1 W.L.R. 681 . . . . 19–015, 19–017
Ball v Druces & Atlee [202] P.N.L.R. 23 16–010
Balston Ltd v Headline Filters Ltd [1987] F.S.R. 330 . . . . 14–017, 14–027
Balu v Dudley Primary Care Trust [2010] EWHC 1208 (Admin) 18–062
Bank of Tokyo Ltd v Karoon [1987] A.C. 45 . . . . 3–179, 12–001
Bankers Trust Co v Shapira [1980] 1 W.L.R. 1274 . . . . 10–008, 12–013
Barclays Bank plc v Taylor [1989] 1 W.L.R. 1066 . . . . 12–001, 12–002, 12–003, 12–005, 12–010,
                           12–012, 12–013
Barings Plc (In Liquidation) v Coopers & Lybrand (No.1) [2000] 1 W.L.R. 2353; [2000] 3 All E.R.
 910 CA 19–059
Barlow Clowes Gilt Managers Ltd, Re [1992] Ch.208 19–083
Barnes v Addy (1874) 9 Ch.App. 244 . . . . 2–091, 3–069, 3–073
Barrett v Ministry of Defence, Times, January 24, 1990 . . . . 19–035, 19–037
Barrymore v News Group Newspapers Ltd [1997] F.S.R. 600 3–091
BBC v HarperCollins Publishers Ltd [2010] EWHC 2424 (Ch); [2011] E.M.L.R. 6 . . 4–023, 4–025
BBC v Sugar (No.2) [2009] UKHL 9; [2009] 1 W.L.R. 430; [2009] 4 All E.R. 111 . 8–027, 13–009
BBC v Sugar [2009] EWHC 2349 (Admin); [2010] 1 All E.R. 782; affirmed [2010] EWCA Civ
 715; [2010] 1 W.L.R. 2278; [2011] 1 All E.R. 101; [2010] E.M.L.R. 24; affirmed [2012] UKSC
 4; [2012] 1 W.L.R. 439 . . . . 8–027, 13–009
Beatson v Skene (1860) 5 H. & N. 838 19–035
Beatty v Guggenheim Exploration Co. (1919) 225 N.Y. 380 . . . . 9–023, 9–024
Beckham v Gibson Unreported April 29, 2005 3–096
Bell v Lever Bros [1932] A.C. 161 19–035
Bellerophon, The (1875) 44 L.J.Adm (N.S.) 5 19–035
Beloff v Pressdram Ltd [1973] 1 All E.R. 241 . . . . 6–016, 6–020, 6–061, 6–063
Bennett v Commissioner of Police of Metropolis [1995] 1 W.L.R. 488 19–095
Bensaid v United Kingdom (2001) 33 E.H.R.R. 208 7–031
Berezovksy v Hine [2011] EWHC 1904 (Ch) 18–004, 18–062
Bishopsgate Investment Management Ltd v Maxwell [1993] Ch. 1 3–019
Black v Taylor [1993] 3 N.Z.L.R. 403 16–008
Bliss v South East Thames Regional Health Authority [1987] I.C.R. 700 9–044
Bluck v Information Commissioner (Information Tribunal, September 17, 2007, Appeal No.
 EA/2006/0090) 11–051
Boat Harbour Holdings Ltd v Steve Mowat Building & Construction Ltd [2012] N.Z.C.A.
 305 9–028
Bodle v Coutts & Co [2003] EWHC 1865 16–010
Bodnar v Townsend [2003] TASSC 148 12–018
Bolam v Friern Barnet Management Committee [1957] 1 W.L.R. 582 11–011
Bonnard v Perryman [1891] 2 Ch. 269; [1891–94] All E.R. Rep. 965 CA 9–006
Bookbinder v Tebbit (No. 2) [1992] 1 W.L.R. 217 19–059
Booth v Eastwood [2005] 1 W.L.R. 567 3–006
Botta v Italy (1998) 26 E.H.R.R. 241 2–009
Bowman v Fels [2005] EWCA Civ 226; [2005] 1 W.L.R. 3083 . . 16–019, 16–020, 16–023, 16–043
Brake Bros Ltd v Ungless [2004] EWHC 2799 (QB) 14–030
Breen v Williams (1996) 186 C.L.R. 71 3–063
Breeze v John Stacey & Sons Ltd, Times, July 8 1999 CA 18–057
Brighton v Australia and New Zealand Banking Group Ltd [2011] NSWCA 152 12–001
British American Tobacco Australia Ltd v Gordon (No.3) [2009] V.S.C. 619 6–069
British and Commonwealth Holdings plc v Barclays de Zoete Wedd Ltd [1999] 1 B.C.L.C.
 86 . . . . 19–067, 19–068
British Coal Corp v Dennis Rye (No. 2) Ltd [1988] 1 W.L.R. 1113 18–069
British Industrial Plastics Ltd v Ferguson [1940] 12 All E.R. 479 HL 3–072
British Sky Broadcasting Plc v Virgin Media Communications Ltd (formerly NTL Communications
 Ltd) [2008] EWCA Civ 612; [2008] 1 W.L.R. 2854 16–011

TABLE OF CASES

British Steel Corporation v Granada Television Ltd [1981] A.C. 1096 . . . . . . 3–171, 5–016, 9–058,
13–002, 13–016,
15–008, 17–001
Broadmoor Special Hospital Authority v Robinson [2000] Q.B. 775 . . . . 3–001, 3–183, 5–016
Brookville Carriers Flatbed GP Inc v Blackjack Transport Ltd (2008) N.S.C.A. 22; 263 N.S.R. (2d)
272 16–005
Broome v Cassell & Co Ltd (No.1) [1972] A.C. 1027; [1972] 2 W.L.R. 645; [1972] 1 All E.R. 801
HL 9–052
Brown v Matthew [1990] 1 Ch.662 19–038
Brown v Rice [2007] EWHC 625 (Ch); [2008] F.S.R. 3 15–018
Brown v Stott [2003] 1 A.C. 681 19–012
Browne v Associated Newspapers Ltd [2007] EWCA Civ 295; [2008] Q.B. 103 . . . . 3–087, 6–076,
9–004
Bullivant v Attorney General for Victoria [1901] A.C. 196 . . . . 3–191, 16–015, 16–016
Bunn v British Broadcasting Corp [1998] 3 All E.R. 552 3–126
Burmah Oil Co. Ltd v Governor and Company of the Bank of England [1098] 1 A.C.
1090 . . . . 19–003, 19–007, 19–015, 19–021, 19–024,
19–032, 19–072
Butler v Board of Trade [1971] 1 Ch. 680 . . . . 18–035, 18–040
C (A Minor) (Wardship: Medical Treatment) (No. 2) [1990] Fam. 39 11–041
C v Holland [2012] NZHC 2155 2–098
Cadbury Schweppes Inc v FBI Foods Ltd (1999) 167 DLR (4th) 577 . . . . 2–090, 9–039
Calcraft v Guest [1898] 1 Q.B. 759 CA 18–014, 18–015, 18–017, 18–018, 18–019,
18–021, 18–022, 18–023, 18–025,
18–026, 18–027, 18–029, 18–030,
18–031, 18–043, 18–063, 18–065,
18–067
Camelot Group plc v Centaur Ltd [1999] Q.B. 124 13–027
Campaign Against Arms Trade v BAE Systems Plc [2007] EWHC 330 (QB) 9–058
Campbell v Frisbee [2002] EWCA Civ 1374; [2003] E.M.L.R. 76 . . . 3–007, 3–124, 4–036, 6–046,
6–047,
14–031
Campbell v MGN Ltd [2002] EWHC 499 (QB); reversed [2002] EWCA Civ 1373; [2003] Q.B.
633; [2003] 2 W.L.R. 80; [2003] 1 All E.R. 224; [2003] E.M.L.R. 2; reversed [2004] UKHL 22;
[2004] 2 A.C. 457 . . . . 1–059, 2–002, 2–011, 2–16, 2–017,
2–021, 2–084, 3–044, 3–075, 3–093,
6–036, 7–019, 7–024, 7–041, 7–053,
7–067, 8–010, 8–011, 8–032, 9–047,
13–007, 13–009
Campbell v Tameside MBC [1982] 1 Q.B. 1065 . . . . 19–038, 19–041, 19–088
Canadian Imperial Bank of Commerce v Sayani (1993) 83 B.C.L.R. (2d) 167 CA (British
Columbia) 12–018
Canham v Jones (1813) 2 V. & B. 218 3–187
Carnduff v Rock [2001] 1 W.L.R. 1786; [2001] EWCA Civ 680 19–090
Carter v Managing Partner, Northmore, Hale, Davy & Leake (1995) 183 C.L.R. 121 18–006
Carter v Northmore Davy Hale and Leaken (1995) 183 C.L.R. 121 . . . . 18–010, 18–011
Castrol Australia Pty Ltd v Emtech Associates Pty Ltd (1980) 33 A.L.R. 31 . . . . 6–062, 6–066
Caterpillar Logistics Services (UK) Ltd v Huesca de Crean [2012] EWCA Civ 156; [2012] I.C.R.
981 14–017
Catt v Marac Australia Ltd (1986) 9 N.S.W.L.R. 639 . . . . 2–085, 2–093
CDE v MGN Ltd [2010] EWHC 3308 (QB); [2011] 1 F.L.R. 1524 . . . . 9–012, 20–017
Centri-Spray Corp v Cera International Ltd [1979] F.S.R. 175 . . . . 20–002, 20–004
Chalmers v Pardoe [1963] 1 W.L.R. 677 9–024
Chase Manhattan Bank NA v Israel-British Bank (London) Ltd [1981] Ch. 105 2–082
Chief Constable of Humberside Police v Information Commissioner [2009] EWCA Civ 1079;
[2010] 1 W.L.R. 1136 8–019
Chief Constable of the Greater Manchester Police v McNally [2002] EWCA Civ 14 19–014,
19–056
Chief Constable, A v County Council, A [2002] EWHC 2198; [2003] 1 F.L.R. 579 16–052
Christofi v Barclays Bank Plc [2000] 1 W.L.R. 937 12–021
Church of Scientology v Kaufman [1973] R.P.C. 627 . . . . 3–001, 6–079
Cleveland Investments Global Ltd v Evans [2010] N.S.W.S.C. 567 16–008

CMI-Centres for Medical Innovation GmbH v Phytopharm plc [1999] F.S.R. 235 . . . 3–087, 9–005
CoCo v AN Clarke Engineers Ltd [1969] R.P.C. 41 . . . . 1–001, 3–001, 3–011, 3–032, 3–067,
3–079, 3–084, 3–091, 3–108, 3–157,
3–163, 5–005, 6–035
Colbeam Palmer Ltd v Stock Affiliates Pty Ltd (1968) 122 C.L.R.25 2–053
Columbia Picture Industries Inc v Robinson [1987] Ch. 38 9–055
Commissioner of Police of the Metropolis v Times Newspapers Ltd [2011] EWHC 2705
(QB) 3–178, 3–186, 6–035, 6–058, 13–003,
13–029, 18–044
Commissioner of Police v Bermuda Broadcasting Co Ltd [2008] UKPC 5 6–057
Common Services Agency v Scottish Information Commissioner [2008] UKHL 47; [2008] 1 W.L.R.
1550 . . . . 8–016, 8–019, 11–010
Commonwealth of Australia v John Fairfax & Sons Ltd [1969] R.P.C. 41 . . . 1–052, 2–048, 3–001,
3–031, 3–115,
3–165, 4–029, 5–005, 5–011, 5–015,
6–001, 6–057, 6–069, 19–025, 19–032
Commonwealth v Northern Land Council (1993) 176 C.L.R. 604 . . . . . . 19–007, 19–027, 19–028
Company's Application, Re [1989] Ch. 477; [1989] 2 All E.R. 248 . . . . 6–024, 6–052, 6–066
Concept Television Productions Pty Ltd v Australian Broadcasting Corp (1988) 12 I.P.R.
129 2–093
Concrete Industries (Monier) Ltd v Gardner Bros & Perrott (WA) Pty Ltd Unreported Vic S.C.,
August 18, 1977 3–034
Conmar Products Corporation v Universal Slide Fastener Co Inc (1949) 172 F.2d 150 4–010
Consul Corfitzon, The [1917] A.C. 550 10–004
Conway v Rimmer [1968] A.C. 910 . . . . 3–022, 5–002, 19–003, 19–007, 19–008,
19–015, 19–017, 19–018, 19–021,
19–024, 19–029, 19–030, 19–032,
19–034, 19–035, 19–041, 19–043,
19–044, 19–045, 19–061
Coogan v News Group Newspapers Ltd [2012] EWCA Civ 48; [2012] 2 W.L.R. 848; [2012] 2 All
E.R. 74; [2012] E.M.L.R. 14 2–029
Co-ordinated Industries Pty Ltd v Elliott (1998) 43 N.S.W.L.R. 282 14–012
Copland v United Kingdom [2007] E.C.H.R. 253 14–035
Cornelius v de Tarranto [2001] E.M.L.R. 12; on appeal [2001] EWCA Civ 1511; [2002] E.M.L.R.
6 . . . . 3–095, 9–046, 11–016
Corrs Pavey Whiting & Byrne v Collector of Customs (1987) 74 A.L.R. 428 . 2–091, 6–013, 6–022,
6–064, 6–066,
6–068
Council of Civil Services Unions v Minister for the Civil Service [1985] A.C. 374 19–017
Cowell v British American Tobacco Australia Services Ltd [2007] V.S.C.A. 301 18–047
Cranleigh Precision Engineering Ltd v Bryant [1966] R.P.C. 81 . . . . . 4–007, 4–011, 4–014, 4–015,
4–024,
4–027
Cream Holdings Ltd v Bannerjee [2005] 1 A.C. 253 . . . . 6–048, 7–050, 9–003
Creation Records Ltd v News Group Newspapers Ltd [1997] E.M.L.R. 444 . . 1–054, 3–001, 3–043,
3–044, 3–106,
3–126, 3–128, 7–084
Crowson Fabrics Ltd v Rider [2007] EWHC 2942 (Ch); [2008] F.S.R. 17 . . . . . . 14–018, 14–019
Cumbria Waste Management v Baines Wilson [2008] EWHC 786 (TCC) 15–018
Cumpana v Romania [2004] E.C.H.R. 692 3–097
Cutts v Head [1984] Ch. 290 . . . . 17–009, 17–010
CVB v MGN Ltd [2012] EWHC 1148 (QB) 20–015
D (Infants), Re [1970] 1 W.L.R. 599 . . . . 19–038, 19–039
D (Minors) (Conciliation: Disclosure of Information), Re [1993] Fam. 231 . . . . . . 15–018, 17–018
D v L [2003] EWCA Civ 1169; [2004] E.M.L.R. 1 7–041
D v NSPCC [1978] A.C. 171 . . . . 3–171, 5–001, 17–001, 17–018, 18–002,
18–065, 19–002, 19–009, 19–015,
19–029, 19–038, 19–039, 19–058,
19–087
Dadourian Group International Inc v Simms [2008] EWHC 1784 (Ch) 16–017
Darlington Building Society v O'Rourke James Scourfield & McCarthy [1999] 1 Lloyd's Rep. (PN)
33 16–028

TABLE OF CASES

David Syme & Co Ltd v General Motors-Holden's Ltd [1984] 2 N.S.W.L.R. 294 6–066
Dawkins v Lord Rokeby (1873) L.R. 8 Q.B. 255 19–035
Dawson, dec'd, Re [1966] 2 N.S.W.R. 211 2–093
De Maudsley v Palumbo [1996] F.S.R. 447 3–086
Dean v MacDowell (1878) 8 Ch.D. 345 . . . . 2–035, 2–036
Department of Economics, Policy and Development of then City of Moscow v Bankers Trust Co
    [2004] EWCA Civ 314; [2005] Q.B. 207 . . . . 20–007, 22–014, 22–018, 22–023
Department of Health v Information Commissioner [2011] EWHC 1430 (Admin); [2011] Med. L.R.
    363 8–016
Derby & Co Ltd v Weldon (No. 8) [1991] 1 W.L.R. 73 . . .3–045, 18–039, 18–043, 18–051, 18–054
Derby & Co Ltd v Weldon (Nos 3 & 4) [1990] Ch. 65 10–002
Dickens, Re [1935] 1 Ch. 267 2–031
Dickson v Earl of Wilton (1859) 1 F. & F. 419 19–035
Dolling-Baker v Merrett [1990] 1 W.L.R. 1205 . . . . 15–015, 20–038, 22–002, 22–007
Donald v Ntuli [2010] EWCA 1276; [2011] 1 W.L.R. 294 . . . . 9–008, 9–011, 20–017
Donaldson v Beckett (1774) 4 Bur. 2408 . . . . 1–007, 1–008
Douglas v Hello! Ltd (No. 3) [2005] EWCA Civ 595; [2006] Q.B. 125; reversed [2007] UKHL 21;
    [2008] 1 A.C. 1 . . . . 1–059, 2–001, 2–016, 2–022, 2–029,
                                                                  2–036, 2–050, 2–060, 2–083, 2–084,
                                                                  3–044, 3–063, 3–106, 3–110, 3–126,
                                                                  3–188, 3–189, 7–001, 7–059, 7–065,
                                                                  7–071, 7–072, 9–043, 9–048
Douglas v Hello! Ltd (No. 1) [2001] Q.B. 967; [2001] 2 W.L.R. 992 CA 13–013
Douglas v Hello! Ltd (No. 6) [2003] EWHC 786 (Ch); [2003] 3 All E.R. 996; [2003] E.M.L.R.
    31 8–032
Dowson & Mason Ltd v Potter [1986] 1 W.L.R. 1419 . . . . 2–068, 2–077, 2–088
Duchess of Kingston's Case (1776) State Trials 355 . . . . 3–171, 11–037, 18–002
Dudgeon v United Kingdom (1981) 4 E.H.R.R. 149 7–032
Duke of Queensbury v Shebbeare (1758) 2 Eden 329 . . . . 1–003, 1–006, 1–008, 1–022
Duncan v Cammell Laird & Co [1942] A.C. 624 . . . . 19–003, 19–018
Duncan v Medical Practitioners Disciplinary Committee [1986] 1 N.Z.L.R. 513 . . . 3–178, 11–007,
                                                                                   11–032, 16–029
Dunford & Elliott v Johnson & Firth Brown [1978] F.S.R. 143 3–082
Durant v Financial Services Authority [2003] EWCA Civ 1746; [2004] F.S.R. 28 . . . 8–013, 8–015,
                                                                                   8–016
E v Channel Four Television Corp [2005] EWHC 1144, Fam; [2005] E.M.L.R. 30 11–046
Edwards and Lewis v United Kingdom [2004] E.H.R.R. 593 19–012
Edwards v United Kingdom; Lewis v United Kingdom [2003] E.C.H.R. 381; [2004] E.C.H.R. 560;
    [2005] 40 E.H.R.R. 593 19–084
EI Du Pont de Nemours Company v Masland (1917) 244 U.S. 100 2–053
El Jawhary v BCCI [1993] B.C.L.C. 396 . . . . 6–041, 12–004, 12–006
Elliott v Chief Constable of Wiltshire, Times, December 5, 196 3–135
Ellis v Home Office [1953] 2 Q.B. 135 19–041
Emerald Construction Co Ltd v Lowthian [1966] 1 W.L.R. 691 3–072
Emmott v Michael Wilson & Partners Ltd [2008] EWCA Civ 184; [2008] C.P. Rep.
    26 . . . . 22–001, 22–014, 22–015, 22–026, 22–027,
                                                                                   22–032, 22–034
English & American Insurance Ltd v Herbert Smith [1988] F.S.R. 232 . . . . . 3–001, 3–045, 3–046,
                                                                                   3–048, 7–008,
                                                                  16–011, 18–023, 18–048, 18–049,
                                                                  18–050, 18–053, 18–066
English v Dedham Vale Properties [1978] 1 W.L.R. 93 2–067
Environmental Defence Society Inc v South Pacific Aluminium Ltd (No. 2) [1981] 1 N.Z.L.R.
    153 19–028
EPI Environmental Technologies Inc v Symphony Plastic Technologies Plc [2004] EWHC 2945;
    upheld on appeal [2006] EWCA Civ 3; [2006] 1 W.L.R. 495 (Note) 3–011
Esal (Commodities) Ltd (No. 2), Re [1990] B.C.C. 708 3–018
Esal (Commodities) Ltd, Re [1989] B.C.L.C. 59 3–018
Essex CC v R. [1994] Fam. 167 . . . . 16–050, 16–052
Esso Australia Resources Ltd v Plowman [1994–1995] 183 C.L.R. 10 . . . . . 3–173, 5–015, 6–067,
                                                                                   22–003, 22–008,
                                                                  22–008, 22–012, 22–024, 22–034

TABLE OF CASES

European Pacific Banking Corp v Television New Zealand Ltd [1994] 3 N.Z.L.R. 43 6–060
Evans v Chief Constable of Surrey [1988] 1 Q.B. 588 . . . . 19–047, 19–094
Evans v Information Commissioner [2012] UKUT 313 (AAC) 8–029
EWQ v GFD [2012] EWHC 2182 (QB) 7–048, 20–017
F v G [2012] I.C.R. 246 20–014
Faccenda Chicken Ltd v Fowler [1987] 1 Ch. 117 . . . . . . 1–036, 3–006, 14–001, 14–008, 14–013,
    14–015, 14–029, 16–011
Farah Constructions Pty Ltd v Say-Dee Pty Ltd [2007] HCA 22; (2007) 81 A.J.L.R.
    1107 2–093
Farm Assist Ltd v Secretary of State for the Environment, Food and Rural Affairs (No.2) [2009]
    EWHC 1102 (TCC); [2009] B.L.R. 399 . . . . 15–018, 17–016
Fayed v Commissioner of Police [2002] EWCA Civ 780; Times, June 17, 2002 . . . 3–045, 18–057,
    18–062, 19–096
Federal Commissioner of Taxation v United Aircraft Corp (1943–44) 68 C.L.R. 525 . 2–032, 2–051
Ferdinand (Rio) v MGN Ltd [2011] EWHC 2454 (QB) 7–053, 13–006
Financial Times Ltd v United Kingdom [2009] E.C.H.R. 2065; (2010) 50 E.H.R.R. 46 9–058,
    13–018, 13–020, 13–026, 13–029
Finers v Miro [1991] 1 W.L.R. 35. . . . . 16–016, 16–017, 16–023
Fitt v United Kingdom [2000] 30 E.H.R.R. 400 . . . . 19–012, 19–084
Flood v Times Newspapers Ltd [2012] UKSC 11; [2012] 2 W.L.R. 760 3–097
Force India Formula One Team Ltd v 1 Malaysia Racing Team Sdn Bhd [2012] EWHC 616
    (Ch) 3–075, 9–041, 14–011
Format Communications MFG Ltd v ITT (United Kingdom) Ltd [1983] F.S.R. 473
    CA 20–002, 20–004
Forrester v Waller, June 13, 1741, cited 4 Burr. 2331 . . . . 1–006, 1–008
Fortex Group Ltd v MacIntosh [1998] 3 N.Z.L.R. 171 9–028
Foskett v McKeown [2001] 1 A.C. 102; [2000] 2 W.L.R. 1299 HL 9–035
Foxley v United Kingdom (2001) E.H.R.R. 637 16–002
Franchi v Franchi [1967] R.P.C. 149 . . . . 3–115, 3–138
Francome v Mirror Group Newspapers [1984] 1 W.L.R. 892 . . 3–033, 6–014, 6–019, 6–020, 6–052,
    13–002
Franklin v Giddins [1978] Qd.R. 72 . . . . 2–043, 3–001, 3–035, 3–042, 9–014
Fraser v Evans [1969] 1 Q.B. 349 . . . . 2–047, 3–001, 3–055, 3–182
Fraser v Thames Television [1984] 1 Q.B. 44. . . . . 2–057, 3–068, 3–086
Fry v Stevens (see Calcroft v Guest). 18–015, 18–016
FSS Travel & Leisure Systems Ltd v Johnson [1999] F.S.R. 505 . . . . 3–087, 14–015
G (A Minor) (Social Worker: Disclosure), Re [196] 1 W.L.R. 1407 19–039
G v E [2010] EWHC 2042 (Fam) 20–009
Gain v Gain [1961] 1 W.L.R. 1469 19–035
Galileo Group Ltd, Re [1999] Ch. 100; [1998] 2 W.L.R. 364 19–059
Gamlen Chemical Co (UK) Ltd v Rochem, Transcript No. 777 of 19079; Unreported December 7,
    1979 CA 16–015, 16–017
Garner v Garner (1920) 36 T.L.R. 196 3–171
Gartside v Outram (1857) 26 L.J.Ch. (N.S.) 113 . . . . 1–030, 6–003, 6–004, 6–005, 6–013,
    6–020, 6–022, 6–060, 6–064, 6–065,
    12–018, 14–007
Gaskin v Liverpool CC [1980] 1 W.L.R. 1549 19–038
Gee v Pritchard (1818) 2 Swans. 402 . . . . 1–009, 1–013
General Billposting Co Ltd v Atkinson [1909] A.C. 118 14–031
General Dental Council v Savery [2011] EWHC 3011 (Admin) 11–020
General Mediterranean Holdings SA v Patel [2000] 1 W.L.R. 272 18–010
General Tire and Rubber Co v Firestone Tyre & Rubber Co Ltd [1975] 1 W.L.R. 819 2–068
Generics (UK) Ltd v Yeda Research and Development Co Ltd [2012] EWCA Civ 726; [2012] C.P.
    Rep. 39 . . . . 14–017, 16–011
Geveran Trading Co Ltd v Skjevesland [2002] EWCA Civ 1567; [2003] 1 W.L.R.
    912 16–008
Gilbert v Star Newspapers Co Ltd (1894) 11 T.L.R. 4 3–188
Giller v Procopets [2008] VSCA 236, 24 V.R. 1 . . . . 2–095, 9–052
Gillick v West Norfolk Area Health Authority [1986] A.C. 112 . . . . 11–038, 11–042
Giumelli v Giumelli [1999] H.C.A. 10; (1999) 196 C.L.R. 101 9–025

TABLE OF CASES

Goddard v Nationwide Building Society [1987] 1 Q.B. 670 . . . . . . 3–045, 3–059, 16–011, 18–024,
18–037,
18–040, 18–048, 18–049, 18–050,
18–053, 18–065
Goldberg v Ng Unreported November 3, 1995 HC Australia 18–070
Goldman v Hesper [1988] 1 W.L.R. 1238 18–069
Goodridge v Chief Constable of Hampshire [1999] 1 W.L.R. 1558 19–047
Goodwin v News Group Newspapers Ltd [2011] EWHC 1437; [2011] E.M.L.R. 27 . 2–017, 13–006,
20–017
Goodwin v United Kingdom (1996) 22 E.H.R.R.123 13–018
Gotha City v Sotheby's [1998] 1 W.L.R. 114 18–004
Gray v News Group Newspapers Ltd [2012] UKSC 28; [2012] 3 W.L.R. 312 17–007
Gray v UVW [2010] EWHC 2367 (QB) 20–017
Green Corns Ltd v Claverly Group Ltd [2005] EWHC 958; [2005] E.M.L.R. 31 . . . 3–001, 3–185,
7–058
Green v Folgham (1823) 1 Sim. & St. 398 . . . . 1–015, 2–033
Greene v Associated Newspapers Ltd [2004] EWCA Civ 1462; [2005] Q.B. 972 9–006
Grosvenor Hotel, London (No. 2), Re [1965] 1 Ch. 1210 19–029
GT Corp Pty Ltd v Amare Safety Pty Ltd [2007] V.S.C. 123 16–011
Guardian News and Media Ltd, Re [2010] UKSC 1; [2010] 2 A.C. 697; [2010] 2 W.L.R.
325 . . . . 9–012, 13–006, 13–009, 20–014
Guinness Peat Ltd v Fitzroy Robinson Partnership [1987] 1 W.L.R. 1027 . . 3–045, 18–049, 18–053,
18–058, 18–067
Gunton v Richmond BC [1981] Ch. 448 14–031
GUS Consulting GmbH v Leboeuf Lamb Greene & Macrae [2006] EWCA Civ 683; (2006)
P.N.L.R. 32 16–010
H v News Group Newspapers Ltd [2011] EWCA Civ 42; [2011] 1 W.L.R. 1645 20–017
Hakendorf v Rosenborg [2004] EWHC 2821 (QB) 16–031
Halewood International Ltd v Addleshaw Booth & Co [2000] Lloyd's Rep. (PN) 298 16–010
Halford v Sharples [1992] 1 W.L.R. 736 19–075
Halford v United Kingdom (1997) 24 E.H.R.R. 523 7–044
Hassneh Insurance v Mew [1993] 2 Ll.Rep. 243 . . . . 3–176, 22–007, 22–011, 22–028
Hayes v Dodd [1990] 2 All E.R. 815 9–044
Health Authority v X [2001] EWCA Civ 2014; [2002] 2 All E.R. 780 11–020
Helitune Ltd v Stewart Hughes Ltd [1994] F.S.R. 422 20–002
Hellewell v Chief Constable of Derbyshire [1995] 1 W.L.R. 804; [1995] 4 All E.R.
473 . . . . 3–001, 3–013, 3–014, 3–085, 7–009,
9–053
Henderson v Merrett Syndicates Ltd [1995] 2 A.C. 145 . . . . . 2–080, 2–100, 3–006, 3–152, 9–041,
14–004
Hennessy v Wright (1888) 21 Q.B.D. 509 19–082
Herbert Morris Ltd v Saxelby [1916] A.C. 688 . . . . 1–036, 1–041, 1–043, 3–006, 3–079,
14–010
Heyman v Darwins Ltd [1942] A.C. 356 4–038
Heywood v Wellers [1976] Q.B. 446 9–044
Hill v Chief Constable of West Yorkshire [1989] A.C. 53 11–025
Hilton v Barker Booth & Eastwood [2005] UKHL 8; [2005] 1 W.L.R. 567 . . 3–006, 3–120, 3–134,
3–151, 3–152,
16–003
Hivac Ltd v Park Royal Scientific Instruments Ltd [1946] 1 Ch. 169 . . . . 3–070, 3–072
Holmes v Walton [1961] W.A.R. 96 2–081
Home v Bentinck (1820) 2 Brod. & B. 130. . . . . 19–035, 19–052, 19–072
Hosking v Runting [2003] 3 N.Z.L.R. 385; [2004] NZCA 34 . . . . 2–016, 2–096, 2–098, 7–041
Hospital Products Ltd v United States Surgical Corp (1984) 156 C.L.R. 41 9–023
Hubbard v Vosper [1971] 1 All E.R. 1023; [1972] 2 Q.B. 84 . . . . 3–001, 6–052, 6–078, 6–079
Hunter v Mann [1974] Q.B. 767 . . . . 11–001, 11–037
Hutcheson v News Group Newspapers Ltd [2011] EWCA Civ 808; [2012] E.M.L.R. 2 7–032
Imerman v Tchenguiz [2010] EWCA Civ 908; [2011] 1 All E.R. 55 . . 2–001, 2–024, 3–044, 3–050,
3–063,
3–087, 3–154, 3–178, 9–017, 13–005,
18–023
Imutran Ltd v Uncaged Campaigns Ltd [2002] 2 All E.R. 385 . . . . 3–001, 6–051

xxiv

TABLE OF CASES

Indata Equipment Supplies Ltd v ACL Ltd [1998] 1 B.C.L.C. 412 9–042
Independent News and Media Ltd v A [2010] EWCA Civ 343; [2010] 1 W.L.R. 2262; [2010] 3 All
   E.R. 32 20–009
Independent Publishing Co Ltd v Attorney General of Trinidad and Tobago [2005] 1 A.C.
   190 20–014
Industrial Furnaces Ltd v Reaves [1970] R.P.C. 605 9–016
Industrial Rollformers Pty Ltd v Ingersoll-Rand (Australia) Ltd [2001] N.S.W.C.A.
   111 3–011
Initial Services Ltd v Putterill [1968] 1 Q.B. 396 . . . . .6–010, 6–039, 6–044, 6–052, 12–018,
                                                                                                    14–002, 14–007
Inquiry under the Company Securities (Insider Dealing) Act 1985, Re [1988] A.C.
   660 13–021
Insurance Company v Lloyd's Syndicate [1995] 1 Lloyd's Rep. 272 22–029
Interbrew v Financial Times Ltd [2002] EWCA Civ 274; [2002] 2 Lloyd's Rep. 229 3–093,
                                                                                                    13–026, 13–029
International Business Machines Corp v Phoenix International (Computers) Ltd [1995] 1 All E.R.
   413 . . . . .18–055, 18–062
Inverugie Investments Ltd v Hackett [1995] 1 W.L.R. 713 2–072
Ismail-Zai v The State of Western Australia [2007] W.A.S.C.A. 150 16–008
Istil Group Inc v Zahoor [2003] EWHC 165 (Ch); [2003] 2 All E.R. 252 18–044
ITC Film Distributors Ltd v Video Exchange Ltd [1982] 1 Ch. 431 18–063
Ixora Trading Inc v Jones [1990] 1 F.S.R. 251 14–017
Jameel v Wall Street Journal Europe Sprl [2006] UKHL 44; [2006] 3 W.L.R. 642 9–052
Jardin and Jardim Investments Pty v Metcash Ltd [2011] NSWCA 409 4–035
Jarvis v Swan Tours Ltd [1973] Q.B. 233 9–044
Jasper v United Kingdom (2000) 30 E.H.R.R. 441 19–084
Jefferys v Boosey (1854) 4 H.L.C. 815 . . . . .1–007, 2–030, 2–051
JIH v News Group Newspapers Ltd [2011] EWHC 2818 (QB); on appeal [2011] EWCA Civ 42;
   [2011] 1 W.L.R. 1645 . . . . .3–127, 4–034, 7–058, 9–012, 20–015
JN Dairies Ltd v Johal Dairies Ltd [2009] EWHC 1331 (Ch) 14–019
John v Express Newspapers [2000] 1 W.L.R. 1931 . . . . .13–022, 13–025
Johnson & Bloy (Holdings) Ltd v Wolstenholme Rink Plc [1987] I.R.L.R. 499 14–009
Johnson v Medical Defence Union Ltd [2006] EWHC 321 . . . . .8–011, 8–020
Jones v Smith [1999] 1 S.C.R. 455 18–009
Jones v Tsige [2012] ONCA 32 2–098
Joseph Hargreaves Ltd, Re [1900] 1 Ch. 347 . . . . .19–015, 19–060, 19–063
JP Morgan Multi-Strategy Fund LP v Macro Fund Ltd [2003] CILR 250 . . . . . . .18–021, 18–045
JXF v York Hospitals NHS Trust [2010] EWHC 2800 (QB) .20–017
K Ltd v National Westminster Bank Plc [2006] EWCA Civ 1039; [2007] 1 W.L.R.
   311 10–013
Kadian v Richards [2004] N.S.W.S.C. 382 11–031
Kallinicos v Hunt [2005] N.S.W.S.C. 1181 16–008
Kaufman v Credit Lyonnais Bank, Times, February 1, 1995 19–050
Kaye v Robertson [1991] F.A.R. 62 . . . . .2–012, 4–021, 7–004, 7–006
Kennedy v Lyell (1883) L.R. 23 Ch. D. 387 18–004
Khashoggi v Smith (1980) 124 S.J. 149 . . . . .3–093, 3–104
Kitchenology BV v Unicor GmbH Plastmaschinen [1995] R.P.C. 765 . . . . .2–008, 2–079
KJO v XIM [2011] EWHC 1768 (QB) 3–127, 3–152
Koch Shipping Inc v Richards Butler [2002] EWCA Civ 1280; [2002] 2 All E.R. (Comm)
   957 16–010
KOO Golden East Mongolia v Bank of Nova Scotia [2007] EWCA Civ 1443; [2008] Q.B.
   717 12–013
Kuwait Airways Corp v Iraqi Airways Co [2005] EWCA Civ 286 . . . . .16–015, 16–017
L (A Child) (Care: Assessment: Fair Trial), Re [2002] 2 F.L.R. 730 19–039
L, Re [1977] A.C. 16 . . . . .16–045, 16–048, 16–049, 16–051, 16–052
LAC Minerals Ltd v International Corona Resources Ltd [1990] F.S.R. 441 . .2–085, 2–086, 9–026
Lamb v Evans [1893] 1 Ch. 218 . . . . .1–033, 1–036, 1–038, 2–100, 3–036,
                                                                                             3–165, 14–001, 14–008
Lancashire Fires Ltd v SA Lyons & Co Ltd [1996] F.S.R. 629 . . . . .3–001, 3–053, 3–075, 3–080,
                                                                                                                      14–027,
                                                                                                                      14–029
Lansing Linde v Kerr [1991] 1 All E.R. 418 . . . . .9–004, 14–014

TABLE OF CASES

Laskey, Jaggard and Brown v United Kingdom [1997] E.C.H.R. 4; (197) 24 E.H.R.R.
39 7–032
Lawrence David Ltd v Ashton [1991] 1 All E.R. 385 . . . . 3–087, 9–005
Leander v Sweden (A/116) (1987) 9 E.H.R.R. 433 7–061
Lee Gleeson Pty Ltd v Sterling Estates Pty Ltd [1992] 1 Bank L.R. 342 New South Wales Supreme
Court 12–023
Leigh v Gladstone (1909) 26 T.L.R. 139 19–040
Lewis v Secretary of State for Health [2008] EWHC 2196 (QB) . . 3–191, 11–022, 11–051, 11–052
Libyan Arab Foreign Bank v Bankers Trust Co [1989] Q.B. 728; [1989] 3 W.L.R.
314 12–015
Lillicrap v Nalder [1993] 1 W.L.R. 94 3–177
Lilly Icos Ltd v Pfizer Ltd (No. 2) [2002] EWCA Civ 2; [2002] 1 W.L.R. 2253 20–002
Lion Laboratories v Evans [1985] Q.B.526 . . . . 3–093, 6–018, 6–020, 6–052, 6–060
Lipkin Gorman v Karpnale Ltd [1991] 2 A.C. 548 . . . . 3–001, 3–060
Lloyd v Mostyn 10 M. & W. 478 18–017
Local Authority v A Mother [2011] EWHC 1764 (Fam) 9–008
Local Authority v W [2005] EWHC 1564 . . . . 3–001, 3–186, 7–064
Lock International plc v Beswick [1989] 1 W.L.R. 1268 9–055
London & Leeds Estates Ltd v Paribas Ltd (No. 2) [1999] 1 W.L.R. 314; [1995] 02 E.G.
134 . . . . 22–033, 22–035
London and County Securities Ltd v Caplan Unreported May 26, 1978 10–009
London Regional Transport v Mayor of London [2001] EWCA Civ 1491; [2003] E.M.L.R.
4 . . . . 3–006, 5–014, 6–046, 6–053, 6–058
Lonrho Ltd v Shell Petroleum Co Ltd [1980] 1 W.L.R. 627 19–059
Lonrho plc v Fayed (No. 4) [1994] Q.B. 775 . . . . 3–012, 19–015, 19–062, 19–063, 19–064,
19–068, 19–069, 19–080, 19–088
Lord Advocate v Scotsman Publications Ltd [1990] 1 A.C. 812 5–007
Loyd v Freshfield (1826) 2 Car. & P. 325 12–013
Lunn Poly Ltd v Liverpool & Lancashire Properties Ltd [2006] EWCA Civ 430; [2006] 2 E.G.L.R.
29 9–043
Lyell v Kennedy (No. 3) (1884) 27 Ch.D.1 16–013
M (A Patient) (Court of Protection: Reporting Restrictions), In re [2011] EWHC 1197 (Fam);
[2012] 1 W.L.R. 287 20–009
MacDonald Estate v Martin 7 D.L.R. (4th) 249 16–009
MacKinnon v Donaldson, Lufkin & Jenrette Corp [1986] 1 Ch. 483 . . . . 10–004, 10–006, 10–009,
10–012
Macmillan Inc v Bishopsgate Investment Trust Plc [1993] 1 W.L.R. 1372 3–171
Maggbury Pty Ltd v Hafele Australia Pty Ltd (2001) 210 C.L.R. 181 3–006
Mahon v Keena [2007] IEHC 348 High Court of Ireland 5–016, 13–006
Mahon v Post Publications [2007] IESC 15 Supreme Court of Ireland 5–016
Mainmet Holdings plc v Austin [1991] F.S.R. 538 14–025
Makanjuola v Commissioner of Police of the Metropolis [1992] 3 All E.R. 617 19–087
Malik v Bank of Credit and Commerce International SA [1997] UKHL 23; [1998] A.C.
20 14–035
Malone v Metropolitan Police Commissioner [1979] 1 Ch. 344 . . . . . 2–066, 2–073, 3–031, 3–033,
9–038,
9–053
Marcel v Commissioner of Police [1992] Ch. 225 . . . . 3–001, 3–015, 3–016, 3–020, 19–044,
19–065, 19–069, 19–082
Marckx v Belgium (1979) 2 E.H.R.R. 330 . . . . 3–184, 7–018
Marfani & Co Ltd v Midland Bank Ltd [1968] 1 W.L.R. 956 2–058
Marks & Spencer Group plc v Freshfields Bruckhaus Deringer [2004] EWCA Civ
741 16–010
Marks v Beyfus (1890) 25 Q.B.D. 494 19–053
Marlwood Commercial Inc v Kozeny [2004] EWCA Civ 798; [2005] 1 W.L.R. 104 3–018
Mars UK Ltd v Teknowledge Ltd [2000] F.S.R. 138 3–010
Marsh v Sofaer [2003] EWHC 3334; (2004) P.N.L.R. 24 16–003
Maxwell Communications Corporation Plc (No. 3) [1995] 1 B.C.L.C. 521 3–018
Maynes v Casey [2011] NSWCA 156 2–095
McE v Prison Service of Northern Ireland [2009] UKHL 15; [2009] 1 A.C. 908 . . 16–035, 16–039,
16–043

McKennitt v Ash [2005] EWHC 3003; [2006] E.M.L.R. 10; upheld on appeal [2006] EWCA Civ
  1714, [2008] Q.B. 73 . . . . 3–091, 3–096, 3–124, 3–127, 7–035,
                                                                          7–048, 7–056, 9–006
McKenzie v McDonald [1927] V.L.R. 134 2–081
McKie v Western Scottish Motor Traction Co Ltd (1952) S.C. 206 19–043
McKillen v Misland (Cyprus) Investments Ltd [2012] EWHC 1158 (Ch) 20–002
McNicol v Sportsman's Book Stores (1930) McG.C.C. 116 . . . . .3–001, 3–090, 6–077
Mechanical and General Inventions Co v Austin [1935] A.C. 346 . . . . 1–044, 14–032
Medcalf v Mardell [2002] UKHL 27; [2003] 1 A.C. 120 . . . . . . 16–029, 16–030, 18–005, 18–007
Merryweather v Moore [1892] 2 Ch. 518 . . . . .1–032, 14–006
Mersey Care NHS v Ackroyd (No. 2) [2006] EWHC 107; [2006] E.M.L.R. 12; upheld [2007]
  EWCA Civ 101; [2008] E.M.L.R. 1 . . . . .3–184, 11–003, 13–020, 13–021, 13–029
Mersey Care NHS v Ackroyd [2003] EWCA Civ 663; [2003] F.S.R. 820 . . . . . . .13–019, 13–029
Messtechnik v Hartley [2012] EWHC 1013 (QB) 14–019
Metall und Rohstoff AG v Donaldson Lufkin & Jenrette Inc [1990] 1 Q.B. 391 . . . . 3–073, 9–028
MGN Ltd v United Kingdom [2011] E.C.H.R. 66 7–025
MGN Ltd's application, Re [2011] 1 Cr. App. R. 31 20–014
Michael Wilson & Partners Ltd v Emmott. See Emmott v Michael Wilson & Partners
  Ltd 20–014
Mid East Trading Ltd, Re [1998] 1 All E.R. 577 10–010
Mid-City Skin Cancer & Laser Centre v Zahedi-Anarak [2006] NSWSC 844 3–187
Miles v Genesys Wealth Advisers Ltd [2009] NSWCA 25 3–088
Millar v Taylor (1769) 4 Bur. 2303 . . . . .1–004, 1–006, 1–007, 1–008, 1–020,
                                                                          1–021, 1–022, 2–027, 2–030
Mills v News Group Newspapers Ltd, June 4, 2001 3–126
Milsom v Ablyazov [2011] EWHC 955 (Ch) 22–034
Minister for Immigration and Citizenship v Kumar [2009] H.A.C. 10; (2009) 238 C.L.R.
  448 . . . . .6–022, 6–069
Ministry of Defence v Griffin [2008] EWHC 1542 (QB) 3–005, 5–013
Missingham v Shamin [2012] NSWSC 288 3–127
Mitsui & Co Ltd v Nexen Petroleum UK Ltd [2005] EWHC 625; [2005] 3 All E.R.
  511 10–004
MMI Research Ltd v Cellxion Ltd [2007] EWHC 2456 (Ch) 18–062
Moorgate Tobacco Co Ltd v Philip Morris Ltd (No. 2) (1982) 64 F.L.R. 387; affirmed (1984) 156
  C.L.R. 414 . . . . .2–026, 2–048, 2–092, 3–089, 3–157,
                                                                          3–164, 3–165, 3–166, 3–187
Morison v Moat (1851) 9 Hare 241 . . . . .1–026, 1–034, 3–056, 3–061, 3–187,
                                                                          11–051
Morris v Director of Serious Fraud Office [1993] B.C.L.C. 580 . . . . .3–018, 6–041
Mortgage Express Ltd v Bowerman & Partners [1996] 2 All E.R. 836 . . . . 16–026, 16–027
Mortgage Express Ltd v Sawali [2010] EWHC 3054 (Ch); [2011] P.N.L.R. 11 . . . . 16–003, 16–028
Mosley v News Group Newspapers Ltd [2008] EWHC 1777 (QB); [2008] E.M.L.R.
  20 . . . . .2–084, 7–032, 9–048, 9–052, 13–009
Mosley v United Kingdom (2003) 53 E.H.R.R. 30 13–006
Mosley v United Kingdom [2011] E.C.H.R. 774 7–052
Mount Murray Country Club Ltd v Macleod [2003] UKPC 53; (2003) S.T.C. 1525 . 3–012, 19–062
MS v Sweden (1997) 28 E.H.R.R. 313 . . . . .11–034, 17–002
Murphy Oil Company Ltd v The Predator Corp Ltd [2006] ABQB 680 Court of Queen's Bench of
  Alberta 9–028
Murray v Express Newspapers Plc [2008] EWCA Civ 446; [2009] Ch. 481; [2008] 3 W.L.R.
  1360 . . . . .2–024, 7–027, 7–041, 8–019, 8–020
Muschinski v Dodds (1985) 160 C.L.R. 583 9–025
Mustad & Son v Dosen [1964] 1 W.L.R. 109 . . . . .2–075, 3–108, 3–189, 4–002, 4–004,
                                                                          4–006, 4–008, 4–009, 4–014, 4–025
Nam Tai v Pricewaterhouse Coopers FACV No. 1 of 2007 3–173
Named person v Vancouver Sun (2007) S.C.C. 43; 285 D.L.R. (4th) 193 19–056
Napier v Pressdram Ltd [2009] EWCA Civ 443; [2009] E.M.L.R. 21 . . . . . .3–009, 5–016, 16–041
National Westminster Bank plc v Bonas [2003] EWHC 1821 16–009
Nationwide Anglia Building Society v Various Solicitors [1999] P.N.L.R. 52 . . . . . 16–003, 16–027
Neilson v Laugharne [1981] Q.B. 736 . . . . .19–049, 19–076
Newbery v James (1817) 2 Mer. 446 1–014
Nichrotherm Electrical Co Ltd v Percy [1957] R.P.C. 207 . . . . .2–032, 2–051, 2–064

Niemietz v Germany (1992) 16 E.H.R.R. 97 . . . . .7–030, 7–077, 7–083
NM v Smith [2007] Z.A.C.C. 6 . . . . .7–026, 7–027
Nocton v Ashburton [1914] A.C. 932 . . . . .2–078, 2–079, 2–081, 11–054
North Shore Ventures Ltd v Anstead Holdings Plc [2011] EWHC 910 (QB); [2011] 1 W.L.R.
   2265 20–013
Northern Rock Plc v The Financial Times Ltd [2007] EWHC 2677 (QB) 3–127, 4–025, 6–058
Norwich Pharmacal Co v Customs & Excise Commissioners [1974] A.C. 133 . . . . .6–074, 9–058,
                                                              10–004, 10–008, 10–020,
                                                              13–020, 13–030, 19–022
NP Generations Pty Ltd v Fenely (2001) 80 S.A.S.R. 151 14–020
O'Brien v Komesaroff (1982) 150 C.L.R. 310 3–086
O'Rourke v Darbishire [1920] A.C. 581 . . . . .16–015, 16–017
O'Sullivan v Commissioner of Police of the Metropolis, Times, July 3, 1995 19–048
Observer and Guardian v United Kingdom (1991) 14 E.H.R.R. 153 4–023
Ofulue v Bossert [2009] UKHL 16; [2009] 1 A.C. 990 . . . . .17–010, 17–011
OPQ v BJM [2011] EWHC 1059 (QB); [2011] E.M.L.R. 23 9–009
Owners and/or Demise Charterers of the Dredger "Kamal XXVI" and the Barge "Kamal XXIV" v
   The Owners of the Ship "Ariela" [2010] EWHC 2531 (Comm) 16–015
Oxford v Moss (1979) 68 Cr. App. R. 183 2–049
Oxfordshire CC v P [1995] Fam. 161 16–051
P v Independent Print Ltd [2011] EWCA Civ 756 20–009
Palmer v Tees Health Authority [2000] P.N.L.R. 87 11–025
Paragon Finance plc v Freshfields [1999] 1 W.L.R. 1183 . . . . .3–177, 11–031, 16–031
Parry-Jones v Law Society [1969] 1 Ch. 1 . . . . .12–013, 16–037, 16–038, 16–041, 16–042
Paterson Zochonis & Co Ltd v Merfarken Packaging Ltd [1986] 3 All E.R. 522 2–058
Peck v United Kingdom (2003) 36 E.H.R.R. 41 . . . . .7–043, 7–083
Pell Frischmann Engineering Ltd v Bow Valley Iran Ltd [2009] UKPC 45; [2010] Bus. L.R.
   73 9–043
Pennwell Publishing (UK) Ltd v Ornstien [2007] EWHC 1570 (QB); [2007] I.R.L.R.
   700 13–002
Percival v Phipps (1813) 35 E.R. 225 . . . . .1–009, 1–010
Peter Pan Manufacturing Corp v Corsets Silhouette Ltd [1963] R.P.C. 45; [1964] 1 W.L.R.
   96 . . . . .4–006, 9–016, 9–018, 9–020
Pfeifer v Austria (2009) 48 E.H.R.R. 8 3–097
Pharaon v BCCI SA [1998] 4 All E.R. 455 10–017
Phillips v Mulcaire [2012] UKSC 28 . . . . .2–029, 3–154
Phipps v Boardman [1967] 2 A.C. 46 . . . . .2–034, 2–035, 2–037, 2–092, 4–027,
                                                              9–029
Photo Production Ltd v Securicor Transport Ltd [1980] A.C. 827 . . . . .4–037, 14–031
Pinnacle Living Pty Ltd v Elusive Image Pty Ltd [2006] V.S.C. 202 16–007
Pizzey v Ford Motor Co Ltd, February 26, 1993, CA; partially reported Times, March 8,
   1993 . . . . .18–039, 18–040, 18–055, 18–057, 18–060
Plon v France [2004] E.C.H.R. 200 . . . . .11–055, 11–056
Pollard v Photographic Company (1888) 40 Ch.D. 34 . . . . .1–031, 1–032, 7–007, 7–010
Polly Peck International plc (No. 2) [1998] 3 All E.R. 812 9–028
Pope v Curl (1741) 2 Atk. 342 . . . . .1–002, 1–006, 1–008
Porton Capital Technology Funds v 3M UK Holdings Ltd [2010] EWHC 114
   (Comm) 14–026
Potters-Ballotini Ltd v Weston-Bake [1977] R.P.C. 202 . . . . . .3–086, 3–087, 4–025, 9–001, 9–005
Practice Direction (Family Proceedings: Case Management) [1995] 1 W.L.R. 332 16–051
Practice Guidance on Interim Non-disclosure Orders [2012] 1 W.L.R. 1003 . . . . . .9–007, 20–006,
                                                              20–007, 20–012, 20–015
Price Waterhouse v BCCI Holdings (Luxembourg) SA [1992] B.C.L.C. 583 .6–041, 6–074, 9–053,
                                                              12–016
Prince Albert v Strange (1849) 1 De G. & Sm. 652; (1849) 1 Mac. & G. 25 .1–001, 1–004, 1–018,
                                                              1–019, 1–022,
                                                              1–025, 1–028, 1–031, 3–001, 3–030,
                                                              3–038, 3–053, 3–055, 5–003, 7–007,
                                                              9–014, 14–006, 20–031
Prince Jefri Bolkiah v KPMG [1999] 2 A.C. 222 . . . . . .3–155, 14–017, 16–005, 16–006, 16–008,
                                                              16–009, 16–010, 16–011

TABLE OF CASES

Prince of Wales v Associated Newspapers [2006] EWCA Civ 1776; [2008] 1 Ch. 57 . 3–007, 3–102, 6–047, 6–058, 7–046, 13–004

Printers & Finishers Ltd v Holloway [1965] R.P.C. 239 . . . . . 1–023, 1–036, 2–057, 3–001, 3–009, 3–055, 3–067, 3–072, 3–075, 3–085, 3–132, 3–155, 3–156, 14–001, 14–009, 14–019, 14–027

Printing and Numerical Registering Co v Sampson (1875) L.R. 19 Eq.462 6–006

Proctor v Bayley (1889) 42 Ch.D. 390 . . . . 2–071, 9–038

Prout v British Gas plc [1992] F.S.R. 478 14–035

PSM International plc v Whitehouse [1992] 1 I.R.L.R. 279 . . . . 9–005, 14–014

QBE Management Services (UK) Ltd v Dymoke [2012] EWHC 80 (QB) 4–004

Quinn Direct Insurance Ltd v Law Society [2010] EWCA Civ 80; [2011] 1 W.L.R.
308 . . . . 16–034, 16–035

Quinton v Peirce [2009] EWHC 912 (QB); [2009] F.S.R. 17 . . . . 8–016, 8–019, 8–032

R. (A Child) (Care: Disclosure: Nature of Proceedings), Re [2002] 1 F.L.R. 755 19–039

R. (on the application of Hafner) v City of Westminster Magistrates' Court [2008] EWHC 524
(Admin); [2009] 1 W.L.R. 1005 10–021

R. v Chief Constable of B County Constabulary (November 1997; reported in the Encyclopedia of
Data Protection and Privacy, at para.6–544) 8–020

R. (AHK) v Secretary of State for the Home Department [2012] EWHC 1117
(Admin) 19–085

R. (Department of Health) v Information Commissioner [2011] EWHC 1430 (Admin) 8–016

R. (Guardian News and Media Ltd) v City of Westminster Magistrates Court [2012] EWCA Civ
420 . . . . 9–010, 20–007, 20–008, 20–011

R. (Jackson) v Attorney General [2007] UKHL 52 2–029

R. (Malik) v Manchester Crown Court [2008] 4 All E.R. 403 19–085

R. (Mohamed) v Secretary of State for Foreign and Commonwealth Affairs (No.2) [2010] EWCA
Civ 65; [2011] Q.B. 218 19–022

R. (Nicholls) v Security Industry Authority [2007] 1 W.L.R. 2067 2–029

R. (Omar) v Secretary of State for Foreign and Commonwealth Affairs [2012] EWHC 1737
(Admin) 19–085

R. (on the application of Ali) v Director of High Security Prisons [2009] EWHC 1732 (Admin);
[2010] 2 All E.R. 82 19–042

R. (on the application of Axon) v Secretary of State for Health [2006] H.R.L.R.12; [2006] EWHC
37 11–042

R. (on the application of British Sky Broadcasting Ltd) v Central Criminal Court [2011] EWHC
3451 (Admin); [2012] 3 W.L.R. 78 19–85

R. (on the application of Countryside Alliance) v Attorney General [2007] UKHL 52; [2008] 1 A.C.
719; [2007] 3 W.L.R. 922 7–032

R. (on the application of Ferguson) v Secretary of State for Justice [2011] EWHC 5
(Admin) 19–042

R. (on the application of Green) v Police Complaints Authority [2004] 1 W.L.R. 725 19–048

R. (on the application of Kent Pharmaceuticals Ltd) v Director of the Serious Fraud Office [2004]
EWCA Civ 1494; [2005] 1 W.L.R. 1302; [2005] 1 All E.R. 449 . . . . 3–023, 7–083

R. (on the application of L) v Commissioner of Police of the Metropolis [2009] UKSC 3; [2010] 1
A.C. 410; [2009] 3 W.L.R. 1056 . . . . 3–152, 4–034, 7–061

R. (on the application of Lord) v Secretary of State for the Home Department [2003] EWHC 2073
(Admin); [2004] Prison L.R. 65 19–042

R. (on the application of Morgan Grenfell Ltd) v Special Commissioner of Income Tax [2002]
UKHL 21; [2003] 1 A.C. 563 . . . . 16–012, 16–035, 16–038, 16–039, 16–041, 16–043, 18–005, 18–008

R. (on the application of Omar) v Secretary of State for Foreign and Commonwealth Affairs [2012]
EWHC 1737 (Admin) 10–020

R. (on the application of Pelling) v Bow CC [2001] UKHRR 165 20–010

R. (on the application of S) v Plymouth CC [2002] EWCA Civ 388; [2002] 1 W.L.R.
2583 11–047

R. (on the application of TB) v Stafford Combined Court [2006] EWHC 1645 17–002

R. (on the application of UMBS Online Ltd) v Serious Organised Crime Agency [2007] EWCA Civ
406; [2008] 1 All E.R. 465 10–013

R. (on the application of Wood) v Commissioner of Police of the Metropolis [2009] EWCA Civ
414; [2010] 1 W.L.R. 123 . . . . 7–032, 7–041, 7–046

TABLE OF CASES

R. (Prudential Plc) v Special Commissioner of Income Tax [2009] EWHC 2494 (Admin); [2011]
 Q.B. 669 . . . . 18–008, 18–009
R. (RMC) v Commissioner of Police of the Metropolis [2012] EWHC 1681 (Admin). 7–032
R. (Youssef) v Secretary of State for Foreign & Commonwealth Affairs [2012] EWHC 2091
 (Admin) 19–085
R. v Ataou [1988] Q.B. 798 18–007
R. v Brady [2004] EWCA Crim 1763; [2004] 1 W.L.R. 3240 3–023
R. v Broadcasting Standards Commission Ex p BBC [2001] Q.B. 885 . . . . . . 2–010, 7–073, 7–084
R. v Brushett [2001] Crim.L.R. 471 19–013
R. v Chief Constable of North Wales Police Ex p. AB [1999] Q.B. 396 3–143
R. v Chief Constable of West Midlands Police Ex p. Wiley [1995] 1 A.C. 274 . . . 19–006, 19–008,
                                                  19–010, 19–031, 19–039,
                                                  19–048, 19–049, 19–050, 19–072,
                                                  19–075, 19–077, 19–088, 19–093,
                                                  19–094
R. v Chief Registrar of Friendly Societies Ex p. New Cross Building Society [1984] Q.B. 227;
 [1984] 2 W.L.R. 370 20–012
R. v Commissioner of Police of the Metropolis Ex p. Hart-Leverton, Times, February 6,
 1990 . . . . 19–074, 19–076, 19–078
R. v Cox and Railton (1884) 14 Q.B.D. 153 . . . . 6–006, 16–013, 16–015
R. v Davis [1993] 1 W.L.R. 613 18–011
R. v Department of Health Ex p. Source Informatics Ltd [2001] Q.B. 424 . . 3–157, 6–050, 11–009
R. v Derbyshire Magistrates' Court Ex p. B [1996] A.C. 487 . . . 16–005, 16–032, 16–033, 16–047,
                                                  16–052,
                                                  18–005, 18–006, 18–007, 18–008,
                                                  18–010, 18–018, 18–021, 18–022
R. v Dica [2004] EWCA Crim 1103 11–029
R. v Directors of Serious Fraud Office Ex p. Smith [1993] A.C. 1 17–007
R. v G [2004] EWCA Crim 1368; [2004] 1 W.L.R. 2932 . . . . . . 18–037, 18–058, 18–070, 19–096,
                                                  20–002
R. v Governor of Brixton Prison Ex p. Osman [1991] 1 W.L.R. 281 19–021
R. v Grossman (1981) 73 Cr.App.R. 302 . . . . 10–005, 10–007, 10–008, 10–009, 10–015
R. v H [2004] UKHL 3; [2004] 2 A.C. 134 . . . . 18–011, 19–012, 19–056, 19–084, 19–085
R. v Hampshire CC [1990] 2 Q.B. 71 16–050
R. v Home Secretary Ex p. Simms [2002] A.C. 115 13–028
R. v Inland Revenue Commissioners Ex p. National Federation of Self-Employed and Small
 Businesses Ltd [1982] A.C. 617 3–012
R. v Inland Revenue Commissioners Ex p. Preston [1985] A.C. 835 3–012
R. v Institute of Chartered Accountants of England and Wales Ex p. Brindle [1994] B.C.C.
 297 . . . . 3–178, 6–041, 16–029
R. v Keane [1994] 1 W.L.R. 746 19–055
R. v Konzani [2005] EWCA Crim 706; [2005] 2 Cr. App. R. 198 11–029
R. v Legal Aid Board Ex p. Kaim Todner [1999] Q.B. 966 . . . . 20–014, 20–016
R. v Lewes Justices Ex p. Home Secretary [1973] A.C. 388 . . . . 19–002, 19–010, 19–057, 19–082,
                                                  19–087,
                                                  19–093
R. v Licensing Authority Established under Medicines Act 1968 Ex p. Smith Kline & French
 Laboratories Ltd [1968] A.C. 910 . . . . 3–001, 3–027
R. v Preston [1994] 2 A.C. 130 3–033
R. v Secretary of State for the Home Secretary Ex p. Benson Unreported November 1,
 1988 19–042
R. v Secretary of State for the Home Secretary Ex p. Duggan [1994] 3 All E.R. 277 19–042
R. v Shayler [2002] UKHL 11; [2003] 1 A.C. 247 13–021
R. v South Worcestershire Magistrates' Ex. p Lilley, Times, February 22, 1995 DC 19–086
R. v Tompkins (1978) 67 Cr. App. R. 181 18–037
R. v Turner [1995] 1 W.L.R. 264 19–055
R. v Uljee [1982] 1 N.Z.L.R. 561 18–021
R. v Ward [1993] 1 W.L.R. 619 18–011
Raab v Associated Newspapers Ltd [2011] EWCA 3375 6–059
Radio France v France [2004] E.C.R. 127; (2005) 40 E.H.R.R. 706 3–097
Rakusen v Ellis, Munday & Clarke [1912] 1 Ch. 831 16–007
Ralli Bros v Compania Naviera a Sota y Aznar [1920] 2 K.B. 287 10–014

Ramsbotham v Senior (1869) L.R. 8 Eq. 575 16–044
Ranson v Customer Systems Plc [2012] EWCA Civ 841; [2012] I.R.L.R. 769 14–004
Rapid Metal Developments (Australia) Pty Ltd v Anderson Formrite Pty Ltd [2005] W.A.S.C.
    255 3–165
Reading v Attorney General [1951] A.C. 507 9–018
Real Estate Opportunities Ltd v Aberdeen Asset Managers Jersey Ltd [2007] EWCA Civ 197;
    [2007] 2 All E.R. 791 . . . . 3–023, 19–059, 19–064
Reed Executive plc v Reed Business Information Ltd [2004] EWCA Civ 887; [2004] 1 W.L.R.
    3026 . . . . 15–018, 17–010
Regal Castings Ltd v Lightbody [2008] N.Z.S.C. 87; [2008] 2 N.Z.L.R. 434 9–028
Reid & Sigrist Ltd v Moss & Mechanism Ltd (1932) 49 R.P.C. 461 . . . . . . 1–035, 9–016, 14–006
Retractable Technologies Inc v Occupational and Medical Innovations Ltd [2007] F.C.A.
    545 . . . . 3–063, 3–087
Reynolds v Times Newspapers Ltd [2001] 2 A.C. 127 13–006
Ridehalgh v Horsefield [1994] Ch. 205 16–030
Robb v Green [1895] 2 Q.B. 315 . . . . 1–037, 1–038, 1–039, 2–063, 2–100,
                                                        3–036, 9–016, 14–001, 14–006, 14–019,
                                                                              14–021, 14–022
Robertson v Canadian Imperial Bank of Commerce [1994] 1 W.L.R. 1493 . . . . . . 12–007, 12–010,
                                                                                        12–013
Robinson State of South Australia [1931] A.C. 704 PC 19–009
Roger Bullivant Ltd v Ellis [1987] F.S.R. 172 . . . . 4–025, 9–001, 14–022, 14–023
Rogers v Television New Zealand Ltd [2007] NZSC 91, [2008] 2 NZLR 277 2–098
Rolls-Royce Ltd v Jeffrey [1962] 1 All E.R. 801 2–052
Rookes v Barnard [1964] A.C. 1129 9–051
Rowe v United Kingdom (2000) 30 E.H.R.R. 1 19–084
Royal Brunei Airlines v Tan [1995] 2 A.C. 378 . . . . 2–082, 3–069, 3–073, 3–075, 9–039
Rush & Tompkins Ltd v Greater London Council [1989] 1 A.C. 1280 . . . 17–008, 17–009, 17–011
S and W (Minors) (Confidential Reports), Re (1983) 4 F.S.L. 290 19–087
S County Council v B [2000] Fam. 76 . . . . 16–048, 16–053
S v United Kingdom (2008) 48 E.H.R.R. 1169 7–032
S, Re [2003] EWCA Civ 963; [2004] Fam. 43; [2003] 3 W.L.R. 1425; affirmed [2004] UKHL 47;
    [2005] 1 A.C. 593; [2004] 3 W.L.R. 1129 . . . . 7–062, 7–064, 9–008
Saltman Engineering Co Ltd v Campbell Engineering Co Ltd (1948) 65 R.P.C. 203 . 1–025, 1–046,
                                                                          1–047, 1–048, 1–049,
                                                  1–051, 2–004, 3–003, 3–038, 3–067,
                                                  3–079, 3–108, 4–005, 5–003, 7–007,
                                                                          9–015, 20–031
Sankey v Whitlam (1978) 142 C.L.R. 1 . . . . 19–005, 19–024, 19–028, 19–093
Satnam Investments Ltd v Dunlop Heywood & Co Ltd [1999] 3 All E.R. 652 9–032
Saunders v Punch Ltd [1998] 1 W.L.R. 986 13–022
Savage v Chief Constable of Hampshire [1997] 1 W.L.R. 1061 19–089
Sayers v Smithkline Beecham Plc [2007] EWHC 1346 (QB) 11–009
Scally v Southern Health and Social Services Board [1992] 1 A.C. 294 22–012
Schering Chemicals Ltd v Falkman Ltd [1982] 1 Q.B. 1 . . . . . 3–117, 3–121, 3–123, 3–125, 3–128
Sciacca v Italy (2005) 43 E.H.R.R. 83 17–032
Science Research Council v Nasse [1980] A.C. 1028 . . . . 3–171, 9–058, 17–001
Scopelight Ltd v Chief Constable of Northumbria Police Force [2010] Q.B. 438 19–071
Scott Paper Co v Drayton Paper Works Ltd (1927) 44 R.P.C. 151 17–009
Scott v Scott [1913] A.C. 417 . . . . 9–010, 20–011, 20–012, 22–020
Seager v Copydex Ltd (No. 2) [1969] 1 W.L.R. 809; [1969] 2 All E.R. 718 . . 2–042, 2–067, 2–075,
                                                                                2–081, 3–035,
                                                                                      9–043
Secretary of State for Defence v Guardian Newspapers Ltd [1985] A.C. 339 13–023
Seager v Copydex Ltd [1967] 1 W.L.R. 923; [1967] 2 All E.R. 415; [1967] R.P.C. 349 2–026,
                                                        2–040, 2–045, 2–046, 2–065,
                                                        2–067, 2–068, 2–070, 2–075, 2–076,
                                                        2–077, 2–081, 3–009, 3–053, 3–075,
                                                                                3–155, 3–157
Secretary of State for the Home Department v AF (No. 3) [2009] UKHL 28; [2010] 2 A.C.
    269 19–084

TABLE OF CASES

Secretary of State for the Home Department v AP (No. 2) [2010] UKSC 26; [2010] 1 W.L.R. 1652 13–005
Secretary of State for the Home Department v British Union for the Abolition of Vivisection [2008] EWHC 892 (QB); [2008] EWCA Civ 870; [2009] 1 W.L.R. 636 . . . . .3–023, 8–029
Secretary of State for the Home Department v MB; Same v AF [2007] UKHL 46; [2008] 1 A.C. 440 19–084
Sectrack NV v Satamatics Ltd [2007] EWHC 3003 (Comm) 4–025
Shah v HSBC Private Bank (UK) Ltd [2010] EWCA Civ 31; [2010] Bus. L.R. 1514; [2010] 3 All E.R. 477 12–013
Shah v HSBC Private Bank (UK) Ltd [2012] EWHC 1283 (QB); [2012] Lloyd's Rep. F.C. 507 12–013
Shelley Films v Rex Features Ltd [1994] E.M.L.R. 134 . . . . . 1–054, 3–001, 3–038, 3–044, 3–105, 7–084
Shellmar Products Co v Allen-Qualley Co (1936) 87 F.2d 104 4–010
Sidaway v Board of Governors of the Bethlem Royal Hospital and the Maudsley Hospital [1985] A.C. 871 11–011
Sinclair Investments (UK) Ltd v Versailles Trade Finance Ltd (In Administration) [2011] EWCA Civ 347; [2012] Ch. 453; [2011] 3 W.L.R. 1153; [2011] Bus. L.R. 1126; [2011] 4 All E.R. 335; [2011] 2 B.C.L.C. 501; [2011] W.T.L.R. 1043; [2011] 2 P. & C.R. DG6 9–035
SJB Stephenson Ltd v Mandy [2000] F.S.R. 286 14–023
SKA v CRH [2012] EWHC 2236 (QB) 20–017
SKA v CRH [2012] EWHC 766 (QB) 7–032, 7–048, 20–017
Smith Kline & French Laboratories (Australia) Ltd v Department of Community Services and Health [1990] F.S.R. 617; affirmed [1991] 28 F.C.R. 291 . . 2–053, 2–091, 2–092, 3–027, 3–157, 3–164, 3–181, 6–050, 6–066, 14–032
Smith Kline & French Laboratories (Australia) Ltd v Secretary to the Department of Community Services and Health (1991) 99 A.L.R. 679 3–085
Smith Kline and French Laboratories Ltd v Attorney General [1989] 1 N.Z.L.R. 385 3–027
Snepp v United States (1980) 444 U.S. 507 . . . . .9–023, 9–036
Societe Colas Est v France [2002] E.C.H.R. 421 . . . . .7–077, 7–083
Solicitor (Disclosure of Confidential Records), Re [1997] 1 F.L.R. 101 20–005
Solicitor-General v Alice [2007] NZHC 48; [2007] 2 N.Z.L.R. 783 . . . . .6–060, 6–075
Solicitors (A Firm), Re [1992] Q.B. 959 16–011
Solicitors, In the matter of a Firm of [2000] 1 Lloyd's Rep. 31 16–010
Solicitors, Re [1997] Ch. 1; [1995] 3 All E.R. 482 16–011
Soulos v Korkontzilas [1997] 2 S.C.R. 217 . . . . .9–027, 9–036
Southey v Sherwood (1817) 2 Mep. 435 . . . . .1–009, 1–012
Speed Seal Products Ltd v Paddington [1985] 1 W.L.R. 1327 . . . . .4–011, 4–015
Spelman v Express Newspapers [2012] EWHC 355 (QB) 7–052, 9–048
Spigelman v Hocken (1934) 150 L.T. 256 . . . . .19–007, 19–043
Spycatcher (No. 1) [1987] 1 W.L.R. 1248 . . . . .3–059, 4–023
"Spycatcher " Case. See Attorney General v Guardian Newspapers Ltd (No. 2) ("Spycatcher") 3–059, 4–023
Squirrell Ltd v National Westminster Bank Plc [2005] EWHC 664; [2006] 1 W.L.R. 637 12–013
Stace v Griffith (1869) L.R. 2 P.C. 420 19–072
Stanke (H) & Sons Pty Ltd v Von Stanke [2006] S.A.S.C. 308 Supreme Court of South Australia 18–046
State of New South Wales v Public Transport Ticketing Corp [2011] NSWCA 60 . . 19–007, 19–028
State of Norway's Application, Re [1990] 1 A.C. 723 10–019
Steel and Morris v United Kingdom (2005) 41 E.H.R.R. 403 9–052
Stephens v Avery [1988] 1 Ch. 449 . . . . .3–091, 6–014
Stevenson Jordan & Harrison Ltd v MacDonald & Evans (1951) 68 R.P.C. 190 3–057
Stiedl v Enyo Law LLP [2011] EWHC 2649 (Comm); [2012] P.N.L.R. 4 16–011
Stjerna v Finland (1997) 24 E.H.R.R. 235 . . . . .3–184, 7–018
Stoke-on-Trent City Council v W & J Wass Ltd [1988] 1 W.L.R. 1406 . . . . .2–070, 2–071
Stoll v Switzerland (2008) 47 E.H.R.R. 59 . . . . .7–052, 13–009, 19–020
Strother v 3464920 Canada Inc [2007] 2 S.C.R. 177 .16–003, 16–005
Sullivan v Sclanders [2000] S.A.S.C. 273 6–068
Sun Valley Foods Ltd v Vincent [2000] F.S.R. 825 . . . . .4–025, 9–001, 9–004
Sunday Times v United Kingdom (No. 2) (1991) 14 E.H.R.R. 229 4–023
Sunderland v Barclays Bank Ltd, Times, November 24, 1938 . . . . .12–021, 12–022

Surface Technology plc v Young [2002] F.S.R. 387 3–055
Sutherland Publishing Co Ltd v Caxton Publishing Co Ltd [1936] Ch. 323 9–018
Sutton v GE Capital Commercial Finance Ltd [2004] EWCA Civ 315 3–020
Swinney v Chief Constable of Northumbria [1997] Q.B. 464 3–161
Talbot v General Television Corp Pty Ltd [1981] R.P.C. 1; [1980] V.R. 224 . . . . . . .2–088, 9–038
Tarasoff v Regents of the University of California (1976) Sup., 131 Cal. Rptr.14 11–025
Target Holdings Ltd v Redferns [1995] 3 W.L.R. 352 2–083
Taylor v Anderton [1995] 1 A.C. 274 19–048
Taylor v Blacklow (1836) 3 Bing. (N.C.) 235 16–001
Taylor v Director of the Serious Fraud Office [1999] A.C. 177 . . . . .3–025, 6–033
Terrapin Ltd v Builders' Supply Company (Hayes) Ltd [1967] R.P.C. 375 . . . 4–004, 4–006, 4–008,
                                                                        4–009, 4–014,
                                                              4–023, 4–024, 4–025
Terry v Persons Unknown [2010] EWHC 119 (QB); [2010] E.M.L.R. 16 . . . . .7–032, 9–006
Theodoropoulas v Theodoropoulas [1964] P. 311 . . . . .15–017, 17–017
Thomas Marshall Ltd v Guinle [1979] 1 Ch. 227 . . . . . . .3–079, 3–132, 4–034, 14–001, 14–014,
                                                                              14–031
Thomas v Farr [2007] EWCA Civ 118; [2007] I.C.R. 932 . . . . .3–088, 14–030
Thomas v Pearce [2000] F.S.R. 718 . . . . .2–057, 3–071, 3–075
Thompson v Stanhope (1774) Amb. 737 1–008
Thorburn v Hermon, Times, May 14, 1992 19–005
Three Rivers DC v Governor and Company of the Bank of England [2002] EWHC
    2309 . . . . .17–002, 18–004, 18–005, 18–009, 18–022
Times Newspaper Ltd v MGN Ltd [1993] E.M.L.R. 443 . . . . .3–088, 3–099, 9–005
Times Newspapers Ltd v R. [2007] EWCA Crim 1925; [2008] 1 W.L.R. 234 20–014
Tipping v Clarke (1843) 2 Hare 383 . . . . .1–017, 14–006
Titchborne Case (1874) 4–022
Torbay BC v News Group Newspapers [2003] EWHC 2927; [2004] E.M.L.R. 18 7–048
Tournier v National Provincial and Union Bank [1924] 1 K.B. 461 . . 3–001, 3–085, 3–133, 3–168,
                                                                                3–171,
                                          3–176, 3–181, 6–008, 6–010, 6–042,
                                          10–013, 11–032, 12–001, 12–002,
                                          12–003, 12–008, 12–009, 12–011,
                                          12–014, 12–015, 12–017, 12–018,
                                          12–020, 16–029, 22–015, 22–028
Townends Grove Ltd v Cobb [2004] EWHC 3432 (Ch) 14–029
Trimingham v Associated Newspapers Ltd [2012] EWHC 1296 (QB) 7–032
Trinity Mirror Plc, In re [2008] Q.B. 770 20–014
Trinity Mirror v Punch Ltd Unreported July 19, 2000 13–020
TSB Bank plc v Robert Irving & Burns [1999] Lloyd's Rep. (PN) 956 16–003
TSE v News Group Newspapers Ltd [2011] EWHC 1308 (QB) 3–127, 20–017
Turner v Royal Bank of Scotland plc [1999] Lloyd's Rep. Bank. 231CA 12–025
TUV v Persons Unknown [2010] EWHC 853 (QB); [2010] E.M.L.R. 19 9–007
Twinsectra Ltd v Yardley [2002] UKHL 12; [2002] 2 A.C. 164; [2002] 2 W.L.R. 802; [2002] 2 All
    E.R. 377 3–075
Under Water Welders & Repairers Ltd v Street & Longthorne [1968] R.P.C. 498 3–086
Unilever plc v Procter & Gamble Co [2000] 1 W.L.R. 2436 . . . . .17–011, 17–015
United Australia Ltd v Barclays Bank Ltd [1941] A.C. 1 9–041
United Co Rusal Plc v HSBC Bank Plc [2011] EWHC 404 (QB) 10–009
United Pan Europe Communications NV v Deutsche Bank AG [2000] EWCA Civ 166 9–035
United Scientific Holdings Ltd v Burnley BC [1978] A.C. 904 9–040
United States Surgical Corp v Hospital Products International Pty Ltd [1983] 2 N.S.W.L.R. 157;
    reversed in the High Court on other grounds (1984) 156 C.L.R. 41 4–026
United Stirling Corp Ltd v Felton and Mannion [1974] R.P.C. 162 14–028
Universal Thermosensor Ltd v Hibben [1992] 1 W.L.R. 840; [1992] F.S.A.R. 361 . . .2–070, 9–006,
                                                                              9–055, 9–056
University of Nottingham v Fishel [2000] I.C.R. 1462; [2000] I.R.L.R. 471 14–004
US Surgical Corp v Hospital Products International Pty Ltd [1982] 2 N.S.W.L.R. 766; reversed on
    other grounds (1984) 156 C.L.R. 41 . . . . .2–081, 9–024
USA v Philip Morris Inc [2004] EWCA Civ 330 10–020
Valeo Vision SA v Flexible Lamps Ltd [1995] R.P.C. 205 . . . . .2–057, 3–074
Varec SA v Belgium [2008] ECR I–581; [2008] 2 C.M.L.R. 24 . . . . .7–083, 7–084

TABLE OF CASES

Venables v News Group Newspapers Ltd [2001] Fam. 430 . . . . .3–149, 7–020
Ventouris v Mountain [1991] 1 W.L.R. 607 . . . . .9–008, 16–013
Veolia ES Nottinghamshire Ltd v Nottinghamshire County Council [2010] EWCA Civ
    1214 . . . . .2–029, 7–083
Vercoe v Rutland Fund Management Ltd [2010] EWHC 424 (Ch); [2010] Bus. L.R.
    D141 . . . . 9–021, 9–036, 9–043
Vernon v Bosley (No. 2) [1999] Q.B. 18 16–049
Vestergaard Franksen A/S v BestNet Europe Ltd [2009] EWHC 1456 (Ch); on appeal [2011]
    EWCA Civ 424 . . . . .2–083, 3–075, 3–085, 4–023
Viagogo Ltd v Myles [2012] EWHC 433 (Ch) 13–009
Victoria Park Racing and Recreation Grounds Co Ltd v Taylor (1937) 58 C.L.R. 479 .2–094, 2–095
Von Hannover v Germany (2005) 40 E.H.R.R. 1 . . . . .1–056, 2–009, 2–015, 3–184, 7–018,
                                                                    7–032, 7–040, 7–041, 7–051, 7–052,
                                                                            13–006, 13–008, 13–028
Von Hannover v Germany (No. 2) [2012] E.M.L.R. 16 .13–006
Vulcan Detinning Co v Assam (1918) 185 N.Y.App.Div. 399 3–115
W v Egdell [1990] 1 Ch. 359 . . . . .3–001, 3–085, 6–029, 6–034, 6–066,
                                                                                    11–021, 11–023
W v Westminster CC [2005] EWHC 102 3–096
Wainwright v Home Office [2004] UKHL 22; [2004] 2 A.C. 406 . . . . .2–012, 2–017, 7–006
Wainwright v United Kingdom [2006] ECHR 807 2–014
Wallace Smith Trust Co v Deloitte Haskins & Sells [1997] 1 W.L.R. 257 19–064
Warner-Lambert Co v Glaxo Laboratories Ltd [1975] R.P.C. 354 20–002
Watson & Ors v Ebsworth & Ebsworth (a firm) & Anor [2010] V.S.C.A. 335 16–005
Watts v Morrow [1991] 1 W.L.R. 1421 9–044
Webb v Rose, May 24, 1732, cited 4 Bur. 2330 .1–006, 1–008
Webster (a child), Re [2006] EWHC 2733 (Fam); [2007] E.M.L.R. 7 13–002
Webster v James Chapman & Co [1989] 3 All E.R. 939 . . 3–045, 3–180, 18–038, 18–040, 18–043,
                                                                                            18–070
Weld-Blundell v Stephens [1919] 1 K.B. 520 CA; affirmed [1920] A.C. 956 HL 3–159, 6–004,
                                                                            6–009, 6–010, 6–012,
                                                                    6–062, 6–072, 11–050, 12–014, 12–018,
                                                                                            16–013
WER v REW [2009] EWHC 1029 (QB); [2009] E.M.L.R. 17 .9–006
Wessex Dairies Ltd v Smith [1935] 2 K.B. 80 . . . . .1–039, 14–018, 14–021
West London Pipeline and Storage Ltd v Total UK Ltd [2008] EWHC 1729 (Comm); [2008] 2
    C.L.C. 258 17–003
Westdeutsche Bank v Islington LBC [1996] A.C. 669 . . . . .9–022, 9–028
Wheatley v Bell [1984] F.S.R. 16; [1982] 2 N.S.W.L.R. 544 3–058
White v Jones [195] 2 A.C. 207 . . . . .2–082, 3–191, 11–054
White v Sweden (42435/02) [2007] E.M.L.R. 1; (2008) 46 E.H.R.R. 3 13–009
Williams v Settle [1960] 1 W.L.R. 1072 9–045
Williams v Star Newspaper Co Ltd (1908) 24 T.L.R. 297 19–040
Williams v Williams (1817) 3 Mer. 157 1–014
Wilson v Rastall (1792) 4 T.R. 753 16–005
Winters v Mishcon de Reya [2008] EWHC 2419 .16–008, 16–010
Woodward v Hutchins [1977] 1 W.L.R. 760 . . . . .3–117, 3–118, 3–123, 3–124, 6–017,
                                                                    6–023, 6–061, 6–063, 6–064, 6–071
Woolgar v Chief of Sussex Police [2000] 1 W.L.R. 25 . . . . . .3–001, 3–024, 6–033, 6–034, 6–037
Worth Recycling Pty Ltd v Waste Recycling and Processing Pty Ltd [2009] N.S.W.C.A.
    354 16–011
Wright v Gasweld Pty Ltd (1991) 22 NSWLR 317 14–029
Wrotham Park Estate Co Ltd v Parkside Homes Ltd [1974] 1 W.L.R. 798 9–043
X (Children) (Morgan and others intervening), In re [2011] EWHC 1157 (Fam), [2012] 1 W.L.R.
    182 20–016
X (formerly Mary Bell) v O'Brien [2003] EWHC 1101 . . . . .3–149, 7–020
X AG v Bank, A [1983] 2 All E.R. 464 10–011
X and Y v Netherlands (1986) 8 E.H.R.R. 235 . . . . .3–184, 7–018
X Ltd v Morgan-Grampion (Publishers) Ltd [1991] 1 A.C. 1 13–024
X v Persons Unknown [2006] EWHC 2783 (QB); [2007] E.M.L.R. 10 . . . . .7–054, 9–007, 9–008
X v Y [1988] 2 All E.R. 648 . . . . .11–030, 1–033, 13–023
Young v Robson Rhodes [1999] 3 All E.R. 524 16–010

TABLE OF CASES

Yovatt v Winyard (1820) 1 Jac. & W. 394 1–014
Z (A Minor) (Identification Restrictions on Publication), Re [1997] Fam. 1 11–041
Z Ltd v A-Z [1982] Q.B. 558; [1982] 2 W.L.R. 288 9–009
Z v Finland (1997) 25 E.H.R.R. 371 11–034
Z, Re [2009] EWHC 3621 (Fam); [2010] 2 F.L.R. 132; [2010] Fam. Law 458 . . . . 16–007, 16–010

TABLE OF STATUTES

1533	Clergy Act (25 Hen.8 c.16) 15–008
1535	Statute of Uses(27 Hen.8
	c.10) 1–001
1709	Statute of Anne. 1–005, 1–007
1858	Lord Cairns's Act (Chancery
	Amendment Act) (21 & 22 Vict.
	c.27) . . 1–038, 1–048, 2–063, 2–064,
	2–066,
	2–069, 2–074, 2–075,
	2–078, 2–081, 2–090,
	2–093, 9–015, 9–037,
	9–038, 9–039
1862	Companies Act (25 & 26 Vict. c.89)
	s.115 19–060
1871	Regulations of Railways Act (34 & 35
	Vict. c.78)
	s.6 19–034
1873	Supreme Court of Judicature Act (36 &
	37 Vict. c.66) 9–040
1879	Bankers' Books Evidence Act (42 & 43
	Vict. c.11) . . 10–006, 10–009, 12–013
	s.7 10–005
1911	Official Secrets Act (1 & 2 Geo.V
	c.28) 4–012
1921	Tribunal of Inquiry (Evidence) Act (11
	& 12 Geo.V c.7) 6–042
1933	Children and Young Persons Act (23 &
	24 Geo.V c.12)
	s.39 . . . . . 21–017, 21–021, 21–022
	(1) 21–005, 21–022
	s.49 21–022
1934	Law Reform (Miscellaneous Provisions)
	Act (25 & 25 Geo.V c.41)
	s.1(1) 3–190
1949	Wireless Telegraphy Act (12, 13 & 14
	Geo.VI c.54) 3–033
1956	Restrictive Trade Practices Act (4 & 5
	Eliz.2 c.68) . . . 6–010, 6–011, 6–012
1957	Solicitors Act (5 & 6 Eliz.2 c.27)
	s.29 16–037
1960	Administration of Justice (8 & 9 Eliz.2
	c.65) 21–024
	s.12 . . . . . 21–013, 21–021, 21–025,
	21–026
	(1) 21–024
	(a) 21–024
	(4) 21–026
1967	Abortion Act (15 & 16 Eliz.2
	c.87) 11–037
1968	Theft Act (c.60)
	s.4 2–049
	Medicines Act (c.67) 3–027
1970	Taxes Management Act
	(c.9) 3–021
	Supreme Court Act
	s.68 2–081

1974	Solicitors Act (c.47)
	s.31(1) 16–040
1975	Evidence (Proceedings in Other
	Jurisdictions) Act
	(c.34) 10–018
1980	Limitation Act (c.58)
	s.32 9–060
1981	Contempt of Court Act (c.49)
	s.4 20–014
	(2) 20–014
	s.10 . . . . . . 3–171, 13–017, 13–020,
	13–021, 13–023,
	13–024, 13–025
	s.11 20–014
	Senior Courts Act (c.54)
	s.34 20–044
	s.50 . . . . 1–038, 2–063, 9–037
	s.51(6) 16–029
	s.72 . . . . 2–029, 17–007
1983	Mental Health Act (c.20) 7–043
	Medical Act (c.54)
	s.35A 11–019
1984	Public Health (Control of Disease) Act
	(c.22) 11–037
	Dentists Act (c.24)
	s.33B 11–019
	County Courts Act (c.28)
	s.53 20–044
	Data Protection Act (c.35) 8–002, 8–007,
	8–020
	Police and Criminal Evidence Act
	(c.60) 3–018, 10–021, 13–015,
	19–071
	ss.8–12 11–037
	s.9 . 12–003, 12–012, 12–013, 13–015
	s.166 7–009
	Sch.1 . . . . 12–013, 13–015
1985	Companies Act (c.6) . . . 3–018, 12–013,
	17–014
	s.432 19–067
	s.452(1A) 12–013
	(1B) 12–013
1986	Animals (Scientific Procedures) Act
	(c.14) 6–051
	s.24 . . . . 3–023, 8–029
	Insolvency Act (c.45) . . . 3–018, 12–013
	s.221 10–010
	ss.234–236 3–020
	s.235 . . . . 3–023, 19–071
	s.236 . 3–019, 3–022, 3–023, 10–010,
	12–013,
	19–071
	s.366 12–013
	Financial Services Act
	(c.60) 6–024, 19–050, 19–051
1987	Banking Act (c.22) 6–041
	s.39 . . . . 6–041, 10–022

TABLE OF STATUTES

s.82	10–022
s.84	10–022
(6)	10–023
s.86	10–023

Criminal Justice Act (c.38). 3–018,
3–021, 3–022
    s.2 19–064
        (3) 3–019, 19–071
        (9) 3–021
        (10) 3–021
    s.3(3) 3–021

1988 Access to Medical Reports Act
    (c.28) 11–036
Criminal Justice Act (c.33)
    s.159 20–014
Road Traffic Act (c.52)
    s.172 11–037

1989 Children Act (c.41) . . .15–018, 16–045,
16–048, 17–018,
19–039,
21–002, 21–024,
21–028
    Pt IV 21–028
    Pt V 21–028
    s.1 21–016
    s.97 . . . . .21–021, 21–023
        (2) 21–025
        (2)–(9) 21–023
    s.98(2) 21–028

1990 Access to Health Records Act
    (c.23) 11–036
Human Fertilisation and Embryology
Act (c.37)
    s.31 8–023
    s.33 8–023

1996 Employment Rights Act
    (c.18) 14–007
    s.43J 14–007
Arbitration Act (c.23) . . 22–017, 22–019
    s.67 22–017
    s.68 . . . . . .22–017, 22–018, 22–020
    s.69 . . . . .22–017, 22–035
Broadcasting Act (c.55) . . 2–010, 7–073
    s.107(1) 13–012
    s.130 13–012

1997 Civil Procedure Act (c.12)
    s.7 9–056

1998 Public Interest Disclosure Act
    (c.23) 14–007
Data Protection Act (c.29) 3–139, 8–003,
8–005, 8–006, 8–008,
8–009, 8–010, 8–012,
8–013, 8–016, 8–019,
8–020, 8–021, 8–026,
8–032, 8–033, 11–010,
11–035
    Pt I 8–021
    Pt II 8–021
    s.1 . . . . .8–011, 8–012, 8–013, 8–015,
8–018
        (1) 8–016
    s.2 8–017

    s.4 8–019
    s.7 . . . . .8–013, 8–020
        (1) 8–020
    s.9A 8–014
    s.10 8–020
    s.11 8–020
    s.12 8–020
    s.13 8–020
    s.14 8–020
    s.17 8–018
    ss.18–20 8–018
    s.21 8–026
    s.27 8–021
    s.28 8–022
    s.29 8–022
    s.30 8–022
    s.31 8–022
    s.32 . . . . .8–022, 8–024
    s.33 8–022
    s.33A 8–014
    s.34 . . . . .3–139, 8–022
    s.35 . . . . .3–139, 8–022
    s.35A 8–022
    s.36 8–021
    s.38 8–023
    s.40 8–008
    s.43 8–008
    s.47 8–026
    s.51 8–009
    s.55 8–026
        (1) 8–026
        (2) 8–026, 8–027
        (ca) 8–027
    s.55A 8–008
    s.60 8–008
    s.68 8–012
    Sch.1, Pt I 8–019
    Sch.1, Pt II 8–019
        paras 2, 3 8–019
    Sch.2 8–019
    Sch.3 8–019
    Schs 1–3 3–139
    Sch.7, para.1 8–022
        para.2 8–022
        para.3 8–022
        para.4 8–022
        para.5 8–022
        para.6 8–022
        para.7 8–022
        para.8 8–022
        para.9 8–022
        para.10 8–022
        para.11 8–022
    Sch.11 8–012
    Sch.12 8–012

Human Rights Act (c.42) . 1–051, 1–055,
                2–001, 2–003, 2–013,
                6–049, 6–052, 7–004,
                7–011, 7–017, 11–047,
                13–003, 13–017,
                13–021, 18–007,
                19–012, 19–014,
                19–090, 21–006
    s.6 . . . . 1–058, 2–016, 7–002, 7–017,
                7–019,
                7–021, 21–029, 21–033
    s.7 . . . . 2–015, 9–049
    s.8 . . . . 2–015, 9–049
    s.12   . . 6–048, 7–003, 9–002, 13–010
        (2) 21–006
        (3) . . 7–003, 7–050, 9–003, 13–010
        (4) 7–003, 7–049, 13–010
        (b) 13–010
1999 Youth Justice and Criminal Evidence
        Act (c.23)
        Sch.2, para.2 21–022
        Greater London Authority Act
        (c.29) 6–053
        s.298(3) 6–053
2000 Financial Services and Markets Act
        (c.8) 3–018
        Pt 11 12–013
        s.146 12–013
        s.147 12–013
        s.175(5) 12–013
        s.348 19–059
        Terrorism Act (c.11) . . . 12–013, 13–015
        Regulation of Investigatory Powers Act
        (c.23) 3–033, 16–043
        Freedom of Information Act
        (c.36) . . 8–004, 8–006, 8–009, 8–032
        Pt 1 8–008
        Pt II 8–028
        Pt IV 8–030
        Pt V 8–031
        Pt VI 8–031
        s.1(1) 8–027
        s.3 8–027
        ss.8–17 8–027
        s.14 8–027
        s.19 8–027
        s.21 8–028
        s.22 8–028
        s.23 8–028
        s.24 8–028
        s.26 8–028
        s.27 8–028
        s.28 8–028
        s.29 8–028
        s.30 8–028
        s.31 8–028
        s.32 8–028
        s.33 8–028
        s.35 8–028
        s.36 8–028
        s.37 8–028
        s.38 8–028

        s.39 . . . . 8–007, 8–028
        s.40 . . . . 8–005, 8–028
        s.41 8–029
        s.42 8–029
        s.43 8–029
        s.44 8–029
        s.47 8–009
        s.50 8–008
        s.52 8–008
        s.54 8–030
        s.56 8–030
        s.77 8–030
        Sch.1 8–027
2001 Health and Social Care Act (c.15)
        s.60 11–022
2002 Proceeds of Crime Act
        (c.29) 9–011, 12–018
        ss.327–329 . 16–018, 16–019, 16–020
        s.328 . . . . 12–013, 16–019
        s.330 . . . . 12–013, 16–021
        (6)(b) 16–021
        (10) 16–021
        (11) 16–021, 16–023
        s.333A 12–013, 16–022
        ss.333B–333E 12–013
        s.333D 16–022
        s.338 . . . . 16–018, 16–020
        Sch.9 16–021
        Police Reform Act (c.30) 19–048
        ss.20, 21 19–048
        Adoption and Children Act
        (c.38) 21–023, 21–024
        Freedom of Information (Scotland) Act
        (asp 13) 8–016, 13–009
2003 Communications Act (c.21)
        s.3 13–012
        (2)(f) 13–012
        Criminal Justice (International
        Co-operation) Act
        (c.32) 10–021
        s.16 10–021
        s.19 10–021
        ss.32–46 10–021
2005 Prevention of Terrorism Act
        (c.2) 19–084
        s.2 13–005
        Sch.1, para.4 19–085
        Mental Capacity Act (c.9) 11–046,
                                        20–008
        Serious Organised Crime and Police Act
        (c.15) 3–018, 12–013, 13–015
2006 National Health Service Act
        s.251 11–022
2007 Legal Services Act (c.29) 16–040
        Sch.4, Pt 1 16–041
2008 Criminal Justice and Immigration Act
        (c.4) 8–027
        Health and Social Care Act (c.14)
        s.64 11–037
2010 Children, Schools and Families Act
        (c.26) 21–024
        Sch.3(2) 21–023

para.3 21–022
Sch.4(2) 21–023
2011 Finance Act (c.11) 12–013
Sch.23 12–013

Terrorism Prevention and Investigation
Measures Act (c.23) 19–085

TABLE OF STATUTORY INSTRUMENTS

1965 Rules of the Supreme Court (SI
1965/1776)
RSC Ord.24, r.14A . . 20–025, 20–034
RSC Ord.85 16–017
1991 Abortion Regulations (SI
1991/499) 11–037
Family Proceedings Rules (SI
1991/1247) 11–020, 21–019
Pt XI 21–027
r.4.16(7) 21–019
r.4.23 21–027
r.10.20A 21–027
(3) 21–027
r.11.4 21–027
(1) 21–027
Family Proceedings Courts (Children
Act 1989) Rules (SI
1991/1395) 21–019
1992 National Health Service (General
Medical Services) Regulations (SI
1992/635)
Sch.2, para.36(6) 11–020
1995 Reporting of Injuries, Diseases and
Dangerous Occurrences Regulations
(SI 1995/3163) 11–037
2000 Data Protection (Notification and
Notification Fees) Regulations (SI
2000/188) 8–018
Data Protection (Subject Access) (Fees
and Miscellaneous Provisions)
Regulations (SI
2000/191) 8–020
Data Protection (Subject Access
Modification) (Health) Order (SI
2000/413) 11–035
Data Protection (Subject Access
Modification) (Education) Order (SI
2000/414) 15–001
Data Protection (Processing of Sensitive
Personal Data) Order (SI
2000/417) 8–025
Data Protection (Miscellaneous Subject
Access Exemptions) Order (SI
2000/419)
Sch. Pt I 8–023
Pt II 8–023
2001 Financial Services and Markets Act
2000 (Disclosure of Confidential
Information) Regulations (SI
2001/2188) 17–006
Financial Services and Markets Act
2000 (Confidential Information)
(Bank of England) Regulations (SI
2001/3648) 17–006

2002 Health Service (Control of Patient
Information) Regulations (SI
2002/1438) 11–022, 11–035
reg.2 11–022
reg.3 11–022
reg.4 11–022
reg.7 11–022
Data Protection (Processing of Sensitive
Personal Data (Elected
Representatives) (SI
2002/2905) 8–025
2003 Electronic Communications (EC
Directive) Regulations (SI
2003/2426) 8–007
2004 National Health Service (General
Medical Services Contracts)
Regulations (SI 2004/291)
Sch.6, Pt 5 11–020
Freedom of Information and Data
Protection (Appropriate Limit and
Fees) Regulations (SI
2004/3244) 8–016
Environmental Information Regulations
(SI 2004/3391) 8–007, 8–028
2005 Education (Pupil Information) (England)
Regulations (SI
2005/1437) 15–001
Family Procedure (Adoption) Rules (SI
2005/2795) 21–019
2006 Data Protection (Processing of Sensitive
Personal Data) Order (SI
2006/2068) 8–025
2007 Court of Protection Rules (SI
2007/1744)
r.90 20–008
rr.90–92 20–008
2009 Data Protection (Processing of Sensitive
Personal Data) Order (SI
2009/1811) 8–025
INSPIRE Regulations (SI
2009/3157) 8–007
2010 Regulation of Investigatory Powers
(Covert Human Intelligence Sources:
Matters Subject to Legal Privilege)
Order (SI 2010/123) 16–043
Health Protection (Notification)
Regulations (SI
2010/659) 11–037
Data Protection (Monetary Penalties)
Order (SI 2010/910) 8–008
Health Protection (Notification) (Wales)
Regulations (SI
2010/1546) 11–037
Family Procedure Rules (SI
2010/2955) . 21–019, 21–021, 21–026
r.12.73 . . . . 21–026, 21–027
(1) 21–026

(c) 21–027
(2) 21–027
r.12.75 . . . . 21–026, 21–027
(1) 21–027
r.14.14 21–026
r.27.10 21–019
r.27.11 21–020
2011 Criminal Procedure Rules (SI
2011/1709)
Pt 28 17–003

2012 Data-gathering Powers (Relevant Data)
Regulations (SI
2012/847) 12–013
Data Protection (Processing of Sensitive
Personal Data) Order (SI
2012/1978) 8–025

TABLE OF CIVIL PROCEDURE RULES

1998   Civil Procedure Rules (SI
     1998/3132) 22–027
     rr.5.4A–5.4D 20–018
     PD12G 21–026
     PD14E 21–026
     Pt 18 20–022
     r.18.1 20–022
     r.18.2 20–022
     Pt 25 . . . . 9–056, 20–022
     r.27.11 21–020
     PD27B, para.2.4 21–020
     PD27C, para.2.4 21–020
     Pt 31 19–082
     r.31 . . . . 20–020, 20–022
     r.31.12 20–027
     r.31.16 17–004
     r.31.17 . . . . 17–004, 20–044, 20–057
     r.31.19 . . . . 17–003, 19–082
     (5), (6) 17–003
     r.31.20 18–057
     r.31.22 . . . . 20–020, 20–022, 20–023,
                   20–024, 20–025,
                    20–039, 20–042,
                    20–043, 20–045,
                    20–049, 20–052,
                    20–053, 20–054,
                    20–056

     (1)(a) 20–055
     (c) 20–026
     (2) 20–034, 20–041, 20–054,
                   20–055, 22–056
     PD31B 21–020
     r.32 20–021
     r.32.12 20–021
     Pt 34 10–018
     r.34 . . . . 20–045, 20–047
     r.34.12 20–047
     r.39.2(1) 20–007
     (3) 20–010, 20–013
     (4) 20–014
     r.48.7 16–029
     r.62.10 22–017

CHAPTER 1

Historical Introduction

EARLY ORIGINS

In *Coco v A.N. Clark (Engineers) Ltd* Megarry J. said[1]:

> "The equitable jurisdiction in cases of breach of confidence is ancient; confidence is the cousin of trust. The Statute of Uses, 1535, is framed in terms of 'use, confidence or trust'; and a couplet, attributable to Sir Thomas More, Lord Chancellor avers that
> 'Three things are to be . . . in Conscience: Fraud, Accident and things of Confidence.'
> (See 1 Rolle's Abridgement 374). In the middle of the last century, the great case of *Prince Albert v Strange* (1849) 1 Mac. & G. 25 reasserted the doctrine."

1–001

It is doubtful, however, whether "confidence" in the time of Sir Thomas More bore any resemblance to its present day meaning. Bacon in his "Essay on the Statute of Uses" explained the meaning of confidence as follows:

> "The special trust lawful is, as when I infeoff some of my friends, because I am to go beyond the seas, or because I would free the land from some statute, or bond, which I am to enter into, or upon intent to be reinfeoffed, or intent to be vouched, and so to suffer a common recovery, or upon intent that the feoffees shall infeoff over a stranger, and infinite the like intents and purposes, which fall out in men's dealings and occasions; and this we call confidence, . . . "

Moreover, for more than a century before *Prince Albert v Strange* courts of equity were decidedly cautious in their approach to cases which would now be regarded as involving confidence and did not proceed on any broad or general jurisdiction.

The early reported cases concerned letters, literary works and recipes for medicines. In *Pope v Curl*[2] Alexander Pope obtained an injunction against the bookseller Curl restraining him from selling a book entitled "Letters from Swift, Pope and others". The Lord Chancellor, Lord Hardwicke, continued the injunction in relation to the letters from Pope to Swift but not vice versa. The basis of the distinction was that property in such letters belonged to the author; that the sending of a letter did not constitute a gift to the receiver; that the receiver had only a "special property", possibly property in the paper and at most joint property with the writer; and that such limited property did not give to the receiver licence to publish to the world.

1–002

---

[1] [1969] R.P.C. 41 at 46.
[2] (1741) 2 Atk. 342.

1

1–003   In *Duke of Queensberry v Shebbeare*[3] the personal representatives of Lord Clarendon obtained an injunction restraining the defendant from publishing a previously unpublished history by Lord Clarendon. Dr Shebbeare's case was that he had acquired the manuscript from his co-defendant Mr Gwynne, whose father had been given it by Lord Clarendon. The injunction was continued on the ground that it was not to be presumed that Lord Clarendon had thereby intended Mr Gwynne to "have the profit of multiplying it in print".

1–004   These and other cases of unauthorised publication of writings were analysed in *Millar v Taylor*.[4] The importance of this copyright case lies in its discussion of common law rights of property and in the reliance placed on it in *Prince Albert v Strange*.[5] The facts were simple. Millar claimed ownership of a book of poems by James Thompson, entitled "The Seasons", copies of which he printed and sold. Taylor also printed and sold copies of the work, acting without Millar's permission. Millar sued for damages for trespass on the case. He brought the action in the Court of King's Bench, presided over by Lord Mansfield.

1–005   The case was argued first in June 1767, but the judges were unable to agree and it was ordered to be re-argued. It was argued for the second time in 1768. Judgment was finally delivered in April 1769, the plaintiff having, in the meantime, died. Lord Mansfield recorded that it was the first occasion since his appointment on which the court had been unable to reach unanimity despite repeated attempts to do so. Lord Mansfield, Willes and Aston JJ. found for the plaintiff. Yates J. dissented.

There were three issues:

(1)   whether copyright existed at common law;
(2)   if it did, whether it was lost on first publication;
(3)   whether any such common law right was removed by the Statute of Anne 1709, under which authors of unpublished works could obtain a copyright for a term of 14 years, renewable for a further 14 years.

On the common law questions, the defendant's argument was that there was no common law right of property detached from a physical object, and therefore no right of literary property. The owner of a document had the right to its use, but once he transferred to another the ownership of the physical document, or a copy of it, that person acquired at common law an equal right to make such use of it as he pleased.

1–006   This argument was rejected by the majority. Lord Mansfield who had great experience of the subject, having (as he said) appeared as counsel in most of the cases cited in Chancery, said[6]:

> "I use the word 'copy' in the technical sense in which that name or term has been used for ages, to signify an incorporeal right to the sole printing and publishing of somewhat intellectual, communicated by letters. It has all along been expressly admitted 'that, by the common law, an author is intitled to the copy of his own work until it has been once printed and published by his authority;' and 'that the four

---

[3] (1758) 2 Eden 329.
[4] (1769) 4 Bur. 2303.
[5] (1849) 1 De G. & Sm. 652, (1849) 1 Mac. & G. 25.
[6] *Millar v Taylor* (1769) 4 Bur. 2303 at 2396.

cases in Chancery,[7] cited for that purpose, are agreeable to the common law; and the relief was properly given, in consequence of the legal right.'

The property in the copy, thus abridged, is equally an incorporeal right to print a set of intellectual ideas or modes of thinking, communicated in a set of words and sentences and modes of expression. It is equally detached from the manuscript, or any other physical existence whatsoever. . . .

From what source, then, is the common law drawn, which is admitted to be so clear, in respect of the copy before publication? From this argument—because it is just, that an author should reap the pecuniary profits of his own ingenuity and labour. It is just, that another should not use his name, without his consent. It is fit that he should judge when to publish, or whether he ever will publish. It is fit he should not only choose the time, but the manner of publication; how many; what volume; what print. It is fit, he should choose to whose care he will trust the accuracy and correctness of the impression; in whose honesty he will confide, not to foist in additions: with other reasonings of the same effect. . . .

But the same reasons hold, after the author has published. He can reap no pecuniary profit, if, the next moment after his work comes out, it may be pirated upon worse paper and in worse print, and in a cheaper volume."

Yates J., dissenting, observed that no logical distinction could be drawn between literary compositions and any other production of the brain, such as mechanical inventions.

The matter was considered by the House of Lords in *Donaldson v Beckett*,[8] on appeal from a decree of the Court of Chancery founded on the decision in *Millar v Taylor*.[9] The opinions of the judges were taken. A majority agreed with *Millar v Taylor* on the common law questions, but not on the effect of the Statute of Anne 1709. The House of Lords voted to reverse the decree. On the common law questions, the views of the majority of the judges in *Millar v Taylor* were ultimately to be reversed by the House of Lords, but not until 80 years later in *Jefferys v Boosey*.[10]   **1–007**

In *Thompson v Stanhope*[11] Lord Apsley L.C. granted an injunction to restrain the publication of letters, following the precedents of *Forrester v Waller*, *Webb v Rose*, *Pope v Curl* and *Duke of Queensberry v Shebbeare*. No reference is made in the report to *Donaldson v Beckett*, decided by the House of Lords four weeks earlier, nor to *Millar v Taylor*.   **1–008**

Those cases and the principles on which they rested were considered in a trio of cases in equity between 1813 and 1818—*Percival v Phipps*, *Southey v Sherwood* and *Gee v Pritchard*.   **1–009**

In *Percival v Phipps*[12] the defendant Phipps had published in a newspaper a letter purportedly written by the plaintiff to the defendant Mitford. The plaintiff had subsequently stated publicly that it was a forgery. Mitford asserted that it was genuine and that he had passed it to Phipps with the plaintiff's consent. To corroborate his version Mitford passed to Phipps a number of other letters from the plaintiff, which Phipps wished to publish in order to rebut the allegation that   **1–010**

---

[7] *Webb v Rose* May 24, 1732, cited 4 Bur. 2330; *Pope v Curl* (1741) 2 Atk. 342; *Forrester v Waller* June 13, 1741, cited 4 Burr. 2331 and *Duke of Queensberry v Shebbeare* (1758) 2 Eden 329.
[8] (1774) 4 Bur. 2408.
[9] (1769) 4 Bur. 2303.
[10] (1854) 4 H.L.C. 815.
[11] (1774) Amb. 737.
[12] (1813) 35 E.R. 225.

he had published false information on spurious authority. The plaintiff sought an injunction to restrain him from doing so. The application was based on grounds both of literary property and that the publication would amount to a breach of confidence. The application failed.

1–011 The Vice-Chancellor expressed doubt whether a court of equity could restrain publication of private correspondence on grounds of breach of confidence, independent of contract or a right of property in the correspondence. He also took a restricted view of the class of correspondence in which there could be a right of property based on the concept of a literary work, and he held that the defendants' reasons for publication were sufficient for a court of equity not to intervene.

1–012 In *Southey v Sherwood*[13] Lord Eldon L.C. refused the poet Southey an injunction to restrain the publication of a poem which he had placed with a publisher 23 years earlier, holding that such injunctions were only granted to prevent the use of that which was the exclusive property of another.

1–013 *Gee v Pritchard*[14] was another case of an injunction to restrain the publication of letters. The plaintiff claimed both that the letters were her property and that their proposed publication would be a breach of private confidence. Lord Eldon granted the injunction, following the precedents of his predecessors Lord Hardwicke and Lord Apsley, but he did so expressly and only on the ground of the plaintiffs' right of property.

1–014 Lord Eldon also took a cautious approach to claims for injunctions to restrain misuse of secret medical recipes for which either there was no patent or the patent had expired. He refused injunctions in *Newbery v James*[15] and *Williams v Williams*,[16] observing in the latter that he did not think that on general principles the court ought to struggle to protect such secrets. In *Yovatt v Winyard*[17] Lord Eldon granted an injunction restraining the defendant from using or communicating certain recipes for veterinary medicines, but on the ground (according to the headnote) that he had obtained knowledge of them by a breach of trust. The defendant had been employed by the plaintiff and during his employment surreptitiously obtained access to the plaintiffs' books of recipes, which he copied. The report does not give Lord Eldon's reasons beyond stating that he granted the injunction upon the ground of there having been a breach of trust and confidence.

1–015 *Green v Folgham*[18] also involved a breach of trust in relation to a medical recipe, but in that case the recipe was the subject of an express trust.

1–016 In *Abernethy v Hutchinson*[19] the plaintiff was a distinguished surgeon and lecturer at St Bartholomew's Hospital. The defendants were publishers and sellers of *The Lancet*. The action was brought for an injunction to restrain them from reproducing the plaintiff's lectures, the text of which must have been taken down in shorthand by a student and supplied to the defendants for publication contrary to the plaintiff's express wishes.

---

[13] (1817) 2 Mep. 435.
[14] (1818) 2 Swans. 402.
[15] (1817) 2 Mer. 446.
[16] (1817) 3 Mer. 157.
[17] (1820) 1 Jac. & W. 394.
[18] (1823) 1 Sim. & St. 398.
[19] (1824) 3 L.J.Ch. 209.

After days of argument, during which various possible grounds of relief were **1–017** canvassed, Lord Eldon finally granted an injunction on the ground that there was an implied contract between the plaintiff and his students that they would not publish his lectures for profit; and that, although there was no implied contract between the plaintiff and the defendants, they must have procured the text of the lectures in an undue manner from those who were under a contract not to publish, and that this was a form of fraud in a third party sufficient to enable the court to grant an injunction against them.[20]

In summary, the cases before *Prince Albert v Strange*[21] did not establish any **1–018** general right of relief in respect of misuse or threatened misuse of confidential information. The cases in which the courts intervened may be classified as cases of actual or threatened:

(1) infringement by the defendant of a right of property recognised at common law;
(2) breach of contract by the defendant;
(3) breach of trust by the defendant; or
(4) use by the defendant of information knowingly obtained from a party who was himself acting in breach of contract or trust in supplying it.

Prince Albert v Strange

In *Prince Albert v Strange*[22] the plaintiff obtained an injunction against the **1–019** defendant restraining him from publishing a catalogue of private etchings made by Queen Victoria and Prince Albert. As well as describing the etchings, the catalogue announced a proposed exhibition of them and implied falsely that the publication had royal consent. The catalogue was compiled from copies surreptitiously made by an employee of a printer in Windsor, to whom plates of the etchings had been sent for the purpose of making copies for the Queen and Prince.

The plaintiff's principal argument was that publication of the catalogue **1–020** infringed their right of property in the etchings on the basis of *Millar v Taylor*[23] and similar authorities. Secondly, it was argued that the information in the catalogue was derived from a breach of trust, and therefore the plaintiff was entitled to an injunction against a knowing recipient by analogy with *Abernethy v Hutchinson*.[24] The defendant's argument was that mere description of the etchings did not infringe any property right of the Queen and Prince at common law and that he was not party to any breach of trust.

The Vice-Chancellor, Sir Knight Bruce, held in favour of the plaintiff on both **1–021** grounds and his judgment was upheld on appeal by Lord Cottenham L.C. On the issue of property, the Vice-Chancellor adopted Yates J.'s argument in *Millar v Taylor* that there was no difference between literary works and other products of

---

[20] See also *Tipping v Clarke* (1843) 2 Hare 383. A person who surreptitiously obtained information which he could only have obtained from a person in breach of contract in communicating it could not be permitted to avail himself of that breach of contract.

[21] (1849) 1 De G. & Sm. 652, (1849) 1 Mac. & G. 25.

[22] (1849) 1 De G. & Sm. 652, (1849) 1 Mac. & G. 25.

[23] (1769) 4 Bur. 2303.

[24] (1824) 3 L.J.Ch. 209.

the brain, such as mechanical or artistic creations. He held also that the owner's common law right of property was infringed as much by description without consent as by copying without consent. On the second issue the Vice-Chancellor regarded the circumstances as so obviously redolent of the etchings having been obtained by a breach of trust as to warrant an injunction on that ground.

1–022   Lord Cottenham L.C. said at the outset of his judgment that the importance attached to the case arose entirely from the exalted station of the plaintiff, and not from the facts, which so clearly fell within established principles as not to cause any difficulty. After summarising the facts, he said[25]:

> "It was said by one of the learned counsel for the Defendant, that the injunction must rest upon the ground of property or breach of trust; both appear to me to exist. The property of an author or composer of any work, whether of literature, art or science, in such work unpublished and kept for his private use or pleasure, cannot be disputed, after the many decisions in which that proposition has been affirmed or assumed."

He continued[26]:

> "Upon the first question, therefore, that of property, I am clearly of opinion that the exclusive right and interest of the Plaintiff in the composition or work in question being established, and there being no right or interest whatever in the Defendant, the Plaintiff is entitled to the injunction of this Court to protect him against the invasion of such right and interest by the Defendant, which the publication of any catalogue would undoubtedly be; but this case by no means depends solely upon the question of property, for a breach of trust, confidence, or contract, would of itself entitle the Plaintiff to an injunction . . .
>
> If, then, these compositions were kept private, except as to some given to private friends and some sent to Mr Brown for the purpose of having certain impressions taken, the possession of the Defendant, or of his intended partner Judge, must have originated in a breach of trust, confidence or contract, in Brown or some person in his employ taking more impressions than were ordered, and retaining the extra number, or in some person to whom copies were given, which is not to be supposed, but which, if the origin of the possession of the Defendant or Judge, would be equally a breach of trust, confidence or contract, Duke of Queensberry v Shebbeare (2 Eden 329); and upon the evidence on behalf of the Plaintiff, and in the absence of any explanation on the part of the Defendant, I am bound to assume that the possession of the etchings by the Defendant or Judge has its foundations in a breach of trust, confidence or contract, as Lord Eldon did in the case of Mr Abernethy's lectures (3 Law J. Chanc. 209); and upon this ground also I think the Plaintiff's title to the injunction sought to be discharged, fully established."

Lord Cottenham's observation that the case fell clearly within established principles did less than justice to the defendant's arguments. On the question of property, there was substantial force in the argument that the case went significantly beyond *Millar v Taylor*[27] or any other precedent and that mere description of the etchings did not involve any usurpation of the plaintiff's ownership. On the question of equity, the case fell within the principle of

---

[25] *Prince Albert v Strange* (1848) 1 Mac. & G. 25 at 42.

[26] *Prince Albert v Strange* (1848) 1 Mac. & G. 25 at 44.

[27] (1769) 4 Bur. 2303.

Abernethy v Hutchinson[28] if the circumstances were such that the defendant must have known of the unlawful conduct of the person showing him the etchings, for in that case (as in *Abernethy v Hutchinson*) his own conduct would be regarded in equity as a form of fraud by a third party. The circumstances were suspicious, but the defendant denied on affidavit any knowledge or suspicion of unlawfulness.

The decision has been treated as authority for the grant of an injunction against someone who has acquired information to which he was not entitled, without notice of any breach of duty on the part of the person who imparted it to him, but who cannot claim to be a purchaser for value.[29] In this respect also the case did not fall within any previously settled principles.

1–023

More generally it has been seen as a landmark case because of the broad statement that "a breach of trust, confidence or contract would of itself entitle the plaintiff to an injunction", although it is questionable whether Lord Cottenham was there intending to lay down three independent categories in which an injunction would be granted, or merely using a compendious phrase wide enough to cover the facts of the case without intending or attempting any precise definition of the legal requirements. The trust or confidence owed by Brown to the plaintiff arose from his contract, and Lord Cottenham's judgment does not suggest that he was intending to consider them in isolation.

1–024

The century after *Prince Albert v Strange*

During the 100 years between *Prince Albert v Strange* and *Saltman Engineering Co Ltd v Campbell Engineering Co Ltd*,[30] the main cases on confidentiality are significant for their lack of any uniform jurisprudential basis. The confidences were mostly commercial and arose generally in the context of contracts, such as contracts of partnership, employment, agency or sale.

1–025

In *Morison v Moat*[31] the action arose from a partnership to manufacture and sell "Morison's Universal Medicine". The medicine was not the subject of any patent. The original partners were the plaintiffs' father, who was the inventor of the medicine, and the defendant's father. The plaintiffs' father disclosed the secret of the recipe to the defendant's father on terms that he was not to tell anyone else. Shortly before his death, the defendant's father gave the recipe to the defendant. After the expiry of the partnership the defendant manufactured and sold the medicine for his own account. The plaintiffs, to whom the recipe had been bequeathed under their father's will, obtained an injunction to restrain the defendant. Turner V.C. said[32]:

1–026

"That the Court has exercised jurisdiction in cases of this nature does not, I think, admit of any question. Different grounds have indeed been assigned for the exercise of that jurisdiction. In some cases it has been referred to property, in others to contract, and in others, again, it has been treated as founded upon trust or confidence, meaning, as I conceive, that the Court fastens the obligation on the conscience of the party, and enforces it against him in the same manner as it

[28] (1824) 3 L.J.Ch. 209.

[29] *Printers & Finishers Ltd v Holloway* [1965] R.P.C. 239 at 253 and 257, per Cross J.

[30] (1948) 65 R.P.C. 203.

[31] (1851) 9 Hare 241, affirmed (1852) 21 L.J.Ch. (N.S.) 248.

[32] (1851) 9 Hare 241 at 255.

enforces against a party to whom a benefit is given the obligation of performing a promise on the faith of which the benefit has been conferred; but, upon whatever grounds the jurisdiction is founded, the authorities leave no doubt as to the exercise of it."

1–027 The approach of taking the jurisdiction as established, without further inquiry into its jurisprudential basis, has been followed in many subsequent cases with the consequence that the uncertainty to which the Vice-Chancellor referred has continued. The Vice-Chancellor did, however, provide the earliest judicial definition of what was meant by "trust or confidence" for the purposes of this jurisdiction.

1–028 The Vice-Chancellor dealt with the defendant's argument that the effect of an injunction would be to give the plaintiffs a better right than that of a patentee by saying that[33]:

> " . . . what we have to deal with here is, not the right of the Plaintiffs against the world, but their right against the Defendant. It may well be that the Plaintiffs have no title against the world in general, and may yet have a good title against this Defendant . . . ."

Despite the language of title, it would seem that the injunction must have been based on a personal obligation of the defendant towards the plaintiffs, rather than a property right in the plaintiffs; for if they had a right of property, it is difficult to see why it would not be good against the world.

1–029 The Vice-Chancellor also commented, without having to decide the point, that it might have been different if the defendant were a purchaser for value of the secret without notice of any obligation affecting it. This too remains an unsettled question.

1–030 *Gartside v Outram*[34] is best known as the origin of the "defence of iniquity", but it also involved consideration of the basis of the jurisdiction. The plaintiff brokers filed a bill for an injunction to restrain a former clerk from disclosing any of their dealings. The defendant in his answer stated that the plaintiffs were in the habit of defrauding their principals, and in support of his answer he filed interrogatories, to which the plaintiffs objected. It was held that there was no privilege to prevent them from answering, the discovery being relevant to the defendant's answer which, if proved, would be a defence to the bill. Wood V.C. said[35]:

> "The equity upon which the bill is founded is a perfectly plain and simple one, recognized by a number of authorities and most salutary to be enforced, by which any person standing in the confidential relation of a clerk or servant is prohibited, subject to certain exceptions, from disclosing any part of the transactions of which he thus acquires knowledge. But there are exceptions to this confidence, or perhaps, rather only nominally, and not really exceptions. The true doctrine is, that there is no confidence as to the disclosure of iniquity. You cannot make me the confidant of a crime or a fraud, and be entitled to close up my lips upon any secret which you have the audacity to disclose to me relating to any fraudulent intention on your part: such a confidence cannot exist."

---

[33] *Prince Albert v Strange* (1851) 9 Hare 241 at 258.

[34] (1857) 26 L.J.Ch. (N.S.) 113.

[35] (1857) 26 L.J.Ch. (N.S.) 113 at 114.

This places the jurisdiction on the relationship between the parties, although at the end of his judgment Wood V.C. said[36]:

"The real ground of the jurisdiction, as it is properly put, is founded first upon property, because the Court attempts not to interfere with morals, except in administering civil rights connected with rights of property. There is the property of the employer in those secrets of his business which he is obliged to communicate to others, and which are not to be trifled with. It is a sacred and solemn deposit, but there is no property in these transactions with this gentlemen which were of the character I have been describing, and in his answer he has made no disclosures except as to these fraudulent transactions."

Although Wood V.C. said that the court was concerned with the administration of civil rights connected with rights of property and not morals, he was clearly influenced by considerations of public interest in holding that there could be no property in secrets of an iniquitous character.

In *Pollard v Photographic Company*[37] North J. took a different approach. The   **1–031** plaintiff had photographs of herself taken by the defendant. Without her consent, the defendant used one of the negatives to make a form of Christmas card and displayed a copy of it in his shop window for sale. The plaintiff obtained an injunction to restrain the defendant from selling copies of the photograph. North J. dismissed as irrelevant the defendant's argument that his conduct did not injure any property right of the plaintiff. He said[38]:

"The right to grant an injunction does not depend in any way on the existence of property as alleged; nor is it worth while to consider carefully the grounds upon which the old Court of Chancery used to interfere by injunction. But it is quite clear that, independently of any question as to the right at law, the Court of Chancery always had an original and independent jurisdiction to prevent what that Court considered and treated as a wrong, whether arising from a violation of an unquestionable right or from breach of contract or confidence, as was pointed out by Lord *Cottenham* in *Prince Albert v Strange*."

North J. compared the photographer to a person who obtained confidential information in the course of his employment and who would not be permitted to make improper use of it; and he held that it was an implied term of the defendant's contract that prints from the negative would be appropriated only to the plaintiff's use.

In *Merryweather v Moore*[39] Kekewich J. cited part of the passage from North   **1–032** J.'s judgment in *Pollard v Photographic Company* set out above and went on to say[40]:

" . . . it is sometimes difficult to say whether the Court has proceeded on the implied contract or the confidence, for I will put aside once for all any cases arising on express contract. Perhaps the real solution is that the confidence postulates an implied contract: that, where the Court is satisfied of the existence of the

---

[36] *Gartside v Outran* (1857) 26 L.J.Ch. (N.S.) 113.
[37] (1888) 40 Ch.D. 345.
[38] (1888) 40 Ch.D. 345 at 354.
[39] [1892] 2 Ch. 518.
[40] [1892] 2 Ch. 518 at 522.

confidential relation, then it at once infers or implies the contract arising from that confidential relation—a contract which thus calls into exercise the jurisdiction to which I have referred."

Implied contract can be a useful device, as in *Abernethy v Hutchinson*,[41] but it is not apparent why a relationship intended to be confidential need involve the postulation of a fictitious contract in order for equity to intervene. On the other hand the terms (whether express or, more usually, implied) on which any confidential relationship came into existence should rightly be regarded as fundamental whether in contract or in equity.

1–033   This approach was taken by the Court of Appeal in *Lamb v Evans*.[42] The plaintiff engaged the defendants on a commission basis to obtain advertisements for publication in a trade directory. The advertisers provided the defendants with blocks for printing their advertisements. The defendants subsequently went to work for a rival publication and used the same blocks for identical advertisements. The plaintiff obtained an injunction to prevent them from doing so.

1–034   The Court of Appeal decided the case on the basis of principles of agency. Lindley L.J. said[43]:

> "What right has any agent to use materials obtained by him in the course of his employment and for his employer against the interest of that employer? I am not aware that he has any such right. Such a use is contrary to the relation which exists between principal and agent. It is contrary to the good faith of the employment, and good faith underlies the whole of an agent's obligations to his principal."

Bowen L.J. went back to the source of the relationship. He said that the plaintiff's entitlement to an injunction[44]:

> " . . . depends entirely, I think, upon the terms upon which the employment was constituted through which the fiduciary relation of principal and agent came into existence. I think my Brothers have already during the course of the argument expressed what I fully believe, that there is no distinction between law and equity as regards the law of principal and agent. The common law, it is true, treats the matter from the point of view of an implied contract, and assumes that there is a promise to do that which is part of the bargain, or which can be fairly implied as part of the good faith which is necessary to make the bargain effectual. What is an implied contract or an implied promise in law? It is that promise which the law implies and authorises us to infer in order to give the transaction that effect which the parties must have intended it to have and without which it would be futile . . . It seems to me that in this case the proper inference to be drawn would be that it was part of the understanding that these materials were not to be used otherwise than for the purposes of the employment in the course of which they were obtained."

---

[41] (1824) 3 L.J.Ch. 209.
[42] [1893] 1 Ch. 218.
[43] [1893] 1 Ch. 218 at 226.
[44] [1893] 1 Ch. 218 at 229.

Lindley and Bowen L.JJ. both referred to the misuse of "materials", a point further emphasised by Kay L.J. After considering *Morison v Moat*,[45] *Abernethy v Hutchinson*[46] and *Prince Albert v Strange*,[47] he said[48]:

> "So that I think the doctrine . . . does extend to every case in which a man has obtained materials (I use the word advisedly, because it would be very difficult indeed to grant an injunction to prevent a man using his knowledge)—where a man has obtained materials while he was in the position of agent for another—materials which were obtained by him in the course of that agency and were to be used for the purposes for which his principal had employed him."

Subsequent development of the law has not been so confined. In *Reid and Sigrist Ltd v Moss and Mechanism Ltd*,[49] for example, Luxmoore J. said: **1–035**

> "Undoubtedly there is a well recognised rule in the law relating to Master and Servant that a servant cannot use to the detriment of his master information of a confidential or secret nature entrusted to the servant or learnt by him in the course of his employment. There are many cases in the books on the subject. In some of them it has been debated what is the precise ground to be assigned for the exercise of the jurisdiction of the Court. Is it to be referred to property or contract, or is it to be founded upon trust or confidence? But whatever may be the true ground on which the jurisdiction is founded there is no doubt as to its existence."

"Information of a confidential or secret nature" is potentially much wider than "materials". In *Printers & Finishers Ltd v Holloway*,[50] Cross J. said: **1–036**

> "The mere fact that the confidential information is not embodied in a document but is carried away by the employee in his head is not, of course, of itself a reason against the granting of an injunction to prevent its use or disclosure by him."

Nevertheless, Kay L.J. touched on a major problem when he referred in *Lamb v Evans* to the difficulty of extending the doctrine to the use of knowledge. There is not only the difficulty of enforcement, but also a potential clash between legitimate competing interests: on the one hand that secrets should be respected, and on the other hand that a skilled person should not be restricted from making use of his skills. The boundary between knowledge of particular secrets derived from confidential sources and more general knowledge may be elusive, particularly since the latter may be derived to a greater or lesser extent from the former. This topic has been considered in many subsequent cases, including notably *Herbert Morris Ltd v Saxelby*,[51] *Printers & Finishers Ltd v Holloway*[52] and *Faccenda Chicken Ltd v Fowler.*[53]

---

[45] (1851) 9 Hare 241.
[46] (1824) 3 L.J.Ch. 209.
[47] (1849) 1 De G. & Sm. 652, (1849) 1 Mac. & G. 25.
[48] [1893] 1 Ch. 218 at 236.
[49] (1932) 49 R.P.C. 461 at 480.
[50] [1965] R.P.C. 239 at 255.
[51] [1916] A.C. 688.
[52] [1965] R.P.C. 239.
[53] [1987] 1 Ch. 117.

1–037   No such problem arose in *Robb v Green*,[54] in which Kay L.J. was again a member of the Court of Appeal. An employee surreptitiously copied his employer's customer list for the purpose of soliciting orders from them after setting up in business on his own account. The claim was for damages, delivery up of the list and an injunction to restrain him from making use of the information so obtained.

1–038   The court followed the analysis of Bowen L.J. in *Lamb v Evans*, but, whilst he had said in that case that there was no distinction between the law and equity as regards the law of principal and agent, the court in *Robb v Green* did distinguish between the remedies available. Kay L.J. said that an injunction ought to be granted "either on the ground of breach of trust or breach of contract", and that "a document surreptitiously made in breach of the trust imposed in the servant clearly ought to be given up to be destroyed." He continued[55]:

> "As to the damages, I think there is more difficulty. The right to them depends on whether the conduct of the defendant can be regarded as a breach of an implied contract. According to the view taken by Bowen L.J. in *Lamb v Evans*, it can; and in the result I come to the conclusion that the judgment in that respect must be upheld."

This is in accordance with classical doctrine that damages cannot be awarded for breach of an equitable obligation except under the jurisdiction derived from Lord Cairns's Act.[56]

1–039   The crucial fact in *Robb v Green* was that the defendant copied the customer list while still in the plaintiff's employment. This point was emphasised in *Wessex Dairies Ltd v Smith*[57] by Maugham L.J., who noted that in *Robb v Green* the defendant was not restrained from sending out circulars to customers whose names he could remember.

1–040   The availability of equitable relief to restrain misuse of confidential information, not only by the confidant but also by a third party recipient, was reaffirmed by the Court of Appeal in *Ashburton v Pape*.[58] Copies of privileged letters written by Lord Ashburton to his solicitor had been obtained by the defendant from a clerk employed by the solicitor. Swinfen Eady L.J. said[59]:

> "The principle upon which the Court of Chancery has acted for many years has been to restrain the publication of confidential information improperly or surreptitiously obtained or of information imparted in confidence which ought not to be divulged. Injunctions have been granted to give effectual relief, that is not only to restrain the disclosure of confidential information, but to prevent copies being made of any record of that information, and, if copies have already been made, to restrain them from being further copied, and to restrain persons into whose possession that confidential information has come from themselves in turn divulging or propagating it."

---

[54] [1895] 2 Q.B. 315.

[55] [1895] 2 Q.B. 315 at 320.

[56] Chancery Amendment Act 1858 (now s.50 of the Senior Courts Act 1981).

[57] [1935] 2 K.B. 80 at 89.

[58] [1913] 2 Ch. 469.

[59] [1913] 2 Ch. 469 at 475.

In *Herbert Morris Ltd v Saxelby*[60] there was no misconduct by the defendant **1–041** during his employment, but the plaintiffs, who were manufacturers of lifting machinery, sought to enforce against him a covenant against being involved as principal, agent or employee, in the sale or manufacture of lifting machinery of various types within the United Kingdom for a term of seven years after the end of his employment. The plaintiffs had a leading position in the market. The defendant was an engineer. The covenant was held to be unenforceable.

The employers' argument was that the covenant was a reasonable provision for **1–042** the protection of their property, namely trade secrets and customer connection. The argument of counsel for the employee conceded that it was permissible for a clause to protect "the filching of the employer's property such as trade secrets or customers' connection" but objected to the covenant on the ground that its real object was to protect against mere competition. This argument was essentially adopted by the various members of the Judicial Committee.

Lord Atkinson contrasted, on the one hand, "trade secrets . . . , such as secret **1–043** processes of manufacture, which may be of great value" and documents containing commercially sensitive information, such as lists of customers and their requirements, all of which were to be regarded as "private and confidential documents, the property of the [plaintiffs]" and, on the other hand, more general employee know-how, saying[61]:

> "The respondent cannot, however, get rid of the impressions left upon his mind by his experience of the appellants' works; they are part of himself; and in my view he violates no obligation express or implied arising from the relation in which he stood to the appellants by using in the service of some persons other than them the general knowledge he has acquired of their scheme of organisation and methods of business."

Lord Parker said that[62]:

> " . . . the reason, and the only reason, for upholding such a restraint on the part of an employee is that the employer has some proprietary right, whether in the nature of trade connection or in the nature of trade secrets, for the protection of which such a restraint is—having regard to the duties of the employee—reasonably necessary. Such a restraint has, so far as I know, never been upheld if directed only to the prevention of competition or against the use of personal skill and knowledge acquired by the employee in his employer's business."

Lord Shaw also used the language of property[63]:

> "Trade secrets, the names of customers, all such things which in sound philosophical language are denominated objective knowledge—these may not be given away by a servant; they are his master's property, and there is no rule of public interest which prevents a transfer of them against the master's will being restrained. On the other hand, a man's aptitudes, his skill, his dexterity, his manual or mental ability—all those things which in sound philosophical language are not objective, but

---

[60] [1916] A.C. 688.
[61] [1916] A.C. 688 at 703.
[62] [1916] A.C. 688 at 710.
[63] *Herbert Morris Ltd v Saxelby* [1916] A.C. 688 at 714.

subjective—they may and they ought not to be relinquished by a servant; they are not his master's property; they are his own property; they are himself."

1–044   In *Mechancial and General Inventions Co v Austin*[64] the plaintiffs were patentees of a system for installing sun roofs in cars. They provided details to the defendants with a view to entering into a licence agreement, which did not materialise. The House of Lords upheld a finding by the jury that there was a contract whereby the information disclosed to the defendants was to be used only under a licence agreement and also its award of £35,000 damages.

1–045   From the note of the defendants' argument,[65] it appears that the contract alleged was an implied contract. It was argued on their behalf that no such contract should be inferred and that,

> "The appellants are really complaining of something in the nature of a breach of trust or confidence, for which relief, if there be any, must be sought in a Court of equity, and not by way of damages at common law."

Lord Atkin said[66]:

> "It is quite sufficient to support the contract averred that the terms upon which the information was disclosed were that it was to be used for a particular purpose only. The giving of the information is ample consideration, and use for any other purpose would be a breach. The analogy of a contract of bailment I think supports this view."

Saltman

1–046   *Saltman Engineering Co Ltd v Campbell Engineering Co Ltd*[67] is a landmark case, both because of its re-affirmation of the equitable doctrine of confidence independent of contract, and because of its attempt to define the quality of confidence necessary for the doctrine to apply. The plaintiffs supplied the defendants with drawings of tools for the manufacture of leather punches. After supplying punches to the plaintiffs, the defendants retained the drawings, which they used for manufacturing and selling other punches to other purchasers. The plaintiffs alleged breach of contract and breach of confidence, and claimed relief including an order for delivery up of the drawings and all tools made from them, an injunction and an inquiry as to damages.

1–047   The Court of Appeal held that it was unnecessary to decide the question of breach of contract, because there was a plain breach of confidence in that the drawings had been supplied for the limited purpose of manufacturing punches for the plaintiffs, and (per Somervell L.J.[68]) that the plaintiffs' relief under that head was as great as it could be under any other.

1–048   Lord Greene M.R. said[69]:

---

[64] [1935] A.C. 346.
[65] [1935] A.C. 346 at 350–351.
[66] [1935] A.C. 346 at 370.
[67] (1948) 65 R.P.C. 203.
[68] *Saltman* (1948) 65 R.P.C. 203 at 217.
[69] *Saltman* (1948) 65 R.P.C. 203 at 215.

"The information, to be confidential, must, I apprehend, apart from contract, have the necessary quality of confidence about it, namely it must not be something which is public property and public knowledge. On the other hand, it is perfectly possible to have a confidential document, be it a formula, a plan, a sketch, or something of that kind, which is the result of work done by the maker upon materials which may be available for the use of anybody; but what makes it confidential is the fact that the maker of the document has used his brain and thus produced a result which can only be produced by somebody who goes through the same process."

The court declined to order the destruction of the tools made by the defendants but ordered an inquiry as to damages, to cover both past and future acts, under Cairns's Lord Act.

The decision in *Saltman* provided a great impetus for the use of the action to prevent industrial piracy,[70] from which its use spread to the protection of personal confidences (*Argyll*[71]) and government secrets (*Attorney-General v Jonathan Cape Ltd*[72]).

1–049

In 1981 the Law Commission produced a report on Breach of Confidence[73] in which it commented on the many uncertainties concerning the ultimate legal foundation of the jurisdiction, its ambit and the remedies available, and recommended that the law be placed on a statutory basis. It drafted a Breach of Confidence Bill, which would have created a statutory tort of breach of confidence and abrogated all principles of equity and common law relating to breach of confidence, except in cases of proceedings for breach of contract or contempt of court. The recommendations were not accepted and the law has continued to develop on a case by case basis.

1–050

Saltman to the Human Rights Act 1998

In the 50 years from *Saltman* (1948) to the Human Rights Act 1998 there was considerable development of the action for breach of confidence, induced by changes in the political and social landscape. Three factors have been particularly significant—the writing of memoirs by ex-spies, spymasters or politicians containing information regarded as secret by the Government; the use of increasingly sophisticated means of obtaining information covertly; and increased media appetite for publishing details of the private lives of well-known figures, often obtained by intrusive methods.

1–051

Public sector confidentiality

A number of cases have resulted from Government attempts to use the law of confidentiality to prevent, or provide a remedy against, publication by former public office holders or employees of material which the Government considered

1–052

---

[70] See Lord Oliver's summary of the history of the breach of confidence action in "Spycatcher: Confidence, Copyright and Contempt", *Israel Law Review* (1989) 23(4) 407.

[71] [1967] Ch. 302.

[72] [1976] 1 Q.B. 752.

[73] Law Com No.110, Cmnd. 8388 (1981).

should be kept secret in the public interest.[74] It is now established that the law of confidentiality is not confined to the private sector, but in the case of public sector confidentiality the Government has to show that the public interest requires the relief claimed to be granted. The *Spycatcher* case is of particular importance for its analysis of the cause of action.[75]

Covert and intrusive ways of obtaining information

1–053   In Britain and elsewhere the use of invasive methods of obtaining information has become common. Kirby J. and Callinan J. referred to it in *Australian Broadcasting Corp v Lenah Game Meats Pty Ltd*.[76]

1–054   Kirby J. said:

> "The phenomena of 'cheque-book journalism', intrusive telephoto lenses, surreptitious surveillance, gross invasions of personal privacy, deliberately deceptive 'stings' and trespass to land 'with cameras rolling' are mainly phenomena of recent times."

Callinan J. said:

> "The means and sources of information (both legitimate and unlawful) available to the media are more numerous and diverse today than ever before; spy cameras, telephone interception devices, access to satellites, night vision equipment, thermal imaging, parabolic listening devices, telephoto lenses, and concealable video cameras to name some only."

The courts have recognised that a person who uses underhand methods to obtain information which he knows that the target intends not to allow to become publicly available (or not until it chooses to do so) may be held to be under a duty of confidentiality. The courts have also recognised that a design may be regarded as a form of information which may be protected from underhand reproduction.[77]

Human Rights Act and personal privacy

1–055   The Human Rights Act has led to the creation of a new cause of action for infringement of personal privacy.

Article 8 of the European Convention on Human Rights provides that everyone has the right to respect for his private and family life, his home and his correspondence.

1–056   In *Von Hannover v Germany*[78] the European Court of Human Rights held that Art.8 imposes on a state both negative and positive obligations. A state must not only abstain from unwarranted interference with the private lives of individuals

---

[74] *Att Gen v Jonathan Cape Ltd* [1976] 1 Q.B. 752; *Commonwealth of Australia v John Fairfax & Sons Ltd* [1969] R.P.C. 41; *Att Gen v Guardian Newspapers Ltd (No.2) ("Spycatcher")* [1990] 1 A.C. 109; *Att Gen v Blake* [2001] 1 A.C. 268.

[75] See especially [1990] 1 A.C. 280–289 (Lord Goff).

[76] (2001) 208 C.L.R. 199 at [172] and [255].

[77] *Shelley Films Ltd v Rex Features Ltd* [1994] E.M.L.R. 134; *Creation Records Ltd v News Group Newspapers Ltd* [1997] E.M.L.R. 444.

[78] (2005) 40 E.H.H.R. 1 at [57].

but must also take appropriate measures to secure respect for private life in the sphere of the relations of individuals between themselves.

The court held that Germany was in breach of Art.8 in that its laws failed to give adequate protection to the applicant from the actions of paparazzi photographers, and that her rights had been breached by the publication of photos showing her in scenes from her daily life, engaged in activities of a purely private nature such as practising sport, walking, leaving a restaurant or enjoying a holiday. **1–057**

The Human Rights Act 1998, s.6 provides that it is unlawful for a public authority (which includes a court) to act in a way which is incompatible with a Convention right. **1–058**

In a series of important cases[79] the courts have given effect to the Act by developing a cause of action, initially under the umbrella of the action for breach of confidence, for infringement of a person's right to privacy under Art.8 by unwarranted publication of material of a personal nature. The full extent and implications of this development have yet to be worked out. **1–059**

---

[79] *A v B Plc* [2002] EWCA Civ 337; [2003] Q.B. 195; *Campbell v MGN Ltd* [2004] UKHL 22; [2004] 2 A.C. 457; *Douglas v Hello! Ltd (No.3)* [2007] UKHL 21; [2008] 1 A.C. 1.

CHAPTER 2

Foundations

DIFFERENT SPECIES OF ACTION

The Law Commission in its 1981 Report[1] observed that there was uncertainty as **2–001** to the nature and scope of the action for breach of confidence owing to its somewhat obscure legal basis, and quoted the words of Professor Gareth Jones[2]:

> "A cursory study of the cases, where the plaintiff's confidence has been breached, reveals great conceptual confusion. Property, contract, bailment, trust, fiduciary relationship, good faith, unjust enrichment, have all been claimed, at one time or another, as the basis of judicial intervention. Indeed some judges have indiscriminately intermingled all these concepts. The result is that the answer to many fundamental questions remains speculative."

Since then the scope of the action has become broader but there is clearer consensus about its foundations. A claimant's action may, but need not necessarily, be based on a breach of confidence in the ordinary sense. Aside from cases where there is an underlying relationship giving rise to a duty of confidentiality, the law may recognise an obligation to treat information with confidentiality if it is obviously of a confidential nature and was obtained by the recipient by dishonest or discreditable means or, possibly, by an obvious accident. Since the Human Rights Act 1998 the action has also become available to protect, within limits, a person's rights under Art.8 of the European Convention to respect for his private and family life, his home and his correspondence. The action can therefore cover very different types of case giving rise to different considerations.

It is necessary to distinguish between breach of confidentiality and infringement of privacy. The same set of facts may give rise to claims under both heads but they are different concepts and rest on different legal foundations. Lord Nicholls summarised the position in *Douglas v Hello! Ltd (No.3)*:

> "As the law has developed breach of confidence, or misuse of confidential information, now covers two distinct causes of action, protecting two different interests: privacy, and secret ('confidential') information. It is important to keep these two distinct. In some cases information may qualify for protection both on grounds of privacy and confidentiality."[3]

---

[1] Law Com No.110, Cmnd. 8388 (1981) at [3.1].

[2] Jones, "Restitution of benefits obtained in breach of another's confidence" (1970) 86 L.Q.R. 463.

[3] [2007] UKHL 21; [2008] 1 A.C. 1 at [255].

The action for infringement of privacy is a form of tort.[4] A duty of confidentiality arises either from contract or from the development of the court's equitable jurisdiction.[5]

2–002   In *Campbell v MGN Ltd*[6] Lord Nicholls observed that the gist of the original cause of action in equity was that information of a confidential character had been disclosed to another in circumstances "importing an obligation of confidence" even though no contract of non-disclosure existed.

2–003   Where there is an underlying relationship of confidentiality, the law has not changed as a result of the Human Rights Act (subject to possible arguments by a defendant under Art.10 of the European Convention, which protects freedom of expression). The basic value which underlies the law in such circumstances is that a person ought to be able to entrust information to another without having that trust abused. This vital concept affects both the range of information which may be protected and the scope of potential defences.

2–004   The jurisprudential basis of a duty of confidence arising from a confidential relationship may be contractual or equitable.[7]

2–005   The range of information which may be protected by reason of such a relationship is potentially wide and certainly wider than information which could be protected under Art.8. It may include information which is not of a personal character, and the claimant may be a business organisation or public authority.

2–006   In cases where there is an underlying relationship of confidentiality, the focus of the court's inquiry is on the requirements properly arising from it. These may vary according to the nature of the relationship but the general principle in such cases, and the value underlying it, were stated by Lord Goff in the *Spycatcher* case[8]:

> "I start with the broad principle (which I do not intend in any way to be definitive) that a duty of confidence arises when confidential information comes to the knowledge of a person (the confidant) in circumstances where he has notice, or is held to have agreed, that the information is confidential, with the effect that it would be just in all the circumstances that he should be precluded from disclosing the information to others. I have used the word 'notice' advisedly, in order to avoid the (here unnecessary) question of the extent to which actual knowledge is necessary; though I of course understand knowledge to include circumstances where the confidant has deliberately closed his eyes to the obvious. The existence of this broad general principle reflects the fact that there is such a public interest in the maintenance of confidences that the law will provide remedies for their protection."

2–007   The same public interest and the same general principle apply to an original confidant and to a subsequent recipient who knows that the information has been passed to him in breach of confidence. As Dillon L.J. said in the *Spycatcher* case[9]:

---

[4] *Imerman v Tchenguiz* [2010] EWCA Civ 908; [2011] 1 All E.R. 55 at [65] (Lord Neuberger, M.R.).
[5] *Douglas v Hello! Ltd (No.3)* [2007] UKHL 21; [2008] 1 A.C. 1 at [276] (Lord Walker, whose statement on this point is not weakened by the fact that he was in a minority as to the result).
[6] [2004] UKHL 22; [2004] 2 A.C. 457 at [13].
[7] *Saltman* (1948) 65 R.P.C. 203; *Att Gen v Guardian Newspapers Ltd (No.2)* [1990] 1 A.C. 109; *Kitchenology BV v Unicor Gmbh Plastmaschinen* [1995] R.P.C. 765 at 778.
[8] [1990] 1 A.C. 109 at 281.
[9] [1990] 1 A.C. 109 at 201.

" . . . anyone who receives information from a person bound by an obligation of secrecy or confidence, and who knows that the information has been passed to him by his informant in breach of that obligation, becomes automatically prima facie himself bound by a like obligation of secrecy or confidence which will prevent his disseminating the information any further, or making any use of it without the consent of the person to whom the obligation of secrecy or confidence was owed by the informant."

It is not difficult to apply by analogy the same principle to a person who obtains what he knows to be confidential information by dishonest or discreditable means or, possibly, by accident. In the *Spycatcher* case Lord Goff deliberately stated the broad principle underlying breach of confidence in terms wide enough to cover such situations, where there was no pre-existing confidential relationship, although he observed that in the vast majority of cases a duty of confidence would arise from a transaction or relationship between the parties.[10]

In cases where there is no such transaction or relationship, but the recipient is alleged to have obtained the information by dishonest or discreditable means, or possibly by accident, the focus of the inquiry will be on the nature of the information and whether the recipient obtained it in such circumstances that he should in conscience be required to treat it as confidential. **2–008**

Where Art.8 is engaged the focus is different. The European Court of Human Rights has stated that the primary purpose of Art.8 is to enable the development, without outside interference, of the personality of each individual in his relations with other human beings.[11] This extends beyond the family circle and includes a social dimension. The court has recognised that there is a "zone of interaction with others, even in a public context, which may fall within the scope of 'private life'".[12] An aspect of a person's right to enjoyment of that zone of privacy is the right to control personal information about himself, including information about his personal relationships with others. **2–009**

The difference between confidentiality and privacy as concepts was discussed by Lord Mustill in *R. v Broadcasting Standards Commission, Ex p. BBC*.[13] It was held that under the Broadcasting Act 1996 a company could make a complaint of unwarranted infringement of its privacy in the obtaining of material included in a broadcast programme. But the court emphasised that this conclusion was based on the particular language of the statute and its underlying purpose, which was concerned with establishing broadcasting standards rather than legal rights. Lord Mustill said: **2–010**

"I do . . . wish to emphasise the degree to which this conclusion is dependent on the language and purpose of this particular statute, for in general I find the concept of a company's privacy hard to grasp. To my mind the privacy of a human being denotes at the same time the personal 'space' in which the individual is free to be itself, and also the carapace, or shell, or umbrella, or whatever other metaphor is preferred, which protects that space from intrusion. An infringement of privacy is an affront to the personality, which is damaged both by the violation and by the demonstration

---

[10] [1990] 1 A.C. 109 at 281.

[11] *Botta v Italy* (1998) 26 E.H.R.R. 241 at [32]; *Von Hannover v Germany* (2005) 40 E.H.R.R. 1 at [50] and [69].

[12] *Von Hannover v Germany* at [50].

[13] [2001] Q.B. 885 at [48]–[49].

that the personal space is not inviolate. The concept is hard indeed to define, but if this gives something of its flavour I do not see how it can apply to an impersonal corporate body, which has no sensitivities to wound, and no selfhood to protect.

There will, it is true, be many occasions where grounds for complaint maintainable by a company will be of the same kind as those which could be presented by an individual as a breach of privacy. For example the clandestine copying of business documents would be actionable by a company and an individual alike as civil wrongs, amounting to a breach of confidentiality, copyright and the like. But privacy and confidentiality are not the same. For example, the reading and copying of personal diaries, letters to relatives or lovers, poems and so on could ground not only an allegation of tortious conduct but also an additional complaint that the privacy of the writer and perhaps also of the recipient have been intruded upon. Such conduct is specially objectionable, not because legal rights have been infringed but because of the insult done to the person as a person. No such complaint would, I believe, be feasible when made by a company, not for the obvious reason that a corporation does not create documents of this kind, but because an intrusion into such matters has an extra dimension, in the shape of the damage done to the sensibilities of a human being by exposing to strangers the workings of his or her inward feelings, emotions, fears and beliefs—a damage which an artificial 'person', having no sensibilities, cannot be made to suffer. A company can have secrets, can have things which should be kept confidential, but I see this as different from the essentially human and personal concept of privacy."

In Art.8 cases concerning disclosure of personal information, the focus of the court's inquiry will be on the extent to which the disclosure interferes, or would interfere, with the objective of Art.8 (when balanced against Art.10).

2–011   As Lord Hoffmann put it in *Campbell v MGN Ltd*,[14]

"The result . . . has been a shift in the centre of gravity of the action for breach of confidence when it is used as a remedy for the unjustified publication of personal information . . . Instead of the cause of action being based upon the duty of good faith applicable to confidential personal information and trade secrets alike, it focuses upon the protection of human autonomy and dignity—the right to control dissemination of information about one's private life and the right to the esteem and respect of other people."

Given the differences in concepts and objectives between breach of confidence and breach of privacy, to attempt to meld the different types of case into a uniform cause of action risks doctrinal and practical confusion.

2–012   It is understandable that courts should be more willing to make new law when it can be viewed as adapting and extending existing doctrine rather than creating a new branch of law. So the law was developed incrementally by expansion of the action for breach of confidence rather than by declaration of a new cause of action for breach of privacy, particularly in view of a strong line of authority denying a cause of action for breach of privacy, of which the high watermark was *Wainwright v Home Office*.[15]

2–013   A mother and son were strip searched for drugs on a prison visit. The search was conducted in a manner which contravened prison rules and was gratuitously humiliating. It included indecent touching of the son. They sued the Home Office.

---

[14] [2004] UKHL 22; [2004] 2 A.C. 457 at [51].
[15] *Kaye v Robertson* [1991] F.S.R. 62; *Wainwright v Home Office* [2003] UKHL 53; [2004] 2 A.C. 406.

The events pre-dated the Human Rights Act but the Act was in force by the time that the case reached the House of Lords. The son recovered damages for battery in respect of the indecent touching, but otherwise their claim in respect of their degrading treatment failed. It was argued that there was a common law tort of invasion of privacy, and that recognition of its existence was necessary for the United Kingdom to conform with its international obligations in respect of Art.8. The House of Lords rejected both parts of this argument.

The Wainwrights took their case to the European Court, which held that there had been a violation of Art.8.[16] Strip searching involved an interference with the applicants' right to personal privacy which required to be justified in terms of the second paragraph of Art.8 by showing that it had a legitimate objective and was proportionate to that objective. The court accepted that the prevention of smuggling drugs into prison was a legitimate objective, but held that the searches were not proportionate to the legitimate objective in the way that they were carried out. Because English law (as held by the House of Lords) did not provide the applicants with a remedy, except in respect of the indecent touching of the son, the United Kingdom was held also to be in breach of Art.13.
 2–014

If the same facts were to occur today, the Wainwrights would be entitled to damages by virtue of ss.7 and 8 of the Human Rights Act for the violation of their Art.8 rights by the prison officers, since their mistreatment was at the hands of public officials. In those circumstances there would therefore no longer be a breach of Art.13. But Art.8 may also impose on the state an obligation to safeguard a person's rights of privacy from interference by companies or private individuals,[17] and ss.7 and 8 of the Act would not provide a remedy in that situation.
 2–015

In relation to the publication of information about a person's private life, the Court of Appeal took a bold approach by declaring in *A v B Plc*[18]:
 2–016

> "[Articles 8 and 10] have provided new parameters within which the court will decide, in an action for breach of confidence, whether a person is entitled to have his privacy protected by the court or whether the restriction of freedom of expression which such protection involves cannot be justified. The court's approach . . . has been modified because, under section 6 of the 1998 Act, the court, as a public authority, is required not to act 'in a way which is incompatible with a Convention right'. The court is able to achieve this by absorbing the rights which articles 8 and 10 protect into the long-established action for breach of confidence."

---

[16] *Wainwright v UK* [2006] ECHR 807.
[17] *Von Hannover v Germany* (2005) 40 E.H.R.R. 1 at para.57.
[18] Para.4 (Lord Woolf, C.J. giving the judgment of the court); [2002] EWCA Civ 337; [2003] Q.B. 195.

This approach was approved by the House of Lords in *Campbell v MGN Ltd*,[19] but there are limitations and difficulties in trying to absorb breach of rights of privacy within breach of confidence, as has been noted by commentators[20] and courts.[21]

2–017   First, for Art.8 rights to be brought under the umbrella of confidentiality, the case must involve use of information of a private character, but there may be invasions of privacy which do not involve publication of information.[22] Secondly, although there is obvious potential overlap in cases concerning personal information between rights of confidentiality founded on pre-Human Rights Act law and rights under Art.8, the concepts of privacy and confidentiality are neither identical nor mutually exclusive. It is therefore right that the courts have now come to recognise explicitly that there are separate (sometimes overlapping) causes of action in contract or equity for breach of confidentiality and in tort for infringement of privacy.

Relationships giving rise to a duty of confidentiality

2–018   A duty of confidentiality may arise from express or implied terms of a contract. Aside from contract, the courts have also long recognised that an equitable duty of confidentiality may arise out of a relationship under which information is imparted. The basis on which breach may give rise to a claim for an injunction or compensation is discussed below.

Information obtained by dishonest or discreditable means

2–019   A person who obtains confidential information by dishonest or discreditable means (such as electronic eavesdropping) should be, and is, in no better legal position than if the information had been imparted to him voluntarily in confidence. Equity acts on the conscience, and the conduct of a person who obtains confidential information improperly is as reprehensible to the conscience as that of a person who violates the confidence in which he received it.

Information obtained by accident

2–020   The law in this area is less developed. The cases considered have been ones where a person has received a document of a confidential nature which was plainly not intended for him. A person has no right to retain or make use of a

---

[19] [2004] UKHL 22; [2004] 2 A.C. 457.

[20] See, for example, G. Phillipson, "Transforming Breach of Confidence? Towards a Common Law Right of Privacy under the Human Rights Act" (2003) 66 M.L.R. 726; N. Moreham, "Privacy and horizontality: relegating the common law" L.Q.R. 2007, 123(Jul), 373-378.

[21] See, in particular, the judgments of the New Zealand Court of Appeal in *Hosking v Runting* [2004] NZCA 34 and *Douglas v Hello! Ltd (No.3)* [2005] EWCA Civ 595; [2006] Q.B. 125 at [53], "We cannot pretend that we find it satisfactory to be required to shoe-horn within the cause of action for breach of confidence claims for publication of unauthorised photographs of a private occasion" (Lord Phillips M.R. giving the judgment of the court).

[22] As Lord Nicholls noted in *Campbell v MGN Ltd* [2004] 2 A.C. 457 at [15], referring to the example of *Wainwright* [2004] UKHL 22; see also *Goodwin v News Group Newspapers Ltd* [2011] EWHC 1437; [2011] E.M.L.R. 27, per Tugendhat J. at [85].

document which does not belong to him and to read what he knows is not intended for him may well be regarded as unconscionable.

Article 8 cases

Cases under Art.8 need not be founded on a relationship of confidentiality, and to use the word "confidential" to describe photographs taken of a person doing something essentially private but open to public view, such as visiting a doctor, is not a natural use of language, as Lord Nicholls commented in *Campbell v MGN Ltd*.[23] In that case the claim for damages for publication of photographs of the claimant leaving premises of Narcotics Anonymous was regarded by him as an action in tort.

2–021

A contrary view was taken by the Court of Appeal in *Douglas v Hello! Ltd*.[24] The court considered the nature of the Douglases' claim for the purpose of determining the appropriate choice of law. It observed that their claim in relation to the invasion of their privacy might seem most appropriately to fall within the law of delict. But it concluded, with hesitation, that the effect of shoe-horning this type of claim into the cause of action for breach of confidence meant that it did not fall to be treated as a tort under English law. It regarded as persuasive the suggestion of *Dicey & Morris on the Conflict of Laws*[25] that a claim for breach of confidence fell to be categorised as a restitutionary claim for unjust enrichment.

2–022

There may well be cases in which an infringement of a person's rights may cause damage, physical or psychological, unrelated to any enrichment of the wrongdoer. Instances might include cases where the publication of the identity and address of a person could place them in physical danger, but there could be less dramatic examples. Indeed, the damages awarded to the Douglasses were based on personal distress, cost and inconvenience, rather than any estimation of enrichment of the defendants. Far from making a profit, the court noted that the defendants made a loss on the whole exercise, and this was one ground on which the court rejected the suggestion of a notional royalty as basis for assessing damages.[26]

2–023

It is suggested that the court's natural inclination towards tort as the basis of the claim was sound, and that the problem which troubled the court about the "shoe-horning" of breach of privacy within breach of confidence is best addressed by recognising the differences between them. This view accords with the more recent approach of the Court of Appeal in *Murray v Express Newspapers Plc*[27] and *Imerman v Tchenguiz*.[28]

2–024

---

[23] [2004] UKHL 22; [2004] 2 A.C. 457 at [14].

[24] [2005] EWCA Civ 595, [2006] Q.B. 125 at [96]–[97].

[25] 13th edn, 2000, para.34–029. See now *Dicey, Morris and Collins*, 15th edn (London: Sweet & Maxwell, 2012), paras 34–091 to 34–092 and 35–141, which now tentatively advances the view that claims based on rights of privacy may perhaps be better categorised as tortious.

[26] [2005] EWCA Civ 595; [2006] Q.B. 125 at [243]–[245].

[27] [2008] EWCA Civ 446; [2008] 3 W.L.R. 1360 at [27].

[28] [2010] EWCA Civ 908; [2011] Fam. 116 at [65].

Conflicting views on information as property

2–025 There has been a long standing debate whether confidential information is or should be regarded by the law as property. If so, it would give rise to proprietorial remedies which could be exercised against a third party, regardless of whether he was or ought to have been aware that the information was confidential.

2–026 In the *Spycatcher* case Lord Goff said[29]:

> "I have . . . deliberately avoided the fundamental question whether, contract apart, the duty lies simply 'in the notion of an obligation of conscience arising from the circumstances in or through which the information was communicated or obtained' (see *Moorgate Tobacco Co. Ltd v Philip Morris Ltd (No. 2)* (1984) 156 C.L.R. 414, 438, *per* Deane J., and see also *Seager v Copydex Ltd* [1967] 1 W.L.R. 923, 931, *per* Lord Denning M.R.), or whether confidential information may also be regarded as property (as to which see Dr Francis Gurry's valuable monograph on *Breach of Confidence* (1984), pp.46–56 and Professor Birks' *An Introduction to the Law of Restitution* (1985), pp.343–344)."

2–027 The question whether (statute apart) there can be property in ideas or information goes back to the issues debated in *Millar v Taylor*[30] (in which the judgments repay reading). Now, as then, opinions are divided.

2–028 The question depends on what is meant by property, a matter of complexity upon which much has been written. As Professor Cornish has commented:

> "The root difficulty of such a question is the flexibility of the property notion in English law and the many ends to which it is employed."[31]

It is therefore not surprising that different views have been expressed. However, there are formidable difficulties in the way of any treatment of the action for breach of confidence as an action in tort based on infringement of a proprietary interest. The objections may be grouped under the headings of precedent, conceptual analysis and logical consequence.

2–029 As a matter of precedent, the recent decisions in *Douglas v Hello! Ltd (No.3)*[32] and *Coogan v News Group Newspapers Ltd*,[33] and the weight of previous authority, are against the proposition that confidential information is to be regarded as property.[34]

---

[29] [1990] 1 A.C. 109 at 281.

[30] (1769) 4 Bur. 2303. See para.1–004 above.

[31] Cornish, Llewellyn & Aplin *Intellectual Property: Patents, Copyright, Trade Marks and Allied Rights* 7th edn (London:Sweet & Maxwell, 2010) para.8-50.

[32] [2005] EWCA Civ 595; [2006] Q.B. 125 at [119]; [2007] UKHL 21; [2008] 1 A.C. 1 at [124] (Lord Hoffmann), [275]–[276] (Lord Walker).

[33] [2012] EWCA Civ 48 at [39]. It was held that confidential commercial information did, however, fall within the statutory definition of "intellectual property" in s.72 of the Senior Courts Act 1981. The decision was upheld by the Supreme Court under the title *Phillips v NewsGroup Newspapers Ltd* [2012] UKSC 28; [2012] 3 W.L.R. 312. Lord Walker said at [20] that the fact that technical and commercial information ought not, strictly speaking, to be described as property could not prevail over clear statutory language, and that it was irrelevant whether confidential information could only loosely, or metaphorically, be described as property.

[34] In *Veolia ES Nottinghamshire Ltd v Nottinghamshire County Council* [2010] EWCA Civ 1214 Rix L.J. said, at [111], that confidential information is "a well recognised species of property, protected by the common law", but the court was not referred to any of the authorities on the point and the

The view held by Lord Mansfield and the majority of the judges in *Miller v Taylor*[35] that the common law recognised an incorporeal right to a set of ideas was ultimately rejected by the House of Lords in *Jefferys v Boosey*.[36] Lord Brougham said[37]:

> "Whatever can be urged for property in a composition, must be applicable to property in an invention or discovery. It is the subject matter of the composition, not the mere writing, the mere collection of words, that constitutes the work. It may describe an invention, as well as contain a narrative or poem, and the right to the exclusive property in the invention, the title to prevent anyone from describing it to others, or using it himself (before it is reduced to writing) without the inventor's leave, is precisely the same with the right of the author to exclude all men from the multiplication of his work. But in what manner has this ever been done or attempted to be done by inventors? Never by asserting a property at common law in the inventor, but by obtaining a grant from the Crown."

Lord Brougham recognised that the author of an unpublished manuscript had a right to the manuscript, and was entitled to publish the composition, or not, as he saw fit.[38] In later authorities it was held that the "so-called copyright that remains in an author in respect of an unpublished work" at common law could be passed to another independently of the manuscript.[39] But the right so recognised was in the *form* of the composition, not the ideas or information which it contained, as was explained by Lord Oliver in a lecture given to the Hebrew University of Jerusalem in 1989[40]:

> "Now the action of confidence is entirely an equitable invention . . . . The common law recognised the right of property of an author in his unpublished work, but what it protected was the mode of expression not the information expressed. The idea that information imparted or acquired in confidence or as a result of a confidential relationship, such as a doctor and a patient, could be legally protected by the courts seems to have arisen only in the early nineteenth century."

He also referred to the basis of the action being[41]:

> " . . . that equity intervenes to preserve the confidentiality of information not because information is susceptible of a *proprietary* claim but because its use in the hands of the defendant is unconscionable."

2–030

2–031

---

observation would appear to be per incuriam. Rix L.J. also said, at [121], that he could not see why valuable confidential information could not fall within the concept of "possessions" in Art.1 of the First Protocol. This is not a straightforward question and there is no authority that Art.1 of the First Protocol has horizontal effect in domestic law. For authorities on the effect of Art.1 of the First Protocol, see *R. (Jackson) v Att Gen* [2007] UKHL 52 at [20]–[21] (Lord Bingham), approving the judgment of Kenneth Parker QC in *R. (Nicholls) v Security Industry Authority* [2007] 1 W.L.R. 2067 at [70]–[76].

[35] (1769) 4 Bur. 2303.

[36] (1854) 4 H.L.C. 814. For a valuable description of Lord Mansfield's contribution to the development of the law of intellectual property, see Professor James Oldham, *The Mansfield Manuscripts* (University of North Carolina Press, 1992) Vol.1, Ch.12.

[37] (1854) 4 H.L.C. 814 at 966.

[38] (1854) 4 H.L.C. 814 at 962.

[39] *Re Dickens* [1935] 1 Ch. 267 at 286.

[40] "Spycatcher: Confidence, Copyright and Contempt", *Israel Law Review* (1989) 23(4) 407, 413.

[41] "Spycatcher: Confidence, Copyright and Contempt", *Israel Law Review* (1989) 23(4) 407, 421.

2–032   In *Nichrotherm Electrical Co Ltd v Percy*[42] Lord Evershed M.R. also rejected the suggestion of property in ideas, saying:

> " . . . a man who thinks of a mechanical conception and then communicates it to others for the purpose of their working out means of carrying it into effect does not, because the idea was his (assuming that it was), get proprietary rights equivalent to those of a patentee. Apart from such rights as may flow from the fact, for example, of the idea being of a secret process communicated in confidence or from some contract of partnership or agency or the like which he may enter into with his collaborator, the originator of the idea gets no proprietary rights out of the mere circumstance that he first thought of it."[43]

2–033   It may be argued that this is hard to reconcile with the concept of a secret recipe as capable of being the subject of a trust (see *Green v Folgham*[44]). But it is perfectly possible to recognise a fiduciary relationship (e.g. between trustee and beneficiary or between partners) involving obligations in relation to confidential information, without regarding such information as property in the strict sense of the word.[45]

2–034   In *Phipps v Boardman*[46] a solicitor to the trustees of a will and a beneficiary under the will trust bought shares in a company in which the trust had a substantial holding. At the time of the negotiations the purchasers were in the position of agents of the trustees and, as such, learned information relevant to the company, which they did not fully report to the trustees. From their special position they gained the opportunity to make a profit from the purchase of the shares and the knowledge that it was there to be made. The House of Lords held by a majority that the purchasers were liable to account for their profits from the purchase as constructive trustees, having used their position to make a personal profit without the full knowledge and consent of their principals.

2–035   The judges were divided on the question whether the information obtained by the purchasers was to be regarded as trust property in the strict sense. Lords Dilhorne,[47] Cohen[48] and Upjohn[49] considered that it was not; Lords Hodson[50] and Guest[51] that it was. Lord Upjohn said[52]:

> "In general, information is not property at all. It is normally open to all who have eyes to read and ears to hear. The true test is to determine in what circumstances the information has been acquired. If it has been acquired in such circumstances that it would be a breach of confidence to disclose it to another then courts of equity will restrain the recipient from communicating it to another. In such cases such

---

[42] [1957] R.P.C. 207 at 209.

[43] See also *Federal Commissioner of Taxation v United Aircraft Corp* (1943–1944) 68 C.L.R. 525 at 534 (High Court of Australia), per Latham C.J.: "I am unable to regard the communication of information as constituting a transfer of property . . . It is only in a loose metaphorical sense that any knowledge as such can be said to be property."

[44] (1823) 1 Sim. & Stu. 398.

[45] *Phipps v Boardman* [1967] 2 A.C. 46 at 102, per Lord Cohen, and at 127–128, per Lord Upjohn.

[46] [1967] 2 A.C. 46.

[47] [1967] 2 A.C. 46 at 89–90.

[48] [1967] 2 A.C. 46 at 102.

[49] [1967] 2 A.C. 46 at 127–128.

[50] [1967] 2 A.C. 46 at 107 and 110.

[51] [1967] 2 A.C. 46 at 115.

[52] [1967] 2 A.C. 46 at 127.

confidential information is often and for many years has been described as the property of the donor, the books of authority are full of such references; knowledge of secret processes, 'know-how', confidential information as to the prospects of a company or of someone's intention or the expected results of some horse race based on stable or other confidential information. But in the end the real truth is that it is not property in any normal sense but equity will restrain its transmission to another if in breach of some confidential relationship."

Lord Hodson disagreed. He said[53]:

" . . . I dissent from the view that information is of its nature something which is not properly to be described as property. We are aware that what is called 'know-how' in the commercial sense is property which may be very valuable as an asset."

Lord Hodson also cited[54] a passage from the judgment of Bowen L.J. in *Aas v Benham*,[55] in which he commented on an observation of Cotton L.J. in *Dean v MacDowell*[56] that:

"Again if he (that is, a partner) makes any profit by the use of any property of the partnership, including, I may say, information which the partnership is entitled to, there the profit is made out of the partnership property."

Bowen L.J. commented: 2–036

"He is speaking of information which a partnership is entitled to in such a sense that it is information which is the property, or is to be included in the property of the partnership—that it to say, information the use of which is valuable to them as a partnership, and to the use of which they have a vested interest."

It is suggested that Lord Upjohn's analysis is to be preferred and it was cited as an accurate summary by the Court of Appeal in *Douglas v Hello! Ltd.*[57] The passages cited by Lord Hodson from *Dean v MacDowell* state the sense in which information has sometimes been referred to as "belonging to" a partnership (i.e. information valuable to the partnership and which the partnership has a right to use), but the basis of such right lies in the relationship between the partners.

The information in *Phipps v Boardman* was of the same character in that its   2–037
use was of potential value to the trustees and it was obtained by the purchasers in the capacity of agents for the trustees.

Similarly in *Bell v Lever Bros*[58] Lord Blanesbury said, in relation to private   2–038
cocoa speculations by directors of a company engaged in the cocoa market, that:

" . . . the company has no concern in his profit and cannot make him accountable for it unless it appears—this is the essential qualification—that in earning that profit he has made use *either* of the property of the company *or* of some confidential information which has come to him as a director of the company." (Emphasis added.)

---

[53] *Phipps v Boardman* [1967] 2 A.C. 46 at 107.
[54] *Phipps v Boardman* [1967] 2 A.C. 46 at 109–110.
[55] [1891] 2 Ch. 244 at 258.
[56] (1878) 8 Ch.D. 345 at 354.
[57] [2005] EWCA Civ 595; [2006] Q.B. 125 at [127].
[58] [1932] A.C. 161 at 194.

2–039   The director's liability in the latter case would arise not from the confidential information constituting property, but from use of his fiduciary position to make a personal profit without his principal's knowledge.

2–040   In *Seager v Copydex Ltd*[59] the plaintiff entered into negotiations with the defendants with a view to their marketing a carpet grip invented by him and for which he had a patent. During the negotiations the plaintiff suggested to the defendants an alternative form of grip. After the negotiations fell through, the defendants marketed a grip closely similar to the plaintiff's suggested alternative. The plaintiff claimed an injunction and damages. The defendants were found to have made use unconsciously of information supplied to them in confidence. The Court of Appeal declined to grant an injunction or an account of profits but ordered an inquiry as to damages.

2–041   Following the precedent of *Mechanical and General Inventions Co v Austin*[60] the plaintiff would appear to have had a good case for relying on breach of an implied contract, but there is no reference to that authority being cited; and the decision of the Court of Appeal was expressly based not on any theory of implied contract, but on the principle of equity that a person who receives information in confidence shall not take unfair advantage of it.

2–042   In *Seager v Copydex Ltd (No.2)*[61] the Court of Appeal directed that the damages be assessed, by analogy with damages for conversion, on the basis of the market value of the information misused by the defendants. Lord Denning M.R. said that just as a satisfied judgment in trover transferred the property in the goods, so the confidential information would belong to the defendants once the damages were paid.

2–043   This has prompted the comment:

> "The Court of Appeal had already held . . . that the confidence was purely equitable. What it was now doing was to hold that equity would condone, nay facilitate, the compulsory acquisition by the defendant of the plaintiff's property; a state of affairs that would have exceeded the comprehension of the masters of equity who spoke in England before darkness enveloped all."[62]

2–044   The analogy of conversion has also been criticised by others including Professor Cornish[63]:

> "Altogether, the analogy to damages for misappropriation of a single tangible article is inept, given in particular the more obvious comparison to patents and copyright and the more flexible approach to damages which applies to their infringement."

2–045   While it seems entirely just that the plaintiff should have been compensated for the fact that information supplied by him to the defendants in confidence was

---

[59] [1967] 1 W.L.R. 923.

[60] [1935] A.C. 346.

[61] [1969] 1 W.L.R. 809.

[62] *Meagher, Gummow and Lehane on Equity: Doctrines and Remedies*, 4th edn (Butterworths LexisNexis, 2002), para.41–090. Contrast also *Franklin v Giddins* [1978] Qd.R. 72 (see para.3–034, below).

[63] Cornish, Llewelyn & Aplin, *Intellectual Property: Patents, Copyright, Trade Marks and Allied Rights*, 7th edn (London: Sweet & Maxwell, 2010) para.8–-48.

used by them without his permission to their commercial advantage, the *Seager v Copydex* decisions present difficulties of analysis.

A possible interpretation of *Seager v Copydex* is that it established a new head **2–046** of tortious liability for breach of confidence, analogous to conversion and based on the plaintiff's proprietary right in the information.[64] However, that is difficult to reconcile with the fact that the judgment of the Court of Appeal on liability was expressly founded on "the broad principle of equity that he who has received information in confidence shall not take unfair advantage of it".[65] That principle does not require any underlying proprietary right.

Lord Denning M.R. expressed the same view in *Fraser v Evans*[66]: **2–047**

> "The jurisdiction is based not so much on property or on contract as on the duty to be of good faith. No person is permitted to divulge to the world information which he has received in confidence, unless he has just cause or excuse for doing so."

A similar view was expressed in the High Court of Australia in *Moorgate* **2–048** *Tobacco Co Ltd v Philip Morris Ltd (No.2)*[67] by Deane J. (with the concurrence of Gibbs C.J. and Mason, Wilson and Dawson JJ.):

> "It is unnecessary, for the purposes of the present appeal, to attempt to define the precise scope of the equitable jurisdiction to grant relief against an actual or threatened abuse of confidential information not involving any tort or any breach of some express or implied contractual provision, some wider fiduciary duty or some copyright or trade mark right. A general equitable jurisdiction to grant such relief has long been asserted and should, in my view, now be accepted: see *The Commonwealth v John Fairfax & Sons Ltd*.[68] Like most heads of exclusive equitable jurisdiction its rational basis does not lie in proprietary right. It lies in the notion of an obligation of conscience arising from the circumstances in or through which the information was communicated or obtained."

It has also been held that the information in an examination paper does not **2–049** constitute "intangible property" capable of falling within s.4 of the Theft Act 1968.[69]

In *Douglas v Hello! Ltd (No.3)* the question arose whether confidential or **2–050** private information, capable of commercial exploitation, constituted as such a form of property. The Douglases (Michael Douglas and Catherine Zeta-Jones) entered into a contract with OK! Magazine giving it the exclusive right to publish pictures of their wedding. Steps were taken to prevent anyone except the authorised photographer from taking pictures of the event, but a freelance photographer escaped the security precautions and took photographs which he sold to Hello! The unauthorised photographs were published by Hello! as a spoiler. The Douglases and OK! brought claims against Hello!

---

[64] For a critique of this interpretation and its problems see Prof. P. M. North, "Breach of Confidence: Is there a New Tort?" 12 J.S.P.T.L. 149.
[65] [1967] 1 W.L.R. 923 at 931, per Lord Denning M.R. Lord Goff in the *Spycatcher* case treated *Seager v Copydex Ltd* as founded on obligation of conscience rather than proprietary rights. See [1990] 1 A.C. 109 at 281.
[66] [1969] 1 Q.B. 349 at 361.
[67] (1984) 156 C.L.R. 414 at 437–438.
[68] (1980) 147 C.L.R. 39 at 50–52.
[69] *Oxford v Moss* (1979) 68 Cr. App. R. 183.

Lindsay J. found that the Douglases had a right to control pictorial information about their wedding because it was a private event; and that because it was commercially exploitable, their right to exclusivity of photographic coverage of the event was a form of property right which could be shared with another and enforced by the other, at any rate where the defendant knew or could be taken to know of the co-ownership before acting in breach and where all entitled to the confidence asserted it. He awarded damages of approximately £15,000 to the Douglases and £1 million to OK! The Court of Appeal upheld the award in favour of the Douglases but allowed the appeal by Hello! It held that the Douglases had a right of protection of information about their wedding because it was private but rejected the argument that their right was based on some form of proprietary interest.[70]

The House of Lords, by a majority, restored the award in favour of OK! but not on the basis that Hello! had infringed a property right. Lord Hoffmann, in the leading judgment, noted that the claim by OK! had nothing to do with the concepts of privacy or Convention rights. Photographs of the wedding were confidential information in that the Douglases had made it clear that no one admitted to the wedding was to make or communicate photographic images. The Douglases were entitled to decide how and through whom such information was to be made public. Everybody at the wedding was therefore under an obligation of confidentiality. There was no reason why OK! should not be able to enforce the benefit of that obligation. The conscience of Hello! was tainted because it had made known to paparazzi in advance that it would pay well for photographs and it deliberately asked no questions about how the photographs which it bought had been obtained. In those circumstances the award of damages against Hello! was straightforward. It did not involve creating an image right or any other unorthodox form of intellectual property.[71]

2–051 Although some forms of confidential information bear some similarity to some forms of intellectual property, any broad concept of confidential information as property would be hard to encapsulate. Confidential information involves information about some fact or idea, but a mere fact or private idea is not susceptible of ownership.[72] It would be a strange form of property which would come into existence on the confidential acquisition of information about a fact or idea and cease to exist on its wider publication.

2–052 As Professor Gareth Jones has commented[73]:

> "Confidential information is conceptually very much *sui generis*. It is an intangible; and, consequently, it would be 'wrong to confuse the physical records with [the information] itself . . . ; for if you put them on a duplicator and produce one hundred copies you have certainly not multiplied your asset in proportion'.[74] It has, too, the quality that it may be transmitted to a limited class without destroying its value; so, know-how 'can be communicated to or shared with others outside the manufacturer's own business,' for example, under licence.[75] Conversely the nature

---

[70] [2005] EWCA Civ 595; [2006] Q.B. 125 at [119], [126]–[127].

[71] [2007] UKHL 21; [2008] 1 A.C. 1 at [114]–[118], [124].

[72] *Jefferys v Boosey* (1854) 4 H.L.C. 814; *Nichrotherm Electrical Co Ltd v Percy* [1957] R.P.C. 207; *Federal Commissioner of Taxation v United Aircraft Corp* (1943) 68 C.L.R. 525 at 534.

[73] "Restitution of benefits obtained in breach of another's confidence" (1970) 86 L.Q.R. 463, 464.

[74] *Rolls-Royce Ltd v Jeffrey (Inspector of Taxes)* [1962] 1 All E.R. 801 at 805, per Lord Radcliffe.

[75] *Rolls-Royce Ltd v Jeffrey (Inspector of Taxes)* [1962] 1 All E.R. 801 at 805.

of confidential information is such that no one, save the person who imparted it, may realise for some time that it has been communicated in breach of confidence. For similar reasons it is not always easy to protect a purchaser of confidential information from his seller who subsequently sells the same information to another innocent third party.

Information is not like other choses in action, such as debt or copyright, which lend themselves more easily to a classical analysis in terms of property."

There is a danger of circularity of reasoning in concluding, because equity intervenes by injunction or other remedy, that the reason for the intervention lies in the protection of a proprietary interest. This point was recognised by Gummow J. in *Smith Kline & French Laboratories (Australia) Ltd v Department of Community Services*,[76] citing *Colbeam Palmer Ltd v Stock Affiliates Pty Ltd*[77] and *E.I. Du Pont de Nemours Powder Company v Masland*,[78] where Holmes J. said: **2–053**

> "The word property as applied to trade-marks and trade secrets is an unanalysed expression of certain secondary consequences of the primary fact that the law makes some rudimentary requirements of good faith."

These objections, powerful though they are, would be no compelling reason for the courts not to recognise confidential information as a form of property, if to do so would resolve problems and assist the development of the law on a principled and rational basis. But, if anything, the opposite would be the case. **2–054**

Professor Finn has observed[79]: **2–055**

> "Certain types of information and particularly trade secrets doubtless can have certain of the attributes of property. Information can for example be intrinsically valuable; it can be the subject matter of a trust; it can be communicated for a consideration; it can be included in the 'property' which passes to a trustee in bankruptcy.
>
> But even if from such similarities one wishes to create a form of abstract property, difficulties immediately arise. If all information is described as property, it is nonetheless meaningless to give a property basis to the jurisdiction relieving against misuse of information. All such 'property' is not protected by the courts. The information, and the circumstances of its communication must, as will be seen, possess certain characteristics before protection will be given. If only some information is described as property, i.e. information protected by the courts, to call that information property is merely to add yet another consequence to a decision taken for reasons quite unrelated to property considerations."

Nowhere are the difficulties of adopting property as a basis of the jurisdiction more acute than in relation to the "innocent" third party. The concept of an action for breach of confidence based on a broad principle that one should not break, or co-operate with another in breaking, a personal duty of confidence is **2–056**

---

[76] [1990] F.S.R. 617 at 673–674; (affirmed (1991) 28 F.C.R. 291).
[77] (1968) 122 C.L.R. 25 at 34, per Windeyer J.
[78] (1917) 244 U.S. 100 at 102.
[79] Finn, *Fiduciary Obligations* (1977) paras 295–296. Note also his comment at para.293, "Perhaps the most sterile of debates which have arisen around the subject of information received in confidence is whether or not such information should be classified as property".

fundamentally different from the concept of an action based on tortious infringement of a property right analogous to trespass to goods.

2–057   If the concept is based on equitable principles, no liability would be expected to attach to a third party recipient of confidential information for acts done by him in ignorance that there had been any breach of confidence. So, it has been held that, in order to be fixed with an obligation of confidence, a third party must know that the information was confidential.[80] On discovering that there had been such breach the third party would ordinarily then come under a duty of confidence, at least if he were a volunteer.[81] On the other hand, it might be unfair to impose such a duty on him if he had paid in good faith for the information, or had subsequently incurred effort or expense in putting it to use, or had otherwise undergone a change of circumstances, except possibly on terms compensating him for the loss or prejudice which he would otherwise suffer.[82]

2–058   However, if the concept is based on a tort of infringement of property analogous to conversion, the mental innocence of the third party would be no defence and he would be liable in damages for his past innocent misuse of the plaintiff's confidential information,[83] a liability analogous to the statutory liability to damages of an infringer of copyright.[84]

2–059   The only way of avoiding strict liability for innocent misuse of confidential information would be for the courts to create a special defence not ordinarily available in cases of tortious infringement of property rights.

2–060   In *Douglas v Hello! Ltd (No. 3)* Lindsay J. tentatively followed this path when he held that the benefit of a confidence could be shared between and be enforceable by co-owners or by a successor in title, but added "at any rate where the defendant knew or could be taken to have known of the co-ownership or sharing before acting in breach".[85] But, as the Court of Appeal held, if the claimants had a proprietary right in information about the events at their wedding, it would be a right which could be exercised against a third party regardless of whether he ought to have been aware that the information was private or confidential.[86]

2–061   As Professor Gareth Jones has said[87]:

"No property theory can satisfactorily determine, even with the aid of equity, the question of the liability of the person who innocently exploits a secret. For example, there may be circumstances where it is just that a volunteer should be free of any liability to account for profits made through the use of confidential information. Conversely, it may not be difficult to imagine a case where even a bona fide purchaser ought to be enjoined, albeit on terms, from using information which he later learns was given him in breach of another's confidence."

---

[80] *Fraser v Thames Television* [1984] 1 Q.B. 44 at 65. *Valeo Vision S.A. v Flexible Lamps Ltd* [1995] R.P.C. 205 at 226–228. *Thomas v Pearce* [2000] F.S.R. 718. See also the Report of the Law Commission, Law Com No.110, Cmnd. 8388 (1981), para.4.12.

[81] *Printers & Finishers Ltd v Holloway* [1965] R.P.C. 239 at 253 and 257, per Cross J. and *Fraser v Thames Television* [1984] 1 Q.B. 44.

[82] See paras 3–068 to 3–075, below.

[83] Compare *Marfani & Co Ltd v Midland Bank Ltd* [1968] 1 W.L.R. 956.

[84] *Paterson Zochonis & Co Ltd v Merfarken Packaging Ltd* [1986] 3 All E.R. 522.

[85] [2005] EWCA Civ 595; [2006] Q.B. 125 at [123].

[86] [2006] Q.B. 125 at [126].

[87] "Restitution of benefits obtained in breach of another's confidence" (1970) 86 L.Q.R. 463, 465.

Some forms of confidential information bear a closer resemblance to intellectual property than others, and that factor may affect the court's view about the most appropriate equitable remedy, but in such cases it is a mistake to reason that property therefore provides the basis of the jurisdiction.

Conflicting views on damages

For a long time there was uncertainty about the foundation on which damages could be awarded for breach of confidence. **2–062**

If a duty of confidentiality arises simply from an equitable obligation of conscience, according to traditional authority the remedies would not include damages (except under the jurisdiction derived from Lord Cairns's Act and now contained in s.50 of the Senior Courts Act 1981). So, for example, in *Robb v Green*[88] the Court of Appeal held that the plaintiff's entitlement to damages depended on whether he could establish a breach of an implied contract or only a breach of an equitable duty of confidence. **2–063**

In *Nichrotherm Electrical Ltd v Percy*,[89] Harman J. ordered an inquiry as to damages for breach of confidence and breach of copyright. In the Court of Appeal the matter proceeded, by agreement, on the basis that the breach of confidence relied upon by the plaintiff involved breach of an implied contract, and on that ground the court did not have to consider further the basis of the enquiry as to damages. But the court was clearly troubled by the form of order at first instance, and Lord Evershed M.R. observed[90]: **2–064**

> "If the confidence, breach of which is alleged or proved, is imposed by or arises out of contract, express or implied, then the remedy would, I assume, be by way of damages at law as upon a breach of contract. If, on the other hand, the confidence infringed is one imposed by the rules of equity, then the remedy would be, prima facie, by way of injunction or damages in lieu of an injunction under Lord Cairns' Act."

In *Seager v Copydex Ltd*[91] the Court of Appeal held that the defendant was in breach of an equitable duty for which it declined to order an injunction or account of profits but ordered an inquiry as to damages, which it later directed should be assessed on the basis of the market value of the information misused.[92] The two decisions caused much academic debate but their historical significance was in setting a precedent for an award of damages for breach of an equitable obligation. **2–065**

In the telephone tapping case of *Malone v Metropolitan Police Commissioner*[93] one of the grounds on which the plaintiff sought, unsuccessfully, a declaration that it was unlawful for the defendant to tap his telephone line was based on a claimed right of confidentiality. Sir Robert Megarry V.C. said[94]: **2–066**

---

[88] [1895] 2 Q.B. 315.
[89] [1956] R.P.C. 272.
[90] [1957] R.P.C. 207 at 213.
[91] [1967] 1 W.L.R. 923.
[92] [1969] 1 W.L.R. 809.
[93] [1979] 1 Ch. 344.
[94] [1979] 1 Ch. 344 at 360.

"This is an equitable right which is still in the course of development, and is usually protected by the grant of an injunction to prevent disclosure of the confidence. Under Lord Cairns' Act 1858 damages may be granted in substitution for an injunction; yet if there is no case for the grant of an injunction, as when the disclosure has already been made, the unsatisfactory result seems to be that no damages can be awarded under this head: see *Proctor v Bayley* (1889) 42 Ch.D. 390. In such a case, where there is no breach of contract or other orthodox foundation for damages at common law, it seems doubtful whether there is any right to damages, as distinct from an account of profits. It may be, however, that a new tort is emerging (see *Goff and Jones, The Law of Restitution* (6th edn 2002), pp.518, 519 and Gareth Jones (1970) 86 L.Q.R. 463, 491), though this has been doubted: see *Street, The Law of Torts* 6th edn (1976), p.377. Certainly the subject raises many questions that are so far unresolved . . . "

2–067　　In its Report on Breach of Confidence in 1981[95] the Law Commission expressed the different view, in para.4.76, that:

"It is a reasonable inference from the decision in *Seager v Copydex Ltd* that damages are awardable for a past breach of confidence."

But it qualified that view by adding:

"On the other hand it can be argued that it is not clear from that case whether the damages which were ordered to be assessed were intended to include loss suffered in respect of the past breach of confidence or only to provide compensation in lieu of an injunction. The subsequent decision in *Seager v Copydex Ltd (No. 2)*, in which the Court of Appeal had to determine the basis of assessment for the damages ordered in the earlier case, has not clarified the position in this respect."

In *English v Dedham Vale Properties*[96] Slade J. said that he read *Seager v Copydex Ltd* as a case in which the court granted damages in lieu of an injunction.

2–068　　In *Dowson & Mason Ltd v Potter*[97] an employee of the plaintiffs in breach of duty divulged confidential information to another company, who used it to compete with his employers. The plaintiffs sued the employee and the company. Both submitted to an order for an inquiry as to damages. Subsequently an issue arose as to the basis on which damages were to be assessed. The company contended that damages should be assessed by reference to the value of the information, following *Seager v Copydex Ltd*. The plaintiffs contended successfully for assessment by reference to their loss of profits. The Court of Appeal held that *Seager v Copydex Ltd* laid down no general rule as to the appropriate basis of assessment in such a case, and applied the principle stated by Lord Wilberforce in *General Tire and Rubber Co v Firestone Tyre & Rubber Co Ltd*[98]:

"As in the case of any other tort (leaving aside cases where exemplary damages can be given) the object of damages is to compensate for loss or injury. The general rule

---

[95]　Law Com No.110, Cmnd. 8388 (1981).

[96]　[1978] 1 W.L.R. 93 at 111.

[97]　[1986] 1 W.L.R. 1419.

[98]　[1975] 1 W.L.R. 819 at 824.

at any rate in relation to 'economic' torts is that the measure of damages is to be, so far as possible, that sum of money which will put the injured party in the same position as he would have been in if he had not sustained the wrong."

However, there was no analysis of the underlying basis of the order for damages, which had not been articulated in any judgment, since the order was made by consent.

In the *Spycatcher* case Lord Goff said[99]:

2–069

"An important section of the law of restitution is concerned with cases in which a defendant is required to make restitution in respect of benefits acquired through his own wrongful act—notably cases of waiver of tort; of benefits acquired by certain criminal acts; of benefits acquired in breach of a fiduciary relationship; and, of course, of benefits acquired in breach of confidence. The plaintiff's claim to restitution is usually enforced by an account of profits made by the defendant through his wrong at the plaintiff's expense. This remedy of an account is alternative to the remedy of damages, which in cases of breach of confidence is now available, despite the equitable nature of the wrong, through a beneficent interpretation of the Chancery Amendment Act 1858 (Lord Cairns' Act) . . . "

In *Universal Thermosensors Ltd v Hibben*[100] Sir Donald Nicholls V.C. referred to *Seager v Copydex Ltd* and, in particular, the passage in Lord Denning's judgment to the effect that a recipient of confidential information should not get a start over others by using it, at any rate without paying for it, even if the case was not one for an injunction. The Vice-Chancellor added:

2–070

"An award of damages in such circumstances would not be a novelty. There are several fields where the courts have awarded damages to a plaintiff whose property is wrongfully used by another even though the plaintiff has not suffered pecuniary loss by such user. The cases concerning this principle, sometimes called 'the "user" principle', can be found gathered together in *Stoke-on-Trent City Council v W & J Wass Ltd* [1988] 1 W.L.R. 1406, 1416–1418."

Stoke-on-Trent City Council v W. & J. Wass Ltd is authority for the proposition that as a general rule damages in tort are to be assessed by reference to the loss sustained by the plaintiff; but that exceptionally in certain cases (such as trespass to land, patent infringement and certain cases of nuisance or detinue) the user principle may apply to enable the plaintiff to recover a reasonable sum for the use made of his property.

2–071

The principle was approved in *Inverugie Investments Ltd v Hackett*,[101] where Lord Lloyd said:

2–072

"The principle need not be characterised as exclusively compensatory, or exclusively restitutionary; it combines elements of both."

It would be deeply unsatisfactory that monetary compensation should be capable of being awarded for past misuse of confidential information only where there was a case for the grant of an injunction (as Sir Robert Megarry V.C.

2–073

---

[99] [1990] 1 A.C. 109 at 286.
[100] [1992] 1 W.L.R. 840 at 856.
[101] [1995] 1 W.L.R. 713 at 718, PC.

observed in *Malone v Metropolitan Police Commissioner*[102]) and, probably because that is so obvious, it has become accepted in practice that compensation can be awarded generally for breach of confidence. The surprise is that the courts should still be grappling for a satisfactory explanation on what basis (other than breach of contract) this may be done.

2–074   Lord Goff's suggestion in the *Spycatcher* case[103] that damages are now available for breach of confidence, despite the equitable nature of the wrong, through a "beneficent interpretation" of Lord Cairns's Act, is not entirely satisfactory.

2–075   In neither *Seager v Copydex Ltd* nor *Seager v Copydex Ltd (No.2)*[104] did the Court of Appeal make any reference to Lord Cairns's Act providing the basis for damages. Further, it is not difficult to imagine cases in which there could be no grounds for the grant of an injunction, for example, because there was no threat to repeat a past breach, or because the information had ceased to be confidential for reasons which might be quite independent of the defendant's breach (as in *Mustad & Son v Dosen*[105]). In such a case, to describe an award of damages for a past breach as being in lieu of an injunction would involve more than a beneficent interpretation of Lord Cairns's Act. It would be a fiction.

2–076   An alternative partial solution might be advanced under the rubric of restitution, under which a wrongdoer may be required to restore benefits obtained through his own wrongful act. In *Spycatcher*[106] Lord Goff recognised this principle as applying to benefits obtained in breach of confidence. This would justify the wrongdoer being ordered to pay over the value of the benefit received, regardless of the availability of an injunction; and so, on the facts of *Seager v Copydex Ltd*, would afford a legitimate basis for the defendants being required to pay the "market value" of the information misused.

2–077   That would have the same effect as a *quantum meruit* award, which previous editions of Goff and Jones[107] suggested would have been a happier basis of the award in *Seager v Copydex Ltd*. However, the authors recognise that it is difficult to square that approach with an award of damages. It would be still more difficult to justify expectation damages (i.e. damages for loss of anticipated profits), as in *Dowson & Mason Ltd v Potter*,[108] on a restitutionary basis.

Equitable compensation

2–078   An alternative solution (not dependent on Lord Cairns's Act or on the developing principles of restitution) is to recognise that equitable compensation may be awarded for breach of an equitable duty of confidence, just as it may be awarded for breach of duty by a fiduciary (*Nocton v Ashburton*[109]).

---

[102] [1979] 1 Ch. 344 at 360.
[103] [1990] 1 A.C. 109 at 286.
[104] [1967] 1 W.L.R. 923; [1969] 1 W.L.R. 809.
[105] [1964] 1 W.L.R. 109.
[106] [1990] 1 A.C. 109 at 286.
[107] *The Law of Restitution* (7th edition, 2009), at para.34–022. The 8th edition (*Unjust Enrichment*, 2011) does not address the topic.
[108] [1986] 1 W.L.R. 1419.
[109] [1914] A.C. 932.

This approach accords with the view expressed by Professor Finn that[110]:　　　　**2–079**

> " . . . no great violence to principle is wrought if they [i.e. awards of damages for breach of an equitable obligation of confidence] are regarded as modern developments in the compensatory jurisdiction of Equity which was so forcefully reaffirmed by Viscount Haldane L.C. in *Nocton v Ashburton*."

It is also consistent with the decision of the Court of Appeal in *Kitchenology BV v Unicor Gmbh Plastmaschinen*.[111] The court held that claims for breach of confidence do not arise in tort and that it was clear beyond doubt that the jurisdiction to "restrain and, if necessary, award damages for breach of confidence" was an equitable jurisdiction.

The law relating to fiduciary relationships is one of the least clearly defined　　**2–080** areas of the law,[112] but there is a close parallel between a person owing an equitable obligation of confidence and a person owing a fiduciary obligation, and there seems no good reason in principle why a person should not be required to provide compensation in equity (sometimes called equitable damages) for breach of an equitable obligation of confidence as in a case of breach of a fiduciary obligation.

Seager v Copydex Ltd was explained in this way in *U.S. Surgical Corporation*　　**2–081** *v Hospital Products International Pty Ltd* by McLelland J., who said[113]:

> "Apart from the limited power to award damages in addition to or in substitution for equitable relief, conferred by the Supreme Court Act, 1970, S.68 (following Lord Cairns' Act), which is of no present relevance, the court has an inherent power to grant relief by way of monetary compensation for breach of a fiduciary or other equitable obligation: see *Nocton v Lord Ashburton* [1914] A.C. 932 at pp.946, 956, 957; *McKenzie v McDonald* [1927] V.L.R. 134 at p.146; *Holmes v Walton* [1961] W.A.R. 96; *cf. Seager v Copydex Ltd* [1967] 1 W.L.R. 923; [1967] 2 All E.R. 415; [1969] 1 W.L.R. 809; [1969] 2 All E.R. 718."

Just as the doctrine of fiduciary duty is not limited to direct relationships[114] but　　**2–082** extends to a person who dishonestly assists in a breach of trust by another (*Royal Brunei Airlines v Tan*[115]), or who receives (by accident or misconduct) assets emanating from another in the knowledge that he was not intended to do so (*Chase Manhattan Bank N.A. v Israel-British Bank (London) Ltd*[116]), there seems no reason in principle why equitable compensation for breach of a duty of confidence should not equally be awarded against a person who knowingly

---

[110] Finn, *Fiduciary Obligations* (1977), para.388.

[111] [1995] F.S.R. 765 at 777–778.

[112] See *Henderson v Merrett Syndicates Ltd* [1995] 2 A.C. 145 at 206, per Lord Browne-Wilkinson.

[113] [1982] 2 N.S.W.L.R. 766 at 816. (Reversed on other grounds (1984) 156 C.L.R. 41.) See also Davidson, "The Equitable Remedy of Compensation", 13 *Melbourne University Law Review* 349.

[114] *White v Jones* [1995] 2 A.C. 207 at 271, per Lord Browne-Wilkinson: " . . . the special relationship (i.e. a fiduciary relationship) giving rise to the assumption of responsibility held to exist in Nocton's case does not depend on any mutual dealing between A and B, let alone on any relationship akin to contract. Although such factors may be present, equity imposes the obligation because A has assumed to act in B's affairs".

[115] [1995] 2 A.C. 378.

[116] [1981] Ch. 105.

assists in a breach of confidence by another,[117] or who knowingly receives confidential information by mistake or misconduct and misuses it.[118]

2–083   Although there is considerable historical authority on the difference between compensation in equity and damages at common law,[119] the House of Lords held in *Target Holdings Ltd v Redferns*[120] that the principles underlying both are the same, the fundamental object being to compensate the innocent party for the loss caused by the wrong.

The award of damages to OK! in *Douglas v Hello! Ltd*[121] accords with this approach. Hello! published photographs which it knew had been taken in breach of a duty of confidentiality owed by those who attended the wedding, for the purpose of causing loss to OK!, and that conduct merited an award of equitable compensation for the loss which it caused. The House of Lords did not explore the distinction between "damages" and "equitable compensation".[122]

Equitable compensation should be capable of accommodating in an appropriate case the restitutionary principle referred to by Lord Goff in *Spycatcher*.[123]

2–084   In Art.8 cases, it is established that damages may be awarded, including damages for distress (as in *Campbell v MGN Ltd*,[124] *Douglas v Hello! Ltd*[125] and *Mosley v News Group Newspapers Ltd*[126]). It is suggested that it is more realistic to regard such damages as based in tort than on a strained concept of an equitable obligation, and the authorities cited by Eady J. in *Mosley*[127] appear to be moving in that direction.

New Zealand, Canada and Australia

2–085   It is instructive to compare the development of the law in New Zealand, Canada and Australia. In *Aquaculture Corp v New Zealand Green Mussel Co Ltd*[128] the defendants misused confidential information, supplied by the plaintiff, in manufacturing and marketing a product. The plaintiff claimed that its own business prospects had been injured by the defendants' irresponsible marketing campaign. Damages for the plaintiff's loss were assessed at $1.5 million, but the

---

[117] See paras 3–066—3–074, below.
[118] See paras 3–030 and 3–043—3–047, below.
[119] See Meagher, Gummow and Lehane, *Equity: Doctrines and Remedies*, 4th edn (LexisNexis Australia, 2002), Ch.23.
[120] [1996] A.C. 421.
[121] [2007] UKHL 21; [2008] 1 A.C. 1.
[122] In *Vestergaard Franksen A/S v BestNet Europe Ltd* [2009] EWHC 1456 (Ch) there was argument whether "damages" or "equitable compensation" was available for breach of confidentiality. Arnold J. did not find it necessary to decide the point but inclined to the latter. His judgment went to appeal ([2011] EWCA Civ 424), but the Court of Appeal did not address the point.
[123] [1990] 1 A.C. 109 at 286.
[124] [2004] 2 A.C. 457; [2004] UKHL 22.
[125] [2005] EWCA Civ 595; [2006] Q.B. 125.
[126] [2008] EWHC 1777 (QB). Eady J. discussed the question whether it is right to attach the label of tort to such a cases when considering a claim for exemplary damages but did not find it necessary to come to a view about it: [181]–[184].
[127] [2008] EWHC 1777 (AB); [2008] EMCR 20.
[128] [1990] 3 N.Z.L.R. 299.

trial judge held that he had no power to award compensatory damages. This ruling was reversed on appeal. Delivering the judgment of the Court of Appeal of New Zealand, Cooke P. said[129]:

> "There is now a line of judgments in this Court accepting that monetary compensation (which can be labelled damages) may be awarded for breach of a duty of confidence or other duty deriving historically from equity . . . In some of these cases the relevant observations were arguably obiter, but we think that the point should now be taken as settled in New Zealand. Whether the obligation of confidence in a case of the present kind should be classified as purely an equitable one is debatable, but we do not think that the question matters for any purpose material to this appeal. For all purposes now material, equity and common law are mingled or merged. The practicality of the matter is that in the circumstances of the dealings between the parties the law imposes a duty of confidence. For its breach a full range of remedies should be available as appropriate, no matter whether they originated in common law, equity or statute."

More recently, the position in New Zealand was summarised by the Court of Appeal in *Hunt v A*:

> "Undoubtedly, New Zealand law recognises the equitable doctrine of breach of confidence...The present law relating to that doctrine can be summarised thus. The leading modern judgments have returned to the proposition asserted by the early chancellors: the jurisdiction is based on a broad principle of good faith. 'He who has received information in confidence should not take unfair advantage of it'...That doctrine does not depend on the existence of a contract between the parties or there being "property" in the subject-matter of the confidence. Nor does it depend on the existence of a fiduciary relationship. Breach of confidence is not a tort. The doctrine is a *sui generic* cause of action."[130]

In *Aquaculture Corp v New Zealand Green Mussel Co Ltd* Cooke P. drew support for his approach not only from New Zealand authorities but also from the decisions of the Supreme Court of Canada in *LAC Minerals Ltd v International Corona Resources Ltd*[131] and of Rogers J. in the Supreme Court of New South Wales in *Catt v Marac Australia Ltd*.[132]

In *Lac Minerals* the plaintiff owned mining rights on land on which it was drilling exploratory holes. In the course of negotiations with a view to a possible partnership or joint venture (which never materialised), the plaintiff revealed to the defendant information about the drilling results, from which it was clear that an adjacent property was likely to have valuable deposits. The plaintiff attempted to acquire the mining rights in the adjacent property but was outbid by the defendant, which developed the mine on its own account. The plaintiff sought a declaration that the defendant held the mining rights on constructive trust for the plaintiff on the grounds either of breach of fiduciary duty or of breach of confidence. It was found that, but for the defendant's use of the relevant information, the plaintiff would have obtained the mining rights and developed the mine for itself.

2–086

---

[129] [1990] 3 N.Z.L.R. 299 at 301.
[130] Glazebrook, Hammond and Wilson JJ., [2007] N.Z.C.A. 332, [2008] 1 N.Z.L.R. 368 at [64].
[131] [1990] F.S.R. 441.
[132] (1986) 9 N.S.W.L.R. 639.

2–087   Three issues therefore arose: first, whether the defendant acquired the mining rights in breach of fiduciary duty (in which case there could be no dispute about the defendant holding the rights on trust for the plaintiff); secondly, whether the defendant acted in breach of confidence; and thirdly, if so, what remedy was available.

2–088   The Supreme Court held (by a majority) that the parties were not in a fiduciary relationship, but (unanimously) that the defendant acted in breach of confidence. On the question of remedy, the majority (La Forest, Lamer and Wilson JJ.) upheld the plaintiff's argument in favour of the imposition of a constructive trust. The minority (Sopinka and McIntyre JJ.) considered damages a more appropriate remedy. There was, however, no difference between the judges as to the range of remedies which it lay within the court's power to award. On this the most detailed analysis was that of Sopinka J. He said[133]:

> "The foundation of action for breach of confidence does not rest solely on one of the traditional jurisdictional bases for action of contract, equity or property. The action is *sui generis* relying on all three to enforce the policy of the law that confidences be respected: see Gurry, *Breach of Confidence* (Clarendon Press, Oxford, 1984) at pp.25–26, and Goff & Jones, *The Law of Restitution*, (3rd edn, Sweet & Maxwell, 1986) at pp.664–667.
>
> This multi-faceted jurisdictional basis for the action provides the court with considerable flexibility in fashioning a remedy. The jurisdictional basis supporting the particular claim is relevant in determining the appropriate remedy . . . . A constructive trust is ordinarily reserved for those situations where a right of property is recognised . . .
>
> Although confidential information has some of the characteristics of property, its foothold as such is tenuous . . .
>
> As a result, there is virtually no support in the cases for the imposition of a constructive trust over property acquired as a result of the use of confidential information . . .
>
> Although unjust enrichment has been recognised as having an existence apart from contract or tort under a heading referred to as the law of restitution, a constructive trust is not the appropriate remedy in most cases . . .
>
> While the remedy of the constructive trust may continue to be employed in situations where other remedies would be inappropriate or injustice would result, there is no reason to extend it to this case.
>
> The conventional remedies for breach of confidence are an accounting of profits or damages. An injunction may be coupled with either of these remedies in appropriate circumstances. A restitutionary remedy is appropriate in cases involving fiduciaries because they are required to disgorge any benefits derived from the breach of trust. In a breach of confidence case, the focus is on the loss to the plaintiff and, as in tort actions, the particular position of the plaintiff must be examined. The object is to restore the plaintiff monetarily to the position he would have been in if no wrong had been committed: see *Dowson & Mason Ltd v Potter* [1986] 2 All E.R. 418 (CA) and *Talbot v General Television Corp. Pty Ltd* [1980] V.R. 224. Accordingly, this object is generally achieved by an award of damages, and a restitutionary remedy is inappropriate."

2–089   The majority considered that the imposition of a constructive trust was the appropriate remedy as the surest way of putting the plaintiff in the position that it would have been in but for the defendant's breach of confidence; and that the

---

[133] [1990] F.S.R. 441 at 495–497.

restitutionary principle, which enables a court to give to a plaintiff something which has been wrongly taken from him (a restitutionary proprietary award), or its monetary value (a personal restitutionary award), should by analogy apply equally in the situation in which the wrongdoer has acquired a benefit which would otherwise have accrued for the benefit of the plaintiff.

In *Cadbury Schweppes Inc v FBI Foods Ltd*[134] Binnie J., delivering the judgment of the Supreme Court, rejected criticisms of Sopinka J.'s sui generis characterisation of the action for breach of confidence. He observed that the concept had been adopted to recognise the flexibility that had been shown by the courts to uphold confidentiality and in crafting remedies for its protection. On the jurisdiction of the court to award damages he said[135]: **2–090**

> "Equity, like the common law, is capable of ongoing growth and development . . . In my view, therefore, having regard to the evolution of the equitable principles apparent in the case law, we should clearly affirm that, in this country, the authority to award financial compensation for breach of confidence is inherent in the exercise of general equitable jurisdiction and does not depend on the niceties of Lord Cairns' Act or its statutory successors. This conclusion is fed, as well, by the *sui generic* nature of the action. The objective in a breach of confidence case is to put the confider in as good a position as it would have been in but for the breach. To that end, the Court has ample jurisdiction to fashion appropriate relief out of the full gamut of available remedies, including appropriate financial compensation."

In Australia there has been searching analysis, particularly by Meagher, Gummow and Lehane[136] and (in his judicial capacity) by Gummow J. in *Corrs Pavey v Collector of Customs*[137] and *Smith, Kline & French Laboratories (Australia) Ltd v Secretary to the Department of Community Services and Health*.[138] Meagher, Gummow and Lehane have observed that[139]: **2–091**

> " . . . the equitable duty of confidence has now sufficiently developed (as has the law of trusts to a much greater degree) to be regarded as occupying a specific field of its own, but subject always to the caveat that where there are questions as to the direction of further development (for example, in dealing with third parties who receive information) these can best be answered by looking to the source whence the stream has sprung. Thus, it will be contended that the third party who participates in breach of a duty of confidence is accountable under the second limb of *Barnes v Addy* (1874) 9 Ch.App. 244 at 251, no less than is a participant in a breach by a delinquent fiduciary within the strict modern acceptance of that term."

In Smith, Kline & French Gummow J. said[140]: **2–092**

> "It seems clear enough that knowledge *per se* is not proprietary in character; see *Moorgate Tobacco Co. Ltd v Philip Morris Ltd* (1982) 64 F.L.R. 387 at 404–405, affirmed (1984) 156 C.L.R. 414; *Boardman v Phipps* [1967] 2 A.C. 46 at 89–92,

---

[134] (1999) 167 D.L.R. (4th) 577 at 591.

[135] (1999) 167 D.L.R. (4th) 577 at 604.

[136] Meagher, Gummow and Lehane, *Equity: Doctrines and Remedies*, 4th edn (LexisNexis Australia, 2002), Ch.41.

[137] (1987) 74 A.L.R. 428.

[138] [1990] F.S.R. 617, affirmed [1991] 28 F.C.R. 291.

[139] Meagher, Gummow and Lehane, 4th edn (LexisNexis Australia, 2002), para.41–035.

[140] [1990] F.S.R. 617 at 673.

102–103, 127–129, but compare 106–107, 115. Further, it is clear in Australia that the equitable jurisdiction to grant relief against an actual or threatened abuse of confidential information, not involving any tort or breach of contract, fiduciary duty, copyright or trade mark, is based not in pre-existing proprietary right, but in an obligation of conscience arising in the circumstances of the case: *Moorgate Tobacco Co Ltd v Philip Morris Ltd (No.2)*."[141]

2–093   Gummow J. also held it to be established law in Australia that the court had an inherent jurisdiction to award monetary compensation, independent of its statutory powers under any derivative of Lord Cairns's Act, for breach of an equitable duty of confidence, as appears from the following part of his judgment[142]:

"I should have hoped that any controversy as to the applicability of Lord Cairns's Act and its derivatives to claims in respect of purely equitable rights (rather than tortious or contractual rights) had been quelled by the recent analysis by Mr Dean in his work, *The Law of Trade Secrets* (1990), pp.317–320, 329. I have indicated my views in *Concept Television Productions Pty Ltd v Australian Broadcasting Corporation* (1988) 12 I.P.R. 129 at 136. This Court is, by statute, a court of equity as regards matters otherwise within its jurisdiction . . . This brings with it, in a case such as the present, the inherent jurisdiction to grant relief by way of monetary compensation for breach of an equitable obligation, whether of trust or confidence. After all, long before the birth of Lord Cairns, delinquent trustees were brought to book in Chancery and, independently of any tracing remedy *in rem*, were obliged to make up from their own pockets the value of trust funds which had been lost: *Re Dawson dec'd* [1966] 2 N.S.W.R. 211. And as to the personal liability of fiduciaries other than trustees, see *Catt v Marac Australia Ltd* (1986) 9 N.S.W.L.R. 639. If it transpires that the applicants are entitled to an inquiry [as to pecuniary loss], it would, in my view, be on this basis in the inherent equitable jurisdiction . . . "

In *Farah Constructions Pty Ltd v Say-Dee Pty Ltd* the High Court of Australia affirmed the approach of Gummow J., observing that the protection given by equitable doctrines and remedies causes confidential information sometimes to be described as having a proprietary character "not because property is the basis upon which that protection is given, but because of the effect of that protection". Certain types of confidential information share characteristics of certain types of property. Thus trade secrets may be transferred, held in trust or charged, but to describe confidential information as property is to confuse the cause and effect of the court's protection.[143]

The courts of Australia, Canada and New Zealand have also considered the relationship between confidentiality and privacy.

2–094   In *Australian Broadcasting Corp v Lenah Game Meats Pty Ltd*[144] trespassers made a secret video recording of the killing of possums at the respondent's abattoir. The film was passed to the appellants, who proposed to broadcast it. The respondent applied for an injunction to prevent the broadcast. The High Court held by a majority of five to one that no injunction should be granted. The

---

[141] (1984) 156 C.L.R. 414.
[142] [1990] F.S.R. 617 at 634.
[143] Gleeson C.J., Gummow, Callinan, Heydon and Crennan JJ., [2007] HCA 22; (2007) 81 A.J.L.R. 1107 at [118], [120].
[144] [2001] HCA 63; (2001) 208 C.L.R. 199.

respondent conceded that it had no claim under the law of confidentiality because the nature of the process filmed was not secret. But it argued among other grounds that the court should recognise a tort of breach of privacy, to which an earlier decision of the High Court in *Victoria Park Racing and Recreation Grounds Co Ltd v Taylor*[145] was generally considered to be an obstacle. The court left the question open.

Gleeson C.J. accepted that the law should be more astute than it had been in the past to identify and protect interests of a kind which fell within the concept of privacy, but expressed caution about declaring a new tort of breach of privacy, partly because of the lack of precision of the concept of privacy and partly because of the availability of breach of confidentiality as a way of protecting images and sounds of private activities. Gummow, Hayne and Gaudron JJ. did not consider that the *Victoria Park* case should stand in the way of the possible development of a tort of breach of privacy, but suggested that any such development should be by adapting recognised forms of action to meet new situations rather than searching to identify ingredients of a generally expressed wrong. Kirby J. described it as a difficult question whether, so many years after *Victoria Park*, the court should declare the existence of an actionable wrong of invasion of privacy. Callinan J. (who would have granted an injunction) was strongly critical of the *Victoria Park* case and considered that the time was ripe for consideration whether a tort of privacy should be recognised.[146]

2–095

In *Hosking v Runting*[147] parents brought an action to prevent publication of pictures of the mother pushing their 18-month old twins in the street. The couple were celebrities who had recently separated. The pictures were taken without the mother's knowledge by a photographer commissioned by a magazine. The claim was brought on the ground that publication of the photographs would amount to a breach of the twins' right of privacy. The Court of Appeal of New Zealand was unanimous in rejecting the claim but divided on the issue of the existence of a cause of action for breach of privacy. The majority (Gault P. and Blanchard and Tipping JJ.) held that there was. Keith and Anderson JJ. disagreed.

2–096

Gault P. (giving the judgment of himself and Blanchard J.) analysed the English authorities and summarised the position as follows:

2–097

> "It seems then that there are now in English law two quite distinct versions of the tort of breach of confidence. One is the long-standing cause of action applicable alike to companies and private individuals under which remedies are available in respect of use or disclosure where the information has been communicated in confidence . . . The second gives a right of action in respect of the publication of personal information of which the subject has a reasonable expectation of privacy

---

[145] (1937) 58 C.L.R. 479.

[146] In *Giller v Procopets* [2008] VSCA 236; 24 V.R. 1, a case involving the defendant's distribution of a video recording of sexual intercourse between himself and the claimant, the Victorian Court of Appeal also declined to express a view whether a tort of invasion of privacy should be recognised by Australian law. Neave JA pointed out, at [452], that the Australian Law Reform Commission had recently recommended that federal legislation should provide a cause of action for serious invasion of privacy. In *Maynes v Casey* [2011] NSWCA 156, the New South Wales Court of Appeal (at [35]) observed (obiter) of previous decisions that "These cases may well lay the basis for development of liability for unjustified intrusion on personal privacy, whether or not involving breach of confidence."

[147] [2004] NZCA 34; [2005] 1 N.Z.L.R. 1.

irrespective of any burden of confidence, but only where that publication is likely to be highly offensive to a reasonable person."[148]

He continued:

" . . . we consider that it will be conducive of clearer analysis to recognise breaches of confidence and privacy as separate causes of action . . . Privacy and confidence are different concepts. To press every case calling for a remedy for unwarranted exposure of information about the private lives of individuals into a cause of action having as its foundation trust and confidence will be to confuse those concepts."[149]

2–098   Tipping J. said:

"In the United Kingdom the Courts have chosen incrementally to develop the equitable remedy of breach of confidence. But, in so doing, it has been necessary for the Courts to strain the boundaries of that remedy to the point where the concept of confidence has become somewhat artificial. The underpinning element of the breach of confidence cause of action has conventionally been that either by dint of a general or a transactional relationship between the parties, one party can reasonably expect that the other will treat the relevant information or material as confidential and will not publicly disclose it.

 . . . It . . . seems to me . . . that it is more jurisprudentially straightforward and easier of logical analysis to recognise that confidence and privacy, while capable of overlapping, are essentially different concepts. Breach of confidence, being an equitable concept, is conscience based. Invasion of privacy is a common law wrong which is founded on the harm done to the plaintiff by conduct which can reasonably be regarded as offensive to human values. While it may be possible to achieve the same substantive result by developing the equitable cause of action, I consider it legally preferable and better for society's understanding of what the Courts are doing to achieve the appropriate substantive outcome under a self contained and stand-alone common law cause of action to be known as invasion of privacy . . .

The result in substantive terms of recognising a separate tort is not significantly different from the extended form of the breach of confidence cause of action as it is being developed in the United Kingdom. What is at stake is really a matter of legal method rather than substantive outcome."

However, in *Rogers v Television New Zealand Ltd* doubts were expressed by some members of the Supreme Court about the law as stated in *Hosking v Runting*.[150] It therefore cannot be regarded as settled.[151] In *Jones v Tsige*[152] the Court of Appeal for Ontario held that breach of privacy (or "intrusion upon seclusion") is a tort under Canadian law.

---

[148] para.42.

[149] paras 45, 48.

[150] [2007] NZSC 91; [2008] 2 N.Z.L.R. 277. Elias CJ expressed doubts about the scope of the tort at [23]–[26]. Anderson expressed doubt about both the existence and the scope of the tort at [144].

[151] In *C v Holland* [2012] NZHC 2155 the defendant made video recordings of the claimant in her bathroom without her knowledge or consent. There was no evidence that the defendant had ever published or showed the video clips to any person. Whata J. held that there was a tort of inclusion upon seclusion in New Zealand law, defining its essential elements as follows "(a) an intentional and unauthorised intrusion; (b) into seclusion (namely intimate personal activity, space or affairs); (c) involving infringement of a reasonable expectation of privacy; (d) that is highly offensive to a reasonable person."

[152] [2012] ONCA 32 at [65]–[70].

Conclusion

Common to the approach adopted in New Zealand, Canada and Australia is the recognition that the essential foundation of the law of confidentiality lies in an obligation arising from the circumstances under which the information was obtained. This is consistent with the historical development of the action for breach of confidence in England.

2–099

In cases of contract, such obligation may arise from an express or implied term of the contract. Such obligation may also arise by imposition of law. Just as a duty of care or a fiduciary duty may arise both under the terms of a contract and by imposition of law,[153] similarly a duty of confidence may arise both under a contract and by imposition of law.[154]

2–100

It may not appear to make a practical difference whether, contract apart, the action for breach of confidence:

2–101

(1)   is founded on an equitable obligation, for breach of which the court may now award monetary compensation in addition to or instead of other equitable remedies, or

(2)   is founded on a multi-faceted jurisdiction under which the court may award a full range of equitable and common law remedies.

It is suggested that the first is the preferable analysis, both historically and conceptually. The action for breach of confidence has come to occupy its own area within the law, and it may in that sense be described as sui generis, but it is desirable for its coherent development that its underlying foundation should be clear.

The circumstances in which a person may obtain confidential information vary widely. Broadly they may be divided into the following classes:

(1)   *Direct receipt.* A discloses confidential information to X. This is the simplest case.

(2)   *Indirect receipt.* A discloses confidential information to B, who passes it to X. X may know that it is confidential at the time or he may not discover that until later, by which time he may have incurred expense or otherwise altered his position in the belief that he was entitled to use the information or he may himself have passed on the information.

(3)   *Accidental receipt.* X obtains information regarded by A as confidential as a result, directly or indirectly, of accident, carelessness or mistake on the part of A or some person to whom A has passed the information.

(4)   *Surreptitious receipt.* X obtains information regarded by A as confidential as a result, directly or indirectly, of reprehensible conduct, to which X may or may not be a party.

---

[153] *Henderson v Merrett Syndicates Ltd* [1995] 2 A.C. 145 at 206, per Lord Browne-Wilkinson:

"The existence of a contract does not exclude the co-existence of concurrent fiduciary duties (indeed, the contract may well be their source); but the contract can and does modify the extent and nature of the general duty that would otherwise arise".

[154] e.g. *Lamb v Evans* [1893] 1 Ch. 218; *Robb v Green* [1895] 2 Q.B. 315.

2–102   It can be seen that in some instances there will be an obvious, direct relationship of confidentiality between A and X; in some instances, there may be said to be an indirect relationship of confidentiality between A and X; in some instances the information has not reached X under or by reason of any relationship of confidentiality.

2–103   Insofar as all these types of case may involve breach of what has been recognised as an equitable obligation, it is established that monetary compensation is now in principle available for all of them.

2–104   There is also now developing in English law a different species of action, introduced under the same name, for the protection of information about a person's private life within the meaning of Art.8. There are conflicting views how this is best classified. It is suggested that it is best seen as an action based in tort, but the content is more important than the classification.

CHAPTER 3

Essential Features of Confidentiality

GENERAL PRINCIPLES

The principles considered in this chapter are those which relate to the law of confidentiality excluding claims for infringement of privacy under Art 8. Aside from cases founded on a person's right to privacy under Art.8, the core principles of the law of confidentiality may be stated in broad terms as follows: **3–001**

(1) A duty to treat information as confidential may arise by the express or implied terms of a contract or as an equitable obligation.
(2) Key factors in establishing an equitable obligation are the nature of the information, the circumstances in which it was obtained and notice of its confidentiality.
(3) The circumstances must have been such as to import an obligation of confidentiality.[1] Such circumstances include cases where information:
   (a) is received in the course of a relationship or venture which a reasonable person would regard as involving a duty of confidentiality[2];
   (b) is received for a limited purpose in the exercise of a legal power or furtherance of a legal duty[3];
   (c) is obtained by improper or surreptitious means[4] or, possibly, by accident or mistake[5];
   (d) is received directly or indirectly from another person under a duty of confidentiality.[6]

---

[1] *Coco v A N Clark (Engineers) Ltd* [1969] R.P.C. 41 at 47; *Att Gen v Guardian Newspapers Ltd (No.2)* [1990] 1 A.C. 109 at 281.
[2] *Coco v A. N. Clark (Engineers) Ltd* [1969] R.P.C. 41 at 48.
[3] *Marcel v Commissioner of Police* [1992] Ch. 225 at 262; *Hellewell v Chief Constable of Derbyshire* [1995] 1 W.L.R. 804 at 807; *R. v Licensing Authority Established under Medicines Act 1968 Ex p. Smith Kline & French Laboratories Ltd* [1968] A.C. 910 at 946; *Woolgar v Chief Constable of Sussex Police* [2000] 1 W.L.R. 25 at [6].
[4] *Lord Ashburton v Pape* [1913] 2 Ch. 469 at 475; *Franklin v Giddins* [1978] Qd. R. 72 at 79–80; *The Commonwealth v John Fairfax* (1980) 147 C.L.R. 39 at 50; *Shelley Films Ltd* [1994] E.M.L.R. 134; *Creation Records Ltd v News Group Newspapers Ltd* [1997] E.M.L.R. 444.
[5] *English & American Insurance Ltd v Herbert Smith* [1988] F.S.R. 232 at 237–238; *Att Gen v Guardian Newspapers Ltd (No.2)* [1990] 1 A.C. 109 at 281.
[6] *Abernathy v Hutchinson* (1824) 3 L.J.Ch. 209; *Prince Albert v Strange* (1848) 1 Mac. & G. 25; *Printers & Finishers Ltd v Holloway* [1965] R.P.C. 239 at 253; *Att Gen v Guardian Newspapers Ltd (No.2)* [1990] 1 A.C. 109 at 201; *Lancashire Fires Ltd v S.A. Lyons & Co Ltd* [1996] F.S.R. 629 at 676.

(4)   The recipient must have notice that the information is confidential.[7] The degree of notice or knowledge required may vary according to the circumstances. Where information is imparted in the course of a relationship or venture which a reasonable person would regard as involving a duty of confidentiality, it is enough that a reasonable person in the recipient's position would regard the information as confidential.[8] Where information claimed to be confidential is received by a person in other circumstances, the question of what knowledge is required to bind the conscience of the recipient is more complicated.

(5)   The nature of the information must be such as to warrant the recipient being under an obligation to treat it as confidential.

(6)   It is an essential ingredient of the action for breach of confidence that confidential information has been, or is threatened to be, misused.[9] What constitutes misuse will depend on the circumstances of the case and the scope of the duty owed.

(7)   A duty of confidentiality may be negated or qualified by public interest.[10]

(8)   A duty of confidentiality may be subject to other qualifications either by agreement or by operation of law.[11]

(9)   Where an action is based on the court's equitable jurisdiction, the court may decline to grant relief (or limit the terms of any relief) on equitable grounds. These may include:
  (a)   that the claim is stale;
  (b)   that the claimant's own conduct is not such as to merit relief[12]; or
  (c)   that the relief claimed would cause injustice to a defendant who has acted in good faith.[13]

(10)   As a general rule an action for breach of confidentiality may be brought only by a person to whom the duty in question is owed, but exceptionally an action for protective relief may be brought by someone having responsibility to protect the welfare of that person.[14]

Contract

3–002   A contract may contain express terms restricting a person's use of information. This may include information about matters which are common knowledge or easily ascertainable.[15]

---

[7] *Att Gen v Guardian Newspapers Ltd (No.2)* [1990] 1 A.C. 109 at 281.

[8] *Printers & Finishers Ltd v Holloway* [1965] R.P.C. 239 at 256; *Coco v A. N. Clark (Engineers) Ltd* [1969] R.P.C. 41 at 48.

[9] *Coco v A. N. Clark (Engineers) Ltd* [1969] R.P.C. 41 at 47.

[10] *Att Gen v Guardian Newspapers Ltd (No.2)* [1990] 1 A.C. 109; *W v Egdell* [1990] 1 Ch. 359 at 419–420; *Imutran Ltd v Uncaged Campaigns Ltd* [2002] 2 All E.R. 385 at [20].

[11] *Tournier v National Provincial and Union Bank* [1924] 1 K.B. 461.

[12] *McNicol v Sportsman's Stores* (1930) McG.C.C. 116 at 125; *Hubbard v Vosper* [1972] 2 Q.B. 84 at 99–101; *Church of Scientology v Kaufman* [1973] R.P.C. 627 at 654–656.

[13] Compare *Lipkin Gorman v Karpnale Ltd* [1991] 2 A.C. 548 at 577–580.

[14] *Fraser v Evans* [1969] 1 Q.B. 344; *Broadmoor Special Hospital Authority v Robinson* [2000] Q.B. 775; *Green Corns Ltd v Claverley Group Ltd* [2005] EWHC 958, QB; *A Local Authority v W* [2005] EWHC 1564, Fam.

[15] As the Law Commission noted in its Report on Breach of Confidence, Law Com. No.110 (Cmnd 8388), 1981, at para.4.15 and fn.140.

In *Saltman*[16] Lord Greene M.R. emphasised that: **3–003**

> "The information, to be confidential, must, I apprehend, apart from contract, have the necessary quality of confidence about it, namely, it must not be something which is public property and public knowledge."

In *Att Gen v Barker*[17] Lord Donaldson M.R. observed that a contractual promise not to publish information, even if not inherently confidential, is a form of negative covenant for consideration which the court will enforce "provided only that the covenant itself cannot be attacked for obscurity, illegality or on public policy grounds such as that it is in restraint of trade".

In *Att Gen v Blake*[18] the House of Lords declared that the Attorney-General   **3–004**
was entitled to an account of profits made by the spy, George Blake, by breach of his contractual undertaking not to divulge any official information gained by him as a result of his employment in the Secret Intelligence Service either in the press or in book form. Blake broke the undertaking by writing his autobiography. At the time of its publication none of the information relating to his activities as a secret service officer was secret, nor was it alleged that the publication would damage the public interest. The contractual undertaking was nevertheless still binding.

In *Ministry of Defence v Griffin* an injunction was granted to enforce a   **3–005**
contractual undertaking by a former soldier and member of the United Kingdom Special Forces (UKSF) not to disclose any information relating to the work of the UKSF without prior authority from the Ministry. Eady J. said:

> "A contract may embrace categories of information within the protection of confidentiality even if, without a contract, equity would not recognise such a duty."[19]

A contract will be unenforceable if and to the extent that: **3–006**

(1)   it would prevent an ex-employee from making proper use of his skills[20] or otherwise amounts to an unreasonable restraint on trade[21];
(2)   it conflicts with English or European competition law;
(3)   it would prevent publication justified in the public interest, including the right to freedom of expression protected by Art.10 of the European Convention[22];
(4)   it would be otherwise unlawful.

Where a relationship of a confidential nature arises from a contract which does not contain an express confidentiality term, the courts will imply a contractual duty of confidentiality,[23] but it is suggested that the scope of the duty will be the

---

[16] (1948) R.P.C. 203 at 215.
[17] [1990] 3 All E.R. 257 at 259.
[18] [2001] 1 A.C. 268.
[19] [2008] EWHC 1542 at [26].
[20] *Herbert Morris Ltd v Saxelby* [1916] A.C. 688; *Faccenda Chicken Ltd v Fowler* [1987] 1 Ch. 117.
[21] *Maggbury Pty Ltd v Hafele Australia Pty Ltd* (2001) 210 C.L.R. 181.
[22] *London Regional Transport v Mayor of London* [2001] EWCA Civ 1429; [2003] E.M.L.R. 4.
[23] *Faccenda Chicken Ltd v Fowler* [1987] 1 Ch. 117 at 135.

same whether viewed as an implied term or an equitable obligation.[24] The duty of confidentiality between a doctor and patient, for example, will be the same whether the patient is treated privately or under the National Health Service. The extent of an equitable obligation of confidentiality arising from a relationship governed by contract will fall to be determined by reference to the underlying contractual relationship.[25]

3–007   It has been suggested[26] that an obligation of confidence expressly assumed under a contract might carry more weight than an obligation that is merely implied or equitable in origin. As stated above, express contractual terms may impose a duty of confidentiality where none would otherwise exist. They may also assist a claimant in identifying and defining information that can properly be characterised as confidential. Otherwise, it is difficult to see on what basis and how a court could attach greater legal force to an express contractual term than to an implied one or an equitable obligation.

Circumstances Importing an Obligation of Confidentiality

Information imparted in the course of a relationship or venture which a reasonable person would regard as involving a duty of confidentiality

3–008   It would be impossible to compile a list of all relationships likely to give rise to duties of confidentiality. They include agents, trustees, partners, directors and employees; professional people; holders of public and private offices; people in close personal relationships; and many others. The common thread is that a reasonable person would understand them as involving an obligation of confidentiality.

3–009   In *Printers & Finishers Ltd v Holloway*[27] Cross J. said that the law would defeat its own object if it sought to enforce standards which would be rejected by the ordinary man. Conversely, it would be defective if it failed to protect information imparted in trust in the course of a relationship which a reasonable person would regard as involving an obligation of confidentiality. Such a relationship may be enduring, or may be limited to a single transaction or may arise where parties are in pre-contractual negotiations.[28]

3–010   In *Mars UK Ltd v Teknowledge Ltd*[29] the claimant company had developed a "Cashflow" machine for testing the validity and denomination of coins. Despite the claimant's use of an encryption system, the defendant had succeeded in reverse engineering the claimant's machine and had used the information thereby

---

[24] This is expressed as a suggestion rather than a dogmatic statement because of dicta in *Hilton v Barker, Booth & Eastwood* [2005] UKHL 8; [2005] 1 W.L.R. 567, discussed below at para.3–134.

[25] As in the case of a fiduciary duty: see *Henderson v Merrett Syndicates Ltd* [1995] 2 A.C. 145 at 206 per Lord Browne-Wilkinson.

[26] *Campbell v Frisbee* [2002] EWCA Civ 1374; [2003] E.M.L.R. 76 at [22]; *HM Att Gen v MGN Ltd* [2002] EWHC 3201 (Ch) at [14] per Lewison J.; *Prince of Wales v Associated Newspapers* [2006] EWCA Civ 1776; [2008] 1 Ch. 57 at [69].

[27] [1965] R.P.C. 239 at 256. See also *Napier v Pressdram Ltd* [2009] EWCA Civ 443; [2009] E.M.L.R. 21 at [42].

[28] *Seager v Copydex Ltd* [1967] 1 W.L.R. 923.

[29] [2000] F.S.R. 138.

gained to compete with the claimant. Jacob J. held that the defendant had infringed the claimant's copyrights and database rights but had not acted in breach of confidence.

Turning to the requirement of communication in circumstances importing a duty of confidence, Jacob J. said:

3–011

> "Mars say that such circumstances are to be inferred from the fact that the student of the Cashflow finds encryption. They say the fact of encryption is equivalent to a notice saying 'confidential—you may not de-encrypt'. And they go on to say that if such an express notice were given, the examiner of the machine would come under a duty of confidence. I think they are wrong on both counts. As pure matter of common sense I cannot see why the mere fact of encryption makes that which is encrypted confidential or why anyone who de-encrypts something in code, should necessarily be taken to be receiving information in confidence. He will appreciate that the source of the information did not want him to have access, but that is all. He has no other relationship with that source. Nor do the circumstances have an analogy with eavesdropping or secret long-lens photography . . . or telephone tapping . . . There is nothing surreptitious in taking a thing apart to find out how it is made. In so holding I am applying the 'reasonable man' test suggested by Megarry J. in *Coco* . . . "[30]

Information received for a limited purpose in the exercise of a legal power or furtherance of a legal duty

Where information of a personal or confidential nature is obtained or received in the exercise of a legal power or in furtherance of a legal duty, the recipient will in general owe a duty to the person from whom it was obtained or to whom it relates not to use it for unrelated purposes. Tax payers, for example, are required to disclose details of their income to the revenue. The revenue owes a duty of confidence to every tax payer in respect of such information.[31] There need not therefore be a voluntary imparting of information in order for the recipient to be under an equitable obligation of confidence arising from the nature of the information and the circumstances of its receipt.

3–012

Just as a photographer employed to take a person's photograph owes a duty of confidence to the customer in respect of the material obtained,[32] so a police authority empowered to take a "mug shot" of an arrested person owes an equitable obligation to that person under the law of confidence not to make improper use of the material obtained.[33]

3–013

The scope of the duty may vary from one case to another according to the circumstances in which, and purpose for which, the material was obtained. In

3–014

---

[30] The use of reverse engineering to analyse products supplied confidentially was considered by Peter Smith J. in *EPI Environmental Technologies Inc v Symphony Plastic Technologies Plc* [2004] EWHC 2945 (Ch) upheld on appeal [2006] EWCA Civ 3; [2006] 1 W.L.R. 495 (Note). See also the decision of the New South Wales Court of Appeal in *Industrial Rollformers Pty Ltd v Ingersoll-Rand (Australia) Ltd* [2001] N.S.W.C.A. 111 at [114]–[116].

[31] *R. v Inland Revenue Commissioners Ex p. National Federation of Self-Employed and Small Businesses Ltd* [1982] A.C. 617 at 654, per Lord Scarman; *R. v Inland Revenue Commissioners Ex p. Preston* [1985] A.C. 835 at 864, per Lord Templeman; *Lonrho Plc v Fayed (No.4)* [1994] Q.B. 775; *Mount Murray Country Club Ltd v Macleod and others* [2003] UKPC 53; (2003) S.T.C. 1525 at [33].

[32] *Pollard v Photographic Co* (1888) 40 Ch.J. 345.

[33] *Hellewell v Chief Constable of Derbyshire* [1995] 1 W.L.R. 804.

Hellewell v Chief Constable of Derbyshire[34] Laws J. held that the police might make reasonable use of the photograph for the purpose of the prevention and detection of crime, the investigation of alleged offences and the apprehension of suspects or persons unlawfully at large. Limited circulation of the mug shot of the plaintiff (who had 32 convictions including 19 for offences of dishonesty) to shopkeepers who were considered to have legitimate cause for apprehension if he were to visit their premises, was not improper use of it.

3–015   The general principle was stated in *Marcel v Commissioner of Police*[35] by Sir Christopher Slade:

> "In my judgment, documents seized by a public authority from a private citizen in exercise of a statutory power can properly be used only for those purposes for which the relevant legislation contemplated that they might be used. The user for any other purpose of documents seized in a draconian power of this nature, without the consent of the person from whom they were seized, would be an improper exercise of the power. Any such person would be entitled to expect that the authority would treat the documents and their contents as confidential, save to the extent that it might use them for the purposes contemplated by the relevant legislation."

The Court of Appeal recognised that the duty in that regard lay not only in public law but also in the private law of confidentiality. But just as the recipient of information voluntarily imparted to him in confidence may be compelled to disclose it by process of law, so may the recipient of information which was itself supplied to him under compulsion.

3–016   In *Marcel's* case a development company sued a purchaser for default in contracts for the purchase of some flats. The purchaser alleged that he was induced to enter the contracts by misrepresentations made by three agents of the company. The three were arrested by the police on suspicion of conspiracy to defraud the purchaser (with which they were later charged, but the charges were dropped) and documents were seized from them. The purchaser served a subpoena *duces tecum* on the police requiring them to produce the seized documents at the trial of the action brought by the company. The police allowed the purchaser's solicitor to inspect and copy some of the documents before the subpoena was formally served. The three agents issued proceedings against the police, the purchaser and his solicitor, to prevent use of the documents in the civil action.

3–017   The Court of Appeal held that voluntary disclosure of the seized documents by the police to the purchaser, without a subpoena, would have been a breach of duty of confidence; but that the police might be compelled to produce them on subpoena, just as the owners of the seized documents might themselves have been compelled to produce them on subpoena. The Court expressed differing views about the propriety of the disclosure of the documents after issue of the subpoena but prior to the requirement for their formal production in court. Dillon L.J. said that he could see the practical sense of producing them prior to the trial so that they could be sifted and administrative arrangements made to facilitate the conduct of the civil proceedings, provided that it was remembered that the

---

[34] *Hellewell v Chief Constable of Derbyshire* [1995] 1 W.L.R. 804.
[35] [1992] Ch. 225 at 262.

documents were not the property of the police. Sir Christopher Slade, while having sympathy with the course taken by the police, said that they should not have disclosed the documents without the consent of the owners or the authority of the court.

The plethora of powers given to different bodies for obtaining information under the Police and Criminal Evidence Act 1984, the Companies Act 1985, the Insolvency Act 1986, the Criminal Justice Act 1987, the Financial Services and Markets Act 2000, the Serious Organised Crime and Police Act 2005 and other statutes, and the potential for the powers of compulsion under one statute to be used to obtain information supplied by compulsion under another, have combined to produce almost as many possible permutations as a football pools coupon. This has given rise to some complex questions of confidentiality, especially in cases where the facts are complicated, the documents are voluminous and various regulatory bodies are involved.[36]

3–018

The principles and potential complexities are illustrated by *Re Arrows Ltd (No.4)*.[37] N was a director and principal shareholder of Arrows Ltd. When the company collapsed he was examined by the liquidators, under s.236 of the Insolvency Act 1986, and transcripts were made. A person examined under that section may not refuse to answer questions on the ground that his answers would be self-incriminating.[38] At the time of his examination N was also under investigation by the Serious Fraud Office (SFO). The SFO subsequently served a notice on the liquidators, under s.2(3) of the Criminal Justice Act 1987 requiring the liquidators to produce the transcripts to the SFO for use as evidence in criminal proceedings against him.

3–019

It was argued on behalf of N that the *Marcel* principle applied, and that the liquidators owed a private law duty to him not to produce the transcripts to the SFO. The House of Lords rejected that argument. They recognised the validity of the *Marcel* principle within its limits, i.e. to prevent voluntary disclosure otherwise than for the purposes for which the information or material was obtained. But, said Lord Browne-Wilkinson[39]:

3–020

> "In my view, where information has been obtained under statutory powers the duty of confidence owed on the *Marcel* principle cannot operate so as to prevent the person obtaining the information from disclosing it to those persons to whom the statutory provisions either require or authorise him to make disclosure."[40]

Moreover, even though the statutory provisions under which the first body (i.e. the liquidators) obtained information by compulsion might not require or authorise that body to pass it on to a second body (i.e. the SFO), the second body might be empowered to require its disclosure under its own statutory powers.

3–021

---

[36] *Re Esal (Commodities) Ltd* [1989] B.C.L.C. 59; *Re Esal (Commodities) Ltd (No.2)* [1990] B.C.C. 708; *Morris v Director of Serious Fraud Office* [1993] B.C.L.C. 580; *Re Maxwell Communications Corp Plc (No.3)* [1995] 1 B.C.L.C. 521; *Marlwood Commercial Inc v Kozeny* [2004] EWCA Civ 798; [2005] 1 W.L.R. 104.

[37] [1995] 2 A.C. 75.

[38] *Bishopsgate Investment Management Ltd v Maxwell* [1993] Ch. 1.

[39] [1995] 2 A.C. 75 at 102.

[40] See also the analysis by the Court of Appeal in *Sutton v GE Capital Commercial Finance Ltd* [2004] EWCA Civ 315 at [39]–[43], of the purposes for which administrative receivers may use documents obtained pursuant to requests under ss.234–236 of the Insolvency Act 1986.

This was so in *Re Arrows Ltd*, where the SFO claimed production under the Criminal Justice Act 1987, under which its powers were wide. Lord Browne-Wilkinson said[41]:

> "Subject to limited exceptions the Act of 1987 expressly overrides any duty of confidence 'imposed by or under' any statute other than the Taxes Management Act 1970: section 3(3) of the Act of 1987. Similarly, the fact that section 2(9) and (10) of the Act of 1987 expressly preserves two specific duties of confidence (legal professional privilege and banking confidence) shows that all other common law duties of confidence are overridden."

3–022   N also relied on public interest immunity.[42] It was argued that although his own *private law* right in the confidentiality of information extracted from him under statutory powers was subject to the statutory powers of the SFO under the Act of 1987, there was a wider *public* interest in ensuring that information extracted was used only for the purpose for which the statutory power to obtain it was conferred (*Conway v Rimmer*[43]; *Alfred Crompton Amusement Machines Ltd v Customs & Excise Commissioners (No. 2)*).[44] So it was submitted that N's transcripts, having been obtained under s.236 of the Insolvency Act 1986, could be used only for the purposes of the liquidation.

3–023   This argument caused the House of Lords to examine the extent of the duty of confidentiality owed by liquidators to persons examined under s.236. They concluded that the Act of 1986 contemplated liquidators disclosing information and documents obtained by them to others, including disclosure for the purposes of criminal proceedings. Accordingly, liquidators could not give any assurance to a person examined under s.236 that his answers would not be disclosed to prosecuting authorities and the claim that the answers enjoyed public interest immunity also failed.[45]

The creation of statutory regulatory bodies is now frequently accompanied by express provisions as to the confidentiality of information provided to, or obtained from, those bodies.[46] In some cases the statutory scheme may also impose criminal sanctions for disclosure of confidential material.[47]

In *R. (Kent Pharmaceuticals Ltd) v Director of the Serious Fraud Office* the Court of Appeal upheld the lawfulness of the SFO's decision, in the exercise of a statutory discretion, to disclose to the Department of Health documents which had been seized during a criminal investigation into the activities of pharmaceutical companies suspected of selling drugs to the National Health

---

[41] *Sutton v GE Capital Commercial Finance Ltd* [2004] EWCA Civ 315 at [99].

[42] For fuller discussion of public interest immunity see Ch.19, below.

[43] [1968] A.C. 910 at 946.

[44] [1974] A.C. 405.

[45] In relation to material obtained under s.235 of the Insolvency Act 1986, see *R. v Brady* [2004] EWCA Crim 1763; [2004] 1 W.L.R. 3240 at [23ff].

[46] Difficulties may remain in determining the effect of such provisions, for example, whether they may require a person to withhold information which he would otherwise be under a duty to disclose to a third party. See *Real Estate Opportunities Ltd v Aberdeen Asset Managers Jersey Ltd* [2007] EWCA Civ 197; [2007] 2 All E.R. 791.

[47] For example, s.24 of the Animals (Scientific Procedures) Act 1986, considered by Eady J. and the Court of Appeal in *Secretary of State for the Home Department v British Union for the Abolition of Vivisection* [2008] EWHC 892 (QB); [2008] EWCA Civ 870; [2009] 1 W.L.R. 636.

Service at artificially high prices. The disclosure was requested by the Department which had brought civil claims against some of the companies.[48]

In *Woolgar v Chief Constable of Sussex Police*[49] the Court of Appeal accepted **3–024** that what a person says to the police during an interview under caution after arrest is confidential, subject to qualifications. It may obviously be used in the course of a trial if charges are brought, since that is a primary purpose of the interview. The court also held in that case that the police were entitled on grounds of public interest to disclose a transcript to a nursing regulatory body in connection with a wider investigation being carried out into the treatment of patients at a nursing home where the claimant was the matron.

A similar duty of confidentiality is owed to a witness who gives voluntary **3–025** information to the police. In *Taylor v Director of the Serious Fraud Office*[50] Millett L.J. said in the Court of Appeal:

> "Members of the public who volunteer information to the police are entitled to expect that it will be used only for the purpose of the investigation and subsequent criminal proceedings. Their expectations should be respected."

Even if the information itself is not of a confidential nature, the fact that the witness has given it may well be so.

There are also cases in which disclosure of otherwise confidential information **3–026** is obligatory if a person wishes to pursue a particular activity (e.g. to carry on a business for which a licence is required). Many examples could be given. Such disclosure may be described as voluntary in one sense but obligatory in another. Whichever way it is classified, the recipient will owe to the confider a duty of confidentiality, the extent of which will depend on the purposes for which it is provided.

In *R. v Licensing Authority Established under Medicines Act 1968 Ex p. Smith* **3–027** *Kline & French Laboratories Ltd*[51] the applicants were manufacturers of a drug used in the treatment of gastric ulcers. The Medicines Act 1968 prohibits the manufacture or sale of any medicinal product except in accordance with a product licence granted by the appropriate licensing authority. By a combination of the provisions of the Act, regulations made under it and EC directives, an application for a licence had to be supported by a large amount of information of an obviously confidential nature. The applicants sought declarations to the effect that the licensing authority was not entitled to have regard to information supplied by the applicants, when considering applications by other companies for licences to market generic versions of the drug. The application failed. Lord Templeman said[52]:

> "If the appellants choose to apply for a product licence under the Act, they choose to provide information to the licensing authority for the purposes of the Act. It is not unconscionable for the licensing authority to make use of that information in the

---

[48] [2004] EWCA Civ 1494; [2005] 1 W.L.R. 1302. A majority of the court held that the SFO had acted unfairly by failing to give adequate notice to the claimant of its intention to release the documents to the Department but that the claimant had not been prejudiced as a result.

[49] [2000] 1 W.L.R. 25 at [6].

[50] [1999] A.C. 177 at 198.

[51] [1990] 1 A.C. 64.

[52] [1990] 1 A.C. 64 at 104.

public interest for the purposes of the Act, although it would be unconscionable for the licensing authority to disclose that information to third parties for other purposes."

Looking at the purposes of the Act, Lord Templeman concluded that,

" . . . it is the right and duty of the licensing authority to make use of all the information supplied by any applicant for a product licence which assists the licensing authority in considering whether to grant or reject any other application, or which assists the licensing authority to perform any of its other functions under the Act of 1968."

A similar question arose under different statutory provisions in New Zealand[53] and in Australia[54] with a similar result in each case.

3–028   In Australia the court rejected "the test of confider's purpose" (argued for by the company) as governing the scope of the confidant's duty in such a case. The confider's purpose in disclosing the information was narrow (to obtain a licence). The authority's purpose was wider (to protect public health and safety). In considering whether the confidant's use of the information was unconscionable, it was necessary to consider the purpose of the regulations under which the information was provided, rather than merely the purpose of the provider.

3–029   In New Zealand, Jeffries J. approached the question whether there had been a breach of a duty of confidentiality by considering the nature of the relationship between the parties. He said[55]:

"It is not a bilateral commercial relationship. It has no contractual base whatsoever. . . . The parties are forced into the relationship by statute law. The Minister and his departmental officers are responsible for consenting to the use of new medicines which if faulty can have catastrophic effects of which thalidomide is an example. The Minister and Department are acting on issues in granting consent of the foremost public importance being the health of the nation . . .

In the circumstances, as disclosed by this case, I would think it wrong to impose such a strict and narrow duty of confidentiality on a Government Department so as to prevent access to its own records of prior applications, and its accumulated knowledge and experience when performing the task of approving another pharmaceutical product which is identical, or nearly so."

Information obtained by improper or surreptitious means

3–030   In *Prince Albert v Strange* the Solicitor-General argued that:

"The information, which has been here made use of by the Defendant was improperly obtained; either there was a breach of contract or there was a crime committed. In neither case could the Defendant obtain a title to use the information so acquired."[56]

---

[53] *Smith Kline and French Laboratories Ltd v Att-Gen* [1989] 1 N.Z.L.R. 385.
[54] *Smith Kline and French Laboratories (Australia) Ltd v Department of Community Services* [1990] F.S.R. 617, per Gummow J.; affirmed (1991) 28 F.C.R. 291 (Full Court of the Federal Court).
[55] [1989] 1 N.Z.L.R. 385 at 396–397.
[56] (1848) 1 Mac. & G. 25 at 38.

Lord Cottenham L.C. said[57] that on the affidavit evidence the collection of royal etchings described in the catalogue published by the defendant could only have been formed by "impressions surreptitiously and improperly obtained", and that since the defendant was unable to suggest any mode by which they could have been properly obtained, so as to entitle the possessor to use them for publication, it must be assumed that the defendant's possession had its foundation in a breach of trust, confidence or contract. The tenor of the judgment does not suggest that he would have taken a more favourable view if the etchings had been surreptitiously obtained in some other way.

The principle in Ashburton v Pape

In *Ashburton v Pape*[58] the defendant surreptitiously obtained copies of letters between the plaintiff and his solicitor from a clerk employed by the solicitor, so there was both surreptitious behaviour and breach of a confidential relationship. Swinfen Eady L.J. expressed the principle as follows:

> "The principle upon which the Court of Chancery has acted for many years has been to restrain the publication of information improperly or surreptitiously obtained or of information imparted in confidence which ought not to be divulged."[59]

3–031

However, as the Law Commission noted in its Working Paper on Breach of Confidence in 1974,[60] in *Ashburton v Pape* there was a breach of duty by one of the parties to the confidence. In its Report in 1981[61] the Law Commission concluded that:

> " . . . under the present law it is very doubtful to what extent, if at all, information becomes impressed with an obligation of confidence by reason solely of the reprehensible means by which it has been acquired, and irrespective of some special relationship between the person alleged to owe the obligation and the person to whom it is alleged to be owed."

The Law Commission's doubts were based partly on the absence of precedent for the imposition of such a duty and partly on the judgment of Sir Robert Megarry V.C. in *Malone v Metropolitan Police Commissioner.*[62]

Malone had sought a declaration that the tapping of his telephone line by the police, on the authority of the Home Secretary, was unlawful on various grounds, including confidentiality. In dismissing the claim, Megarry V.C. said that one of the requirements of the action for breach of confidence was that information must have been "imparted in circumstances importing an obligation of confidence" and in this connection he contrasted the facts with those of *Coco v A. N. Clark*

3–032

---

[57] (1848) 1 Mac. & G. 25 at 41–45.
[58] [1913] 2 Ch. 469 at 475.
[59] Cited by Mason J. (later Mason C.J.) in *Commonwealth of Australia v John Fairfax & Sons Ltd* (1980) 147 C.L.R. 39 at 50.
[60] Working Paper No.58 at para.21.
[61] Law Com. No.110: Breach of Confidence (Cmnd. 8388) at para.4.10.
[62] [1979] 1 Ch. 344.

(Engineers) Ltd,[63] where his own decision had been based on the communication by an inventor to a manufacturer of information which the manufacturer misused. He continued[64]:

> "In the present case, the alleged misuse is not by the person to whom the information was intended to be communicated, but by someone to whom the plaintiff had no intention of communicating anything: and that, of course, introduces a somewhat different element, that of the unknown overhearer.
>
> It seems to me that a person who utters confidential information must accept the risk of any unknown overhearing that is inherent in the circumstances of communication. Those who exchange confidences on a bus or a train run the risk of a nearby passenger with acute hearing or a more distant passenger who is adept at lip-reading. Those who speak over garden walls run the risk of the unseen neighbour in a tool-shed nearby. Office cleaners who discuss secrets in the office when they think everyone else has gone run the risk of speaking within earshot of an unseen member of the staff who is working late. Those who give confidential information over an office intercommunication system run the risk of some third party being connected to the conversation. I do not see why someone who has overheard some secret in such a way should be exposed to legal proceedings if he uses or divulges what he has heard. No doubt an honourable man would give some warning when he realises that what he is hearing is not intended for his ears; but I have to concern myself with the law, and not with moral standards. There are, of course, many moral precepts which are not legally enforceable.
>
> When this is applied to telephone conversations, it appears to me that the speaker is taking such risks of being overheard as are inherent in the system. . . .
>
> No doubt a person who uses a telephone to give confidential information to another may do so in such a way as to impose an obligation of confidence on that other: but I do not see how it could be said that any such obligation is imposed on those who overhear the conversation, whether by means of tapping or otherwise."

3–033   The contrast drawn in this passage between a person to whom confidential information is consciously confided and the unintended overhearer suggests that Megarry V.C. considered that a duty of confidentiality required some deliberate act of confiding. If so, subsequent authorities show that the duty is not so confined.

Malone was distinguished by the Court of Appeal in *Francome v Mirror Group Newspapers*.[65] The plaintiff, a well-known jockey, sought and obtained an interlocutory injunction to restrain the defendants from publishing information derived from unauthorised tapping of his telephone. The tapping was a criminal offence under the Wireless Telegraphy Act 1949.[66] The defendants contended that there could be no right of action against them, or against the eavesdroppers who recorded the plaintiff's conversations, and relied for that proposition on *Malone*. Sir John Donaldson M.R. described it as a "rather surprising proposition". The court rejected the argument that the decision in *Malone* negatived the right to confidentiality alleged by the plaintiff, and stressed that Megarry V.C. had been dealing only with a case of authorised tapping by the police; but because the

---

[63] *Coco v A. N. Clark (Engineers) Ltd* [1969] R.P.C. 41.
[64] *Coco v A. N. Clark (Engineers) Ltd* [1969] R.P.C. 41 at 376.
[65] [1984] 1 W.L.R. 892.
[66] See now the Regulation of Investigatory Powers Act 2000.

matter was before the court on an interlocutory application, it was unnecessary for it to make a final decision whether there had been a breach of a duty of confidentiality.[67]

In Australia the courts have recognised the applicability of an equitable   3–034
obligation of confidentiality to a person who obtained confidential information by improper or surreptitious means. In *Concrete Industries (Monier) Ltd v Gardner Bros & Perrott (WA) Pty Ltd*[68] Fullager J. said that it is not a defence that the plaintiff did not impart the information to the defendant and that he got it by stealing it from the plaintiff's safe.

Obtaining confidential information through trespass

In *Franklin v Giddins*[69] the defendant trespassed on the plaintiff's orchard and   3–035
stole some budwood cuttings from a new and commercially valuable strain of nectarine (called "Franklin Early White"), which the plaintiff had developed by selective cross-breeding over a considerable number of years. The plaintiff could have sued in trover, but the consequence of judgment being satisfied would have been that property in the subject-matter would then have vested in the defendant (see the observations of Lord Denning M.R. in *Seager v Copydex (No.2)*[70]), and this would have given the defendant an unassailable right thereafter to propagate trees from the cuttings and sell them in competition with the plaintiff. The plaintiff sued for delivery up of all trees in the defendant's possession which had been propagated from the stolen cuttings and for injunctive relief, basing his claim on misuse of confidential material by the defendant.

If the defendant had been employed by the plaintiff to work in the orchard,   3–036
there could be no doubt that the plaintiff would have been entitled to such relief. The case would have fallen squarely within such authorities as *Lamb v Evans*[71] (misuse of printers' blocks for use in compiling a trade directory) and *Robb v Green*[72] (surreptitious copying of the employer's customer list). The plaintiff's budwood was not for sale, precisely because he wished to preserve to himself the technique which he had developed for propagating Franklin Early White nectarines, as the defendant knew. By stealing the budwood the defendant acquired the ability to use that technique by dishonest means. The judge accepted that the parent tree could be likened to a safe in which were locked a number of copies of a formula for making a nectarine tree with special characteristics, and when budwood was stolen it was as if a copy of the formula was taken out of the safe. The formula was genetic, the result of cross-breeding, and was contained in (and inseparable from) the budwood.

The defendant relied on the absence of any consensual relationship between   3–037
himself and the plaintiff, and he contended that an equitable obligation of confidence could only arise from the imparting of confidential matter by the plaintiff. It would be most unsatisfactory if that were so in relation to a formula of

---

[67] See also *R. v Preston* [1994] 2 A.C. 130 at 150.
[68] Vic S.C., August 18, 1977, unreported, at pp.6–7.
[69] [1978] Qd.R. 72.
[70] [1969] 1 W.L.R. 809 at 813.
[71] [1893] 1 Ch. 218.
[72] [1895] 2 Q.B. 315.

commercial value, which the plaintiff was not prepared to impart to the defendant, and which the defendant therefore resorted to dishonest means to obtain.

3–038   Dunn J. upheld the plaintiff's claim. After reference to *Prince Albert v Strange*,[73] *Saltman*[74] and *Argyll*,[75] he said[76]:

> "[Counsel for the defendants] argued that the budwood twigs were not 'information confidentially imparted' and that therefore no obligation of confidence deserving of protection had arisen, challenging the proposition that 'it would be extraordinary if a defendant, who acquired by eavesdropping or other improper covert means the secrets of the plaintiff because he would not have been able to get them by consensual arrangement, could defend proceedings by the plaintiff on the ground that no obligation of confidence could arise without communication of the information by the plaintiff.' (Meagher, Gummow and Lehane's book, at p.719.)
>
> I find myself quite unable to accept that a thief who steals a trade secret, knowing it to be a trade secret, with the intention of using it in commercial competition with its owner, to the detriment of the latter, and so uses it, is less unconscionable than a traitorous servant. The thief is unconscionable because he plans to use and does use his own wrong conduct to better his position in competition with the owner, and also to place himself in a better position than that of a person who deals consensually with the owner.
>
> I have already expressed the opinion that, when the male defendant stole budwood from the plaintiff's orchard, what he got was a trade secret. The secret was the technique of propagating Franklin Early White nectarines, using budwood from the plaintiff's orchard. The technique of budding was no secret, but the budwood existed only in the plaintiff's orchard, where the plaintiffs guarded it by exercising general surveillance over fruit-pickers and visitors, and by bruiting it abroad that it was theirs and theirs alone. The 'information' which the genetic structure of the wood represented was of substantial commercial value, much time and effort had been expended by the male plaintiff in evolving it and it could not be duplicated by anybody whatsoever."

More recent authorities in England have followed the same approach. In *Shelley Films Ltd v Rex Features Ltd*[77] an injunction was granted on the ground of breach of an equitable duty of confidence against use of photographs surreptitiously taken of a confidential costume design.

3–039   The plaintiffs were producers of a film, *Mary Shelley's Frankenstein*, starring the actor Robert De Niro as the Frankenstein "creature". He wore a highly distinctive costume made up of prostheses described as analogous to a rubber sculpture. The plaintiffs, who had invested over $40 million in the film, were anxious that the appearance of the creature should remain a secret until the film was released. Filming took place in a secure area, manned by security guards and with notices stating that the taking of photographs was not permitted. A freelance photographer managed to gain access to the set and took photographs depicting the "creature" on the scaffold, which he supplied to the defendant photographic agency. A picture of the scene was published in the *Sunday People*.

---

[73] (1848) 1 Mac. & G. 25.
[74] (1948) 65 R.P.C. 203.
[75] [1967] Ch. 302.
[76] [1978] Qd.R. 72 at 79–80.
[77] [1994] E.M.L.R. 134.

Two days later the plaintiffs obtained, ex parte, an order against the defendants **3–040** requiring them to disclose the identity of the photographer, but Rattee J. set aside the order, on an inter partes hearing, on the ground that the information relating to the film which the plaintiffs sought to protect could not be said to have been communicated to the photographer in confidence, when it was the plaintiffs' case that he had obtained it clandestinely and without the plaintiffs' knowledge. The judge appears not to have been referred to any of the authorities showing that a duty of confidence may be owed by a person who obtains confidential information surreptitiously or by accident or mistake.

The plaintiffs continued with the action and applied for an interlocutory **3–041** injunction restraining the defendants from publishing any photograph or reproduction depicting any costume design made for use in the film. The injunction was granted after fuller argument.

The judge, Martin Mann QC, cited *Franklin v Giddins* and added: **3–042**

> "Although Dunn J. characterised the information involuntarily imparted to the defendant as a trade secret, there is in my judgment no relevant distinction for present purposes between such information and less secret information similarly or analogously obtained provided always that it is properly to be regarded as confidential."

He further held that the steps taken by the plaintiffs to maintain security and prevent photography, the circumstances in which the photographs were taken, and the plaintiffs' evidence about the value which they attached to keeping the film costumes secret for commercial reasons, established against the defendant agency a serious issue to be tried that it was under an equitable obligation not to publish the photographs, sufficient for the grant of an interlocutory injunction.

In *Creation Records Ltd v News Group Newspapers Ltd* [78] the plaintiffs had a **3–043** recording contract with the pop group Oasis and planned to take photographs for an album sleeve featuring a white Rolls Royce in a swimming pool with members of the group around it. The filming was to be done at a hotel. Security staff were employed to see that members of the public who were at the hotel did not take photographs of the set, but a newspaper photographer managed to take photographs of it which were published. Lloyd J. granted an interlocutory injunction against further publication of the photographs, holding that it was arguable on the evidence that the photographer must have acted surreptitiously, knowing that there was no consent to the taking of photographs, and that the album design was a form of confidential information. It was not entirely secret since members of the public would be able to describe what they had seen, but still had significant confidentiality because they were not permitted to record it photographically.

Douglas v Hello! Ltd[79] was another case of surreptitious photography. After **3–044** citing *Shelley Films Ltd v Rex Features Ltd* and *Creation Records Ltd v News Group Newspapers Ltd*, the Court of Appeal stated:

> "Where an individual ('the owner') has at his disposal information which he has created or which is private or personal and to which he can properly deny access to

---

[78] [1997] E.M.L.R. 444.
[79] [2005] EWCA Civ 595; [2006] Q.B. 125 at [118].

third parties, and he reasonably intends to profit commercially by using or publishing that information, then a third party who is, or who ought to be, aware of these matters and who has knowingly obtained the information without authority, will be in breach of duty if he uses or publishes the information to the detriment of the owner. We have used the term 'the owner' loosely."

The only member of the House of Lords to refer to *Shelley Films Ltd v Rex Features Ltd* and *Creation Records Ltd v News Group Newspapers Ltd* was Lord Walker. He queried whether photographs of a white Rolls Royce in a swimming pool were not too trivial to attract the protection of the law but did not otherwise criticise the reasoning that surreptitious obtaining of information intended to be confidential could give rise to a duty of confidentiality.[80]

In *Tchenguiz v Imerman* during the course of divorce proceedings the wife's brothers accessed the husband's computer and copied confidential materials which were then sent to the wife's forensic accountants and solicitors. The motive was concern that the husband would not make frank disclosure of his financial position in ancillary proceedings. The Court of Appeal held that the accessing, copying and dissemination of the documents was a breach of confidentiality. Lord Neuberger M.R., delivering the judgment of the court, stated the principles as follows:

"It was only some 20 years ago that the law of confidence was authoritatively extended to apply to cases where the defendant had come by the information without the consent of the claimant. That extension…was established in the speech of Lord Goff of Chievely in [*Spycatcher*]. He said (…[1990] 1 AC 109 at 281) that confidence could be invoked where "an obviously confidential document is wafted by an electric fan out of a window…or…is dropped in a public place, and is then picked up by a passer-by…

If confidence applies to a defendant who adventitiously, but without authorisation, obtains information in respect of which he must have appreciated that the claimant had an expectation of privacy, it must, a fortiori, extend to a defendant who intentionally, and without authorisation, takes steps to obtain such information. It would seem to us to follow that intentionally obtaining such information, secretly and knowing that the claimant reasonably expects it to be private, is itself a breach of confidence…

The fact that the law of confidentiality was extended in *Campbell v Mirror Group Newspapers Ltd* …for the purpose of giving effect to art. 8 in English law, cannot, as we see it, mean that the law of confidentiality has somehow been circumscribed in other respects."[81]

The court also recognised that a claim based on confidentiality is an equitable claim. Accordingly, while a court would normally be expected to grant injunctive relief in the type of case under discussion, it retained a discretion whether to grant relief and in what form. As it observed, "equity fashions the appropriate relief to fit the rights of the parties, the facts of the case, and, at least sometimes, the wider merits".[82]

There is today no doubt of the general principle that the equitable doctrine of confidentiality applies where a person improperly or surreptitiously obtains

---

[80] [2007 UKHL 21; [2008] 1 A.C. 1 at [289]–[291].
[81] [2010] EWCA Civ 908; [2011] Fam. 116 at [64], [68], [71].
[82] At [74].

confidential information. If a duty of confidence can be owed by the recipient of obviously confidential information obtained by accident (discussed below), the same must apply with added force where it has been obtained improperly, as the court held in *Tchenguiz v Imerman*. It would be absurd if a duty were owed in equity by a finder of a private diary dropped in the street, but not by a pickpocket, whose conscience should be more greatly affected.

Extension of *Ashburton v Pape* to mistake

A series of cases have now confirmed the principle stated by Swinfen Eady L.J.   3–045
in *Ashburton v Pape*[83] and have extended it to information obtained by mistake known to the recipient.[84]

In *English & American Insurance Ltd v Herbert Smith*[85] papers which a   3–046
barrister intended to be sent to solicitors instructing him in litigation were by a clerical error sent instead to the defendants, who were the solicitors acting for the other side. The defendants read them and took copies before sending on the original documents to the intended recipients, acting upon guidance given by the Law Society and in the belief that their paramount duty was to their clients. Sir Nicolas Browne-Wilkinson V.C. held that their conduct was in breach of an equitable obligation of confidentiality. He rejected the argument that the jurisdiction did not apply where there was "an accidental escape of information to the third party" or that the recipient need be "improperly implicated in the leakage of the information".

He also drew a distinction between innocent receipt of a document and   3–047
innocent receipt of the information contained in it, saying:

> "If somebody is handed a letter addressed to another marked 'Private and Confidential', that letter having been handed to him in error, and he chooses to read it notwithstanding seeing that it is marked 'Private and Confidential', and as a result acquires the information contained in that letter, I find it difficult to say that he is not implicated in the leakage of the information contained in that letter."[86]

In *Spycatcher* Lord Goff, after stating the general principle that a duty of   3–048
confidence arises when confidential information comes to the knowledge of a person in circumstances where he has notice that the information is confidential, with the effect that it would be just in all the circumstances that he should be precluded from disclosing the information to others, added[87]:

> "I realise that, in the vast majority of cases, in particular those concerned with trade secrets, the duty of confidence will arise from a transaction or relationship between the parties—often a contract, in which event the duty may arise by reason of either

---

[83] [1913] 2 Ch. 469 at 475.
[84] *Goddard v Nationwide Building Society* [1987] 1 Q.B. 670; *Guiness Peat Ltd v Fitzroy Robinson* [1987] 1 W.L.R. 1027; *English & American Insurance Ltd v Herbert Smith* [1988] F.S.R. 232; *Webster v James Chapman & Co* [1989] 3 All E.R. 939; *Derby & Co Ltd v Weldon (No. 8)* [1991] 1 W.L.R. 73; *Fayed v Commissioner of Police of the Metropolis* [2002] EWCA Civ 780; *The Times*, June 17, 2002.
[85] [1988] F.S.R. 232.
[86] [1988] F.S.R. 232 at 238.
[87] [1990] 1 A.C. 109 at 281.

an express or an implied term of that contract. It is in such cases as these that the expressions 'confider' and 'confidant' are perhaps most aptly employed. But it is well settled that a duty of confidence may arise in equity independently of such cases; and I have expressed the circumstances in which the duty arises in broad terms, not merely to embrace those cases where a third party receives information from a person who is under a duty of confidence in respect of it, knowing that it has been disclosed by that person to him in breach of his duty of confidence, but also to include certain situations, beloved of law teachers—where an obviously confidential document is wafted by an electric fan out of a window into a crowded street, or where an obviously confidential document, such as a private diary, is dropped in a public place, and is then picked up by a passer-by."

In *English & American Ltd v Herbert Smith* and the hypothetical cases instanced by Lord Goff there would be no room for doubt in the recipient's mind that the document was not meant to be read by him before he read its contents.

3–049   Other cases have occurred where there has been an intended delivery to the recipient, but there has been a mistake in the document enclosed. The mistake may not be apparent to the recipient until after he has read it or until sometime later. In such situations an equitable obligation of confidentiality may still arise when the recipient realises that he has been sent a confidential document by mistake, but whether it does will depend on all the circumstances of the case. The yardstick is what standard of behaviour is reasonably and practicably to be expected of the recipient. There may be cases where it is reasonable and practicable to expect the recipient to return the document and make no use of it, but there may be other cases where this would be unrealistic or unjust. Suppose, for example, that a company managing director wrote a document addressed to its head of human resources stating that he had decided to terminate the employment of a senior employee, X, and discussing how this could be done most cheaply and with least damage, but inadvertently sent the document to X. It would be obvious to X at once that the document was intended to be confidential and that he was the last person who was meant to see it, but to expect him to return it unread would be to expect an unreal standard of behaviour.

3–050   There is, however, now no doubt that as a matter of general principle the law of confidentiality applies to a person who receives accidentally a document which he knows to be confidential, and in *Tchenguiz v Imerman* the Court of Appeal used that principle as a stepping stone to its ruling that the law of confidentiality similarly applies as a matter of general principle to a person who deliberately and secretly obtains information which he knows to be confidential.[88]

3–051   There is a complex body of case law on the relationship of confidentiality and legal professional privilege, particularly where one party in the course of litigation mistakenly discloses privileged documents to an opposing party. This subject is discussed in Ch.18.

---

[88] [2010] EWCA Civ 908; [2011] Fam. 116 at [64], [68].

Information received directly or indirectly from another person under a duty of confidentiality

Information properly disclosed

A third party may receive confidential information or material for a proper **3–052** purpose. A general practitioner might, for example, provide medical information about a patient to a consultant for the purpose of obtaining the consultant's opinion or send a specimen of the patient's blood to a laboratory for the purpose of testing. The consultant or analyst receiving the information or specimen would as a general proposition be under a duty of confidentiality to the patient not to use the information or material otherwise than for the purpose for which it was provided.

Information improperly disclosed

A third party may also receive confidential information or material in **3–053** circumstances where the supplier is in breach of a duty of confidence to another (the confider). Where the third party receives information knowing that it has been disclosed by his informant in breach of confidence, he will himself owe a duty of confidence to the confider.[89] This principle is derived from the doctrine that it is equitable fraud in a third party knowingly to assist in a breach of trust, confidence or contract by another: *Abernethy v Hutchinson*[90] and *Prince Albert v Strange*.[91] In *Lancashire Fires Ltd v S. A. Lyons & Co Ltd*[92] Sir Thomas Bingham M.R. said:

> "In *Seager v Copydex Ltd* [1967] 1 W.L.R. 923 Lord Denning M.R. at p.931 considered the nature of a claim for breach of confidence and stated 'The law on this subject does not depend on any implied contract. It depends on the broad principle of equity that he who has received information in confidence shall not take unfair advantage of it.'
>
> That principle would be defeated if a third party to whom the secret information had wrongfully been disclosed could as a matter of course make use of it."

Innocent recipient with subsequent knowledge of improper disclosure

The position of a third party who receives confidential information innocently **3–054** and subsequently learns that it was supplied to him in breach of confidence is more difficult. In principle, lack of notice at the time of its receipt that the information was subject to a duty of confidence should not prevent the recipient from himself coming under such a duty as from the time of his discovering the true position, *provided* that he had not in good faith incurred detriment by paying for the information or perhaps by incurring expense of money or effort in consequence of obtaining it (for example, in further research or development).

---

[89] *Spycatcher* [1990] 1 A.C. 109 at 201, per Dillon L.J. at 261, per Lord Keith at 281, per Lord Goff.
[90] (1824) 3 L.J.Ch. 209.
[91] (1848) 1 Mac. & G. 25.
[92] [1996] F.S.R. 629 at 676.

3–055   Leaving the proviso aside, the principle accords with authority. In *Printers & Finishers Ltd v Holloway*[93] Cross J. said:

> "If authority is needed for the grant of an injunction against someone who has acquired—or may have acquired—information to which he was not entitled without notice of any breach of duty on the part of the man who imparted it to him but who cannot claim to be a purchaser for value, I think that it can be found in the case of *Prince Albert v Strange* (1850) 1 MacN. and G. 25. There the court granted an injunction against a defendant who was not—or at all events was assumed by the court not to have been—implicated in the breach of confidence in question. There again, however, the precise wording of any injunction will require careful consideration."

Where the proviso applies, the position is unclear.

"Bona fide purchase" and change of position

3–056   In *Morison v Moat*[94] Turner V.C. in granting an injunction against the defendant, observed,

> "It might indeed be different if the Defendant was a purchaser for value of the secret without notice of any obligation affecting it; and the Defendant's case was attempted to be put upon this ground . . . but I do not think that this view of the case can avail him . . . So far as the secret is concerned he is a mere volunteer deriving under a breach of trust or of contract."

3–057   In *Stevenson Jordan & Harrison Ltd v MacDonald & Evans*[95] the defendant publishers resisted a claim for an injunction to prevent publication of a book allegedly containing material obtained in breach of confidence on the grounds that they were bona fide purchasers for value. At first instance Lloyd-Jacob J. ruled against the existence of such a defence and granted an injunction. His decision was reversed on other grounds and the Court of Appeal declined to express an opinion on the point, although Lord Evershed M.R. observed,[96] obiter, that it would be "somewhat shocking" if a third party purchaser persisted in plans to implement use of confidential material after becoming aware of the breach of duty by which it had been supplied to him.

3–058   In *Wheatley v Bell*[97] Helsham C.J. in the Supreme Court of New South Wales granted an injunction against a bona fide purchaser, holding that the defence of bona fide purchase only applied to property rights and that there were no property rights attached to equities involved in the protection of confidence.

3–059   In *Spycatcher (No.1)* Nourse L.J. said in interlocutory proceedings:

> "As for the newspapers and any other third party into whose hands the confidential information comes, an injunction can be granted against them on the simple ground

---

[93] [1965] R.P.C. 239 at 253; see also *Fraser v Evans* [1969] 1 Q.B. 349 at 361 and *Surface Technology Plc v Young* [2002] F.S.R. 387 at 399, per Pumfrey J.
[94] (1851) 9 Hare 241 at 263–264.
[95] (1951) 68 R.P.C. 190.
[96] (1952) 69 R.P.C. 10 at 16.
[97] [1984] F.S.R. 16; [1982] 2 N.S.W.L.R. 544. See also *AG Australia Holdings Ltd v Burton* [2002] N.S.W.S.C. 170 at [224]–[227] per Campbell J.

that equity gives relief against all the world, including the innocent, save only a bona fide purchaser for value without notice."[98]

This passage was cited at first instance by Sir Nicolas Browne-Wilkinson V.C. in *Spycatcher (No.1)*[99] and by Lord Donaldson M.R. in *Spycatcher (No.2)*, who said[100]:

"Since the right to have confidentiality maintained is an equitable right, it will (in legal theory and practical effect if the aid of the court is invoked) 'bind the conscience' of third parties, unless they are bona fide purchasers for value without notice (*per* Nourse L.J. on 25 July, 1986 in the interlocutory proceedings: *Attorney General v Observer Ltd* Court of Appeal (Civil Division) Transcript No.696 of 1986)."

Professor Gareth Jones, in an article entitled "Restitution of Benefits Obtained in Breach of Another's Confidence", observed:[101]

"Judicial dicta, and the Reporters of the *Restatement of Torts*, accept that a good-faith purchaser who has no notice of any breach of confidence should be free to use and exploit confidential information even though he is subsequently told that it has been sold to him in breach of another's confidence.

Superficially this is an attractive conclusion which marks off the position of the bona fide purchaser from that of the innocent volunteer, such as the donee. Moreover, it preserves the certainty of commercial transactions. Bona fide purchase would certainly be a good defence if the plaintiff's action was based on the defendant's infringement of the plaintiff's equitable property in the particular information. But it is questionable whether the mere payment of money should, in itself, defeat a restitutionary claim whose essence is a duty of good faith, a duty not to take unfair advantage of the plaintiff's confidence. Contrast these two cases,

(a)   D, a business man, pays R for some information which, unknown to D, R has imparted to D in breach of P's confidence. Two weeks later P discovers the true facts and tells D, at which time D has incurred no further expenditure.

(b)   D, a business man, pays R for certain information which, unknown to D, R has imparted to D in breach of P's confidence. D begins to develop a grip, using this information. His expenditure on plant, machinery and leasehold premises has been very substantial. D is then told by P, who has just discovered R's duplicity, the true facts. Three years have elapsed since he paid R for the information.

If bona fide purchase is accepted as a defence, then P will fail in both these cases. In (b) it is right that he should do so. But is there not a great deal to be said for granting him relief in (a), on the terms that he reimburses D his expenditure? This expenditure apart, there has been no detrimental change of position. In such a case, certainty of transaction can be preserved by the recognition of a strong rebuttable presumption that a good-faith purchaser is deemed to have changed his position to his detriment; and the financial interests of the defendant can be safeguarded by the condition that the plaintiff reimburses him his expenditure, with interest, before he

---

[98] Nourse L.J. used the same words in *Goddard v Nationwide Building Society* [1987] 1 Q.B. 671 at 685.
[99] [1987] 1 W.L.R. 1248 at 1265.
[100] [1990] 1 A.C. 109 at 177.
[101] (1970) 86 L.Q.R. 463 at 478–479.

is granted relief. The application of a flexible notion of change of position may, it is suggested, balance more effectively than an absolute defence of bona fide purchase the competing equities of the honest purchaser and the deceived plaintiff."

Other writers have also argued for a flexible approach in cases where an innocent third party has suffered detriment by expending resources in obtaining or exploiting information supplied to him in breach of another's confidence.[102]

3–060   In *Lipkin Gorman v Karpnale Ltd*[103] the House of Lords held that in principle a defence of detrimental change of position is available in restitutionary claims to:

> "a person whose position has so changed that it would be inequitable in all the circumstances to require him to make restitution, or alternatively to make restitution in full",[104]

the explanation being that:

> "where an innocent defendant's position is so changed that he will suffer an injustice if called upon to repay or repay in full, the injustice of requiring him so to repay outweighs the injustice of denying the plaintiff restitution."[105]

If that defence is available to one who has received money belonging to another, there is at least as strong an argument for saying that it should be available to one who has received information in breach of a duty of confidence owed to another. Indeed, the case for the latter may be stronger, because (as Lord Goff recognised in *Lipkin Gorman*) a claim to recover money at common law is made as a matter of right, whereas the obligation of the third party recipient of confidential information supplied in breach of confidence to another is founded on an obligation of conscience, which *ex hypothesi*, cannot bind him to do (or abstain from doing) that which it would in all the circumstances be inequitable to require him to do (or abstain from doing).

3–061   Although the expression "purchaser for value" of confidential information is of respectable antiquity, going back to *Morison v Moat*,[106] and has been used by distinguished judges, it is apt to mislead because of its implication of transfer of property.

3–062   If confidential information were a form of equitable property, there would be logic in affording to the bona fide purchaser of such property an absolute defence to any claim based on his use of the property, regardless of the adequacy of the consideration which he paid or any other circumstances.

3–063   Since confidential information is not a form of equitable property in English law,[107] "bona fide purchaser" is merely a loose description of a person who pays

---

[102] Cornish, Llewelyn & Aplin, *Intellectual Property: Patents, Copyright, Trade Marks and Allied Rights*, 7th edn (London: Sweet & Maxwell, 2010), paras 8–032 to 8–033; Meagher, Gummow and Lehane, *Equity: Doctrines and Remedies* 4th edn (LexisNexis Australia, 2002), para.41–110.

[103] [1991] 2 A.C. 548 at 577–580.

[104] [1991] 2 A.C. 548 at 577–580.

[105] [1991] 2 A.C. 548 at 580.

[106] (1851) 9 Hare 241.

[107] *Douglas v Hello! Ltd* [2005] EWCA Civ 595; [2006] Q.B. 125 at [119] and [126]. See Ch.2 for a fuller discussion.

money for the supply of information in ignorance that it is being supplied to him in breach of another's confidence. In principle, his position on discovering the truth should be governed by considerations of conscience rather than misleading analogies with transfer of property rights.

It does not follow that the fact that the third party has paid for the information in good faith is of no significance, as Greenwood J. rightly concluded in *Retractable Technologies Inc v Occupational and Medical Innovations Ltd* after a valuable review of the authorities.[108] He noted that the cases contain statements at a "reasonably high level of abstraction" and do not deal "definitively or comprehensively" with the various factors which should ultimately determine the just outcome in a particular case. Whilst "in some circumstances the restraint of an apprehended or continued breach of confidence may involve enjoining third parties" (citing Gummow J. in *Breen v Williams*[109]), he stated:

> "...the circumstance that the third party has acted innocently in reliance on a contract, altered its position and conducted its commercial affairs on a particular footing (perhaps with great prejudice and no real ease of adjustment) are factors...that a court would closely examine either in framing the scope of the relief fashioned appropriately to particular conduct or from or to a particular time; or, in determining the respective positions of the parties having regard to the equity asserted by the claimant primary disclosor on the one hand and the innocent purchaser for value without notice on the other.
>
> In that sense, I do not accept the ubiquity of the proposition that the whole notion of the position of a bona fide purchaser for value has no role to play in the discourse upon the right to or scope of relief that might be granted against an innocent third party put on notice that its conduct involves use of another's confidential information, simply because the jurisdictional foundation of relief lies in enforcing an obligation of confidence rather than an order in support of a proprietary interest."

The fact that a person innocently acts to his detriment by paying for the supply of the information should not automatically afford him an absolute right in all circumstances to continue to use the information after discovering the truth, but is, and should be regarded as, a form of detrimental change of position. In any case where there has been a detrimental change of position in good faith by the recipient of information supplied in breach of another's confidence, it is a question of judgment for the court to decide in all the circumstances whether, balancing the parties' respective interests and the justice or injustice which would result to each from the grant or refusal of the relief claimed, any such relief should be granted and, if so, on what terms. **3–064**

Notice of confidentiality

In *Spycatcher*[110] Lord Goff stated in his formulation of the general principle that a duty of confidence arises when confidential information comes to the knowledge of a person in circumstances where he "has notice or is held to have agreed" that the information is confidential. He added that he used the word **3–065**

---

[108] [2007] F.C.A. 545 at [67]–[87]. See also the reference to bona fide purchasers without notice in *Tchenguiz v Imerman* [2010] EWCA Civ 908; [2011] Fam. 116 at [74].
[109] (1996) 186 C.L.R. 71 at 129.
[110] [1990] 1 A.C. 109 at 281.

"notice" advisedly in order to avoid the question of the extent to which actual knowledge is necessary, although he understood knowledge to include circumstances where the confidant has deliberately closed his eyes to the obvious.

Direct relationship between confider and confidant

3–066 Where information is imparted in the course of a relationship or venture which a reasonable person would regard as involving a duty of confidentiality, it is enough that a reasonable person in the recipient's position would regard the information as confidential.

3–067 Cross J. in *Printers & Finishers Ltd v Holloway*,[111] gave the following example in the case of an ex-employee:

> "Suppose such a man to be told by his new employers that at this or that stage in the process they encounter this or that difficulty. He may say to himself: 'Well, I remember that on the corresponding piece of machinery in the other factory such-and-such a part was set at a different angle or shaped in a different way': or again, 'When that happened we used to do this and it seemed to work,' 'this' being perhaps something which he had been taught when he first went to the other factory, or possibly an expedient which he had found out for himself by trial and error during his previous employment.
>
> Recalling matters of this sort is, to my mind, quite unlike memorising a formula or list of customers or what was said (obviously in confidence) at a particular meeting. The employee might well not realise that the feature or expedient in question was in fact peculiar to his late employer's process and factory; but even if he did, such knowledge is not readily separable from his general knowledge of the flock printing process and his acquired skill in manipulating a flock printing plant, and I do not think that any man of average intelligence and honesty would think that there was anything improper in his putting his memory of particular features of his late employer's plant at the disposal of his new employer. The law will defeat its own object if it seeks to enforce in this field standards which would be rejected by the ordinary man."

The same concept is echoed in the judgment of Megarry J. in *Coco v Clark*[112]:

> "It seems to me that if the circumstances are such that any reasonable man standing in the shoes of the recipient of the information would have realised that upon reasonable grounds the information was being given to him in confidence, then this should suffice to impose upon him the equitable obligation of confidence. In particular, where information of commercial or industrial value is given on a business-like basis and with some avowed common object in mind, such as a joint venture or the manufacture of articles by one party for the other, I would regard the recipient as carrying a heavy burden if he seeks to repel a contention that he was bound by an obligation of confidence: see the *Saltman*[113] case at 216."

---

[111] [1965] R.P.C. 239 at 256.
[112] [1969] R.P.C. 41 at 48.
[113] (1948) 65 R.P.C. 203.

Third party recipient

In order to be fixed with an obligation of confidence, a third party must know that the information was confidential; knowledge of a mere assertion of confidentiality is not sufficient.[114]

3–068

There has been debate over what constitutes sufficient knowledge for the conscience of a third party to be bound. The relevant equitable principle is the same as applies to accessories to a breach of trust. In *Royal Brunei Airlines v Tan*[115] the Privy Council re-examined the principle in relation to that subject and reviewed the authorities, including the much cited judgment of Lord Selborne L.C. in *Barnes v Addy*.[116] Lord Nicholls, delivering the judgment of the Board, held that failure to exercise reasonable diligence was insufficient to establish liability against a third party who procured or assisted in a breach of trust, and that it was necessary to establish that he had failed "to observe the standard which would be observed by an honest person" placed in his circumstances. He preferred that formulation to posing the test in terms of whether the third party had "knowingly" assisted in a breach of trust, because a question posed in the latter form led too often into tortuous convolutions about the sort of knowledge required.

3–069

Dishonesty is a natural word to use in relation to misappropriation of trust assets. It is an equally natural word to use in relation to misuse of confidential information of a commercially valuable kind. In the case of confidential information of a non-commercial character other expressions might more naturally be used to convey the gravity of misconduct required, such as wilful or reckless disregard of its confidentiality.[117] Unconscionable is another word which reflects the root of the jurisdiction in an equitable duty of conscience, but suffers from the disadvantage referred to by Lord Nicholls of not being in everyday use by non-lawyers and requiring its own definition.

3–070

The important thing is that for a third party to be held liable in equity for a breach of confidence, more is required than merely careless, naive or stupid behaviour; there must be awareness of the fact that the information was confidential or willingness to turn a proverbial blind eye. This test was applied by the Court of Appeal in *Thomas v Pearce*.[118]

3–071

Where the supply of confidential information to a third party involves the supplier in a breach of a contractual duty of confidence, the third party will be liable for the tort of inducement of breach of contract if he makes himself party to the receipt of the information with knowledge that the supplier is acting in breach

3–072

---

[114] *Fraser v Thames Television* [1984] 1 Q.B. 44 at 65.

[115] [1995] 2 A.C. 378.

[116] (1874) L.R. 9 Ch.App. 244.

[117] In *Hivac Ltd v Park Royal Scientific Instruments Ltd* [1946] 1 Ch. 169 at 172 Lord Greene M.R. said, "The defendants and the employees on the evidence appear quite clearly to have known exactly what they were doing, and they knew that, at any rate, it was morally reprehensible, if not legally wrong".

[118] [2000] F.S.R. 718.

of contract.[119] Conversely, the third party will not be liable if he lacks that knowledge, unless he deliberately shuts his eyes to suspicion.[120]

3–073 There is no action in tort for inducement of a breach of trust or, by analogy, breach of an equitable duty of confidence, but this is not a deficiency because the position of secondary parties to a breach of an equitable duty is adequately dealt with by the principles developed in *Barnes v Addy*[121] and *Royal Brunei Airlines v Tan*.[122] The Court of Appeal so held in relation to inducement of breach of trust in *Metall und Rohstoff A.G. v Donaldson Lufkin & Jenrette Inc.*[123] The effect is similar whether the information was supplied in breach of a contractual or equitable duty of confidentiality, and it is just that it should be so.

3–074 In *Valeo Vision S.A. v Flexible Lamps Ltd*[124] the plaintiffs supplied confidential information to M, who wrongly disclosed it to the defendants. The defendants, unaware of M's breach of confidence, used the information in competition with the plaintiffs. The plaintiffs claimed damages from the defendants, not on the basis that the defendants were party to M's misconduct, but on the simple basis that it was inequitable that they should retain the benefit of their innocent misuse of confidential information. Aldous J. dismissed the claim, holding that the conscience of the defendants could not be bound, and therefore any claim against them in equity failed, in circumstances in which they had no knowledge of the breach of confidence.

3–075 In *Thomas v Pearce*[125] a letting agency sued a former employee and her new employer, another letting agency, for breach of confidence. On changing her employment the employee took with her a list of landlord clients of the first firm and showed it to P, another employee of the second firm. P arranged for letters to be written to some of those on the list to tell them that the employee had joined the second firm. The trial judge found that the employee had acted in breach of confidence but dismissed the claim against the second firm. His assessment of P's evidence was that she had not acted dishonestly, and, although a reasonable estate agent in her position would have made further inquiries, she had not deliberately refrained from asking questions in case she learned something which she would rather not know. The judge accepted her evidence that it did not enter her mind and that the incident happened during the course of a busy day. On his findings of fact the Court of Appeal upheld his judgment.

The thrust of the argument advanced by the appellant was that the judge should have asked himself whether an honest person in the position of the defendant would have acted differently if she had known what she ought objectively to have appreciated.[126] It has been suggested by some authors that the

---

[119] *Hivac Ltd v Park Royal Scientific Instruments Ltd* [1946] 1 Ch. 169. *Ansell Rubber Co Pty Ltd v Allied Rubber Industries Pty Ltd* [1972] R.P.C. 811.

[120] *British Industrial Plastics Ltd v Ferguson* [1940] 12 All E.R. 479, (HL). *Printers & Finishers Ltd v Holloway* [1965] R.P.C. 239. *Compare Emerald Construction Co Ltd v Lowthian* [1966] 1 W.L.R. 691 at 700.

[121] (1874) L.R. 9 Ch.App. 244.

[122] [1995] 2 A.C. 378.

[123] [1990] 1 Q.B. 391.

[124] [1995] R.P.C. 205; see too *B v H Bauer Publishing Ltd* June 14, 2001, QBD, per Eady J. at [23].

[125] [2000] F.S.R. 718.

[126] [2000] FSR 718 at 723–724.

case was wrongly decided.[127] It is argued by them that it is wrong to apply the same approach as applies to accessory liability for a breach of trust; P should have been held liable not for participating in the ex-employee's breach of confidentiality but for her own use of material which objectively she should have realised was confidential. However, the same argument could be made in the case of a recipient of funds paid in breach of trust. It could be argued that a recipient who has used the funds honestly should be liable to the principal if he ought reasonably to have made inquiries which should have led him to realise that the funds were proceeds of a breach of trust. Critics of the Court of Appeal's decision would place a higher burden on an honest person who uses information which he ought reasonably to have appreciated or discovered had been supplied to him in breach of another's confidence than the law places on an honest person who uses funds which he ought reasonably to have appreciated or discovered had been supplied to him in breach of trust. (Relief will of course be granted to an honest recipient of funds received in breach of trust if he still has them, subject to special defences, but that is another matter.)

The position in English law was restated by the Court of Appeal in *Campbell v MGN Ltd*:

"Where a third party receives information that has been disclosed by his informant in breach of confidence owed to the confider, the third party will come under a duty of confidence to the confider if he knows that the information has been obtained in breach of confidence. This principle is derived from the doctrine that it is equitable fraud in a third party knowingly to assist in a breach of trust, confidence or contract by another...

The mental element necessary to render a defendant liable as an accessory to a breach of trust has been refined by the decisions of the House of Lords in *Royal Brunei Airlines Sdn Bhd v Tan* [1995] 2 AC 378 and *Twinsectra Ltd v Yardley* [2002] 2 AC 164."[128]

Based on that jurisprudence, an "ambitious submission" was advanced that a third party would only be liable if he not only knew that the information was confidential, but knew also that its publication could not be justified on the ground of public interest. This submission was rejected.[129]

The submission was not renewed in the House of Lords. In those circumstances, and since there was no challenge to the judge's finding that the Mirror must have known that the information about Ms Campbell's attendance at Narcotics Anonymous was confidential, there was no issue about the correctness of Court of Appeal's statement of the law in the passage set out above and it remains the law. However, two passages in the judgments of the House of Lords have been identified by critics of the Court of Appeal's approach.

---

[127] Arnold, "Circumstances importing an obligation of confidence" [2003] L.Q.R. 193, Stanley, *The Law of Confidentiality: A Restatement* (Oxford: Hart, 2008), 30, and Gurry, *Breach of Confidence*, 2nd edn (Oxford University Press, 2012), 7.106–1.110.

[128] [2002] EWCA Civ 1373; [2003] Q.B. 633 at [66]–[68]. In *Force India Formula One Team Ltd v 1 Malaysia Racing Team Sdn Bhd* [2012] EWHC 616 (Ch) at [251] Arnold J. seems to have interpreted this part of the Court of Appeal's judgment as rejecting the analogy between accessory liability for breach of trust and for breach of confidence. If that is indeed what he meant, we disagree.

[129] [2002] EWCA Civ 1373; [2003] QB 633 at [68]–[69].

Lord Nicholls said that "the law imposes a 'duty of confidence' whenever a person receives a piece of information he knows or ought to know is fairly and reasonably to be regarded as confidential."[130] There is a difference between saying that a person ought to have appreciated on the facts of which he was aware that the information was confidential and saying that a person ought to have acquired knowledge from which he would or should have appreciated the confidential nature of the information. The House of Lords was not concerned with the position of a third party recipient, but it is suggested that if Lord Nicholls had intended to disapprove of the Court of Appeal's statement of principle about the mental element necessary for liability on the part of a third party recipient he would have said so explicitly.

The same applies to Lord Hofmann's statement that equity imposes an obligation of confidentiality upon anyone who receives information "with actual or constructive knowledge of the duty of confidence".[131] That could be read as imposing a duty of inquiry on the recipient to make such inquiries as a reasonable person would have made. If so, it would be inconsistent with the law as stated by the Court of Appeal. It can also be read as meaning that equity imposes a duty on the conscience of a person who receives information which he ought to treat as confidential on the facts known to him. That would be consistent with the law as stated by the Court of Appeal. "Constructive knowledge" is a notoriously difficult expression.

A purely objective approach in the case of an indirect recipient was rejected by the Court of Appeal in *Vestergaard Frandsen A/S v BestNet Europe Ltd*.[132] The claimants made insecticidal fabrics. Their head of production and their European sales manager, Mrs Sig, surreptitiously embarked on a project to develop a competing product in association with a scientist who was a consultant to the claimants. They subsequently left the claimants and set up a group of companies to market the rival product. Arnold J. found that the scientist used a confidential data base of the claimants in developing the new product. He found that although Mrs Sig was not personally involved in devising the recipes for the rival product, she had taken part in misuse of confidential information by her involvement in setting up the new companies and was constructively liable even if she was not conscious that what she was doing amounted to using confidential information. In support of his reasoning he cited *Seager v Copydex Ltd*.[133] Jacob, L.J., held, in a short judgment with which the other members of the court agreed, that the facts found by the judge were insufficient to justify finding Mrs Sig liable for breach of confidentiality although she had behaved reprehensibly in a number of ways.

In *Hunt v A* the New Zealand Court of Appeal reviewed certain of the authorities in this area (but not *Campbell v MGN Ltd*). After observing that the equitable doctrine of confidentiality is broad and flexible, the court said:

> "In the current state of the law in New Zealand, it appears to us that the most satisfactory principle to proceed on is to determine whether a third party recipient of confidential information has acted unconscionably in relation to the acquisition of the information or the way it has been employed...When so approached, the factors

---

[130] para.14.

[131] para.44.

[132] [2011] EWCA Civ 424 on appeal from [2009] EWHC 1456 (Ch).

[133] [1967] 1 W.L.R. 923.

to be considered in a given case will include: the nature of the information; the state of knowledge of the acquirer of the confidential information; what kind of detriment has resulted or might result to the other parties; and the degree of "culpability", as it were, of the third party acquirer and discloser. This is not, of course, a closed list of the considerations which may be appropriate in a given case."[134]

The difficulty with that approach, with respect, is that while it is certainly "broad and flexible", it might be considered so broad and flexible as to be nebulous. The court added that the most critical factor in the vast majority of cases will be the defendant's state of knowledge. In the instant case, it said that the defendant "may not have acted wisely, but she acted in good faith". For a combination of that and other reasons, it concluded that she had not acted unconscionably.

However, the ultimate question in each case is whether equity should intervene to grant the relief claimed, and that may permit flexibility in order to do justice. It is always important to have in mind the context in which the question of "unconscionability", which lies at the heart of the doctrine of confidentiality, is posed. More particularly, the questions "Did, or does, X have sufficient notice of the confidential nature of the information to make it equitable to grant an injunction or compensation in lieu of an injunction?" and "Ought equitable compensation (or other relief) to be awarded against X for their past use of confidential information?" may yield different answers. This was recognised by Sir Thomas Bingham M.R. in *Lancashire Fires Ltd v SA Lyons & Co Ltd*. He found that the third defendant had been sufficiently involved in the operations of a company which used a secret process of her former employer that it was right to grant injunctive relief against her, but he made clear that whether financial relief should be awarded against her was a different issue on which the court would need to hear further argument before deciding the point.[135] A third party recipient may not have acted unconscionably in the receipt of confidential information, but may subsequently not be entitled in good conscience to retain or use it.[136]

Accidental recipient

Although there is no direct authority on the point, an accidental recipient of confidential information should not be under an equitable obligation unless he knows that the information is confidential or is deliberately blind to the likelihood of it being confidential. The absence of authority is unsurprising. If the confidential nature of the document is truly obvious, the court is likely to conclude that the recipient must have known it. But the recipient should be entitled to explain why its confidentiality was not obvious to him; and if he is believed, he should not be held to have acted unconscionably. To hold otherwise would be to set a standard of behaviour higher than the ordinary person would expect. It is also difficult to see why there should be a more onerous obligation on a person who unwittingly receives confidential information by accident than on a person who unwittingly receives confidential information from someone who is under a duty of confidentiality.

3–076

---

[134] [2008] 1 N.Z.L.R. 368 at [91]–[94].
[135] [1996] F.S.R. 629, 677–678.
[136] See *Printers & Finishers v Holloway* [1965] RPC 239 at 253 and the discussion under "Innocent recipient with subsequent knowledge of improper disclosure" at paras 3–054 to 3–064, above.

Improper or surreptitious receipt

3–077   A person who obtains confidential information improperly or surreptitiously behaves in a way which by its nature is contrary to "a properly formed and instructed conscience" (to use the expression of Gleeson C.J. in *Australian Broadcasting Corporation v Lenah Game Meats Pty Ltd*[137]). It is hard to imagine circumstances in which such a person could resist the application of the equitable jurisdiction on grounds of lack of notice of the confidentiality.

Confidential nature of the information

3–078   The requirements for a duty of confidentiality that the information must be confidential, and that it must be obtained in circumstances giving rise to a duty of confidentiality, are closely linked. Both are determined from the viewpoint of a reasonable person; and the circumstances in which information is received may be relevant to whether a reasonable person would regard the subject matter as confidential. But it does not necessarily follow that information will have the objective quality of confidentiality because it is imparted in the course of a confidential relationship.

3–079   Sir Robert Megarry V.C. referred to the difficulties of definition, in a commercial setting, in *Thomas Marshall Ltd v Guinle*[138]:

> "It is far from easy to state in general terms what is confidential information or a trade secret. Certain authorities were cited, but they did not carry matters very far. Plainly 'something which is public property and public knowledge' is not confidential: see *Saltman Engineering Co. Ltd v Campbell Engineering Co. Ltd* (1948) 65 R.P.C. 203, 215, *per* Lord Greene M.R. On the other hand, 'something that has been constructed solely from materials in the public domain may possess the necessary quality of confidentiality: for something new and confidential may have been brought into being by the application of the skill and ingenuity of the human brain. Novelty depends on the thing itself, and not upon the quality of its constituent parts': *Coco v A. N. Clark (Engineers) Ltd* [1969] R.P.C. 41, 47, a case that was not cited, but in part draws on the *Saltman* case, which was. Costs and prices which are not generally known may well constitute trade secrets or confidential information: see *Herbert Morris Ltd v Saxelby* [1916] 1 A.C. 688, 705, referring to prices."

He went on to suggest, as a matter of principle, certain elements which might assist in identifying confidential information in an industrial or trade setting—the party claiming confidentiality must believe that release of the information would be injurious to him or of advantage to his rivals or others; the party claiming confidentiality must believe that the information is confidential, i.e. not already in the public domain; his belief under the two previous heads must be reasonable; and the information must be judged in the light of the usage and practices of the particular industry or trade concerned.

3–080   In *Lancashire Fires Ltd v S A Lyons & Co Ltd*[139] (also a trade secret case) Carnwath J. noted the "subjective emphasis" of that approach and said that:

---

[137]   (2001) 208 C.L.R. 199 at [45].
[138]   [1979] 1 Ch. 227 at 248.
[139]   [1996] F.S.R. 629 at 646, 656.

"The subjective view of the owner cannot be decisive. There must be something which is not only objectively a trade secret, but something which was known, or ought to have been known, by both parties to be so."

Adapted for more general application, the following elements may be suggested:

3–081

(1) There must be some value to the party claiming confidentiality (not necessarily commercial) in the information being treated as confidential;
(2) The information must be such that a reasonable person in the position of the parties would regard it as confidential; and in considering reasonableness, usage and practices in the relevant sector (for example, industrial or professional) are to be taken into account.

These elements are expressed in positive terms. The courts have also identified particular factors which negate confidentiality, and these can be seen as instances where one or more of the positive elements is lacking.

Confidentiality and reasonableness

In *Dunford & Elliott v Johnson & Firth Brown*[140] Lord Denning M.R. held that the courts would recognise confidentiality only to the extent that it was reasonable to do so.

3–082

This principle has not been explicitly followed in later cases, but there is no doubt that the concept of what is reasonable has influenced the development of the law of confidentiality.

3–083

First, in *Coco v Clark*[141] itself Megarry J. pressed into service "that hard-worked creature, the reasonable man" in determining whether information should be regarded as confidential.

3–084

Secondly, in many cases the difficult question has been not whether there is any duty of confidence but what are its limits. In determining that question the court is bound to be influenced by consideration of what is reasonable, and there are plenty of examples among the cases.[142]

3–085

Necessity of identification of information claimed to be confidential

Information alleged to be confidential must be specific in the sense that it is clear and identifiable as confidential.[143] The problem arises especially with alleged trade secrets, where elements of the information for which protection is sought

3–086

---

[140] [1978] F.S.R. 143 at 148.
[141] [1978] F.S.R. 143 at 148.
[142] *Tournier v National Provincial and Union Bank* [1924] 1 K.B. 461; *Printers & Finishers Ltd v Holloway* [1965] R.P.C. 239 at 256; *Smith Kline & French Laboratories (Australia) Ltd v Secretary to the Department of Community Services and Health* (1991) 99 A.L.R. 679 at 691–692; *R. v Department of Health, Ex p. Source Informatics Ltd* [2001] Q.B. 424; *W v Egdell* [1990] 1 Ch. 359; *Hellewell v Chief Constable of Derbyshire* [1995] 1 W.L.R. 804 at 810.
[143] *Amway Corp v Eurway International Ltd* [1974] R.P.C. 82 at 86–87; *Potters-Ballotini Ltd v Weston-Baker* [1977] R.P.C. 202 at 205–206; *O'Brien v Komesaroff* (1982) 150 C.L.R. 310 at 324–328; *Fraser v Thames Television Ltd* [1984] 1 Q.B. 44 at 63; and *De Maudsley v Palumbo* [1996] F.S.R. 447.

may be in the public domain or within a former employee's general expertise. In some cases there may be confidentiality about a system even if it is made up of parts which are familiar. In *Under Water Welders & Repairers Ltd v Street and Longthorne* Buckley J. said[144]:

> "The fact that all the individual units of equipment that are employed in a particular operation may be articles that can be obtained in the general market and the fact that systems are well known to those concerned in whatever sort of activity is involved, does not mean that there cannot be *some degree of confidentiality* about the way in which they are used to achieve a particular result." (Emphasis added.)

It is, however, for the claimant to establish with particularity what is alleged to be confidential.

3–087   Further, it is a cardinal rule that an injunction must be framed in such a way that the party affected can know with certainty what he is or is not allowed to do.[145] In *Potters-Ballotini Ltd v Weston-Baker*,[146] *Lawrence David Ltd v Ashton*[147] and *CMI-Centres for Medical Innovation GmbH v Phytopharm Plc*[148] applications for interlocutory injunctions to restrain alleged misuse of confidential information, which was insufficiently defined, were refused for that reason.[149] However, it does not follow that the claimant necessarily has to identify each and every document which is said to be confidential.[150]

3–088   Those cases concerned alleged trade secrets, but the problem also arose in *Times Newspapers Ltd v MGN Ltd*,[151] in which an unsuccessful attempt was made to restrain the unauthorised, advance publication of extracts from Lady Thatcher's memoirs. Leggatt L.J. said:

> "It is a matter of regret that because the plaintiffs are constrained to concede that vital parts of the book should be excepted from the scope of any injunction, and because the drafting of such an exception could not, in my judgment, be satisfactorily achieved, as the plaintiffs' draft demonstrates, the continued pirating of passages from the book cannot be effectually restrained by the plaintiffs, whatever prospects they may enjoy of eventually recovering damages."

By contrast, a clause in an employment contract restraining the employee from post-employment competitive activity in order to protect the employer's confidential information may be valid although the employer may not be able to

---

[144] [1968] R.P.C. 498 at 506–507.
[145] *Att Gen v Punch Ltd* [2003] 1 A.C. 1046 at 1055 (Lord Nicholls). See also *Browne v Associated Newspapers Ltd* [2007] EWCA Civ 295; [2008] Q.B. 103 at [65] (Sir Anthony Clarke M.R.).
[146] [1977] R.P.C. 202 at 206.
[147] [1991] 1 All E.R. 385 at 393.
[148] [1999] F.S.R. 235.
[149] In *FSS Travel and Leisure Systems Ltd v Johnson* [1999] F.S.R. 505 the Court of Appeal upheld Ronald Walker QC's refusal of a final injunction on the grounds (among others) that the pleadings and evidence were insufficiently specific, precise and cogent. See also *Retractable Technologies Inc v Occupational and Medical Innovations Ltd* [2007] F.C.A. 545 at para.90 (Greenwood J.).
[150] *Tchenguiz v Imerman* [2010] EWCA Civ 908; [2011] Fam. 116 at [78].
[151] [1993] E.M.L.R. 443 at 448.

identify with precision the line between that which is confidential and non-confidential. The potential difficulty in drawing the line may be a ground for regarding the clause as reasonable.[152]

Trivial or useless information

The rule that confidentiality does not attach to trivial or useless information reflects the underlying rationale of the jurisdiction. The reasoning was expressed by Deane J. in *Moorgate Tobacco Co Ltd v Philip Morris Ltd (No.2)*[153] as follows:

    3–089

> "Like most heads of exclusive equitable jurisdiction, its rational basis does not lie in proprietary right. It lies in the notion of an obligation of conscience arising from the circumstances in or through which the information was communicated or obtained. Relief under the jurisdiction is not available, however, unless it appears that the information in question has 'the necessary quality of confidence about it' (*per* Lord Greene M.R., *Saltman*[154]) and that it is significant, not necessarily in the sense of commercially valuable (see *Argyll v Argyll*[155]) but in the sense that the preservation of its confidentiality or secrecy is of substantial concern to the plaintiff."

In *Spycatcher*[156] Scott J. referred as an example to *McNicol v Sportsman's Book Stores*,[157] where the plaintiff was the originator of a betting system based on the age of the moon. Maugham J. refused an injunction to protect its alleged confidentiality. Scott J. said that:

    3–090

> "The ground for the refusal was that the information was 'perfectly useless'."

In *Stephens v Avery*[158] the plaintiff revealed to a friend details of a lesbian relationship with a woman who was murdered. The friend passed the information to a newspaper, which published it. Sir Nicolas Browne-Wilkinson V.C. refused to strike out a claim against the confidant and the newspaper for damages for breach of confidence. One of the grounds unsuccessfully relied upon by the newspaper was that the information was mere gossip or "trivial tittle-tattle" outside the protection of the law.[159] Rejecting this argument, Sir Nicolas Browne-Wilkinson said[160]:

    3–091

> "As to the submission that there is no confidentiality in tittle-tattle and gossip, Mr. Wilson relied on a passage in the *Coco* case [1969] R.P.C. 41, 48, where Megarry, J. said:

---

[152] *Thomas v Farr* [2007] EWCA Civ 118; [2007] I.C.R. 932 at [41]–[42] (Toulson L.J.); *Miles v Genesys Wealth Advisers Ltd* [2009] NSWCA 25 at [22]–[27] (Hodgson J.A.).
[153] (1984) 156 C.L.R. 414 at 438.
[154] [1948] 65 R.P.C. 203 at 215.
[155] [1967] Ch. 302 at 329.
[156] [1990] 1 A.C. 109 at 149.
[157] (1930) McG.C.C. 116.
[158] [1988] 1 Ch. 449; followed by Jacob J. in *Barrymore v News Group Newspapers Ltd* [1997] F.S.R. 600.
[159] [1988] 1 Ch. 449 at 452.
[160] [1988] 1 Ch. 449 at 454.

' . . . I doubt whether equity would intervene unless the circumstances are of sufficient gravity; equity ought not to be invoked merely to protect trivial tittle-tattle, however confidential.'

Since the *Coco* case was exclusively concerned with information which was of industrial value, those remarks were plainly obiter dicta. Moreover, I have the greatest doubt whether wholesale revelation of the sexual conduct of an individual can properly be described as 'trivial' tittle-tattle. Again, although it is true that the passage I have quoted occurs in that part of the judgment which deals with the nature of information which can be protected, it is to be noted that the judge appeared to be considering when equity would give a remedy, not dealing with the fundamental nature of the legal right. If, as I think he was, Megarry J. was saying that the discretion to grant an injunction or to award damages would not be exercised in a case which was merely trivial, I agree. But the exercise of such a discretion can only be decided in the light of all the circumstances. Those cannot be known until there has been a trial.

Although Sir Nicolas Browne-Wilkinson V.C. saw the question of triviality as a factor going to the exercise of the court's discretion, rather than to the principle whether a duty of confidence was owed, in *Spycatcher* Lord Goff recognised it as a "limiting principle . . . that the duty of confidence applies neither to useless information, nor to trivia."[161]

In *McKennitt v Ash* Eady J. refused to grant an injunction in respect of certain items of information because he considered them too anodyne to merit protection.[162]

3–092   If a matter is not such that the preservation of its confidentiality would be thought by a person of ordinary honesty and intelligence to be of any substantial concern to the plaintiff, there is sense in not attaching to it any duty of confidence.

Falsity of information

3–093   It has sometimes been argued that there can be no confidentiality in false information or, to put it more fully, that the publication of information said to be inaccurate cannot give rise to a claim for breach of confidentiality.[163] The argument is based on the distinction between defamation and breach of confidentiality referred to by Sir David Cairns in *Khashoggi v Smith*[164]:

> "It seems to me that there is a fundamental distinction between the two types of action, in that in the one case the plaintiff is saying 'Untrue and defamatory statements have been made about me,' and in the other case the plaintiff is saying 'Statements which are about to be published are statements about events which have happened and have been disclosed as a result of a breach of confidence.' "

---

[161] [1990] 1 A.C. 109 at 282.

[162] [2005] EWHC 3003 (QB); [2006] E.M.L.R. 10, discussed at paras 7–035 to 7–038, below. Eady J.'s judgement was upheld on appeal, although Buxton L.J. commented that in some cases he might have taken a different view: [2006] EWCA Civ 1714; [2008] 1 Q.B. 73 at [26].

[163] See *Campbell v MGN Ltd* [2002] EWHC 499 (QB) at [55] (Morland J.), [2003] Q.B. 633 at [56]–[57], CA; *Interbrew v Financial Times Ltd* [2002] EWCA Civ 274; [2002] 2 Lloyd's Rep. 229 at [38].

[164] (1980) 124 S.J. 149, cited by the Court of Appeal in *Lion Laboratories v Evans* [1985] Q.B. 526 at 538 (Stephenson L.J.), 548 (O'Connor L.J.).

However, a claimant might say with good cause, "Statements which are about to be published are about a subject matter which ought properly to be treated as confidential and also contain inaccuracies". In such a case there is no just or logical reason why the inaccuracies should obliterate the confidential nature of the subject matter. If, for example, one party to a marriage proposed to publish what purports to be an intimate account of their sexual life, the other party ought to be able to apply for an order restraining the publication on the grounds of the confidentiality of the subject matter, regardless of the accuracy of the details. Or if a disgruntled former spy proposed to publish the alleged identities of other agents, the security service ought to be able to apply for an order restraining the publication without having to accept the accuracy of the identifications.

An account about a confidential subject may not be less injurious to the interests which are intended to be protected by its confidentiality because it contains falsehoods.   3–094

In *Cornelius v de Tarranto*[165] a psychiatrist was instructed for a fee to provide a medical report on the claimant for legal purposes. On ordinary principles the psychiatrist owed a contractual and equitable duty to the claimant not to make improper disclosure of the report. Without the claimant's consent, she disclosed her report to other medical staff. It contained some defamatory statements. The claimant sued the psychiatrist for defamation and breach of confidentiality. Morland J. dismissed the claim for defamation on grounds of justification but found for the claimant on the issue of breach of confidentiality. If, however, the defence of justification had failed, it would be odd to suppose that the defamatory nature of the report would have afforded a defence to the claim for breach of confidentiality, whether in contract or in equity, although it would have been necessary to avoid double counting in the assessment of damages.   3–095

It would also run counter to the object of confidentiality if a party had to disclose the extent to which he accepted the account of the other party on a confidential subject in order to be able to claim that the subject should be treated as confidential. This point was made by Eady J. in *McKennitt v Ash*[166]:   3–096

> "Although there is no claim for defamation or malicious falsehood, Ms McKennitt has indicated, in respect of certain parts of the evidence, that the account which Ms Ash has chosen to give is untrue, distorted or misleading. It is not in my judgment, however, permissible to respond by advancing the somewhat simplistic proposition that a reasonable expectation of protection, or a duty of confidence, as the case may be, *cannot* arise in relation to false allegations. As I observed in the case of *Beckham v Gibson*, 29 April 2005 (unreported), the protection of the law would be illusory if a claimant, in relation to a long and garbled story, was obliged to spell out which of the revelations are accepted as true, and which are said to be false or distorted: see also *W v Westminster City Council* [2005] EWHC 102; Q.B. Tugendhat J."

The Court of Appeal agreed.[167]

---

[165] [2002] E.M.L.R. 6.
[166] [2005] EWHC 3003 (QB) at [78].
[167] [2006] EWCA Civ 1714; [2008] 1 Q.B. 103 at [78]–[80] (Buxton L.J.) and [85]–[86] (Longmore L.J.).

3–097 The European Court of Human Rights has gone further. In *Cumpana v Romania*[168] two journalists were convicted of criminal defamation after they published an article in virulent terms making false allegations of corruption against two public officials. The European Court rejected a complaint that their convictions violated their rights under Art.10,[169] holding that the protection of the reputation of those against whom the allegations had been made was "a right which, as an aspect of private life, is protected by Article 8 of the Convention".[170] In *Radio France v France*[171] and *Pfeifer v Austria*[172] the court reiterated that a person's right to a reputation is among the rights guaranteed by Art.8.

3–098 Where a publication goes unacceptably into a person's private life, and is also defamatory, Art.8 is breached in both respects. The wronged party is entitled to complain of one or other or both.

Intention to publish

3–099 In *Times Newspapers Ltd v MGN Ltd*[173] Sir Thomas Bingham M.R. expressed doubt whether the necessary quality of confidence could attach to Lady Thatcher's memoirs in circumstances in which the book was shortly due to be published, although he expressed no final view and regretted that because of the timescale the decision whether to grant an interlocutory injunction had had to be made after brief argument and without full time for reflection.

3–100 The fact that somebody intends to publish material may in some circumstances be inconsistent with an intention to regard it as confidential but that will by no means always be so.

3–101 Many examples could be given. A company may intend to apply for a patent. That involves publication of the secret. It would be surprising if an employee or other person to whom the details were imparted in confidence, or a third party who obtained them from such a person, could contend that the information lacked the quality of confidence because the company intended to publish it.

3–102 As the Court of Appeal observed in *Prince of Wales v Associated Newspapers Ltd*,[174] there can be no doubt that if a dishonest typist tried to sell a copy of the Chancellor's budget speech to a newspaper before it was delivered to Parliament, it would be a breach of confidentiality for the newspaper to purchase and publish it.[175]

3–103 The same would apply to a company's yearly or half-yearly results in advance of publication.

---

[168] [2004] E.C.H.R. 692; (2005) 41 E.H.R.R. 14.

[169] The court considered that the convictions were sufficient to restore the balance between the various competing interests at stake and that sentences including imprisonment and a year's ban on working as journalists were manifestly excessive: [115]–[122], [129].

[170] ibid. at [91].

[171] [2004] E.C.R. 127; (2005) 40 E.H.R.R. 706 at [31].

[172] (2009) 48 E.H.R.R. 8 at [35]. See also *Flood v Times Newspapers Ltd* [2012] UKSC 11; [2012] 2 W.L.R. 760, at [44].

[173] [1993] E.M.L.R. 443.

[174] [2006] EWCA 1776; [2008] 1 Ch. 57 at [67].

[175] Or take the D-day landing plans referred to by Bingham L.J. in *Spycatcher* in the Court of Appeal [1990] 1 A.C. 109 at 215. See para.3–113, below.

In *Khashoggi v Smith*[176] the Court of Appeal (Roskill L.J. and Sir David **3–104** Cairns) did not consider that that the plaintiff had lost her claimed right to confidentiality because she had been negotiating with a newspaper for the sale of her memoirs (although their observations were obiter because the claim failed on other grounds). Sir David Cairns said:

> "It seems to me that a person may well be entitled, in an ordinary case, to say: 'I am willing for the details of my private life to be made known to the public by me in the form which I choose and for my financial benefit; but not for them to be published through information disclosed by my confidential servant in a form chosen by her and others and to the profit of her and others.' "

In *Shelley Films Ltd v Rex Features Ltd*[177] an injunction was granted to **3–105** restrain disclosure of details of a film costume prior to the film's release.

In *Creation Records Ltd v News Group Newspapers Ltd*[178] an injunction was **3–106** granted to restrain premature publication of photos of the design for an album sleeve.

In *Douglas v Hello! Ltd* it was argued by Hello! that there could be no confidentiality in photographic images of the Douglases' wedding when they intended such images to be published to the world by OK! The argument was rejected by a majority of the House of Lords. The Douglases were entitled to require others to treat the information conveyed by photographic images as confidential until such time as they chose to permit its publication.[179]

It is accordingly now settled that an intention to publish is not inconsistent **3–107** with maintaining a right of confidentiality until the intended publication.

Public domain

The law regarding confidentiality and "public domain" began simply but has **3–108** become more complicated. In *Saltman*[180] Lord Greene M.R. said:

> "The information, to be confidential, must, I apprehend, apart from contract, have the necessary quality of confidence about it, namely it must not be something which is public property and public knowledge.""Public domain" has come to be the expression most often used in this context, but other phrases used in the cases include "common knowledge"[181] and "information generally available to the public".[182]

In the *Spycatcher* case Lord Goff observed that the equitable duty of **3–109** confidentiality is subject to certain limiting principles. He continued:

> "The first limiting principle (which is rather an expression of the scope of the duty) is . . . that the principle of confidentiality only applies to information to the extent

---

[176] (1980) 124 S.J. 149.
[177] [1994] E.M.L.R. 134.
[178] [1997] E.M.L.R. 444.
[179] [2007] UKHL 21; [2008] 1 A.C. 1 at [120] (Lord Hoffmann) and 307 (Baroness Hale).
[180] (1948) 65 R.P.C. 203 at 217.
[181] *Mustad & Son v Dosen* [1963] R.P.C. 41 at 43; *Coco v A N Clark (Engineering) Ltd* [1969] R.P.C. 41 at 47.
[182] *Ackroyds (London) Ltd v Islington Plastics Ltd* [1962] R.P.C. 97 at 104.

that it is confidential. In particular, once it has entered what is usually called the public domain (which means no more than that the information in question is so generally accessible that, in all the circumstances, it cannot be regarded as confidential) then, as a general rule, the principle of confidentiality can have no application to it."[183]

3–110   Because there has been a misleading tendency at times to treat the question of public domain as if it involves a free standing rule to be mechanistically applied, three points are to be noted about the principle as set out in this passage. First, it is expressed as a general and not an absolute rule. This is reflected in the statement of the Court of Appeal in *Douglas v Hello! Ltd (No.3)* that "In general, once information is in the public domain, it will no longer be confidential or entitled to the protection of the law of confidence, though this may not always be true".[184] Secondly, it is seen to be an aspect of the scope of the duty of confidentiality—or in other words a factor affecting the question whether a person's conscience ought to require him to treat information as confidential. Thirdly, the statement that the principle of confidentiality cannot generally apply to information so generally accessible that it cannot be regarded as confidential might be considered somewhat circular, but its value lies in the flexibility of the guidance which it provides. Read as a whole, the passage highlights that in each case the question for the court is whether the degree of accessibility of the information is such that, in all the circumstances, it would not be just to require the party against whom a duty of confidentiality is alleged to treat it as confidential.

3–111   It is relevant to consider why the fact of information being publicly accessible should affect that issue. The reasons correspond, negatively, with the positive elements of confidential information previously identified: that there is value to the party claiming confidentiality in the information being treated as confidential; and that a reasonable person in the position of the parties would regard the information as confidential.

3–112   The first reason is that the essence of the law of confidentiality is that it is designed to protect secrecy. The essence of a secret is that it is not publicly known. If information is known to the public at large, it would be idle (both in the sense of unreal and in the sense of purposeless) to seek to regard it as confidential.

3–113   Bingham L.J. gave a vivid illustration in the *Spycatcher*[185] case in the Court of Appeal:

> "Forty-four years ago there can have been few, if any, national secrets more confidential than the date of the planned invasion of France. Any Crown servant who divulged such information to an unauthorised recipient would plainly have been in flagrant breach of his duty. But it would be absurd to hold such a servant bound to treat the date of the invasion as confidential on or after (say) 9 June 1944 when the date had become known to the world. A purist might say that the Allies, as confiders and owners of the information, had by their own act destroyed its

---

[183] [1990] 1 A.C. 109 at 282.
[184] [2005] EWCA Civ 595; [2006] Q.B. 125 at [105].
[185] [1990] 1 A.C. 109 at 215.

confidentiality and so disabled themselves from enforcing the duty, but the common sense view is that the date, being public knowledge, could no longer be regarded as the subject of confidence."

In the same case Dillon L.J. said that it would be "futile and just plain silly" to maintain an injunction against further distribution of *Spycatcher* when it had been widely circulated in the English language throughout the world.[186]

The House of Lords upheld the Court of Appeal in concluding (by a majority) that the extensiveness of the publication of *Spycatcher* abroad and the availability of copies in the UK had resulted in all possible damage being already done and all confidentiality in the subject matter effectively destroyed, so there was no purpose in preventing further publication.[187]   **3–114**

In less extreme cases there may be significant value to a person in being able to claim confidentiality despite some loss or lack of secrecy. Cross J. said in *Franchi v Franchi*[188]:   **3–115**

> "Clearly a claim that the disclosure of some information would be a breach of confidence is not defeated simply by proving that there are other people in the world who know the facts in question besides the man as to whom it is said that his disclosure would be a breach of confidence and those to whom he has disclosed them.
>
> There appear to be no English cases on this branch of the law of trade secrets, but the plaintiffs referred me to the United States case of *Vulcan Detinning Co. v Assam* (1918) 185 N.Y. App. Div. 399 . . . where it was held that the fact that a German and a Dutch firm had complete knowledge of the process in question which one of the defendants (an employee of the plaintiffs) had disclosed to the other defendant was no bar to the plaintiff's success. If it is not impertinent for me to say so, that seems to me sound sense. It must be a question of degree depending on the particular case, but if relative secrecy remains, the plaintiff can still succeed."[189]

The question of confidentiality has sometimes arisen where the information relates to an event which happened in public or is accessible to the general public, although the degree of public knowledge about it is limited.

The Law Commission discussed the issue and posed an example in its Working Paper on Breach of Confidence[190]:   **3–116**

> "Much information which is technically available to the public is not generally known and may in fact be known only to a handful of people. For example, the back files of a local newspaper may, if properly and assiduously searched, yield a good deal of information not generally known about a person who spent his early life in the area—his family and educational background, his business connections, his political beliefs and his personal and social problems. Perhaps they show that he was at the centre of an unfortunate affair at his school, that he attempted to take his own life, that he took part in a political demonstration in favour of an unpopular cause, that he associated in his business or private life with someone later convicted

---

[186] [1990] 1 A.C. 109 at 205.

[187] [1990] 1 A.C. 109 at 259–260, 265–267, 290–291, 293.

[188] [1967] R.P.C. 149 at 152–153.

[189] See also *Spycatcher* [1990] 1 A.C. 109 at 260, per Lord Keith; *Commonwealth of Australia v John Fairfax & Sons Ltd* (1980) 147 C.L.R. 39 at 54, per Mason J.; *Artedomus v Del Casale* [2006] N.S.W.S.C. 146 at [23]–[26], per Burchett A.J.

[190] No.58, 1974, at [102].

of grave crimes against society or even that he 'helped the police' with their inquiries into an offence with which he was never charged. These facts will, of course, be known to and remembered by those who were directly involved, but if the publication took place a long time ago it is quite possible that nobody now knows or remembers them solely by reason of the publication in the local newspaper. If the person concerned subsequently discloses any of these facts in confidence to another in the course of a relationship in which absolute frankness is essential, is it right that the person who accepts the confidence should be able, solely on the ground that the facts are technically accessible to the public, to disclose them to others in breach of his duty of confidence?"

The confidant would surely owe a duty of confidentiality to the confider on grounds that the information was communicated in confidence as well as on the ground that he would be entitled to respect for his private life under Art.8.

3–117   In this context it is instructive to contrast the decisions of the Court of Appeal in *Woodward v Hutchings*[191] and *Schering Chemicals Ltd v Falkman Ltd.*[192]

3–118   In *Woodward v Hutchins* the Court of Appeal discharged an injunction against a former press relations agent to a group of singers who had embarked on the publication in the media of details of the group's lives, including what was described by Lord Denning M.R. as "a very unsavoury episode in a Jumbo Jet". The plaintiffs failed on two grounds.

3–119   First, it was held that since the group had retained the press agent "to have themselves presented to the public in a favourable light", they could not complain afterwards if he revealed unfavourable details, it being in the public interest that the truth should be known.

3–120   Secondly, it was held that the information was not confidential because it was in the public domain. Lord Denning said[193]:

> "But what is confidential? As Bridge L.J. pointed out in the course of the argument, Mr Hutchins, as a press agent, might attend a dance which many others attended. Any incident which took place at the dance would be known to all present. The information would be in the public domain. There could be no objection to the incidents being made known generally. It would not be confidential information. So in this case the incident on the Jumbo Jet was in the public domain. It was known to all passengers on the flight. Likewise with several other incidents in the series."

But suppose instead that the defendant had been a solicitor, instructed by one or more of the group in connection with the incident in the aircraft. It is hard to conceive that the court would in that case have refused an injunction restraining him from selling the story to the media.[194]

3–121   In *Schering Chemicals Ltd v Falkman Ltd*[195] the plaintiffs manufactured a pregnancy testing drug marketed as "Primodos". An issue arose as to its safety and it was withdrawn from the market. Schering retained Falkman to give media and public relations training to Schering's executives in order to counteract bad publicity, and for this purpose they supplied to Falkman a large amount of

---

[191] [1977] 1 W.L.R. 760.
[192] [1982] 1 Q.B. 1.
[193] [1977] 1 W.L.R. 760 at 764.
[194] See the discussion of *Hilton v Barker Booth & Eastwood* [2005] UKHL 8; [2005] 1 W.L.R. 567 at para.3–151 below.
[195] [1982] 1 Q.B. 1.

information about the drug. Falkman retained for a daily fee the second defendant, Elstein, to give instruction to its staff, and he too was provided with information supplied by Schering. He subsequently, without Schering's permission, approached a television company and gave them information from which they made a documentary on the drug. It was contended on their behalf that the information on which the film was based was all available to the public. The Court of Appeal by a majority (Lord Denning M.R. dissenting) upheld an injunction against Elstein and the television company to prevent the broadcasting of the film.

Templeman L.J. said[196]:   **3–122**

> "In my judgment, when Mr Elstein agreed for reward to take part in the training course and received and absorbed information from Schering, he became under a duty not to use that information and impliedly promised Schering that he would not use that information for the very purpose which Schering sought to avoid, namely, bad publicity in the future, including publicity which Schering reasonably regarded as bad publicity."

He continued:

> "The information supplied by Schering to Mr. Elstein had already been published, but it included information which was damaging to Schering when it was first published and which could not be re-published without the risk of causing further damage to Schering."

In both *Woodward v Hutchins* and *Schering Chemicals Ltd v Falkman Ltd* the   **3–123**
defendants' professional skills were engaged to produce good publicity for the plaintiffs and were used by them to produce bad publicity. This was regarded as a reason for refusing an injunction in the former case; but for granting it in the latter case (where paradoxically, the public interest in knowing the truth about Primodos was far greater than any public interest in the private lives of a group of singers). Unless the engagement was in some way disreputable, it is suggested that the approach in *Schering Chemicals Ltd v Falkman Ltd* is to be preferred. But the more important difference is in their approach to the question of confidentiality and the public domain.

The simplest and most satisfactory explanation of *Woodward v Hutchins* is   **3–124**
that there was nothing in the defendant's engagement which required him to regard as confidential the behaviour of the plaintiffs in a public place. If, on the other hand, the plaintiffs had consulted a solicitor about the incident in the aircraft, he would have been under a duty to use the information given to him for the purpose for which it was given and not otherwise.[197] On that basis *Woodward v Hutchins* may be seen as turning on its own particular facts. Although it has never been overruled, its authority is doubtful.

---

[196] [1982] 1 Q.B. 1 at 37.
[197] See *Australian Football League v The Age Co Ltd* [2006] VSC 308, per Kellam J. at [42]. In *Campbell v Frisbee* [2002] EWCA Civ 1374 at [34] Lord Phillips M.R. commented, obiter, that Lightman J. might well be right to suggest that *Woodward v Hutchins* should no longer be applied. See also *McKennitt v Ash* [2005] EWHC 3003 (QB) at [101]–[105] (Eady J.) , [2007] EWCA Civ 1714; [2008] 1 Q.B. 73, at [33]–[36] (Buxton L.J.); and Tugendhat & Christie, *The Law of Privacy and the Media*, 2nd edn (2011), at paras 12–27 to 12–31 and 12–59 to 12–60.

3–125   In *Schering Chemicals Ltd v Falkman Ltd* information was given to the defendants in confidence, and although such information might be obtained from other sources, it was nevertheless perceived by the plaintiffs (reasonably in the eyes of the court) that the defendants would do harm to the plaintiffs if the programme, compiled from information supplied in confidence, were broadcast on a major television network, using information supplied in confidence as a springboard. It is, however, questionable whether the court considered sufficiently the public interest in the facts about Primados and whether a court would reach the same decision today.

3–126   In *Creation Records Ltd v News Group Newspapers Ltd*[198] Lloyd J. granted an injunction to prevent publication in poster form of photographs which the defendants had already published in three editions of *The Sun* (as the judge said "in no doubt millions of copies"), holding that the degree of publication was not a reason in itself for refusing to restrain a further publication of a different kind which the claimants reasonably believed would cause them further damage.[199] The decision was cited with implicit approval by the Court of Appeal in *Douglas v Hello! Ltd (No.3)*.[200]

Lord Hoffmann summarised the modern approach to public domain in *Douglas v Hello! Ltd*:

> "...it is certainly the case that once information gets into the public domain, it can no longer be the subject of confidence. Whatever the circumstances in which it was obtained, there is no point in the law providing protection. But whether this is the case or not depends on the nature of the information. Whether there is still a point in enforcing the obligation of confidence depends on the facts."[201]

3–127   The possibility of further publication causing further damage is particularly likely to arise where the information is personal and the damage is to the person's feelings. In *Spycatcher*[202] Lord Keith envisaged the possibility of cases where, even in the light of widespread publication, a person might still be entitled to restrain further publication if it would cause them further damage, and he gave disclosure of marital secrets as an example. In *McKennitt v Ash*[203] Eady J. commented on Lord Keith's remarks, observing that:

> "there are grounds for supposing that the protection of the law will not be withdrawn unless and until it is clear that a stage has been reached where there is no longer anything left to be protected. For example, it does not necessarily follow that because personal information has been revealed impermissibly to one set of

---

[198] [1997] E.M.L.R. 444.

[199] See also *Mills v News Group Newspapers Ltd*, June 4, 2001, per Lawrence Collins J. at [25]. Contrast *Bunn v British Broadcasting Corp* [1998] 3 All E.R. 552.

[200] [2005] EWCA Civ 595; [2006] Q.B. 125, at [105].

[201] [2007] UKHL 21; [2008] 1 A.C. 1 at [122].

[202] [1990] 1 A.C. 109 at 260.

[203] [2005] EWHC 3003 (QB); [2006] E.M.L.R. 10 at [80]. See also *Northern Rock Plc v The Financial Times Ltd* [2007] EWHC 2677 (QB); *JIH v News Group Newspapers Ltd* [2011] EWHC 2818 (QB) at [58]–[59] (Tugendhat J.), repeated in *TSE v News Group Newspapers Ltd* [2011] 1308 (QB) at [29], and *KJO v XIM* [2011] EWHC 1768 (QB) at [21]–[22] ("The test which has been applied to public domain arguments...is whether, in the light of such accessibility as there is, it is realistic to regard the information as no longer capable of any protection": Tugendhat J.), and *Missingham v Shamin* [2012] NSWSC 288 at [55]–[68].

newspapers, or to readers within one jurisdiction, there can be no further intrusion upon a person's privacy by further revelations. Fresh revelations to different groups of people can still cause distress and damage to an individual's emotional or mental well-being."

To summarise the discussion of the first reason identified for the accessibility of information being relevant to the issue whether a person may justly be required to treat it as confidential, it is a question of fact in each case whether the degree of public accessibility is such that it that it would be senseless to try to protect it as confidential. The distinction between *Spycatcher*, on the one hand, and *Schering Chemicals Ltd v Falkman Ltd* and *Creation Records Ltd v News Group Newspapers Ltd*, on the other hand, is that in the former the courts considered that further publication could do no further damage but in the latter they considered that it could do further damage.   **3–128**

The second, and linked, factor is that the accessibility of information may affect whether a reasonable person in the position of the parties would regard it as confidential. The position of the parties, as well as the accessibility of the information, is important in this regard.   **3–129**

Accessibility may itself depend on the skills and knowledge of the particular defendant, which may therefore also be a relevant factor. Suppose, for example, that a company, C, consulted a solicitor, S, with a view to litigation on its behalf against an ex-employee, E, to restrain him from using certain technical know-how in his employment by another company. Suppose that another company in the industry, hearing of the dispute, approached S or an employee of S and offered him money to provide it with details of the same know-how. Suppose further that the technical know-how was not exclusive to C, and was capable of being acquired from other legitimate sources by a person with E's skills, but only by someone with his skills. E might well be entitled to regard the know-how as non-confidential, since he knows that he could acquire it by his own skills and knowledge from another public source, whereas S (or his employee) could say no such thing.   **3–130**

If E were obliged to continue to treat the information as confidential, it could inhibit his proper ability to develop and use his own skills, and might place him under a disadvantage compared with others in his sphere of employment. No such considerations would apply to S (or his employee).   **3–131**

In each case the decision should accord with the usage and practices of the relevant industry or profession (factors which Megarry V.C. in *Thomas Marshall Ltd v Guinle*[204] regarded as pertinent to the question whether the information possessed the necessary quality of confidence) and the standards of the man of average intelligence and honesty (invoked by Cross J. in *Printers & Finishers Ltd v Holloway*[205]).   **3–132**

As Bankes L.J. said in Tournier v National Provincial and Union Bank of England[206]:   **3–133**

"The privilege of non-disclosure to which a client or a customer is entitled may vary according to the exact nature of the relationship between the client or the customer

---

[204] [1979] 1 Ch. 227 at 248.
[205] [1965] R.P.C. 239 at 256.
[206] [1924] 1 K.B. 461 at 474.

and the person on whom the duty rests. It need not be the same in the case of the counsel, the solicitor, the doctor, and the banker, though the underlying principle may be the same."

Hilton v Barker Booth & Eastwood

3–134   More recently it has been suggested that solicitors may owe duties of confidentiality which do not form part of the ordinary concept of confidentiality and the law relating to it. In *Hilton v Barker Booth & Eastwood*[207] a firm of solicitors in breach of professional duty acted for both the claimant and another client, B, in a property development transaction. Unknown to the claimant, but known to the solicitors, B had recently been released from prison after serving a sentence for offences of fraudulent trading and obtaining credit while an undischarged bankrupt. It was held that their duty to the claimant required the solicitors to disclose these facts to him, and it was no excuse that in so doing they would have breached their duty to B. The solicitors through their own fault had placed themselves in a situation where they were bound to be in breach of their duty to one client or the other, whatever they did. The relevance of the case for present purposes is in the comments made, obiter, about the nature of the duty owed by the solicitors to B not to divulge his previous bankruptcy and criminal convictions.

3–135   Lord Scott[208] doubted whether "a matter of public record, such as a bankruptcy or a criminal conviction", could justify being described as confidential; and that the reason why it would have been a breach of the solicitors' duty to have disclosed those facts to the claimant was not that the information was confidential, but that they owed B a duty to do their best to further his interests in the proposed transaction and that disclosure of those facts would have frustrated it.

3–136   Lord Walker said[209]:

"In my opinion the notion of confidentiality, as generally understood by lawyers, is not really relevant to the issues in this case. It is a solicitor's duty to act in his client's best interests and not to do anything likely to damage his client's interests, so far as this is consistent with the solicitor's professional duty. To disclose discreditable facts about a client, and to do so without the client's informed consent, is likely to be a breach of duty, even if the facts are in the public domain. Some of the references in the Court of Appeal judgments to confidential information must, I think, be understood in this looser sense."

These comments raise questions of substance and classification. The question of substance is whether and in what circumstances a person can be under a duty to treat as confidential information about something which is a matter of "public record".

---

[207] [2005] UKHL 8; [2005] 1 W.L.R. 567.
[208] [2005] UKHL 8 at [7]. See also his decision, when Vice-Chancellor, in *Elliott v Chief Constable of Wiltshire, The Times*, December 5, 1996.
[209] [2005] UKHL 8 at [34].

Public record

The phrase "public record" is itself a loose expression. The Law Commission in   **3–137**
its Working Paper on Breach of Confidence[210] proposed that the test of public
domain should be broader in the case of commercial than private information and
that in the case of private information it should be a defence to an action for
breach of confidence to prove that

> "1. the information can be ascertained by recourse to any register kept in
>   pursuance of any Act of Parliament which is open to inspection by the public
>   or to any other document which is required by the law of any part of the
>   United Kingdom to be open to inspection by the public; or
> 2.   the information was disclosed in the course of any proceedings, judicial or
>   otherwise, which the public were by the law of any part of the United
>   Kingdom entitled to attend."

However, there appears to have been an internal inconsistency in the Working
Paper (illustrative of the problem of hard rules in this area) because in referring to
the types of case where the Commission considered that a person should be able
to obtain damages for pecuniary loss resulting from disclosure of private
information, supplied in confidence, it stated[211]:

> "An example would be where the defendant publishes information in breach of
> confidence that the plaintiff is divorced in circumstances where the defendant
> knows or ought to know that, owing to the attitude of the plaintiff's employer,
> publication of this information will lead to the plaintiff's dismissal."

But pronouncement of a divorce would have been a judicial act done in open
court.

In its final report[212] the Law Commission stated that, after consultation and   **3–138**
reconsideration of the matter, it was departing from its provisional recommendation. It considered that it should be for the courts to decide in the circumstances
of the individual case whether the information at the time of the alleged breach of
confidence was "relatively secret"[213] or "available to the public",[214] and it did not
think that it would be practical or desirable to impose a more rigid standard of
what constitutes "the public domain" in respect of personal information than in
respect of purely commercial information.

Since the Law Commission considered the matter, technological developments   **3–139**
have led to changes in practice and in statutory provisions affecting the ways in
which information is stored and used by public and private bodies. The electronic
processing of personal data as part of a filing system (by public bodies or others)
is subject to control under the Data Processing Act 1998. "Processing" of
information or data for the purposes of the Act includes use or disclosure by
transmission or otherwise making it available. The provisions of the Act are

---

[210] No. 58, 1974 at [103]. (See more generally [94]–[105] et seq.)
[211] No. 58, 1974 at [63].
[212] Law Com. No.110 (Cmnd 8388), 1981, at para.6.69.
[213] *Franchi v Franchi* [1967] R.P.C. 149 at 152–3.
[214] *Ackroyds (London) Ltd v Islington Plastics Ltd* [1962] R.P.C. 97 at 104.

complex, reflecting the complexity of the European Directive[215] which it implements. The topic is discussed more fully in Ch.8. The point of relevance for present purposes is that it is likely to be misleading and oversimplified to speak of personal data being a matter of public record (with the implication that the information is generally available), if the record is electronically maintained, because the criteria for permissible disclosure of personal data electronically stored as part of a filing system are intricate. Personal data are exempt from the non-disclosure provisions of the Act where the data consist of information which the data controller is obliged by or under any enactment to make available to the public[216] or the particular disclosure is required by any enactment, rule of law or order of the court,[217] but generally such data can only be disclosed without the consent of the person concerned where there is an identifiable public interest in doing so.[218]

3–140   Information about matters which are contained in a recorded form available to the public or have been stated in open court can vary in many respects. It may be known to many or to few or possibly only to the person concerned. It may be fresh or stale. The subject matter may or may not affect the wider public. It may relate to misconduct, of which the person concerned may have been the perpetrator or the victim, or to misfortune.

3–141   A rule which provided that a person who confides information to another about some matter which is contained in a recorded form technically available to the public, or has been stated in open court, can never be entitled to have the confidence respected, could produce surprising and unfair results.

3–142   Consider the following examples:

1.   A person is illegitimate and had an unhappy childhood, involving a sibling who committed suicide and a drunken, violent stepfather who used to beat his mother and himself. These facts have left emotional scars. He discloses them in confidence to a doctor or a counsellor or a close friend. No one else knows about them, although his illegitimacy could be deduced from his birth certificate, his sibling's suicide was the subject of a coroner's inquest and evidence was given about his stepfather's violence when the stepfather was prosecuted for an assault.

2.   A person was convicted as a student for possession of drugs. Years later he discloses it in a job application because he is required to state if he has ever had any criminal conviction. No one else knows about it.

In these circumstances a reasonable person would expect the information to be treated in confidence and the idea that the recipient could sell it to a newspaper would be shocking.

3–143   In *R. v Chief Constable of North Wales Police Ex p. AB*[219] the applicants, a married couple ("AB" and "CD"), were released from prison after serving long sentences for sexual offences against children. They bought a caravan and moved onto a caravan site. The local police tried unsuccessfully to persuade them to

---

[215] Council Directive 95/46/EC.

[216] s.34.

[217] s.35.

[218] Schs 1–3 set out principles to be applied in processing personal data or sensitive personal data.

[219] [1999] Q.B. 396.

leave and then informed the site owner of their records. The site owner ordered them to move on. The applicants sought judicial review by way of declarations that the decision to inform the site owner of their convictions was unlawful. Their grounds included breach of confidence and breach of their rights under Art.8.

The claim was rejected by the Divisional Court. Lord Bingham C.J.[220] accepted the principle that when in the course of performing its public duties a public body comes into possession of information regarding a member of the public, being information not generally available and damaging to that member of the public if disclosed, the body ought not to disclose such information save for the purpose of and to the extent necessary for performance of its public duty or enabling some other public body to perform its duty. He stated that the principle rested in his view on a fundamental rule of good public administration and not on the existence of a duty of confidence owed by the public body to the member of the public, but he added that "it might well be that such a duty of confidence might in certain circumstances arise". On the facts, the police had not acted in breach of that principle because they had legitimate ground for disclosing the information.

3–144

Buxton J. agreed that the police's knowledge that the applicants had committed serious crimes was not something that they were free to impart to others without restraint, but that the restraint was not based on the law of confidence. His reasoning was that the information did not come to the police through any relationship with AB and CD; was not imparted to them by AB and CD; and was not acquired by the police subject to any express obligation of confidence.[221]

3–145

He also said[222]:

3–146

> " . . . counsel for the Secretary of State and also, I think, counsel for the police authority were disposed to argue that issues of disclosure of confidential or private information could not arise in any event on the facts of this case, because the fact of AB and CD's convictions were by concession and self-evidently neither confidential nor private, and the identity of AB and CD and their presence on the caravan site was already known to the person to whom disclosure was made. I do not think that the matter can be turned away so easily. What in this case might at least be argued to have the basic attribute of inaccessibility (see *Gurry, Breach of Confidence* (1984), p.70, cited in *Attorney-General v Guardian Newspapers Ltd (No. 2)* [1990] 1 A.C. 109, 215) was the *conjunction* of those various facts. It was that conjunction that the police deliberately brought to the attention of the site owner, when otherwise he would not, or probably would not, have found it out. As I have said, I very much doubt whether the subject of even that conjunction of information can claim confidence in it, because none of that information has come into the possession of its holder in circumstances that impart an obligation of confidence. I do however consider that a wish that certain facts in one's past, however notorious at the time, should remain in that past is an aspect of the subject's private life sufficient at least potentially to raise questions under article 8 of the Convention . . . "

The decision of the Divisional Court was upheld by the Court of Appeal. The applicants did not pursue their arguments based on breach of confidence.

---

[220] [1999] Q.B. 396 at 409–410.
[221] [1999] Q.B. 396 at 414–415.
[222] [1999] Q.B. 396 at 415–416.

3–147   Although the Divisional Court did not consider that the police owed any duty of confidentiality to the applicants on the facts, neither Bingham C.J. nor Buxton J. excluded the possibility that information of the kind with which the court was concerned could be imparted in circumstances which would give rise to a duty of confidentiality.

3–148   The passage from Buxton J.'s judgment set out above (and cited in part in the judgment of the Court of Appeal[223]) is significant for two other reasons. The first is his point about the conjunction of facts. As with trade secrets, so with personal information, individual pieces of a jigsaw may be accessible but the whole may not. The second is his anticipation of the potential effect of Art.8. His remarks pre-dated the incorporation of the Convention in domestic law by the Human Rights Act and were prescient.

3–149   Under the species of action for breach of confidentiality based on a person's right to respect for his private life, injunctions were granted in *Venables v News Group Newspapers Ltd*[224] and *X (formerly Mary Bell) v O'Brien*[225] to prevent publication of the present names and addresses of the claimants, who had been convicted of murder or manslaughter when they were children and whose names the trial judge had in each case permitted to be published.

3–150   It is now established that information about a person's convictions stored in central records can be within the scope of Art.8, especially when it concerns a person's distant past.[226] There is a difference between information which is received in circumstances giving rise to a duty of confidentiality and information which is private within the meaning of Art.8, but the same information may fall into both categories and it would be contradictory to hold that information which is sufficiently private to fall within Art.8 is incapable of being the subject of a duty of confidentiality on the ground that it is (or was) in the "public domain"..

3–151   In *Hilton v Barker Booth & Eastwood*[227] the House of Lords recognised that the defendant solicitors owed a duty to their client B not to disclose his past bankruptcy and criminal convictions to the claimant, but (obiter) treated the duty as unrelated to the ordinary law relating to confidentiality. If the law of confidentiality is circumscribed so that it cannot apply to information imparted in confidence about anything which has occurred in open court or is contained in a record theoretically available to the public, regardless of how secret or accessible it may be in practical terms, then the defendants' duty of non-disclosure could only be explained on some other basis. For the reasons discussed above, it is suggested that this is an over narrow view of the law. If not, it gives rise to difficult issues of classification.

Where contracting parties are in a confidential relationship, it is common place for a court to imply a duty of confidentiality in relation to information about which there is relative secrecy. It is also established law[228] that there can be an express contractual duty to refrain from publicising information about which there is no element of secrecy.

---

[223] [1999] Q.B. 396 at 425.

[224] [2001] Fam. 430.

[225] [2003] EWHC 1101.

[226] *R(L) v Commissioner of the Police of the Metropolis* [2009] UKSC 3; [2010] 1 A.C. 410 at [27].

[227] [2005] UKHL 8; [2005] 1 W.L.R. 567.

[228] *Att Gen v Blake* [2001] 1 A.C. 268.

The approach in *Hilton v Barker Booth & Eastwood* seems to involve a new   **3–152**
classification of duty—an implied duty of non-disclosure of information said to
lack the quality of inaccessibility which is necessary for a duty of confidentiality
in the normal sense. The result of this approach would be a category of cases
where there is a duty of confidentiality but not so described. The cases would be
those where the duty to treat information as confidential is a consequence or part
of a wider duty. But that is typical of a large number of confidential relationships,
such as doctor–patient, employer–employee, banker–customer, trading partners
and the like. Just as it has been said that the phrase "fiduciary duties" is a
dangerous one, giving rise to a mistaken assumption that all fiduciaries owe the
same duties in all circumstances, and that the extent and nature of the fiduciary
duties owed in any particular case fall to be determined by reference to any
underlying contractual relationship between the parties,[229] so the same may be
said about duties of confidentiality. The precise scope of the duty of
confidentiality in each case depends on the nature of the relationship and its
underlying purpose. As the Law Commission observed in its Working Paper on
Breach of Confidence,[230]

> "to compile an exhaustive list of such relationships would not be practicable, and,
> even if it were, the list would be of limited value because the extent of the
> obligation of confidence varies according to the exact nature of the relationship."

In *R (L) v Commissioner of Police of the Metropolis* a majority of the Supreme
Court considered that information about a person's criminal convictions which
was stored in police central records long after the time when everyone other than
the person concerned was likely to have forgotten about it should be regarded as
part of their private life to which Art. 8 would apply.[231] There is no logical or just
reason why such information should not equally be capable of being the subject
of an equitable duty of confidentiality.

In *KJO v XIM* Eady J. rightly commented that information in a "public record"
may not be in the "public domain" because provision may be made prohibiting
information in a record maintained by a public body from being made available
to the general public.[232]

Conclusion on public record

It is suggested that whether information is, or was once upon a time, a matter of   **3–153**
"public record" (whatever the meaning intended by that expression, as compared
with the broader expression "public domain") is simply a factor in determining
whether it is so generally accessible that it would not be just to require the party
against whom a duty of confidentiality is alleged to treat it as confidential.

---

[229] *Henderson v Merrett Syndicates Ltd* [1995] 2 A.C. 145 at 206 per Lord Browne-Wilkinson.
[230] (1974), Working Paper No. 58, p.14.
[231] [2009] UKSC 3; [2010] 1 A.C. 410 at [27] (Lord Hope) and [71] (Lord Neuberger).
[232] [2011] EWHC 1768 (QB) at [21].

Misuse

3–154 It is an essential ingredient of the action for breach of confidence that confidential information has been or is threatened to be, misused. The principle is self-evident, but determining what is misuse can present difficult questions. A more accurate word might be abuse, but misuse is the term commonly used in the authorities and it should be understood as sufficiently broad to include any form of abuse.

Surreptitiously to examine, copy or take a confidential document is itself a form of misuse and a breach of confidentiality. There does not have to be further misuse for the court to have power to grant relief.[233] Many cases have been brought by victims of phone hacking by journalists without need to prove that the private information wrongly obtained has been published.[234]

3–155 Misuse will typically take the form of disclosure to another, but it need not do so.[235] Where a duty of confidentiality exists, misuse need not be intentional in order to found liability.[236] This is not to be confused with the situation where the nature of the information and position of the parties are such that someone of ordinary intelligence and honesty in the shoes of the recipient would be likely to use the information, consciously or unconsciously, without any apprehension of being under restraint; in such a case the recipient's defence to an allegation of breach of confidence would not be that the alleged breach was unintentional, but that he owed no duty or only a qualified duty.[237] What constitutes misuse is necessarily dependent on the scope of the duty owed in the particular relationship.

3–156 Cross J.'s observation in *Printers & Finishers v Holloway*[238] that the law would defeat its own object if it sought to enforce in this field standards which would be rejected by the ordinary person is pertinent when considering questions of the scope of a duty of confidentiality and whether particular conduct constitutes misuse.

3–157 In *Smith Kline & French v Community Services*[239] a question arose as to the extent of the duty owed by a government department to a pharmaceutical company in relation to confidential information supplied for the purpose of obtaining approval of a drug. The court referred to Megarry J.'s suggested test in *Coco v Clark*[240] for determining whether a duty of confidence existed (whether a reasonable person in the shoes of the recipient would have realised that, on reasonable grounds, the information was being given to him in confidence) and continued[241]:

---

[233] *Tchenguiz v Imerman* [2010] EWCA Civ 908; [2011] Fam. 116 at [69]–[71].

[234] None has yet come to trial, but a large number have been settled (as noted by the Supreme Court in *Phillips v Mulcaire* [2012] UKSC 28).

[235] *Prince Jefri Bolkiah v KPMG* [1999] 2 A.C. 222 at 235, where Lord Millett said in a case about a solicitor and a former client, "It [the duty] is not merely a duty not to communicate the information to a third party. It is a duty not to misuse it that is to say, without the consent of the former client to make any use of it or cause any use to be made of it by others otherwise than for his benefit.".

[236] *Seager v Copydex Ltd* [1967] 1 W.L.R. 923.

[237] *Printers & Finishers Ltd v Holloway* [1965] R.P.C. 239 at 256–257.

[238] [1965] R.P.C. 239 at 256.

[239] (1991) 28 F.C.R. 291.

[240] [1969] R.P.C. 41 at 48.

[241] [1969] R.P.C. 41 at 303–304.

"However, this test does not give guidance as to the scope of an obligation of confidence, where one exists. Sometimes the obligation imposes no restriction on use of the information, as long as the confidee does not reveal it to third parties. In other circumstances, the confidee may not be entitled to use it except for some limited purpose. In considering these problems, and indeed the whole question, it is necessary not to lose sight of the basis of the obligation to respect confidences:

'It lies in the notion of an obligation of conscience arising from the circumstances in and through which the information was communicated or obtained.'

This is quoted from *Moorgate Tobacco Co. Ltd v Philip Morris Ltd (No. 2)* (1984) 156 C.L.R. 414 at 438, per Deane J., with whom the other members of the court agreed . . . . Similar expressions recur in other cases: see *Seager v Copydex Ltd* [1967] R.P.C. 349 at 368:

'The law on this subject . . . depends on the broad principle of equity that he who has received information in confidence shall not take unfair advantage of it.'

To avoid taking unfair advantage of it does not necessarily mean that the confidee must not use it except for the confider's limited purpose. Whether one adopts the 'reasonable man' test suggested by Megarry J. or some other, there can be no breach of the equitable obligation unless the court concludes that a confidence reposed has been abused, that unconscientious use has been made of the information."

This passage was cited by Simon Brown L.J. in *R. v Department of Health, Ex p. Source Informatics Ltd.*[242] He applied the test whether a reasonable person's conscience would be troubled by the proposed use of the relevant information.[243]

Misuse and negligence

The Law Commission in its Report on Breach of Confidence[244] considered whether a person under an obligation of confidentiality could be liable if disclosure or use of a confidential document or information occurred, not through his direct disclosure or use, but through his failure to take reasonable care to prevent its disclosure or use by someone else.

A person may undoubtedly owe a contractual duty to take reasonable care to safeguard the confidentiality of a document or information entrusted to him,[245] but the Law Commission said that:

3–158

3–159

"There does not appear to be any clear answer in the present state of the law to the question whether . . . a person who is under a duty of confidence, but is not in any contractual relationship with the person to whom it is owed, can be liable for breach of confidence if the information to which the duty relates is disclosed or used owing to his negligence."

There is a distinction between an equitable duty of confidentiality and a duty to take care to prevent confidential information or documents from falling into the hands of someone else. The former is an obligation of conscience, which requires the recipient not to misuse the information or documents. The latter is a duty of a different character and is not an automatic concomitant of the former. In

3–160

---

[242] [2001] Q.B. 424 at [24].

[243] [2001] Q.B. 424 at [31].

[244] Law Com. No.110, Cmnd. 8388 (1981), at para.4.14.

[245] In *Weld-Blundell v Stephens* [1919] 1 K.B. 520; [1920] A.C. 956, it was conceded that a firm of accountants owed a duty to take reasonable care of their client's documents as a bailee for reward: [1919] 1 K.B. at 523.

the absence of a relevant contract, it will arise only if there is a special relationship between the parties giving rise to a duty of care under the law of negligence.[246]

3–161   The question of the existence of such a duty arose in *Swinney v Chief Constable of Northumbria.*[247] An informant gave information to a police officer about the identity of the driver of a vehicle which had hit and killed another police officer. Details of the information and the informant's name and address were recorded in a document which was stolen from a police vehicle and came into the hands of the alleged driver. As a result, the informant and her husband were threatened with violence and arson. They sued the chief constable, alleging that they had suffered psychological damage and economic loss because of failure by the police to take proper care of the information. On an application to strike out the claim, the Court of Appeal held that it was arguable that there was a special relationship between the parties so as to give rise to a duty of care on the part of the police.[248]

Misuse and detriment

3–162   The question has from time to time been raised whether misuse, actual or threatened, must be detrimental in order to give rise to a cause of action for breach of confidentiality.

3–163   In *Coco v A N Clark (Engineering) Ltd*[249] Megarry J. observed:

> "Some of the statements of principle in the cases omit any mention of detriment; others include it. At first sight, it seems that detriment ought to be present if equity is to be induced to intervene; but I can conceive of cases where a plaintiff might have substantial motives for seeking the aid of equity and yet suffer nothing which could fairly be called detriment to him, as when the confidential information shows him in a favourable light but gravely injures some relation or friend of his whom he wishes to protect. The point does not arise for decision in this case, for detriment to the plaintiff plainly exists."

In the *Spycatcher* case[250] opinions were divided. Lord Keith[251] said:

> " . . . as a general rule, it is in the public interest that confidences should be respected, and the encouragement of such respect may in itself constitute a sufficient ground for recognising and enforcing the obligation of confidence even where the confider can point to no specific detriment to himself . . . So I would think it a sufficient detriment to the confider that information given in confidence is to be disclosed to persons whom he would prefer not to know of it, even though the disclosure to him would not be harmful to him in any positive way. The position of the Crown, as representing the continuing government of the country may, however, be regarded

---

[246] *B v A County Council* [2006] EWCA Civ 1388; [2007] 1 F.L.R. 1189.
[247] [1997] Q.B. 464.
[248] At the trial before Jackson J. (1999) 11 Admin L.R. 811, it was conceded by the police that they owed a duty of care to the informant, but the judge found that there was no negligence. In *An Informer v A Chief Constable* [2012] EWCA Civ 197 it was accepted that the police owed a duty of care for the safety of the informer.
[249] [1969] R.P.C. 41 at 48.
[250] [1990] 1 A.C. 109.
[251] [1990] 1 A.C. 109 at 255–256.

as being special . . . . The Crown . . . as representing the nation as a whole, has no private life or personal feelings capable of being hurt by the disclosure of confidential information. In so far as the Crown acts to prevent such disclosure or to seek redress for it on confidentiality grounds, it must necessarily, in my opinion, be in a position to show that the disclosure is likely to damage or has damaged the public interest."

Lord Griffiths[252] considered that detriment, or potential detriment, to the confider must be established before a private individual was entitled to a remedy for breach of confidence, since the remedy was fashioned to protect the confider and not to punish the confidant, and therefore there was little point in extending it to a confider who did not need protection. Lord Goff[253] wished to keep the point open, but observed that it might depend on how wide a meaning could be given to the word "detriment".

In *Smith Kline & French Laboratories (Australia) Ltd v Department of Community Services*[254] Gummow J., after reviewing the authorities, noted that the issue remained open in Australia but expressed his view that:

3–164

> "The basis of the equitable jurisdiction to protect obligations of confidence lies . . . in an obligation of conscience arising from the circumstances in or through which the information, the subject of the obligation, was communicated or obtained: *Moorgate Tobacco Co. Ltd v Philip Morris Ltd (No.2)*[255] . . . . The obligation of conscience is to respect the confidence, not merely to refrain from causing detriment to the plaintiff. The plaintiff comes to equity to vindicate his right to observance of the obligation, not necessarily to recover loss or to restrain infliction of apprehended loss. To look into a related field, when has equity said that the only breaches of trust to be restrained are those that would prove detrimental to the beneficiaries?"

In *Rapid Metal Developments (Australia) Pty Ltd v Anderson Formrite Pty Ltd*,[256] Johnson J., sitting in the Supreme Court of Western Australia, followed Gummow J. in stating:

3–165

> "In my view, the requirement for proof of detriment is inconsistent with the established notion that the basis for the exercise of equitable jurisdiction is to enforce the obligation of confidence."

It is suggested that the key, whether the case is approached in equity or in contract, lies in correctly identifying in each set of circumstances the nature of the obligation and the interest which it is intended to protect. This was the approach taken by Scott J. at first instance in the *Spycatcher* case. After citing *Moorgate Tobacco Co Ltd v Philip Morris Ltd (No. 2)*[257] and *Commonwealth of Australia v John Fairfax & Sons Ltd*,[258] he said[259]:

---

[252] *Att Gen v Guardian Newspapers Ltd (No.2)* [1990] 1 A.C. 109 at 270.
[253] *Att Gen v Guardian Newspapers Ltd (No.2)* [1990] 1 A.C. 109 at 281–282.
[254] [1990] F.S.R. 617 at 664.
[255] (1984) 156 C.L.R. 414 at 438.
[256] [2005] W.A.S.C. 255 at [78].
[257] (1984) 156 C.L.R. 414.
[258] (1980) 147 C.L.R. 39.
[259] [1990] 1 A.C. 109 at 147–148.

"The dicta in these two cases place the origin of the duty of confidence not in contract, express or implied, but in equity. But the ambit of the duty of confidence imposed by equity will depend, in my view, on the same type of judicial approach to the surrounding circumstances of the case as that adopted where an implicit term is treated as the basis of the duty. As long ago as 1893 the Court of Appeal concluded that there was no distinction between the duty of confidence placed on an agent by implied contract and that imposed on him by equity; see *Lamb v Evans* [1893] 1 Ch. 218."

3–166   In the case of private confidences, the confider may have an interest in the information being kept confidential, regardless of whether disclosure would be positively harmful to him, for reasons which may be perfectly understandable (and which would be understood by any reasonable person in the position of the confidant). If so, for the reasons suggested by Lord Keith in the *Spycatcher* case, that should be sufficient to found a cause of action; and the question whether unauthorised disclosure in such circumstances is considered to involve "detriment" is an exercise in semantics. If on the other hand the confider has no substantial interest in the information being kept confidential, it would follow that the information would not possess the necessary quality of confidence to found an obligation of confidentiality.[260]

3–167   In the case of public confidences, the interest intended to be protected is the public interest, and it is therefore logical that the jurisdiction should only come into play in circumstances where disclosure would be injurious to the public interest. It is for that reason that cases of public confidence involve what Lord Goff referred to in the *Spycatcher* case as the additional requirement of establishing that the public interest would be harmed by publication.[261] Conversely, it is misleading in such cases to speak of a public interest defence, since the injurious effect of publication on the public interest is an ingredient required to be established in order for the jurisdiction to arise.

Qualifications to a duty of confidentiality

3–168   In *Tournier v National Provincial and Union Bank*[262] the Court of Appeal held that the duty of confidence owed by a banker to his customer is impliedly subject to qualifications, which Bankes L.J. said could not be exhaustively defined, but could be classified under four headings:

(1)   where disclosure was made with the express or implied consent of the customer;
(2)   where disclosure was made under compulsion of law;
(3)   where there was a duty to the public to disclose;
(4)   where the interests of the bank required disclosure.

Such factors are not unique to the relationship of banker and customer, but involve considerations of wider application. Although Bankes L.J. referred to the qualifications as implied qualifications of an implied contractual duty of secrecy,

---

[260] *Moorgate Tobacco Co Ltd v Philip Morris Ltd (No.2)* (1984) 156 C.L.R. 414 at 438.
[261] [1990] 1 A.C. 109 at 283.
[262] [1924] 1 K.B. 461 at 473.

the underlying considerations are equally relevant to the parallel jurisdiction in equity. Bankes L.J. also observed that[263]:

> "The privilege of non-disclosure to which a client or customer is entitled may vary according to the exact nature of the relationship between the client or the customer and the person on whom the duty rests. It need not be the same in the case of the counsel, the solicitor, the doctor and the banker, though the underlying principle may be the same."

Express or implied consent

A person cannot be in breach of a duty of confidence to another by disclosure of information or material to which the other consents. Consent to disclosure may be express or implied, and general or limited. A person seeking life insurance, who gives information about his health to his insurance broker, impliedly consents to the broker passing on the information to the underwriter, but not to the press.   **3–169**

Disclosure required by law

The law cannot at the same time require a person to treat information as confidential and compel him to disclose it, and therefore disclosure required by law cannot be misuse.[264] Such requirement may arise in a variety of ways.   **3–170**

A number of statutory provisions require the disclosure of information otherwise confidential.[265] In litigation, a duty of confidence to another is generally no bar to disclosure, although the court in its discretion will only compel the production of otherwise confidential documents if it considers it necessary to do so.[266] Nor is duty of confidence to another a ground for refusal by a witness to answer questions or produce documents if ordered to do so by a court or tribunal of competent jurisdiction, although again a court will require a witness to disclose otherwise confidential information only if disclosure is necessary for attainment of justice in the particular case.[267]   **3–171**

Duty to the public

Public interest as a justification for disclosure is an important topic on which much has been written. It is considered in Ch.6.   **3–172**

---

[263] [1924] 1 K.B. 461 at 474.

[264] The subject of confidentiality and foreign law raises separate problems as to which see Ch.10, below.

[265] In *Tournier v National Provincial & Union Bank* [1924] 1 K.B. 461 at 473 Bankes L.J. gave the example of the Bankers Books Evidence Act 1879.

[266] *D. v N.S.P.C.C.* [1978] A.C. 171; *Science Research Council v Nasse* [1980] A.C. 1028; *British Steel Corp v Granada Television Ltd* [1981] A.C. 1096. See para.17–001, below.

[267] *Duchess of Kingston's Case* (1776) 20 St.Tr. 355 at 386–391; *Garner v Garner* (1920) 36 T.L.R. 196; *Att Gen v Mulholland and Foster* [1963] 2 Q.B. 477; *Att Gen v Clough* [1963] 1 Q.B. 773; *D v N.S.P.C.C.* [1978] A.C. 171 at 238 and 243; *British Steel Corp v Granada Television Ltd* [1981] A.C. 1096; *Macmillan Inc v Bishopsgate Investment Trust Plc* [1993] 1 W.L.R. 1372. See also Contempt of Court Act 1981 s.10.

Disclosure required in the interests of the confidant

3–173 Disclosure or use of confidential information will often be motivated by self-interest, without being in any sense necessary. A duty of confidentiality would be of little value if it could be easily trumped by the interests of the confidant. But there may be circumstances in which the confidant has a real need to be permitted to disclose or use information otherwise confidential and where the courts will not imply or impose an obligation preventing him from doing so. Brennan J. captured the flavour when he referred in *Esso Australia Resources Ltd v Plowman*[268] to cases "where disclosure of the material is fairly required for the protection of the party's legitimate interests". What is "fairly required" and what are "legitimate interests" will necessarily depend on the circumstances and the nature of the relationship between the confider and confidant. In *Nam Tai v Pricewaterhouse Coopers* the Court of Final Appeal of Hong Kong held that "defensive disclosure" would be permissible if it was made in response to an allegation made by a former client to others about the discloser, provided that the disclosure did not exceed what was fairly required to rebut the allegation.[269]

3–174 One type of case which may be seen as falling within this category is that of the ex-employee who has learned confidential information during his employment, which has become inseparable from the general skill and knowledge that he needs to use for earning his living.

3–175 Another purpose for which it may be necessary for a party to refer to information otherwise confidential is in order to establish or protect his legal rights against other parties or to defend himself.

3–176 In *Hassneh Insurance v Mew*[270] Colman J. held that the implied contractual duty of confidence which arises between the parties to an arbitration agreement is subject to the qualification that it does not prevent disclosure of the award "if it is reasonably necessary for the establishment or protection of an arbitrating party's legal rights *vis-à-vis* a third party". In so holding Colman J. drew on the judgments of the Court of Appeal in *Tournier*.[271]

3–177 In *Lillicrap v Nalder*[272] property developers sued their solicitors for negligently failing to advise them on rights of way affecting their title to property which they bought when the defendants were acting for them. Negligence was admitted, but the solicitors disputed the plaintiffs' claim that, if properly advised, they would not have entered into the transaction. They sought to allege that on previous occasions they had advised the plaintiffs on similar matters affecting other properties and that their advice had been ignored. On an interlocutory application the judge refused to allow the solicitors to refer in their pleadings to previous retainers, and ordered that they deliver up to the plaintiffs all confidential documents relating to those retainers and refrain from publishing them. He said:

---

[268] [1994–1995] 183 C.L.R. 10 at 36.
[269] FACV No. 1 of 2007, paras 58–61, 65–66.
[270] [1993] 2 Ll.Rep. 243 at 249. See further discussion at paras 22–028 to 22–032, below.
[271] [1924] 1 K.B. 461.
[272] [1993] 1 W.L.R. 94.

"The bringing of a claim for negligence in relation to a particular retainer will normally be a waiver of privilege and confidence for facts and documents relating to that retainer, but not without more for those relating to other discrete retainers."

The Court of Appeal agreed with that statement of principle, saying that the waiver could only extend to matters relevant to an issue in the proceedings. But, said Dillon L.J.[273]:

"the waiver must go far enough, not merely to entitle the plaintiff to establish his cause of action, but to enable the defendant to establish a defence to the cause of action if he has one."

The Court of Appeal accordingly reversed the judge's decision. A confider cannot therefore rely on confidence to prevent the confidant from defending himself against subsequent attack by the confider.[274]

Suppose, however, that the attack had come from someone other than the confider. Supppose, for example, that criticism of a hospital consultant's treatment of a case (e.g. involving alleged euthanasia) by other members of staff led to his prosecution, or to professional disciplinary proceedings,[275] or to the health authority taking steps under his contract to suspend or dismiss him. Grave injustice might be done to the doctor if he were not free to disclose matters concerning the patient which he would otherwise be required to treat as confidential.

Commissioner of Police of the Metropolis v Times Newspapers Ltd[276] provides an analogy. The defendant published an article about a man who was reported to be the head of a criminal network so vast that the police were unable to take him on. The article was based on documents from files of the police and the Serious Organised Crime Agency which were leaked to the newspaper. The police brought a claim against the newspaper for an injunction to restrain further breaches of confidence and delivery up of the leaked documents. It was accepted that there was a proper public interest in the story, but the police wished to prevent any further use of the leaked documents because of legitimate concern for the safety of those who had provided information to the police or might be suspected of having done so. After the publication of the article the person named in the article brought an action against the newspaper for libel. The newspaper wished to use the information in the leaked documents to plead defences of justification defence and Reynolds privilege. It had no other intention of making further use of the information in the documents. Tugendhat J. held that it would be wrong to prevent the newspaper from using the information to the extent that was necessary for that purpose.

3–178

---

[273] [1993] 1 W.L.R. 94 at 99.

[274] The Court of Appeal gave further guidance in *Paragon Finance Plc v Freshfields* [1999] 1 W.L.R. 1183 as to the scope of the waiver of privilege effected by a claim against one's former solicitors.

[275] In *Duncan v Medical Practitioners Disciplinary Committee* [1986] 1 N.Z.L.R. 513 (N.Z. High Court) and *R. v Institute of Chartered Accountants of England and Wales Ex p. Brindle* [1994] B.C.C. 297 at 312, per Hirst L.J., it was recognised that a professional person was entitled to use confidential information to defend himself against disciplinary charges.

[276] [2011] EWHC 2705 (QB).

In *Imerman v Tchenguiz*[277] the court was faced with a particularly difficult clash between a husband's interest in preserving confidential information about his finances and his wife's interest in obtaining a just outcome to her claims for ancillary relief on the breakdown of their marriage. Anticipating that he would not come clean about his assets, the wife's brothers accessed information stored by the husband on a computer in premises which they shared. Several files of documents were passed to the wife's solicitors, who sent them on to the husband's solicitors after making copies. This all took place after divorce proceedings had begun but before the wife made an application for ancillary relief. The husband was alleged to have said in the past that she would never be able to find his money because it was well hidden. A practice had developed in the family courts of permitting the use of documents obtained by wives in similar circumstances. The Court of Appeal held that there was no justification for applying special rules in matrimonial cases and that there was no reason why the husband should not be entitled to protect his private financial information as between himself and his wife. Her proper course, if she had reason to believe that he would suppress relevant information in the ancillary relief proceedings, would have been to apply for a search order. The court ordered that the documents retained by the wife's solicitors should be returned to the husband's solicitors. Significantly, however, it imposed terms that the husband's solicitors were not to part with any of the documents without the permission of the wife's solicitors or an order of the court, and it noted that they would be under a duty to ensure that the husband complied with his disclosure duty in the ancillary relief proceedings.

An argument might have been advanced that although the relationship between married parties does not prevent either from owing to the other a duty of confidentiality in relation to the other's financial affairs, the special nature of their partnership may have the effect that such a duty is subject to qualifications which would not arise in the absence of such a relationship. More particularly, it may not be right to regard one party's financial affairs as entirely separate from the legitimate interest of the other, and the right of one party to a fair and effective determination of any financial issues between them might limit the right to confidentiality which the court will enforce against that party in relation to their financial affairs, depending on the factual circumstances. That argument does not appear to have been advanced, but the court did limit the relief which it granted to the husband by the terms on which it ordered delivery up of the documents, with the practical consequence that they were available to the court in the ancillary relief proceedings, and to that extent the object of the conduct of the wife and her brothers was achieved.

3–179
It is suggested that the legitimate interests of the confidant may in appropriate cases include disclosure to another party who has a legitimate interest in the matter, for example, disclosure by a wholly owned subsidiary to its holding company.[278]

3–180
A possible approach is to say that it is all a matter for the court's discretion. In *Webster v James Chapman & Co* Scott J. said[279]:

---

[277] [2010] EWCA Civ 908; [2011] Fam. 116.
[278] The distinction between parent companies and their subsidiaries from the point of view of confidentiality was emphasised by the Court of Appeal in *Bank of Tokyo Ltd v Karoon* [1987] A.C. 45.
[279] [1989] 3 All E.R. 939 at 945.

"The court must, in each case where protection of confidential information is sought, balance on the one hand the legitimate interests of the plaintiff in seeking to keep the confidential information suppressed and on the other hand the legitimate interests of the defendant in seeking to make use of the information. There is never any question of an absolute right to have confidential information protected. The protection is the consequence of the balance to which I have referred coming down in favour of the plaintiff."

The decision whether to grant a particular form of equitable relief may involve an exercise in discretion. But an essential ingredient of the action for breach of confidence, before reaching any question of discretion, is that there must be actual or threatened misuse of confidential information. What constitutes misuse depends on the scope of the duty, which is not a matter of discretion but a matter of law, requiring analysis of the facts and application of principle.

In so far as a contractual duty is relied upon, determining its scope is a matter of contractual analysis. In so far as an equitable duty is relied upon, there is force in the observation that:

3–181

"equitable principles are best developed by reference to what conscionable behaviour demands of the defendant not by 'balancing' and then overriding those demands by reference to matters of social or political opinion."[280]

Preservation of confidentiality may affect the interests of the confider, the confidant and other people (including the public at large). There has been more discussion of the extent to which duties of confidence should be qualified so as to permit disclosure in cases of potential harm to others than in cases of potential harm to the confidant. But the judgment of Bankes L.J. in *Tournier v National Provincial and Union Bank*[281] illustrates that there is scope for the courts to recognise a qualification of a duty of confidence, not only where disclosure is necessary to prevent harm to others, but also where disclosure is necessary for the protection of the confidant.

Who may sue?

As a general principle, the person suing must be someone to whom the relevant duty of confidence is owed. In *Fraser v Evans*[282] the plaintiff prepared a confidential report for the Greek Government. A copy of the report was leaked to a newspaper and the plaintiff sought an injunction to prevent publication or use of its contents. It was held that the plaintiff had no standing to complain. Lord Denning M.R. said[283]:

3–182

"The jurisdiction is based not so much on property or on contract as on the duty to be of good faith. . . . But the party complaining must be the person who is entitled to the confidence and to have it respected. He must be a person to whom the duty of good faith is owed. . . . There is no doubt that Mr Fraser was himself under an

---

[280] *Smith Kline & French Ltd v Department of Community Services* [1990] F.S.R. 617 at 663, per Gummow J.
[281] [1924] 1 K.B. 461.
[282] [1969] 1 Q.B. 349.
[283] [1969] 1 Q.B. 349 at 361.

obligation of confidence to the Greek Government. . . . The Greek Government entered into no contract with Mr Fraser to keep it secret. . . . They were the people to say aye or no whether it should be communicated elsewhere, or be published generally. It follows that they alone have any standing to complain if anyone obtains the information surreptitiously or proposes to publish it."

3–183   In *Broadmoor Special Hospital Authority v Robinson*[284] the defendant, who had been convicted of manslaughter and ordered to be detained in a secure hospital, wrote a book which included information about other inmates, their mental condition, treatment and progress in hospital. The hospital authority sought to prevent him from publishing it. The Court of Appeal held that it could not bring proceedings to protect other patients' rights to privacy or confidentiality.[285]

3–184   Since the European Court of Human Rights has held[286] that the obligations of the state under Art.8 may involve a positive obligation to adopt measures designed to secure respect for private life, it is arguable that a court could be acting in breach of the Convention if it refused on jurisdictional grounds to entertain proceedings begun by a hospital authority to safeguard respect for the private lives of its patients, whose privacy the authority would owe them a duty to protect.[287]

3–185   In *Green Corns Ltd v Claverley Group Ltd*[288] Tugendhat J. granted an injunction to a children's home provider to restrain a newspaper from publishing the addresses of homes provided for troubled children in order to prevent the risk of serious harm to the children and carers occupying the addresses concerned.

3–186   In *A Local Authority v W*[289] Sir Mark Potter P. granted an injunction on the application of a local authority to prevent the media from publishing information which would be likely to cause prejudice to the welfare of children who were the subject of care proceedings.

In *Commissioner of Police of the Metropolis v Times Newspapers Ltd* Tugendhat J. accepted that the police were entitled to invoke the Art.8 rights of members of the public (not parties to the action) to whom they owed a duty to protect those rights.[290]

3–187   The question what happens when the right to use confidential information, e.g. technical know-how, is shared or "assigned" was once controversial but is now settled. It has been suggested in the past that, if confidential information is not property, the "assignor" cannot pass to the "assignee" his personal right to have

---

[284] [2000] Q.B. 775.

[285] [2000] Q.B. 775 at [30] (Lord Woolf M.R.) and 54 (Waller L.J.).

[286] *Marckx v Belgium* (1979) 2 E.H.R.R. 330 at [31]; *X and Y v Netherlands* (1986) 8 E.H.R.R. 235 at [23]; *Stjerna v Finland* (1997) 24 E.H.R.R. 195 at [38]; *Von Hannover v Germany* (2005) 40 E.H.H.R. 1 at [57].

[287] See *Mersey Care NHS Trust v Ackroyd* [2006] EWHC 17 (QB), Tugendhat J., at [96]: "The hospital is not suing on behalf of any patient. It could not do that. But it is suing to safeguard the respect for the private lives of all its patients. It would be unlawful for the court to act in a way which would be incompatible with the rights of the patients at Ashworth."

[288] [2005] EWHC 958 (QB).

[289] [2005] EWHC 1564 (Fam).

[290] [2011] EWHC 2705 (QB) at [53] and [60]–[61]. In *K v News Group Newspapers Ltd* [2011] EWCA Civ 439; [2011 1 W.L.R. 1827, the Court of Appeal took into account not only the Art.8 rights of the claimant, but also those of his wife and children and the work colleague with whom he had conducted an affair.

the information treated as confidential, and therefore the "assignee" cannot sue to enforce a duty of confidence,[291] but has at most a right to compel the "assignor" to take action.

In *Morison v Moat*[292] the defendant was held to owe a duty of confidence to the plaintiff in respect of the recipe for "Morison's Universal Medicine", details of which were supplied by the plaintiff's father to the defendant's father. Turner V.C. stressed that:

> "what we have to deal with here is, not the right of the Plaintiffs against the world, but their right against the Defendant."[293]

He distinguished *Canham v Jones*[294] as a case (unlike *Morison v Moat*[295]) based on property and not confidence. The injunction against the defendant was therefore based not on an assignment of a proprietary right, but on the principle that the defendant owed a duty in conscience towards the plaintiff to respect the original confidence in which the information was supplied, although the plaintiff had not been the original confider of the information, but had himself been originally a confidant (from his father).

In *Gilbert v Star Newspaper Co Ltd*[296] the plot of a Gilbert comic opera was   **3–188** leaked to the defendant newspaper, probably by a member of the cast or theatre employee whose contract was with the theatre manager. Gilbert brought a claim for an injunction to prevent further disclosure by the newspaper. As an indirect recipient of confidential information, with knowledge of its confidentiality, on ordinary principles the newspaper's source owed an equitable duty of confidentiality to Gilbert, but Chitty J. required the joinder as plaintiff of the theatre manager, and granted an interlocutory injunction to both Gilbert and the manager. The decision to grant an injunction to the manager necessarily implied that he too was owed a duty of confidentiality in respect of the libretto. In *Douglas v Hello! Ltd (No.3)*[297] the Court of Appeal observed that:

> "This decision supports the proposition that, where the benefit of confidential information is shared between A and B, B can claim that disclosure of that information will constitute a breach of confidence owed to B."

In *Mustad & Son v Dosen*[298] the defendant was employed as a skilled   **3–189** mechanic by a firm which went into liquidation. His contract of employment contained a confidentiality clause. The plaintiffs paid the liquidator for the business, including the benefit of any trade secrets and pledges of confidentiality.

---

[291] See the judgment of Hope J.A. in the New South Wales Court of Appeal in *Moorgate Tobacco Co Ltd v Philip Morris Ltd* (1982) 64 F.L.R. 387 at 404. The point was not referred to in the judgment of Deane J. in the High Court of Australia (1984) 156 C.L.R. 414. In *Mid-City Skin Cancer & Laser Centre v Zahedi-Anarak* [2006] NSWSC 844, Campbell J. declined to follow the Court of Appeal's decision in *Moorgate*.

[292] (1851) 9 Hare 241; (affirmed (1852) 21 L.J. Chanc. (N.S.) 248).

[293] (1851) 9 Hare 241 at 258.

[294] (1813) 2 V. & B. 218.

[295] (1851) 9 Hare 241; (affirmed (1852) 21 L.J. Chanc. (N.S.) 248).

[296] (1894) 11 T.L.R. 4.

[297] [2005] EWCA Civ 595; [2006] Q.B. 125, at [129].

[298] [1964] 1 W.L.R. 109n.

The defendant went to work for new employers and in the course of his new employment gave them some information about the construction of a machine about which he had acquired in his previous employment. The plaintiffs applied for an injunction to restrain him from disclosing any further details. Lord Buckmaster observed that it was essential for the plaintiffs to prove that the defendant had obtained "special information" during his first employment which he was prevented from disclosing, and that he either had disclosed it or had threatened to do so. The claim failed for an injunction failed on the ground that by the time the case reached the House of Lords all the relevant information was in the public domain, but not on the ground that the defendant could not owe a duty of confidentiality to the plaintiffs.

The question was settled by the decision of the House of Lords in *Douglas v Hello! Ltd*.[299] A majority held that OK!, having paid for the exclusive rights to publish photographs of the Douglases' wedding, was entitled to the benefit of the obligation of confidentiality owed to the Douglases.

3–190   If therefore the original confider has passed confidential information to another person, with the intention that the latter shall enjoy the benefit of it, that person will have standing to enforce the confidentiality.

The Law Commission[300] considered the effect of death on duties of confidentiality. By s.1(1) of the Law Reform (Miscellaneous Provisions) Act 1934 all causes of action, except for defamation, subsisting against or vested in any person on his death survive against or, as the case may be, for the benefit of the estate. But there may be situations falling outside the scope of that section, as illustrated by the following example from the Law Commission's Report[301]:

> " . . . there is the situation in which a person who has imparted information in confidence to another dies before any breach of confidence has taken place. His personal representatives will have a right of action for any subsequent breach only if the information is of a 'quasi proprietorial' character—such as information relating to 'know-how'—which can be regarded as an asset of the deceased person's estate. The personal representatives of a deceased patient cannot employ the action for breach of confidence to protect the relations or friends of the deceased from distress resulting from the doctor's disclosure of his deceased patient's confidences."

3–191   It is doubtful whether that would be a correct statement of law today. "Quasi-proprietorial" is not a familiar term in the law of confidentiality and its meaning is unclear. If it is meant to include information which could be used for financial profit, it would include much beside technical know-how, for example, intimate confidences of a celebrity. If a doctor who treated a celebrity suffering from AIDS during his final illness were subsequently to sell to a newspaper intimate details which had been revealed to him by his former patient in confidence, and in the expectation that the doctor would continue to respect that confidence after the patient's death, it is likely that a court would regard the obligation of confidence as subsisting after his death[302]; and would grant to the personal representatives (depending on the circumstances) an injunction and/or

---

[299] *OBG Ltd v Allen* [2007] UKHL 21; [2008] 1 A.C. 1.
[300] *Breach of Confidence*, Law Com. No.110, Cmnd. 8388 (1981), paras 4.105–4.107.
[301] *Breach of Confidence*, Law Com. No.110, Cmnd. 8388 (1981), para.4.107.
[302] See para.11-051, below.

an account of profits as the only effective means of enforcing the obligation.[303] In such a case it could not be said that the deceased would suffer detriment from the publication, but it would seem contrary to justice that the doctor should make a windfall from his breach of his obligation. Privilege may survive in favour of a deceased's estate[304] and it is hard to see why a court should not recognise the survival of an obligation of confidentiality. The period for which any duty of confidentiality could reasonably be expected to continue would depend on many circumstances, including the nature of the relationship, the nature of the information and any harm which might be caused to the deceased's estate or, possibly, those whom the deceased would reasonably have wished to protect, as well as any grounds for justifying disclosure.[305]

---

[303] Compare *White v Jones* [1995] 2 A.C. 207 at 268, where the House of Lords held that a solicitor whose negligence in drawing a will led to the inability of an intended beneficiary to inherit as the testator had intended, was liable to the intended beneficiary, because otherwise there would be no effective means of enforcing the obligation owed by the solicitor to the deceased.

[304] *Bullivant v Att Gen for Victoria* [1901] A.C. 196.

[305] In *Lewis v Secretary of State for Health* [2008] EWHC 2196 (QB) at [18]–[27], Foskett J. considered that it is arguable that a doctor's duty of confidentiality may survive the death of his patient; it was unnecessary for him to decide more.

CHAPTER 4

Duration of Confidentiality

GENERAL PRINCIPLE

In principle a duty of confidentiality should cease if the information loses the **4–001** quality of confidence, whether through passage of time, loss of secrecy or other change of circumstances. Most of the reported cases concern loss of secrecy.

LOSS OF SECRECY

In 1928 the House of Lords held in *Mustad & Son v Dosen*[1] that an injunction **4–002** could not be granted to restrain misuse of confidential information about a "secret" process after the plaintiffs had applied for a patent for it, since by that publication, in the words of Lord Buckmaster, "The secret, as a secret, had ceased to exist".[2]

In later cases the courts have also considered whether publication by a third **4–003** party or by the defendant has the same effect as publication by the plaintiff.

TERRAPIN AND THE SPRINGBOARD THEORY

Because *Mustad* was not reported until 1964, it was not cited in *Terrapin Ltd v* **4–004** *Builders' Supply Company (Hayes) Ltd*, decided by Roxburgh J. in 1959.[3] *Terrapin* is significant for the introduction of the so-called "springboard doctrine".[4]

The defendants manufactured portable buildings to the plaintiffs' design. The **4–005** plaintiffs disclosed to the defendants in confidence details of proposed modifications. Subsequently the defendants sold in competition with the plaintiffs a form of portable building containing many of the plaintiffs' revised features. It was argued for the defendants that the plaintiffs' conduct in selling buildings and publishing brochures which disclosed all their features discharged any obligation of confidentiality by the defendants, since the information could no longer be

---

[1] [1964] 1 W.L.R. 109.
[2] [1964] 1 W.L.R. 109 at 111.
[3] But not fully reported at first instance until [1967] R.P.C. 375, although the decision of the Court of Appeal was reported at [1960] R.P.C. 128.
[4] Haddon-Cave J. provided a convenient summary of the principles behind "springboard" relief in *QBE Management Services (UK) Ltd v Dymoke* [2012] EWHC 80 (QB) at [239]–[247].

regarded as secret. Roxburgh J. rejected this argument. Founding on Lord Greene's judgment in *Saltman's* case, he said[5]:

> "As I understand it, the essence of this branch of the law, whatever the origin of it may be, is that a person who has obtained information in confidence is not allowed to use it as a spring-board for activities detrimental to the person who made the confidential communication, and spring-board it remains even when all the features have been published or can be ascertained by actual inspection by any member of the public. The brochures are certainly not equivalent to the publication of the plans, specifications, other technical information and know-how. The dismantling of a unit might enable a person to proceed without plans or specifications, or other technical information, but not, I think, without some of the know-how, and certainly not without taking the trouble to dismantle. I think it is broadly true to say that a member of the public to whom the confidential information had not been imparted would still have to prepare plans and specifications. He would probably have to construct a prototype, and he would certainly have to conduct tests. Therefore, the possessor of the confidential information still has a long start over any member of the public . . . It is, in my view, inherent in the principle upon which the *Saltman* case rests that the possessor of such information must be placed under a special disability in the field of competition in order to ensure that he does not get an unfair start . . . "

THE *MUSTAD* AND *TERRAPIN* DEBATE

4–006   In *Peter Pan Manufacturing Corp v Corsets Silhouette Ltd*[6] the relationship between the reasoning of Roxburgh J. in the *Terrapin* case and of Lord Buckmaster in *Mustad's* case arose for consideration, but Pennycuick J. did not find it necessary to decide the issue, which he referred to as one of considerable general importance and difficulty.

4–007   The point arose again in *Cranleigh Precision Engineering Ltd v Bryant*.[7] The defendant, as managing director of the plaintiffs, invented an above-ground swimming pool with two unique features. While still in the plaintiffs' employment, he learned of a Swiss patent for a similar pool but lacking the two special features. After leaving the plaintiffs' employment the defendant obtained an assignment of the Swiss patent. The plaintiffs brought two actions against him. In the first action, they obtained an injunction to restrain him from using the knowledge he had gained in confidence about the plaintiffs' product, in particular the two unique features. In the second action they claimed an injunction to prevent the defendant from using the information obtained by him about the Swiss patent and sought damages.

Roskill J. summarised the plaintiffs' arguments in the second action as follows:

> " . . . it was not what appeared in [the Swiss patent] itself which was confidential. It was the knowledge of the possible effect to and upon the plaintiffs of the existence and publication of this specification which was confidential in the hands of the one

---

[5] [1967] R.P.C. 375 at 391–392.

[6] [1963] R.P.C. 45; [1964] 1 W.L.R. 96. *Peter Pan* is interesting on a separate point for its recognition of an account of profits as a remedy available for breach of confidence.

[7] [1966] R.P.C. 81.

person who was in a position to assess its true significance because of the knowledge which he, as the plaintiffs' managing director, possessed of all the facts of the plaintiffs' swimming pool and of their business connected therewith."[8]

The defendant argued that confidentiality ceased when information entered the public domain; that all confidentiality concerning the Swiss patent ended on its publication; and that in so far as *Terrapin* provided a precedent for injunctive relief after the supposed secret had ceased to be secret as a result of publication, it was inconsistent with *Mustad*'s case. **4–008**

Roskill J. found that the defendant acted in breach of his duty to the plaintiffs in concealing from them the information which he had learned about the Swiss patent and in taking no steps to protect the plaintiffs against its possible consequences; and that he acted in breach of confidence in using, after he left the plaintiffs, the information which he had acquired about the Swiss patent and its possible effect on the plaintiffs' business for his own advantage. He distinguished *Mustad*'s case on the ground that in that case the plaintiffs had themselves been the publishers of the specification, whereas in the present case the publishers were the Swiss applicants. He accordingly followed *Terrapin* and granted an injunction and damages. **4–009**

The reasoning of Roskill J. was criticised by the Law Commission in its Report on Breach of Confidence[9]:

"Notwithstanding the view of *Mustad* taken by Roskill J., however, it is doubtful whether an obligation of confidence, as distinguished from any express or implied contractual obligation which may exist between the parties, can persist after the information in question has reached the public domain, irrespective of the way in which it has come into the public domain. Suppose an inventor has given particulars of a certain device to a draughtsman who accepts an obligation in respect of that information. The draughtsman passes on that information to a third party, who knows that he is obtaining the information in breach of the draughtsman's obligation of confidence. Subsequently all the details of the device are independently published in a trade journal. Is the third party thereafter subject to indefinite restraint in making and marketing the device at a time when any of his trade rivals are free to exploit the information in the article?"

The Law Commission also referred to divergent opinions in the American courts between those which followed "*the Rule in Shellmar*",[10] according to which a defendant could be enjoined in perpetuity from using what he had once misused, and those which followed "*the Rule in Conmar*",[11] under which a defendant who had misused information might nevertheless legitimately use it once it had passed into the public domain. The Law Commission preferred the latter. **4–010**

In *Speed Seal Products Ltd v Paddington*[12] the defendants were an engineer and a company under his control. He had formerly worked for the plaintiffs and been a member of their design committee. It was alleged that the committee designed a novel cam-operated coupling device, that the information about its **4–011**

---

[8] At p.93.
[9] Law Com. No.110; Cmnd. 8388 (1981), at para.4.29.
[10] *Shellmar Products Co v Allen-Qualley Co* (1936) 87 F.2d 104.
[11] *Conmar Products Corp v Universal Slide Fastener Co Inc* (1949) 172 F.2d 150.
[12] [1985] 1 W.L.R. 1327.

design was confidential and that the defendants had wrongly used that information to market a rival product. The defendants applied to strike out the claim for injunctions on the ground that they had published the design in a brochure and in a European patent application, and that even if they had acted wrongly in doing so, they could be under no continuing duty of confidentiality. It was not in dispute for the purposes of the appeal that the alleged confidential information had been "published to the world", but the plaintiffs argued that a wrongdoer could not rely on his own wrongdoing and that an injunction could be granted under the springboard principle. The Court of Appeal refused to strike out the claim. Founding on the reasoning of Roskill J. in *Cranleigh Precision Engineering*,[13] they held that publication of confidential information by a third party does not necessarily release from his obligations a person who previously owed a duty of confidentiality. The defendants could be in no better position than if publication had been made by a third party. In considering the question of an injunction Fox L.J. said[14]:

> "The purpose of an injunction is protection. Whether a plaintiff, in circumstances such as the present, needs protection might depend upon the state of the market. If, for example, the only traders seriously competing in the market are the plaintiff and the defendant (the latter being a person who, in breach of duty to the plaintiff, wrongfully published the information to the world) it may be a matter of continuing importance to the plaintiff that the defendant should not continue to get the benefit of the wrongdoing. If, on the other hand, the publication has produced a market with a large number of traders, the elimination of one trader (the defendant) might not be of consequence."

SPYCATCHER

4–012   Peter Wright, a former intelligence officer, in breach of his contract of service with the Crown and of the provisions of the Official Secrets Act 1911, contracted with Australian publishers for the publication of his memoirs of his service in MI5. The book was distributed world wide. The *Sunday Times* bought the serialisation rights and published the first instalment shortly before the book went on sale in the USA. The Attorney General sought an injunction to restrain the *Sunday Times* from serialising further extracts. The House of Lords held unanimously that the *Sunday Times* had acted in breach of duty of confidence in publishing the first extract, but refused by a majority to grant an injunction to prevent further serialisation because the entire book was now in the public domain.[15]

4–013   In considering the position of the *Sunday Times*, the House also considered the position of Peter Wright, although he was not a party to the proceedings. It was necessary to do so, because the argument on behalf of the Crown was that an English court would grant an injunction against Peter Wright, on the ground that an obligation of confidence still attached to him, and that such duty continued to attach in conscience to third parties. This was described by Lord Goff as a

---

[13] [1966] R.P.C. 81.
[14] [1985] 1 W.L.R. 1327 at 1332.
[15] *Att Gen v Guardian Newspapers Ltd (No.2)* [1990] 1 A.C. 109.

"formidable argument"[16] and caused him to consider the premise on which it was based, viz. the continuing duty of confidence said to be owed by Peter Wright.

Lord Goff approached the issue from the starting point that a duty of **4–014** confidence can only apply in respect of information which is confidential; from which the logical consequence should be that, if confidential information ceases to be confidential, the duty of confidence should end (as held in *Mustad*). Referring to *Cranleigh Precision Engineering* Lord Goff said[17]:

> " . . . it seems to me that the true basis of the decision was that, in reliance on the well known judgment of Roxburgh J. in the 'springboard' case, *Terrapin Ltd v Builders' Supply Co. (Hayes) Ltd* [1967] R.P.C. 375, the defendant was in breach of confidence in taking advantage of his own confidential relationship with the plaintiff company to discover what a third party had published and in making use, as soon as he left the employment of the plaintiff company, of information regarding the third party's patent which he had acquired in confidence."

Lord Goff did not consider that *Cranleigh Precision Engineering*[18] supported **4–015** any general principle that, if it is a third party who puts the confidential information into the public domain, the confidant would not be released from his duty of confidence. He therefore disapproved the reasoning in *Speed Seal*.[19] Lord Goff reserved the question (since it had not been fully argued) whether some more limited obligation (analogous to the springboard doctrine) might nevertheless continue to rest on a confidant who, in breach of confidence, destroyed the confidential nature of the information entrusted to him, whilst he rejected the broader argument of the Crown that a confidant who publishes confidential information to the world can remain under a further obligation not to disclose it, simply because it was he who wrongly destroyed its confidentiality. This rejection of the Crown's main argument forms an essential part of the ratio of Lord Goff's speech, because, in Lord Goff's words, it enabled him to "consider the specific issues in the case unfettered by its otherwise considerable force".[20]

Lord Keith and Lord Brightman dealt with the matter more concisely. Lord **4–016** Keith cited Lord Widgery's judgment in *Att Gen v Jonathan Cape Ltd*,[21] in which he held that the confidential character of public confidences lapsed when publication would no longer do public harm. Lord Keith said that the question whether Mr Wright would be at liberty to publish *Spycatcher* in England did not arise for immediate consideration, but, since such publication would cause no further harm:

> " . . . the case for an injunction now against publication by or on behalf of Mr Wright would in my opinion rest upon the principle that he should not be permitted to take advantage of his own wrongdoing."[22]

---

[16] *Att Gen v Guardian Newspapers Ltd (No.2)* [1990] 1 A.C. 109 at 285.
[17] *Att Gen v Guardian Newspapers Ltd (No.2)* [1990] 1 A.C. 109 at 285.
[18] [1966] R.P.C. 81.
[19] [1985] 1 W.L.R. 1327.
[20] *Att Gen v Guardian Newspapers Ltd* (No.2) [1990] 1 A.C. 109 at 289.
[21] [1976] 1 Q.B. 752 at 771.
[22] [1990] 1 A.C. 109 at 259.

Lord Brightman said[23]:

> "In my opinion the reason why the court would, or might, grant an injunction against Wright if he now brought himself within the jurisdiction and sought to publish *Spycatcher* here, is not that such an order would recognise a subsisting duty of confidence, but that it would impede the unjust enrichment of Wright, or preclude him from benefiting, tangibly or intangibly, from his own wrongdoing; or perhaps that the copyright of the work would in equity be vested in the Crown, as suggested by three of Your Lordships."

He added[24]:

> "The Crown is only entitled to restrain the publication of intelligence information if such publication would be against the public interest, as it normally will be if theretofore undisclosed. But if the matter sought to be published is no longer secret, there is unlikely to be any damage to the public interest by re-printing what all the world has already had the opportunity to read. There is no possible damage to the public interest if Tom, Dick or Harry, or "The Sunday Times" reprints in whole or part what is already printed and available within the covers of *Spycatcher*. Therefore it seems to me that no injunction should be granted to restrain further serialisation."

A majority of the House therefore rejected the concept of a duty of confidentiality subsisting after the information had so lost the quality of confidence that further publication would do no harm, while leaving open the possibility of an injunction against repetition of disclosure by the wrongdoer, based not on a continuing duty but either on the desirability of preventing him from profiting from his past breach or on an application of the springboard principle.

4–017 Lord Griffiths, dissenting, considered that an injunction would have been granted against Mr Wright on the basis of a continuing duty of confidence and ought to have been granted against the *Sunday Times*.

4–018 Lord Jauncey considered that an injunction would have been granted against Peter Wright, and should have been granted also against the *Sunday Times* if to do so would have been effective to prevent further serialisation, but that the grant of such an injunction would be a vain act in circumstances in which that any other newspaper could publish whatever extracts it wished.

4–019 In *Att Gen v Blake*[25] the proposition that a former member of the security services, who had turned traitor, owed a continuing fiduciary duty not to publish information which had once been confidential, but had lost its confidentiality, was rejected by Sir Richard Scott V.C. and the Court of Appeal.[26] Lord Woolf M.R. stated that[27]:

> "Equity . . . does not impose a duty to maintain the confidentiality of that which has ceased to be confidential."

---

[23] [1990] 1 A.C. 109 at 266.
[24] [1990] 1 A.C. 109 at 267.
[25] [1987] Ch. 84; [1988] Ch. 439; [2001] 1 A.C. 268.
[26] The argument was not pursued in the House of Lords.
[27] [1988] Ch. 439 at 453.

INJUNCTION TO PREVENT PROFIT FROM PAST MISCONDUCT?

The concept of granting injunctive relief, not for the purpose of preventing a threatened breach of duty, but for the purpose of preventing a wrongdoer from profiting from past misconduct, presents problems. Since it is not based on any continuing duty of confidence, but on the broader principle that wrongdoers should not be allowed to take advantage of their wrongdoing, there would be no justification for limiting it to cases of breach of confidence; but it is unclear whether it would apply to all forms of civil liability, or only to deliberate acts, or to acts involving some form of moral obliquity (and, if so, how they are to be defined).

4–020

If an injunction could be granted on the broad principle that a wrongdoer should not be permitted to profit from his wrongdoing, an exceptionally strong case on the facts arose in *Kaye v Robertson*.[28] In that case a journalist entered without permission a hospital room where the plaintiff was recovering from brain injuries and took photographs of him without his fully informed consent. The defendants not only obtained the photographs by trespass, but their conduct towards the plaintiff was a "monstrous invasion of his privacy" (per Bingham L.J.[29]) committed for commercial gain. However, the Court of Appeal (Glidewell, Bingham and Leggatt L.JJ.) held that it had no power in law to grant an injunction prohibiting the defendants from publishing the photographs so as to prevent them from profiting from the taking of the photographs, i.e. from their own trespass, attractive though the argument might appear to be.[30]

4–021

In the *Spycatcher* case Lord Goff gave the example of convicted criminals being invited to sell their stories on release from prison.[31] He observed that this is highly offensive to many people; but doubted whether that fact provided an appropriate basis for defining the scope of a confidant's civil obligations at common law.

4–022

Further, if the object is to prevent commercial profiteering from past misconduct, why should injunctive relief be limited to the wrongdoer and not extend to those co-operating with him for commercial profit? If the *Sunday Times* was guilty of breach of confidence in publishing Peter Wright's first instalment, why should it not itself have been prohibited from publishing further extracts in order to prevent it too from continuing to exploit a prior wrong to which it had been party? Only one of their Lordships, Lord Griffiths, would have gone that far.[32]

4–023

---

[28] [1991] F.S.R. 62.

[29] [1991] F.S.R. 62 at 70.

[30] [1991] F.S.R. 62 at 69.

[31] [1990] 1 A.C. 109 at 289. It is not a novel practice. In 1874 the imposter in the *Titchborne* case, Arthur Orton (otherwise Thomas Castro, otherwise Sir Roger Titchborne, Bart.) was finally sent to prison for 14 years. On his release, encouraged by a newspaper, he published his story.

[32] See also the judgment of the European Court of Human Rights in *Observer and Guardian v United Kingdom* (1991) 14 E.H.R.R. 153 at 195–196 and *Sunday Times v United Kingdom (No.2)* (1991) 14 E.H.R.R. 229 at 243–244, echoing Lord Oliver's objections in his dissenting speech in *Spycatcher (No.1)* [1987] 1 W.L.R. 1248 at 1318.

In *Vestergaard Frandsen A/S v BestNet Europe Ltd*,[33] Arnold J. analysed the principal authorities on the springboard doctrine and injunctions to prevent profit from past misconduct. He concluded that its proper foundation was that information might possess a limited degree of confidentiality even though it could be ascertained from non-confidential sources, thus supporting an injunction for an appropriate period. He considered that it was doubtful whether mere prevention of profit from a past breach of confidentiality could be a sound basis for the grant of an injunction, and that in general the remedy for past misuse of confidential information was financial.

In *BBC v Harper Collins Publishing Ltd*,[34] the actor Ben Collins played a character in a BBC television series. The identity of the actor was intended to be kept a mystery from the public and Mr Collins contracted with the BBC not to reveal it. He disclosed the secret to Harper Collins (without the BBC's permission) with a view to its inclusion in an autobiography, which Harper Collins was intending to publish, and he tried unsuccessfully to obtain the BBC's agreement to the inclusion of the information in his book. When several press articles appeared, stating that Mr Collins was the actor who played the character, the BBC applied for an injunction to restrain the publishers and Mr Collins from publishing the fact. Morgan J. found that Mr Collins had acted in breach of confidentiality but that the effect of the press coverage was that his identity as the actor had become so generally accessible as public knowledge that it was no longer confidential. He refused to grant an injunction. He distinguished cases such as *Terrapin*, where the object of an injunction was to protect the claimant from harm caused by the defendant using an improper springboard advantage. By contrast, in Mr Collins' case the only purpose of an injunction would be to prevent him and the publishers from profiting from his past breach. He held that this would not be a proper use of the court's power to grant an injunction. The proper remedy for the past breach was a financial remedy.[35]

CONCLUSIONS ON SPRINGBOARD

4–024   It is noteworthy that the House of Lords expressed no disapproval of the decision in *Cranleigh Precision Engineering*,[36] nor of the springboard doctrine stated in *Terrapin*.[37] On the contrary, Lord Goff impliedly considered both to be right, although in relation to the former only as he interpreted it, i.e. as a springboard case.

4–025   As the Law Commission argued in its report on Breach of Confidence,[38] the springboard doctrine is not in total conflict with the principle that information cannot enjoy the protection of the action for breach of confidence once it has entered the public domain, but rather is a limited qualification of it. The object of

---

[33] [2009] EWHC 1456 (Ch): [2010] F.S.R. 2 at [76]–[78] and [93]. Arnold J.'s observations on the springboard doctrine were not affected by the Court of Appeal's subsequent decision on appeal ([2011] EWCA Civ 424).

[34] [2010] EWHC 2424 (Ch).

[35] [2010] EWHC 2424 at [65].

[36] [1966] R.P.C. 81.

[37] [1967] R.P.C. 375.

[38] Cmnd. 8388 (1981), para.4.31.

the springboard doctrine is merely to ensure that the recipient of confidential information does not obtain an unfair start by misuse of information received in confidence. Subsequent decisions have confirmed that the protection given should be related to the unfair advantage which the defendant would otherwise obtain, and, accordingly, that an injunction should not normally extend beyond the period for which the unfair advantage is likely to continue.[39] In *Sun Valley Foods Ltd v Vincent*,[40] Jonathan Parker J. held that it was a further requirement for the grant of an injunction that, as at the date of the court's order, the unfair advantage should still exist and be continuing to have effect. In *Sectrack NV v Satamatics Ltd*, Flaux J. took into account, in continuing an injunction, the fact that the defendant's failure to provide proper disclosure made it currently difficult to assess accurately the extent of the unfair advantage gained by it.[41]

The question whether information originally obtained by a person in confidence has become so freely accessible to the world at large that it is unrealistic to regard it as confidential any more requires a fact specific assessment. At one end of the spectrum are cases like *BBC v Harper Collins Ltd*, where a simple fact (the identity of an actor in a television series) had become widespread public knowledge, but there are less obvious and more difficult cases. The information gained in confidence might not be so readily apparent from the material later published, which might take time and effort to assimilate, or from which it might need a process of inquiry and deduction to arrive at the information provided in confidence. In such cases the court will need to make a quantative and qualitative assessment of the information publicly available.[42]

It may be relevant whether the disclosure has come from the party claiming confidentiality or from someone else (the defendant or a third party). Where it has come from the party seeking confidentiality, that party could not complain of anyone making use of what it has chosen to publish; but if the information provided by it in confidence went beyond that which would be immediately apparent from the information made public (as in *Terrapin* but not in *Mustad*), it is in principle entitled to protection against the recipient of the confidential information using the advantage of having received that information to obtain a head start (the springboard principle). To that extent, the confidentiality of the original disclosure will not have been lost, although no complaint could be made of the recipient doing as anyone else might do.

---

[39] *Potters-Ballotini Ltd v Weston-Baker* [1977] R.P.C. 202 at 206, per Lord Denning M.R. ("Although a man must not use such information as a springboard to get a start over others, nevertheless that springboard does not last for ever.") *Roger Bullivant Ltd v Ellis* [1987] F.S.R. 172 at 184, per Nourse L.J. ("All these observations support the view that the injunction should not normally extend beyond the period for which the unfair advantage may reasonably be expected to continue. That is in my judgment the period for which an injunction should normally be granted in springboard cases.")
[40] [2000] F.S.R. 825 at 834–837.
[41] [2007] EWHC 3003 (Comm) at [69].
[42] *Northern Rock Plc v Financial Times Ltd* [2007] EWHC 2677 (QB) at [15], per Tugendhat J.: "Whether or not the fact that information has already become available to the public should lead to the refusal of an injunction requires a qualitative and not just quantitative assessment. For example, material sought to be restrained may, depending on the facts of each case, already have become available to the public by no more than a single publication, say on an obscure website. Another example may be mass distribution through multiple media. And different items of information from a single confidential source may likewise have received different degrees of publication."

Where the disclosure has come from someone other than the party claiming confidentiality, the party claiming confidentiality may still rely on the springboard principle. It may also be in a stronger position to resist the argument that the information publicly disclosed should be regarded as non-confidential, having regard to the extent of its availability, than if it had voluntarily made the disclosure itself.

As a general principle, an injunction ought not to be granted for the purpose only of preventing a person from profiting from a past breach of confidentiality, as distinct from the prevention of future harm to the wronged party or the enforcement of a continuing right. There are other more appropriate remedies for past wrongdoing.

4–026   Although the springboard doctrine is in itself narrow, it can also be seen as part of a wider principle. In *United States Surgical Corp v Hospital Products International Pty Ltd*[43] the New South Wales Court of Appeal held:

> "It is a principle applied in conformity with the more general principle that a person misusing confidential information must answer for his default according to his gain. A headstart may often be the gain in these cases. If it is the gain, damages will be assessed accordingly and any other relief, such as injunction, will be moulded. If it is not the gain the method of assessing damages or the appropriateness of some other remedy has to be considered in the light of what that gain is."

4–027   In the *Cranleigh Precision Engineering* case two features were particularly relevant in considering what fairness required. The first was that not only did the defendant's knowledge of the third party's patent come to him in his capacity as the company's managing director from its patent agents, but he immediately realised its significance for the company from facts which were not in the public domain. The second is that, although he was under a duty to the company to bring his knowledge of the patent to the board's attention, he deliberately concealed it in order to make use of it to his advantage and against the interests of the company. Roskill J. emphasised these matters in his judgment. Typically cases of breach of confidence involve the passing by A to B of confidential information, which B wrongly divulges to C. *Cranleigh Precision Engineering* does not fall into that pattern, but is rather a case of an agent using his position as agent to acquire information which is pertinent to his principal's affairs and which is not known to his principal, and then using that information for his personal benefit without the principal's fully informed consent. This is a classic example of breach of fiduciary duty by an agent, for which the courts will grant an injunction, damages or an account of profits. It is analogous in its essential elements to *Phipps v Boardman*.[44]

---

[43] [1983] 2 N.S.W.L.R. 157 at 233 (reversed in the High Court on other grounds (1984) 156 C.L.R. 41).

[44] [1967] 2 A.C. 46. See para.2–039, above.

PASSAGE OF TIME AND CHANGE OF CIRCUMSTANCES

In *Attorney-General v Jonathan Cape Ltd*[45] Lord Widgery C.J. recognised in the case of public confidences that:

    4–028

> "There must, however, be a limit in time after which the confidential character of the information, and the duty of the court to restrain publication, will lapse."

He added that:

> "It may, of course, be intensely difficult in a particular case, to say at what point the material loses its confidential character, on the ground that publication will no longer undermine the doctrine of Cabinet responsibility."

The principle that, on information losing its confidential character, the duty of confidence ceases must apply equally in the case of private confidences. In applying that principle, due attention must be paid in each case to the original purpose of the duty of confidence. In the case of private confidence, the duty exists "to protect the personal, private and proprietary interests of the citizen".[46] The duration of such duty will vary according to the nature of the information and the nature of the relationship.

    4–029

It may be difficult, as in the case of public confidences, to identify the point at which such information loses its confidential character, and any statement of principle can only be expressed in general terms. The remarks which follow are intended merely to be illustrative.

    4–030

The General Medical Council states in its advice to doctors that the obligation to keep personal information confidential does not end with the patient's death.[47]

    4–031

The implication of the G.M.C.'s advice is that it regards the duty to a living patient as lifelong (subject to other qualifications, which are discussed in the chapter on medical confidence).

    4–032

In the case of employees it is well recognised that termination of the employment will bring to an end the duty of confidence in relation to some forms of information (that is, information which has become part of the employee's general skill and knowledge), but not in relation to the narrower band of information which may qualify for continued protection under the head of trade secrets.[48]

    4–033

Trade secrets, too, may lose their confidentiality by other means than by entering the public domain. In *Thomas Marshall Ltd v Guinle*[49] Sir Robert Megarry V.C. suggested, inter alia, that, for information to constitute a trade secret, the party claiming confidentiality must reasonably believe that the release of the information would be injurious to him or of advantage to his rivals or others. A trade secret may cease to have that quality, for example, through changes in the confider's business or through technological advances rendering the trade secret obsolescent.

    4–034

---

[45] [1976] 1 Q.B. 752 at 771.

[46] *Commonwealth of Australia v John Fairfax & Sons Ltd* (1980) 147 C.L.R. 39 at 51, per Mason J.

[47] *Confidentiality* (2009), at para.51; see the discussion at para.11–051, below.

[48] See Ch.14, below.

[49] [1979] 1 Ch. 227 at 248.

Other considerations apply in relation to information which involves privacy, as distinct from confidentiality.[50] The subject is discussed in Ch.7.

CONTINUING CONTRACTUAL OBLIGATIONS

4–035   It is possible for a party to be subject to a contractual obligation not to publish information even though it does not have or may have ceased to have the quality of confidentiality.[51] In *Jardin and Jardim Investments Pty v Metcash Ltd*[52] the Court of Appeal of New South Wales contrasted contractual and equitable obligations of confidence in the context of an application for springboard relief.

EFFECT OF A REPUDIATORY BREACH OF CONTRACT

4–036   In *Campbell v Frisbee*[53] the claimant applied for summary judgment for breach of a confidentiality clause in a contract for the provision of management services. The defendant had supplied information about the claimant's sex life to a newspaper, contrary to the provisions of the confidentiality clause. The defendant argued that the clause was not binding because the claimant had acted in repudiatory breach of the contract. Lightman J. held:

> "In the case of a contract for services, there can be no conceivable basis for the suggestion that a repudiatory breach by the client entitles the independent contractor to a release from the obligations of confidentiality. It is plain beyond question that the obligation of confidence of e.g. a lawyer, doctor or security consultant survives acceptance by the service provider of the repudiation of his contract by the client. Indeed that is surely the premise on which the relationship between client and service provider is created. Likewise the law protects marital confidence notwithstanding repudiation of the marriage vows, adultery and divorce: none of these events operate to release the "innocent" spouse from the obligation to preserve these earlier confidences: *Argyll v Argyll* [1967] Ch. 302 at 332–3."

The Court of Appeal allowed an appeal by the defendant. Lord Phillips M.R. said[54]:

> "We do not believe that the effect on duties of confidence assumed under contract when the contract in question is wrongfully repudiated is clearly established. While we do not think that it is likely that Miss Frisbee will establish that Lightman J. erred in his conclusions in a manner detrimental to her case, it cannot be said that she has no reasonable prospect of success on the issue."

---

[50] Passage of time may in some cases diminish a person's right to protection of information under Art.8 but in others it may increase it: see, for example, *R(L) v Commissioner of Police of the Metropolis* [2009] UKSC 3; [2010] 1 A.C. 410 at [27] and [71]. See also the comments of Tugendhat J. in *JIH v News Group Newspapers Ltd* [2010] EWHC 2818 (QB); [2011] E.M.L.R. 9 at [58]–[59] about Art.8 and republication of information previously published.

[51] *Att Gen v Barker* [1990] 3 All E.R. 256 and *Att Gen v Blake* [2001] 1 A.C. 268. See also the discussion at paras 3-002 ff., above.

[52] [2011] NSWCA 409 at [108]–[119], per Meagher J.

[53] [2002] EWCA Civ 1374.

[54] [2002] EWCA Civ 1374 at [22].

The issue remains open.

Lord Diplock's speech in *Photo Production Ltd v Securicor Transport Ltd*[55] is the leading modern authority on the effect of a repudiatory breach of contract (although he did not use that expression) on the innocent party's obligations. He held that it entitled the innocent party to elect to put an end to all primary obligations of both parties remaining unperformed (and to claim monetary compensation for loss caused by the guilty party's non-performance of its primary obligations). However, this general principle did not mean that the parties could not validly contract for what should happen in such a situation.

4–037

Arbitration or choice of forum clause are examples.[56] The validity of such a clause can be analysed on the basis that the arbitration is a collateral agreement or more simply it may be seen as a qualification to the general principle based on the parties' intention that the clause should apply in cases of alleged repudiatory breach of contract.

4–038

Clauses limiting liability for damages are another example. It is artificial to try to analyse such a clause as a collateral contract. The true reason for giving effect to such a clause even after a repudiatory breach is that to do so gives effect to the parties' intention.

4–039

Arbitration, choice of forum and limitation of liability clauses have in common that they can be described as ancillary rather than core contractual terms, but so can a confidentiality clause. Whatever the main purpose of a contract, a confidentiality clause is ancillary to it in that its purpose is to protect a party who provides confidential information during a contract against its use by the other party for other purposes. It is hard to see why a confidentiality clause should not continue to be effective after a repudiatory breach if on the proper construction of the contract that represents the parties' intention. If, however, that view is wrong, or if the party claiming confidentiality is unable to establish as a matter of construction that a confidentiality clause was intended to have contractual effect after repudiation of the contract, it does not follow that the other party should cease to be under an obligation of conscience. It is the receipt of confidential information which gives rise to an obligation of confidentiality, whether contractual or equitable, and there is no reason why an obligation of conscience should necessarily cease just because the other party has subsequently been guilty of a repudiatory breach of contract.

4–040

There may be particular circumstances in which it would be unfair to hold the innocent party under a continuing obligation of confidentiality. For example, if two parties agreed to carry out a joint venture, which one party repudiated after disclosing confidential information relevant to the venture to the other, the effect of the innocent party being required not to use the information for purposes other than the joint venture could be to prevent that party from attempting to carry out the venture on its own, and so leave the field clear for the party in repudiation to do so. In such a case a reasonable person would not regard it as fair for the innocent party to be under a continuing obligation of confidentiality, but that would be because on those facts it would result in an unjust disadvantage.

4–041

---

[55] [1980] A.C. 827 at 848–850.
[56] *Heyman v Darwins Ltd* [1942] A.C. 356.

CHAPTER 5

Public Sector Confidentiality

The application of the doctrine of confidence to government secrets should not be **5–001** confused with the doctrine of public interest immunity, which is part of the law of evidence.[1] Public interest immunity (or Crown privilege as it used to be known) has a long history. Under this doctrine, documents which would otherwise be disclosable in litigation may be immune from production if wider public interest so requires.

In *Conway v Rimmer*[2] the House of Lords adopted the principle expressed by **5–002** Lord Reid:

> "I would therefore propose that the House ought now to decide that Courts have and are entitled to exercise a power and duty to hold a balance between the public interest, as expressed by a Minister, to withhold certain documents or other evidence, and the public interest in ensuring the proper administration of justice."

Lord Reid also observed that:

> "Virtually everyone agrees that Cabinet minutes and the like ought not to be disclosed until such time as they are only of historical interest."

Fortuitously, the first case in which the courts were asked to apply the **5–003** equitable doctrine of confidentiality to the workings of Government in fact concerned the publication of details of cabinet discussions. In *Att Gen v Jonathan Cape Ltd*[3] the Attorney General sought an injunction restraining publication of Richard Crossman's *Diaries of a Cabinet Minister*. It was argued, unsuccessfully, by the defendants that the principle underlying such cases as *Prince Albert v Strange*,[4] *Saltman*[5] and *Argyll*[6] should be restricted to private relationships and not extend to Government secrets.

Lord Widgery C.J. said[7]: **5–004**

> "I cannot see why the courts should be powerless to restrain the publication of public secrets, while enjoying the *Argyll* powers in regard to domestic secrets. Indeed, as already pointed out, the court must have power to deal with publication which

---

[1] *D v N.S.P.C.C.* [1978] A.C. 171 at 241, per Lord Simon. Public interest immunity is discussed in Ch.19, below.
[2] [1968] A.C. 910 at 952.
[3] [1976] 1 Q.B. 752.
[4] (1848) 1 Mac. & G. 25.
[5] (1948) 65 R.P.C. 203.
[6] [1967] Ch. 302.
[7] [1976] 1 Q.B. 752 at 769–770.

threatens national security, and the difference between such a case and the present case is one of degree rather than kind. I conclude, therefore, that when a Cabinet Minister receives information in confidence the improper publication of such information can be restrained by the court, and his obligation is not merely to observe a gentleman's agreement to refrain from publication."

Lord Widgery went on to hold as a matter of principle that:

"The Attorney-General must show

(a)   that . . . publication would be a breach of confidence;
(b)   that the public interest requires that the publication be restrained; and
(c)   that there are no other facts of the public interest contradictory of and more compelling than that relied upon."

This required a balancing exercise. Lord Widgery refused an injunction because 10 years and three general elections had passed since the events described in the diaries, and he concluded after reading the book that:

"I cannot believe that the publication at this interval of anything in volume one would inhibit free discussion in the Cabinet of today, even though the individuals involved are the same, and the national problems have a distressing similarity with those of a decade ago."[8]

5–005   Lord Widgery's approach was followed by Mason J. in *Commonwealth of Australia v John Fairfax & Sons Ltd.*[9] He said:

"However, the plaintiff must show, not only that the information is confidential in quality and that it was imparted so as to import an obligation of confidence, but also that there will be 'an unauthorised use of that information to the detriment of the party communicating it' (*Coco v A. N. Clark (Engineers) Ltd*).[10] The question then, when the executive government seeks the protection given by equity, is: What detriment does it need to show?

The equitable principle has been fashioned to protect the personal, private and proprietary interests of the citizen, not to protect the very different interests of the executive government. It acts, or is supposed to act, not according to standards of private interest, but in the public interest. This is not to say that equity will not protect information in the hands of the government, but it is to say that when equity protects government information it will look at the matter through different spectacles.

It may be a sufficient detriment to the citizen that disclosure of information relating to his affairs will expose his actions to public discussion and criticism. But it can scarcely be a relevant detriment to the government that publication of material concerning its actions will merely expose it to public discussion and criticism. It is unacceptable in our democratic society that there should be a restraint on the publication of information relating to government when the only vice of that information is that it enables the public to discuss, review and criticise government action.

---

[8] *Att Gen v Jonathan Cape Ltd* [1976] 1 Q.B. 752 at 771.
[9] [1969] R.P.C. 41 at 47.
[10] (1980) 147 C.L.R. 39 at 51–52.

Accordingly, the court will determine the government's claim to confidentiality by reference to the public interest. Unless disclosure is likely to injure the public interest, it will not be protected."

This principle was approved and applied in the *Spycatcher* case.[11] In that case Peter Wright's book had been disseminated world wide to the extent of over a million copies and was freely available in the United Kingdom. There was therefore no longer a secret to protect, and any damage which might be caused had already been caused.

5–006

While the *Spycatcher* case was working its way through the English courts, *Lord Advocate v The Scotsman Publications Ltd*[12] was proceeding through the Scottish courts, reaching the House of Lords after the *Spycatcher* decision. The case concerned the memoirs of another former member of the security service, Anthony Cavendish. After permission to publish had been requested, and refused, he had 500 copies printed at his own expense. He provided 279 copies to private individuals, before giving an undertaking to the Crown not to distribute any further copies without advance notice. A copy came into the hands of *The Scotsman* newspaper, which published an article including some of the material.

5–007

The Government brought proceedings for an injunction to restrain further publication. They sought to distinguish *Spycatcher* on the grounds that Anthony Cavendish's memoirs, unlike Peter Wright's, were not in general circulation. It was conceded by the Government that the contents of the book did not include any material damaging to national security. But it was argued that publication was damaging, irrespective of the innocuous nature of the contents, because it would lower morale, encourage copy cats, and cause foreign security powers to lose confidence in the ability of the British security and intelligence services to protect their own secrets.

5–008

The House of Lords held that the combination of circumstances (that the book did not contain any material damaging to national security and that publication on a limited scale had already taken place) meant that the Government had no arguable case that further publication would do any material damage to the public interest. The contents were not going to be harmful, and in so far as the fact of publication might be harmful, it had already happened.

5–009

Lord Keith (with whose speech Lord Griffiths and Lord Goff agreed)[13] added:

5–010

"It was argued for the appellant that the dismissal of this appeal would have the effect that any newspaper which received an unsolicited book of memoirs by a present or former member of the Security or Intelligence Service would be free to publish it. That is not so. If there had been no previous publication at all and no concession that the contents of the book were innocuous the newspaper would undoubtedly itself come under an obligation of confidence and be subject to restraint. If there had been a minor degree of prior publication, and no such concession it would be a matter for further investigation whether further publication would be prejudicial to the public interest, and interim interdict would normally be appropriate."

---

[11] [1990] 1 A.C. 109 at 258, per Lord Keith; 270, per Lord Griffiths and 283, per Lord Goff. See also para.4–012, above.

[12] [1990] 1 A.C. 812.

[13] [1990] 1 A.C. 812 at 822–823.

5–011   It is implicit that it would be for the Government to have to establish that further publication would be detrimental to the public interest, following the judgments of Mason J. in *Commonwealth of Australia v John Fairfax & Sons Ltd*[14] and of the House of Lords in the *Spycatcher* case.[15]

5–012   In *Att Gen v Blake*[16] the defendant was a former member of the intelligence service and Russian agent. He was caught and sent to prison, but escaped and fled to Moscow. Over 20 years later he wrote an autobiography. He had given a contractual undertaking not to divulge in press or book form, during or after his period of service, any official information gained by him as a result of his employment. At the time of the book's publication none of the information contained in it was secret and its disclosure was therefore harmless. The Attorney General brought a claim to recover the proceeds of the publication.

5–013   At the trial it was accepted on behalf of the Attorney General that in writing the book Blake had not committed any breach of duty of confidence, but it was argued that he owed a continuing fiduciary duty not to use his position as a former public servant to generate a profit for himself. This argument was rejected by Scott V.C. and by the Court of Appeal. In the judgment of the Court of Appeal, given by Lord Woolf M.R., it was noted that Blake had committed a clear breach of contract in submitting the book for publication without clearance by the Government but that the Attorney General had decided not to advance a claim to the profits of the book on that ground, while wishing to keep the point open for a higher court.[17] The claim was advanced in the House of Lords and succeeded. Most of the argument was about the availability of an account of profits as a remedy for breach of contract. The fact that publication was harmless to the public interest did not prevent the Government from succeeding in a claim for breach of contract. Lord Nicholls (with whom Lord Goff and Lord Browne-Wilkinson agreed) said[18]:

> "The Crown had and has a legitimate interest in preventing Blake profiting from the disclosure of official information, whether classified or not, while a member of the service and thereafter. Neither he, nor any other member of the service, should have a financial incentive to break his undertaking."

In *Ministry of Defence v Griffin*[19] the government obtained an injunction compelling a former member of the United Kingdom Special Forces (UKSF) to comply with a contractual obligation not to disclose any information relating to the work of the UKSF, obtained by virtue of his position as a member, without prior authority from the ministry. Eady J. accepted that much of the information which the defendant had so far published was anodyne, and that an unreasonable refusal of authorisation by the ministry could be challenged by judicial review, but he held that the ministry was properly entitled under the contract to advance notice of any proposed disclosure in order to have the opportunity of considering it. Because of the special nature of the work of the UKSF, the state was entitled to

---

[14] (1980) 147 C.L.R. 39.
[15] [1990] 1 A.C. 109.
[16] [2001] 1 A.C. 268.
[17] [1998] Ch. 439 at 455–456.
[18] [2001] 1 A.C. 268 at 287.
[19] [2008] EWHC 1542 (QB).

impose a proper system for controlling disclosure about it by members and former members. The judge observed that it was important to remember that the relief sought was not a blanket ban on the defendant's right to publish relevant information, but only to require him to go through the clearance procedure prescribed by the contract.[20]

There seems no reason to suppose that the principles relating to public sector confidentiality are limited to central government. They may equally apply, it is suggested, to local government.

In March 2009 there were nearly 800 public bodies classified by the UK government. They included 192 executive and 405 advisory NDPBs (Non-Departmental Public Bodies),[21] the Bank of England, 23 NHS bodies and various other public corporations. The classification is conservative because it does not include bodies that are the responsibility of devolved government, various lower tier boards (for example, within the NHS) and other boards operating in the public sector (for example, police authorities).   **5–014**

Insofar as such bodies are carrying out functions comparable to those of government, comparable principles should apply to them.[22]

In *Esso Australia Resources Ltd v Plowman*[23] Mason C.J. (with whom Dawson and McHugh JJ. agreed) went further. The case arose from contracts for the supply of natural gas by oil companies to two public utilities. Disputes under the contracts were referred to arbitration. The oil companies wished to prevent commercially sensitive information from being disclosed outside the arbitration. Mason C.J. rejected the oil companies' argument that a duty of confidence was owed to them by virtue of the fact that information was provided in, and for the purposes of, the arbitration. He went on to suggest, obiter, that if such a duty were owed, the case should be viewed as one involving governmental secrets, rather than personal or commercial secrets, and therefore it would have to be established that the public interest demanded non-disclosure. He explained his reasoning as follows[24]:   **5–015**

> "The approach outlined in John Fairfax[25] should be adopted when the information relates to statutory authorities or public utilities because, as Professor Finn notes,[26] in the public sector '[t]he need is for compelled openness, not for burgeoning secrecy.' The present case is a striking illustration of this principle. Why should the consumers and the public of Victoria be denied knowledge of what happens in these arbitrations, the outcome of which will affect, in all probability, the prices chargeable to consumers by the public utilities?"

Mason C.J.'s approach differed from that adopted by the majority of the House of Lords in *British Steel Corp v Granada Television Ltd*,[27] as he recognised.   **5–016**

---

[20] [2008] EWHC 1542 at [19]–[25].
[21] Cabinet Office *Public Bodies 2009*. The Cabinet Office no longer publishes annual statistics of all NDPBs but only those sponsored by the Cabinet Office.
[22] *London Regional Transport v Mayor of London* [2001] EWCA Civ 1491 provides a good example on its facts, but the point was not raised. The case is discussed at para.6–053 below.
[23] [1994–1995] 183 C.L.R. 10.
[24] [1994–1995] 183 C.L.R. 10 at 32.
[25] *Commonwealth of Australia v John Fairfax & Sons Ltd* (1980) 147 C.L.R. 39.
[26] Finn, "Confidentiality and the 'Public Interest' " (1984) 58 *Australian Law Journal* 497, 505.
[27] [1981] A.C. 1096.

Moreover, whether or not the principles relating to public sector confidentiality should apply to a public utility seeking to enforce an obligation of confidentiality, it is difficult to see why such principles should apply where a commercial organisation seeks to enforce an obligation of confidentiality against a public utility in order to protect its commercial secrets. There is, it is suggested, a fallacy in viewing the information which the oil companies were seeking to protect as government secrets.

Subject to any relevant statutory provision, a public body has no power unilaterally to impose on others a duty of confidentiality to protect its own functioning beyond the ordinary principles of confidentiality.[28]

---

[28] *Mahon v Post Publications* [2007] IESC 15 (Supreme Court of Ireland) and *Mahon v Keena* [2007] IEHC 348 (High Court of Ireland), concerning a tribunal of inquiry. See also *Broadmoor Special Hospital Authority v Robinson* [2000] Q.B. 775 at [30] (Lord Woolf M.R.) and [55] (Waller L.J.), and *Napier v Pressdram Ltd* [2009] EWCA Civ 443; [2009] E.M.L.R. 21.

CHAPTER 6

Public Interest

There is a distinction between private and public sector confidentiality. Public interest is potentially relevant to both, but different principles are involved. Where confidentiality is invoked in support of Government, it is for the Government to establish not only that there has been a breach or threatened breach of confidentiality, but also that publication is contrary to the public interest.[1] The topic is considered in Ch.5.

6–001

In other cases, a duty of confidentiality may be negated or circumscribed by overriding public interest considerations. That topic is considered in the present chapter.

6–002

THE DEFENCE OF INIQUITY

The earliest manifestation of what has come to be referred to as the public interest defence was the so-called defence of iniquity, which owed its origin to the judgment of Sir William Page-Wood V.C. in *Gartside v Outram*.[2]

6–003

Gartside v Outram was reinterpreted, and the beginnings of a broader principle recognised, in *Weld-Blundell v Stephens*.[3] The plaintiff sent a letter to the defendant, an accountant, instructing him to investigate the affairs of a company, with which he had dealings, and making libellous statements about those responsible for running the company. The defendant's partner carelessly left the letter at the company's office. Libel actions were successfully brought against the plaintiff by persons defamed in the letter (one of whom he described as "an ingenious thief"). The plaintiff sued the accountant for negligence.

6–004

The defendant argued that there was no duty of confidence in relation to the letter, since the libels amounted to a malicious wrong. The argument failed. Warrington and Scrutton L.JJ. interpreted *Gartside v Outram* (questionably, perhaps) as a case in which the court had declined to exercise its equitable jurisdiction in favour of the plaintiffs and left them to their remedy at law. Bankes and Warrington L.JJ. considered that there could be circumstances in which the duty of confidence would be overridden by a duty to the public, and they drew a distinction between a document concerning a past crime and a crime in contemplation.

6–005

---

[1] *Att Gen v Jonathan Cape Ltd* [1976] 1 Q.B. 752; *Commonwealth of Australia v John Fairfax & Sons Ltd* (1980) 147 C.L.R. 39; *Att Gen v Guardian Newspapers Ltd (No.2)* [1990] 1 A.C. 109.
[2] (1857) 26 L.J.Ch. (N.S.) 113. See para.1–030 above.
[3] [1919] 1 K.B. 520, affirmed [1920] A.C. 956.

6–006   Scrutton L.J. said[4]:

> "Under the decision in *Reg. v Cox and Railton*[5] when the accused has consulted his solicitor after the commission of a crime for the legitimate purpose of being defended the communication is privileged, the privilege being that of the client. If then the solicitor in breach of this confidence and privilege announced his intention of informing the prosecution of the contents of his client's communication, I cannot believe that the Court would not restrain him before communication or give damages against him for breach of his contract of employment after communication, even though those damages were based on his having provided evidence to prove the client guilty of a crime he had in fact committed. The reason would be that the public policy that crime should be punished would be outweighed by the public policy that accused persons should be properly defended, and contracts necessary for their defence observed. There is a public policy in not lightly interfering with freedom of contract: *per* Jessel M.R. in *Printing and Numerical Registering Co. v Sampson.*"[6]

Scrutton L.J., however, was in a minority on the plaintiff's entitlement to damages, the majority (both in the Court of Appeal and in the House of Lords) holding that he was entitled to nominal damages only, since the damages which he had been ordered to pay in the libel actions were to be regarded as caused by his own wrongful acts.

6–007   In the House of Lords,[7] the defendant limited his argument to the latter issue of causation, but Viscount Finlay commented:

> "It would be startling if it were the law that an agent who is negligent in the custody of a letter handed to him in confidence by his principal might plead in defence that the letter was libellous. There may, of course, be cases in which some higher duty is involved. Danger to the State or public duty may supersede the duty of the agent to his principal. But nothing of that nature arises in this case."

6–008   In *Tournier v National Provincial and Union Bank of England*[8] the Court of Appeal had to consider what duty of confidentiality was owed by a bank to its customer. The Court (Bankes, Scrutton and Atkin L.JJ.) held that there was necessarily implied into the contract between them a duty of confidentiality, but subject to qualifications.

6–009   Bankes L.J. said[9]:

> "On principle I think that the qualifications can be classified under four heads: (a) Where disclosure is under compulsion by law; (b) where there is a duty to the public to disclose; (c) where the interests of the bank require disclosure; (d) where the disclosure is made by the express or implied consent of the customer."

In relation to the second qualification Bankes L.J. said:

---

[4] [1919] 1 K.B. 520 at 544–545.
[5] (1884) 14 Q.B.D. 153 at 175.
[6] (1875) L.R. 19 Eq. 462 at 465.
[7] [1920] A.C. 956 at 965.
[8] [1924] 1 K.B. 461.
[9] [1924] 1 K.B. 461 at 473.

"Many instances of the second class might be given. They may be summed up in the language of Lord Finlay in *Weld-Blundell v Stephens*,[10] where he speaks of cases where a higher duty than the private duty is involved, as where 'danger to the State or public duty' may supersede the duty of the agent to his principal."

Scrutton and Atkin L.JJ.[11] agreed that the term necessarily to be implied into the contract between a bank and its customer must be subject to qualifications, entitling the bank to make disclosure in certain circumstances, including for prevention of or protection against frauds or crimes.

THE CONTRACTUAL ANALYSIS

The contractual analysis begun in *Weld-Blundell* and *Tournier* was further developed in *Initial Services Ltd v Putterill*.[12] The plaintiffs ran a laundry. The defendant, who had been their sales manager, resigned and took with him various documents which, according to him, were part of or related to a price fixing agreement entered into between the plaintiffs and other launderers, but not registered, contrary to the Restrictive Practices Act 1956. The defendant passed the documents to a newspaper, which published two articles on the subject. The plaintiffs sued the defendant for breach of an implied term of his contract of employment not to disclose to third parties confidential information relating to the plaintiffs obtained during his employment. The defendant alleged in his defence that the plaintiffs were part of a cartel conducting business in breach of statute, and he denied that his disclosure of their activities was in breach of the implied term of the contract relied on by the plaintiffs. The plaintiffs applied, unsuccessfully, to strike out the paragraphs of the defence containing the defendant's allegations as disclosing no defence.   **6–010**

Breach of the provisions of the Restrictive Practices Act was not a criminal offence, and it was argued by the plaintiffs that the relevant qualification to the implied duty of confidentiality owed by an employee was limited to crime or fraud. This argument was rejected.   **6–011**

Lord Denning M.R. accepted that every contract of employment contained an implied obligation that the employee would not, during or after his employment, disclose information or documents received in confidence; but the obligation was subject to exceptions. As to the scope of the relevant exception, he said[13]:   **6–012**

"In *Weld-Blundell v Stephens*,[14] Bankes L.J. rather suggested that the exception is limited to the proposed or contemplated commission of a crime or a civil wrong. But I should have thought that was too limited. The exception should extend to crimes, frauds and misdeeds, both those actually committed as well as those in contemplation, provided always—and this is essential—that the disclosure is justified in the public interest. . . .

The disclosure must, I should think, be to one who has a proper interest to receive the information. Thus it would be proper to disclose a crime to the police; or a

---

[10] [1920] A.C. 956 at 965.
[11] [1924] 1 K.B. 46 at 480–481, 483–484 and 486.
[12] [1968] 1 Q.B. 396.
[13] [1968] 1 Q.B. 396 at 405–406.
[14] [1919] 1 K.B. 520 at 527.

breach of the Restrictive Trade Practices Act to the registrar. There may be cases where the misdeed is of such a character that the public interest may demand, or at least excuse, publication on a broader field, even to the press."

Salmon L.J. said[15]:

"Suppose the servant had entered into a contract with the master not to disclose certain information, would that contract be enforceable or would it be illegal? To my mind that must depend on the circumstances of the particular case. Consider this case: the Restrictive Trade Practices Act, 1956, is an Act which certainly was very much concerned with the public interest. It imposed an obligation upon these plaintiffs to disclose to the registrar the agreements into which they had entered with their fellow launderers in relation to the supply of goods. That obligation was imposed in the public interest . . . .
Suppose the master had said to the servant,
'We, of course, appreciate that these agreements into which we have entered ought in the public interest to be disclosed to the registrar, but we hope that the registrar will never find out about them. We propose to ignore our statutory obligation to disclose these agreements. You must agree with us that you will never make any disclosure about them to anyone.'
Suppose that the servant had agreed. I am by no means convinced that any court would do other than regard such an agreement as illegal on the ground that it was clearly contrary to the public interest. I do not think that the law would lend assistance to anyone who is proposing to commit and to continue to commit a clear breach of a statutory duty imposed upon him in the public interest."

Winn L.J. adopted the same approach, saying[16]:

"I agree with both of the judgments delivered by my Lords. I desire to say that for my own part my approach to this problem has been in substance identical with that of Salmon L.J. It seems to me that the proper function of an implied term of a contract is either to dot the i's and cross the t's of the express terms or to fill in some lacuna left by the contracting parties which must properly be filled by the implied term in order to give business efficacy, and produce the true intent of those contracting parties. As my Lord has said, the question whether or not a term properly to be implied in a contract is enforceable in law must be decided by asking whether it would have been enforced had it been an express term. I entirely agree, if I may respectfully say so, with that approach, which has been my own approach also to this problem."

To pose the question whether a term "properly to be implied" is enforceable may be said to be tortuous in that there cannot be "properly implied" into a contract a term which would be unenforceable; but the sense is clear, namely that the court should not imply a term requiring secrecy in circumstances where, if there were an express term to that effect, the court would refuse to enforce it as contrary to public policy.

6–013 The same analysis was advanced by Gummow J. in the Federal Court of Australia in *Corrs Pavey Whiting & Byrne v Collector of Customs*.[17] Referring to *Gartside v Outram*, he said that:

---

[15] [1968] 1 Q.B. 396 at 409–410.
[16] [1968] 1 Q.B. 396 at 410–411.
[17] (1987) 74 A.L.R. 428 at 449.

" . . . any court of law or equity would have been extremely unlikely to imply in a contract between master and servant an obligation that the servant's good faith to his master required him to keep secret details of his master's gross bad faith to his customers. Likewise, before any express contractual obligation of confidence is enforced at law or in equity the term relied on must be valid at law."

He added[18] that where the plaintiff asserted a contractual right of confidence, the law of contract (supplemented by equitable defences where equitable relief was sought) sufficiently dealt with the matter. Where the plaintiff asserted an equitable duty of confidence, the principle applicable was no wider than that:

" . . . information will lack the necessary attribute of confidence if the subject matter is the existence or real likelihood of the existence of an iniquity in the sense of a crime, civil wrong or serious misdeed of public importance, and the confidence is relied upon to prevent disclosure to a third party with a real and direct interest in redressing such crime, wrong or misdeed."

In other words equity, following the law, would not impose an equitable obligation to do that which in contract would be unenforceable.

Misdeeds may include "anti-social" conduct in the sense of "activities which, whilst not in breach of the law, are seriously contrary to the public interest".[19] But that has to be judged according to generally accepted standards, as was emphasised by Sir Nicolas Browne-Wilkinson V.C. in *Stephens v Avery*[20] in relation to alleged sexual "wrongdoing":

6–014

"If it is right that there is now no generally accepted code of sexual morality applying to this case, it would be quite wrong in my judgment for any judge to apply his own personal moral views, however strongly held, in deciding the legal rights of the parties. The court's function is to apply the law, not personal prejudice. Only in a case where there is a generally accepted moral code can the court refuse to enforce rights in such a way as to offend that generally accepted code."

SERIOUS HARM TO THE PUBLIC

The reasoning which applies in cases of serious misdeeds has been extended to cases where there is serious danger of harm, without misconduct necessarily being the cause, but differing views have been expressed about the scope of the principle involved.

6–015

In *Beloff v Pressdram Ltd*[21] Ungoed-Thomas J. said:

6–016

"The defence of public interest clearly covers and, in the authorities does not extend beyond, disclosure, which . . . must be disclosure justified in the public interest, of matters carried out or contemplated, in breach of the country's security, or in breach of law, including statutory duty, fraud, or otherwise destructive of the country or its people, including matters medically dangerous to the public; and doubtless other misdeeds of similar gravity."

---

[18] (1987) 74 A.L.R. 428 at 450.
[19] *Francome v Mirror Group Newspapers Ltd* [1984] 1 W.L.R. 892 at 895–896.
[20] [1988] 1 Ch. 449 at 454.
[21] [1973] 1 All E.R. 241 at 260.

6–017   In *Woodward v Hutchins*[22] Lord Denning M.R. took an altogether broader approach. He said:

> "There is no doubt whatever that this pop group sought publicity. They wanted to have themselves presented to the public in a favourable light so that audiences would come to hear them and support them . . . . If a group of this kind seek publicity which is to their advantage, it seems to me that they cannot complain if a servant or employee of theirs afterwards discloses the truth about them. If the image which they fostered was not a true image, it is in the public interest that it should be corrected. *In these cases of confidential information it is a case of balancing the public interest in maintaining the confidence against the public interest in knowing the truth.*" (Emphasis added.)

This approach did not involve considering the seriousness of the need for public disclosure but amounted to an unstructured balancing exercise. In effect, the court assumed a general discretion whether or not to enforce confidentiality. In that respect it went further than previous authorities and has not generally been supported by later authorities.

6–018   In *Lion Laboratories Ltd v Evans*[23] Griffiths L.J. said:

> "I am quite satisfied that the defence of public interest is now well established in actions for breach of confidence . . . .
>
> I can see no sensible reason why this defence should be limited to cases in which there was been wrongdoing on the part of the plaintiffs. I believe that the so-called iniquity rule evolved because in most cases where the facts justified a publication in breach of confidence, it was because the plaintiff had behaved so disgracefully or criminally that it was judged in the public interest that his behaviour should be exposed. No doubt it is in such circumstances that the defence will usually arise, but it is not difficult to think of instances where, although there has been no wrongdoing on the part of the plaintiff, it may be vital in the public interest to publish a part of his confidential information."

6–019   In *Francome v Mirror Group Newspapers Ltd*[24] the Court of Appeal recognised that there may be public interest grounds for limited but not general disclosure. It upheld an interlocutory injunction restraining the defendants from general publication of tapped telephone conversations, which allegedly revealed breaches by a well-known jockey of the rules of racing and possibly the criminal law, but the court was willing for them to be disclosed to the Jockey Club and the police.

SPYCATCHER

6–020   In the *Spycatcher* case, Lord Goff said[25]:

> " . . . although the basis of the law's protection of confidence is that there is a public interest that confidences should be preserved and protected by the law, nevertheless

---

[22] [1977] 1 W.L.R. 760 at 763–764. See para.3–115, above.
[23] [1985] Q.B. 526 at 550.
[24] [1984] 1 W.L.R. 892.
[25] [1990] 1 A.C. 109 at 282–283.

that public interest may be outweighed by some other countervailing public interest which favours disclosure. This limitation may apply, as the learned judge pointed out, to all types of confidential information. It is this limiting principle which may require a court to carry out a balancing operation, weighing the public interest in maintaining confidence against a countervailing public interest favouring disclosure.

Embraced within this limiting principle is, of course, the so called defence of iniquity. In origin, this principle was narrowly stated, on the basis that a man cannot be made 'the confidant of a crime or a fraud': see *Gartside v Outram* (1857) L.J.Ch. 113 at 114, *per* Sir William Page Wood V.C. But it is now clear that *the principle extends to matters of which disclosure is required in the public interest*: see *Beloff v Pressdram Ltd* [1973] 1 All E.R. 241 at 260, *per* Ungoed-Thomas J., and *Lion Laboratories Ltd v Evans* [1985] Q.B. 526 at 550, *per* Griffiths L.J. It does not however follow that the public interest will in such cases *require* disclosure to the media, or to the public by the media. There are cases in which a more limited disclosure is all that is *required*: see *Francome v Mirror Group Newspapers Ltd* [1984] 1 W.L.R. 892. A classic example of a case where limited disclosure is *required* is a case of alleged iniquity in the Security Service. Here there are a number of avenues for proper complaint; these are set out in the judgment of Sir John Donaldson M.R." (Emphasis added.)

The limiting principle recognised by Lord Goff applies to matters of which disclosure is required in the public interest, but only to such form of disclosure as the public interest requires. The word "required" is instructive. It is not enough to show that disclosure would be interesting to the public. It has to be shown that disclosure is required to serve some important public interest, such as the interest in public safety, health, the exposure of serious wrongdoing, or the proper conduct of public affairs.

The limitation is consistent with the underlying notion of confidentiality as an obligation of conscience in recognising that there may be circumstances in which a conscientious recipient of confidential information would reasonably consider it right as a responsible citizen to make some form of disclosure of the information.   **6–021**

Something may present a serious risk to the medical health of the public, national security, the administration of justice or a matter of comparable public importance such that it may fairly be regarded as necessary in the public interest that a person possessing such information should be free to disclose it to an appropriate third party, whether or not the matter involves individual wrongdoing (by the claimant or anyone else). As in the case of "iniquity", so also in the case of such information, it may be said that no court would imply a contractual obligation prohibiting such disclosure, or enforce an express contractual prohibition, and that such information would be regarded both at common law and in equity as lacking the necessary attribute of confidence to prevent such disclosure. It is perfectly possible to accommodate such an extension to *Gartside v Outram*[26] within the framework of the analysis favoured by Gummow J. in the *Corrs Pavey* case, and there are strong grounds to do so. It would be wholly unsatisfactory if, for example, a hospital doctor were prevented by his contract of   **6–022**

---

[26] [1857] 26 L.J.Ch. (N.S.) 113.

employment from notifying the Department of Health of an imminent risk to public health detected by him in the course of his hospital duties, whether misconduct was involved or not.[27]

6–023   That is very different from the approach adopted by the Court of Appeal in *Woodward v Hutchins*.[28] It could hardly be suggested that the group's desire to foster a good public image presented a danger to the public. Notwithstanding the absence of any such danger, the Court of Appeal considered that it was free to balance generally "the public interest in maintaining the confidence against the public interest in knowing the truth" and resolved in favour of the latter. It may be that the true explanation for the decision was not so much any real public interest in revealing the group's behaviour as the court's distaste for it, which made the court regard it as unworthy of protection. If so, it is not a case from which any general principle can be drawn.

APPLICATION OF THE LIMITING PRINCIPLE

6–024   Lord Goff's statement of the limiting principle has been influential. In *Re A Company's Application*[29] Scott J. considered the scope of an employee's duty of confidentiality in the context of disclosure to an industry regulator. A company which carried on a business regulated under the Financial Services Act 1986 dismissed its compliance officer. In discussions about compensation for alleged unfair dismissal he mentioned that he intended to report the company to the financial services regulator, FIMBRA, for breach of the regulatory scheme introduced under the Act, and to the Inland Revenue for misfeasances by the company's directors.

6–025   The company applied for an injunction to restrain him from making use of any confidential documents or information relating to the company's affairs. The defendant volunteered an undertaking not to disclose his placing of information with FIMBRA or the Inland Revenue to other persons apart from his legal advisers. The issue was whether the defendant was to be restrained, pending trial, from making the threatened disclosures to FIMBRA and the Inland Revenue. The company argued that it was a case of naked blackmail. The defendant denied any blackmailing attempt.

6–026   Scott J. refused to restrain the defendant from disclosing the matters in question to FIMBRA or the Inland Revenue. He observed[30] that if there were any threat of general disclosure by the defendant of confidential information concerning the way in which the plaintiff carried on its business or the affairs of any of its clients, there could be no answer to a claim for an injunction, but that the question was whether an employee of a company carrying on the business of giving financial advice and of financial management to members of the public under the regulatory umbrella provided by FIMBRA owed a duty of confidentiality that extends to barring disclosure of information to FIMBRA.

---

[27] See *Minister for Immigration and Citizenship v Kumar* [2009] H.A.C. 10; (2009) 238 C.L.R. 448, at 27.

[28] [1977] 1 W.L.R. 760.

[29] [1989] Ch. 477. For a review of the case, see Lomnicka, "The Employee Whistleblower and the Duty of Confidentiality" (1990) 106 L.Q.R. 42.

[30] [1989] Ch. 477 at 481.

He concluded[31]:   6–027

> "I think it would be contrary to the public interest for employees of financial services companies who thought that they ought to place before FIMBRA information of possible breaches of the regulatory system, or information about possible fiscal irregularities before the Inland Revenue, to be inhibited from so doing . . . "

Scott J. also held that it was not for him to conduct a preliminary investigation into the merits of the allegations where the disclosure was proposed to be made to a body which itself had responsibility for investigating such matters.

The judge accepted that the company might be right in its assertion that the   6–028
proposed disclosure was a blackmailing ploy. But if the defendant owed no contractual duty not to disclose information to FIMBRA, malicious motivation could not make the proposed disclosure a breach of contract.

In *W v Egdell*[32] the plaintiff, a paranoid schizophrenic, shot and killed five   6–029
people and injured two others. He pleaded guilty to manslaughter on the ground of diminished responsibility and was ordered to be detained in a secure hospital. For the purpose of an application to a mental health review tribunal with a view towards his ultimate release, the plaintiff, through his solicitors, retained the defendant, a consultant psychiatrist, to report on his state of mental health. The defendant formed a more serious view of the plaintiff's condition than had been taken by the medical officer responsible for his treatment, and his report was adverse to the plaintiff's application. After considering the report, the plaintiff, through his solicitors, withdrew his application. The defendant was so concerned about the difference between his views and those formed by the medical officer that, without the plaintiff's consent, he forwarded a copy of his report to the assistant medical director at the hospital. The plaintiff brought an action against the defendant alleging breach of confidence. The claim failed before Scott J. and on appeal.

Scott J. sought to identify the scope of the relevant duty owed by the defendant   6–030
to the plaintiff. He said[33]:

> "It is convenient for me first to ask myself what duty of confidence a court of equity ought to regard as imposed on Dr Egdell by the circumstances in which he obtained information from and about W. and prepared his report. It is in my judgment plain, and the contrary has not been suggested, that the circumstances did impose on Dr Egdell a duty of confidence. If, for instance, Dr Egdell had sold the contents of his report to a newspaper, I do not think any court of equity would hesitate for a moment before concluding that his conduct had been a breach of his duty of confidence. The question in the present case is not whether Dr Egdell was under a duty of confidence; he plainly was. The question is as to the breadth of that duty. Did the duty extend so as to bar disclosure of the report to the medical director of the hospital?"

He concluded[34]:

---

[31] [1989] Ch. 477 at 483.
[32] [1989] Ch. 359.
[33] [1989] Ch. 359 at 389.
[34] [1989] Ch. 359 at 392.

"True it is that Dr. Egdell was engaged by W. He was the doctor of W.'s choice. Nonetheless, in my opinion, the duty he owed to W. was not his only duty. W. was not an ordinary member of the public. He was, consequent upon the killings he had perpetrated, held in a secure hospital subject to a regime whereby decisions concerning his future were to be taken by public authorities, the Home Secretary or the tribunal. W.'s own interests would not be the only nor the main criterion in the taking of those decisions. The safety of the public would be the main criterion. In my view, a doctor called upon, as Dr. Egdell was, to examine a patient such as W. owes a duty not only to his patient but also a duty to the public. His duty to the public would require him, in my opinion, to place before the proper authorities the result of his examination if, in his opinion, the public interest so required. This would be so, in my opinion, whether or not the patient instructed him not to do so."

6–031   In the Court of Appeal the plaintiff criticised the judge's approach for leaving the question whether disclosure was justified to the subjective judgment of the doctor. Bingham L.J. agreed with the criticism, but added that in judging whether the disclosure was justified in law the court would attach weight to the doctor's considered judgment.[35] In considering the public interest qualification to the duty of confidence owed to the plaintiff, Bingham L.J. stated that only the most compelling circumstances could justify a doctor in acting in a way which would injure the immediate interests of the patient, as the patient perceived them, without obtaining his consent, but he concluded[36]:

"Where a man has committed multiple killings under the disability of serious mental illness, decisions which may lead directly or indirectly to his release from hospital should not be made unless a responsible authority is properly able to make an informed judgment that the risk of repetition is so small as to be acceptable. A consultant psychiatrist who becomes aware, even in the course of a confidential relationship, of information which leads him, in the exercise of what the court considers a sound professional judgment, to fear that such decisions may be made on the basis of inadequate information and with a real risk of consequent danger to the public is entitled to take such steps as are reasonable in all the circumstances to communicate the grounds of his concern to the responsible authorities."

6–032   Dr Egdell was clearly fearful of the risk to the public from the possible premature release into the community of a dangerous schizophrenic who had, according to his report, a seriously abnormal interest in the making of home-made bombs. If the plaintiff had confided to the doctor that he planned to commit murder, no court would have held that there was an implied obligation on the part of the defendant to keep that information to himself, nor would it have upheld an express agreement to do so. Should different principles apply because the perceived danger to the public arose from illness? It would be surprising if any court had thought so. As Meagher Gummow and Lehane observe[37]:

"A contract not to disclose to the responsible authorities the continued murderous propensities of the plaintiff would have offended public policy: *A v Hayden*."[38]

---

[35] [1989] Ch. 359 at 422.

[36] [1989] Ch. 359 at 423–424.

[37] Meagher, Gummow & Lehane's *Equity: Doctrines and Remedies*, 4th edn (LexisNexis Australia, 2002) at para.41–115.

[38] (1984) 156 C.L.R. 532.

As to the criticism made of Scott J.'s approach that it left the question whether **6–033** disclosure was justified to the subjective judgment of the doctor (in saying that the doctor's "duty to the public would require him to place before the proper authorities the result of his examination if, in his opinion, the public interest so required"), a similar point arose in *Woolgar v Chief Constable of Sussex Police.*[39] A nurse who was the matron of a nursing home was arrested and interviewed by the police after the death of a patient. The police concluded that there was insufficient evidence to charge her with any offence. The health authority then referred the matter to the council which was the regulatory body for nursing. The nursing council asked the police for any relevant information. The police asked the nurse for her consent to disclosure of a transcript of her interview under caution, which she refused. On being told that the police solicitor would listen to the tape and then decide whether it should be disclosed to the nursing council, the nurse applied for an injunction to restrain the police from disclosing the transcript on ground that it was confidential. Kennedy L.J. stated the issue as follows[40]:

> "Undoubtedly when someone is arrested and interviewed by the police what he or she says, is confidential. Plainly it may be used in the course of a criminal trial if charges are brought arising out of that investigation, but if it is not so used the person interviewed is entitled to believe that, generally speaking, his or her confidence will be respected. If authority be required for that proposition, it can be found in *Taylor v Director of the Serious Fraud Office* [1999] 2 A.C. 177, but, as all of the authorities cited to us indicate, there are exceptional circumstances which justify the disclosure by the police, otherwise than in the course of a criminal trial, of what has been said by a suspect during the course of an interview, in circumstances where the suspect, or former suspect, does not consent to such disclosure. The question which arises in this case is whether, if the regulatory body of the profession to which the suspect belongs is investigating serious allegations and makes a formal request to the police for disclosure of what was said in interview, the public interest in the proper working of the regulatory body is or may be such as to justify disclosure of the material sought. If the answer to that question is in the affirmative how, as a matter of procedure, should contentious issues in relation to disclosure be resolved?"

He concluded[41] that where a regulatory body operating in the field of public health and safety seeks access to confidential material, which the police are reasonably persuaded is relevant to the subject matter of an inquiry being conducted by the regulatory body, a public interest is shown to exist which entitles the police to release the material to the regulatory body on the basis that, save insofar as it may be used by the regulatory body for its own inquiry, the confidentiality which attaches to the material will be maintained. He added:

> "Even if there is no request from the regulatory body, it seems to me that if the police come into possession of confidential information which, in their reasonable view, in the interests of public health or safety, should be considered by a professional or regulatory body, then the police are free to pass that information to the relevant regulatory body for its consideration.

---

[39] [2000] 1 W.L.R. 25.
[40] [2000] 1 W.L.R. 25 at [6].
[41] [2000] 1 W.L.R. 25 at [9].

Obviously in each case a balance has to be struck between competing public interests, and at least arguably in some cases the reasonableness of the police view may be open to challenge. If they refuse to disclose, the regulatory body can, if aware of the existence of the information, make an appropriate application to the court. In order to safeguard the interests of the individual, it is, in my judgment, desirable that, where the police are minded to disclose, they should, as in this case, inform the person affected of what they propose to do in such time as to enable that person, if so advised, to seek assistance from the court. In some cases that may not be practicable or desirable, but in most cases that seems to me to be the course that should be followed. In any event, in my judgment, the primary decision as to disclosure should be made by the police who have the custody of the relevant material, and not by the court."

6–034   The patterns of thought involved in this approach contain a mixture of private and public law. It was held that the police owed a legal duty of confidentiality to the nurse in relation to what she told them in her interview, subject to a qualification enabling the police to disclose the transcript to the nursing regulatory authority if it was reasonable to consider that it was in the interests of public health and safety to do so. But the court did not consider that it was for itself to decide whether disclosure should be made. Rather, this was a matter for the decision of the police, subject "arguably in some cases" to review in the way that a court may review the legality of a decision of a public body as a matter of public law. In this respect the court's approach differed from *W v Egdell,* where Bingham L.J. said[42]:

"Where, as here, the relationship between doctor and patient is contractual, the question is whether the doctor's disclosure is or is not a breach of contract. The answer to that question must turn not on what the doctor thinks but on what the court rules. But it does not follow that the doctor's conclusion is irrelevant. In making its ruling the court will give such weight to the considered judgment of a professional man as seems in all the circumstances to be appropriate."

While at a technical level the difference may be explained because there was no contract involved in *Woolgar v Chief Constable of Sussex Police,* nevertheless if the police owed the nurse an obligation of confidentiality the question whether there was a breach or threatened breach of that duty was one for the court.

6–035   In considering whether the interests of public health or safety should permit a doctor or the police to disclose information given in circumstances importing an obligation of confidentiality, without the consent of the person to whom the obligation is owed, it does not seem satisfactory to draw a distinction according to whether there was an underlying contract. It is suggested that in either case it is for the court to rule on the legal criteria which govern the question whether and in what circumstances public interest may justify disclosure. Within those criteria, a person should not be held to have acted unconscionably if their decision was reasonable.[43]

---

[42] [1990] 1 Ch. 359 at 422.

[43] Cited by Tugendhat J. in *Commissioner of Police of the Metropolis v Times Newspapers Ltd* [2011] EWHC 2705 (QB) at [107]. At [106] he said "In summary, the law of confidentiality is part of the law of equity. In equity conscience is not the equivalent of a personal judgment or preference, however deeply held. Conscience sets an objective standard that must be met by everyone...On some questions there may be only one possible answer a reasonable person can give. On other questions there may be a range of answers within which reasonable people may differ...But difficulty of ascertaining a right answer does not mean that there is no right answer, but only opinions. Nor does it mean that the court

The suggestion that an unreasonable but honestly held belief that publication **6–036** is justified should provide a defence to a claim for breach of confidence was rejected by the Court of Appeal in *Campbell v MGN Ltd*[44] and was not pursued on appeal to the House of Lords.

An applicant for an injunction to prevent a disclosure on grounds of **6–037** confidentiality has to satisfy the court that there is a threatened breach of duty. In *Woolgar v Chief Constable of Sussex Police* the applicant was not in a position to do so (since the police solicitor had not listened to the tape or made a decision on the nursing council's request for disclosure) unless she could establish that disclosure would necessarily be wrongful. Having rejected that argument, it would have been premature for the court to rule whether a decision to disclose the nurse's interview would be justifiable, and it did not have the material on which to do so.

There is some uncertainty whether it may make a difference if the party **6–038** claiming confidentiality is relying on an express term rather than on an implied term or an equitable obligation when considering the issue of public interest.

In *Initial Services Ltd v Putterill*[45] Salmon and Winn L.JJ. considered that the **6–039** proper test in deciding if an implied contractual obligation or an equitable obligation of confidentiality arising from an employment contract extended to the disclosure in question was to ask whether an express term prohibiting the disclosure would have been contrary to public policy.

In *Spycatcher* Scott J. followed the same approach[46]: **6–040**

> "The court would obviously never, by means of an implied term, impose on an ex-employee a duty which would have been unenforceable if it had been incorporated into an express term. But in deciding upon the ambit of the implied term the same considerations will, in my view, be relevant as would be relevant to an examination of whether an express term was enforceable."

In *Price Waterhouse v BCCI*[47] Millett J. arguably took a different approach. **6–041** An inquiry into the supervision of BCCI under the Banking Act 1987 was set up under the Chairmanship of Bingham L.J. by the Treasury and the Bank of England. The inquiry had no statutory power to enforce the attendance of witnesses or to compel the production of documents, and the judge rejected the argument that the Bank of England could have required production of documents for the purposes of the inquiry under s.39 of the Banking Act (since that section empowered the Bank of England to require the production of documents only if necessary for the performance of its supervisory function, not for the purpose of

---

must give equal respect to all views as to what the answer is." See also *Coco v A.N. Clark (Engineers) Ltd* [1969] R.P.C. 41 at 48: "It may be that that hard-worked creature, the reasonable man, may be pressed into service once more; for I do not see why he should not labour in equity as well as at law." (Megarry J.).

[44] [2002] EWCA Civ 1373; [2003] Q.B. 633 at [66]–[70].

[45] [1968] 1 Q.B. 368 at 409 per Salmon L.J. and 411 per Winn L.J.

[46] [1990] 1 A.C. 109 at 146.

[47] [1992] B.C.L.C. 583. The collapse of BCCI and subsequent litigation and inquiries gave rise to various confidentiality problems. See also *El Jawhary v BCCI* [1993] B.C.L.C. 396; *R. v Institute of Chartered Accountants of England and Wales Ex p. Brindle* [1994] B.C.C. 297; *Morris v Director of Serious Fraud Office* [1993] B.C.L.C. 580.

enabling the inquiry to review its performance). The inquiry requested the accountants Price Waterhouse to submit evidence and produce documents.

6–042   The accountants performed various functions in relation to the bank, including co-ordinating the worldwide audits of the companies in the group. They were concerned that most of the information in their possession was confidential to the bank, and that much of it was also covered by a duty of banking confidentiality owed by the bank to its customers, of which the accountants had notice. They sought a declaration that they were not precluded from supplying information or documents to the inquiry. There was unquestionably a relationship of confidentiality between the bank and its customers (of which the accountants had notice), and between the accountants and the bank, but the issue was whether the scope of the accountants' obligations to the bank and its customers was such as to preclude them from cooperating with the inquiry.

After citing passages from the speeches of Lord Griffiths and Lord Goff in the *Spycatcher* case[48] and from the judgment of Bankes L.J. in *Tournier*,[49] Millett J. said[50]:

> "In all the cases cited to me in which the public interest in favour of disclosure has prevailed, it has been the public interest in the detection or prevention of wrong-doing, or in preventing a miscarriage of justice, or in the maintenance of public safety. An express contractual undertaking not to make disclosure in such circumstances would be against public policy. However, if those who set up the inquiry had thought that the public interest required that all relevant material should be made available to it, they could have set it up under the Tribunal of Inquiries and Evidence Act 1921. No doubt there were good reasons for not doing so. But they were content to rely upon the voluntary submission of evidence by those willing to co-operate with the inquiry. Where the information is confidential, the choice whether to volunteer it ought prima facie in my view to rest with the person to whom the duty of confidence is owed, rather than with the person who owes it. An express contractual undertaking not to co-operate with the inquiry would not, I apprehend, be contrary to public policy. That, however, is not the test which has been laid down by the authorities. The duty of confidentiality, whether contractual or equitable, is subject to a limiting principle. It is subject to the right, not merely the duty, to disclose information where there is a higher public interest in disclosure than in maintaining confidentiality.
>
> I have reached the conclusion that in the particular circumstances of the present case the public interest in favour of disclosure ought to prevail."

6–043   When the judge said that an express contractual undertaking not to help the inquiry would not have been contrary to public policy, but that this was not the test laid down by the authorities, it is unclear whether he meant: (a) that even if there had been such an undertaking he would have made the declaration sought, because he judged that there was a higher public interest in disclosure, or (b) that although such an express undertaking would not have been contrary to public policy, and therefore would have been enforceable, that was irrelevant to the question whether the court should imply or impose a contractual or equitable obligation precluding the accountants from helping the inquiry. Either approach presents difficulties.

---

[48] [1990] 1 A.C. 109 at 268 and 282.
[49] [1924] 1 K.B. 461 at 472–473.
[50] [1992] B.C.L.C. 583 at 601.

The difficulty with the first approach is that it is one matter to hold (as in **6–044** *Initial Services Ltd v Putterill*[51]) that public policy would require a court to declare a term unenforceable because its enforcement would be contrary to public policy; it is another matter to declare in advance, on grounds of public interest, that a party is free not to comply with a contractual undertaking, even though public policy does not require the undertaking to be treated as unenforceable. The difficulty with the second approach is that it is inconsistent with previous authorities.

The proceedings were most unusual in that the judge was being asked in effect **6–045** to give a negative declaration as to the accountants' obligations towards the bank's customers (or possibly a dispensation from complying with them), without having details of the information which might be disclosed and without the customers having the opportunity to make representations. Because all the parties to the action supported the relief claimed, the judge did not have the benefit of contrary argument as to the appropriateness of the declaration. It is suggested that it would be unsafe to draw any general conclusions from the case.

In *Campbell v Frisbee*[52] Lord Phillips M.R. said: **6–046**

> "We consider it arguable that a duty of confidentiality that has been expressly assumed under contract carries more weight, when balanced against the right of freedom of expression, than a duty of confidentiality that is not buttressed by express agreement—contrast the observations of Walker L.J. in *London Regional Transport v The Mayor of London* [2001] EWCA Civ 1491 at paragraph 46 with those of Lord Donaldson of Lymington M.R. in *Attorney-General v Barker* [1990] 3 All E.R. 257 at p 260."

The court expressed no further view on the matter. The two cases mentioned by Lord Phillips shared the significant feature that they concerned publication of material which was not intrinsically confidential. Because of the lack of intrinsic confidentiality, no question of an implied contractual obligation not to publish the material could have arisen in either case. In each case the claimants' attempts to prevent publication were entirely dependent on express contractual undertakings.

In *Associated Newspapers v Prince of Wales* the Court of Appeal adhered to **6–047** the view expressed in *Campbell v Frisbee* but added that the extent to which a contract added weight to a duty of confidence arising out of a confidential relationship would depend on the facts of the individual case.[53] Where information is of an intrinsically confidential nature, it is not easy to see as a general principle why it should be more easily overridden by a public interest defence on account of the duty of confidentiality not being expressed in a written term, but there may be cases in which a written agreement would fortify the existence and scope of a duty which might otherwise be open to possible doubt.

ARTICLE 10

Article 10 of the European Convention provides as follows: **6–048**

---

[51] [1968] 1 Q.B. 396.
[52] [2002] EWCA Civ 1374 at [22].
[53] [2006] EWCA Civ 1776; [2008] Ch. 57 at [69].

"(1)   Everyone has the right to freedom of expression. This right shall include freedom to hold opinions and to receive and impart information and ideas without interference by public authority and regardless of frontiers. This Article shall not prevent States from requiring the licensing of broadcasting, television or cinema enterprises.

(2)   The exercise of these freedoms, since it carries with it duties and responsibilities, may be subject to such formalities, conditions, restrictions or penalties as are prescribed by law and are necessary in a democratic society, in the interests of national security, territorial integrity or public safety, for the prevention of disorder or crime, for the protection of health or morals, for the protection of the reputation or rights of others, for preventing the disclosure of information received in confidence, or for maintaining the authority and impartiality of the judiciary."

Section 12 of the Human Rights Act 1998 prohibits a court from granting an injunction before trial which might affect the exercise of the Convention right to freedom of expression unless it is satisfied that the applicant is likely to establish that publication should not be allowed. In *Cream Holdings Ltd v Bannerjee*[54] the House of Lords held that the word likely should be interpreted with some flexibility and that the court should not make an interim restraint order unless satisfied that the applicant's prospects of success at the trial are sufficiently favourable to justify such an order being made in all the circumstances of the case.

6–049   In the *Spycatcher* case Lord Goff considered Art.10, although the Convention had not yet been incorporated into domestic law. He said[55]:

" . . . I can see no inconsistency between English law on this subject and article 10 of the European Convention on Human Rights. This is scarcely surprising, since we may pride ourselves on the fact that freedom of speech has existed in this country perhaps as long as, if not longer than, it has existed in any other country in the world . . . . The exercise of the right to freedom of expression under article 10 may be subject to restrictions (as are prescribed by law and are necessary in a democratic society) in relation to certain prescribed matters, which include 'the interests of national security' and 'preventing the disclosure of information received in confidence'. It is established in the jurisprudence of the European Court of Human Rights that the word 'necessary' in this context implies the existence of a pressing social need, and that interference with freedom of expression should be no more than is proportionate to the legitimate aim pursued. I have no reason to believe that English law, as applied in the courts, leads to any different conclusion."

Except in the area of privacy (discussed in Ch.7), the incorporation of the Convention by the Human Rights Act 1998 has not led to a change of substance in the approach of the courts to issues of confidentiality and public interest, but in some cases the courts have used the language of Art.10 as reinforcement of the relevant principles.

6–050   In *R. v Department of Health Ex p. Source Informatics Ltd*[56] arguments were based both on domestic jurisprudence and on Art.10. In his judgment (with which the other members of the court agreed) Simon Brown L.J. recognised

---

[54] [2004] UKHL 44; [2005] 1 A.C. 253.

[55] [1990] 1 A.C. 109 at 283–284.

[56] [2001] Q.B. 424 at 444.

"the importance of confining any public interest defence in this area of the law within strict limits—lest, as Gummow J. put it at first instance in *Smith Kline and French Laboratories (Australia) Ltd v Department of Community Services and Health* [1990] F.S.R. 617, 663, it becomes 'not so much a rule of law as an invitation to judicial idiosyncracy by deciding each case on an ad hoc basis as to whether, on the facts overall, it is better to respect or to override the obligation of confidence' ".

He also commented on the need to avoid a starting point of an overwide equitable obligation of confidence.

In *Imutran Ltd v Uncaged Campaigns Ltd*[57] the claimant was a pharmaceutical   **6–051** company engaged in research into organ transplantation. The research involved experiments on pigs. The work was subject to regulatory control by the Home Secretary under the Animals (Scientific Procedures) Act 1986 and by a section of the Department of Health called the Good Laboratory Practice Monitoring Authority (GLPMA). The defendants were a body which campaigned against animal experimentation and one of its directors. The defendants received a large number of leaked documents belonging to the claimant, which were obviously confidential. The defendants considered that they raised extremely serious questions about animal welfare and the public regulation of research. From the leaked documents they compiled a dossier, which was placed on websites, but the websites were soon closed down by the service providers. The dossier was also supplied to the Home Office, GLPMA and the RSPCA.

Sir Andrew Morritt V.C. granted the claimants' application for an injunction to   **6–052** prevent its general publication pending trial, considering that they were likely to establish at the trial that publication of the leaked documents should not be allowed. The defendants relied on public interest and Art.10. The judge said[58]:

"I have been referred to the well-known line of cases consisting of *Initial Services Ltd v Putterill* [1967] 3 All E.R. 145, [1968] 1 Q.B. 396, *Hubbard v Vosper* [1972] 1 All E.R. 1023, [1972] 2 Q.B. 84, *Francome v Mirror Group Newspapers Ltd* [1984] 2 All E.R. 408, [1984] 1 W.L.R. 892, *Lion Laboratories Ltd v Evans* [1984] 2 All E.R. 417, [1985] Q.B. 526, *Re a Company's application* [1989] 2 All E.R. 248, [1989] Ch. 477 and *A-G v Guardian Newspapers Ltd (No.2)* [1988] 3 All E.R. 545, [1990] 1 A.C. 109. Each of them demonstrates that the public interest in disclosure may outweigh the right of the plaintiff to protect his confidences. They demonstrate that the court will also consider how much disclosure the public interest requires; the fact that some disclosure may be required does not mean that disclosure to the whole world should be permitted.

In addition the 1998 Act requires the court, as a public authority, to take into account the right of freedom of expression conferred by art 10 of the convention . . . The effect of that article for present purposes is that any injunction, which by definition is a restriction on the exercise of the right to freedom of expression, must be justified as being no more than is necessary in a democratic society."

The judge was unimpressed by the argument that because the issue of animal welfare was of public importance the defendants should be able to make general disclosure of the documents. In considering what was necessary in a democratic society, he observed that Parliament had considered the issue of animal

---

[57] [2001] 2 All E.R. 385.
[58] [2001] 2 All E.R. 385 at [20]–[21].

experimentation and laid down a licensing and inspection system. The form of the injunction meant that the defendants would be able to communicate the leaked information to the regulatory bodies denoted by Parliament as having responsibility in the field. The defendants had a democratic right to campaign for the abolition of animal experimentation but not with the claimants' confidential documents.

6–053   In *London Regional Transport v Mayor of London*[59] the first claimant (LRT) was a public body established by the London Regional Transport Act 1984. The second claimant, London Underground Ltd (LUL), was a wholly owned subsidiary of LRT. The Greater London Authority Act 1999 provided for LRT to be replaced by a new statutory body, Transport for London (TfL), whose chairman would be the Mayor of London. LUL's functions were to be restricted to operating underground railway services, and the responsibilities for the infrastructure of the system were to be transferred to three newly created subsidiaries of LUL, whose shares were then to be sold to the private sector. In the transitional period the Mayor, LRT and TfL were under a statutory duty (by s.298(3) of the 1999 Act) to consult and co-operate with one another and to provide such information as might reasonably be required by one another for the purpose of discharging any of its functions. K was appointed as chairman of LRT and was also appointed by the Mayor as Commissioner of TfL. LUL had confidentiality agreements with all bidders. LUL supplied information about the bids to TfL under a confidentiality agreement which included the provision:

> "All information related to the review of bids . . . being undertaken by [K] . . . must be held in the strictest confidence and not used for any purpose other than for the purpose of enabling TfL and the Mayor to discharge their duties pursuant to Section 298(3) of the Greater London Authority Act 1999."

K on behalf of TfL commissioned a firm of accountants to report on the value for money exercise conducted by LUL and its advisers. The accountants were given access to the bids. Their report was highly critical. K wrote to the Prime Minister saying that in his opinion the public-private partnership project was not feasible. K was about to present the accountants' report to the board of LRT when he was removed from his chairmanship of LRT by the Secretary of State. On the following day the Mayor announced his intention of publishing the contents of the report. The claimants immediately applied for an injunction against TfL and the Mayor.

6–054   After a short injunction the defendants produced a redacted version of the report which excluded all sensitive price information. On a resumed hearing the judge did not accept that publication of the redacted version would cause significant harm to LRT, LUL, or successful or unsuccessful bidders and he refused to stop its publication. His decision was upheld on appeal.

6–055   The position was summarised by Sedley L.J.[60]:

> "The discharge of the injunction by Sullivan J. is justified on the straightforward ground that there is nothing of genuine commercial sensitivity in the redacted

---

[59] [2001] EWCA Civ 1491.
[60] [2001] EWCA Civ 1491 at [53].

version of the Deloittes report and nothing therefore to justify the stifling of public information and debate by the enforcement of a bare contractual obligation of silence."

While the report had been written as a result of studying confidential bid information, it did not disclose any bid information which could be identified as confidential. The claim that its publication would be a misuse of confidential information therefore rested entirely on the terms of TfL's contractual undertaking. It is possible for parties to contract for non-disclosure of information even though the information in question is not intrinsically confidential,[61] but a contractual undertaking of that kind will not be enforced if to do so would be contrary to the public interest.

The claimants argued that the test was to be found in the passage from Lord Goff's speech in the *Spycatcher* case, where he referred to "matters of which disclosure is required in the public interest" in his summary of the public interest limitation on the principle of confidentiality.[62] However, Lord Goff was considering information which possessed the quality of confidentiality. He was not considering "a bare contractual obligation of silence".   **6–056**

There would also have been a strong case for saying that since the claimants were public bodies (and were not acting in support of any confidentiality of private bodies), it was incumbent on them to establish that publication would be harmful to the public interest, adopting the principles which apply to public sector confidentiality,[63] but this point does not appear to have been argued. The question whether the intended public-private partnership represented good value for money was obviously important to the population of London (if not beyond), and the accountants' report was capable of informing public debate on the issue. There was a strong public interest in its disclosure and no public interest in its non-disclosure.   **6–057**

In the Court of Appeal, Robert Walker L.J. dealt with the matter in terms of principles of confidentiality. He cited, without express approval or disapproval,[64] the following passage from a previous edition of this book: **6–058**

"the true principle is not (as dicta in some cases suggest) that the court will permit a breach of confidence whenever it considers that disclosure would serve the public interest better than non-disclosure, but rather that no obligation of confidence exists in contract or equity, in so far as the subject matter concerns a serious risk of public

---

[61] *Att Gen v Blake* [2001] 1 A.C. 268.

[62] [1990] 1 A.C. 109 at 282–283.

[63] *Att Gen v Jonathan Cape Ltd* [1976] 1 Q.B. 752; *Commonwealth of Australia v John Fairfax & Sons Ltd* (1980) 147 C.L.R. 39; *Att-Gen v Guardian Newspapers Ltd (No.2)* [1990] 1 A.C. 109. In *Commissioner of Police v Bermuda Broadcasting Co Ltd* [2008] UKPC 5; *The Times*, January 24, 2008, the police failed to establish that it would be contrary to public interest for the broadcasting company to use sensitive documents which had been taken from the police headquarters and supplied to the press. The court considered, at [10], that it was irrelevant how the documents had been removed from the police station because it was not suggested that the press was complicit in their removal. That is understandable on the facts of that case, since the question was whether publication was against the public interest. However, there could be cases where the circumstances under which the information was obtained could be relevant to that question.

[64] [2001] EWCA Civ 1491; [2003] E.M.L.R. 4 at [36]. In *Commissioner of Police of the Metropolis v Times Newspaper Ltd* [2011] EWHC 2705 (QB) at [137], Tugendhat J. said that Robert Walker L.J. cited the passage with approval, but that may be reading more than is justified.

harm (including but not limited to cases of 'iniquity') and the alleged obligation would prevent disclosure appropriate to prevent such harm."

Sedley L.J. agreed with his approach but added that the conclusion was reinforced by Art.10.[65] He went on to suggest that an Art.10 approach based on a test of proportionality might provide a more certain guide than the test of the reasonable recipient's conscience. However, the reasonable recipient's conscience is a standard well established in determining the existence and scope of a duty of confidentiality, and the existence of such a duty is an important limitation on a person's Art.10 right to freedom of expression, because there is a public interest in duties of confidentiality being observed.

In *Associated Newspapers Ltd v Prince of Wales*[66] the Prince of Wales brought an action for breach of confidence in relation to journals written by him during foreign expeditions. The journals were provided to the newspaper, via an intermediary, by an employee in breach of her contract of employment. The newspaper relied on Art.10. The Prince of Wales' claim was presented under Art.8, but the Court of Appeal pointed out that this was unnecessary in a case where there was a breach of confidentiality under ordinary principles. It noted that the importance of private duties of confidence in the context of Art.10 rights was not much explored by either English or Strasbourg authorities and set out its view on the matter as one of general principle:

> "There is an important public interest in the observance of duties of confidentiality-...Before the Human Rights Act came into force the circumstances in which the public interest in publication overrode a duty of confidence were very limited...To-day the test is different. It is whether a fetter of the right of freedom of expression is, in the particular circumstances, 'necessary in a democratic society'. It is a test of proportionality. But a significant element to be weighed in the balance is the importance in a democratic society of upholding duties of confidence that are created between individuals. It is not enough to justify publication that the information in question is a matter of public interest...
>
> For these reasons, the test to be applied when considering whether it is necessary to restrict freedom of expression in order to prevent disclosure of information received in confidence is not simply whether the matter is a matter of public interest but whether, having regard to the nature of the information and all the relevant circumstances, it is in the public interest that the duty of confidence should be breached."[67]

This passage was cited and applied by Tugendhat J. in *Northern Rock Plc v Financial Times Ltd*.[68] It was widely known that the claimant bank was in financial difficulty. It attempted to mount a lifeboat operation and sent a briefing memorandum to a number of financial institutions in the hope of enlisting their support. Before the document was delivered, the recipient was required to agree to keep certain information confidential. The memorandum was leaked and some of its contents appeared in the press. The Financial Times then posted a much larger section on its website. Northern Rock applied for an injunction to prevent continued publication of the leaked material. The Financial Times relied on

---

[65] [2001] EWCA Civ 1491 at [54]–[58].

[66] [2006] EWCA Civ 1776; [2008] Ch. 57.

[67] [2008] Ch. 57 at 31 and 65–68.

[68] [2007] EWHC 2677 (QB).

Art.10 and argued that there was a public interest in the disclosure. It submitted that shareholders should know where they stood and that the grant of an injunction would expose the public to the risk of deception and the creation of a false market. Tugendhat J. rejected the argument. He drew a distinction between the extensive copying of whole sections of the briefing memorandum and the earlier much less precise disclosures in other media. The detailed information published by the Financial Times was the kind of commercially sensitive information which it was necessary in a democratic society for a company to be entitled to protect. He distinguished the *LRT* case, in which the published material had been in a carefully redacted form, and he described the detailed commercial information in the briefing memorandum as much closer to the example of a Budget speech. He considered that the information published in media other than the Financial Times website had become so publicly available that the grant of an injunction would be futile, but that the information published by the Financial Times was qualitatively and quantitatively different. There was a real possibility that further publication would do harm, and an injunction was granted to prevent it.

In summary, Art.10 requires any qualification preventing the disclosure of information received in confidence to be prescribed by law. In English law that prescription is to be found in the established principles of confidentiality, and it must be for the claimant in any case to bring the claim within those principles. In so far as the claim is based on the equitable doctrine of confidentiality, it involves the conscience test. The principles include recognition that in some cases a duty of confidentiality may be negated or qualified by public interest. Proportionality in this context is an aspect of the relevant principles rather than a separate principle.

6–059

For publication of information obtained in confidence or through a breach of confidence to be justified on grounds of public interest, the information must not only be a matter of public interest, but it must be of real importance such that the public should know the information despite the confidential nature of the relationship through which it was obtained. In such a case it is not strictly right to say that the law permits a breach of confidentiality, but rather that the duty of confidentiality is subject to a limiting factor.[69] In that way the law recognises that there may be circumstance in which a conscientious recipient of confidential information may have a higher responsibility to society to make some form of disclosure of the information.

A more generalised defence of freedom of speech would be undesirable in principle. The essence of confidentiality is that a person who receives confidential information on trust that they will respect its confidentiality should do so. There may be cases where the public importance of disclosure is greater than the importance of maintaining respect for confidentiality, but to adopt a test of mere desirability of the information being public knowledge would be one-sided and vague, leaving too much to the personal opinion of the judge about what he considers to be desirable for the public to know.

---

[69] See *Raab v Associated Newspapers Ltd* [2011] EWCA 3375 (QB) at [43], Tugendhat J.

NEW ZEALAND

6–060   In New Zealand it has been held by the Court of Appeal that:

> "What has been called ever since *Gartside v Outram* (1856) 26 L.J.Ch. 113 the defence of iniquity is an instance, and probably the prime instance, of the principle that the law will not protect confidential information if the publication complained of is shown to be in the overriding public interest: see generally *Lion Laboratories Ltd v Evans* [1985] Q.B. 526; *Attorney-General for the United Kingdom v Wellington Newspapers Ltd* [1988] 1 N.Z.L.R. 129, at 176–177, 178; *Attorney-General v Observer Ltd* [1990] 1 A.C. 109, at 268–269 and at 282–283."[70]

In *Solicitor-General v Alice* the High Court of New Zealand described as a "valuable synthesis" an earlier version of the principles set out in para.6–075, below.[71] In that case the court held that the respondent lawyer had acted in contempt of court when he disclosed to the media documents which he had obtained in litigation under the terms of a memorandum containing an express confidentiality undertaking. The court recognised that whistle-blowing can be "an ultimate response to systemic oppression and injustice", but stated that where legal remedies were available to be pursued, there could as a rule be no room either for whistle-blowing or any other remedy of self-help, because self-help was in such circumstances the very antithesis of the rule of law.[72] It was open to the respondent to have applied to the court to be released from his undertaking but he had chosen not to do so.

AUSTRALIA

6–061   Australian courts have generally preferred the narrower "public interest defence" enunciated in such cases as *Beloff v Pressdram Ltd*[73] to the broader version put forward by Lord Denning M.R. in *Woodward v Hutchins*,[74] but there have been different judicial views about the preferred approach.

6–062   In *Castrol Australia Pty Ltd v Emtech Associates Pty Ltd*[75] Rath J. observed that the public interest "exception" could not universally be extended to all crimes committed, as Bankes L.J. pointed out in *Weld-Blundell v Stephens*[76]; but that exclusion from protection of designs "to destroy the public welfare" expressed a concept authoritatively expressed by Viscount Finlay in the same case, when he referred to cases where some "higher duty is involved" and said that "danger to the state or public duty may supersede the duty of the agent to his principal".[77]

---

[70] *European Pacific Banking Corp v Television New Zealand Ltd* [1994] 3 N.Z.L.R. 43 at 46.
[71] [2007] NZHC 48; [2007] 2 N.Z.L.R. 783 at [58].
[72] [2007] 2 N.Z.L.R. 783 at [60]–[64].
[73] [1973] 1 All E.R. 241 at 260.
[74] [1977] 1 W.L.R. 760.
[75] (1980) 33 A.L.R. 31 at 54.
[76] [1919] 1 K.B. 520 at 527 and 528.
[77] [1920] A.C. 956 at 965.

Rath J. also cited with agreement Ungoed-Thomas J.'s summary in *Beloff v*   **6–063**
Pressdram Ltd[78] (approved by Lord Goff in *Spycatcher*[79]), saying that it
expressed no more than a reasonable elaboration of Viscount Finlay's "higher
duty" concept and was an acceptable statement of the law as to the defence of
public interest in an action for breach of confidence. He added[80]:

> "What is particularly important in Ungoed-Thomas J.'s formulation of principle is
> his emphasis on the gravity of the conduct that may give rise to the defence. If there
> is to be a defence labelled public interest, some such confinement of its vague
> boundaries is in my view essential."

Rath J. declined to follow the broader test applied by Lord Denning M.R. in
Woodward v Hutchins,[81] saying that[82]:

> "If Lord Denning's quoted statement is taken literally the court will test the
> legitimacy of breach of confidence by its conception of the balance of public
> interest in the particular circumstances of the case."

He went on to say that the court[83]:

> " . . . must have regard to matters of a more weighty and precise kind than a public
> interest in the truth being told . . . . In a sense [the plaintiffs'] image was a matter of
> 'public interest', but not in the sense that as a matter of public policy the defendants
> were entitled, or required, to break confidence."

In *Corrs Pavey Whiting & Byrne v Collector of Customs*[84] Gummow J. was   **6–064**
also critical of *Woodward v Hutchins* and, like Rath J., rejected a broad "public
interest defence". He considered that if there were some principle of general
application inspired by *Gartside v Outram* it was no wider than that

> "information will lack the necessary attribute of confidence if the subject matter is
> the existence or real likelihood of the existence of an iniquity in the sense of a
> crime, civil wrong or serious misdeed of public importance, and the confidence is
> relied upon to prevent disclosure to a third party with a real and direct interest in
> redressing such crime, wrong or misdeed."

Kirby P. took a broader approach in the *Spycatcher* litigation in Australia,[85]   **6–065**
describing *Gartside v Outram* as

> "an instance of the wider category of the public interest which may sometimes, even
> if rarely, outweigh the public interest in confidentiality and secrecy: *cf.* Gibbs C.J. in
> *A v Hayden (No.2)* (1984) 156 C.L.R. 532 at 545 *et seq.*"

---

[78] [1973] 1 All E.R. 241 at 260.
[79] [1990] 1 A.C. 109 at 282.
[80] (1980) 33 A.L.R. 31 at 55.
[81] [1977] 1 W.L.R. 760.
[82] (1980) 33 A.L.R. 31 at 56.
[83] (1980) 33 A.L.R. 31 at 56.
[84] (1987) 74 A.L.R. 428 at 445–450.
[85] *Att-Gen (UK) v Heinemann Publishers Australia Pty Ltd* (1987) 147 C.L.R. 39 at 57.

6–066   In *Smith Klein & French Laboratories (Australia) Ltd v Department of Community Services*[86] Gummow J. drew a distinction between factors which may qualify a duty of confidentiality and the question of a public interest defence. A court of equity would not impute to a party an obligation which would restrict him in his performance of public responsibilities, but the question was what was the content of the obligation at its inception, rather than whether there was a public interest defence to a breach of obligation. He noted that this had been the approach of Scott J. at first instance in the *Spycatcher* case[87] (and, he might have added, in *In Re A Company's Application*[88] and *W v Egdell*[89]). As to the question of a public interest defence, he said:

> "My views upon the wisdom of adopting in Australia the English authorities in which the 'public interest' defence has been constructed in recent years from what may be thought inadequate historical and doctrinal materials, have been expressed in *Corrs Pavey Whiting & Byrne v Collection of Customs (Vic)* . . . , at 451–458. Those views are consistent with what was said by Rath J. in *Castrol Australia Pty Ltd v EmTech Associates Pty Ltd*, . . . , at 210–216 and by Hutley A.P. in *David Syme & Co. Ltd v General Motors-Holden's Ltd* [1984] 2 N.S.W.L.R., 294 at 305–306 . . .
>
> Further, I would accept the submissions by counsel for the applicants in the *SK&F* proceedings that (i) an examination of the recent English decisions shows that the so-called 'public interest' defence is not so much a rule of law as an invitation to judicial idiosyncrasy by deciding each case on an *ad hoc* basis as to whether, on the facts overall, it is better to respect or to override the obligation of confidence, and (ii) equitable principles are best developed by reference to what conscionable behaviour demands of the defendant not by 'balancing' and then overriding those demands by reference to matters of social or political opinion."

6–067   In *Esso Australia Resources Ltd v Plowman*,[90] a case concerning arbitration proceedings, Brennan J. observed that in determining the scope of an implied obligation of confidentiality a party will not be taken to have intended that it would keep confidential documents or information when that party had an obligation, albeit not a legal obligation, to satisfy a public interest—more than mere curiosity—in knowing what was contained in the documents or information. Mason C.J. (with whom Dawson and McHugh JJ. concurred) said that the precise scope of the public interest exception to a duty of confidentiality remained unclear.

6–068   In *Sullivan v Sclanders*[91] the Supreme Court of South Australia reviewed the Australian authorities and preferred the approach of Gummow J. in *Corrs Pavey v Collector of Customs*.[92] Gray J. said[93]:

> "Equitable principles are best developed by reference to what conscionable behaviour demands of the defendant rather than by balancing those demands with

---

[86] [1990] F.S.R. 617 at 662–663.
[87] [1988] 3 All E.R. 545 at 582–584.
[88] [1989] Ch. 477 at 481.
[89] [1989] Ch. 359 at 389.
[90] [1994–1995] 183 C.L.R. 10.
[91] [2000] S.A.S.C. 273.
[92] (1987) 74 A.L.R. 428.
[93] [2000] S.A.S.C. 273 at para.45.

matters of public interest. This approach avoids the ad hoc judicial idiosyncracy associated with deciding whether, on the facts overall, it is better to respect or override the obligation of confidence."

In *AG Australia Holdings Ltd v Burton*[94] Campbell J. concluded, after a lengthy review of the authorities, that the status of a public interest defence in Australia where the plaintiff relies on an equitable duty of confidentiality was not clear, but the tendency of the courts has since been to adopt Gummow J.'s approach.[95] **6–069**

In *Minister for Immigration and Citizenship v Kumar*[96] the High Court of Australia cited (obiter, but with apparent approval) a passage from para.6–022, above.

CONCLUSIONS ON PUBLIC INTEREST

In any country which professes the rule of law and places value on the rights of individuals, those rights should not be lightly overridden in the name of public interest or freedom of expression. Courts should do so only with caution, taking care that they act on clearly identified principles. **6–070**

Whether English law recognises a "defence of public interest" as broad as its critics have suggested is therefore a question of considerable importance. The concept of such a broad defence appears to have originated in *Woodward v Hutchins*,[97] which does suggest that it is for the court to decide in each case on an ad hoc basis whether, on the facts, it is better to respect or override the obligation of confidence; and the result in that case may well be regarded as an instance of judicial idiosyncrasy. There are also dicta in later cases which support the same general approach, but other authorities suggest that the true principle is narrower. **6–071**

Courts have sometimes referred to public interest as a factor negating or circumscribing a duty of confidentiality and sometimes as a factor justifying a breach of a duty of confidentiality. It is a limiting factor which may operate as a defence because it may negate or circumscribe a duty of confidentiality. This does not mean that the public interest factor must have arisen at the inception of the duty, for, as Viscount Finlay said in *Weld-Blundell v Stephens*,[98] "danger to the state or public duty may supersede the duty of the agent to his principal". **6–072**

No duty of confidentiality can be said to be absolute in all circumstances, because it is always subject to the possibility that public interest may require disclosure. However, the law of confidentiality is based on the recognition that people who are entrusted with confidential information (or obtain it in circumstances where they should regard it as confidential) ought as a general principle to respect that confidentiality. That principle and the ability to depend **6–073**

---

[94] [2002] N.S.W.S.C. 170 at para.177. See too *Australian Football League v The Age Company Ltd* [2006] V.S.C. 308.

[95] See *British American Tobacco Australia Ltd v Gordon (No.3)* [2009] V.S.C. 619, per Kaye J. at [103]–[118], and *AMI Australia Holdings Pty Ltd v Fairfax Media Publications Pty Ltd* [2010] NSWSC 1395, per Brereton J. at [20]–[25].

[96] [2009] H.C.A. 10; (2009) 238 C.L.R. 448 at [27].

[97] [1977] 1 W.L.R. 760.

[98] [1920] A.C. 956 at 965.

on it would be weakened if the public interest limitation became too broad or, as has been said of some decisions, idiosyncratic in its operation.

6–074   The Law Commission in its Working Paper on Breach of Confidence[99] discussed the difficulties of trying to define the criteria:

> "Our provisional view is . . . that the range of circumstances in which the defence might properly be used is so wide and so variable that it is not practicable to define in general terms all the criteria to be used and that it would be misleading to single out particular issues (such as the existence of misconduct) for consideration. There is also a further point, which is perhaps even more important. The public interest is a developing concept which changes with the social attitudes of the times: many things are regarded as being in the public interest today which would not have been so regarded in the last century, or even twenty years ago, and it would be unrealistic to suppose that the concept will not undergo further changes in the years ahead. If this fact is recognised, it seems to us that the only prudent course is to frame the defence in terms which are flexible enough to enable each case to be judged on its individual merits. There is, of course, a substantial public interest in the reservation of confidences and the task of the court would therefore be to balance this against the public interest in disclosing the information to which a confidence related. This is a function which the courts already discharge in other spheres: *Norwich Pharmacal Co v Customs and Excise Commissioners*[100] and *Alfred Crompton Amusement Machines Ltd v Customs and Excise Commissioners (No.2)*[101] are recent examples of cases in which the House of Lords considered the question of where the balance of the public interest lay in relation to a claim for an order of discovery."

Where public interest is relied on to justify disclosure of otherwise confidential information, the courts have drawn no distinction between the position in equity and in contract. In the case of an express contractual non-disclosure term the question is whether it is unenforceable as contrary to public policy. In cases of an alleged implied contractual obligation or an equitable obligation the question is as to the existence and scope of the obligation. The approach of the courts is the same in each case.[102]

6–075   Although each case has to be examined on its own facts, the following general principles are suggested:

(1)   Respect for confidentiality is itself a matter of public interest.

(2)   To justify disclosure of otherwise confidential information on the grounds of public interest, it is not enough that the information is a matter of public interest. Its importance must be such that the duty otherwise owed to respect its confidentiality should be overridden.

(3)   In broad summary either the disclosure must relate to serious misconduct (actual or contemplated) or it must otherwise be important for safeguarding the public welfare in matters of health and safety, or of comparable public importance, that the information should be known by those to whom it is disclosed or proposed to be disclosed.

---

[99] No.58, 1974, at para.93.

[100] [1974] A.C. 133.

[101] [1974] A.C. 405.

[102] *Price Waterhouse v BCCI* [1992] B.C.L.C. 583 suggests otherwise, but the observation was (arguably) obiter. The case is discussed at para.6–041, above.

(4)

    (i)   Even if the information meets that test, it does not necessarily follow that it would be proper for the defendant to disclose it.

    (ii)   The court must consider the relationship between the parties and the risks of harm which may be caused (or avoided) by permitting or prohibiting disclosure, both in the particular case and more generally. For example, if the law inhibits a doctor from disclosing information about a patient which may affect another person, it may lead to risk of avoidable injury or death; but if it permits a doctor to do so, it may impair a patient's willingness to confide in the doctor and receive treatment.

(5)   Ultimately the court has to decide what is conscionable or unconscionable, which will depend on its view of what would be acceptable to the community as a fair and proper standard of behaviour. This requires the court to make an evaluative judgment, but it does not have an unfettered discretion.

(6)   In cases where the party claiming confidentiality is a branch of Government, or a body performing a governmental function, a separate principle applies. In such cases detriment to the public interest is an essential ingredient of the cause of action.[103]

Some degree of unpredictability is inevitable, but the courts should avoid the charge of idiosyncracy if the concept of public interest is approached in accordance with these principles.

CLEAN HANDS

The so-called "public interest" defence is not to be confused with the discretion of the court to refuse equitable relief in cases where the plaintiff is not seen to come with clean hands. That discretion has applied in the past as much to confidentiality cases as to any other.   **6–076**

In *Browne v Associated Newspapers* Eady J. questioned whether the clean hands principle was compatible with Art.6.[104] The claimant had told a lie when first seeking injunctive relief. The judge held that he would not refuse to grant an injunction on that account. The Court of Appeal considered that the effect of a lie told to the court might vary depending on the facts, but there was no general discussion of the clean hands principle.[105] The principle has more usually been relied on in cases where there is something disreputable about the claimant's conduct relevant to the subject matter of the claim.

A colourful illustration is provided by *McNicol v Sportsman's Book Stores*.[106] The plaintiff sold to subscribers a supposedly successful method of predicting horse-race winners by the age of the moon, on express terms that each purchaser would treat the information as private and confidential for his own personal use.   **6–077**

---

[103] See *Solicitor-General v Alice* [2007] NZHC 48 at [58].

[104] [2007] EWHC 202 (QB) at 67.

[105] [2007] EWCA 295; [2008] Q.B. 103 at 66–81.

[106] (1930) McG.C.C. 116.

The defendant intended to publish a review of results of using the system, without divulging its precise rules. The plaintiff's application for an injunction to restrain the defendant from doing so failed before Maugham J., among other reasons because he did not consider that the assistance of the court should be given to the plaintiff in circumstances in which:

" . . . the poor people all over this country who are deceived into paying two guineas for this system are getting something which is perfectly worthless."[107]

6–078 Sometimes both concepts may be invoked in the same case, as, for example, in *Hubbard v Vosper*.[108] The defendant had been a member of the Church of Scientology for 14 years. He attended a course, for which he paid a fee, and signed an undertaking not to divulge course materials to those not entitled to receive them. He later wrote a book criticising the teaching and practice of scientology. The Church (and its founders) sued the defendant, alleging breach of a contractual duty of confidence, and sought an interlocutory injunction restraining publication of his book.

6–079 Lord Denning M.R. considered that an injunction should be refused because, on the material before the court, the courses appeared to contain such dangerous medical quackery that no confidence could be claimed to keep them secret.[109]

Megaw L.J. agreed with Lord Denning M.R., but he also referred to evidence that the plaintiffs sought to enforce secrecy on cult members by improper methods. He accepted the defendant's proposition[110]:

"that there is here evidence that the plaintiffs are or have been protecting their secrets by deplorable means . . . and, that being so, they do not come with clean hands to this court in asking this court to protect these secrets by the equitable remedy of an injunction."

In *Church of Scientology v Kaufman*[111] Goff J. followed both approaches.

---

[107] (1930) McG.C.C. 116 at 125. In *Spycatcher* [1990] 1 A.C. 109 at 149 Scott J. cited *McNicol* as a case where the information lacked the quality of confidence because it was trivial.
[108] [1972] 2 Q.B. 84.
[109] *Hubbard v Vosper* [1972] 2 Q.B. 84 at 95–96.
[110] *Hubbard v Vosper* [1972] 2 Q.B. 84 at 101.
[111] [1973] R.P.C. 627.

CHAPTER 7

Confidentiality and Privacy

English law now has a partial law of privacy. Its boundaries are uncertain and it is **7–001** at a transitional stage. It has developed in a curious way involving a hybridisation of Art.8 of the European Convention and the cause of action for breach of confidence. This has resulted in there being two forms of confidentiality, which may overlap although their ingredients are separate. There is the traditional action for breach of confidentiality, based on the principles discussed in earlier chapters, and there is the action based on Art.8. This chapter considers the latter.

The distinction between the two causes of action was summarised by Lord Nicholls in *Douglas v Hello! Ltd*:[1]

> "As the law has developed breach of confidence, or misuse of confidential information, now covers two distinct causes of action, protecting two different interests: privacy and secret ('confidential') information. It is important to keep these two distinct. In some instances information may qualify for protection both on grounds of privacy and confidentiality. In other instances information may be in the public domain, and not qualify for protection as confidential, and yet qualify for protection on the grounds of privacy. Privacy can be invaded by further publication of information or photographs already disclosed to the public. Conversely, and obviously, a trade secret may be protected as confidential information even though no question of personal privacy is involved."

Articles 8 and 10 of the European Convention provide as follows: **7–002**

"*Article 8*

(1) Everyone has the right to respect for his private and family life, his home and his correspondence.
(2) There shall be no interference by a public authority with the exercise of this right except such as is in accordance with the law and is necessary in a democratic society in the interests of national security, public safety or the economic well-being of the country, for the prevention of disorder or crime, for the protection of health or morals, or for the protection of the rights and freedoms of others.

Article 10

(1) Everyone has the right to freedom of expression. This right shall include freedom to hold opinions and to receive and impart information and ideas

---

[1] [2007] UKHL 21; [2008] 1 A.C. 1 at [255].

without interference by public authority and regardless of frontiers. This Article shall not prevent States from requiring the licensing of broadcasting, television or cinema enterprises.

(2) The exercise of these freedoms, since it carries with it duties and responsibilities, may be subject to such formalities, conditions, restrictions or penalties as are prescribed by law and are necessary in a democratic society, in the interests of national security, territorial integrity or public safety, for the prevention of disorder or crime, for the protection of health or morals, for the protection of the reputation or rights of others, for preventing the disclosure of information received in confidence, or for maintaining the authority and impartiality of the judiciary."

Section 6 of the Human Rights Act 1998 provides that it is unlawful for a public authority to act in a way which is incompatible with a Convention right. A public authority includes a court.

7–003   Section 12 of the Act applies where a court is considering whether to grant relief which might affect the exercise of a Convention right to freedom of expression. Section 12(3) provides that there should be no pre-trial restraint on publication unless the court is satisfied that the applicant is likely to establish that publication should not be allowed. Section 12(4) provides that:

"The court must have particular regard to the importance of the Convention right to freedom of expression and, where the proceedings relate to material which the respondent claims, or which appears to the court, to be journalistic, literary or artistic material (or to conduct connected with such material), to—

(a)   the extent to which—
    (i)   the material has, or is about to, become available to the public; or
    (ii)   it is, or would be, in the public interest for the material to be published;
(b)   any relevant privacy code."

HISTORICAL BACKGROUND: CASE LAW

7–004   Before the introduction of the Human Rights Act the courts held that the development of rights of privacy was not a matter for the courts but for Parliament. In *Kaye v Robertson*[2] a journalist interviewed and took photographs of the plaintiff, a well-known actor, while he was in hospital suffering from severe brain injury and in no fit condition either to be interviewed or to give informed consent to be interviewed. The journalist ignored notices at the entrance to the hospital ward and on the plaintiff's door asking visitors to see a member of the medical staff before visiting. The Court of Appeal held with regret that in English law there was no right to privacy and therefore no right of action for breach of privacy.

7–005   Leggatt L.J. said[3]:

"This right has so long been disregarded here that it can be recognised now only by the legislature."

---

[2] [1991] F.S.R. 62.
[3] [1991] F.S.R. 62 at 71.

Bingham L.J. said[4]:

> "This case . . . highlights, yet again, the failure of both the common law of England and statute to protect in an effective way the personal privacy of individual citizens . . . . If ever a person has a right to be let alone by strangers with no public interest to pursue, it must surely be when he lies in hospital recovering from brain surgery and in no more than partial command of his faculties. It is this invasion of his privacy which underlies the plaintiff's complaint. Yet it alone, however gross, does not entitle him to relief in English law."

The court granted limited relief, under the tort of malicious falsehood, in the form of an injunction prohibiting the defendants from publishing an article which implied that the plaintiff had been interviewed and photographed with his consent. The court also held that it could not, as a matter of law, grant an injunction prohibiting the publication of the photographs so as to prevent the defendants from profiting from their own trespass.

Kaye v Robertson was followed by the House of Lords in *Wainwright v Home Office*.[5] Lord Hoffmann distinguished between privacy as a value underlying the existence of some legal right and privacy as a legal right in itself,[6] holding that any protection of privacy as such was a matter for Parliament.   **7–006**

At the same time there was a growing body of case law in which the law of confidentiality was used to protect aspects of privacy. It has long been accepted that the law of confidentiality may apply to information and materials of a personal and private nature. They may include etchings made in private[7] and photographs taken in private.[8] Such materials have about them "the necessary quality of confidence" (in the words of Lord Greene M.R. in *Saltman*[9]) to be capable of protection by an equitable obligation of confidence.   **7–007**

In *Argyll v Argyll*[10] an injunction was granted against the revelation of marital confidences. Commenting on that decision in *Spycatcher*,[11] Lord Keith said: **7–008**

> "The right to personal privacy is clearly one which the law should in this field seek to protect."

When material has the necessary quality of confidence, equitable protection is not limited to cases in which it passes to a recipient under a consensual transaction, but is in principle available in cases in which the material is disclosed to the recipient under compulsion of law or is obtained by mistake known to the recipient or by improper means. If private photographs were accidentally delivered to the wrong house, the recipient who knew that they were not meant for him would be under an obligation of conscience not, for example, to sell them

---

4 [1991] F.S.R. 62 at 70.
5 [2003] UKHL 53; [2004] 2 A.C. 406.
6 [2003] UKHL 53; [2004] 2 A.C. 406 at [31].
7 *Prince Albert v Strange* (1849) 2 De G. & S.M. 652.
8 *Pollard v Photographic Company* (1889) 40 Ch.D. 345.
9 (1948) 65 R.P.C. 203 at 215.
10 [1967] Ch. 302.
11 [1990] 1 A.C. 109 at 255.

to a magazine, just as much as the recipient of a letter meant for somebody else and marked "Private and Confidential" would be constrained by an equitable obligation of confidence.[12]

7–009   In *Hellewell v Chief Constable of Derbyshire*[13] the plaintiff sued for breach of confidence in relation to the use made by the police of a "mugshot" photograph of the plaintiff, taken while he was in police custody (acting under a code of practice issued by the Secretary of State under s.166 of the Police and Criminal Act 1984). The Chief Constable denied that the police owed any duty of confidence to the plaintiff in relation to the photograph. The judgment dealt with three connected issues: whether a photograph was capable of being the subject of a duty of confidence, whether the plaintiff was owed any such duty by the defendant, and what was the scope of the duty (although the judge also analysed the third issue in terms of the public interest defence).

7–010   In relation to the first matter Laws J. said[14]:

> "I entertain no doubt that disclosure of a photograph may, in some circumstances, be actionable as a breach of confidence. If a photographer is hired to take a photograph to be used only for certain purposes but uses it for an unauthorised purpose of his own, a claim may lie against him (*Pollard v Photographic Co.* (1888) 40 Ch.D. 345). That case concerned portrait photographs of a lady taken for her private use by a hired photographer who then used one of the pictures for a Christmas card which was put on sale in his shop. North J. upheld the plaintiff's claim, both in contract and breach of confidence. If someone with a telephoto lens were to take from a distance and with no authority a picture of another engaged in some private act, his subsequent disclosure of the photograph would, in my judgment, as surely amount to a breach of confidence as if he has found or stolen a letter or diary in which the act was recounted and proceeded to publish it. In such a case, the law would protect what might reasonably be called a right of privacy, although the name accorded to the cause of action would be breach of confidence."

As to the duty of the defendant, the judge held that the fact that the police took a photograph of the plaintiff, in custody and without freedom of choice, constrained them in the use to which they might lawfully put it. The circumstances in which they acted imposed a duty of confidence, breach of which would be actionable as a matter of private law. The scope of the duty was governed by what was reasonable.

7–011   There were therefore signs before the Human Rights Act of a broadening of the law of confidentiality in the area of privacy, but it was still necessary to show either that there was a breach of an underlying relationship of confidentiality or that the defendant had obtained the information in circumstances (in particular, by improper or surreptitious means, by accident or by legal compulsion) which gave rise to an equitable obligation of confidentiality.

---

[12] *English & American Insurance v Herbert Smith* [1988] F.S.R. 232; per Sir Nicolas Browne-Wilkinson V.C.
[13] [1995] 1 W.L.R. 804.
[14] [1995] 1 W.L.R. 804 at 807.

HISTORICAL BACKGROUND: PROPOSALS FOR REFORM

The possibility of a statutory right of privacy was the subject of various reports by committees and various unsuccessful parliamentary bills.[15] The Report of the Law Commission in 1981 on Breach of Confidence[16] was an indirect sequel to the 1972 Report of the Younger Committee on Privacy. The Younger Committee rejected proposals that there should be a general remedy for the protection of privacy, but it recommended new remedies to cover certain specific ways in which privacy might be invaded and it drew attention to the action for breach of confidence, which it considered was potentially capable of affording greater protection to privacy than had hitherto been realised. The Committee also recommended that the action for breach of confidence should be referred to the Law Commission.   **7–012**

The Younger Committee was particularly concerned at the covert use of surveillance devices and recommended the creation of a criminal offence of surreptitious surveillance by means of a technical device, i.e. an electronic or optical extension of the human senses.[17] This recommendation was not implemented.   **7–013**

The Law Commission considered the same subject in the context of civil liability for breach of confidence and commented as follows[18]:   **7–014**

> "To turn now to the principles which in our view should govern the imposition of an obligation of confidence upon someone who obtains information by means of a surveillance device, we believe that a distinction must be made between (i) devices which are primarily designed *for the purpose of surveillance* and (ii) the wide range of devices which are not in themselves designed or adapted solely or primarily for that purpose, although they are *capable of being so used*. Examples of devices falling within the second category are ordinary binoculars, and an ordinary tape-recorder which may be used to record the conversation of participants at a meeting, either openly or secretly by hiding it under the table. There may be situations when surveillance devices of the latter kind are used to which those subject to that surveillance should not reasonably take exception, if they are or ought reasonably to be aware of it and if they could without undue inconvenience take precautions to avoid the surveillance in question. Thus, on the one hand, it may be thought that two people, who meet secretly in a secluded corner of a large railway station throughout which clear notices are displayed that television cameras are being used to detect criminal activities (such as malicious damage), cannot reasonably expect the fact of their meeting to be treated as confidential. On the other hand, it may well be that the use of an ordinary camera with a telephoto lens to obtain from the street a picture of a confidential document lying on a desk in a private house would go far beyond the reasonable expectations of the person who left it there, and that the taker of the picture should be subject to an obligation of confidence in respect of the information so obtained.
> We can summarise our views on the use of surveillance devices as follows. We think that an obligation of confidence should cover information obtained by the use of *any* surveillance device, provided that such information would not have been acquired without the use of that device. However, in the case of devices which,

---

[15] Bills were introduced by Lord Mancroft in 1961, Alexander Lyon in 1967, Brian Walden in 1969, William Cash in 1987 and John Browne in 1989.

[16] Cmnd. 8388 (1981), para.1.2.

[17] Cmnd. 5012 (1972), paras 503 and 563.

[18] Cmnd. 8388 (1981), paras 6.37–6.38.

though not designed or adapted primarily for surreptitious surveillance, enable information to be obtained which would not otherwise have been acquired, liability for the subsequent disclosure or use of that information should arise only if the person from whom the information has been obtained was not or ought not reasonably to have been aware of the use of the device, and ought not reasonably to have taken precautions to prevent the information from being acquired in the way in question."

The Law Commission's draft Breach of Confidence Bill contained provisions to that effect,[19] but its recommendation that the law of breach of confidence should be made statutory was not adopted.

7–015   In 1989 the Government responded to a private member's bill, which attracted wide support in the House of Commons, by appointing a committee under the chairmanship of David Calcutt QC to consider the introduction of a statutory law of privacy. The Calcutt Report[20] concluded that it would be possible to create a statutory tort of infringement of privacy. It could specifically relate to publication of personal information (including photographs). Personal information could be defined in terms of an individual's personal life, that is to say, those aspects of life which reasonable members of society would respect as being such that an individual is ordinarily entitled to keep them to himself, whether or not they relate to his body or mind, to his home, to his family, to other personal relationships, or to his correspondence or other documents. The committee did not see advantage in laying down a more detailed statutory definition of personal information. It expressed serious reservations about a general defence labelled merely "public interest". It considered that some form of public interest defence would be necessary, but that it should be limited to cases where the defendant had reasonable grounds for believing that:

(a)   publication of the personal information would contribute to the prevention, detection or exposure of any crime or other seriously anti-social conduct; or

(b)   it would be necessary for the protection of public health or safety; or

(c)   there would, but for the publication, be a real risk that the public, or some section of the public, would be materially misled by a statement previously made public by or on behalf of any individual whose privacy would otherwise be infringed.[21]

In 1993 Sir David Calcutt published a further report[22] recommending that the Government should give further consideration to the introduction of a statutory tort of invasion of privacy.

7–016   In 1995 the Government rejected proposals for a statutory right of privacy, but stated that the Lord Chancellor was reconsidering the Law Commission's recommendations concerning the introduction of legislation on breach of confidence.[23]

---

[19] Clause 5.

[20] *Report on Privacy and Related Matters* (1990) Cmnd. 1102, para.12.17.

[21] *Report on Privacy and Related Matters* (1990) Cmnd. 1102 at paras 12.22–12.23.

[22] *Review of Press Self-Regulation*, Cmnd. 2135.

[23] White Paper on "*Privacy and Media Intrusion*", July 1995, Cmnd. 2918.

HUMAN RIGHTS ACT 1998

The Human Rights Act presented a conundrum both because of the terms of Art.8 and because of the terms of s.6 of the Act. Article 8 recognises a right to respect for private life (in terms far more general than would be expected in a statute), but the direct obligations created by the Convention are obligations on the part of states. The Act makes it unlawful for any public authority to act in a way which is incompatible with the Convention, but it does not on its face create rights against private individuals or bodies. A direct interference by a public authority with a person's rights under Art.8 would undoubtedly be a statutory tort, but the controversial question which arose from the Act was whether the court as a public authority would be acting in a way which was incompatible with the Convention if it failed to recognise and enforce rights under Art.8 against private individuals or bodies. This question involved issues not only about the scope of the Act but about the scope of the Convention, that is to say whether and to what extent there may be a positive obligation on states to ensure that their laws protect people against infringement of Art.8 rights by other people (and not merely by the state itself).   7–017

The European Court of Human Rights had previously held that Art.8 may require the adoption of measures to secure respect for private life between individuals.[24] This principle was reiterated and developed in *Von Hannover v Germany*,[25] where the court said that: 7–018

> "although the object of Article 8 is essentially that of protecting the individual against arbitrary interference by public authorities, it does not merely compel the State to abstain from such interference: in addition to this primary negative undertaking, there may be positive obligations inherent in an effective respect for private or family life. These obligations may involve the adoption of measures designed to secure respect for private life even in the sphere of relations between individuals themselves. That also applies to the protection of a person's picture against abuse by others.
>
> The boundary between the State's positive and negative obligations in this respect does not lend itself to precise definition. The applicable principles are, nevertheless, similar. In both contexts regard must be had to the fair balance that must be struck between the competing interests of the individual and of the community as a whole; and in both contexts the State enjoys a certain margin of appreciation."

The courts have not in terms decided the question of the extent of the duty imposed on courts by s.6 of the Human Rights Act, and in *Campbell v MGN Ltd*[26] Lord Nicholls said that it was unnecessary to do so. Instead they have finessed the question by holding that the law of confidentiality has absorbed the rights protected by Art.8 in regard to the use of information.   7–019

In *Venables and Thompson v News Group Newspapers Ltd*[27] Dame Elizabeth Butler-Sloss P. granted injunctions against the whole world prohibiting publication of information about the appearance, whereabouts and new names of   7–020

---

[24] *X and Y v Netherlands* (1986) 8 E.H.R.R. 235 at [23]; *Stjerna v Finland* (1997) 24 E.H.R.R. 195 at [38]; see also *Marckx v Belgium* (1979) 2 E.H.R.R. 330 at [81].
[25] (2005) 40 E.H.R.R. 1 at [57].
[26] [2004] UKHL 22; [2004] 2 A.C. 457 at [18].
[27] [2001] Fam. 430.

the claimants on their release from custody after they had served periods of detention for the murder of a small boy, which they had committed when they were aged 10. The President held that the law of confidentiality could cover the injunctions sought and that they were necessary to protect the claimants from the risk of death or serious injury. A similar injunction was granted in *X (formerly Mary Bell) v O'Brien*.[28]

7–021
In *A v B Plc*[29] a footballer applied for an injunction to prevent a newspaper publishing lurid accounts by two women of brief affairs which he had with them after they had met in bars. The Court of Appeal held that it was able to achieve the objective of s.6 of the Human Rights Act by "absorbing the rights which articles 8 and 10 protect into the long-established action for breach of confidence."[30] There was therefore no need in the court's view to consider in relation to events after the Human Rights Act came into force "the vexed question of whether there is a separate action based upon a new tort involving the invasion of privacy".[31]

7–022
Adapting Lord Goff's statement of general principle in *Spycatcher*,[32] the court held that:

> "A duty of confidence will arise whenever the party subject to the duty is in a situation where he either knows or ought to know that the other person can reasonably expect his privacy to be protected."[33]

This test does not of itself help to determine the border between what is public and private.

7–023
On this issue the court observed that usually the question whether there was a private interest worthy of protection would be obvious; and that, if it was not obvious, an answer would often be unnecessary, because the weaker the claim for privacy the more likely it was to be outweighed by the right to freedom of expression.[34] It added:

> "The advantage of not having to distinguish between acts which are public and those which are private in a difficult case is made clear by what Gleeson CJ had to say on the subject in *Australian Broadcasting Corpn v Lenah Game Meats Pty Ltd* (2001) 185 A.L.R. 1. He explained the difficulty of distinguishing between public and private information when he said at p.13, para.42:
>
> > 'There is no bright line which can be drawn between what is private and what is not. Use of the term "public" is often a convenient method of contrast, but there is a large area in between what is necessarily public and what is necessarily private. An activity is not private simply because it is not done in public. It does not suffice to make an act private that, because it occurs on private property, it has such measure of protection from the public gaze as the characteristics of the property, the nature of the activity, the locality, and the disposition of the property owner combine to afford. Certain kinds of

---

[28] [2003] EWHC 1101.
[29] [2002] EWCA Civ 337; [2003] Q.B. 195.
[30] [2002] EWCA Civ 337 at [4].
[31] [2002] EWCA Civ 337 at [11(vi)].
[32] [1990] 1 A.C. 109 at 281.
[33] [2003] Q.B. 195 at [11(ix)].
[34] [2003] Q.B. 195 at [11(vii)].

information about a person, such as information relating to health, personal relationships, or finances, may be easy to identify as private; as may certain kinds of activity, which a reasonable person, applying contemporary standards of morals and behaviour, would understand to be meant to be unobserved. The requirement that disclosure or observation of information or conduct would be highly offensive to a reasonable person of ordinary sensibilities is in many circumstances a useful practical test of what is private.'"

The Court of Appeal rejected A's claim for an injunction, saying that:

"Relationships of the sort which A had with C and D are not the categories of relationships which the court should be astute to protect when the other parties to the relationships do not want them to remain confidential."[35]

In *Campbell v MGN Ltd*[36] a newspaper published reports and pictures of a famous fashion model attending meetings of a self-help group for drug addiction. She had previously courted media attention and had claimed untruthfully not to have a drug problem. She accepted that in those circumstances the newspaper was entitled to publish the fact that she was receiving treatment for drug addiction, but she claimed damages for breach of confidentiality in publishing the details of the meetings and the pictures, which had been taken covertly. She won her claim and was awarded £3,500 damages. The judgment was reversed by the Court of Appeal but reinstated by the House of Lords.   **7–024**

The decision of the House of Lords was by a majority of three to two, but there was agreement on the following principles: **7–025**

(1)   The action for breach of confidentiality now covers infringement of a person's right to respect for his private life under Art.8 where the infringement is in the form of disclosure of information (including pictures).

(2)   The principles involved apply as much between individuals or between individuals and non-governmental bodies as they do between individuals and public authorities.

(3)   Article 8 is engaged when the person publishing the information knows or ought to know that the other person can reasonably expect the information to be kept confidential because of its private nature.[37]
Subsumed within this last proposition are two factors—that the information relates to a person's private life and that the person concerned has a reasonable expectation that it will therefore be kept confidential, as the person publishing it knows or should know.

(4)   Where Arts 8 and 10 are both relevant, the court has to balance the competing considerations, neither being presumed to have priority over the other.

---

[35] [2003] Q.B. 195 at [45].
[36] [2004] UKHL 22; [2004] 2 A.C. 457.
[37] This is a distillation of what was said by Lord Nicholls at [20]–[21], Lord Hope at [85] and Baroness Hale at [134].

The Strasbourg court dismissed a complaint by the newspaper that the decision in favour of Ms Campbell violated its rights under Art.10. It said that, having regard to the margin of appreciation accorded to the decisions of national courts in this area, it would require strong reasons to substitute its view for that of the final decision of the House of Lords and that it did not find any reason, let alone a strong reason, to substitute its view for that of the majority of the House of Lords. It also said that it considered the reasons for the decision of the majority to be convincing.[38]

7–026   On the question how the courts should differentiate between what is private and what is public Lord Hope followed the approach of the Court of Appeal in *A v B Plc.*[39] Echoing Gleeson C.J.'s test in *Australian Broadcasting Corp v Lennah Game Meats Pty Ltd,* cited by the Court of Appeal in *A v B Plc,* Lord Hope said that where the answer to the question whether the information was private or public was not obvious,

> "the broad test is whether disclosure of the information about the individual ('A') would give substantial offence to A, assuming that A was placed in similar circumstances and was a person of ordinary sensibilities."[40]

Lord Nicholls and Baroness Hale took a different approach. Lord Nicholls considered that Gleeson C.J.'s "highly offensive" formula suggested an over-strict test of what was private and that it was liable to conflate the question what was private with issues which went to proportionality (the degree of intrusion into private life and the extent to which publication was a matter of proper public concern).[41] Baroness Hale considered that an objective reasonable expectation test was simpler and clearer than Gleeson C.J.'s formula, but she emphasised that the reasonable expectation of privacy test was merely a threshold test which brought into play issues of proportionality and the countervailing rights of others.[42]

7–027   Although at one level Lord Nicholls and Baroness Hale were agreed in trying to separate (a) the issue whether the claimant had a reasonable expectation of privacy and (b) issues of proportionality and countervailing interests, they disagreed about what fell within the first issue. Lord Nicholls considered that by repeatedly asserting in public that she did not use drugs Ms Campbell could no longer have a reasonable expectation that this aspect of her life should be kept private. Her claim therefore in his opinion failed at the first stage.[43] Baroness Hale considered that all the information about Ms Campbell's addiction and treatment was private, because it related to an important aspect of her physical and mental health, and confidential, because it had been received from an insider in breach of confidence.[44] Her public statements about drugs were relevant only

---

[38] *MGN Ltd v United Kingdom* [2011] E.C.H.R. 66.

[39] [2004] UKHL 22; [2004] 2 A.C. 457 at [92]–[94].

[40] In South Africa, the Constitutional Court has adopted a similar test, describing private facts as "those matters the disclosure of which will cause mental distress and injury to anyone possessed of ordinary feelings and intelligence in the same circumstances and in respect of which there is a will to keep them private": *NM v Smith* [2007] Z.A.C.C. 6 at [34] (Madala J.).

[41] At [22]. *Campbell v MGN Ltd* [2004] VKHL 22; [2004] 2 A.C. 457.

[42] At [135]–[137].

[43] At [24]–[26].

[44] At [147].

to the second stage inquiry whether there was justification for publication of the information. The difference serves to demonstrate that behind the apparent simplicity of the "reasonable expectation" test lurk questions about the meaning of private life and the protection which the person concerned may legitimately expect.

In *Murray v Express Newspapers Plc*[45] the Court of Appeal said in relation to the reasonable expectation test:

> "As we see it, the question whether there is a reasonable expectation of privacy is a broad one, which takes account of all the circumstances of the case. They include the attributes of the claimant, the nature of the activity in which the claimant was engaged, the place at which it was happening, the nature and purpose of the intrusion, the absence of consent and whether it could be known or could be inferred, the effect on the claimant and the circumstances in which and the purposes for which the information came into the hands of the publisher."

In that case a newspaper published a photograph of the author, JK Rowling, her husband and their young son, taken as they were out walking in an Edinburgh street with the child in a buggy. The parents brought an action against the newspaper and the photographic agency in the name of the child, alleging a breach of his privacy right under Art.8. The claim against the newspaper was compromised but the claim against the photographic agency was contested. The agency applied to strike out the claim and succeeded at first instance, but the action was reinstated by the Court of Appeal. The facts (assumed to be correct for the purpose of the application) were that the photographer kept a watch on the family from a stationary vehicle, as they were visiting and leaving a café, and used a camera with a long range lens to photograph them. The court considered that the child was entitled to be protected from intrusive media attention.[46]

In considering how far Art.8 protects a person against publication of **7–028** information about them or pictures of them, there are the following issues:

(1) What does Art.8 mean by "private life"?
(2) What does "respect" for private life require and how is it to be balanced against the interests either of other individuals or of the public in general?

THE CONCEPT OF PRIVATE LIFE IN ARTICLE 8

The European Court of Human Rights has adopted a broad concept of private life, **7–029** based on the need to protect a person's autonomy and relationships with others from unjustifiable outside interference.

In *Niemietz v Germany*[47] a lawyer's offices were searched by police looking **7–030** for information about a suspect. In holding that the search violated Art.8, the Court said[48]:

---

[45] [2008] EWCA Civ 446; [2009] Ch. 481 at [36].
[46] [2009] Ch. 481 at [57].
[47] (1992) 16 E.H.R.R. 97.
[48] (1992) 16 E.H.R.R. 97 at [29].

"The Court does not consider it possible or necessary to attempt an exhaustive definition of the notion of 'private life'. However, it would be too restrictive to limit the notion to an 'inner circle' in which an individual may choose to live his personal life as he chooses and to exclude entirely the outside world not encompassed within that circle. Respect for private life must also comprise to a certain degree the right to establish and develop relationships with other human beings.

There appears, furthermore, to be no reason in principle why this understanding of the notion of 'private life' should be taken to exclude the activities of a professional or business nature since it is, after all, in the course of their working lives that the majority of people have a significant, if not the greatest opportunity of developing relationships with the outside world."

7–031   In *Bensaid v United Kingdom*[49] the Court said:

"'Private life' is a broad term not susceptible to exhaustive definition. The Court has already held that elements such as gender identification, name and sexual orientation and sexual life are important elements of the personal sphere protected by Article 8 . . . Mental health must also be regarded as a crucial part of private life associated with the aspect of moral integrity. Article 8 protects a right to identity and personal development, and the right to establish and develop relationships with other human beings and the outside world."

7–032   In *Von Hannover v Germany*[50] the German courts held that the claimant's private life was confined to what happened when she was in her home or some other secluded place out of the public eye. The European Court of Human Rights rejected this approach as too narrow. It held that the object of Art.8 is to protect the development of every human being's personality, which includes a social dimension.[51] It said:

"There is, therefore, a zone of interaction of a person with others, even in a public context, which may fall within the scope of 'private life'."[52]

The case concerned photos of the claimant in scenes from her daily life—on horseback, playing tennis, cycling, visiting a horse show, on a skiing holiday, at a beach club, leaving her house, in a restaurant and shopping. The court held that these were all activities of a purely private nature and therefore fell within the scope of her private life, even if they occurred in places which could not be described as secluded.

In *R. (Countryside Alliance) v Att Gen*[53] supporters of fox-hunting contended that its statutory prohibition was incompatible with their Art.8 rights. They argued that their shared pastime of fox-hunting was part of their social identity and therefore part of their private lives. The House of Lords rejected the argument. It regarded the activity as a noisy and colourful form of public spectacle, liable by its nature to attract on-lookers, rather than an activity of a

---

[49] (2001) 33 E.H.R.R. 208 at [47].
[50] (2005) 40 E.H.R.R. 1.
[51] (2005) 40 E.H.R.R. 1 at [50], [69] and [74].
[52] (2005) 40 E.H.R.R. 1 at [50].
[53] [2007] UKHL 52; [2008] 1 A.C. 719.

private nature, although taking place in a public context, as in the case of *Von Hannover v Germany*. Lord Rodger explained the difference in this way[54]:

> "Princess Caroline succeeded in her claim for protection for her private life because she was riding or cycling or playing tennis simply for her own enjoyment – for the development of her personality, to put it in formal terms. So, even though she was doing these things 'in a public context', they fell within the scope of her 'private life'...In my view, the position would have been different if, say, she and her tennis partner had taken part in a charity tennis tournament where spectators would have come to watch them...They would have stepped outside the sphere of their private life in order to pursue a public purpose."

Lord Rodger considered that the description of hunting in the judgment of the lower court reflected the reality that "When followers are taken into account, the hunt takes on the character of a spectator sport", and he concluded:

> "The huntsmen and women are taking part in what they know is not just a private activity but a much admired public spectacle. I therefore conclude that they are not entitled to the protection for their private life in article 8(1)."

In *Sciacca v Italy* the Strasbourg court found that there was a breach of Art.8 when the Italian police released photographs of the applicant, who was under a criminal investigation, at a press conference. Referring to its decision in *Von Hannover v Germany*, the court stated that "the concept of private life includes elements relating to a person's image".[55]

In *S v United Kingdom* the Strasbourg court held that the UK's policy of retention of finger prints and DNA of acquitted defendants violated Art.8. In considering the scope of Art.8 the court said:[56]

> "The court recalls that the concept of 'private life' is a broad term not susceptible to exhaustive definition. It covers the physical and psychological integrity of a person...It can therefore embrace multiple aspects of the person's physical and social identity."

In *R (Wood) v Commissioner of Police for the Metropolis*[57] the claimant was a member of an anti-arms trade protest group. He bought one share in a company which held trade fairs for the arms industry. He attended the company's annual general meeting. He behaved in a perfectly proper manner. He was photographed by the police in the street after leaving the meeting. He was followed by police officers who tried to establish his identity. The photographs were retained by the police. The Court of Appeal was unanimous that both the taking and the retention of the photographs of the claimant in those circumstances was an interference with his right to respect for his private life within Art.8(1). It held by a majority that the interference was not justified under Art.8(2).

---

[54] [2007] UKHL 52; [2008] 1 A.C. 719 at [107]–[108].
[55] (2005) 43 E.H.R.R. 83 at [29].
[56] (2008) 48 E.H.R.R. 1169 at [66].
[57] [2009] EWCA Civ 414; [2010] 1 W.L.R. 123.

There was a valuable analysis of the scope of Art.8 in the judgment of Laws L.J., with which the other members of the court agreed. After reviewing a number of Strasbourg decisions he said:

> "These and other cases show that the content of the phrase 'private life' is very broad indeed. Looking only at the words of the article, one might have supposed that the essence of the right was the protection of close personal relationships. Whilst that remains a core instance, and perhaps the paradigm case of the right, the jurisprudence has accepted many other facets…
>
> The phrase 'physical and psychological integrity' of a person…is with respect helpful. So is the person's 'physical and social identity'…These expressions reflect what seem to me to be the central value protected by the right. I would describe it as the personal autonomy of every individual."[58]

Laws L.J. identified three safeguards or qualifications designed to prevent Art.8 from being read so widely that its claims became unreal and unreasonable. First, the interference must attain "a certain level of seriousness" in order to engage the article. Secondly, the claimant had to show on the facts that he had "a reasonable expectation of privacy". Thirdly, the breadth of the article might be greatly curtailed by the scope of the justifications available to the state under Art.8.2.[59]

As to photography, he held that the bare taking of a person's photograph in the street would not amount to an interference with their private life, unless there were aggravating circumstances. On the other hand, the circumstances in which a photograph was taken in a public place might turn the event into one in which Art.8 was engaged and violated. Examples would be where the act of taking the picture was intrusive or even violent, conducted by pursuit, confrontation, pushing, shoving or use of bright lights. On the particular facts, the police action was a sufficient intrusion into the claimant's own space, his integrity, as to be an interference with his private life. It was of sufficient seriousness and he had a reasonable expectation that his privacy would not be thus invaded.[60]

The criterion of a reasonable expectation requires modification in cases concerning the retention, rather than the acquisition, of photographs or other personal information about an individual, such as fingerprints or DNA samples taken by the police in the course of a criminal investigation, Lengthy retention of such information after the conclusion of the criminal proceedings is liable to require justification under Art.8.2, whether or not the original obtaining of the data was contrary to the individual's reasonable expectation.[61] Such data clearly falls within the category of private information, and the citizen has a reasonable expectation that police powers to collect and retain such information will be exercised with due regard for the person's Art.8 rights.

Intimate sexual behaviour between consenting adults in private falls within the concept of private life. At one time the English courts were inclined to exclude sexual activity of a casual kind, or with a prostitute, or within a relationship which the court did not consider to be worth protection, from the scope of Art.8, but whether consensual sexual conduct is considered by others to be moral is not

---

[58] [2009] EWCA Civ 414; [2010] 1 W.L.R. 123 at [19]–[20].

[59] [2009] EWCA Civ 414; [2010] 1 W.L.R. 123 at [22], cited in *Hutcheson v News Group Newspapers Ltd* [2011] EWCA Civ 808; [2012] E.M.L.R. 2 at [24].

[60] [2009] EWCA Civ 414; [2010] 1 W.L.R. 123 at [34]–[36] and [44]–[46].

[61] *R (RMC) v Commissioner of Police of the Metropolis* [2012] EWHC 1681 (Admin).

a criterion for excluding such conduct from the concept of a person's private life, as the Strasbourg court and (more recently) the English courts have recognised. Whether there is justification for unauthorised disclosure of such information is a separate question, which requires a balancing of the right to respect for private life against the arguments for permitting disclosure.

In *Dudgeon v United Kingdom*,[62] a case concerning the criminal law of Northern Ireland and buggery, the Strasbourg court referred to consensual sexual behaviour as "an essentially private materialisation of the human personality" engaging Art.8.

In *ADT v United Kingdom* [63] the applicant was convicted of an offence of gross indecency. He and four others took part in group homosexual activities of a non-violent kind at his home, which were filmed. His complaint that his conviction violated his right to respect for his private life was upheld by the European Court. The Government argued[64] that his activities did not fall within Art.8 because of the filming and the number of people involved. The court rejected the argument, saying that the only matter which could cast doubt on whether Art.8 applied was the filming of the activities, but that the evidence did not suggest that there was any likelihood of the films being made public.[65] The court considered that the applicant's activities were genuinely private, and it held that only a narrow margin of appreciation should be afforded to national authorities in an area involving intimate aspects of private life.[66] It accepted that at some point sexual activities could be carried out in such a way that state interference could be justified, but in the absence of public health considerations there was no justification for interference in the applicant's case.

In *Mosley v News Group Ltd* [67] the claimant hired five prostitutes to take part in sexual and sado-masochistic activities on private property. One of the five was paid by the defendant to make a covert video recording of the event. It published photographs and a lurid account, alleging that the event had a Nazi concentration camp theme, which Eady J. found to be untrue. As to the applicability of Art.8, he said:

> "The modern approach to personal privacy and to sexual preferences and practices is very different from that of past generations. First, there is a greater willingness, and especially in the Strasbourg jurisprudence, to accord respect to an individual's right to conduct his or her personal life without state interference or condemnation. It has now to be recognised that sexual conduct is a significant aspect of human life in respect of which people should be free to choose. That freedom is one of the matters which Art.8 protects: governments and courts are required to afford remedies when that right is breached.
>
> Secondly, as Lord Nicholls at [17]-[18] and Lord Hoffmann at [50] observed in *Campbell* in 2004, remedies should be available against private individuals and corporations (including the media) because, absent any serious element of public interest, they are obliged to respect personal privacy as much as public bodies."[68]

---

[62] (1982) 4 E.H.R.R. 149 at [60]. The case has been cited in many subsequent decisions.
[63] [2000] E.C.H.R. 402; (2000) 31 E.H.R.R. 303.
[64] Relying on *Laskey, Jaggard and Brown v UK* [1997] E.C.H.R. 4; (1997) 24 E.H.R.R. 39.
[65] [2000] E.C.H.R. 402 at [25].
[66] [2000] E.C.H.R. 402 at [37].
[67] [2008] EWHC 1777 (QB); [2008] E.M.L.R. 20.
[68] [2008] E.M.L.R. 20 at [125]-[126].

Eady J. found that the claimant had a reasonable expectation of privacy and that his Art.8 right had been breached. He rejected an argument that the claimant had no reasonable expectation of privacy because of the numbers involved and because there was evidence that the claimant liked to record such events, with the consent of all those present, as a private record. In so ruling, Eady J. relied on *ADT v United Kingdom*. He also found that the woman who made the video recording and supplied it to the defendant committed an "old fashioned breach of confidence" as well as a violation of the Art.8 rights of all those involved.[69]

In *Mosley v United Kingdom* the Strasbourg court described the case as "a flagrant and unjustified invasion of the applicant's private life".[70]

The courts have drawn a distinction in a number of cases between publishing the details of a sexual relationship and publishing the "bare fact" of such a relationship.[71] Depending on the facts about how the relationship has been conducted and how widely it is known, the complainant may not have a reasonable expectation of the existence of the relationship being kept private, but may have reasonable grounds for objecting to public disclosure of intimate details. There may also be circumstances which would justify disclosure of the fact of the relationship, for example to counter a false image portrayed by the complainant, without justifying a detailed description of sexual behaviour in private or the publication of intimate photographs.

RESPECT FOR PRIVATE LIFE AND JUSTIFIABILITY OF INTERFERENCE

7–033   Unauthorised disclosure or use of information about a person's private life will be a violation of Art.8 only if the following conditions are satisfied:

(1)   it is sufficiently serious to cause substantial offence to a person of ordinary sensibilities; and

(2)   there is no good and sufficient reason for it—"good" meaning a reason capable of justifying the interference, and "sufficient" meaning sufficient to outweigh the person's Art.8 rights on a balance of the legitimate competing interests.

---

[69] [2008] E.M.L.R. 20 at [105]–[109].

[70] [2011] E.C.H.R. 774; (2011) 53 E.H.R.R. 30 at [104].

[71] In *Terry v Persons Unknown* [2010] EWHC 119 (QB); [2010] E.M.L.R. 16 at [11]–[14] and [67]–[68] Tugendhat J. said, when refusing to grant an injunction to prevent publication of the fact of the claimant having had an affair, that he would have granted an injunction to prevent publication of photographs or intrusive details if there had been sufficient evidence of a threat to do so. See also *SKA v CRH* [2012] EWHC 766 (QB), per Tugendhat J. at [26]–[28] and [64]–[70]; *Trimingham v Associated Newspapers Ltd* [2012] EWHC 1296 (QB), per Tugendhat J. at [285], and the authorities there referred to.

SERIOUS INTERFERENCE AND THE ORDINARY INCIDENTS OF SOCIAL LIVING

Not every disclosure of information about a person's private or family life or home will necessarily cross the threshold of interfering with their rights under Art.8. The disclosure may be too limited or trivial. **7–034**

In *McKennitt v Ash*[72] the claimant was a celebrated composer and performer of folk music. The defendant was a close friend, who sometimes worked with the claimant in connection with her business and on one occasion accompanied her on a foreign tour under a contract containing a confidentiality clause. They fell out, particularly over a property bought by the defendant and her partner with the claimant's help. The dispute resulted in High Court proceedings, which were settled privately through the mechanism of a Tomlin order. The defendant then published a book entitled "Travels with Loreena McKennitt: My life as a Friend". The claimant sued for breach of privacy and confidentiality, relying both on the nature of their confidential relationship and on Art.8. **7–035**

Eady J. described some of the disclosures as anodyne and held that they were insufficiently intimate or intrusive to require protection from disclosure. For example, he said about the description of a shopping trip[73]: **7–036**

> "It is trivial and of no consequence, and unlike relatively trivial but intrusive descriptions of a person's home, there is no need for the law to step in and offer protection. Nor is it likely to cause significant distress or other harm to, say, a celebrity or anyone else, that a friend accompanied her on a shopping trip and managed to bargain with vendors to save money. It is anodyne and not such as to attract any obligation of confidence. I do not even need to ask whether there is any public interest—although, of course, there is not."

As indicated in that passage, the judge took a stricter view of descriptions of the claimant's home. He held that even relatively trivial details would fall within the protection of Art.8, because of the traditional sanctity accorded to hearth and home, and he observed[74]: **7–037**

> "To describe a person's home, the décor, the layout, the state of cleanliness, or how occupiers behave inside it, is generally regarded as unacceptable. To convey such details, without permission, to the general public is almost as objectionable as spying into the home with a long distance lens and publishing the resulting photographs."

The judge upheld complaints about disclosures regarding the claimant's health, her relationship with her fiancé and her reaction to his death by drowning.

He also upheld her complaint about disclosure of details regarding the acquisition of the property which had led to previous litigation. He held that she was entitled to expect that the arrangements by which she advanced money to the defendant and her partner would be kept private, and that the confidentiality had not been lost by proceedings which had resulted in a private settlement. **7–038**

---

[72] [2005] EWHC 3003 (QB); [2006] E.M.L.R. 178; upheld [2006] EWCA Civ 1714; [2008] Q.B. 73.
[73] [2005] EWHC 3003 (QB); [2006] E.M.L.R. 178 at [139].
[74] [2005] EWHC 3003 (QB); [2006] E.M.L.R. 178 at [135].

The need to take a reasonably down to earth view in considering whether information about a person's private life is sufficiently sensitive to require the protection of Art.8 was recognised by Lord Neuberger M.R. in *Ambrosiadou v Coward*. He said:

"Just because information relates to a person's family and private life, it will not be automatically protected by the courts: for instance, the information may be of slight significance, generally expressed, or anodyne in nature. While respect for family and private life is of fundamental importance, it seems to me that the courts should, in the absence of special facts, generally expect people to adopt a reasonably robust and realistic approach to living in the 21st century."[75]

7–039   Although a person's private life is not confined to activities which take place in seclusion, the level of privacy which a person can reasonably expect to enjoy for private activities carried on in public surroundings will vary according to the nature of the activities and their context. A person is entitled to enjoy social relationships without undue outside interference, but not to protection from the ordinary incidents of social living.

7–040   A person, for example, who attends a sporting event could not complain if his face appears on television in a picture of the crowd. By contrast, in *Von Hannover v Germany* a photograph of the claimant visiting a horse show was held to infringe her right to respect for her private life, but that was in the context of her being targeted by paparazzi. The European Court of Human Rights observed that "photos appearing in the tabloid press are often taken in a climate of continual harassment that induces in the persons concerned a very strong sense of intrusion into their private life or even of persecution".[76] The court rejected the view that public figures are required to accept such intrusion as an ordinary part of daily life. It also stated[77]:

"Furthermore, increased vigilance in protecting private life is necessary to contend with new communication technologies which make it possible to store and reproduce personal data. This also applies to the systematic taking of specific photos and their dissemination to a broad section of the public."

7–041   *Von Hannover v Germany, Campbell v MGN Ltd, Murray v Big Pictures Ltd*[78] and *R. (Wood) v Commissioner of Police for the Metropolis*[79] all demonstrate the courts' sensitivity to the particularly intrusive effect which the use of cameras can

---

[75] [2011] EWCA Civ 409; [2011] E.M.L.R. 21; [2011] Fam Law 690 at [30]. The parties were married, had a child and also ran a joint business. Their relationship broke down and the wife began divorce proceedings in Greece. She applied for an injunction from the English court to prevent the defendant from disclosing the contents of an application notice filed in the divorce proceedings. The document contained, for example, unparticularised complaints by the defendant that the claimant had damaged their relationship by high-handed behaviour at work and had obstructed access to their child, but the court did not consider that it contained information in respect of which the claimant had a reasonable expectation of privacy.

[76] (2005) 40 E.H.R.R. 1 at [59].

[77] (2005) 40 E.H.R.R. 1 at [70].

[78] [2008] EWCA Civ 446; [2009] Ch. 481.

[79] [2009] EWCA Civ 414; [2010] 1 W.L.R. 123.

have on a person's sense of privacy.[80] In *Campbell v MGN Ltd* Lord Hope addressed the difference between the ordinary incidents of social living and subjection to intrusive photography[81]:

> "The taking of photographs in a public street must, as Randerson J. said in *Hosking v Runting* [2003] 3 N.Z.L.R. 385, 415, para.138, be taken to be one of the ordinary incidents of living in a free community. The real issue is whether publicising the content of the photographs would be offensive: Gault and Blanchard JJ. in the Court of Appeal [2004] N.Z.C.A. 34, para.165 . . .
>
> Miss Campbell could not have complained if the photographs had been taken to show the scene in the street by a passer-by and later published simply as street scenes. But these were not just pictures of a street scene where she happened to be when the photographs were taken. They were taken deliberately, in secret and with a view to publication with the article. The zoom lens was directed at the doorway of the place where the meeting had been taking place. The faces of others in the doorway were pixelated so as not to reveal their identity. Hers was not, the photographs were published and her privacy was invaded . . .
>
> Any person in Miss Campbell's position, assuming her to be of ordinary sensibilities but assuming also that she had been photographed surreptitiously outside the place where she had been receiving treatment for drug addiction, would have known what they were and would have been distressed on seeing the photographs. She would have seen their publication, in conjunction with the article which revealed what she had been doing when she was photographed and other details about her engagement in the therapy, as a gross interference with her right to respect for her family life."

In such a case the interference with private life is not confined to the act of publication of intrusive photographs. If a person is targeted by photographers, whether at home or when out and about, in a way which a person of ordinary sensibilities would consider intrusive, that in itself will constitute an interference with their right to respect for their private life.[82]   7–042

Technological surveillance for security purposes in shops and other public places has become an ordinary incident of life in many situations, but that does not give the organisers carte blanche in the use made of the material recorded. *Peck v United Kingdom*[83] illustrates the distinction in this context between the ordinary incidents of social living and a serious interference with respect for a person's private life. Late one evening the claimant, who was suffering from depression, tried to commit suicide in the street by cutting his wrists with a kitchen knife. The incident was partially recorded on a CCTV system which had been installed by the local council and was linked to the police. Police officers came and took him to the police station, where he was detained under the Mental Health Act. He was later released without charge after examination and treatment by a doctor. The council released footage of the incident to the media, and   7–043

---

[80] See also *D v L* [2003] EWCA Civ 1169; [2004] E.M.L.R. 1 at 10, where Waller L.J. said that a court may restrain the publication of an improperly obtained photograph even if the taker is free to describe the information which the photograph provides or if the information portrayed by the photograph is already in the public domain.

[81] [2004] 2 A.C. 457; [2004] UKHL 22 at [122]–[124].

[82] *R. (Wood) v Commissioner of Police for the Metropolis* [2009] EWCA Civ 414; [2010] 1 W.L.R. 123.

[83] (2003) 36 E.H.R.R. 41.

pictures from which the claimant could be identified were shown in newspapers and on television. The European Court of Human Rights said[84]:

> "As a result, the relevant moment was viewed to an extent which far exceeded any exposure to a passer-by or to security observation and to a degree surpassing that which the applicant could possibly have foreseen . . .
>
> Accordingly, the Court considers that the disclosure by the Council of the relevant footage constituted a serious interference with the applicant's respect for his private life."

7–044   In *Halford v United Kingdom*[85] the court was concerned with electronic surveillance of a different kind. Personal calls made by the claimant on her office telephone were covertly intercepted by her employer. The court held that calls made from business premises as well as from the home could be covered by the concept of private life. It rejected the argument that an employer was entitled to intercept calls made by an employee on a telephone provided by the employer as an ordinary incident of their relationship.

JUSTIFICATION FOR INTERFERENCE

7–045   An individual's interest in not having information about his private life published has to be set against the freedoms of others, particularly the right to freedom of expression under Art.10, and the interests of the general public.

7–046   In some cases, the person by or to whom the information is being disclosed may have a personal interest in it, which may justify its disclosure independently of any wider public interest. In other cases, the information may have nothing to do with the person disclosing it or the person to whom it is being disclosed, but freedom of speech and public interest may be advanced as sufficient justification for the disclosure.

There is no single test or formula for deciding whether an interference with a person's Art.8 right to respect for private and family life is outweighed by the right to freedom of speech protected by Art.10. It is necessary in each case to consider, on the one hand, the particular aspect of a person's private life which is or would be affected by the publication, and the degree of harm which would be caused; and, on the other hand, the public interest which publication would serve, and the degree of harm which would be caused by prohibiting it.

Despite the superficial similarity,[86] the exercise is not identical to the one which has to be carried out when considering the impact of Art.10 on conduct which would otherwise amount to a breach of a confidential relationship. Both involve balancing exercises, but what is being balanced is not the same. Article.8(1) has been given a very broad interpretation, and it may require a correspondingly liberal approach to Art.10 to provide an acceptable and realistic

---

[84] (2003) 36 E.H.R.R. 41 at [62]–[63].

[85] (1997) 24 E.H.R.R. 523.

[86] The distinction was recognised by the Court of Appeal in *Associated Newspapers Ltd v Prince of Wales* [2006] EWCA Civ 1776; [2008] Ch. 57 at [67]–[68].

balance in a democratic society.[87] The expanded interpretation of Art.8(1) means that some aspects of a person's private life (for example, details of their personal health) may require a higher degree of protection than others. Put simply, some forms of interference with a person's private life may involve a much greater intrusion than others. Where information has been obtained through a confidential relationship, the situation is different. Disclosure of such information will be, on the face of things, a breach of a form of trust, and that should not be permitted merely on an evaluation that on balance it would be beneficial for the information to be published. There is a public, as well as a private, interest in requiring that duties arising out of confidential relationships should be observed, although there may be exceptions where the information is of sufficient public importance to override the normal requirement of the law.

Disclosure by or to someone with a personal interest in the disclosure being made

Freedom of expression includes the right of people not only to express their own views but to talk about their own experiences (regardless of any general public interest), provided that it does not involve breaking a trust or confidence.   7–047

In *McKennitt v Ash*[88] the defendant argued that she should be permitted to tell her own story. The argument was weakened by the description of the book on its cover as "a must for every Loreena McKennitt fan" and Eady J.'s conclusion (which was not challenged by the defendant in her appeal) that much of its content would have been of no interest to anyone but for the fact that the claimant was its central character. It was not an autobiography in which disclosures about the claimant were merely incidental. As the Court of Appeal put it, the defendant had no story to tell that was her own as opposed to the claimant's.[89] In any case, as Eady J. observed[90]:   7–048

> "It does not follow, because one can reveal one's own private life, that one can also expose confidential matters in respect of which others are entitled to protection if their consent is not forthcoming."

The right of a person to tell their own story has sometimes been invoked by the media as a ground for publishing "kiss and tell" stories but generally without success, because it is not just that person's story to tell. If the story concerns activities between two (or more) people in respect of which there was a reasonable expectation of privacy, unless there is a wider public interest in the publication of the story, it is hard to see why one party should be justified in disclosing what was private to the world at large through the media.

There may be far stronger reason for the person to be able to tell the story to another person or group as part of their own personal development. Sharing life's experiences, romantic or otherwise, with friends and family is a normal part of

---

[87] See *R. (Wood) v Commissioner of Police for the Metropolis* [2009] EWCA Civ 414; [2010] 1 W.L.R. 123.
[88] [2005] EWHC 3003 (QB); [2006] E.M.L.R. 178 (Eady J.); [2006] EWCA Civ 1714; [2008] Q.B. 73 (Buxton, Latham and Longmore L.JJ.).
[89] At [51].
[90] At [13].

social living, because people naturally look to those who are close to them for support and interest in each other's affairs. It falls within the "zone of interaction of a person with others" which Art.8 is intended to support.[91] Another sufficient reason for limited disclosure might be for the purpose of seeking help or advice. Disclosures of that kind on a limited scale as part of ordinary living must be common and unsurprisingly have not given rise to caselaw, as opposed to cases where tales of personal intimacy are sold to the media.

A difficult balancing act may be required in cases of disclosure, or threatened disclosure, to someone with a personal interest in the subject matter by reason of their own relationship with one of the parties involved. Article 10 includes the right to receive information without interference by public authority. A person who deceives a partner by having an affair with someone else may hope and expect not to be caught out, but it is questionable whether they would have a legitimate expectation meriting protection under Art.8 from disclosure to the other person concerned, and an order of the court prohibiting disclosure to the deceived party might be considered a breach of that person's Art.10 rights. Whether an employer or business partner would fall into the category of someone with a right not to be prevented from being given such information, and how such a right should be balanced against the Art.8 right of the party seeking confidentiality, would depend on the particular facts and might be a hard question. For example, the partners in a medical practice would have a strong interest in knowing that one of them was having an affair with a patient, but not in knowing otherwise about their private life.

In *ASG v GSA*[92] a well-known person, married with children, had an adulterous relationship with a girl he met at a night club. He claimed that she was attempting to blackmail him by threatening to tell the press or his wife if he did not pay her money. The Court of Appeal granted a temporary injunction prohibiting her from informing either the press or the claimant's wife. Waller L.J. said that the claimant's likelihood of succeeding in obtaining a permanent injunction at the trial might be different as between informing the press and informing the claimant's wife and that, but for the blackmail element, he doubted whether there was a case for restraining the defendant from informing the claimant's wife. The defendant was not represented at the hearing and no reference was made to the claimant's wife's rights under Art.10.

Blackmail is abhorrent and a crime, but it is hard to see its relevance to the question whether the claimant had a *reasonable* expectation of hiding his infidelity from his wife, or to the question of the wife's Art.8 and Art.10 rights to receive the information relating to her husband's behaviour which the informant was threatening to give her.[93] The court was nevertheless entitled to regard it as relevant to the question of the blackmailer's Art.10 right and what weight, if any, should be given to it.[94] Moreover, where publication would be in breach of a

---

[91] See *Torbay Borough Council v News Group Newspapers* [2003] EWHC 2927 (Fam); [2004] E.M.L.R. 18 at [35], per Munby J.

[92] [2009] EWCA Civ 1574.

[93] *SKA v CRH* [2012] EWHC 766 (QB) at [87] and [98] (Tugendhat J.).

[94] *AMM v HXW* [2010] EWHC 2457 (QB) at [38] (Tugendhat J.). In weighing the defendant's Art.10 right in *EWQ v GFD* [2012] EWHC 2182 (QB) at [105] Tugendhat J. commented: "On the evidence as it now is, it seems probable that she does have a conditional wish to tell her story, but that is not her preferred option. Her preferred option would be not to tell the story, provided that her demands are

claimant's right to privacy and there is an additional element of blackmail, the blackmail factor may be a good reason for granting anonymity[95] and for not requiring notice of an application for an injunction to be given to the blackmailer until the order has been made and notice of it given to the media.[96]

Public interest

Cases in which public interest is advanced most commonly involve either public authorities or the media. The grounds available to public authorities are limited by Art.8(2). In cases involving the media, s.12(4) of the Human Rights Act requires the court to have particular regard not only to the importance of the Convention right to freedom of expression, but also to the extent to which it is or would be in the public interest for the material to be published and to any relevant privacy code. The codes of practice for journalists and broadcasters published by the Press Complaints Commission and Ofcom are considered in greater detail in Ch.13.

7–049

The court is also prohibited by s.12(3) from restraining publication before trial unless satisfied that the applicant is likely to establish that publication should not be allowed. This provision was interpreted by the House of Lords in *Cream Holdings Ltd v Banerjee*[97] as having the effect that a court should not make an interim restraint order unless satisfied that the applicant's prospects of success at trial were sufficiently favourable to justify the order being made in the light of all the other circumstances; and that in general the court should be exceedingly slow to make such an order unless satisfied that the applicant would probably succeed at trial, although this was not a rigid test.

7–050

The European Court of Human Rights and domestic courts recognise the vital role of the press in a democratic society both as a watchdog and as a medium for public education and the dissemination of ideas. In *Von Hannover v Germany* the European Court of Human Rights held that the decisive factor in balancing the protection of private life against freedom of expression should lie in the contribution that the published photos and articles made to a debate of general interest.[98]

7–051

It said[99]:

7–052

> "The Court considers that a fundamental distinction needs to be made between reporting facts—even controversial ones—capable of contributing to a debate in democratic society relating to politicians in the exercise of their functions, for example, and reporting details of the private life of an individual who, moreover, as in this case, does not exercise official functions. While in the former case the press

---

met. Of course, the right to free speech is a right to speak not just what you want, but when you want. However, if the defendant really did want to tell her story, she has had over a year to do so since she first raised the possibility. All that an interim injunction will do is to defer her right to do so for what is expected to be the few months until trial."

[95] *AMM v HXW* [2010] EWHC 2457 (QB) at [21]–[29] and [39].

[96] *SKA v CRH* [2012] EWHC 766 (QB) at [47].

[97] [2004] UKHL 44; [2005] 1 A.C. 253.

[98] (2005) 40 E.H.R.R. 1 at [76].

[99] (2005) 40 E.H.R.R. 1 at para.76 at [63]–[65].

exercises its vital role of 'watchdog' in a democracy by contributing to imparting information and ideas on matters of public interest it does not do so in the latter case.

Similarly, although the public has a right to be informed, which is an essential right in a democratic society that, in certain special circumstances, can even extend to aspects of the private life of public figures, particularly where politicians are concerned, this is not the case here. The situation here does not come within the sphere of any political or public debate because the published photos and accompanying commentaries relate exclusively to details of the applicant's private life.

As in other similar cases it has examined, the Court considers that the publication of the photos and articles in question, of which the sole purpose was to satisfy the curiosity of a particular readership regarding the details of the applicant's private life, cannot be deemed to contribute to any debate of general interest to society despite the applicant being well known to the public."

In subsequent cases the Strasbourg court has repeatedly emphasised the importance of the question whether the disclosure will make a contribution to a debate on a subject of general interest.[100] The question is important when considering not only the nature but the detail of the publication.[101]

Where information of a personal and intimate nature is concerned, it is not sufficient that members of the public would find it interesting, as the court stated in *Mosley v United Kingdom*[102]:

"The Court... reiterates that there is a distinction to be drawn between reporting facts – even if controversial – capable of contributing to a debate of general public interest in a democratic society, and making tawdry allegations about an individual's private life... In respect of the former, the pre-eminent role of the press in a democracy and its duty to act as 'public watchdog' are important considerations in favour of a narrow construction of any limitations on freedom of expression. However, different considerations apply to press reports concentrating on sensational and, at times, lurid news, intended to titillate and entertain, which are aimed at satisfying the curiosity of a particular readership regarding aspects of a person's strictly private life (*Von Hannover, Hachette Filipichi Associes (ICI PARIS)* and *MGN Limited*). Such reporting does not attract the robust protection of Article 10 afforded to the press. As a consequence, in such cases, freedom of speech requires a more narrow interpretation (see *Societe Prisma Presse v France; Von Hannover; Leempoel & S.A. ED. Cine Revue v Belgium; Hachette Filipacchi Associes (ICI PARIS)*; and *MGN Limited*). While confirming the Article 10 rights of members of the public to have access to a wide range of publications covering a variety of fields, the Court stresses that in assessing in the context of a particular publication whether there is a public interest which justifies an interference with the right to respect for private life, the focus must be on whether the publication is in the interest of the public and not whether the public might be interested in reading it."

---

[100] See, for example, *Stoll v Switzerland* (2008) 47 E.H.R.R. 59 and *Axel Springer AG v Germany* (2012) 55 E.H.R.R. 6 at [90]–[93].

[101] In *Spelman v Express Newspapers* [2012] EWHC 355 (QB) Tugendhat J. refused to grant an interim injunction to prevent the newspaper from publishing a story about the pressures on a young international sportsman, but he gave a warning that his decision was not a licence to publish anything which the newspaper wished and that "much would depend on the style of any article, and how intrusive or offensive it might be."

[102] [2011] E.C.H.R. 774 at [114].

The court was highly critical of the conduct of the newspaper in that case, saying that:

> "...the conduct of the newspaper in the applicant's case is open to severe criticism. Aside from publication of articles detailing the applicant's sexual activities, the News of the World published photographs and video footage, obtained through clandestine recording, which undoubtedly had a far greater impact than the articles themselves...
>
> The Court, like the Parliamentary Assembly, recognises that the private lives of those in the public eye have become a highly lucrative commodity for certain sectors of the media... The publication of news about such persons contributes to the variety of information available to the public and, although generally for the purposes of entertainment rather than education, undoubtedly benefits from the protection of Article 10. However, as noted above, such protection may cede to the requirements of Article 8 where the information at stake is of a private and intimate nature and there is no public interest in its dissemination."[103]

The role of the press as a medium for public education may include putting the record straight when a person has previously presented a false public picture. In *Campbell v MGN Ltd* the claimant's treatment for drug addiction would have been a private matter which the press had no right to publicise but for the fact that she had presented herself to the public as someone who was not involved in drugs. The mode of disclosure went beyond what a majority of the House of Lords considered to be justified because of the publication of photographs taken of her outside the place where she had been receiving treatment.   **7–053**

Rio Ferdinand v MGN Ltd is an example of a public interest defence succeeding largely because of the way in which the claimant had previously presented himself. The claimant was a successful footballer and captain of the England team. He presented himself in press interviews as someone who had been irresponsible in the past, but had matured, and said that his priorities had become a stable family life and fatherhood. The defendant published an article saying that he had resumed contact with a woman with whom he had previously had a sexual relationship, but it did not go into excessive prurient detail. Nicol J. observed that one facet of the public interest could be the correction of a false image, and he considered that the claimant's conduct might legitimately be used to question his suitability for the role of England captain. He concluded that these considerations outweighed the claimant's privacy right.[104]

If a person has not set out to present a false picture, it is not part of the watchdog role of the press to seek to obtain information about their private life and then put it to them in order to place them in the dilemma of admitting it (thereby giving voluntary disclosure), refusing to comment (thereby seeming to be evasive) or denying it (thereby risking publication in order to rebut the denial).[105]   **7–054**

Where the justification put forward for publication of personal information is not that the person concerned has made false factual statements but has been   **7–055**

---

[103] [2011] E.C.H.R. 774 at [130]–[131].

[104] [2011] EWHC 2454 (QB) at [65], [96]–[99] and [105].

[105] *X v Persons Unknown* [2006] EWHC 2783 (QB); [2007] E.M.L.R. 10 at [36]: "...if someone asks "How's married life treating you?" and the response is "Fine", that does not mean that the public is entitled to a ringside seat when stresses and strains emerge." (Eady J.)

guilty of hypocrisy in advocating a set of standards and behaving differently, much will depend on the particular circumstances, including the person's role (for example, whether he holds or is a candidate for public office) and to what extent the conduct is truly hypocritical.

7–056   In *McKennitt v Ash*[106] the defendant sought to justify publication on the basis that the claimant's conduct belied the standards of behaviour set out on her website as her "compass points". These included a number of goals such as "Be compassionate and never forget how to love". The judge described them as a fragile peg on which to hang a public interest defence, and the Court of Appeal agreed with this description.[107] The claimant recommended them as goals to which she and others could aspire, but had never claimed to have fulfilled them throughout her life. He observed that it could not be right that any person in the public eye who chose to share his or her aspirations with fans or the general public would immediately become vulnerable to having every detail in their private lives exposed to public scrutiny.

Public domain

7–057   This subject has been considered in Ch.3. Publication of information which would otherwise be protected by Art.8 will only be justified on the ground that it is in the public domain if it has been so fully publicised that further publication could not reasonably be expected to cause damage or distress to the person concerned.

7–058   For example, in *Green Corns Ltd v Claverly Group Ltd*[108] a children's home provider applied for an injunction to restrain a local newspaper from publishing the addresses of homes provided for troubled children. The newspaper had published a number of articles reporting that homes had been bought by the claimants to house sex offenders and troubled teenagers in the local community and the addresses of the homes were included. Tugendhat J. rejected the argument that an injunction should be refused on the ground that the information was already in the public domain. He said[109]:

> "I conclude that the information as to the addresses which is sought to be restrained is not in the public domain to the extent, or in the sense, that republication could have no significant effect, or that the information is not eligible for protection at all. The information as to the addresses linked with information as to the business of the applicant and thus to the likely disabilities and other characteristics of the occupants of the addresses brings together matters which together amount to new information which was previously available to the public only in a limited and theoretical sense. Publication or republication risks causing serious harm to the children and carers who occupy, or are about to occupy, the addresses concerned."

In *JIH v News Group Newspapers Ltd*[110] Tugendhat J. expressed the principle in this way:

---

[106] [2005] EWHC 3003 (QB); [2006] E.M.L.R. 10 at [98]–[100].

[107] [2006] EWCA Civ 1714; [2008] Q.B. 73 at [68].

[108] [2005] EWHC 958 (QB); [2005] E.M.L.R. 31.

[109] [2005] EWHC 958 (QB); [2005] E.M.L.R. 31 at [81].

[110] [2010] EWHC 2818 (QB); [2011] E.M.L.R. 9 at [58]–[59]. The case went to the Court of Appeal but not on this point.

"It is important to bear in mind what privacy injunctions are intended to achieve. In some cases the information sought to be protected will be truly secret... Such cases bear some comparison to cases about trade or official secrets: if the secret is revealed there is nothing the court can do to undo what has been done...

But in many privacy cases the information sought to be protected is not secret in that sense, or, even if it is, there is still something to be achieved by an injunction. Art.8 is about interference with a person's private and family life. There may be such interference by repetition in the press of information even when that information is not secret or unknown."

In *Douglas v Hello! Ltd (No.3)*[111] the Douglases contracted with OK! magazine to give it exclusive rights to publish photographs of their wedding. The Douglases were to control which photographs could be published, but they undertook to use their best endeavours to prevent any other media from having access to the wedding and to prevent any guests from taking photographs. Despite elaborate security arrangements, a paparazzo succeeded in gate crashing the event and took photographs which were sold to OK!'s rival Hello! The Douglases and the publishers of OK! sued the publishers of Hello!

      7–059

It was argued by Hello! that after the Douglases entered into their contract with OK! publication of other photographs of the event could not infringe their rights under Art.8, since they had chosen that the event should be publicised. The Court of Appeal rejected the argument, observing that it was wrong to suppose that a person who authorised the publication of selected personal photographs taken on a private occasion would not reasonably feel distress at the publication of unauthorised photographs taken on the same occasion.[112] (The case went to the House of Lords, but not in relation to the Douglases' claim under Art.8.)

      7–060

The court also commented more generally on the propensity of unauthorised personal photographs to cause distress not only on publication but on re-publication[113]:

      7–061

"Once intimate personal information about a celebrity's private life has been widely published it may serve no useful purpose to prohibit further publication. The same will not necessarily be true of photographs. Insofar as a photograph does more than convey information and intrudes on privacy by enabling the individual to focus on intimate personal detail, there will be a fresh intrusion of privacy when each additional viewer sees the photograph and even when one who has seen a previous publication of the photograph is confronted with a fresh publication of it. To take an example, if a film star were photographed, with the aid of a telephoto lens, lying naked by her private swimming pool, we question whether widespread publication of the photograph by a popular newspaper would provide a defence to a legal challenge to repeated publication on the ground that the information was in the public domain."

A person may have a reasonable expectation of privacy in relation to personal matters which occurred in the past, albeit that they may at one time have been public knowledge, as the Supreme Court recognised in *R. (L) v Commissioner of*

---

[111] [2005] EWCA 595; [2006] Q.B. 125.

[112] [2005] EWCA 595; [2006] Q.B. 125 at [106]–[107].

[113] [2005] EWCA 595; [2006] Q.B. 125 at [105].

Police of the Metropolis.[114] The case concerned police records. After citing *Leander v Sweden*[115] and other Strasbourg decisions, Lord Hope said:

"This line of authority from Strasbourg shows that information about an applicant's convictions which is collected and stored in central records can fall within the scope of private life within the meaning of article 8(1), with the result that it will interfere with the applicant's private life when it is released. It is, in one sense, public information because the convictions took place in public. But the systematic storing of this information in central records means that it is available for disclosure under [the Police Act] long after the event when everyone other than the person concerned is likely to have forgotten about it. As it recedes into the past, it becomes a part of the person's private life which must be respected."

The ultimate balancing exercise

7–062   In *Re S*[116] Lord Steyn (with whom the other members of the House of Lords agreed) reiterated that neither Art.8 nor Art.10 as such has priority over the other. When both are engaged, "an intense focus on the comparative importance of the specific rights being claimed in the individual case is necessary". The justifications for interfering with each right must be taken into account and an ultimate balancing exercise carried out.[117]

7–063   The case concerned an eight-year-old boy, who was the subject of care proceedings brought by his local authority. His mother faced trial for murder of his older brother by allegedly poisoning him with salt. The issue was whether an order should be made prohibiting the press from publishing the names or photographs of the mother or the deceased child so as to prevent avoidable distress to the boy from the publicity surrounding the trial. The court accepted that Art.8 was engaged and that the trial with its publicity was bound to be deeply painful for him, but in measuring the impact Lord Steyn observed that it was essentially indirect. There would be no reference at the trial to the boy, his private life or his upbringing. On the other hand, an injunction preventing the press from identifying the mother or the deceased child would be a direct interference with the freedom of the press to perform the important function of reporting criminal trials. The function is important because full contemporaneous reporting of criminal trials promotes public confidence in the administration of justice and the values of the rule of law. A report of the trial without revealing the identity of the defendant would be a "very much disembodied trial". The court concluded that the arguments under Art.8 were insufficient to outweigh the arguments under Art.10.

7–064   The case may be contrasted on its facts with *A Local Authority v W*,[118] where the issue was similar but the result was different. A mother of two small children was due to be sentenced for knowingly infecting the father of one of them with

---

[114] [2009] UKSC 3; [2010] 1 A.C. 410 at [27].

[115] (1987) 9 E.H.R.R. 433 at [48]: "Moreover, public information can fall within the scope of private life where it is systematically collected and stored in files held by the authorities. This is all the truer where such information concerns a person's distant past."

[116] [2004] UKHL 47; [2005] A.C. 593.

[117] [2004] UKHL 47; [2005] A.C. 593 at [17].

[118] [2005] EWHC 1564; [2006] 1 F.L.R. 1, Fam. See Ch.21 for further discussion of *Re S* and *A Local Authority v W*.

the HIV virus. The children were the subject of care proceedings. Sir Mark Potter P. granted an injunction on the application of the local authority to prevent the publication of the identities of the parents or any other information likely to lead to the identification of the children. Although the children were too young to be aware themselves of any publicity, the judge accepted that there was a serious risk of short term and long term prejudice to their welfare if their association with the parties involved in the criminal proceedings became known in the communities where they were living or where the local authority might seek to place them.

Privacy and commercialism

Douglas v Hello! Ltd (No. 3)[119] raised novel issues about personal privacy and commercial exploitation. The purpose of Art.8 is to protect a person from unwanted intrusion into his private life. A person may choose to reveal details about his private life, either in photographic form or otherwise, for commercial purposes. The Douglases did so by their contract with OK! The case raised questions about the extent to which (a) the Douglases and (b) OK! were entitled to use the law of confidentiality to protect their commercial interests.

7–065

Lindsay J. awarded the Douglases £3,750 each for their personal distress and £7,000 jointly for the labour and expense in expediting their selection of photographs because of the impending publication by Hello!.[120] The Court of Appeal commented that this sum could only have reflected damage or the cost of mitigating damage to their commercial interest in the information about their wedding. He awarded £1,033,156 to OK! as damages for lost revenue resulting from Hello! spoiling OK!'s opportunity to exploit exclusive photographic coverage of the wedding. The basis of his reasoning was that the case was analogous to commercial confidence cases where it was common for the benefit of the confidentiality to be shared with another person who could thereafter enforce it.

7–066

The Court of Appeal upheld the award in favour of the Douglases but reversed the decision in favour of OK! In relation to the Douglases's claim, the court acknowledged that recognition of the right of a celebrity to make money out of publicising private information about himself, including photographs taken on a private occasion, broke new ground and had echoes of the "image rights" recognised by French and German law, but it saw no reason in principle why equity should not protect the opportunity to profit from commercial information about oneself in the same circumstances that it protects the opportunity to profit from confidential information in the nature of a trade secret.[121]

7–067

In relation to OK!'s claim, the court rejected the argument that there could be any proprietary interest in information about the wedding. The Douglases' right to protection depended not on any property right, but on the effect on the conscience of a third party's knowledge of the nature of the information and the circumstances in which it was obtained.[122]

7–068

---

[119] [2005] EWCA 595; [2006] Q.B. 125; [2007] UKHL 21; [2008] 1 A.C. 1.
[120] [2005] EWCA 595; [2006] Q.B. 125 at [36].
[121] [2005] EWCA 595; [2006] Q.B. 125 at [113].
[122] [2005] EWCA 595; [2006] Q.B. 125 at [126]–[127].

7–069   The court appears to have accepted the proposition that

> "where the benefit of confidential information is shared between A and B, B can claim that disclosure of that information will constitute a breach of duty of confidence owed to B."[123]

However, it held that the contract between the Douglases and OK! had not purported to transfer to, or share with, OK! the right to use any photographic information about the wedding other than the approved photographs released to OK! by the Douglases for publication. Although the Douglases retained a residual right of privacy or confidentiality in those details of the wedding which were not portrayed by the official photographs released to OK!, it was the Douglases and not OK! who had the sole right to protect that area of privacy or confidentiality.[124] OK!'s claim therefore failed.

The House of Lords reversed the decision of the Court of Appeal and restored the judgment of Lindsay J. Lord Hoffmann said that the analysis of the Court of Appeal lacked commercial sense in confining the confidential rights of OK! to the photographs supplied to it. The purpose of the prohibition of unauthorised photography was to impose an obligation of confidentiality in respect of any pictures of the wedding.[125]

7–070   This was surely right. The terms of the contract provided that the Douglases would procure the taking of photographs of the wedding (described as the official photographs); that they would provide OK! with approved photographs selected from the official photographs; that OK! should have exclusive rights to publish the approved photographs for a period of nine months; and that the Douglases would use their best efforts to ensure that nobody else took photographs of the wedding. The aim, in summary, was that OK! should have exclusive rights to publish photographs of the wedding for nine months, and that the published photographs should be only ones which the Douglases had approved.

7–071   The novel feature of *Douglas v Hello Ltd!* was that, leaving aside the personal distress to the Douglases from the publication of the unauthorised photographs (which the judge considered to be modest in that the damages awarded to them under that head were £3,750 each), the case was not about the Douglases' enjoyment of personal privacy but about Hello!'s interference with the commercial exploitation of an event in their private lives which the Douglases had decided to commercialise in a particular way.

7–072   It is right that the law should protect a person from unwanted exposure of his private life to the scrutiny of the general public. To that end, English law treats photographs of private activities as information protected by the law of confidentiality. The particular characteristic of photographs is, as the Court of Appeal put it,[126] that

> "They enable the person viewing the photograph to act as a spectator, in some circumstances voyeur would be the more appropriate noun, of whatever it is that the photograph depicts."

---

[123] [2005] EWCA 595; [2006] Q.B. 125 at [129].

[124] [2005] EWCA 595; [2006] Q.B. 125 at [131]–[136].

[125] [2007] UKHL 21; [2008] 1 A.C. 1 at [123].

[126] [2005] EWCA Civ 595; [2006] Q.B. 125 at [84].

Applied to celebrities, that characteristic and the public appetite for it can create not only vulnerability to intrusive and unwanted publicity but also valuable commercial opportunities. *Douglas v Hello! Ltd (No. 3)* is authority that a person who chooses to allow disclosure to the general public of selected photographs of an otherwise private event, for commercial purposes, is entitled to rely on the law of confidentiality for protection against commercial damage resulting from unauthorised disclosure of improperly obtained similar material by another. It is important to understand that this right is not itself based on Art.8. As Lord Hoffmann said:

> " OK! has no claim to privacy under article 8 nor can it make a claim which is parasitic upon the Douglases' right to privacy. The fact that the information happens to have been about the personal life of the Douglases is irrelevant. It could have been information about anything that the newspaper was willing to pay for. What matters is that the Douglases, by the way they arranged their wedding, were in a position to impose an obligation of confidence."[127]

The Douglases right to privacy was personal to them, and the only compensation to which they were entitled for breach of their Art.8 right was the award for distress. Their right to commercial exploitation of their wedding stemmed from their ability to control it in such a way as to impose a duty of confidentiality on others, and they were entitled to transfer the benefit of that obligation to OK!

Privacy and companies

In *R v Broadcasting Standards Commission Ex p. BBC*[128] it was held that a **7–073** company could make a complaint under the Broadcasting Act 1996 of unwarranted infringement of its privacy, but that was because of the particular language of the statute and its underlying purpose. Commenting more generally, Lord Mustill observed[129] that an infringement of privacy is an affront to the personality in a sense which cannot be applied to an impersonal corporate body. Many things which could be presented by an individual as a breach of privacy could also amount to wrongs to a company, such as clandestine copying of documents, but when done to a company such conduct would lack the extra dimension of intrusion into the personal space of an individual. A company may have secrets, but that is different from the essentially human concept of privacy.[130]

In *Australian Broadcasting Corporation v Lennah Game Meats Pty Ltd*[131] the **7–074** High Court of Australia considered, but did not need to decide, whether Australian law recognises a cause of action for breach of privacy and, if so, whether it may be available to a company.

Gleeson C.J. observed[132] that he could see no reason why some internal **7–075** corporate communications were any less private than those of a partnership or an

---

[127] [2007] UKHL 21; [2008] 1 A.C. 1 at [118].
[128] [2001] Q.B. 885.
[129] [2001] Q.B. 885 at [48]–[49].
[130] See Emberland, *The Human Rights of Companies* (Oxford University Press, 2006), especially pp.113–117.
[131] [2001] H.C.A. 63; 208 C.L.R. 199.
[132] [2001] H.C.A. 63; 208 C.L.R. 199 at [43].

individual; but that the foundation of much of what is protected, where rights of privacy are acknowledged, is human dignity.

7–076   Gaudron,[133] Gummow and Hayne JJ. examined the development of authority in the United States[134] and considered that any development in Australia of a tort of invasion of privacy should be for the benefit of natural, not artificial, persons.[135] Kirby J. was also doubtful whether a company was apt to enjoy any common law right to privacy, but refrained from expressing a final view.[136] Callinan J. was more favourable to the possibility that in some circumstances a company might be able to enjoy the same or similar rights to privacy as a natural person.[137]

7–077   The broad statements of the European Court of Human Rights about the object of Art.8 being to protect an individual's personal development and relationships with other human beings from unjustifiable outside interference are by their nature applicable only to human beings, not inanimate entities. However, in *Societe Colas Est v France*[138] the court upheld complaints by a number of companies under Art.8, stating that[139]:

> "Building on its dynamic interpretation of the Convention, the Court considers that the time has come to hold that in certain circumstances the rights guaranteed by Art.8 of the Convention may be construed as including the right to respect for a company's registered office, branches or other business premises (see, *mutatis mutandis, Niemietz*)."

The complaints arose from raids by Government officials of the applicants' offices, during which documents were seized. The raids were part of an investigation into suspected corruption in the construction industry. The purpose was to find evidence of unlawful agreements between public works contractors in the award of roadwork contracts. The court accepted that this was a legitimate purpose for interfering with the companies' right to respect for their premises, but it held that the circumstances and manner in which the raids were conducted made the interference disproportionate to the legitimate aims pursued. The seizure of the documents resulted in the companies being fined for breaches of competition law. The companies asked the court to award them reimbursement of the fines. It refused to do so, but awarded each company €5,000 as compensation for "non-pecuniary damage".

7–078   It is not easy to understand what "non-pecuniary" damage the companies suffered. The companies were entities with legal but not human personality, created for the economic purposes of the shareholders. The awards of damages seem more like fines, designed to mark the court's disapproval of what had happened, than true compensation for damage to the companies.

7–079   In its argument the French Government accepted that the inspection of the companies' documents amounted to interference with their right to respect for their home ("domicile" in the French version of the Convention, which the court

---

[133] [2001] H.C.A. 63; 208 C.L.R. 199 at [58].
[134] [2001] H.C.A. 63; 208 C.L.R. 199 at [120].
[135] [2001] H.C.A. 63; 208 C.L.R. 199 at [130]–[132].
[136] [2001] H.C.A. 63; 208 C.L.R. 199 at [190]–[191].
[137] [2001] H.C.A. 63; 208 C.L.R. 199 at [328].
[138] [2002] E.C.H.R. 421.
[139] [2002] E.C.H.R. 421 at [41].

said has a broader connotation than "home"[140]). However, it submitted that, while juristic persons could enjoy similar rights under the Convention to those afforded to natural persons, they could not claim a right to protection of their business premises "with as much force" as an individual, and that the inspections had been carried out within the law.[141]

Possibly because of the French Government's concession, the judgment does **7–080** not attempt a detailed analysis of how the accordance of rights to a non-natural person under Art.8 fits with the purpose of the article, as explained by the court in other cases.

In the case of an individual, it might be argued that the rights protected by **7–081** Art.8 include a proprietorial dimension, because a person's home and his correspondence are forms of property in which he has an interest that he is entitled to enjoy, as well as being essential to his private life. But the heading to the Article is "Right to Respect for Private and Family Life", and it has been interpreted as having a very broad purpose based on the need of human beings for a zone of freedom from outside interference in which to be able to develop their personality and relationships with others. A home and the ability to correspond with others are especially important ingredients of this zone of freedom. Seen in this context, the protection given by Art.8 to a person's home and correspondence is merely a part (but an important part) of this freedom, and not a free standing right available to any legal entity (natural or artificial) in possession of premises or correspondence.

Property rights are protected elsewhere under the Convention. Article 1 of the **7–082** First Protocol provides that every *natural or legal* person is entitled to the peaceful enjoyment of his possessions. Possessions have been interpreted as including immovable and movable property, intellectual property, contractual rights and the goodwill of a business.[142]

In stating that the rights guaranteed by Art.8 may be construed as including **7–083** respect for a company's registered office or other business premises, the European Court of Human Rights cited its previous decision in *Niemietz v Germany*.[143] In that case the court held that a search of a lawyer's offices by police looking for information about the whereabouts of a criminal suspect violated Art.8, but its reasoning was that an individual's private life may include activities of a business or professional nature. The search of the lawyer's offices was therefore an intrusion into his private life. If anything, the reasoning in that case would tend to negate the extension of rights under Art.8 to an inanimate entity, because the court approached the construction of the article from the standpoint that respect for private life is about the right of an individual to live his personal life as he chooses, and that this must comprise the right to establish and develop relationships with other human beings.

In *R (Kent Pharmaceuticals Ltd) v Director of the Serious Fraud Office*[144] the claimant company unsuccessfully challenged the lawfulness of a decision of the Director of the SFO to disclose documents to the Department of Health which

---

[140] [2002] E.C.H.R. 421 at [40].

[141] [2002] E.C.H.R. 421 at [30] and [32].

[142] For further study of this subject, see Clayton & Tomlinson, *The Law of Human Rights* (Oxford University Press, 2nd edn, 2009), Ch.18.

[143] (1992) 16 E.H.R.R. 97.

[144] [2004] EWCA Civ 1494; [2005] 1 W.L.R. 1302 at [5].

had been seized by the SFO under four search warrants. The parties named in the warrants were the company and two of its directors or former directors. The documents were seized as part of a criminal investigation into suspected unlawful price fixing. The Court of Appeal accepted that the company and the directors enjoyed a right to respect for their correspondence under Art.8. The question whether the company had such a right does not appear to have been argued and may have been academic since the individuals concerned clearly had such rights.

The right of a company to rely on Art.8 was considered by the Court of Justice of the EU in *Varec SA v Belgium*.[145] The Belgian defence ministry invited tenders for the supply of equipment for tanks. Two tenderers submitted bids, Varec and Diehl. The ministry decided that Varec's tender did not satisfy the criteria and awarded the contract to Diehl. Varec brought an action for annulment of the decision and sought disclosure of the details of Diehl's bid. Diehl objected to disclosure of what it considered to be confidential and commercially sensitive data. The Belgian court referred the issue to the Court of Justice.

The relevant Council Directive contained a provision that the contracting authorities were obliged to respect the confidential nature of any information provided by a supplier. As the court observed, the effectiveness of the provision would be undermined if an unsuccessful competitor could obtain unrestricted access to such information by mounting a legal challenge to the contracting authority's decision. That would be a compelling reason for holding that the whole tendering scheme was predicated on maintaining respect for commercial confidentiality, but the court expressed its reasoning in broader terms. Observing that the right to a fair hearing ordinarily requires that a party should be able to inspect and comment on the evidence submitted to the court, but in some cases it may be necessary for certain information to be withheld from the parties in order to preserve the "fundamental rights" of a third party, the court stated[146]:

> "One of the fundamental rights capable of being protected in this way is the right to private life, enshrined in Article 8 of the ECHR, which flows from the common constitutional traditions of the Member States…It follows from the case-law of the European Court of Human Rights that the notion of 'private life' cannot be taken to mean that the professional or commercial activities of either natural or legal persons are excluded (see *Niemetz v Germany*…; *Societe Colas Est v France*…; and also *Peck v United Kingdom*…Those activities can include participation in a contract award procedure."

Of the cases cited by the court, only *Societe Colas Est* was concerned with the position of a company. Moreover, the Strasbourg court's comment in that case related to respect for a company's business premises in the context of a police search and followed a concession by the French government in argument that Art.8 was engaged. It was therefore doubtful authority for the broad statement of the Court of Justice.

Varec v Belgium was cited in *Veolia ES Nottinghamshire Ltd v Nottingham-shire County Council* [147] by Rix L.J., who commented that *Niemetz v Germany*

---

[145] [2008] ECR I–581; [2008] 2 C.M.L.R. 24.
[146] [2008] ECR I–581; [2008] 2 C.M.L.R. 24 at [48].
[147] [2010] EWCA Civ 1214; [2011] Env. L.R. 12 at [118].

"might suggest that art.8 is a proper home for the legitimacy of state interference in access to private information, albeit its particular facts are more narrowly concerned with a state prosecutor's search of a lawyer's office."

It was not necessary for the Court of Appeal to reach any decision on the question because it was conceded in that case by the defendant that either Art.8 or Art.1 of Protocol 1 of the Convention was engaged.

Article 8 is essentially a protection of human autonomy and dignity. It is about **7–084** preserving a space for the individual which others should respect. It is capable of embracing aspects of a person's business life, which may be conducted through a company, and it is easy to see that a police raid on a company's premises may impact on the privacy of its owners, employees and customers. It may therefore be a way of protecting those persons' right of privacy to permit the company to invoke Art.8 in such a case. There remains, however, a real distinction between privacy and corporate confidentiality (as Lord Mustill explained in *R v Broadcasting Standards Commission Ex p. BBC*). A company may be owed duties of confidentiality which do not impact on the privacy of its owners, or others, in any ordinary sense. To regard Art.8 as a protection of a company's rights of confidentiality (as the Court of Justice seems to have considered that it was in *Varec v Belgium*) would be to blur the distinction between confidentiality and privacy.

It remains to be seen how the Strasbourg court will approach claims by companies under Art.8 in future cases, but the outcome may not make a significant difference to English law, since English law already protects companies against the obtaining of confidential information by improper means.[148]

---

[148] *Shelley Films Ltd v Rex Features Ltd* [1994] E.M.L.R. 134; *Creation Records Ltd v News Group Newspapers Ltd* [1997] E.M.L.R. 444.

CHAPTER 8

Data Protection and Freedom of Information

THE DPA AND THE FOIA: INTRODUCTION

Data Protection

The statutory development of data protection legislation in the United Kingdom, as elsewhere, has been a response to the rapid technological advances made in the last quarter of the 20th century and subsequently—in particular, in the field of computers.   **8–001**

On January 28, 1981, the member states of the Council of Europe signed the Convention for the Protection of Individuals with regard to Automatic Processing of Personal Data. The Data Protection Act 1984, since repealed, reflected the provisions of the Convention.   **8–002**

The present United Kingdom legislation, in particular the Data Protection Act 1998 ("DPA"), is a consequence of Directive 95/46/EC, on the protection of individuals with regard to the processing of personal data and on the free movement of such data, which was authorised by the European Parliament and Council on October 24, 1995. The DPA came into force on March 1, 2000, but contains extensive transitional provisions.   **8–003**

Freedom of information

While complementing the DPA in a number of respects, the Freedom of Information Act 2000 ("the FOIA") has rather different origins. Its legislative history dates back to the Government's white paper in December 1997, entitled "Your right to know", which set out the Government's proposals for a Freedom of Information Act. The Government expressed its intention to promote openness in government and referred to the similar measures already in existence in a number of other countries (including the USA, Canada, Australia, New Zealand, Sweden, France and the Netherlands).   **8–004**

The FOIA received royal assent in November 2000, but the Act did not come into force for most substantive purposes until January 1, 2005. In order to avoid overlap with the DPA, s.40 of the FOIA ensures that all requests by a data subject for access to personal data relating to him fall under the subject access provisions of the DPA, by expressly exempting such information from the FOIA regime.   **8–005**

The DPA and the FOIA together represent a considerable accretion to the law of confidentiality in the United Kingdom. A full examination of the two Acts is   **8–006** beyond the scope of this work and the reader is referred to the textbooks that address them specifically.[1] There follows merely an outline introduction to the structure of the Acts.

The Information Commissioner

8–007   The Data Protection Act 1984 established a Data Protection Registrar, whose title was changed, under the DPA, to Data Protection Commissioner. With effect from January 30, 2001, the Data Protection Commissioner took over responsibility also for the FOIA and his title changed again, to Information Commissioner. As well as the DPA and the FOIA, the Information Commissioner also enforces and oversees the Privacy and Electronic Communications (EC Directive) Regulations 2003[2] and the Environmental Information Regulations 2004[3] and has acquired a further enforcement role in relation to the INSPIRE Regulations 2009 (which impose obligations on public authorities, among other things, to make "spatial data" available to the public).

8–008   The powers of the Information Commissioner include the service of enforcement notices, where there has been a breach of the data protection principles,[4] the service of information notices, by which information relating to compliance can be required,[5] and the prosecution of those who commit criminal offences under the DPA.[6] The Information Commissioner also has the power to impose monetary penalties on a data controller in respect of serious contraventions of the data protection principles which are of a kind likely to cause substantial damage or substantial distress[7]. Under the FOIA, the Information Commissioner is empowered to issue decision notices (having investigated a complaint against a public authority)[8] and enforcement notices,[9] requiring a public authority to address its failure to comply with Pt 1 of the FOIA.

Appeals from the Information Commissioner's notices are now heard by the First-tier Tribunal (Information Rights), part of the General Regulatory Chamber Information Tribunal.

---

[1] See, for example: Boardman, Gaskill & Grant's *Encyclopedia of Data Protection and Privacy* (loose-leaf, Sweet & Maxwell), Peter Carey's *Data Protection,* 3rd edn (Oxford University Press, 2009), Macdonald, Crail and Jones's *Law of Freedom of Information,* 2nd edn (Oxford University Press, 2009) and Carey and Turle's *Freedom of Information Handbook,* 2nd edn (the Law Society, 2008).

[2] These make further provision in relation to such matters as the use of "cookies", the processing of "traffic data" (i.e. information relating to electronic communications), itemised telephone bills, the identification of incoming/outgoing calls or the geographical location of mobile telephones, subscriber directories, the use of automated calling systems, and telephone or electronic marketing.

[3] These provide a parallel freedom of information regime for environmental information, which is accordingly exempted from the scope of the FOIA (s.39).

[4] See s.40 of the DPA.

[5] See s.43 of the DPA.

[6] See s.60 of the DPA.

[7] See s.55A of the DPA, applicable to breaches committed on or after April 6, 2010, and the Data Protection (Monetary Penalties) Order 2010 (SI 2010/910).

[8] See s.50 of the FOIA.

[9] See s.52 of the FOIA.

The Information Commissioner's statutory functions include the dissemination of information about the operation of the DPA and the FOIA.[10] Guidance is to be found on the web-site of the Commissioner's Office, as well as copies of the Commissioner's decisions.

8–009

The DPA

The DPA is a complex statute and its drafting has not escaped judicial criticism.[11] In *Campbell v MGN Ltd*,[12] the Court of Appeal said:

8–010

> "In interpreting the Act it is appropriate to look to the Directive for assistance. The Act should, if possible, be interpreted in a manner that is consistent with the Directive. Furthermore, because the Act has, in large measure, adopted the wording of the Directive, it is not appropriate to look for the precision in the use of language that is usually to be expected from the parliamentary draftsman. A purposive approach to making sense of the provisions is called for."

The DPA governs the *processing* of *personal data*, but there has been surprising difficulty in identifying the scope even of these central concepts.

Processing

The definition in s.1 of "processing" appears on its face to be very broad:

8–011

> "(1)   ... 'Processing', in relation to information or data, means obtaining, recording or holding the information or data or carrying out any operation or sets of operations on the information or data, including:
> (a)   organisation, adaptation or alteration...
> (b)   retrieval, consultation or use...
> (c)   disclosure..., or
> (d)   alignment, combination, blocking, erasure or destruction...
> (2)   ...
> (a)   'obtaining' or 'recording', in relation to personal data, includes obtaining or recording the information to be contained in the data, and
> (b)   'using' or 'disclosing', in relation to personal data, includes using or disclosing the information contained in the data..."

Automatic manipulation of data is clearly covered by this definition, but the significance of such automatic manipulation often lies in the manner in which the data was selected in the first place, or in the manner in which it is subsequently used. In *Campbell v MGN Ltd*,[13] the Court of Appeal stated that:

> "The Directive and the Act define processing as 'any operation or set of operations'. At one end of the process 'obtaining the information' is included, and at the other end 'using the information'. While neither activity in itself may sensibly amount to

---

[10] See s.51 of the DPA and s.47 of the FOIA.
[11] The Court of Appeal in *Campbell v MGN Ltd* [2003] EWCA Civ 1373; [2003] Q.B. 633 described it at [72] as a "cumbersome and inelegant piece of legislation".
[12] [2003] EWCA Civ 1373; [2003] Q B. 633 at [96]. (The DPA did not receive separate consideration by the House of Lords.)
[13] [2003] 1 Q B. 633 at [103].

processing, if that activity is carried on by, or at the instigation of, a 'data controller', as defined, and is linked to automated processing of the data, we can see no reason why the entire set of operations should not fall within the scope of the legislation. On the contrary, we consider that there are good reasons why it should."

In *Johnson v Medical Defence Union*,[14], the claimant surgeon complained that an employee of the defendant mutual society had made an unfair selection of information relating to him in preparing a computerised "Risk Assessment Review" form, as a result of which the claimant's membership of the defendant (and access to the defendant's insurance scheme) had been wrongfully terminated. Rimer J., at first instance referred[15] to the Court of Appeal's dicta in *Campbell v MGN Ltd* and rejected the defendant's argument that the selection by the defendant's employee had involved the application of her own, non-automatic judgment, and therefore did not constitute processing within the meaning of the DPA. He held that the selection of material and its inputting into a computer amounted to "processing" for the purposes of the Act.

The majority of the Court of Appeal (with Arden L.J. dissenting on this point) took a different view.[16] Buxton L.J., with whom Longmore L.J. agreed, concluded from his analysis of both the language of the Data Protection Directive and the statutory definition of "data" in s.1 that the DPA was intended to govern only automated processing, on the one hand, and processing of material in a relevant filing system, on the other. Moreover, the purpose of the Directive was to protect the privacy of individuals and not to provide them with new causes of action arising from the loss of employment rights or insurance cover. Arden L.J., however, took the view that the restrictive approach favoured by the majority was not justified by the language of the Directive or the DPA.

The Court of Appeal was unanimous in its conclusion that any processing by the defendant that might have taken place had not been unfair in any event and rejected the claimant's request for a reference to the European Court of Justice. However, the issues raised in relation to the intended scope of the Directive and the DPA are both important and complex and have not yet been fully resolved.

Data

8–012   The courts have sought to set limits to the scope of the DPA by careful scrutiny both of what constitutes "data" and of what data is "personal". "Data" is defined in s.1 as:

> " . . . information which—
>
> (a)   is being processed by means of equipment operating automatically in response to instructions given for that purpose,
> (b)   is recorded with the intention that it should be processed by means of such equipment,
> (c)   is recorded as part of a relevant filing system or with the intention that it should form part of a relevant filing system,

---

[14] [2006] EWHC 321 (Ch).
[15] [86]—[97].
[16] [2007] EWCA Civ 262; [2007] 3 C.M.L.R. 9.

(d)   does not fall within paragraph (a), (b) or (c) but forms part of an accessible record as defined by section 68[17]; or

(e)   is recorded information held by a public authority and does not fall within paragraphs (a) to (d)."

Durant v Financial Services Authority[18] concerned the extent of the rights of   **8–013**
an individual, who had brought unsuccessful proceedings against his bank, to gain access under s.7 to information about him that was held by the Financial Services Authority in its capacity as the bank's regulator. The Court of Appeal considered a number of issues relating to the construction of the DPA, including the question whether the FSA's manual files fell within the scope of para.(c) of the DPA's definition of "data". The DPA's definition of "a relevant filing system"[19] is:

> "any set of information relating to individuals to the extent that, although the information is not processed by means of equipment operating automatically in response to instructions given for that purpose, the set is structured, either by reference to individuals or by reference to criteria relating to individuals, in such a way that specific information relating to a particular individual is readily accessible."

Auld L.J., who gave the leading judgment, observed[20] that: **8–014**

> "It is clear from those provisions that the intention is to provide, as near as possible, the same standard or sophistication of accessibility to personal data in manual filing systems as to computerised records."

Auld L.J. considered that any wider approach would be impractical and unfair to data controllers:

> "To leave it to the searcher to leaf through files, possibly at great length and cost, and fruitlessly, to see whether it or they contain information relating to the person requesting information and whether that information is data within the Act bears . . . no resemblance to a computerised search."[21]

He concluded[22] that "a relevant filing system" was one:

> "(1)   in which the files forming part of it are structured or referenced in such a way as clearly to indicate at the outset of the search whether specific information capable of amounting to personal data of an individual . . . is held within the system and, if so, in which file or files it is held; and (2) which has, as part of its own structure or referencing mechanism, a sufficiently sophisticated and detailed means of readily indicating whether and where in an individual file or files specific criteria or information about the applicant can be readily located."

---

[17] As defined at s.68 and in Schs 11 and 12, "accessible records" include health records, educational records and local authority housing and social services records.
[18] [2003] EWCA Civ 1746; [2004] F.S.R. 28.
[19] At s.1.
[20] At [34].
[21] At [48].
[22] At [50].

By virtue of paragraph (e) of the DPA's definition of "data",[23] this significant limitation in respect of information stored manually no longer applies to information held by public authorities. However, protection for public authorities is achieved instead by s.33A, which provides exemptions for manual data held by public authorities. Moreover, s.9A now provides that a public authority is not obliged to comply with a data subject's request for access to "unstructured personal data" (as defined in s.9A), unless the request contains a description of the data; and even then the authority is not obliged to comply if the cost of compliance exceeds either £450 or £600.[24]

Personal data

8–015   In *Durant v Financial Services Authority* the Court of Appeal also adopted a restrictive approach to the meaning of *personal* data. Section 1 defines personal data as:

" . . . data which relates to a living individual who can be identified—

(a)   from those data, or
(b)   from those data and other information which is in the possession of, or is likely to come into the possession of, the data controller,

and includes any expression of opinion about the individual and any indication of the intentions of the data controller or any other person in respect of the individual."

8–016   Observing that the ultimate purpose of an individual's right to have access to information in the form of "personal data" was the protection of privacy, Auld L.J. rejected the suggestion that all information retrieved from a computer search against an individual's name or unique identifier was personal data within the DPA. He concluded[25]:

"It seems to me that there are two notions that may be of assistance. The first is whether the information is biographical in a significant sense, that is, going beyond the recording of the putative data subject's involvement in a matter or an event that has no personal connotations, a life event in respect of which his privacy could not be said to be compromised. The second is one of focus. The information should have the putative data subject as its focus rather than some other person with whom he may have been involved or some transaction or event in which he may have figured or have had an interest, for example, as in this case, an investigation into some other person's or body's conduct that he may have instigated. In short, it is information that affects his privacy, whether in his personal or family life, business or professional capacity."

The Court of Appeal's tethering of the meaning of personal data to the concept of privacy is immediately attractive, but does not resolve all problems in this area.

One possible difficulty in applying the second notion referred to by the Court—that of focus—is that (since the DPA relates not to documents but to

---

[23] Introduced by amendment with effect from January 1, 2005.

[24] At para.3 of the Freedom of Information and Data Protection (Appropriate Limit and Fees) Regulations 2004 (SI 2004/3244).

[25] At para.28.

information) much information is likely to be composite and capable of being broken down into more specific items of information. For example, the fact that 100 named individuals attended a meeting includes within it at least 100 further separate pieces of information, namely that X attended the meeting, that Y attended the meeting, that Z attended the meeting, etc. The overall list of attendance at the meeting may not be information that has X as its focus, but it is less easy to say that the specific information that X attended the meeting clearly does not have X as its focus.

It has also been said that the Court of Appeal's approach requires too proximate a link between the relevant data and the putative data subject, resulting in a test that is more restrictive than is warranted by the words of the underlying Directive.[26] In *Department of Health v Information Commissioner*[27] Cranston J. summarised the conclusions which were reached by a European Commission Data Protection Working Party[28]:

> "It noted that the proposal of the European Commission for a directive had been amended to meet the wishes of the European Parliament, that the definition of personal data should be as general as possible so as to include all information concerning an identifiable individual. It also noted the objective of the rules in the directive as being to protect individuals. The working party stated that the better option was not to restrict unduly the interpretation of the definition of personal data, but rather to note that there was considerable flexibility in the application of the rules to the data. National authorities should endorse a definition which was wide enough so that it would catch all 'shadow zones' within its scope, while making legitimate uses of the flexibility contained in the directive. The text of the directive invited a development of policy which combined a wide interpretation of the notion of personal data and an appropriate balance in the application of the directive's rules.
> The working party report continued that, in general terms, information could be considered to relate to an individual when it was about that individual."

The difference between this approach and the Court of Appeal's reference in *Durant v Financial Services Authority* to biographical focus might be regarded as a distinction of degree, rather than kind. However, it is suggested that as a matter of common sense some restrictions on the scope of the Act are desirable if absurdity is to be avoided.

Anonymisation

A further difficulty arises from the definition of personal data in s.1(1) of the DPA.[29] In *Common Services Agency v Scottish Information Commissioner*[30] a researcher for a member of the Scottish Parliament requested disclosure from a health authority, under the Freedom of Information (Scotland) Act 2002, of data about the incidence of childhood leukaemia in Dumfries and Galloway. The principal issue was whether the effect of anonymising the data in such a way that

---

[26] Eady J. discussed these difficulties of interpretation in *Quinton v Peirce* [2009] EWHC 912 (QB); [2009] F.S.R. 17 at [60]–[68].
[27] [2011] EWHC 1430 (Admin) at [21]–[22].
[28] *Opinion 4/2007 on the concept of personal data* (adopted on June 20, 2007).
[29] Set out at para.8–015 above.
[30] [2008] UKHL 47; [2008] 1 W.L.R. 1550.

it could not lead to identification of the subjects would render it no longer personal information within the meaning of DPA for the purposes of disclosure to the researcher. The House of Lords ordered that the application for disclosure should be remitted to the Scottish Information Commissioner for him to determine whether the information could be sufficiently anonymised for it not to be "personal data" but there were different strands of reasoning in the judgments, and Lord Hope's judgment (with which Lord Hoffmann and Lord Mance was inclined to agree) has given rise to arguments about the proper understanding of his analysis.[31]

In *All Party Parliamentary Group on Extraordinary Rendition v Information Commissioner* it was argued that the effect of the House of Lords' decision was that even where no recipient could identify the individuals concerned, the fact that the data controller (which had done the anonymisation) would be able to do so had the effect that the information remained personal data and that disclosure could therefore only be justified by showing that it was in accordance with data protection principles. Blake J. accepted that this appeared to result from part of Lord Hope's reasoning, but he rejected the argument. He accepted that this construction would give rise to absurdities.[32] He concluded that:

"...the best analysis is that disclosure of fully anonymised information is not a breach of the protection of the Act because at the moment of disclosure the information loses its character as personal data. It remains personal data in the hands of the data controller, because the controller holds the key, but it is not personal data in the hands of the recipients, because the public cannot identify any individual from it."[33]

On his analysis the relevant "processing" was the publication of the anonymised data:

"We consider that the publication of fully anonymised data, or other plain vanilla data from which other individuals cannot be identified, does not involve a processing of personal data."[34]

Blake J.'s reasoning is cogent. It accords with the underlying purpose of the Act, with the summary in the law reporter's headnote and with the form of order made

---

[31] *All Party Parliamentary Group on Extraordinary Rendition v Information Commissioner* [2011] UKUT 153 (AAC) and *R. (Department of Health) v Information Commissioner* [2011] EWHC 1430 (Admin).

[32] At [126]: "...on the MOD's construction, the number of individuals who have died of heart disease in the UK over the last decade would amount to "personal data" if this number were in the hands of data controller that held the underlying records identifying each individual concerned, however large that number might be, but it would plainly not be a sensible construction of the DPA to require all processing of such a wholly general piece of information to comply with the data protection principles".

[33] *All Party Parliamentary Group on Extraordinary Rendition v Information Commissioner* [2011] UKUT 153 at [128].

[34] *All Party Parliamentary Group on Extraordinary Rendition v Information Commissioner* [2011] UKUT 153 at [130].

by the House of Lords. It was a necessary foundation of the order that it was a legal possibility that the information might be sufficiently anonymised for it not to be "personal data".[35]

In any event, it is apparent that, on whatever grounds they proceed, the courts are reluctant to inhibit the use of properly anonymised statistical data—especially in circumstances where such use may be of real importance to medical and other forms of scientific research.

Sensitive personal data

Sensitive personal data attract a higher level of protection. Section 2 defines sensitive personal data as data consisting of information as to: **8–017**

(a)   the racial or ethnic origin of the data subject,
(b)   his political opinions,
(c)   his religious beliefs or other beliefs of a similar nature,
(d)   whether he is a member of a trade union,
(e)   his physical or mental health or condition,
(f)   his sexual life,
(g)   the commission or alleged commission by him of any offence, or
(h)   any proceedings for any offence committed or alleged to have been committed by him, the disposal of such proceedings or the sentence of any court in any such proceedings.

The data protection principles

The DPA imposes duties on a data controller[36] and gives rights to an individual who is the subject of personal data. Section 17 prohibits the processing of computerised data[37] except by registered data controllers and ss.18 to 20 contain further provisions relating to registration.[38]   **8–018**

Section 4 requires all data controllers to comply with the DPA's data protection principles. These are set out in Pt I of Sch.1[39]:   **8–019**

"1.   Personal data shall be processed fairly and lawfully and, in particular, shall not be processed unless—
    (a)   at least one of the conditions in Schedule 2 is met, and
    (b)   in the case of sensitive personal data, at least one of the conditions in Schedule 3 is also met.

---

[35] In *R. (Department of Health) v Information Commissioner* [2011] EWHC 1430 (Admin) Cranston J. considered Blake J.'s reasoning to be attractive, but not open to him. We prefer Blake J.'s approach for the reasons set out above.

[36] i.e. "any person who (either alone or jointly or in common with other persons) determines the purposes for which and the manner in which any personal data are, or are to be, processed": s.1 of the DPA.

[37] i.e. data falling within paragraphs (a) or (b) of the definition of data in s.1 of the DPA.

[38] See also the Data Protection (Notification and Notification Fees) Regulations 2000 (SI 2000/188), as subsequently amended.

[39] As elaborated upon in Pt II of Sch.1.

2. Personal data shall be obtained only for one or more specified and lawful purposes, and shall not be further processed in any manner incompatible with that purpose or those purposes.
3. Personal data shall be adequate, relevant and not excessive in relation to the purpose or purposes for which they are processed.
4. Personal data shall be accurate and, where necessary, kept up to date.
5. Personal data processed for any purpose or purposes shall not be kept for longer than is necessary for that purpose or those purposes.
6. Personal data shall be processed in accordance with the rights of data subjects under this Act.
7. Appropriate technical and organisational measures shall be taken against unauthorised or unlawful processing of personal data and against accidental loss or destruction of, or damage to, personal data.
8. Personal data shall not be transferred to a country or territory outside the European Economic Area unless that country or territory ensures an adequate level of protection for the rights and freedoms of data subjects in relation to the processing of personal data."

Schedules 2 and 3 set out detailed conditions relevant for the purpose of the first data protection principle. By way of example, the first condition in Sch.2 (relating to the processing of personal data) is that the data subject has given his consent to the processing, while the first condition in Sch.3 (relating to the processing of sensitive personal data) is that the data subject has given his *explicit* consent to the processing of the personal data.

The concept of "fairness" for the purposes of the first data protection principle is explained in Pt II of Sch.1. In *Common Services Agency v Scottish Information Commissioner*,[40] at [30], Lord Hope summarised it in this way:

"It is concerned essentially with the method by which the information is obtained, and in particular with whether the person from whom it was obtained was deceived or misled. In this case the processing which is in issue is the disclosure of statistical information in the possession of the agency, and there is no suggestion that any unfairness of that kind will be involved."

Paragraph 2 of Pt II of Sch.1 also appears on its face to impose an obligation on data processors, not only to avoid deceiving or misleading data subjects, but also to take positive steps to inform data subjects of such matters as the purpose or purposes for which the data are intended to be processed. This potentially very onerous obligation on data processors is at least subject to a "practicability" qualification.[41]

Condition 5 of Sch.3 is that the information contained in the personal data has been made public as a result of steps deliberately taken by the data subject. In *Murray v Express Newspapers Plc*,[42] Patten J. held that the infant claimant could not complain that the publication of photographs revealing his racial or ethnic origin infringed the data protection principles because, through his parents, the

---

[40] [2008] 1 W.L.R. 1550

[41] In *Quinton v Peirce* [2009] EWHC 912 (QB); [2009] F.S.R. 17 at [93], Eady J. rejected in robust terms an argument based on a literal interpretation of paras 2 and 3 of Pt II of Sch.1 to the Act: "I decline, however, to interpret the statute in a way which results in absurdity". See also *Chief Constable of Humberside Police v Information Commissioner* [2009] EWCA Civ 1079; [2010] 1 W.L.R. 1136, per Waller L.J. at [48].

[42] [2007] EWHC 1908 (Ch).

claimant had deliberately exposed his image to the public by appearing in a public place. In allowing the claimant's appeal against Patten J.'s decision to strike out the claimant's claim (both at common law and under the DPA),[43] the Court of Appeal did not find it necessary expressly to address Patten J.'s views on this point.[44]

Data subject rights

The rights of data subjects under the DPA include the following: **8–020**

(1)   Under s.7, a right of access to personal data.
(2)   Under s.10, a right to prevent processing that is likely to cause damage or distress, if the damage or distress is "unwarranted".
(3)   Under s.11, a right to prevent processing for the purposes of direct marketing.
(4)   Under s.12, a right to restrain the automated taking of decisions that significantly affect the individual, for example in relation to his performance at work, his creditworthiness, his reliability, or his conduct.
(5)   Under s.14, a right to apply to the court for an order to rectify, block, erase, or destroy inaccurate personal data relating to the applicant (and any expression of opinion based on that data).

Of these rights, the first is probably the one to which appeal is most often made. Under subs.7(1),[45] an individual is entitled:

"(a)   to be informed by any data controller whether personal data of which that individual is the data subject are being processed by or on behalf of that data controller,

(b)   if that is the case, to be given by the data controller a description of—
   (i)   the personal data of which that individual is the data subject,
   (ii)   the purposes for which they are being or are to be processed, and
   (iii) the recipients or classes of recipients to whom they are or may be disclosed,

(c)   to have communicated to him in an intelligible form—
   (i)   the information constituting any personal data of which that individual is the data subject, and
   (ii)   any information available to the data controller as to the source of those data, and

(d)   where the processing by automatic means of personal data of which that individual is the data subject for the purpose of evaluating matters relating to him such as, for example, his performance at work, his creditworthiness, his reliability or his conduct, has constituted or is likely to constitute the sole basis for any decision significantly affecting him, to be informed by the data controller of the logic involved in that decision-taking."

---

[43] [2008] EWCA Civ 446; [2009] Ch. 481.
[44] See also *Quinton v Peirce* [2009] EWHC 912 (QB) at [69], in which Eady J. described as "formidable" an argument that an election leaflet relating to the claimant's public record contained only information which the claimant had himself put in the public domain.
[45] Upon payment of any proper fee required, in accordance with the Data Protection (Subject Access) (Fees and Miscellaneous Provisions) Regulations 2000 (SI 2000/191) (as amended).

An individual is not entitled to nominate specific categories of personal data to which he or she requires access. There is on the data controller only "a simple duty to supply the data subject with the whole of the information held upon him by way of personal data when he requests it".[46] However, there is nothing to prevent the data controller and the data subject agreeing voluntarily to limit the scope of a request and response.

Further effect is given to the rights of data subjects by s.13 of the DPA, which provides a right to compensation for damage or distress caused by contravention of a requirement of the DPA, subject to a defence that the defendant took reasonable care to comply with the requirement. In *Johnson v Medical Defence Union*,[47] the Court of Appeal confirmed the correctness of Rimer J.'s view at first instance that s.13 does not permit recovery of damages for loss of reputation.

In *Murray v Express Newspapers Plc*,[48] Patten J. held that where data processing contravened a provision of the Act, a claimant's entitlement to compensation under s.13 should be calculated by reference to his loss arising from the contravention, rather than his loss arising from the processing. Thus the Claimant's compensation claim arising from the Defendant's failure to inform him of the use to be made of his photographs depended on whether that failure had caused him loss, and not on whether the subsequent (deemed unfair) processing had caused him loss. However, on appeal,[49] the Court of Appeal held that it was at least arguable that Patten J. had adopted too narrow an approach, having regard to the fact that the purpose of the DPA was to enact the provisions of the relevant Directive.

Exemptions

8–021   The DPA contains a large number of exemptions for specified categories of information from some or all of the data protection principles or provisions of the DPA.[50] Some of these are couched in terms of considerable complexity. One of the most briefly expressed and (as it affects the scope of the Act) most significant of the exemptions is that provided by s.36:

> "Personal data processed by an individual only for the purposes of that individual's personal, family or household affairs (including recreational purposes) are exempt from the data protection principles and the provisions of Parts I and II."

8–022   Other exemptions relate to national security (s.28), crime and taxation (s.29), health, education and social work (s.30), regulatory activity (s.31), journalism, literature and art (s.32), research, history and statistics (s.33), information available to the public by or under an enactment (s.34), disclosures required by law or made in connection with legal proceedings (s.35), Parliamentary privilege

---

[46] per Laws J. in *R. v Chief Constable of B County Constabulary* (November 1997; reported in the Encyclopedia of Data Protection and Privacy, at para.6–544), a case relating to the Data Protection Act 1984, rather than the DPA.
[47] [2007] EWCA Civ 262; [2007] 3 C.M.L.R. 9, per Buxton L.J. at [78].
[48] [2007] EWHC 1908 (Ch).
[49] [2009] Ch. 481 at [63].
[50] Categorised as "subject information provisions" and "non-disclosure provisions", as defined at s.27.

(s.35A), confidential references (para.1 of Sch.7), the armed forces (para.2 of Sch.7), judicial appointments and honours (para.3 of Sch.7), Crown employment and Crown or Ministerial appointments (para.4 of Sch.7), management forecasts (para.5 of Sch.7), corporate finance (para.6 of Sch.7), negotiations (para.7 of Sch.7), examination marks (para.8 of Sch.7), examination scripts (para.9 of Sch.7), legal professional privilege (para.10 of Sch.7) and self-incrimination (para.11 of Sch.7).

Moreover, under s.38, the Secretary of State has the power to make further exemption orders. Part II of the Data Protection (Miscellaneous Subject Access Exemptions) Order 2000[51] exempts information, the disclosure of which is prohibited or restricted by ss.31 and 33 of the Human Fertilisation and Embryology Act 1990 (Pt I of the Schedule to the Order), and adoption records, statements of special education needs and parental order records and reports (Pt II of the Schedule to the Order). 8–023

Public interest

Section 32 largely excludes from the data protection principles the processing of personal data with a view to the publication of journalistic, literary or artistic material, where the data controller reasonably believes that publication would be in the public interest, having regard in particular to the special importance of the public interest in freedom of expression. 8–024

The Data Protection (Processing of Sensitive Personal Data) Order 2000[52] lists a number of circumstances in which sensitive personal data may be processed in the public interest. The provisions are complex. 8–025

Offences

The DPA creates a number of criminal offences, punishable by fine. Among the relevant sections are s.21 (registration-related offences) and s.47 (offences in relation to enforcement notices or information notices). Section 55 creates offences in relation to the unlawful obtaining or disclosure of personal data. Under subs.55(1): 8–026

> "A person must not knowingly or recklessly, without the consent of the data controller—
>
> (a)   obtain or disclose personal data or the information contained in personal data, or
> (b)   procure the disclosure to another person of the information contained in personal data."

The effect of this prohibition is mitigated under subs.55(2) by disapplying subs.55(1) to:

> " . . . a person who shows—

---

[51] SI 2000/419.
[52] SI 2000/417. Further circumstances are listed in subsequent orders (SI 2002/2905, SI 2006/2068, SI 2009/1811 and SI 2012/1978).

(a) that the obtaining, disclosing or procuring—
  (i) was necessary for the purpose of preventing or detecting crime,
  (ii) was required or authorised by or under any enactment, by any rule of law or by the order of a court,
(b) that he acted in the reasonable belief that he had in law the right to obtain or disclose the data or information or, as the case may be, to procure the disclosure of the information to the other person,
(c) that he acted in the reasonable belief that he would have had the consent of the data controller if the data controller had known of the obtaining, disclosing or procuring and the circumstances of it, or
(d) that in the particular circumstances the obtaining, disclosing or procuring was justified as being in the public interest."[53]

The FOIA

8–027   Subsection 1(1) of the FOIA provides that:

"Any person making a request for information to a public authority is entitled—

(a) to be informed in writing by the public authority whether it holds information of the description specified in the request, and
(b) if that is the case, to have that information communicated to him."

Public authorities are defined in s.3. Their ranks are from time to time augmented or reduced by statutory instrument. Although the definition proceeds by way of reference to a list in Schedule 1 to the Act, it has not been without its difficulties, as has been demonstrated by the decision of the House of Lords in *British Broadcasting Corp v Sugar*[54] and the subsequent decision of the Court of Appeal in *British Broadcasting Corp v Sugar (No.2)*.[55]

Sections 8 to 17 are largely procedural, providing for the manner in which requests must be made and answered. Of particular significance, s.14 provides that a public authority is not obliged to comply with vexatious or (until a reasonable interval has elapsed) repeated requests. Section 19 requires public authorities to maintain publication schemes, setting out what classes of information they intend to publish, how they intend to publish them and whether they intend to make them available to the public free of charge.

8–028   Part II of the FOIA contains numerous total or partial exemptions, including exemptions for:

- information accessible by other means (s.21),
- information intended for future publication (s.22),
- information supplied by or relating to "security" organisations, such as MI5, MI6, GCHQ, special forces, etc. (s.23),
- information the exemption of which is required for the purpose of safeguarding national security (s.24),

---

[53] Pursuant to an amendment effected by the Criminal Justice and Immigration Act 2008 (but not yet in force), the scope of subs.55(2) will be broadened from a date to be appointed by a new subs.55(2)(ca).
[54] [2009] UKHL 9; [2009] 1 W.L.R. 430.
[55] [2010] EWCA Civ 715; [2010] 1 W.L.R. 2278.

- information the disclosure of which would be likely to prejudice defence or the operation of the armed forces, or forces cooperating with the armed forces (s.26),
- information the disclosure of which would be likely to prejudice international relations (s.27), or relations between the devolved government administrations of Scotland, Northern Ireland and Wales and/or the United Kingdom government (s.28),
- information the disclosure of which would be likely to prejudice the economy (s.29),
- information relating to certain investigations and proceedings conducted by public authorities (s.30),
- information the disclosure of which would be likely to prejudice various law enforcement matters, such as the prevention or detection of crime, or the administration of justice (s.31),
- information in court records, etc. (s.32),
- information held by public auditors (s.33),
- information bearing on the formulation of government policy (s.35),
- information the disclosure of which would be likely to prejudice the effective conduct of public affairs, by (for example) inhibiting the free and frank provision of advice, or the free and frank exchange of views for the purposes of deliberation (s.36),
- information relating to communications with members of the Royal Family or the honours system (s.37), and
- information the disclosure of which would be likely to endanger the health or safety of an individual (s.38).

Sections 39 and 40 (in broad terms) exempt information available under the Environmental Information Regulations 2004 or the DPA.

Section 41 provides a significant and wide-ranging exemption for information if: **8–029**

> "(a) it was obtained by the public authority from any other person (including another public authority), and
> (b) the disclosure of the information to the public (otherwise than under this Act) by the public authority holding it would constitute a breach of confidence actionable by that or any other person."

Section 42 exempts legally privileged information. Section 43 exempts trade secrets and information the disclosure of which would be likely to prejudice the commercial interests of any person (including the authority holding it). Finally, under s.44, information is exempted if its disclosure is prohibited by or under any enactment, is incompatible with any Community obligation, or would constitute or be punishable as a contempt of court.[56]

Exemptions may be expressed by the legislation to be absolute or qualified in their effect and, when they are qualified, the court may be required to balance competing public interests in favour of disclosure or non-disclosure. A good

---

[56] See, for example, *Secretary of State for the Home Office v British Union for the Abolition of Vivisection* [2009] 1 W.L.R. 636 (disclosure prohibited under s.24 of the Animals (Scientific Procedures) Act 1986).

example of the potential complexity of this exercise is provided by the decision of the Upper Tribunal (Administrative Appeals Chamber) in *Evans v Information Commissioner*,[57] in which the Tribunal held that the Information Commissioner had been wrong to uphold refusals by seven government departments to disclose correspondence between Prince Charles and ministers in the departments.

8–030   Part IV of the FOIA deals with enforcement. Section 56 provides that the FOIA does not confer any right of action in civil proceedings in respect of any failure to comply with any duty imposed by or under the Act. However, s.54 provides that a public authority that fails to comply with the Information Commissioner's notices may be dealt with by the High Court as if it had committed a contempt of court.[58]

8–031   Part V covers appeals from the Information Commissioner's notices and decisions, while Pt VI contains provisions relating specifically to historical and public records.

The DPA and the FOIA in confidentiality cases

8–032   To date, the impact of the DPA and the FOIA in cases relating to the general law of confidentiality has been limited. This may be due to a combination of two factors: the availability of remedies for breach of confidence at common law and in equity, as extended under human rights jurisprudence,[59] and the daunting complexity of the legislation, particularly the DPA. Where, for example, issues of public interest are raised, the parties may well surmise that the court is likely to arrive at the same result whether by applying common law or Art.8 principles or by following the more tortuous routes of the DPA and the regulations made under it. Thus, in the House of Lords in *Campbell v MGN Ltd*,[60] the parties simply agreed that Naomi Campbell's claim under the DPA stood or fell with the outcome of the main claim.

---

[57] [2012] UKUT 313 (AAC).

[58] See also s.77, which creates a specific offence of altering, defacing, blocking, erasing, destroying, or concealing, any record held by a public authority with the intention of preventing the disclosure of information to which the applicant would have been entitled.

[59] In *Douglas v Hello! Ltd* [2003] EWHC 786, (Ch); [2003] 3 All E.R. 996 at [230]–[239], Lindsay J. found that there was a breach of the DPA but that this did not provide a separate route to the recovery of damages beyond those to which the claimants were entitled for breach of confidentiality. No point was raised under the DPA when the case went to appeal. Similarly, in *Quinton v Peirce* [2009] EWHC 912 (QB) [2009] F.S.R. 17 at [87], Eady J. said of the DPA: "I am by no means persuaded that it is necessary or proportionate to interpret the scope of this statute so as to afford a set of parallel remedies when damaging information has been published about someone, but which is neither defamatory nor malicious."

[60] [2004] UKHL 22; [2004] 2 A.C. 457. See [32] and [130].

CHAPTER 9

Remedies

INJUNCTION

A final injunction may be granted to a successful claimant in an action for breach   **9–001**
of confidence (whether arising in contract or from an equitable obligation of
confidence) or for inducement of breach of contract, in order to prevent
continuation of the wrongful conduct. It may also be granted, quia timet, to
prevent threatened breach of confidence. In all such cases the court has a
discretion whether to grant an injunction and, if so, on what terms and for what
period. The question of duration arises particularly in "springboard" cases,[1]
where the injunction should not normally extend beyond the period for which
unfair advantage may reasonably be expected to continue.[2]

The Human Rights Act 1998 s.12, requires the court to have particular regard   **9–002**
to the importance of the right to freedom of expression under Art.10 of the
European Convention in considering whether to grant relief which might affect
the exercise of that right.[3]

An interim injunction may be granted on the principles set out in *American*   **9–003**
Cyanamid v Ethicon,[4] except in a case where Art.10 may be engaged. In those
circumstances s.12(3) provides that no such relief may be granted unless the court
is satisfied that the applicant is likely to establish at the trial that publication
should not be allowed. This provision has been construed by the House of Lords
as meaning that the court should not make an interim restraint order unless
satisfied that the applicant's prospects of success at trial are sufficiently
favourable to justify the order being made in all the circumstances; and that
generally this will require the applicant to satisfy the court that it would probably
find that publication should not be allowed, but that there could be circumstances
in which a lesser degree of likelihood would be sufficient.[5] Where an interim
restraining injunction is sought urgently without notice, the test is whether the
court considers that there is a sufficient degree of likelihood that the claimant will
succeed at the trial to justify an injunction for a short period until the court can
consider the matter at a hearing between the parties.[6]

---

[1] See Ch.4, above.
[2] *Potters-Ballotini Ltd v Weston-Baker* [1977] R.P.C. 202 at 206; *Roger Bullivant Ltd v Ellis* [1987]
F.S.R. 172 at 183–184; *Sun Valley Foods Ltd v Vincent* [2000] F.S.R. 825.
[3] See paras 6–048 above and 13–010, below.
[4] [1975] A.C. 396.
[5] *Cream Holdings Ltd v Banerjee* [2004] UKHL 44; [2005] 1 A.C. 253.
[6] *ASG v GSA* [2009] EWCA Civ 1574 at [5].

9–004   Independently of Convention considerations, where the period for which interlocutory relief is sought would be likely to expire before the trial, it is proper for the court to take into account the claimant's prospects of success at trial.[7]

9–005   Any injunction must be framed in terms sufficiently specific to leave no uncertainty what the affected person is or is not allowed to do.[8] In *Times Newspaper Ltd v MGN Ltd*,[9] the Court of Appeal held that no injunction could be granted to prevent premature publication of a pirated version of Lady Thatcher's memoirs, because the plaintiffs had to concede that vital parts of the book would have to be excepted from the scope of any injunction and the drafting of such an exception could not be satisfactorily achieved.

9–006   *Universal Thermosensor Ltd v Hibben*[10] provides salutary warning against obtaining an interlocutory injunction in too wide terms. In that case the plaintiff succeeding in establishing breach of duty of confidence, but, having obtained an interlocutory injunction in excessively wide terms which led to the collapse of the defendants' business, it had to pay damages to the defendants on its cross undertaking. Sir Donald Nicholls V.C. recognised that he had a discretion not to enforce the undertaking, and also found that the defendants had acted dishonestly, but he rejected the plaintiff's argument that the undertaking should for that reason not be enforced. He said[11]:

> "Punishment of the defendants is not my function. If the defendants have suffered material loss by reason of excessive width in the terms of the injunction sought and obtained by the plaintiff in July 1990, in my view they are entitled to look to the plaintiff for damages pursuant to its undertaking. Plaintiffs, and those who advise them, know or ought to know that there is a risk in obtaining interlocutory injunctive relief: the risk is that the plaintiff may have to pay compensation to the defendant if it turns out at the trial that, having regard to the facts and law as established at the trial, the effect of the injunction was to restrain a defendant from activities which it ought to have been at liberty to pursue."

If it appears to the court that a claim, ostensibly brought for the protection of the claimant's privacy, is in substance a claim to protect the claimant's reputation, it will not grant an injunction unless satisfied that the claimant will establish that the damage to reputation will be unjustified, by analogy with the rule in *Bonnard v Perryman*.[12] However, this approach should not be taken too far. It is no

---

[7] *Lansing Linde v Kerr* [1991] 1 All E.R. 418; *Sun Valley Foods Ltd v Vincent* [2000] F.S.R. 825; *Browne v Associated Newspapers Ltd* [2007] EWCA Civ 295; [2008] Q.B. 103 at [63]–[65].

[8] *Potters-Ballotini Ltd v Weston-Baker* [1977] R.P.C. 202; *Lawrence David Ltd v Ashton* [1991] 1 All E.R. 385; PSM *International Plc v Whitehouse* [1992] 1 I.R.L.R. 279; *Times Newspaper Ltd v MGN Ltd* [1993] E.M.L.R. 442; *CMI-Centres for Medical Innovation GmbH v Phytopharm Plc* [1999] F.S.R. 235; *Att Gen v Punch Ltd* [2002] UKHL 50; [2003] 1 A.C. 1046, especially per Lord Nicholls at [33]–[37] and per Lord Hope at [111].

[9] [1993] E.M.L.R. 443.

[10] [1992] 1 W.L.R. 840.

[11] [1992] 1 W.L.R. 840 at 858.

[12] [1891] 2 Ch. 269, followed in *Greene v Associated Newspapers Ltd* [2004] EWCA Civ 1462; [2005] Q.B. 972. The approach was applied in *Terry v Persons Unknown* [2010] EWHC 119 (QB); [2010] E.M.L.R. 16 at [95] and [123]. The claimant, a leading footballer, applied to the court to restrain publication concerning an adulterous relationship. There was no evidence from the claimant himself, but the application was supported by a statement from his solicitor based on information supplied by the claimant's "business partners". No information was provided about the nature of their business relationship, but the evidence included a statement that the claimant had a number of high

defence to a claim for misuse of confidential information that the claimant disputes the truthfulness of the defendant's account.[13] A claimant may also have legitimate reasons not to wish to be drawn into addressing the truth or falsity of the alleged private information.[14]

The problem of the unidentified defendant

A person may become aware of a threatened breach of confidentiality without knowing the source of the leak. In *X v Persons Unknown*[15] a celebrity model and her husband had cause for concern that an anonymous friend was leaking private details about their marriage to a number of media organisations. In *TUV v Persons Unknown*[16] a laptop computer belonging to the claimant was stolen in a burglary of her home. On it were stored a number of private pictures of the claimant and others, which she feared were likely to be circulated to the media. In both cases the court granted an interim injunction against persons identified only by a general description, sometimes known as a John Doe injunction.

9–007

The injunctions were granted on applications made without notice to the defendants, since their identity was unknown. However, since the purpose was to enable the claimants to give notice of the orders to media organisations, Eady J. considered what advance notice ought to be given to them in such circumstances. He recognised that this would depend on the facts of each case, but in general he considered that the claimant should be obliged to give advance notice to any media organisation which was believed to have shown an interest in publishing the material, unless this was impracticable or there were compelling reasons for not doing so.[17]

In *X v Persons Unknown* Eady J. referred to the problem of identifying the information to be protected in a way which distinguished between "matters which are naturally accessible to outsiders and those which are known only to the protagonists". He suggested that the solution might be, as in that case, to attach to the order a confidential schedule containing specific allegations of a private character which there was reason to suppose would be made public in the absence of protective relief.[18] However, in many cases claimants might wish for understandable reasons not to have to set out in explicit detail the precise nature of rumoured allegations about their private lives, which they are seeking to restrain media organisations from publishing, and they may not know precisely what the source has said to the media. It should generally be possible to describe the category or categories of information to be protected in a way which is not so

9–008

---

profile sponsorship or endorsement deals. The evidence also included a written confidentiality agreement signed by the woman concerned, in consideration of payment of £1, but there was no explanation of the circumstances in which the agreement came to be made. Tugendhat J. concluded on the evidence available to him that the real basis of the claimant's concern was the effect of the proposed publication on the business of earning sponsorship, rather than any other aspect of his life, and he refused to grant an injunction. The judgment contains a full review of the relevant authorities.

[13] *McKennitt v Ash* [2006] EWCA Civ 1714; [2008] Q.B. 73.

[14] *WER v REW* [2009] EWHC 1029 (QB); [2009] E.M.L.R. 17.

[15] [2006] EWHC 2783 (QB); [2007] E.M.L.R. 10.

[16] [2010] EWHC 853 (QB); [2010] E.M.L.R. 19.

[17] See *Practice Guidance on Interim Non-disclosure Orders* [2012] 1 W.L.R. 1003 at [18]–[23].

[18] [2006] EWHC 2783 (QB); [2007] E.M.L.R. 10 at [38]–[40].

broad or loose as to include matters which are anodyne or otherwise readily accessible, but without having to go into full details.[19]

On such an application there is a duty on the applicant to reveal to the court, so far as is practicable in the circumstances, any material which is reasonably likely to assist the respondents' probable counter-arguments. That does not mean that there is a duty to put before the court everything which a respondent might dredge up, but the applicant's advocate must make a conscientious determination as to which points he or she would wish to make, if instructed to represent media organisations on the other side.[20]

The court has jurisdiction to grant a permanent injunction against the world at large, sometimes called a *contra mundum* injunction, but such injunctions are exceptional.[21]

9–009   More conventionally, the court may grant a permanent injunction against a person who has threatened to commit a breach of confidentiality, and it is difficult to see any reason in principle why notice of the injunction should not be served on third parties.

In *OPQ v BJM*[22] a woman negotiated with a newspaper group to sell intimate photographs of the claimant obtained in circumstances which were clearly private and in respect of which she owed the claimant a duty of confidentiality. At the same time someone acting on her behalf contacted the claimant's solicitors to say that she would rather do "a deal" with him. It was in Eady J.'s words "a straightforward and blatant blackmail case". The claimant was granted an interim injunction and the parties reached an agreement including provision for the defendant to give a permanent undertaking not to publish any of the confidential material. The claimant also applied to the court for what was described as a *contra mundum* injunction, which Eady J. granted.

It is understandable that the claimant wished to make sure of the position, but on the facts he would have been unquestionably entitled to a permanent injunction against the defendant, and he should not have needed any additional order to enable him to serve notice of the injunction on third parties.

Eady J. referred to the so-called "Spycatcher doctrine", named after *Attorney-General v Newspaper Publishing Plc*. In that case the Court of Appeal held that third parties who know that the court has made orders or accepted undertakings designed to protect the confidentiality of information pending trial are guilty of contempt if they take action to damage or destroy the confidentiality which the court is seeking to protect and so render the legal process ineffectual.[23]

---

[19] For example, in *Donald v Ntuli* [2010] EWCA 1276; [2011] 1 W.L.R. 294 at [26]–[34], the Court of Appeal rejected an argument that the phrase "any intimate, personal or sexually explicit details about the [parties'] relationship" lacked sufficient clarity.

[20] *X v Persons Unknown* at [42]–[53]. See also *Practice Guidance (Interim Non-disclosure Orders)* [2012] 1 W.L.R. 1003 at [30].

[21] *Venables v News Group Newspapers Ltd* [2001] Fam. 430 at [98]–[100]. An injunction was granted to protect the identities of two individuals who murdered a small boy when they were aged 10. The judge was satisfied that the injunction was necessary to protect them from the real risk of suffering serious injury or death on their release into the community. The jurisdiction was recognised in *Re S (a child)* by the Court of Appeal at [2003] EWCA Civ 963; [2004] Fam. 43 at [98]–[99] (Lord Phillips M.R.) and the House of Lords at [2004] UKHL 47; [2005] 1 A.C. 593. See also *A Local Authority v A Mother* [2011] EWHC 1764 (Fam), per Baker J. at [22].

[22] [2011] EWHC 1059 (QB).

[23] [1988] Ch. 333 at 375E per Sir John Donaldson M.R.

Eady J. said that it is generally thought that once a permanent injunction has been granted the *Spycatcher* doctrine will no longer apply. However, there is a wider principle that it is a contempt for a non-party to aid and abet a contempt of court by a party, and that includes assisting a breach of an injunction of which the non-party has notice.[24] A newspaper which bought the pictures in *OPQ v BJM* and published them, with knowledge of an injunction prohibiting the supplier from publishing them, would be liable to be held in contempt. There is no good reason for restricting that principle to the period during which the injunction was temporary, and it would be absurd if the claimant's protection were reduced by the injunction being made permanent.

Superinjunctions and anonymity[25]

A "superinjunction" is an injunction which includes an order prohibiting a person on whom it is served from disclosing the fact that the injunction has been made.   **9–010**

The principle of open justice requires that court proceedings, including the making of an order, should be public unless an exception is justified by some even more important principle, the most common exception being where the particular circumstances are such that openness would put at risk the achievement of justice which is the purpose of the proceedings.[26]

Superinjunctions originated with orders such as freezing orders, search orders and orders made under the Proceeds of Crime Act 2002 against a suspect's bank or professional adviser, which may commonly include a superinjunctive provision intended to prevent the person suspected of serious wrongdoing from being tipped off about the order before it has been executed. From the establishment of the jurisdiction to grant a superinjunction, the practice developed of applicants asking that the making of orders restraining the publication of confidential information should be kept secret, for fear that if it became public knowledge that such an order had been made there would be speculation as to the nature of the confidential information, a likelihood of versions of it (true or false) appearing on the internet, and a danger of jigsaw identification.   **9–011**

In *Donald v Ntuli*[27] the Court of Appeal emphasised that while a claimant is entitled to expect that the proceedings will be conducted in such a way as not to undermine the confidentiality which he is seeking to protect, the open justice principle requires that any restriction should be the least that is necessary.

An order that the existence of legal proceedings should be kept secret is so contrary to the fundamental principle of open justice that it is hard to envisage circumstances in which a court would consider such an order to be proper, except where a temporary embargo may be needed so as to enable the proceedings to be effective.   **9–012**

Alternative measures include anonymisation of the proceedings or restriction of disclosure of the nature or subject matter of the action. The test is what degree

---

[24] *Z v A-Z* [1982] Q.B. 558.

[25] In these paragraphs we summarise the principles. There is a fuller discussion of the case law in Ch.20 below.

[26] *Scott v Scott* [1913] A.C. 417; *R. (Guardian News and Media Ltd) v City of Westminster Magistrates Court* [2012] EWCA Civ 420.

[27] [2010] EWCA Civ 1276; [2011] 1 W.L.R. 294.

of protection is required for the purposes of the proper administration of justice. Before granting an application that the order of the court should not include the names of the parties, or that there should be a restriction on the extent to which the proceedings may be reported, it is essential that (a) the judge is satisfied that the facts and circumstances are sufficient to justify encroaching on the open justice rule, and (b) the judge ensures that the restrictions on publication are fashioned so as to satisfy the need for the encroachment in a way which minimises the extent of any restrictions.[28]

Wherever possible, the judge should give an open judgment, with such redactions as may be necessary, for the reason given by Eady J. in *CDE v MGN Ltd*:

> "The most important element of open justice in this case, as with many other privacy and confidentiality cases, is that interested observers and legal practitioners should be able to monitor the court's processes and form a view as to whether judges are applying a consistent, fair and balanced approach in the application of this recently developed jurisprudence to the facts of individual cases."[29]

Although it is more likely to be the claimant who asks for an injunction to be anonymised, such an application may be made by a defendant. In *Re Guardian News and Media Ltd*[30] anonymity was sought by persons against whom freezing orders were made under anti-terrorism legislation. The basis of the application was that naming them publicly as persons suspected of being involved in terrorism would cause infringement of their rights under Art.8. The Supreme Court considered the interplay between Art.8 and Art.10 and concluded that there was a powerful, public interest in permitting identification.

Destruction or delivery up

9–013   The court has power to order delivery up or destruction of material containing confidential information or derived from misuse of confidential information, unless possibly the material has substantial intrinsic value independently of the misuse of confidential information.

---

[28] *JIH v News Group Newspapers Ltd* [2011] EWCA Civ 42; [2011] 1 W.L.R. 1645 at [22], on appeal from [2010] EWHC 2818 (QB). Tugendhat J. and the Court of Appeal were agreed that on the facts of the case the choice lay between not allowing the public to know the claimant's identity but allowing them to know what the action was about, or allowing them to know the claimant's identity but not allowing them to know anything of the subject matter. Tughendhat J. concluded that the claimant had not passed the high test necessary for anonymity, but that the information which could be published about the nature of the action should be strictly limited. The Court of Appeal took the opposite approach and allowed the claimant's application for anonymity, but in its judgment set out what the action was about. Both judgments contain a valuable discussion of the issues and demonstrate that the point was arguable either way. It is perhaps surprising that the court interfered with the judge's exercise of his discretion in those circumstances,

[29] [2010] EWHC 3308 (QB) at [84]. The judgment contains a detailed commentary on the principles and the competing considerations.

[30] [2010] UKSC 1; [2010] 2 A.C. 697.

In *Prince Albert v Strange* the defendant opposed an order for delivery up or destruction of the catalogues and the impressions of the royal etchings which were in his possession. Knight-Bruce V.C. said[31]: 9–014

> "It is then said that neither the copies of the catalogue, nor the impressions that have been taken, can be delivered, or be directed to be delivered up, inasmuch as the Defendant contends that he is entitled to the property in the materials on which they are printed. With regard to catalogues, no such question, I think, arises. They must be either cancelled or destroyed; and without destruction they can hardly be cancelled. With regard to the impressions, it might possibly be right to attend to the Defendant's claim, had the impressions been upon a material of intrinsic value—upon a material not substantially worthless, except for the impressions which, by the wrongful act of the Defendants, have been placed there. That case, however, does not arise. The material here is substantially worthless, except for that in which the Defendant has no property. There consequently can be no reason why the effectual destruction of subject should not be directed by the Court."

This passage was cited and applied by Dunn J. in *Franklin v Giddins*, where he ordered the delivery up for destruction of fruit trees propagated by the defendant from budwood cuttings stolen from the plaintiff's orchard.[32]

The court's power is discretionary. In *Saltman*, where the defendants misused confidential drawings of tools for the manufacture of leather punches, the report records that[33]: 9–015

> "In the course of the discussion as to the relief to be given to the Plaintiffs, their Lordships expressed reluctance to make any order which would involve the destruction or sterilisation of tools which would serve a useful purpose, since under Lord Cairns's Act the Court could award damages, to cover both past and future acts, in lieu of an injunction."

The order finally agreed was that the defendants should deliver up the drawings, and that there should be an inquiry as to the damages suffered by the plaintiffs by reason of the defendants' conduct in using the drawings for the construction of leather punches for sale on their own account.

Where the successful plaintiff seeks an order for delivery up of material containing confidential information it will usually be granted, especially if the defendant cannot be relied on to destroy it.[34] In *Robb v Green*,[35] for example, the defendant was ordered to deliver up for destruction a customer list which he had surreptitiously copied while employed by the plaintiff, and an injunction was granted restraining him from making use of the information so obtained.[36] 9–016

In *AG Australia Holdings Ltd v Burton*[37] a former employee of a company involved in litigation gave confidential information to solicitors acting for the opposing party. The court ordered that materials, including draft witness 9–017

---

[31] (1849) 2 De G. & S.M. 652 at 716. The point does not appear to have been argued on the defendant's appeal before Cottenham L.C.

[32] [1978] Qd.R. 72 at 81–83. See para.3–035, above.

[33] (1948) 65 R.P.C. 203 at 219.

[34] *Industrial Furnaces Ltd v Reaves* [1970] R.P.C. 605 at 627.

[35] [1895] 2 Q.B. 315.

[36] See also *Reid & Sigrist Ltd v Moss* [1932] 49 R.P.C. 461; and *Peter Pan Manufacturing Corp v Corsets Silhouette Ltd* [1964] 1 W.L.R. 96.

[37] [2002] N.S.W.S.C. 170.

statements or affidavits, relating to the disclosures made by the employee should be placed in store in sealed containers marked with notices that they were not to be opened without permission of the court.

In *Tchenguiz v Imerman*,[38] during divorce proceedings the wife's brothers accessed the husband's computer and made copies of documents, because they feared that he would conceal his assets in ancillary relief proceedings. The court ordered that the documents should be delivered up to the husband's solicitors, but it imposed terms that the documents were to be preserved and should remain in solicitors' possession, unless otherwise agreed by the wife's solicitors or ordered by the court, so that the husband could not dispose of them before the determination of the wife's claim for ancillary relief.

Account of profits

9–018　　Account of profits is an established form of equitable relief. In the *Spycatcher* case the *Sunday Times* was held liable to account to the Crown for profits from its breach of duty of confidence in publishing material from Mr Wright's memoirs, before the information had entered the public domain, knowing that Mr Wright was acting in breach of duty of confidence in disclosing the information. Lord Keith said[39]:

> "An account of profits made through breach of confidence is a recognised form of remedy available to a claimant (*Peter Pan Manufacturing Corporation v Corsets Silhouette Ltd* [1964] 1 W.L.R. 96; *cf. Reading v Attorney-General* [1951] A.C. 507). In cases where the information disclosed is of a commercial character an account of profits may provide some compensation to the claimant for loss which he has suffered through the disclosure, but damages are the main remedy for such loss. The remedy is, in my opinion, more satisfactorily to be attributed to the principle that no one should be permitted to gain from his own wrongdoing. Its availability may also, in general, serve a useful purpose in lessening the temptation for recipients of confidential information to misuse it for financial gain. In the present case 'The Sunday Times' did misuse confidential information and it would be naive to suppose that the prospect of financial gain was not one of the reasons why it did so. I can perceive no good ground why the remedy should not be made available to the Crown in the circumstances of this case, and I would therefore hold the Crown entitled to an account of profits in respect of the publication on 12 July, 1987."

Lord Goff expressed reservations about a general statement that a man is not to be allowed to profit from his own wrong and preferred to place the remedy of an account on a restitutionary basis. He said:[40]

> "The statement that a man shall not be allowed to profit from his own wrong is in very general terms, and does not of itself provide any sure guidance to the solution of a problem in any particular case. That there are groups of cases in which a man is not allowed to profit from his own wrong, is certainly true. An important section of the law of restitution is concerned with cases in which a defendant is required to make restitution in respect of benefits acquired through his own wrongful act—notably cases of waiver of tort; of benefits acquired by certain criminal acts; of

---

[38] [2010] EWCA Civ 908; [2011] Fam. 116.
[39] [1990] 1 A.C. 109 at 262.
[40] [1990] 1 A.C. 109 at 286.

benefits acquired by certain criminal acts; of benefits acquired in breach of a fiduciary relationship; and, of course, of benefits acquired in breach of confidence. The plaintiff's claim to restitution is usually enforced by an account of profits made by the defendant through his wrong at the plaintiff's expense. This remedy of an account is alternative to the remedy of damages, which in cases of breach of confidence is now available, despite the equitable nature of the wrong, through a beneficent interpretation of the Chancery Amendment Act 1858 (Lord Cairns' Act), and which by reason of the difficulties attending the taking of an account is often regarded as a more satisfactory remedy, at least in cases where the confidential information is of a commercial nature, and quantifiable damage may therefore have been suffered."

The rule that the remedy of an account is an alternative remedy to damages was historically explained on the basis that by seeking an account the plaintiff adopted the defendant's acts,[41] and he therefore could not claim both. A better explanation is that both are forms of compensation for wrongful conduct at the plaintiff's expense and that to allow both would lead to over-compensation.

In *Att Gen v Blake*[42] Lord Nicholls said that if the information disclosed by the former intelligence officer had still been confidential at the time of his book's publication, an account of profits would have been ordered "almost as a matter of course".
9–019

The distinctive features of the case were that the loss of confidentiality was largely a result of his own past treachery, of which the book was an autobiographical account, and that he was in breach of contract in publishing the book even though its contents were no longer confidential. The House of Lords held that an account of profits was an appropriate remedy for the breach of contract. It recognised that for a breach of contract the remedies normally appropriate are damages for the loss suffered by the innocent party, an injunction or specific performance. But Lord Nicholls observed[43]:
9–020

"Sometimes the injured party is given the choice: either compensatory damages or an account of the wrongdoer's profits. Breach of confidence is an instance of this. If confidential information is wrongfully divulged in breach of a non-disclosure agreement, it would be nothing short of sophistry to say that an account of profits may be ordered in respect of the equitable wrong but not in respect of the breach of contract which governs the relationship between the parties. With the established authorities going thus far, I consider that it would be only a small step for the law to recognise openly that, exceptionally, an account of profits may be the most appropriate remedy for breach of contract."

An account may be combined with other remedies apart from damages. In *Peter Pan Manufacturing Corp v Corsets Silhouette Ltd*,[44] where the defendants misused confidential design information to produce two styles of bra, Pennycuick J. granted an injunction restraining the defendants from manufacturing, using or distributing those styles, an order for destruction or delivery up of existing stocks and an account of profits made from those styles.

---

[41] *Sutherland Publishing Co Ltd v Caxton Publishing Co Ltd* [1936] Ch. 323 at 336.
[42] [2001] 1 A.C. 268 at 287.
[43] [1990] 1 A.C. 109 at 285.
[44] [1964] 1 W.L.R. 96.

9–021   A breach of confidentiality does not give to the claimant an automatic right to an account of profits in preference to compensatory damages. The question is one for the court's discretion, as was held in *Vercoe v Rutland Fund Management Ltd*.[45] The claimants approached the defendant venture capital enterprises with a view to a management buy in acquisition of a pawnbroker's business. They entered into a written confidentiality agreement which the defendants broke by proceeding with the idea but cutting out the claimants. It was agreed that if damages were the appropriate remedy, they should be assessed by reference to the notional fee which the defendants would have paid to be released from their obligation of confidentiality on the information known to the parties and in the commercial context at the time, on the assumption that both parties had been willing to negotiate reasonably, but the claimants argued for an account of profits. The argument was rejected.

Sales J. observed that Lord Nicholls' speech in *Att Gen v Blake* had opened the way to a principled examination of the circumstances in which it would be appropriate to award an account of profits. The question was whether the claimant's interest in the performance of the obligation (whether contractual or equitable) made it just and equitable that the defendant should receive no benefit from his conduct. Where the right infringed was similar to a property right of a kind which is regularly bought and sold in a market, damages assessed by a notional buy-out fee may often represent a fair remedy. By contrast, there may be cases in which it would not be reasonable to expect that the right could be bought out by a fee, such as the promise to keep state secrets which was in issue in *Att Gen v Blake* or a right under a fiduciary relationship, where the central obligation of the fiduciary is to act in the interests of the beneficiary. The law of confidentiality covered a wide range of different relationships and the strength of the argument in favour of a particular remedy might vary across the range. In some cases the nature of the relationship would be very close to a fiduciary relationship, where the appropriate remedy might be the same as for a breach of trust; in some it would be a commercial relationship at arm's length, in which the appropriate remedy might be similar to the ordinary remedies for breach of contract; and in some cases, where the law of confidentiality was used to protect private information obtained by a stranger, the most appropriate analogy might be with the law of tort.[46]

Constructive trust

9–022   In some jurisdictions (notably Australia, Canada and the USA) the courts have developed the concept of a constructive trust as a discretionary remedy. The difference between an "institutional" and a "remedial" constructive trust is that the former arises by operation of law as from the date of the circumstances which give rise to it, and the function of the court is merely to declare that it has arisen; the latter arises when the court decides that it is the most appropriate remedy for unconscionable behaviour.[47]

---

[45] [2010] EWHC 424 (Ch) at [333]–[334].
[46] [2010] EWHC 424 at [337]–[344].
[47] *Westdeutsche Bank v Islington London Borough Council* [1996] A.C. 669 at 714–715 (Lord Browne-Wilkinson).

In *Beatty v Guggenheim Exploration Co*[48] Cardozo J. said: **9–023**

> "A court of equity in decreeing a constructive trust is bound by no unyielding formula. The equity of the transaction must shape the measure of relief."

In *U.S. Surgical Corp v Hospital Products International Pty Ltd*[49] the **9–024** defendants, who were exclusive distributors in Australia of surgical stapling instruments manufactured by the plaintiffs, marketed their own similar product in circumstances which were found by the trial judge, McLelland J., to amount to a breach of a fiduciary duty owed to the plaintiffs. The plaintiffs sought relief on the basis of a constructive trust over the defendants' assets. McLelland, J. said[50]:

> "Liability for breaches of equitable obligations may be of either a restitutionary or a compensatory nature. Restitutionary relief may be given by way of the imposition of a constructive trust over specific property (specific restitution) or by an accounting for profits. The imposition of a liability to account for profits is essentially a personal rather than a proprietary remedy, but it may in some cases be appropriate to impose an equitable lien over specific property by way of security for such accounting. In the area of relief against what used to be called equitable fraud, of which profiting from a fiduciary position is one example, the precise form of relief must be moulded to satisfy the demands of justice and good conscience in the particular case: 'the court must look at the circumstances in each case to decide in what way the equity can be satisfied' (*Chalmers v Pardoe* [1963] 1 W.L.R. 677 at 682; [1963] 3 All E.R. 552 at 555; 'the equity of the transaction must shape the measure of the relief': *Beatty v Guggenheim Exploration Co.* 122 N.E. 378 [1919], at 381; 225 N.Y. 380, at 389)."

He held that the assets of the defendants' manufacturing business were not property the obtaining or pursuing of which was or ought to have been an incident of the defendants' fiduciary duty, and therefore it would not be right to impose a constructive trust over those assets in favour of the plaintiffs. Instead he ordered an account of profits from sales of the defendants' rival products. He also directed that the defendants' liability to account should be secured by an equitable lien over the defendants' assets, holding that the imposition of such a lien was a matter within the discretion of the court.[51]

In *Muschinski v Dodds*[52] a constructive trust was imposed from the date of the **9–025** court's order by a majority of the High Court of Australia (Gibbs C.J., Deane and Mason JJ.).[53]

---

[48] (1919) 225 N.Y. 380 at 389, cited by Mason J. in *Hospital Products Ltd v U.S. Surgical Corp* (1984) 156 C.L.R. 41 at 108. See also *Snepp v United States* (1980) 444 U.S. 507, in which the Supreme Court of the United States imposed a constructive trust on the proceeds of sale of a book written by a former CIA agent and—in breach of an express contractual obligation—not submitted for pre-publication review.

[49] [1982] 2 N.S.W.L.R. 766, reversed in the High Court on the ground that no fiduciary relationship existed between the parties ((1984) 156 C.L.R. 41).

[50] [1982] 2 N.S.W.L.R. 766 at 812–813.

[51] Citing Goff and Jones, *The Law of Restitution,* 2nd edn (1978), pp.47, 48 and 61, but see now Goff and Jones, 8th edn (London: Sweet & Maxwell, 2011), Chs 37 and 38.

[52] (1985) 160 C.L.R. 583 at 615, 623.

[53] See also *Giumelli v Giumelli* [1999] H.C.A. 10; (1999) 196 C.L.R. 101, where the court said that a constructive trust should not be imposed if there is an adequate alternative remedy.

9–026   In *LAC Minerals Ltd v International Corona Resources Ltd*[54] the defendant acquired mining rights through misuse of information given to it in confidence by the plaintiff, which would otherwise have obtained the mining rights and developed the mine for itself. The trial judge declared that the defendant held the property on trust for the plaintiff, and he ordered it to deliver up the property on being compensated for the value of improvements it had made to the property in developing the mine. The order was upheld (by a majority) by the Supreme Court of Canada. La Forest J. said[55]:

> "The issue then is this. If it is established that one party (here LAC) has been enriched by the acquisition of an asset, the Williams property, that would have, but for the actions of that party, been acquired by the plaintiff (here Corona) and if the acquisition of that asset amounts to a breach of duty to the plaintiff, here either a breach of fiduciary obligation or a breach of a duty of confidence, what remedy is available to the party deprived of the benefit? In my view the constructive trust is one available remedy, and in this case it is the only appropriate remedy.
>
> In my view the facts present in this case make out a restitutionary claim, or what is the same thing, a claim for unjust enrichment. When one talks of restitution, one normally talks of giving back to someone something that has been taken from them (a restitutionary proprietary award), or its equivalent value (a personal restitutionary award). As the Court of Appeal noted in this case, Corona never in fact owned the Williams property, and so it cannot be 'given back' to them. However, there are concurrent findings below that, but for its interception by LAC, Corona would have acquired the property. In *Air Canada v British Columbia* (judgment pronounced May 4, 1989 [now reported at 59 D.L.R. (4th) 161 at pp.193–194, B.C.L.R. (2d) 145; [1989] 4 W.W.R. 97]), I said that the function of the law of restitution 'is to ensure that where a plaintiff has been deprived of wealth that is either in his possession *or would have accrued for his benefit*, it is restored to him. The measure of restitutionary recovery is the gain the [defendant] made at the [plaintiff's] expense.' In my view the fact that Corona never owned the property should not preclude it from the pursuing [of] a restitutionary claim: see Birks, *An Introduction to the Law of Restitution* (1985), at pp.133–139. LAC has therefore been enriched at the expense of Corona."

The minority would have awarded damages as the appropriate remedy.

9–027   In *Soulos v Korkontzilas*[56] the defendant real estate broker entered into negotiations on behalf of the claimant for the purchase of a property. The defendant failed to inform the claimant of a counter-offer by the vendor, which the claimant would have accepted, but instead purchased the property through a nominee. At the time of the trial the value of the property had fallen. The claimant sought an order imposing a constructive trust over the property on terms that he should pay the defendant the purchase price subject to adjustments for its fall in value and for losses incurred on it since its purchase. He claimed to have a special interest in the property. The trial judge refused the claim for a constructive trust on the ground that the defendant had paid the market value of the property and there had been no unjust enrichment. The claimant succeeded on appeal and the Court of Appeal's decision was upheld by a majority of the Supreme Court.

---

[54] [1990] F.S.R. 441; (1989) 61 D.L.R. (4th) 14. See para.2–091, above.
[55] [1990] F.S.R. 441 at 469.
[56] [1997] 2 S.C.R. 217.

The minority would have limited the remedy of constructive trust to cases of unjust enrichment. The majority held that, under the broad umbrella of good conscience, a constructive trust might be imposed for wrongful acts such as fraud and breach of a duty of loyalty as well as in cases of unjust enrichment. In cases of unjust enrichment the court identified four conditions which generally should be satisfied:

(1)   The defendant must have been under an equitable obligation in relation to the activities giving rise to the assets in his hands;

(2)   The assets in the hands of the defendant must have resulted from activity in breach of his obligation to the claimant;

(3)   The claimant must show a legitimate reason for seeking a proprietary remedy, either personal or related to the need that others like the defendant should remain faithful to their duties; and

(4)   There must be no factors which would render the imposition of a remedial trust unjust in all the circumstances (for example, the interests of intervening creditors).[57]

In *Murphy Oil Company Ltd v The Predator Corp Ltd* [58] Nation J. reviewed the Canadian authorities and commented: **9–028**

"Generally, the cases about the misuse of confidential information, and breach of confidence, establish that if the wrongdoer acquires actual property that would otherwise have been acquired by the plaintiff, an *in rem* remedy such as a constructive trust may well be suited to right the wrong, especially if it directs the title of the property to the party in whose name it would have been 'but for' the breach. On the other hand, where the nature of the detriment is that a competitor obtained a time advantage in getting into the market with a competitive product, then the best remedy may be damages for the loss of dominance of the market for that period of time."

The ability of the court to impose a remedial constructive trust was provisionally recognised by the Court of Appeal of New Zealand in *Fortex Group Ltd v MacIntosh*[59] and its provisional conclusion was supported by Tipping J. in the Supreme Court in *Regal Castings Ltd v Lightbody.*[60]

English courts have been cautious about the concept of a remedial constructive trust.[61] In *Westdeutsche Bank v Islington London Borough Council*[62] Lord

---

[57] [1997] 2 S.C.R. 217 at [43]–[45].

[58] [2006] ABQB 680 at [121] (Court of Queen's Bench of Alberta).

[59] [1998] 3 N.Z.L.R. 171 at 172–173.

[60] [2008] N.Z.S.C. 87; [2008] 2 N.Z.L.R. 434 at [162]. The case itself was unrelated to confidentiality and there was no discussion of the general principles on which such a remedy might be appropriate. In *Boat Harbour Holdings Ltd v Steve Mowat Building & Construction Ltd* [2012] N.Z.C.A. 305 at [51], Ellen France J. described the availability of a remedial constructive trust as a matter of debate. See also Jessica Palmer, *Attempting Clarification of Constructive Trusts* (2010) 24 NZULR 113 (cited by Ellen France J.).

[61] *Metall und Rohstoff AG v Donaldson Lufkin & Jenrette Inc* [1990] 1 Q.B. 391 at 478–480; *Westdeutsche Bank v Islington London Borough Council* [1996] A.C. 669; *Re Polly Peck International Plc (No.2)* [1998] 3 All E.R. 812 at 823–825. For a general discussion, see Matthew Conaglen, "Thinking about proprietary remedies for breach of confidence" (I.P.Q. 2008, 1, 82–109). Conaglen questions the foundation for a constructive trust based on a breach of confidentiality and argues that,

Browne-Wilkinson observed that a remedial constructive trust might provide a satisfactory remedy against a holder of property of which the claimant had been unjustly deprived, and, since the remedy could be tailored to the facts of the particular case, injustice to innocent parties could be avoided and restitutionary defences, such as change of position, could be given effect, but he left open for future decision whether English law should follow the courts of the USA and Canada in this area.

9–029   *Phipps v Boardman*[63] was a case of misuse of information by a fiduciary. The defendants bought shares in a company in which a trust had a substantial holding. They used their own money to buy the shares, but they were held to be in breach of fiduciary duty because they gained the opportunity to make the purchase from information acquired as agents of the trustees and they acted without full disclosure to the trustees. Wilberforce J. made an order declaring that they held the shares as constructive trustees, and his judgment was upheld by the House of Lords.[64]

9–030   In the *Spycatcher* case Dillon L.J. said[65]:

> "It has seemed to me throughout the hearing of this appeal that there could have been strong arguments for saying that, as Mr Wright wrote and published *Spycatcher* in breach of his duty of secrecy to the Crown and was only able to do so by the misuse of secret information which had come to him in the course of his employment as an officer in the Security Service of the Crown, the copyright in *Spycatcher* belongs in equity to the Crown and is held on constructive trust for the Crown with whatever consequences may follow from that."

The point was not argued by the Crown, but in the House of Lords a majority commented on it in terms suggesting that it might well be right.[66] None of the judges who referred to the point suggested that it would depend on the information being classified as property.

9–031   The House of Lords held in that case that the Sunday Times was liable to account to the Crown for profits from its breach of confidence in publishing information which it knew had been supplied to it by Mr Wright in breach of his duty of confidence. He was also a fiduciary, but none of the judgments suggest that the remedy of an account against the Sunday Times was dependent on that additional factor. The Crown did not argue (and would not have gained from arguing) that the Sunday Times was a constructive trustee of its profits, but the commentar in the 6th edition of Goff & Jones on the case included the suggestion that "in principle, a third party who instigates, or [sci. knowingly] participates in, a breach of trust should be deemed to be liable as if he were a trustee of any benefits directly or indirectly thereby gained".[67]

---

if such a remedy is to be developed, its exercise should be guided by principles and not left to a broad judicial discretion. See also Sir Terence Etherton, "A New Model For Equity and Unjust Enrichment" (2008) C.L.J. 265.

[62] [1996] A.C. 996 at 714–715.

[63] [1967] 2 A.C. 46.

[64] See para.2–039, above.

[65] [1990] 1 A.C. 109 at 211.

[66] [1990] 1 A.C. 109 at 263 (Lord Keith), 275–276 (Lord Griffiths), 288 (Lord Goff).

[67] *The Law of Restitution,* 6th edn (London: Sweet & Maxwell, 2002), para.33–033. The 8th edition (*Unjust Enrichment*, 2011) no longer comments on the case.

As a matter of justice, it is an attractive proposition. The same might also be argued in the case of a person who knowingly misuses confidential information, or who instigates or knowingly participates in the misuse of confidential information. The latter proposition was accepted by Chadwick J. but rejected by the Court of Appeal in *Satnam Investments Ltd v Dunlop Heywood & Co Ltd.*[68]   9–032

Satnam had an option to buy a site with development potential but the option could be terminated if it went into receivership, which it did. A surveyor who had been acting for Satnam disclosed to a rival company, M Ltd, that Satnam had an interest in the site, that it had gone into receivership and that the local planning authority was well disposed to development of the site. M Ltd bought the site. Chadwick J. found (and these findings were upheld by the Court of Appeal) that the surveyors acted in breach of their duty of confidentiality to Satnam as a fiduciary and that M Ltd knew this at the time of the disclosure. He held that Satnam lost its opportunity to acquire the site because of M Ltd's breach of duty and he declared that the site was held by M Ltd on trust for Satnam.   9–033

The Court of Appeal reversed his judgment for essentially three reasons. First, they found as a fact that the disclosure did not cause M Ltd to act in any way differently from the way in which it would have acted without the disclosure, because it would in any event have learned the facts disclosed to it within two weeks, well before it made an approach to the site owners. Secondly, it held that although M Ltd knew of the surveyors' breach of duty in making the disclosure it did not participate in it. Thirdly, it held that M Ltd could only be constructive trustees of the site if it was trust property or trust property could be traced into it.   9–034

The first reason presents no legal difficulty. If the disclosure made no material difference to M Ltd's behaviour, its acquisition of the site cannot be said to have been a benefit resulting from the disclosure. The second and third reasons are more difficult. The second reason could be explained as a corollary of the first (i.e. that M Ltd cannot be said to have participated in the surveyors' breach of duty if it neither solicited the breach of duty nor acted in any different way because of it), but that is not how it was expressed. The court held that the allegation that M Ltd had unconscionably used and taken advantage of the information could not be treated as one of dishonesty, and that dishonesty was required. But unconscionable (i.e. knowing) misuse of information supplied in breach of a duty by the surveyors should be enough to put M Ltd in the same position as the surveyors. The third reason involves a narrow approach. On this approach the suggestion canvassed by several judges in *Spyycatcher* that Mr Wright held the copyright in his book on constructive trust for the Crown would be unsustainable, except on the notion (not advanced in *Spycatcher* and now discredited) that the information disclosed by him was property owned by the Crown.   9–035

In *United Pan-Europe Communications NV v Deutsche Bank AG*, on an application for an interim injunction, the Court of Appeal accepted that where property was obtained through misuse of confidential information by a party owing a fiduciary duty of loyalty, the imposition of a constructive trust might be appropriate whether or not the innocent party would have acquired the property

---

[68] [1999] 3 All E.R. 652.

but for the wrongdoing. Morritt L.J. said that in such a case the purpose of the constructive trust was to ensure that the fiduciary did not profit from his breach of duty.[69]

In *Sinclair Investments (UK) Ltd v Versailles Trade Finance Ltd* Lord Neuberger M.R. said:

> "Whether a proprietary interest exists is a matter of property law, and is not a matter of discretion: see *Foskett v McKeown* [2001] 1 AC 102, 109 per Lord Browne-Wilkinson. It follows that the courts of England and Wales do not recognise a remedial constructive trust as opposed to an institutional constructive trust."[70]

This statement appears to have been undisputed and a repetition of what had been described by the trial judge as an uncontroversial proposition. The court was therefore not concerned with circumstances in which English law might recognise a remedial constructive trust. In *Foskett v McKeown*, to which reference was made, Lord Browne-Wilkinson described it as crucial to appreciate the nature of the purchasers' claim. The claim was not based on unjust enrichment, and the case did not involve any question of constructive trust. It is apparent from his remarks in *Westdeutsche Bank v Islington London Borough Council*, cited above, that Lord Browne-Wilkinson was not averse in principle to the possibility of a remedial constructive trust in appropriate circumstances.

9–036   Breach of confidentiality cases may differ widely in their nature.[71] They may also differ widely in their consequences. Both factors are relevant when considering in principle whether a constructive trust should be an available remedy. In some cases such an order will be the most direct way of compensating the claimant for his loss, where the result of the defendant's wrong has been to deprive the claimant of property which he would otherwise have obtained. In such a case a constructive trust ought to be an available remedy on a compensatory principle, although if the property was of a kind for which there was a readily available market and the case presented no special features, it is likely that damages would be a sufficient remedy. Such cases would fall into McLaughlin J.'s unjust enrichment category in *Soulos v Korkontzilas*.[72] It is more debatable whether and, if so, when a constructive trust should be available in order to deprive the wrongdoer of his profit, rather than as the fairest means of compensating the innocent party. This was the issue which divided the court in *Soulos v Korkontzilas*. There is a good case for such a remedy being available where the relationship is fiduciary or akin to a fiduciary relationship. In such a case an account of profits may be ordered against a person who has misused confidential information, and it is hard to see in principle why a court should not have jurisdiction to decree a constructive trust where property represents the profit. In *Att Gen v Blake*,[73] in which the House of Lords made an order for an account of profits, Lord Nicholls cited *Snepp v United States*,[74] in which the US

---

[69] [2000] EWCA Civ 166 at [47].

[70] [2011] EWCA Civ 347; [2011] 3 W.L.R. 1153.

[71] As Sales J. discussed in *Vercoe v Rutland Fund Management Ltd* [2010] EWHC 424 (Ch) in the context of a claim for an account of profits.

[72] [1997] 2 S.C.R. 217.

[73] [2001] 1 A.C. 268.

[74] (1980) 444 US 507.

Supreme Court imposed a constructive trust. Lord Nicholls observed that the facts of the two cases were very similar and described the order of an account of profits as "a different means to the same end". That being so, deciding which is the more appropriate form of remedy on a particular set of facts should be a matter of practicality.

It would be undesirable to extend the availability of a constructive trust beyond (a) cases where it would serve a compensatory purpose or (b) cases of or akin to a fiduciary relationship, at least in the absence of some special justification, not only because English law does not generally allow civil remedies aimed at punishing a wrongdoer, but also because it would lead to uncertainty and to the exercise of a general discretion in an area where the courts ought to be guided by established principles.

Damages

Damages are available at common law for breach of a contractual duty of confidence or inducement of breach of contract. Under the jurisdiction derived from Lord Cairns's Act 1858 (now contained in s.50 of the Senior Courts Act 1981) the court has a discretionary jurisdiction to award damages in addition to or in substitution for an injunction.   **9–037**

In *Malone v Metropolitan Police Commissioner*[75] Sir Robert Megarry V.C. said in relation to the right of confidentiality: **9–038**

> "This is an equitable right which is still in course of development, and is usually protected by the grant of an injunction to prevent disclosure of the confidence. Under Lord Cairns's Act 1858 damages may be granted in substitution for an injunction; yet if there is no case for the grant of an injunction, as when the disclosure has already been made, the unsatisfactory result seems to be that no damages can be awarded under this head: see *Proctor v Bayley* (1889) 42 Ch.D. 390. In such a case, where there is no breach of contract or other orthodox foundation for damages at common law, it seems doubtful whether there is any right to damages, as distinct from an account of profits."

The Law Commission said in its Report on Breach of Confidence[76] that, so far as the repetition of a past, or anticipation of a future, breach of confidence is concerned, the courts have been empowered since Lord Cairns's Act to award damages in addition to or in substitution for an injunction. Lord Goff also referred in the *Spycatcher* case, in the passage cited above,[77] to damages being available under the Act for breach of an equitable duty of confidence.[78]

A more problematical question has been the availability of damages in the situation instanced by Megarry V.C. where there is no case for the grant of an injunction. This is considered in Ch.2, dealing with the foundation[79] of the courts' jurisdiction in relation to breach of confidence. It is suggested that, quite apart from Lord Cairns's Act, compensation in equity (also known as equitable   **9–039**

---

[75] [1979] 1 Ch. 344 at 360.
[76] Law Com. No.110, Cmnd. 8388 (1981), para.4.73.
[77] See paras 2–074 and 9–018 above.
[78] The same approach was taken by the Full Court of the Victorian Supreme Court in *Talbot v General Television Corp Pty Ltd* [1981] R.P.C. 1; [1980] V.R. 224.
[79] Where alternatives including a tortious theory of liability are discussed.

damages) may be awarded generally for breach of an equitable duty of confidence, just as for breach of duty by a fiduciary; and that the same compensatory principles underlie compensation or damages in equity as underlie damages at common law.[80] Despite past doubts, it is now accepted that damages are available for breach of duty of confidence, whether in contract or in equity. These may in an appropriate case include loss of anticipated profits or "expectation damages".

9–040   In *United Scientific Holdings Ltd v Burnley Borough Council*[81] Lord Diplock said:

> "Your Lordships have been referred to the vivid phrase traceable to the first edition of *Ashburner, Principles of Equity* where, in speaking in 1902 of the effect of the Supreme Court of Judicature Act he says (p.23) 'the two streams of jurisdiction' (sc. law and equity)—'though they run in the same channel, run side by side and do not mingle their waters.' My Lords, by 1977 this metaphor has in my view become both mischievous and deceptive. The innate conservatism of English lawyers may have made them slow to recognise that by the Supreme Court of Judicature Act 1873 the two systems of substantive and adjectival law formerly administrated by courts of law and Courts of Chancery (as well as those administered by courts of admiralty, probate and matrimonial causes), were fused. As at the confluence of the Rhone and Saône, it may be possible for a short distance to discern the source from which each part of the combined stream came, but there comes a point at which this ceases to be possible. If Professor Ashburner's fluvial metaphor is to be retained at all, the waters of the confluent streams of law and equity have surely mingled now."

Lords Simon and Fraser made similar observations.[82]

9–041   In *Henderson v Merrett Syndicates Ltd*,[83] Lord Browne-Wilkinson, dealing with the relationship of law and equity in a different context, warned of the need to ensure that the law did not "become again manacled by 'clanking chains'[84] this time represented by causes, rather than forms of action". Similarly the court's power to award monetary compensation for breach of confidence should not differ according to whether the cause of action lies in contract or in an equitable obligation of confidence.[85]

9–042   In *Indata Equipment Supplies Ltd v ACL Ltd*[86] a financial broker agreed to arrange finance for a company which wanted to buy a new fleet of cars. The structure of the transaction was that the broker would buy the fleet from the manufacturer and sell it to a finance company, which would supply the fleet to the end user under a financial lease. The broker approached a finance company and gave it details of the end user's financial requirements, the price which the broker was paying to the supplier and its profit margin. Armed with this information, the

---

[80] *Royal Bank of Brunei v Tan* [1995] 2 A.C. 378. See the discussion by the Supreme Court of Canada in *Cadbury Schweppes Inc v FBI Foods Ltd* (1999) 167 D.L.R. (4th) 577, at paras 55–61.

[81] [1978] A.C. 904 at 924.

[82] [1978] A.C. 904 at 944 and 957.

[83] [1995] 2 A.C. 145 at 206.

[84] *United Australia Ltd v Barclays Bank Ltd* [1941] A.C. 1 at 29, per Lord Atkin. "When these ghosts of the past stand in the path of justice clanking their mediaeval chains the proper course for the judge is to pass through them undeterred".

[85] *Force India Formula One Racing Team v 1 Malaysia Racing Team Sdn Bhd* [2012] EWCA Civ 616 (Ch) at [424].

[86] [1998] 1 B.C.L.C. 412.

finance company approached the end user with an offer of better terms by cutting out the broker. The end user accepted the offer. The Court of Appeal held that (1) the finance company acted in breach of an equitable obligation of confidentiality to the broker; (2) the broker was entitled to damages; and (3) the correct measure of damages was "on the tortious basis, ie such sum as would have put the plaintiff into the position it would have been in had it not been for the tort or breach of confidence".[87] Two members of the court considered that the finance company committed the tort of unlawful interference with the broker's business, as well as breach of an equitable obligation, but the case shows that the court considered that the measure of compensation for breach of the equitable obligation of confidence was the same as for tort.

Where confidential information of a commercial nature has been misused, damages may be assessed by reference to its commercial value.[88] Such damages represent the amount which might reasonably have been paid for a licence to use the information as between a willing licensor and licensee (described as "negotiating damages" by Neuberger L.J. in *Lunn Poly Ltd v Liverpool & Lancashire Properties Ltd*[89] and also referred to as *Wrotham Park* damages[90]). Damages on this basis have been awarded in cases of breach of commercial confidentiality.[91] This approach is less likely to be justified in cases involving a domestic context. In *Douglas v Hello! Ltd (No.3)*,[92] the Court of Appeal upheld Lindsay J.'s refusal to award the Douglases damages equivalent to the notional licence fee that they would have charged Hello! to permit them to publish unauthorised photographs. The Court of Appeal made particular reference to the fact that, having sold the exclusive rights to publish photographs to OK!, the Douglases would not have been in a position to grant a licence to Hello!, but also observed[93]:

9–043

> "First, the whole basis of their . . . complaint about Hello!'s publication of the unauthorised photographs is upset and affront at invasion of privacy, not loss of the opportunity to earn money . . . That factor alone would not prevent an assessment on a notional licence fee basis, but it is not a good start. Secondly, the Douglases would never have agreed to any of the unauthorised photographs being published. The licence fee approach will normally involve a fictional negotiation, but the unreality of the fictional negotiation in this case is palpable."

Where misuse of confidential information relates to personal matters, damages can be awarded for mental stress or injury to feelings as well as for economic loss.

Although damages cannot ordinarily be recovered for injury to reputation or feelings,[94] there are exceptions. Defamation has always been an exception, because injury to reputation is the essence of the wrong. The courts have also

9–044

---

[87] [1998] 1 B.C.L.C. 412 at 425–427.
[88] *Seager v Copydex (No.2)* [1969] 1 W.L.R. 809 at 813 per Lord Denning M.R.
[89] [2006] EWCA Civ 430; [2006] 2 E.G.L.R. 29 at [22]–[25].
[90] *Wrotham Park Estate Co Ltd v Parkside Homes Ltd* [1974] 1 W.L.R. 798.
[91] *Pell Frischmann Engineering Ltd v Bow Valley Iran Ltd*[2009] UKPC 45; [2010] Bus. L.R. 73; *Vercoe v Rutland Fund Management Ltd* [2010] EWHC 424 (Ch).
[92] [2005] EWCA Civ 595; [2006] Q.B. 125 at [243]–[249].
[93] At [246].
[94] *Addis v Gramophone Co Ltd* [1909] A.C. 488.

made an exception in cases of contract where the subject matter of the contract is the provision of pleasure[95] or protection from distress,[96] as distinct from other contracts where mental distress is a foreseeable consequence of breach.[97] It is right that there should be a similar exception in the case of misuse of confidential information relating to personal matters, because here the law is intended to protect personal feelings.

9–045   In *Williams v Settle*[98] the defendant, a professional photographer, was employed to take photographs of the plaintiff's wedding. The copyright in the photographs vested in the plaintiff. Two years later the plaintiff's father-in-law was murdered. The defendant sold some of the photographs to the press, one of which, showing a wedding group, was published prominently in national newspapers. The trial judge awarded damages of £1,000, and this was upheld by the Court of Appeal.

9–046   In *Cornelius v de Taranto*[99] Morland J. awarded damages for distress caused by a doctor wrongly disclosing a medical report on her to other medical staff.

9–047   In *Campbell v MGN Ltd*[100] the claimant was awarded damages for distress caused by the publication of an article with photographs showing her leaving therapy session for drug addicts.

9–048   In *Douglas v Hello! Ltd*[101] the Court of Appeal upheld an award of damages for personal distress and economic loss resulting from the publication of surreptitiously taken photographs of the claimants' wedding.

In the past, awards of compensation for distress caused by publication of private information have been low, but more recently the courts have shown a willingness to make larger awards particularly in bad cases.

In *Armonas v Lithuania*[102] the applicant complained of the "derisory sum" of damages available in domestic proceedings for the wrongful disclosure of her husband's HIV-positive status. The court said that:

> "in a case of outrageous abuse of press freedom, as in the present application, the Court finds that the severe legislative limitations on judicial discretion in redressing the damage suffered by the victim and sufficiently deterring the recurrence of such abuses, failed to provide the applicant with the protection that could have legitimately been expected under Article 8 of the Convention."

In *Mosley v News Group Newspapers Ltd*[103] Eady J. awarded £60,000 damages for personal distress caused by the publication of photographs and a luridly misleading account of sexual activities in private.

---

[95] *Jarvis v Swan Tours Ltd* [1973] Q.B. 233.
[96] *Heywood v Wellers* [1976] Q.B. 446.
[97] *Bliss v South East Thames Regional Health Authority* [1987] I.C.R. 700 at 718; *Hayes v Dodd* [1990] 2 All E.R. 815 at 826; *Watts v Morrow* [1991] 1 W.L.R. 1421 at 1439.
[98] [1960] 1 W.L.R. 1072.
[99] [2001] E.M.L.R. 12. The defendant's appeal on liability failed: [2001] EWCA Civ 1511; [2002] E.M.L.R. 6.
[100] [2004] UKHL 22; [2004] 2 A.C. 457 .
[101] [2005] EWCA Civ 595; [2006] Q.B. 125.
[102] [2008] E.C.H.R. 1526; [2009] E.M.L.R. 7 at [47].
[103] [2008] EWHC 1777 (QB); [2008] E.M.L.R. 20.

In *Spelman v Express Newspapers*[104] Tugendhat J. referred to *Armonas* and *Mosley*, and said that damages for wrongful disclosure of private information may, in an appropriate case, include aggravated damages.

Section 7 of the Human Rights Act 1998 provides a right of action for a person who claims that a public authority has acted in a way which is incompatible with his Convention rights. Under s.8, the court is empowered to award damages if such an award is necessary to afford just satisfaction to the person in whose favour it is made.[105]   **9–049**

The Court of Appeal of New Zealand expressed the view in *Aquaculture Corp v New Zealand Green Mussel Co Ltd*[106] that there is no reason in principle why exemplary damages should not be awarded for actionable breach of confidence in a case where a compensatory award would not adequately reflect the gravity of the defendant's conduct.   **9–050**

The law as to exemplary or punitive damages was laid down by the House of Lords in *Rookes v Barnard*.[107] The situations in which such damages may be awarded include conduct calculated to give the defendant a profit likely to exceed the compensation payable to the plaintiff.   **9–051**

The type of case most likely to give rise to a claim for exemplary damages would be where confidential information of a personal nature is leaked to, or surreptitiously obtained by, the media and published in disregard of the rights of the person concerned under Art.8. However, the imposition of a liability on the defendant which was not based on an assessment either of the damage to the claimant or of the profit to the defendant (through the taking of an account) would potentially involve a disproportionate balance between Arts 8 and 10.[108]   **9–052**

In *Mosley v News Group Newspapers Ltd* Eady J. considered the view expressed by Sir Robin Cooke in *Aquaculture Corp v New Zealand Green Mussel Co*, but he ruled that exemplary damages were not available in a claim for breach of privacy, because there was no existing authority to justify it and because it would fail the test of being necessary and proportionate. He accepted the defendant's submission that since a claim for invasion of privacy involves a direct application of Convention values, it would be eccentric to graft onto Convention jurisprudence an alien anomaly from the common law.[109] On the facts, he concluded that the defendant's judgment was casual and cavalier, but not that it had acted from a cynical calculation that its profit would exceed any award of damages. In arriving at a figure of £60,000 for compensatory damages, which was far greater than the usual level of awards for infringement of privacy, he cited the words of Lord Reid, in the context of a defamation claim, in *Broome v Cassell & Co Ltd*[110]

---

[104] [2012] EWHC 355 (QB).

[105] See the Court of Appeal's guidance in *Anufrijera v Southwark LBC* [2003] EWCA Civ 1406; [2004] Q.B. 1124.

[106] [1990] 3 N.Z.L.R. 299 at 301, per Sir Robin Cooke P.

[107] [1964] A.C. 1129 at 1226–1227.

[108] See *Steel and Morris v United Kingdom* (2005) 41 E.H.R.R. 403 at paras 96 to 98; *Jameel v Wall Street Journal Europe Sprl* [2006] UKHL 44; [2007] A.C. 359, especially per Lord Bingham at [18]–[19].

[109] [2008] EWHC 1777 (QB); [2008] E.M.L.R. 20 at [196]–[197].

[110] [1972] A.C. 1027 at 1085.

"It has long been recognised that in determining what sum within that bracket should be awarded, a jury, or other tribunal, is entitled to have regard to the conduct of the defendant. He may have behaved in a highhanded, malicious, insulting or oppressive manner in committing the tort or he or his counsel may at the trial have aggravated the injury by what they there said. That would justify going to the top of the bracket and awarding as damages the largest sum that could fairly be regarded as compensation."

In *Giller v Procopets*[111] the Court of Appeal of Victoria arrived at a similar conclusion. It held that exemplary damages were not available for breach of an equitable duty of confidentiality but that there was no bar to an award of aggravated damages.

In *Mosley* the judge's conclusion that the defendant had not acted from a cynical calculation that its profit would exceed any award of damages was a good reason for not awarding exemplary damages. However, in worst instances of publication of sensitive personal information, where the court is satisfied that the defendant acted in wilful disregard of any relevant journalistic code of conduct, from a cynical calculation that its profit would exceed the likely damages, there remains a case for allowing exemplary damages. Proportionality is essential, but the courts should not rule out the possibility that in some cases such an award may properly be considered necessary and proportionate in order to deter such behaviour and provide adequate protection for the individual or individuals concerned.

Declaration

9–053   The court has a discretionary power to grant declaratory relief, and this may be an appropriate way of determining questions of confidentiality.[112] Such relief is normally sought by a person complaining of breach of confidence. However, there is no reason in principle why a person who is threatened with proceedings for breach of confidence if he makes use of information alleged to be confidential should not bring proceedings for a declaration of non-confidentiality, just as a party threatened, for example, with an action for passing off may seek a declaration of non-liability.[113] In *Price Waterhouse v BCCI Holdings (Luxembourg) SA*[114] the plaintiffs applied for, and were granted, a declaration that they were not precluded by confidence owed to the defendant or its customers from supplying information and documents to an inquiry into the supervision of BCCI, although it is doubted whether the court was right to do so without the customers being represented.

---

[111] [2008] VSCA 236 at [157]–[159] per Ashley J.A. and [437]–[442] per Neave J.A.
[112] See, for example, *Malone v Metropolitan Police Commissioner* [1979] 1 Ch. 344 and *Hellewell v Chief Constable of Derbyshire* [1995] 1 W.L.R. 804.
[113] Compare *Bulmer Ltd v Bollinger S.A.* [1974] Ch. 401; [1978] R.P.C. 79.
[114] [1992] B.C.L.C. 583. See para.6–041, above.

Search order

Anton Piller KG v Manufacturing Processes Ltd[115] was an action for infringement of copyright and misuse of confidential information. The action began with orders made ex parte, authorising the plaintiffs to inspect the defendants' premises and seize relevant documents. The procedure was approved by the Court of Appeal, with the warning that such an order was only to be made where it was essential so that justice could be done between the parties and when, if the defendant were forewarned, there would be grave danger that vital evidence would be destroyed or hidden.

9–054

Concern that such orders were being made too readily, and executed in a way which amounted to abuse, led to stricter controls being imposed by the courts: see *Columbia Picture Industries Inc v Robinson*[116] per Scott J.; *Lock International Plc v Beswick*[117] per Hoffmann J.; and *Universal Thermosensors Ltd v Hibben*[118] per Nicholls V.C.

9–055

In *Universal Thermosensors Ltd v Hibben*, Nicholls V.C. commented that the case illustrated both the virtues and the vices of Anton Piller orders. The plaintiff was enabled to recover stolen documents containing confidential information, which the judge considered would in all probability otherwise have been destroyed; but this result was achieved at a high price. Irregularities in the execution of the order led to claims against the plaintiff and the plaintiff's solicitors which were settled during the trial. The jurisdiction of the High Court to make such orders, now called search orders, was put on a statutory basis by the Civil Procedure Act 1997 s.7.[119]

9–056

A search order remains a valuable weapon, but one which requires the utmost care by the court and by the claimant both in making the application and in executing any order. The fact that such applications are usually made in a hurry makes it all the more important for the claimant to take care to ensure that all relevant matters are drawn to the attention of the court.

9–057

Action for discovery

A person whose confidence has been breached, but who does not know who was responsible, may be able to bring an action against a recipient of the confidential information to compel him to disclose the identity of the informer. This form of action is derived from the ancient bill of discovery in equity, which was given new life by the decision of the House of Lords in *Norwich Pharmacal Co v Customs and Excise Commissioners*[120] and applied by the House of Lords in *British Steel Corp v Granada Television Ltd.*[121] In the latter case the action was brought to compel the disclosure of the source of confidential documents which had been leaked to Granada and used in a television programme. Granada relied

9–058

---

[115] [1976] Ch. 55.

[116] [1987] Ch. 38.

[117] [1989] 1 W.L.R. 1268.

[118] [1992] F.S.R. 361.

[119] The procedure for making an application and a draft form of order are set out in a practice direction on interim injunctions which supplements CPR Pt 25.

[120] [1974] A.C. 133.

[121] [1981] A.C. 1096 at 1171.

on its own obligation of confidentiality to its source, whose identity it had promised not to reveal. The House of Lords ordered disclosure, but recognised that the remedy of an action for discovery, being equitable, was discretionary,[122] and that the court ought not to compel confidence bona fide given to be breached unless necessary in the interests of justice.[123]

In *Campaign Against Arms Trade v BAE Systems Plc*[124] the claimant was granted a *Norwich Pharmacal* order against the defendant, which had received a leaked copy email disclosing legal advice obtained by the claimant in relation to proposed judicial review proceedings. The advice discussed tactics and costs. The defendant had an opposing interest in the proceedings, and the claimant feared that without knowing the source it would be hampered by the fear of further leaks. The case raised no issue of journalistic freedom. In response to an argument by the defendant that the claimant had not exhausted all other practicable means of obtaining the information, King J. observed that in determining what was practicable the court was entitled to have regard to all the circumstances, including the size and resources of the applicant and the urgency of its need to obtain the information.[125]

In *Financial Times Ltd v United Kingdom* the Strasbourg court accepted that the aim of preventing further leaks might justify an order compelling disclosure of journalistic sources in circumstances if, but only if, there was no other reasonable way of averting the risk posed and the risk threatened was sufficiently serious and defined to override the ordinary right of journalists to protect their sources under Art.10.[126]

9–059   The subject of disclosure of journalistic sources is discussed more fully in Ch.13.

Delay

9–060   In accordance with ordinary principles of equity, a person seeking equitable relief against breach of confidence will risk refusal if he fails to act with reasonable promptness once he knows of the breach. He cannot, for example, stand by while the party in breach exploits the information and then claim an account of profits. For actions based on breach of contract the limitation period is six years, subject to the provisions of s.32 of the Limitation Act 1980 relating to fraud, concealment or mistake.

---

[122] *British Steel Corp v Granada Television Ltd* [1981] A.C. 1096 at 1174, per Lord Wilberforce.
[123] *Science Research Council v Nasse* [1980] A.C. 1028.
[124] [2007] EWHC 330 (QB).
[125] [2007] EWHC 330 at [20].
[126] [2009] E.C.H.R. 2065; (2010) 50 E.H.R.R. 46 at [69].

CHAPTER 10

Confidentiality and Foreign Law

A conflict of laws problem arises if the law of one country is invoked to obtain disclosure of documents or information within the jurisdiction of another, a fortiori if such disclosure would be contrary to the law of the country in whose jurisdiction they are[1].   **10–001**

There is generally accepted and well founded dislike of laws which have extra-territorial effect, both on grounds of respect for the jurisdiction of other countries and to avoid injustice in the form of a party being subject to mutually contradictory edicts. The risk is particularly great for companies, like banks, operating across frontiers. But there is another side to the picture. Neill L.J. observed in *Derby & Co Ltd v Weldon (Nos 3 & 4)*[2] that "assets, like the Cheshire cat, may disappear unexpectedly", and that modern technology and the ingenuity of its beneficiaries can make assets depart at a speed which would make the disappearance of the Cheshire cat look sluggish.   **10–002**

There may, therefore, be cases in which strict adherence by the courts to the principle of territoriality may play into the hands of fraudsters. The authorities may be divided into three groups: **10–003**

(1)   cases where English courts are asked to make an order requiring production of documents of a confidential nature which are outside the jurisdiction;

(2)   cases where foreign courts make an order requiring production of documents of a confidential nature which are within the United Kingdom; and

(3)   cases where English courts or regulatory authorities are asked to assist the courts or regulatory authorities of another country.

---

[1] For general consideration of the status of equitable causes of action for the purpose of conflict of laws, see Dicey, Morris and Collins on *The Conflict of Laws,* 15th edn (London: Sweet & Maxwell, 2012). For consideration of the status of the action for breach of confidence for jurisdictional purposes under the Brussels Convention on Jurisdiction and Enforcement of Judgments in Civil and Commercial Matters 1968 and Regulation 44/2001, see Christopher Wadlow's "Bugs, spies and paparazzi: jurisdiction over actions for breach of confidence in private international law" EIPR 2008, 30(7), 269-279. His further article, "Trade secrets and the Rome II Regulation on the law applicable to non-contractual obligations," EIPR 2008, 30(8), 309–319, considers the law applicable to actions relating to the misuse of trade secrets under Reg.864/2007 (Rome II).

[2] [1990] Ch. 65 at 95.

CASES WHERE ENGLISH COURTS ARE ASKED TO ORDER PRODUCTION OF CONFIDENTIAL DOCUMENTS OUTSIDE THE JURISDICTION

10–004   It is necessary to distinguish between:

(1)   cases where the person against whom the order is sought is a party to litigation in the United Kingdom[3] (otherwise than merely for the purpose of obtaining disclosure of information under the Norwich Pharmacal[4] procedure); and

(2)   cases where the person against whom the order is sought is not a party to the litigation or has been joined in an action only for the purpose of obtaining disclosure of information.

In the former class the ordinary rules of disclosure make no distinction between documents inside and outside the jurisdiction, so long as they are within the possession, custody or power of the party from whom disclosure is sought. This involves no breach of comity, because disclosure in the ordinary course of litigation is a matter of procedure, not substance, and the principle that procedure is governed by the lex fori is of general application and universally admitted.[5]

10–005   In cases where the party against whom a production order is sought is not a party to the action, or has been joined for the purpose of discovery, an order for production is not merely an incidental matter of procedure but is the substance of the relief sought. In *R. v Grossman*[6] an order was made, ex parte, against Barclays Bank Ltd at its London head office requiring it to allow the Inland Revenue to inspect and take copies of its books relating to the account of an Isle of Man company at its Isle of Man branch, under s.7 of the Bankers' Books Evidence Act 1879. The order was set aside by the Court of Appeal. Lord Denning M.R. said[7]:

> "I think that the branch of Barclays Bank in Douglas, Isle of Man, should be considered in the same way as a branch of the Bank of Ireland or an American Bank, or any other bank in the Isle of Man which is not subject to our jurisdiction. The branch of Barclays Bank in Douglas, Isle of Man, should be considered as a different entity separate from the head office in London. It is subject to the laws and regulations of the Isle of Man. It is licensed by the Isle of Man government. It has its customers there who are subject to the Manx laws. It seems to me that the court here ought not in its discretion to make an order against the head office here in

---

[3] This category also includes cases in which an application for pre-action disclosure is made against a person *likely* to be made a party to litigation in the United Kingdom: see *Mitsui & Co Ltd v Nexen Petroleum UK Ltd* [2005] EWHC 625 (Ch); [2005] 3 All E.R. 511, per Lightman J. at [30]–[32].

[4] *Norwich Pharmacal Co v Customs & Excise Commissioners* [1974] A.C. 133.

[5] Dicey, Morris & Collins, *The Conflict of Laws,* 15th edn (London: Sweet & Maxwell, 2012), paras 8–068 to 8–071; *The Consul Corfitzon* [1917] A.C. 550 at 555–556; *MacKinnon v Donaldson, Lufkin & Jenrette Corp* [1986] 1 Ch. 483 at 494–495, per Hoffmann J., "I am not concerned with the discovery required by R.S.C., Ord. 24 from ordinary parties to English litigation who happen to be foreigners. If you join the game you must play according to the local rules. This applies not only to plaintiffs but also to defendants who give notice of intention to defend".

[6] (1981) 73 Cr. App. R. 302.

[7] (1981) 73 Cr. App. R. 302 at 307.

respect of the books of the branch in the Isle of Man in regard to the customers of that branch. It would not be right to compel the branch—or its customers—to open their books or to reveal their confidences in support of legal proceedings in Wales. Any order in respect of the production of the books ought to be made by the courts of the Isle of Man—if they will make such an order. It ought not to be made by these courts. Otherwise there would be danger of a conflict of jurisdictions between the High Court here and the courts of the Isle of Man. That is a conflict which we must always avoid."

In *MacKinnon v Donaldson, Lufkin and Jenrette Securities Corporation*[8] the **10–006** plaintiff in an action involving allegations of international fraud obtained an order ex parte under the Bankers' Books Evidence Act requiring an American bank, which was not a party to the action, to produce books held at its head office in New York relating to one of the defendants, a defunct Bahamian company. The plaintiff also issued a supoena *duces tecum* against an officer of the bank at its London office. Hoffmann J. set aside both orders.

The plaintiff attempted to distinguish *Grossman* on the ground that in that case **10–007** the Isle of Man court had previously refused a similar application and had granted an injunction restraining the bank from disclosing the information. It was also argued that the American bank, by carrying on business in London, had submitted to the jurisdiction of the English court and should be required to comply with the *subpoena* unless production would be unlawful by the law of the place where the documents were kept.

Hoffmann J. rejected that argument. He said[9]: **10–008**

"I think that this argument confuses personal jurisdiction, i.e. who can be brought before the court, with subject matter jurisdiction, i.e. to what extent the court can claim to regulate the conduct of those persons. It does not follow from the fact that a person is within the jurisdiction and liable to be served with process that there is no territorial limit to the matters upon which the court may properly apply its own rules or the things which it can order such a person to do. As Dr Mann observed in a leading article 'The Doctrine of Jurisdiction in International Law', (1964) 111 *Recueil de cours* 146,

'The mere fact that a state's judicial or administrative agencies are internationally entitled to subject a person to their personal or "curial" jurisdiction does not by any means permit them to regulate by their orders such person's conduct abroad. This they may do only if the state of the forum also had substantive jurisdiction to regulate conduct in the manner defined in the order. In other words, for the purpose of justifying, even in the territory of the forum, the international validity of an order, not only its making, but also its content must be authorised by substantive rules of legislative jurisdiction.'

See also by the same author 'The Doctrine of International Jurisdiction Revisited after Twenty Years' (1984) 196 *Recueil des cours* 9, 19.

The content of the subpoena and order is to require the production by a non-party of documents outside the jurisdiction concerning business which it has transacted outside the jurisdiction. In principle and on authority it seems to me that the court should not, save in exceptional circumstances, impose such a requirement upon a

---

[8] [1986] 1 Ch. 482.
[9] [1986] 1 Ch. 482 at 493.

foreigner, and, in particular, upon a foreign bank. The principle is that a state should refrain from demanding obedience to its sovereign authority by foreigners in respect of their conduct outside the jurisdiction."

The plaintiff also attempted to distinguish *Grossman* by arguing that he would be entitled to join the bank as a defendant under *Norwich Pharmacal*[10] and *Bankers Trust Co v Shapira*[11] and that the case should not therefore be regarded as an attempt to enforce discovery against a non-party.

10–009 Hoffmann J. rejected that distinction, holding that for jurisdictional purposes such cases were much more akin to a subpoena directed to a witness than to discovery required of an ordinary defendant, and that the court should recognise the same international jurisdictional limits in such cases as in cases of a subpoena *duces tecum* or an order under the Bankers' Books Evidence Act 1879. He accordingly held, following *Grossman*, that an order for production of documents held at a bank's foreign branch or head office should not be made save in very exceptional circumstances. He also expressed the opinion that, where alternative procedures were available (as by way of letters rogatory), an infringement of sovereignty could seldom be justified except perhaps on the grounds of urgent necessity relied upon by Templeman J. in *London and County Securities Ltd v Caplan*.[12]

10–010 In *Re Mid East Trading Ltd*[13] the Court of Appeal held that, since the courts had been given the power to wind up overseas companies under s.221 of the Insolvency Act 1986, the legislature must be taken to have intended the courts in appropriate circumstances to make such assertion of sovereignty as might be required in making an order under s.236 of the Act to produce documents situated abroad. Where compliance with such an order would or might expose the respondent to civil claims or criminal penalties in the jurisdiction in which the documents were situated, that would be an important factor, to be weighted with others; but there was no special hurdle of "exceptional circumstances" to be overcome by the applicant.

CASES WHERE FOREIGN COURTS HAVE ORDERED PRODUCTION OF CONFIDENTIAL DOCUMENTS WITHIN THE UNITED KINGDOM

10–011 The same reasoning applies in reverse in cases of orders by foreign courts for production of confidential documents in the United Kingdom. In *X AG v A Bank*[14] a subpoena was issued in the United States District Court for the Southern District of New York against an American bank requiring it to produce documents relating to accounts maintained at its London branch by X, a Swiss corporation

---

[10] [1974] A.C. 133.
[11] [1980] 1 W.L.R. 1274.
[12] Unreported, May 26, 1978. In *United Co Rusal Plc v HSBC Bank Plc* [2011] EWHC 404 (QB) at [73], Tugendhat followed Hoffmann J.'s dicta in *MacKinnon v Donaldson, Lufkin and Jenrette Securities Corp*, observing that "what applies to banks with offices in more than one jurisdiction must apply to law firms with offices in more than one jurisdiction."
[13] [1998] 1 All E.R. 577 at 592–593.
[14] [1983] 2 All E.R. 464.

with no business in the United States, and Y, a subsidiary of X which was also incorporated in Switzerland, but had a major office in New York. The subpoena was returnable before a federal grand jury investigating alleged tax evasion. The bank declared its intention to comply with the subpoena. X and Y obtained an injunction in the English High Court restraining the bank from doing so on the ground that it would be in breach of duty of confidence. An order was then made by the New York District Court, ex parte and in camera, requiring the bank to comply with the subpoena. The bank applied to set aside the High Court injunction. Leggatt J. refused to do so.

Since the injunction was interlocutory, Leggatt J. decided the matter on *American Cyanamid* principles and did not have to reach a final determination of the points of law raised. However, he referred to the order enforcing the subpoena as "the exercise by the United States court in London of powers which, by English standards, would be regarded as excessive"[15] and stated that in relation to the merits he was firmly on the side of the plaintiffs.   **10–012**

After referring to the qualifications to the duty of banking confidentiality recognised in *Tournier v National Provincial and Union Bank of England*,[16] the first being where disclosure is by compulsion of law, the judge observed that to apply foreign law in relation to banking business conducted in the City of London would be "to allow a fairly large cuckoo in the domestic nest".[17]   **10–013**

It was also argued by the bank that an English court would not enforce a contract if performance required the doing of an act which violates the law of the place of performance (*Ralli Bros v Compania Naviera a Sota y Aznar*[18]), and therefore the contract was unenforceable in so far as it sought to require confidentiality in New York.   **10–014**

If, following the approach in *Grossman*, a bank's London and overseas branches are to be regarded as separate entities, the performance which the English order was seeking to enforce was performance in England. Disclosure in New York could only happen if the London branch breached its duty of confidentiality in London by disclosure of documents to its New York branch for production in New York. The fact that a consequence of the contract being performed in its place of performance (England) was that the documents would not reach New York did not make the English order an extra-territorial order.[19]   **10–015**

Legatt J. rejected the argument that to continue the injunction would be to enforce a contract in a manner contrary to the law of the place of performance on a different ground, that the subpoena and order made without argument on the merits were not to be equated with legislation or a final judgment, and could not be said to have rendered the keeping of secrecy by the bank illegal, particularly since the evidence suggested the bank was most unlikely in the circumstances to be held in contempt by the New York court.   **10–016**

---

[15] Cited by Hoffmann J. in *Mackinnon v Donaldson, Lufkin & Jenrette Corp* [1986] 1 Ch. 482 at 494.
[16] [1924] 1 K.B. 461 at 473.
[17] [1983] 2 All E.R. 464 at 478.
[18] [1920] 2 K.B. 287.
[19] Nor would an order requiring an English company to bring back documents relating to a domestic subject matter, which it had sent out of the jurisdiction (as in *Director of Public Prosecutions v Channel Four Television* [1993] 2 All E.R. 517), be regarded as assuming extra-territorial subject matter jurisdiction.

10–017   In *A v B Bank*[20] Morland J. made an order both restraining the defendant bank from delivering up to a grand jury in New York any documents held at their London branch relating to the plaintiffs' accounts, and also requiring the bank to return to their London branch any documents already removed from the jurisdiction in connection with the grand jury subpoena. By contrast, in *Pharaon v BCCI SA*[21] Price Waterhouse sought the permission of the court to comply with a subpoena issued in New York that required it to produce documents relating to BCCI's activities in the United States. Rattee J. held that the public interest in making documents available in US proceedings that arose out of alleged fraud on the part of BCCI outweighed the public interest in upholding the duty of confidentiality owed by Price Waterhouse to BCCI, its customers and its shareholders.

ASSISTANCE BY ENGLISH COURTS OR REGULATORY AUTHORITIES TO FOREIGN COURTS OR REGULATORY AUTHORITIES

10–018   The United Kingdom is a party to the Hague Convention on the *Taking of Evidence Abroad in Civil and Commercial Matters* (1970)[22] and to a number of bilateral civil procedure conventions. English courts have jurisdiction to assist in obtaining evidence for foreign courts or tribunals under the Evidence (Proceedings in Other Jurisdictions) Act 1975 and CPR Pt 34.

10–019   The question of confidentiality arose in *Re State of Norway's Application*.[23] Norwegian proceedings involved an issue whether a deceased tax payer was the settlor of a trust. On the request of the Norwegian court an order was made by the English court for examination of two directors of the trust's London bank on a number of matters including the identity of the settlor. The Court of Appeal[24] held, by a majority, that the order should be set aside on the grounds that its terms were too wide and that the directors should not be required to disclose banking confidences, which might affect unknown people, in a case where there was no allegation of fraud or crime.

10–020   On a second request by the Norwegian court, in more limited terms, a further order was made and was upheld by the judge, with the qualification that the witnesses were not to be asked the identity of the settlor unless either of them first gave evidence that the settlor was the agent or nominee of the deceased tax payer. The judge's order was reversed by the Court of Appeal on a point of jurisdiction but restored by the House of Lords. On the issue of confidentiality, Woolf L.J. said[25] that in deciding whether to assist in obtaining the evidence requested in the

---

[20] Unreported, August 13, 1990. The order is recited in the later judgment of Hirst J. reported at [1993] Q.B. 311.

[21] [1998] 4 All E.R. 455.

[22] Cmnd. 3991 (1970). The Convention came into force in the United Kingdom on September 14, 1976. In relation to Member States, see Council Regulation (EC) No.1206/2001 of May 28, 2001 on co-operation between the courts of the Member States in the taking of evidence in civil or commercial matters.

[23] [1990] 1 A.C. 723.

[24] [1987] 1 Q.B. 433.

[25] [1990] 1 A.C. 723 at 782.

proceedings, where a question of confidentiality arose, the English court should adopt the same approach as if the proceedings were taking place before the English court. That required a balancing exercise which the judge had properly performed. The judge's approach was approved in the House of Lords by Lord Goff, with whom the other members of the appellate committee agreed.[26]

It is possible to use *Norwich Pharmacal* proceedings to obtain *information* for the purpose of bringing proceedings overseas but, outside the statutory scheme, the courts have no jurisdiction to use their processes for the purpose of providing *evidence* for proceedings in foreign states.[27]

In relation to criminal law the United Kingdom is a party to various **10–021** conventions, including the Convention on Mutual Assistance in Criminal Matters (2000). The Crime (International Co-operation) Act 2003 s.16, provides that the powers of entry, search and seizure under the Police and Criminal Evidence Act 1984 are extended to enable evidence to be obtained at the request of bodies including a foreign court or prosecuting authority, or the International Criminal Police Organisation, in cases which would be serious arrestable offences if they occurred in the United Kingdom, and s.19 provides for seized evidence to be sent directly to the requesting authority. Other provisions of the Act include measures, subject to judicial authorisation, for the monitoring of bank accounts and supply of banking information to assist foreign authorities investigating serious criminal offences.[28]

In considering the procedure to be followed on an application for legal assistance under the Criminal Justice (International Co-operation) Act 2003, Lord Phillips C.J. observed in *R. (on the application of Hafner) v City of Westminster Magistrates' Court*[29]:

> "As a general principle privacy rights under Article 8(1) are unlikely to prevail in the face of Article 8(2) where disclosure of documents or information is necessary for the prevention of crime, but the court should protect documents or information that go beyond what is necessary for this purpose."

A regulatory body which has power to require disclosure of confidential **10–022** material may also have a right to disclose it to a foreign counterpart. In *A v B Bank*,[30] after the U.S. Federal Reserve Board had failed to secure the documents which it wanted from the defendant bank by grand jury *subpoena* (because the bank was restrained from disclosing them by injunction), it approached the Bank of England with information which caused the latter to serve a notice on the defendant bank, under s.39 of the Banking Act 1987, requiring production of documents relating to the plaintiffs' accounts. Section 82 of the Act placed restrictions on the Bank of England's power to disclose information which it obtained under the Act about a person's affairs to another person; but, by s.84,

---

[26] See *USA v Philip Morris Inc* [2004] EWCA Civ 330, in which, notwithstanding possible issues of legal professional privilege, the Court of Appeal acceded to a letter of request seeking the examination of a lawyer who had previously acted for the appellant tobacco company, which was now a defendant to proceedings in the United States.

[27] *R. (on the application of Omar) v Secretary of State for Foreign and Commonwealth Affairs* [2012] EWHC 1737 (Admin).

[28] See ss.32–46.

[29] [2008] EWHC 524 (Admin); [2009] 1 W.L.R. 1005 at [26].

[30] [1993] Q.B. 311. See para.10–017, above.

those restrictions did not preclude it from disclosing such information for the purpose of assisting an authority with corresponding functions in another country. So there was nothing to prevent the Bank of England from supplying the documents to the Federal Reserve Board.

10–023   Hirst J. rejected the plaintiffs' argument that the injunction previously granted by Morland J. precluded the defendant bank from complying with the Bank of England's notice. He also rejected the allegation that the notice was invalid because the Bank of England was acting for a collateral purpose, as an evidence gathering agency for a foreign supervisory body. His judgment suggests that the courts will incline to a broad view of a supervisory authority's functions in matters involving international co-operation. He said[31]:

> "[Counsel for the plaintiffs] seeks in effect to draw a line down the centre of the Atlantic, and to suggest that in some way the supervisory operations of the Federal Reserve Board and those of the Bank of England are separate and unconnected. In fact, in the world of international banking today, supervisory authorities in various countries can, should, and no doubt do regularly co-operate on matters of mutual supervisory concern as sections 84(6) and 86 confirm."

---

[31] [1993] Q.B. 311 at 327.

CHAPTER 11

Medical Advisers[1]

The modern version of the Hippocratic Oath introduced by the World Medical Association as the Declaration of Geneva (as amended at Sydney in 1968) includes the statement:

"I will respect the secrets which are confided in me, even after the patient has died."

There is no doubt that the relationship of doctor[2] and patient carries with it a legal obligation of confidence in respect of confidential information concerning the patient gained by the doctor in his professional capacity,[3] whether directly from the patient or, for example, from medical records. The scope of the duty can present particularly difficult questions.

A wide array of published guidance now exists (much of it available online) to assist health professionals in the assessment and performance of the duties of confidentiality owed by them to patients and others, including (for example):

(1) The General Medical Council's *Confidentiality* (in effect from October 12, 2009), together with supplemental guidance on a variety of specific topics including disclosure: (a) to the DVLA or DVA; (b) for financial and administrative purposes; (c) of gunshot and knife wounds; (d) about serious communicable diseases; (e) for insurance, employment and similar purposes; (f) for education and training purposes; and (g) for the purpose of responding to criticism in the press;

(2) The Department of Health's *Confidentiality NHS Code of Practice* (November 2003), with supplementary guidance on public interest disclosures (November 2010);

(3) The Royal College of Nursing's *Confidentiality: guidance for occupational health nurses* (2005);

(4) The Royal College of Psychiatrists' *Good Psychiatric Practice: Confidentiality and information sharing*, 2nd edn (2010);

(5) The Royal College of Psychiatrists and the Princess Royal Trust for Carers' *Carers and confidentiality in mental health: Issues involved in information-sharing* (revised, May 2010);

---

[1] On confidentiality and the medical profession, see Grubb, *The Principles of Medical Law,* 3rd edn (Oxford University Press, 2010), Ch.12, and Mason and McCall Smith, *Law and Medical Ethics,* 8th edn (Oxford University Press, 2010), Ch.6.

[2] This chapter concentrates on doctors, but duties of confidentiality are owed by all concerned in advising and treating patients.

[3] *Hunter v Mann* [1974] Q.B. 767 at 772. *W v Egdell* [1990] Ch. 359.

(6) The General Medical Council's *Protecting children and young people: the responsibilities of all doctors* (taking effect from September 3, 2012);

(7) The General Dental Council's *Principles of Patient Confidentiality* (May 2005);

(8) The British Psychological Society's *Generic Professional Practice Guidelines,* 2nd edn (2008), s.3 (*Confidentiality*).

11–003 Although a patient may be the most obvious, he or she is not the only person entitled to assert the confidentiality of medical information. Health organisations and individual health professionals may also have independent rights of confidentiality.

In *Ashworth Hospital Authority v MGN Ltd*[4] the health organisation responsible for Ashworth Security Hospital obtained an order requiring the defendant newspaper publisher to disclose the identity of the source of confidential information that the *Daily Mirror* had obtained in relation to the medical records of Ian Brady, the notorious "Moors murderer". In the Court of Appeal, Lord Phillips M.R. said[5]:

> "Though they were personal to Brady, I consider that Ashworth had a clear independent interest in retaining their confidentiality. The Department of Health published, on 7 March 1996, Guidance on the Protection and Use of Patient Information. This includes the following guidance under the heading, 'Who has a duty of confidence?': Everyone working for or with the NHS who records, handles, stores, or otherwise comes across information has a personal common law duty of confidence to patients *and to his or her employer.*" [Emphasis added by Lord Phillips]

The *Daily Mirror*'s source, disclosed after the decision of the House of Lords, turned out to be an intermediary journalist, Mr Robin Ackroyd. A subsequent action, brought to require him in turn to reveal his own source, failed before Tugendhat J.[6] However, Tugendhat J. confirmed the hospital's standing to seek protection for the relevant information, saying[7]:

> "Ian Brady is the subject of that information. A patient has a right to disclose to the public at large information that he has previously given in confidence to a doctor. He also has certain rights of access to information recorded about him by the doctor or hospital. But he does not have an unrestricted right to seize the records kept by the doctor or hospital and publish them to the world. Nor would he have an unrestricted right to authorise any doctor or nurse to disclose the contents of those records. The hospital, as the body responsible for keeping and controlling those records, and other individuals referred to in them, have rights and responsibilities in respect of the information contained in those records."

11–004 A doctor may wish, or feel that he may be under a duty, to disclose information about a patient for a wide variety of purposes. They include:

---

[4] [2002] UKHL 29; [2001] 1 W.L.R. 515 CA; [2002] 1 W.L.R. 2033 HL.

[5] At para.52.

[6] *Mersey Care NHS Trust v Ackroyd (No.2)* [2006] EWHC 107, QB; [2006] E.M.L.R. 12. The decision of Tugendhat J. was upheld by the Court of Appeal: [2007] EWCA Civ 101; [2008] E.M.L.R. 1.

[7] At [94].

(1)   diagnosis, advice and treatment;
(2)   clinical audit and regulation;
(3)   advancement of medicine;
(4)   protection of others;
(5)   protection of himself;
(6)   management and record keeping;
(7)   compliance with a requirement of law.

He is plainly at liberty to disclose information if required by law or with consent properly given.

11–005 Consent may be expressed or implied. Whether it is to be implied will depend on the nature and purpose of the disclosure. But there may be situations in which, for one reason or another, the doctor acts deliberately without consent.

11–006 Difficulties may also arise in relation to minors or persons under a disability and disclosures within the family. Medical confidence is one incident of the relationship between the doctor and his patient and exists for the benefit of the patient. It is not absolute, not only because it would defeat the object for which it exists if it precluded the doctor from making disclosure in circumstances where, in the exercise of a proper professional judgment, he considered it in the patient's best interests to do so, but also because its preservation could in some circumstances be harmful for other reasons.

11–007 The fullest judicial statement is to be found in *Duncan v Medical Practitioner's Disciplinary Committee*, where Jeffries J. attempted to summarise both the principle of medical confidence and certain qualifications. He said[8]:

> "The Court now addresses directly what is medical confidence? It is not difficult to grasp the broad concept of professional confidence for it is fundamental to the relationship of a professional man with a lay person. On a strict analysis of legal relationships, it is probably contractually based, as several cases have suggested . . .
>
> Without trust [the doctor/patient relationship] would not function properly so as to allow freedom for the patient to disclose all manner of confidences and secrets in the practical certainty that they would repose with the doctor. There rests with a doctor a strong ethical obligation to observe a strict confidentiality by holding inviolate the confidences and secrets he receives in the course of his professional ministerings. If he adheres to that ethical principle then the full scope of his ability to administer medical assistance to his patient will develop.
>
> The foregoing embodies the principle of medical confidence, but it cannot be left there without identifying the existence of qualifications and modifications for I have described, not defined exhaustively the concept. Confidentiality is not breached by private discussions with colleagues in pursuance of treatment, but this may require full disclosure and consent. The confidentiality may be waived by the patient. The doctor may be required by law to disclose. A doctor may be in a group practice where common filing systems are used. Staff who have access to information must be impressed with the requirement of confidence. Limited information to some outside agencies may be made available by a doctor from his files for statistical, accounting, data processing or other legitimate purposes. A doctor may be treating more than one person that requires, or mandates, exchange of information, but here caution and prudence must be carefully observed and consents obtained. As this very case demonstrates a doctor may reveal confidences and secrets if he is required to defend himself, or others, against accusations of wrongful conduct. There may be

---

[8] [1986] 1 N.Z.L.R. 513 at 520, N.Z. High Court.

occasions, they are fortunately rare, when a doctor receives information involving a patient that another's life is immediately endangered and urgent action is required. The doctor must then exercise his professional judgment based upon the circumstances, and if he fairly and reasonably believes such a danger exists then he must act unhesitatingly to prevent injury or loss of life even if there is to be a breach of confidentiality. If his actions later are to be scrutinised as to their correctness, he can be confident any official inquiry will be by people sympathetic about the predicament he faced. However, that qualification cannot be advanced so as to attenuate, or undermine, the immeasurably valuable concept of medical confidence. If it were applied in that way it would be misapplied, in my view, because it would be extravagant with what is essentially a qualification to the principle. Some might say that is line-drawing and if they do then so be it. The line-drawing is not arbitrary but based upon reason and experience, and is the exercise of professional judgment which is part of daily practice for a doctor. The foregoing, either in the description or the qualifications, is not advanced as anything but an outline."

ANONYMISATION

11–008 Problems relating to patients' consent or to disclosure without such consent need not arise if the information is disclosed in such a manner as to ensure that the patients to whom it relates cannot be identified. Information may be "coded" (for example by the use of pseudonyms), or more thoroughly anonymised (by the removal of all information which might be capable of identifying an individual). The General Medical Council's *Confidentiality*[9] sets out a general principle that, when disclosing information about a patient, doctors should use anonymised or coded information if practicable and if it will serve the purpose.

11–009 In *R. v Department of Health, Ex p. Source Informatics Ltd*,[10] the Court of Appeal held that the applicant company committed no breach of confidence in purchasing information from the computerised prescription records of pharmacists and passing that information on to pharmaceutical companies, which used it for marketing purposes. Crucially, the information provided by the applicant was in anonymised form. Giving the only judgment, Simon Brown L.J. agreed[11] with submissions, advanced on behalf of the General Medical Council, that patients could not be taken to have impliedly consented to the use made by the applicant of information relating to them. Nevertheless, he concluded:

> "The concern of the law here is to protect the confider's personal privacy. That and that alone is the right at issue in this case. The patient has no proprietorial claim to the prescription form or to the information it contains. Of course he can bestow or withhold his custom as he pleases . . . But that gives the patient no property in the information and no right to control its use provided only and always that his privacy is not put at risk."[12]

The decision of the Court of Appeal has been criticised[13] on the basis that it adopts too narrow a view of a patient's interest in preserving the confidentiality

---

[9] (2009), at para.9.
[10] [2001] Q.B. 424. See also *Sayers v Smithkline Beecham Plc* [2007] EWHC 1346 (QB), per Keith J.
[11] At para.51.
[12] At para.34.
[13] For example, in Grubb's *Principles of Medical Law,* 3rd edn (OUP, 2010), at para.12.26.

of medical information: a patient may object not only to the disclosure but also to the collateral use of such information. It is suggested that the Court of Appeal's decision was sound. Once information has been anonymised, the patient's legitimate interest in preventing its further disclosure *or other use* is limited, if it exists at all; in effect, the information no longer relates to the individual patient. It would be unfortunate if medical research of public importance were unnecessarily impeded by exaggerated sensitivities in respect of a patient's "ownership" of anonymised information.

Annex B of the Department of Health's *NHS Code of Practice: Confidentiality*[14] states that, once information is effectively anonymised, it is no longer confidential, but warns:

11–010

> "Effective anonymisation generally requires more than just the removal of name and address. Full postcode can identify individuals, NHS Number can be a strong identifier and other information, e.g. date of birth, can also serve as an identifier, particularly if looked at in combination with other data items."

Disclosure of partly or wholly anonymised personal data may also give rise to difficult questions under the complex terms of the Data Protection Act 1998. See the discussion of the House of Lords in *Common Services Agency v Scottish Information Commissioner*[15].

DIAGNOSIS, ADVICE AND TREATMENT

In *Sidaway v Board of Governors of the Bethlem Royal Hospital and the Maudsley Hospital*[16] the plaintiff underwent an elective operation which carried a very small risk of damage to the spinal column. This occurred. The surgeon had not advised her of the risk. The judge found that in refraining from doing so he was following a practice which would have been accepted as proper by a responsible body of skilled and experienced neuro-surgeons, and, applying the test formulated in *Bolam v Friern Barnet Management Committee*,[17] he held that the surgeon was not liable. His judgment was upheld by the House of Lords.

11–011

It was argued by the plaintiff that the surgeon's failure to inform should be regarded as a breach of duty, independently of any medical opinion or practice. The House of Lords preferred to view the matter in the context of the doctor's professional duty to his patient. Lord Bridge said that a doctor's professional functions may broadly be divided into three phases: diagnosis, advice and treatment, each requiring the exercise of professional judgment. He also said,[18]

11–012

> "A very wide variety of factors must enter into a doctor's clinical judgment not only as to what treatment is appropriate for a particular patient, but also as to how best to communicate to the patient the significant factors necessary to enable the patient to make an informed decision whether to undergo the treatment. He may take the view, certainly with some patients, that the very fact of his volunteering, without being

---

[14] November 2003, at p.29
[15] [2008] 1 W.L.R. 1550; further considered at para.8–016 above.
[16] [1985] A.C. 871.
[17] [1957] 1 W.L.R. 582.
[18] [1985] A.C. 871.

> asked, information of some remote risk in the treatment proposed, even though he described it as remote, may lead to that risk assuming an undue significance in the patient's calculations."

11–013 For purposes of diagnosis, advice or treatment, a doctor might wish to discuss a patient's case with colleagues or to have tests done. Investigative procedures involving the taking of samples or invasive techniques clearly require the patient's consent, whether they are performed for the purpose of routine screening (as in pregnancy) or for the more specific purpose of differential diagnosis.

11–014 A more difficult question is to what extent the patient's explicit consent is needed for a sample to be tested in a particular way which the patient may not appreciate is intended. A doctor might not wish to go into the precise forms of testing with his patient in advance, for reasons similar to those referred to by Lord Bridge, i.e. to avoid causing possibly undue alarm.

11–015 It is suggested that, in general, a patient who consults a doctor impliedly consents to the doctor disclosing such information about the patient to other appropriately skilled staff (whether by sending a sample for analysis or otherwise) as may be necessary to enable the doctor to decide how best to perform the three phases of diagnosis, advice and treatment. But that is a general, not a universal, proposition. It may be displaced by other considerations.

11–016 The scope of any implied consent may vary according to the purpose for which the doctor is consulted. For example, a doctor instructed to provide a medico-legal report for the purpose of possible legal proceedings may commit a breach of confidence if he or she discloses the report for therapeutic purposes, without the client's express consent, to the client's general practitioner, or to other medical practitioners.[19]

11–017 Even where a patient's consent to disclosure for the purposes of diagnosis, advice, or treatment can be implied, it is good practice to inform the patient expressly that such disclosure is possible. The GMC's advice[20] is that:

> "Most people understand and accept that information must be shared within the health care team in order to provide their care. You should make sure information is readily available to patients explaining that, unless they object, personal information about them will be shared within the healthcare team, including administrative and other staff who support the provision of their care."

CLINICAL AUDIT AND REGULATION

11–018 Doctors are professionally obliged to participate in clinical audit and to comply with the regulatory requirements of the General Medical Council. Although it is for the courts, not a professional body, to determine the scope of a doctor's duty of confidentiality, in doing so the courts will have close regard to any professional guidance or requirements promulgated by a responsible professional or regulatory body. A court would be likely to conclude that a doctor's duty of

---

[19] *Cornelius v de Taranto* [2001] E.M.L.R. 12, Morland J.; largely upheld by the Court of Appeal [2001] EWCA Civ 1511; [2002] E.M.L.R. 6, CA.
[20] GMC: *Confidentiality* (2009), at para.25.

confidentiality would be qualified so as to permit him to participate properly in clinical audit or to comply with reasonable requirements of the General Medical Council, provided that steps are taken (by way of anonymisation or otherwise) to ensure that the confidential information thereby disclosed is reduced to the minimum level that is consonant with the doctor's professional obligations. In framing those obligations, the General Medical Council itself has taken account of patients' rights of confidentiality. Thus, for the purposes of a clinical audit conducted by the patient's own care team, doctors are advised that they may assume the patient's implied consent to disclosure, so long as the patient has ready access to information that explains that their personal information may be disclosed for local clinical audit. However, for the purposes of a clinical audit conducted outside the patient's own care team, doctors are required to obtain the patient's express consent to disclosure of any information which is not anonymised or coded.[21]

The General Medical Council has statutory powers under s.35A of the Medical **11–019** Act 1983 to require a practitioner or any other person to supply information or produce documentation which appears relevant to the discharge of its functions in respect of professional conduct, professional performance or fitness to practise. The General Dental Council has similar powers under s.33B of the Dentists Act 1984.

In *A Health Authority v X*,[22] the Court of Appeal considered the circumstances **11–020** in which a doctor should comply with a health authority's request for patient records, made pursuant to para.36(6) of Sch.2 to the National Health Service (General Medical Services) Regulations 1992.[23] At first instance, Munby J. had said[24]:

> "Now of course in the final analysis Dr X's ultimate obligation is to comply with whatever order the court may make. But prior to that point being reached his duty, like that of any other professional or other person who owes a duty of confidentiality to his patient or client, is to assert that confidentiality in answer to any claim by a third party for disclosure and to put before the court every argument that can properly be put against disclosure. All the more so when, as in the present case, he knows, because he has asked, that his patient or client is refusing to consent to disclosure."

On appeal, it was argued by the health authority that a doctor's duty was rather to comply with a para.36(6) request unless he had reason to doubt the health authority's right to make it. Giving the only judgment, Thorpe L.J. emphasised that the Court of Appeal's decision should not be construed or used as laying down any general propositions beyond the context of Children Act proceedings and their aftermath, but said[25]:

> "However I would add that I am not persuaded that Munby J. overstated the doctor's duty to his patient."

---

[21] GMC: *Confidentiality* (2009), at paras 30 to 32.

[22] [2001] EWCA Civ 2014; [2002] 2 All E.R. 780.

[23] Since repealed. See now Pt 5 of Sch.6 to the National Health Service (General Medical Services) Contracts) Regulations 2004.

[24] See para.7 of the report.

[25] At [25].

Leaving aside the provisions of the Family Proceedings Rules 1991 that were engaged in *A Health Authority v X*, Munby J.'s dictum may be very relevant to the question whether a doctor has acted properly in disclosing confidential information to a third party with a legitimate interest in receiving it. He ought not to make such disclosure without considering the interests of the patient or client, and, if he is uncertain whether the patient or client might legitimately object to the disclosure, he would be well advised to insist upon an order of the court. However, if a regulator *is* entitled to the disclosure of information by a regulated person, then the regulator can lawfully require such disclosure (and the regulated person can lawfully provide it) without the intervention of the court—even in the absence of the relevant patient's consent.[26]

ADVANCEMENT OF MEDICINE

11–021 In *W v Egdell* Bingham L.J. said[27]:

> "It has never been doubted that the circumstances here were such as to impose on Dr Edgell a duty of confidence owed to W. He could not lawfully sell the contents of his report to a newspaper, as the judge held. . . . Nor could he, without a breach of the law as well as professional etiquette, discuss the case in a learned article or in his memoirs or in gossiping with friends, unless he took appropriate steps to conceal the identity of W."

The same principle must apply to the use of patient information for medical research unless with the patient's consent.

11–022 The Health Service (Control of Patient Information) Regulations 2002 (made pursuant to s.60 of the Health and Social Care Act 2001[28]) provide for the processing of confidential patient information for purposes related either to the diagnosis or treatment of neoplasia (reg.2), or to communicable disease and other risks to public health (reg.3). Under reg.4, the processing of information in accordance with the Regulations is deemed to be lawful, notwithstanding any obligation of confidentiality that may exist. Regulation 7 imposes a number of obligations on the possessors of confidential patient information, including an obligation to anonymise such information, so far as it is practical to do so. The limits on the scope of the Regulations were considered by Foskett J. in *Lewis v Secretary of State for Health.*[29] He held that the Regulations did not extend to the disclosure of medical records to a confidential inquiry into the removal of tissues from the remains of deceased workers in the nuclear industry. However, the court was able to authorise such disclosure by means of its general declaratory jurisdiction.

---

[26] *General Dental Council v Savery* [2011] EWHC 3011 (Admin), in which Sales J. added (at [64]) that it was, however, arguable that there was a legal obligation to notify the patient in advance of the proposed disclosure.

[27] [1990] 1 Ch. 359 at 419.

[28] Since repealed and replaced by s.251 of the National Health Service Act 2006.

[29] [2008] EWHC 2196 (QB).

PROTECTION OF OTHERS

It is clear from *W v Egdell*[30] that disclosure of information about a patient, even contrary to his wishes and contrary to his interests, may be lawful for the protection of others potentially at risk. It is equally clear that the risk must be grave. Reference was made both by the trial judge and in the judgments of Sir Stephen Brown P. and Bingham L.J. (with which the third member of the court agreed) to the advice at that time published by the GMC that: **11–023**

> "Rarely, disclosure may be justified on the ground that it is in the public interest which, in certain circumstances such as, for example, investigation by the police of a grave or very serious crime, might override the doctor's duty to maintain his patient's confidence."

The Department of Health's *NHS Code of Practice: Confidentiality*[31] addresses directly one of the difficult questions to which this guidance[32] gives rise: **11–024**

> "The definition of serious crime is not entirely clear. Murder, manslaughter, rape treason, kidnapping, child abuse or other cases where individuals have suffered serious harm may all warrant breaching confidentiality. Serious harm to the security of the state or to public order and crimes that involve substantial financial gain or loss will also generally fall within this category. In contrast, theft, fraud or damage to property where loss or damage is less substantial would generally not warrant breach of confidence."

The General Medical Council's *Confidentiality: reporting gunshot and knife wounds*[33] is undoubtedly correct in its advice that the police should be told whenever a person has arrived at a hospital with a gun shot wound or an injury from an attack with a knife. The General Medical Council's Guidance advises that a professional judgment then requires to be made as to whether disclosure of the patient's identity is justified in the public interest. However, it is difficult to envisage circumstances in which the identification of such a patient at the request of the police would be unjustified.

American courts have gone further. In *Tarasoff v Regents of the University of California*[34] the parents of a girl killed by a man, who two months earlier told a psychologist employed at the university of his intention to kill her, were held to have an arguable claim against the university authorities for negligent failure to warn the deceased of the danger, although they did warn the police. It is unlikely that an English court would entertain such a claim.[35] **11–025**

It is not only violent criminals who may present a serious risk to the life or health of others. A motorist who suffers from blackouts obviously ought not to drive and is under a duty to inform the licensing authority of his disability. What **11–026**

---

[30] [1990] 1 Ch. 359.
[31] Annex B, Figure 7.
[32] For the GMC's current guidance, see paras 53 to 56 of *Confidentiality* (2009).
[33] September 2009.
[34] (1976) Sup., 131 Cal. Rptr. 14.
[35] See *Hill v Chief Constable of West Yorkshire* [1989] A.C. 53; *Palmer v Tees Health Authority* [2000] P.N.L.R. 87.

is the position of his doctor if he advises the patient of his duty, but the patient ignores his advice and continues to drive? A motorist who drives in disregard of a serious disability is an obvious danger to the life of others, and it would be surprising if the doctor's duty of confidentiality extended to keeping secret the fact that he was doing so.

11–027   A controversial question is whether a specialist who diagnoses a serious communicable disease (for example, HIV, tuberculosis, or hepatitis B or C) is at liberty to inform other health care professionals, who are or may be involved in the patient's care, and the patient's spouse or other sexual partner.

11–028   The GMC's Confidentiality: disclosing information about serious communicable diseases (September 2009) requires that the patient's consent to such disclosure should be sought where possible, but advises that in the last resort it would not be improper to make such disclosure, without the patient's consent, where the doctor judges that such disclosure is necessary to protect others.

11–029   This advice is consistent with the principle that a doctor's duty of confidentiality is subject to the qualification that a doctor who learns in his professional capacity of matters which cause serious risk to others is not prevented from making such disclosure as may be necessary to safeguard those at risk, and it is likely that a court would support it. A person who knows that he is infected with a serious sexually transmissible disease and recklessly passes it to another person by sexual activity, without disclosing his condition to the other person, is guilty of a serious criminal offence.[36]

11–030   In X v Y[37] the plaintiff health authority obtained injunctions against a newspaper reporter and the publishers of a newspaper, restraining publication of information about two doctors in general practice suffering from AIDS, which was supplied to the reporter by an employee or employees of the health authority from access to hospital records. Both doctors had sought medical advice and were being properly and effectively counselled. The judge found that the small theoretical risk of their infecting a patient was, in practice, removed by counselling. The sole justification sought to be advanced by the defendants for publication was not that it was necessary to protect individuals at risk, but that the subject was one of public interest and that publication would contribute to public debate. This was no defence.

SELF-PROTECTION

11–031   If a patient sues a doctor or makes a complaint about him, for example, to the Health Services Ombudsman or the GMC, he would no doubt be taken to waive confidentiality to the extent necessary to enable the doctor to defend himself.[38] However, the General Medical Council's supplementary guidance, Confidentiality: Responding to criticism in the press (September 2009) warns that doctors should not disclose confidential information for the purpose of conducting a dispute with a patient in the media.

---

[36] Contrary to the Offences against the Person Act 1861 s.20: see R. v Dica [2004] EWCA Crim 1103; [2004] Q.B. 1257; R. v Konzani [2005] EWCA Crim 706; [2005] 2 Cr. App. R. 198.

[37] [1988] 2 All E.R. 648.

[38] Compare Paragon Finance Plc v Freshfields [1999] 1 W.L.R. 1183 (claim against solicitor). As to the limits on such waiver, see Kadian v Richards [2004] N.S.W.S.C. 382 (Campbell J.).

A doctor might have equal need to use information gained about a patient in **11–032** his professional capacity for the protection of his own position in circumstances resulting, not from a complaint by a patient but, for example, from allegations by other staff. Just as the Court of Appeal has recognised an implied qualification of the implied duty of confidence owed by a banker to his customer where disclosure is required in the interests of the banker,[39] it would be surprising if there was no similar qualification in the case of a doctor and if he had to rely simply on a discretion of the court to enable him to safeguard his own professional position.[40]

MANAGEMENT AND RECORD KEEPING

General practitioners and hospitals have to maintain computerised and other **11–033** records. The storing of information, whether manually or on computer, to which as a matter of practical reality others may have access involves actual or potential loss of secrecy. Moreover information may be stored not merely for medical but for management purposes, e.g. in the case of a private hospital patient so that the accounting department bills the patient correctly. The legal justification may be put in alternative ways. Since no medical practice or hospital could operate properly or efficiently without maintaining medical records, it may be said that the patient impliedly consents to it. Alternatively it may be said that the keeping of records is in part for the purpose of the patient's present or future treatment and in part for the protection of the doctor's or hospital's proper interests, and therefore does not in itself infringe upon any duty of confidentiality to the patient. Infringement will occur if records are leaked for other purposes, for example, by disclosure to the press (as in *X v Y*[41] or the *Ashworth Hospital* case[42]).

The European Court of Human Rights has emphasised the importance of **11–034** protecting the confidentiality of a person's medical data. In *Z v Finland*[43] the court said:

> " . . . the protection of personal data, not least medical data, is of fundamental importance to a person's enjoyment of his or her right to respect for private and family life as guaranteed by Article 8 of the Convention. Respecting the confidentiality of health data is a vital principle in the legal systems of all Contracting Parties to the Convention. It is crucial not only to respect the sense of privacy of a patient but also to preserve his or her confidence in the medical profession and health services in general. Without such protection, those in need of medical assistance may be deterred from revealing such information of a personal and even intimate nature as may be necessary in order to receive appropriate treatment and, even, from seeking such assistance, thereby endangering their own health, and, in the case of transmissible diseases, that of the community."

---

[39] *Tournier v National Provincial and Union Bank of England* [1924] 1 K.B. 461.

[40] See *Duncan v Medical Practitioner's Disciplinary Committee* [1986] 1 N.Z.L.R. 513, per Jeffries J. ("As this very case demonstrates a doctor may reveal confidences and secrets if he is required to defend himself, or others, against accusations of wrongful conduct".)

[41] [1988] 2 All E.R. 648.

[42] See para.11–003, above.

[43] *Z v Finland* (1997) 25 E.H.R.R. 371 at [95]. See also *MS v Sweden* (1997) 28 E.H.R.R. 313

11–035   The Data Protection Act 1998 imposes obligations on health organisations and health professionals in relation to the processing (which includes holding) of personal data,[44] as do the Health Service (Control of Patient Information) Regulations 2002.[45] A patient who is concerned what may be in his medical records has a right of access to them, subject to certain exceptions, under the Data Protection Act 1998. Special exceptions in the case of personal data consisting of information as to the physical or mental health or condition of the data subject were created by the Data Protection (Subject Access Modification) (Health) Order 2000.

11–036   For some limited purposes (for example, in relation to deceased patients) the Access to Health Records Act 1990 also continues to be relevant, as does the Access to Medical Reports Act 1988 (in relation to medical reports for employment or insurance purposes).

DISCLOSURE REQUIRED BY LAW

11–037   A number of statutory provisions compel disclosure of otherwise confidential information and material. Some apply specifically to doctors; others apply more generally but would include doctors. The following are examples:

(1)   Abortion Act 1967 and Abortion Regulations 1991 (SI 1991/499).
        Any practitioner terminating a pregnancy is required to provide specified information to the Chief Medical Officer.

(2)   Health and Social Care Act 2008 s.64.
        The Care Quality Commission is empowered to require identified categories of person to provide information and documents which it requires for the purposes of its regulatory functions.

(3)   Police and Criminal Evidence Act 1984 ss.8 to 12.
        Medical records are excluded from powers of search under a magistrates' warrant, but a constable may obtain access to such records for the purposes of a criminal investigation by order of a circuit judge.

(4)   Public Health (Control of Diseases) Act 1984 and Health Protection (Notification) Regulations 2010 (SI 2010/659) and Health Protection (Notification) (Wales) Regulations 2010 (SI 2010/1546).
        These require a doctor to notify actual or suspected cases of patients suffering various forms of infectious disease to the proper officer of the local authority.

(5)   Reporting of Injuries, Diseases and Dangerous Occurrences Regulations 1995 (SI 1995/3163).
        These require notification of industrial accidents and diseases.

(6)   Road Traffic Act 1988 s.172.
        Under this section any person may be required to give information which may lead to the identification of a driver alleged to be guilty of certain offences. In *Hunter v Mann*[46] a doctor who refused to give such

---

[44] See Ch.8 above.

[45] See para.11–022, above.

[46] [1974] Q.B. 767.

information under the equivalent section of the previous Act on grounds of confidentiality was held by the Divisional Court to have been rightly convicted.

A doctor may also be required as a witness to answer questions about matters learned confidentially in his professional capacity.[47]

CHILDREN

The relationship and rights of parent and child in connection with medical treatment and advice, and the duties of the doctor, were considered by the House of Lords in *Gillick v West Norfolk Area Health Authority*.[48] The Department of Health and Social Services issued to health authorities a memorandum of guidance on family planning services, including a section on contraceptive advice and treatment for young people. It recommended that clinics should be available for people of all ages; that if a girl under 16 wanted contraception the doctor should do his best to persuade her to inform her parents or guardian; but that if she refused, the doctor might exceptionally, in the exercise of his clinical judgment, prescribe contraceptive treatment, without parental knowledge or consent; and the document referred to the doctor's duty of confidentiality to patients, including those under 16.   **11–038**

The Court of Appeal declared that the advice was unlawful, but the House of Lords (by a majority) reversed the decision. The central reasoning of the majority was that parental rights existed only for the benefit of the child and diminished gradually as the child acquires the ability to make decisions for himself. The pace of that development will vary from child to child. Lord Scarman said[49]:   **11–039**

> "The law relating to parent and child is concerned with the problems of the growth and maturity of the human personality. If the law should impose upon the process of 'growing-up' fixed limits where nature knows only a continuous process, the price would be artificiality and a lack of realism in an area where the law must be sensitive to human development and social change."

It was held that the parental right to decide whether or not a child under 16 should have medical treatment terminates if and when the child has sufficient understanding and intelligence to enable him or her to understand fully what is involved.

The doctor's duty is to act in accordance with what he believes to be in the patient's best interest. That duty involves satisfying himself whether the patient has a sufficiently mature understanding to have the capacity to consent to the treatment in question. In assessing whether the patient has such capacity and what is in his or her best interests, the doctor must exercise his professional judgment.   **11–040**

The same considerations must govern the doctor's approach to the question of confidentiality. The doctor stands in a confidential relationship to every patient of   **11–041**

---

[47] *Duchess of Kingston's Case* (1776) State Trials 355 at 571–572; see also at 586–591; *Garner v Garner* (1920) 36 T.L.R. 196.
[48] [1986] A.C. 112.
[49] [1986] A.C. 112 at 186.

whatever age including a baby,[50] but the purpose of the relationship is the welfare of the patient. Information relevant to matters within the parent's responsibility for decision-making can and should ordinarily be disclosed to the parent in the child's interests, and to do so would not involve a breach of duty.

11–042 The House of Lords' decision in *Gillick* was considered and applied in *R. (Axon) v Secretary of State for Health*[51] by Silber J., who upheld the lawfulness of guidance issued by the Department of Health in relation to the provision of advice and treatment to children on contraception and sexual and reproductive health. Silber J. provided guidelines as to the circumstances in which a medical professional is entitled to provide medical advice and treatment on sexual matters without the knowledge or consent of parents.

11–043 Whatever the age of the child, special considerations would arise if the doctor had reason to believe that the parent was abusing the child, or neglecting the child, or that disclosure to the parent would for some reason be harmful to the child. In those cases it might be the doctor's duty not to inform the parent but, for example, to inform the police or the social services department. Paragraph 63 of the GMC's *Confidentiality* (2009) warns that:

> "If you believe that a patient may be a victim of neglect or physical, sexual or emotional abuse, and that they lack capacity to consent to disclosure, you must give information promptly to an appropriate responsible person or authority, if you believe that the disclosure is in the patient's best interests . . . "

11–044 In matters where the doctor is satisfied that the patient has sufficient responsibility to make his or her own judgment, the doctor should respect the patient's confidentiality and should accordingly not disclose information to the patient's parent against the patient's wishes, save in exceptional circumstances.[52]

11–045 Because development is a continuous process, there may be grey areas in which the doctor can only be guided by his professional judgment in considering whether the interests of the patient require that information should or should not be disclosed.

PERSONS LACKING CAPACITY TO CONSENT TO DISCLOSURE

11–046 The relationship between persons rendered incapable of consent to disclosure by age, illness or accident, and those who care for them will obviously vary according to the nature and extent of the disability, but the same general principles should apply in relation to invalid and carer as in relation to minor and

---

[50] *Re C (A Minor) (Wardship: Medical Treatment) (No.2)* [1990] Fam 39. See also *Re Z (A Minor) (Identification Restrictions on Publication)* [1997] Fam. 1.

[51] [2006] EWHC 37; [2006] H.R.L.R. 12.

[52] See para.11–048, below. The General Medical Council's *0–18 years: guidance for all doctors* (2007), at para.49, advises that "you should disclose information if this is necessary to protect the child or young person, or someone else, from risk of death or serious harm".

parent or guardian.[53] Relevant guidance may be found online in the Code of Practice issued in respect of the Mental Capacity Act 2005 by the Lord Chancellor on April 23, 2007.

In *R. (S) v Plymouth City Council*,[54] the respondent local authority had made a **11–047** guardianship order in respect of the claimant, an adult with mental difficulties. The claimant's mother, his nearest relative, sought disclosure of the material on which the guardianship order had been made, for the purpose of applying for discharge of the guardianship order. The Court of Appeal recognised that the claimant had an interest, independent of his mother, in protecting the confidentiality of personal information about himself, but concluded that:

> " . . . both at common law and under the Human Rights Act 1998, a balance must be struck between the public and private interests in maintaining the confidentiality of this information and the public and private interests in permitting, indeed requiring, its disclosure for certain purposes."

The Court of Appeal took into account the mother's Art.6 and Art.8 rights and observed that there was no suggestion that the claimant had any objection to his mother and her advisers being properly informed about his health and welfare. By a majority (Hale L.J. and Clarke L.J., with Kennedy L.J. dissenting as to where the balance lay), the court held that the claimant's mother was entitled to the disclosure sought by her.

DISCLOSURE TO A RELATIVE

Aside from patients of limited capacity, disclosure of information gained by the **11–048** doctor in his professional capacity should in normal circumstances only be made to another member of the patient's family with the patient's express or implied consent.[55] But there may be cases where a doctor believes that it would be in the patient's interests, for example, to inform the patient's husband or wife of something unknown to the patient. It is likely that the courts would regard that as a matter for the doctor's professional judgment, and would not hold him to be in breach of duty to the patient provided that he acted in what he reasonably believed to be in the patient's best interest, with the purpose of avoiding serious harm to the patient. The principle is not confined to disclosure within the circle of the patient's family, but that is where it is most likely to apply.

The circumstances would have to be still more exceptional to justify a doctor **11–049** disclosing confidential information about a patient from concern for his best medical interests but contrary to the patient's express wishes. The General Medical Council's *Confidentiality*[56] states that "...you should usually abide by a competent adult patient's refusal to consent to disclosure, even if their decision

---

[53] See *E v Channel Four Television Corp* [2005] EWHC 1144 (Fam); [2005] E.M.L.R. 30, per Munby J. at [115]–[120].

[54] [2002] EWCA Civ 388; [2002] 1 W.L.R. 2583.

[55] The General Medical Council's *Confidentiality* (2009), at para.65, points out that, "Unless they indicate otherwise, it is reasonable to assume that patients would want those closest to them to be kept informed of their general condition and prognosis."

[56] (2009), at para.51.

leaves them, but nobody else, at risk of serious harm". However, it is difficult to say that disclosure against the express wishes of a patient could never be justified.

11–050   In *Weld-Blundell v Stephens*[57] Bankes L.J. took the example of a patient informing his doctor that he intended to commit suicide at a particular place and time, and he implied that a contract to keep that communication secret would be an illegal contract. Attempted suicide was then a criminal offence, and a different justification would now be required for the doctor to warn others if forbidden by the patient to do so, although it is still an offence to assist in another's suicide. Suppose that the patient was suffering from clinical depression. The doctor might well feel that it was his duty to warn someone close to the patient in order to try to avert the possibility of suicide. It is suggested that a court would be unlikely to hold that the doctor's duty of confidentiality extended to prevent him from taking what he believed to be necessary action for the purpose of saving the patient's life.

THE DEAD

11–051   The ethical obligation recognised in the Declaration of Geneva ("I will respect the secrets which are confided in me, even after the patient has died") is repeated in the General Medical Council's *Confidentiality*[58]:

> "Your duty of confidentiality continues after a patient has died. Whether and what personal information may be disclosed after a patient's death will depend on the circumstances . . . "

Equity may impose a duty of confidentiality towards another after the death of the original confider.[59] The question is not one of property (whether a cause of action owned by the deceased has been assigned) but of conscience.

11–052   It is open to the courts to regard divulgence by a doctor of information supplied in confidence by a patient who has since died as being unconscionable as well as unprofessional. If so, there is no reason in principle why equity should not regard the doctor as owing a duty of confidence to the deceased's estate, consonant with the maxim that equity will not suffer a wrong to be without a remedy.[60]

11–053   It is possible also that a doctor might owe a duty in conscience towards others. A patient might disclose to his doctor information about X, another member of his family (who might or might not also be his patient), publication of which would be damaging or embarrassing to X, in the understandable belief that there

---

[57] [1919] 1 K.B. 520 at 527.

[58] (2009), at para.70

[59] *Morison v Moat* (1851) 9 Hare 241; affirmed (1852) 21 L.J. Chanc. 248. In *Lewis v Secretary of State for Health* [2008] EWHC 2196 at [18], Foskett J. observed that *Morison v Moat* was not a case concerning purely private, non-commercial, information. But see also *Bluck v Information Commissioner (Information Tribunal*, September 17, 2007, Appeal No. EA/2006/0090).

[60] In *Lewis v Secretary of State for Health* [2008] EWHC 2196, Foskett J. reviewed the discussion in the 2nd edn of this text and the authorities referred to, before holding that it was at least arguable that a doctor's duty of confidentiality is capable of surviving the patient's death.

was no risk to X of the doctor making the information public. It would be most unsatisfactory if, on the patient being killed the next day, the doctor became free to make disclosure.

If the doctor knew that the patient was concerned for X and did not want the information to get out for X's sake, it would be open to a court to hold that publication by the doctor on the patient's death would be unconscionable conduct towards X. *White v Jones*,[61] although not a case on confidentiality, nevertheless provides an interesting parallel. If under concepts derived from *Nocton v Lord Ashburton*[62] a solicitor may owe a duty in respect of the economic well-being of his client's surviving intended beneficiary,[63] so should the doctor's conscience move him to continue to respect his former patient's confidence on behalf of X.

11–054

In *Plon v France*[64] the European Court of Human Rights considered the question whether publishers should be permitted to distribute a book by President Mitterrand's doctor entitled "Le Grand Secret". Mitterrand was diagnosed with cancer in 1981, only a matter of months after beginning the first of his two seven-year terms as president of France. The public was not officially informed until 1994. The book went into the details of his health and treatment, and the steps taken by the president and his medical team to keep the truth from the public. Mitterrand died on January 8, 1996. Two days later *Le Monde* published an article saying that he had been suffering from cancer from the beginning of his first term, and soon afterwards Mitterrand's brother complained publicly that he had not received proper treatment. These matters generated wide public interest. Publication of the book was planned for January 17 and 40,000 copies were distributed, but on the same day the Paris Tribunal de Grande Instance granted an interlocutory injunction on the application of Mitterrand's widow and children to restrain further distribution pending a full hearing. Between the interlocutory and the full hearing the doctor was prosecuted for a criminal offence of breaking a professional confidence, convicted and sentenced to a suspended term of imprisonment and a fine. In October 1996, on the full hearing of the civil action, the court awarded damages to Mitterrand's widow and children and ordered that the ban on distribution of the book should remain in force indefinitely. The ban was upheld by the French courts on appeal.

11–055

The European Court of Human Rights distinguished between the interim and the final injunction, observing that a need to interfere with freedom of expression may be present initially but subsequently cease to exist.[65] It concluded that the interim injunction did not violate Art.10. It was imposed for a limited period (until the full hearing) at a time of great grief to Mitterrand's family, which could only have been intensified by publication so soon after his death.[66] But as his death became more remote, this factor became less important. The more time elapsed, the more the public interest in discussion of the history of Mitterrand's two terms of office prevailed over protecting the president's right to medical confidence. This did not mean that the requirements of historical debate may release doctors from a duty of medical confidentiality save in strictly exceptional

11–056

---

[61] [1995] 2 A.C. 207.
[62] [1914] A.C. 932.
[63] *White v Jones* [1995] 2 A.C. 207 at 270–272 and 275–276, per Lord Browne-Wilkinson.
[64] [2004] E.C.H.R. 200.
[65] [2004] E.C.H.R. 200 at [45].
[66] [2004] E.C.H.R. 200 at [47].

circumstances. But by the time of the final order, not only had 40,000 copies been sold but there had been discussion on the internet and considerable media comment, as a result of which the book was to a large extent no longer confidential in practice. The doctor had also been subject to criminal sanctions.[67] Taking all these factors into account, the court concluded that at the time of the final order there was not a pressing social need for a permanent ban.[68]

---

[67] [2004] E.C.H.R. 200 at [53].
[68] [2004] E.C.H.R. 200 at [55].

CHAPTER 12

Bankers

THE GENERAL PRINCIPLE

Tournier v National Provincial and Union Bank of England[1] is the leading **12–001** authority on the duty of confidence owed by a bank to its customer. The Court of Appeal held that a bank owes to its customer an implied contractual duty to keep his affairs secret, but that the duty is qualified. The duty arises at the commencement of the relationship and continues after the customer has closed his account in relation to information gained during the period of the account. It covers information about the customer's affairs gained by virtue of the banking relationship and is not limited to information from or about the account itself.[2] The duty may prevent a bank from communicating information to other companies in the same group, including its own direct subsidiaries.[3]

In *Brighton v Australia and New Zealand Banking Group Ltd*[4] the New South Wales Court of Appeal declined to find an implied obligation of confidentiality in the contractual relationship between a bank and individuals who had provided the bank with personal guarantees but accepted that:

> "It might possibly be the case that if a guarantor were to supply to a bank information concerning his or her own financial circumstances (as could fairly readily happen if the bank needed assurance that the guarantor had the wherewithal to meet the guarantee) there would be either an implied contractual obligation of confidentiality, or an equitable obligation of confidentiality concerning that information."

The appeal in *Tournier* arose from a jury trial, in which the judge had directed **12–002** the jury that disclosure of the state of a customer's account by a banker to a third party was not a breach of contract if made "justifiably, that is to say, if, under the circumstances of the particular case, it was reasonable and proper that he should make the communication". This was held to be an inadequate explanation of a difficult area of law. Atkin L.J. commented that[5]:

---

[1] [1924] 1 K.B. 461.
[2] See also *Barclays Bank Plc v Taylor* [1989] 1 W.L.R. 1066 at 1070 per Lord Donaldson M.R., "The banker-customer relationship imposes upon the bank a duty of confidentiality in relation to information concerning its customer and his affairs which it acquires in the character of his banker".
[3] *Bank of Tokyo Ltd v Karoon*: (Note) [1987] A.C. 45 CA.
[4] [2011] NSWCA 152 at [53]–[60]
[5] *Tournier v National Provincial and Union Bank of England*[1924] 1 K.B. 461 at 485.

"... to leave to the jury what is 'justifiable' or 'proper' is merely to tell them that the bank may not divulge information except on occasions when they may divulge it, and that of what those occasions are the jury are the judges. This appears to me to treat as fact what is matter of law . . . ."

The fullest judgment on the qualifications to the implied obligation of secrecy is that of Bankes L.J. who said[6]:

"At the present day I think it may be asserted with confidence that the duty is a legal one arising out of contract, and that the duty is not absolute but qualified. It is not possible to frame any exhaustive definition of the duty. The most that can be done is to classify the qualification, and to indicate its limits. . . .
On principle I think that the qualifications can be classified under four heads: (a) Where disclosure is under compulsion by law; (b) where there is a duty to the public to disclose; (c) where the interests of the bank require disclosure; (d) where the disclosure is made by the express or implied consent of the customer."

These four qualifications were reaffirmed by the Court of Appeal in *Barclays Bank Plc v Taylor*.[7]

12–003   The true effect of the qualifications is not to excuse a breach of duty, but to identify certain limits to the duty itself. In this regard the judgment of Lord Donaldson M.R. in *Barclays Bank Plc v Taylor* is to be preferred to that of Croom-Johnson L.J. Lord Donaldson M.R. said[8]:

"The duty to maintain confidentiality is not all-embracing, subject to exceptions. It does not exist in four exceptional circumstances . . . ."

Croom-Johnson L.J. said[9]:

"Faced with those orders [under section 9 of the Police and Criminal Evidence Act 1984], the banks complied with them, thereby necessarily breaching the duties of confidence which they owed to Mr and Mrs Taylor.
The four circumstances in which a banker is justified in breaking that duty are set out in *Tournier v National Provincial and Union Bank of England* [1924] 1 K.B. 461, 473 in the judgment of Bankes, L.J. The first is 'disclosure . . . under compulsion by law'. That means that, in complying with the orders under section 9, the banks were not in breach of that implied term in their contracts with Mr Taylor."

It is contradictory to speak of the banks "necessarily breaching their duty of confidence" owed to the customer, and at the same time to say that "the banks were not in breach of that implied term of their contracts".

12–004   In *El Jawhary v BCCI*[10] Sir Donald Nicholls V.C. followed the approach taken by Lord Donaldson, saying:

"Where the case is within one of the qualifications to the duty of confidence, the duty, ex hypothesi, does not exist . . . ."

---

[6] *Tournier v National Provincial and Union Bank of England* [1924] 1 K.B. 461 at 471–472 and 473.
[7] [1989] 1 W.L.R. 1066 at 1070, per Lord Donaldson M.R.
[8] [1989] 1 W.L.R. 1066 at 1074.
[9] [1989] 1 W.L.R. 1066 at 1075.
[10] [1993] B.C.L.C. 396 at 400.

In *Barclays Bank Plc v Taylor* it was argued by the customer that a bank   **12–005**
served with notice of an application for an order under the Police and Criminal
Evidence Act, requiring disclosure of documents relating to his affairs, owed him
a duty to resist the application and to inform him. The court held that the contract
between banker and customer did not contain any such implied duty on the part
of the bank; and that, once an order valid on its face was made, the bank was
obliged to comply with it.

The same principle applies after disclosure as before it. In *El Jawhary v BCCI*   **12–006**
Sir Donald Nicholls V.C. held that, where a bank disclosed information to a third
party in circumstances within one of the qualifications to the duty of confidence,
there was no basis for implying an obligation on the bank to tell the customer
what it had done.

In *Robertson v Canadian Imperial Bank of Commerce*[11] a subpoena was   **12–007**
served on a bank requiring it to give evidence and produce bank statements in an
action to which the customer was not a party. The bank manager, having tried
unsuccessfully to contact the customer before complying with the subpoena,
produced the bank statements and gave evidence as required, without protest and
without informing the court that he had been unable to contact the customer. The
customer sued the bank, alleging breach of confidence in disclosing the
information without having first consulted the client or voiced objection. At first
instance the judge found that the defendant had breached its duty, but that the
action failed because the bank manager's evidence, including the production of
the information, was covered by absolute privilege.

The Privy Council held that the first of the *Tournier* qualifications applied   **12–008**
(disclosure under compulsion by law), so that there was no duty, and expressed
no opinion whether the bank, if it had been in breach of duty, would have been
protected by the absolute immunity which attaches to the testimony of witnesses.

In concluding that the first of the *Tournier* qualifications applied, the Board   **12–009**
left unanswered a number of questions. Lord Nolan said that the Board had much
sympathy with the argument by the customer that he should have been notified of
the issue of the subpoena. He added[12]:

> "In the ordinary way a customer in good standing could reasonably expect, *if only as
> a matter of courtesy and good business practice*, to be told by his bank that a
> subpoena had been received . . . . Their Lordships accept that the bank was
> compelled by law to produce the bank statement to the court, but it was under no
> compulsion to withhold knowledge of the subpoena from the customer." (Emphasis
> added.)

Although observing that there was no compulsion to withhold knowledge, the
Board refrained from holding that there was a duty to inform. Lord Nolan
recognised that it would be difficult to formulate the terms of any duty to be
implied, and that it could not go beyond a duty to use best endeavours, in which
case on the judge's findings there had been no breach.

On the question of the bank's failure to object to production, Lord Nolan said   **12–010**
that there was no head of privilege which the customer, or the bank, could have
claimed, and that it would be difficult to formulate the terms of any contractual

---

[11] [1994] 1 W.L.R. 1493.
[12] [1994] 1 W.L.R. 1493 at 1498.

duty to inform the court that the bank was producing the bank statement without the customer's consent. In any event, the customer had not established that the bank's omission to do so had caused him any loss, but Lord Nolan added[13]:

> "Their Lordships would not exclude the possibility that a particular banker/customer relationship would include some such implied term or duty of care as that for which the customer has contended, and that damages might be recoverable as a result of its breach by the bank concerned, but this is not such a case."

There is no reason to differentiate between a bank given notice of an intention to apply for an order for discovery[14] and a bank served with a witness summons. *Barclays Bank Plc v Taylor* was cited in argument in *Robertson*,[15] but regrettably is not referred to in the judgment. The judgment of the Privy Council leaves open the question whether a bank served with notice requiring production of documents owes any, and if so what, duty to try to inform the customer, or to object to the order (if there are potential grounds for objection), or to inform the court of the absence of the customer's consent.

12–011   In *Tournier* Atkin L.J. emphasised that it would not be right to imply an obligation of secrecy into the contract between a bank and its customer merely because it would be a reasonable term to include, but only if it was a necessary term; and that, whilst it was necessary to imply some term, there must be "important limitations" to the term required to be implied, one being that it was "plain that there is no privilege from disclosure enforced in the course of legal proceedings".[16]

12–012   That limitation plainly applies to documents produced pursuant to a witness summons or other compulsory process. That being so, as Lord Donaldson M.R. said in *Barclays Bank Plc v Taylor*[17]:

> "The real question is whether, in order to give business efficacy to the relationship of banker and customer, there must be an implied obligation to contest a section 9 application or to probe it or to inform its customer."

It may be that a customer in good standing would reasonably expect, "as a matter of courtesy and good business practice", to be informed by the bank of any notice requiring it to produce documents regarding the customer's affairs. Courtesy and good business practice are no doubt the basis on which many commercial relationships are expected to be conducted, and in fact conducted, but they are not the basis for the imposition of an implied term. Although a customer might be displeased at his bank complying with an order for discovery without informing him or seeking to oppose the order, it is difficult to see how a term requiring the bank to do so could be said to be necessary. Moreover the difficulty which the Privy Council recognised about any attempt to formulate such an implied contractual term is argument against it.

---

[13]   [1994] 1 W.L.R. 1493 at 1500.
[14]   *Barclays Bank v Taylor* [1989] 1 W.L.R. 1066.
[15]   [1994] 1 W.L.R. 1493.
[16]   [1924] 1 K.B. 461 at 483 and 486.
[17]   [1989] 1 W.L.R. at 1074.

COMPULSION BY LAW

Apart from obligations of disclosure which are of general application (e.g. to answer questions in the witness box[18]), compulsion may arise in various ways particularly relevant to banks. They include the following,[19]   **12–013**

(1) *Bankers' Books Evidence Act 1879*, under which orders for inspection may be made in civil or criminal proceedings.

(2) *Finance Act 2011.* Banks may be compelled to disclose certain information to Revenue and Customs (for example, in relation to interest payments) under Sch.23 to the Finance Act 2011 and the Data-gathering Powers (Relevant Data) Regulations 2012.

(3) *The Proceeds of Crime Act 2002.* Section 328 creates an offence of entering into or becoming concerned in defined arrangements relating to criminal property.[20] Section 330 creates an offence for bankers and others in the regulated sector of failing to disclose their knowledge or suspicions of money laundering activities. Section 333A creates (subject to ss.333B to 333E) a "tipping off" offence of making a disclosure prejudicial to money laundering investigations.

(4) *Insolvency Act 1986.* A bank may be compelled to disclose information about the affairs of insolvent customers under ss.236 (companies) and 366 (individuals).

(5) *Financial Services and Markets Act 2000.* Sections 146 and 147 of the Act empower the Financial Services Authority to make rules about, respectively, money laundering and the disclosure and use of information held by an authorised person. Rules under these sections appear in the Financial Service Authority's handbook. Part 11 of the Act contains a number of further provisions in relation to the Financial Services Authority's information gathering powers (see especially s.175(5)).

(6) *Companies Act 1985.* Inspectors appointed under the Act may require a bank to disclose information or produce documents relating to the affairs of a customer, where the customer is the company under investigation, or where the requirement is authorised by the Secretary of State, or where the bank is itself under investigation: s.452(1A), (1B).

(7) *Police and Criminal Evidence Act 1984.* Under s.9 and Sch.1, a bank may be ordered to produce documents for the purposes of a criminal investigation, as illustrated by *Barclays Bank Plc v Taylor*.[21] The Terrorism

---

[18] *Loyd v Freshfield* (1826) 2 Car. & P. 325 at 329; *Parry-Jones v Law Society* [1969] 1 Ch. 1 at 9; *Robertson v Canadian Imperial Bank of Commerce* [1994] 1 W.L.R. 1493.

[19] See Paget, *Law of Banking*, 13th edn (LexisNexis Butterworths, 2007), at Ch. 27.

[20] The risk to bank customers of an injustice caused by the operation of s.328 was identified by Laddie J. in *Squirrell Ltd v National Westminster Bank Plc* [2005] EWHC 664; [2006] 1 W.L.R. 637, at [7]. See also the discussion of the draconian effects of the relevant provisions in *K Ltd v National Westminster Bank Plc* [2006] EWCA Civ 1039; [2007] 1 W.L.R. 311; *R. (on the application of UMBS Online Ltd) v Serious Organised Crime Agency* [2007] EWCA Civ 406; [2008] 1 All E.R. 465, and *Shah v HSBC Private Bank (UK) Ltd* (both the Court of Appeal's decision on the defendant's summary judgment application—[2010] EWCA Civ 31; [2010] 3 All E.R. 477, especially per Longmore L.J. at [32]; and Supperstone J.'s final judgment after trial—[2012] EWHC 1283 (QB), especially at [38]).

[21] [1989] 1 W.L.R. 1066.

Act 2000 and the Serious Organised Crime and Police Act 2005 also contain disclosure provisions relating to their subject-matter.

(8)   Disclosure orders may be made in support of a tracing claim in equity, or in support of a freezing injunction, requiring a bank to disclose information relating to its customer.[22] In *Koo Golden East Mongolia v Bank of Novia Scotia*,[23] Sir Anthony Clarke M.R. said, "A court should be very reluctant to make a Norwich Pharmacal order which involves a breach of confidence as between a bank and its customer." Although it might be said that, strictly speaking, a bank's compliance with an order of the court could not amount in law to a breach of confidence, the Master of the Rolls's dictum serves to illustrate the importance that is attached by the courts to obligations of banking confidentiality.

Confidentiality and foreign law is considered in Ch.10.

DUTY TO THE PUBLIC

12–014   In *Tournier* Banks L.J. said[24]:

> "Many instances . . . might be given. They may be summed up in the language of Lord Finlay in *Weld-Blundell v Stephens*,[25] where he speaks of cases where a higher duty than the private duty is involved, as where 'danger to the State or public duty may supercede the duty of the agent to his principal'."

Scrutton L.J. thought it clear that the bank might disclose the customer's account and affairs to prevent fraud or crimes.[26]

12–015   Atkin L.J. also thought it safe to say that the bank's obligation was subject to the qualification that it had the right to disclose information relating to its customer's affairs when and to the extent to which it was reasonably necessary for protecting the bank, or other interested persons, or the public, against fraud or crime.[27]

The scope of the public interest exception to banking confidentiality is uncertain. Staughton J. adopted a broad approach in *Libyan Arab Foreign Bank v Bankers Trust Co*,[28] in which the defendant bank's branch in London had informed the New York Federal Reserve Board of fund movements which were being effected by its Libyan clients. Staughton J. said obiter:

> "...presuming (as I must) that New York law on this point is the same as English law, it seems to me that the Federal Reserve Board, as the central banking system in the United States, may have a public duty to perform in obtaining information from

---

[22]   *A v C (Note)* [1981] Q.B. 956; *Banker's Trust Co v Shapira* [1980] 1 W.L.R. 1274; *A.J. Bekhor & Co Ltd v Bilton* [1981] Q.B. 923.

[23]   [2008] Q.B. 717, at [49].

[24]   [1924] 1 K.B. 461 at 473.

[25]   [1920] A.C. 956 at 965.

[26]   [1924] 1 K.B. 461 at 481.

[27]   *Tournier v National Provincial and Union Bank of England* 1 K.B. 461 at 486.

[28]   [1989] Q.B. 728 at 771.

banks. I accept the argument that higher public duty is one of the exceptions to a banker's duty of confidence, and I am prepared to reach a tentative conclusion that the exception applied in this case."

In *Price Waterhouse v B.C.C.I.*[29] Millett J. had to consider banking confidence **12–016** at one remove. The issue was whether Price Waterhouse was at liberty to disclose information, obtained in the course of acting for B.C.C.I. as auditors and professional advisers, to an inquiry set up by the Government and the Bank of England, under the chairmanship of Bingham L.J., to investigate the supervision of B.C.C.I. under the Banking Act and to make recommendations.

On the subject of banking confidentiality and public duty of disclosure, Millett **12–017** J. said that[30]:

" . . . there seems no reason to doubt the general correctness of the statement in Paget's *Law of Banking* (10th edn, 1989) p.256, based on a remark of Bankes L.J. in the *Tournier* case [1924] 1 K.B. 461 at 474 . . . that

'The giving of information to the police, for instance in regard to a customer suspected of a crime would be unwarranted.'"

What Bankes L.J. said in *Tournier* was[31]:

"I cannot think that the duty of non-disclosure is confined to information derived from the customer himself or from his account. To take a simple illustration. A police officer goes to a banker to make an inquiry about a customer of the bank. He goes to the bank, because he knows that the person about whom he wants information is a customer of the bank. The police officer is asked why he wants the information. He replies, because the customer is charged with a series of frauds. Is the banker entitled to publish *that* information? Surely not. He acquired the information in his character of banker." (Emphasis added.)

The point which Bankes L.J. was making was that in his simple illustration the banker would not be entitled to publish to the world the information which he gained about his customer *from* the police that the customer was charged with a number of frauds, because he acquired that information "in his character of banker" (albeit not from the customer himself). Bankes L.J. was not there addressing the scope of the public duty qualification and whether the banker would be entitled to assist the police.

An express undertaking by a bank to a customer to keep secret the fact that the **12–018** customer was presently engaged, or intending to engage, in a criminal or fraudulent course of conduct would be unenforceable as contrary to public policy; and a bank would not be under an implied obligation to keep such information secret (see the judgments of Scrutton and Atkin L.JJ. in *Tournier* referred to above).[32] The situation may be different where a customer discloses the

---

[29] [1992] B.C.L.C. 583. For a fuller discussion, see paras 6–041 to 6–045, above.
[30] [1992] B.C.L.C. 583 at 598.
[31] [1924] 1 K.B. 461 at 474.
[32] [1924] 1 K.B. 461 at 481 and 486. See also *Gartside v Outram* [1857] 26 L.J.Ch. (N.S.) 113; *Initial Services Ltd v Patterill* [1968] 1 Q.B. 396; *Canadian Imperial Bank of Commerce v Sayani* (1993) 83 B.C.L.R. (2d) 167, Court of Appeal of British Columbia.

commission of a past offence. In *Weld-Blundell v Stephens*[33] the Court of Appeal drew a strong distinction between confiding in a professional man an intention to commit a crime and confessing a past crime, and between voluntary disclosure and disclosure under process of law. However, recent statutory interventions, such as the Proceeds of Crime Act 2002,[34] have significantly eroded this distinction—certainly in cases where previous criminal conduct has not yet come to the attention of the proper authorities.

12–019   The subject of public interest is considered further in Ch.6.

INTEREST OF THE BANK

12–020   In *Tournier* Bankes and Scrutton L.JJ. instanced disclosure in collecting or suing for an overdraft.[35] Atkin L.J. referred to the bank having the right to disclose information when, and to the extent to which, it is reasonably necessary for the protection of the bank's interests, either as against its customer or as against third parties in respect of transactions of the bank for or with its customer.[36]

12–021   In *Sunderland v Barclays Bank Ltd*[37] the defendants dishonoured a cheque drawn by the plaintiff in favour of her dressmaker at a time when her account was overdrawn. The bank manager's real reason was not the fact of the account being overdrawn, but that most of the cheques drawn on it had been to bookmakers. The plaintiff complained about the return of the cheque to her husband, who spoke to the bank manager. He told the plaintiff's husband about the cheques to the bookmakers. The plaintiff sued for breach of duty of confidence. Du Parcq L.J. dismissed her claim, holding that when the bank received an implied demand for an explanation of its apparent discourtesy in dishonouring the cheque, it was entitled in its own interests to explain the circumstances.[38]

CONSENT

12–022   In *Sunderland v Barclays Bank Ltd*, Du Parcq L.J. also held that there was implied consent to disclosure in that when the plaintiff's husband took over the conduct of the matter of the dishonoured cheque, the plaintiff impliedly consented to the bank giving him the explanation.

12–023   *Lee Gleeson Pty Ltd v Sterling Estates Pty Ltd*[39] provides another example of implied consent. A builder entered into a contract with a site owner for the development of a site. The owner ran into financial difficulties and the builder stopped work for non-payment. Negotiations took place involving the builder, owner and owner's bank. The builder and the owner came to an arrangement for the builder to complete the work and for the owner to pay by staged instalments.

---

[33] [1919] 1 K.B. 521 at 527, per Bankes L.J. and 544–545, per Scrutton L.J. See also *Bodnar v Townsend* [2003] TASSC 148, per Blow J. at [8].

[34] See para.12–013, above.

[35] [1924] 1 K.B. 461 at 473 and 481.

[36] [1924] 1 K.B. 461 at 486.

[37] *The Times*, November 24, 1938, 5 Legal Decisions Affecting Bankers 163.

[38] See also *Christofi v Barclays Bank Plc* [2000] 1 W.L.R. 937 (CA).

[39] [1992] 1 Bank L.R. 342 (New South Wales Supreme Court).

At the owner's request, the bank wrote to the builder confirming that the owner had authorised the bank to make payments in accordance with the arrangement. The owner subsequently countermanded the bank's instructions. The bank did not inform the owner. The owner sued the bank under an Australian statutory provision relating to misleading or deceptive conduct in trade or commerce.

The bank contended that it could not have informed the builder of the revocation of the owner's instructions without placing itself in breach of confidence to its customer. Brownie J. rejected the bank's argument, holding that by authorising the bank to write to the builder, making a statement as to its authority to make payments to the builder, the customer impliedly authorised the bank to inform the owner of the change to those instructions.   **12–024**

In *Turner v Royal Bank of Scotland Plc*,[40] the defendant bank answered third party status enquiries in relation to its customer, without informing its customer that it was doing so. The bank argued that its approach had been in accordance with universal banking practice and that its customer had impliedly consented to such disclosures being made. The Court of Appeal rejected the bank's argument, observing that the evidence suggested that the bank had deliberately withheld knowledge of its practice from its customers.   **12–025**

---

[40] [1999] Lloyd's Rep. Bank. 231.

CHAPTER 13

Broadcasting and Journalism

The law of confidentiality affects the media in two separate ways—(1) in limiting **13–001** their freedom to publish, and (2) in providing qualified protection against disclosure of sources.

FREEDOM TO PUBLISH

There are innumerable dicta which emphasise the importance in a democracy of a **13–002** free press, but also that it must operate within the rule of law.[1] The principles of the law of confidentiality therefore apply to the press as they apply to others, but with recognition of the particular role of the press.[2] Many of the most important recent cases in which the general law of confidence has been developed have required the courts to assess rights of confidentiality or privacy in the context of publication in the media.

Since the introduction of the Human Rights Act 1998 and the statutory **13–003** incorporation of Arts 8 and 10 of the European Convention into English domestic law, the decisions of the European Court of Human Rights on issues of press freedom have become increasingly important in the English courts.

In *Commissioner of Police of the Metropolis v Times Newspapers Ltd*,[3] Tugendhat J. engaged in an interesting analysis of the status of journalism under European human rights law. He observed that, since the advent of the internet, journalism can no longer be regarded simply as the activity which is carried on by professional "journalists", since it is to an increasing extent carried on by amateurs. He concluded[4]:

---

[1] e.g. *British Steel Corp v Granada Television* [1981] A.C. 1096 at 1168 per Lord Wilberforce,"First, there were appeals, made in vigorous tones to such broad principles as the freedom of the press, the right to a free flow of information, the public's right to know. In Granada's printed case we find quotations from pronouncements of Sheridan in Parliament and from declarations of eminent judges in cases where the freedom of the press might be involved. I too would be glad to be counted among those whose voice was raised in favour of this great national possession—a free press: who indeed would not?. . . Freedom of the press imports, generally, freedom to publish without pre-censorship, subject always to the laws relating to libel, official secrets, sedition and other recognised inhibitions".

[2] *Francome v Mirror Group Newspapers Ltd* [1984] 1 W.L.R. 892. For the importance of the media to the administration of justice, see also *Re Webster (a child)* [2006] EWHC 2733 (Fam); [2007] E.M.L.R. 7, per Munby J. at [29]ff. For consideration of the difference between an employed journalist's list of contacts and an employed salesman's list of contacts, see *Pennwell Publishing (UK) Ltd v Ornstien* [2007] EWHC 1570 (QB); [2007] I.R.L.R. 700, per Justin Fenwick QC at [113] and [114].

[3] [2011] EWHC 2705 (QB), especially at [122]–[135].

[4] [2011] EWHC 2705 at [130].

"The distinction between journalism and mere self-expression must be made on the basis of the nature of the speech in question."

Tugendhat J. pointed out that, in both English and Strasbourg jurisprudence, it is the activity of journalism, rather than the status of the journalist, which enjoys special protection. He also suggested that form is less important than content:

"The type of speech to which [Strasbourg jurisprudence] gives most protection is that which is directed to informing public debate (or, as it sometimes put, imparting information and ideas on political questions and on other matters of public interest). It is that type of speech which is referred to by a figure of speech as 'the press', or as journalism, in that body of case law. The Strasbourg jurisprudence does not look to the form in which the speech is published, and, if it is in a particular form, categorise it as journalism even if its content is no more than gossip which does not inform public debate."[5]

RELATIONSHIP BETWEEN ARTICLE 10 AND RIGHTS OF CONFIDENTIALITY

13–004   Article 10, containing the right to freedom of expression, is expressly subject to such restrictions as are prescribed by law and necessary in a democratic society (in the well-established sense of involving a pressing social need) for, among other things, preventing the disclosure of information received in confidence. The manner in which Art.10 rights are to be balanced against Art.8 rights to privacy has been the subject of numerous decisions.[6] On the other hand, it is not immediately obvious how Art.10 rights are to be taken into account in the context of a traditional action for breach of an equitable duty of confidence. The tendency of the courts in this regard (as elsewhere) has been to seek to assimilate the traditional action for breach of confidence and the modern action for misuse of private information. In *Prince of Wales v Associated Newspapers Ltd*[7] the Court of Appeal said:

"Whether a publication, or threatened publication, involves a breach of a relationship of confidence, an interference with privacy or both, it is necessary to consider whether these matters justify the interference with article 10 rights that will be involved if the publication is made the subject of a judicial sanction. A balance has to be struck."

13–005   In some cases, the publishing of information may give rise to a threat to the physical safety of an individual.[8] If so, the court's balancing exercise may have to take account of not only Art.8 rights to privacy, but also the Art.3 prohibition on inhuman or degrading treatment, or even the Art.2 right to life.

---

[5] [2011] EWHC 2705 at [132].
[6] See the discussion in Ch.7, above.
[7] [2008] Ch. 57 at [65]. See also *Imerman v Tchenguiz* [2011] Fam. 116 (CA) at [67].
[8] See, for example, *Secretary of State for the Home Department v AP (No.2)* [2010] UKSC 26; [2010] 1 W.L.R. 1652 (concerning the identification of an individual subject to a control under s.2 of the Prevention of Terrorism Act 2005).

ARTICLE 10 AND ITS APPLICATION TO DIFFERENT KINDS OF INFORMATION

Article 10 states that everyone has the right to freedom of expression, but the European Court of Human Rights has emphasised its particular importance in relation to the press. In *Von Hannover v Germany*,[9] Princess Caroline of Monaco complained of the failure of the German courts to protect her from the publication of photographs taken of her acting in a private capacity, though in public locations. Referring to previous similar expressions of principle, the Court observed:

13–006

> " . . . freedom of expression constitutes one of the essential foundations of a democratic society . . . In that connection the press plays an essential role in a democratic society. Although it must not overstep certain bounds, in particular in respect of the reputation and rights of others, its duty is nevertheless to impart—in a manner consistent with its obligations and responsibilities—information and ideas on all matters of public interest."[10]

However, the Court considered that the importance to be attached to the press's freedom of expression varied in accordance with the nature of the information that it sought to convey. Where the sole purpose of publication was to satisfy the curiosity of a particular readership regarding the details of a person's private life, "freedom of expression calls for a narrower interpretation".[11] Finding in favour of Princess Caroline, the Court concluded:

> " . . . the decisive factor in balancing the protection of private life against freedom of expression should lie in the contribution that the published photos and articles make to a debate of general interest. It is clear in the instant case that they made no such contribution since the applicant exercises no official function and the photos and articles related exclusively to details of her private life."[12]

In *Mosley v United Kingdom*[13] the European Court of Human Rights said:

> "The Court also reiterates that there is a distinction to be drawn between reporting facts — even if controversial — capable of contributing to a debate of general public interest in a democratic society, and making tawdry allegations about an individual's private life...In respect of the former, the pre-eminent role of the press in a democracy and its duty to act as a 'public watchdog' are important considerations in favour of a narrow construction of any limitations on freedom of expression. However, different considerations apply to press reports concentrating

---

[9] *Von Hannover v Germany* [2005] 40 E.H.R.R. 1 ("*Von Hannover v Germany (No.1)*"); a later, second, application to the ECHR was unsuccessful: *Von Hannover v Germany* [2012] 55 E.H.R.R. 15 ("*Von Hannover v Germany (No.2)*").

[10] *Von Hannover v Germany (No.1)* (2005) 40 E.H.R.R. 1 at [58]; *Von Hannover v Germany (No.2)* [2012] E.M.L.R. 16 at [101]–[102]. See also *Reynolds v Times Newspapers Ltd* [2001] 2 A.C. 127, per Lord Nicholls at 200.

[11] At [66].

[12] At [76]. Cited by the Supreme Court in *In re Guardian News and Media Ltd* [2010] UKSC 1; [2010] 2 A.C. 697 at [49].

[13] (2003) 53 E.H.R.R. 30 at [114]. The contrary observations made by Fennelly J. (representing a majority of the Supreme Court of Ireland) in *Mahon v Post Publications* [2007] I.E.S.C. 15, at [42] and [43], must now be regarded as doubtful.

on sensational and, at times, lurid news, intended to titillate and entertain, which are aimed at satisfying the curiosity of a particular readership regarding aspects of a person's strictly private life....Such reporting does not attract the robust protection of Article 10 afforded to the press. As a consequence, in such cases, freedom of expression requires a more narrow interpretation....While confirming the Article 10 right of members of the public to have access to a wide range of publications covering a variety of fields, the Court stresses that in assessing in the context of a particular publication whether there is a public interest which justifies an interference with the right to respect for private life, the focus must be on whether the publication is in the interest of the public and not whether the public might be interested in reading it."

Even "tawdry allegations about an individual's private life" may contribute to a debate of genuine public interest. In *Ferdinand v MGN Ltd*,[14] Nicol J. dismissed a claim brought by the former English football captain against the Mirror newspaper in respect of his relationship with a woman who had been paid £16,000 by the Mirror for her story. Nicol J. held:

"In my judgment there was a public interest in this article. At one level it was a 'kiss and tell' story. Even less attractively, it was a 'kiss and paid for telling' story, but stories may be in the public interest even if the reasons behind the informant providing the information are less than noble."

The claimant had consciously presented an image of himself in the media as a reformed "family man" and there was a public interest in demonstrating (if it were the case) that the image was false.

Similarly, in *Goodwin v News Group Newspapers Ltd*,[15] Tugendhat J. held obiter that:

"...it is in the public interest that there should be public discussion of the circumstances in which it is proper for a chief executive (or other person holding public office or exercising official functions) should be able to carry on a sexual relationship with an employee in the same organisation. It is in the public interest that newspapers should be able to report upon cases which raise a question as to what should or should not be a standard in public life. The law, and standards in public life, must develop to meet changing needs. The public interest cannot be confined to exposing matters which are improper only by existing standards and laws, and not by standards as they ought to be, or which people can reasonably contend that they ought to be."

13–007 The value of information may lie in a variety of different spheres. It is possible that at least a partial and informal hierarchy of types of media publication is emerging from judicial decisions. In *Campbell v MGN Ltd*,[16] Baroness Hale said:

"There are undoubtedly different types of speech, just as there are different types of private information, some of which are more deserving of protection in a democratic society than others. Top of the list is political speech. The free exchange of information and ideas on matters relevant to the organisation of the economic,

---

[14] [2011] EWHC 2454 (QB). See also the judgment of the European Court of Human Rights in *Axel Springer AG v Germany* [2012] E.M.L.R. 15 at [90]–[91].
[15] [2011] EWHC 1437 (QB); [2011] E.M.L.R. 27 at [133].
[16] [2004] UKHL 22; [2004] 2 A.C. 457 at [148]. See also per Lord Hope, at [117].

social and political life of the country is crucial to any democracy. Without this, it can scarcely be called a democracy at all. This includes revealing information about public figures, especially those in elective office, which would otherwise be private but is relevant to their participation in public life. Intellectual and educational speech and expression are also important in a democracy, not least because they enable the development of individuals' potential to play a full part in society and in our democratic life. Artistic speech and expression is important for similar reasons, in fostering both individual originality and creativity and the free-thinking and dynamic society we so much value."

The courts also recognise that even responsible journalism of real value may well require a degree of colour if it is to reach an audience of any size. Thus, in *Von Hannover (No.1)*, the court accepted that: **13–008**

"Journalistic freedom also covers possible recourse to a degree of exaggeration, or even provocation."[17]

Similarly, in *Campbell v MGN Ltd*,[18] Lord Hope (although finding in favour of the appellant claimant) observed: **13–009**

"There is no doubt that the presentation of the material that it was legitimate to convey to the public in this case without breaching the duty of confidence was a matter for the journalists. The choice of language used to convey information and ideas, and decisions as to whether or not to accompany the printed word by the use of photographs, are pre-eminently editorial matters with which the court will not interfere. The respondents are also entitled to claim that they should be accorded a reasonable margin of appreciation in taking decisions as to what details needed to be included in the article to give it credibility. This is an essential part of the journalistic exercise."

In *Re Guardian News & Media Ltd*,[19] Lord Rodger elaborated on the reasons for the latitude allowed to media organisations:

"Writing stories which capture the attention of readers is a matter of reporting technique, and the European Court holds that article 10 protects not only the substance of ideas and information but also the form in which they are conveyed ... This is not just a matter of deference to editorial independence. The judges are recognising that editors know best how to present material in a way that will interest the readers of their particular publication and so help them to absorb the information. A requirement to report it in some austere, abstract form, devoid of much of its human interest, could well mean that the report would not be read and the information would not be passed on. Ultimately, such an approach could threaten the viability of newspapers and magazines, which can only inform the public if they attract enough readers and make enough money to survive."

However, in *Stoll v Switzerland*,[20] the majority of the European Court of Human Rights added a warning:

---

[17] At [58].

[18] At [112]. See also the dicta of Eady J. in *Mosley v News Group Newspapers Ltd* [2008] EWHC 1777 (QB); [2008] E.M.L.R. 20 at [135]–[171], discussed in more detail at para.7–032, above.

[19] [2010] 2 A.C. 697 at [63]; see also *Viagogo Ltd v Myles* [2012] EWHC 433 (Ch) (Hildyard J.).

[20] (2008) 47 E.H.R.R. 59 at [103]–[104]; see also *White v Sweden* (2008) E.H.R.R. 3 at [21], and *Springer Axel AG v Germany* (2012) 55 E.H.R.R. 6 at [93] and [102]–[107].

"...the safeguard afforded by Art.10 to journalists in relation to reporting on issues of general interest is subject to the proviso that they are acting in good faith and on an accurate factual basis and provide 'reliable and precise' information in accordance with the ethics of journalism ... These considerations play a particularly important role nowadays, given the influence wielded by the media in contemporary society: not only do they inform, they can also suggest by the way in which they present the information how it is to be assessed. In a world in which the individual is confronted with vast quantities of information circulated via traditional and electronic media and involving an ever-growing number of players, monitoring compliance with journalistic ethics takes on added importance."

Although the journalistic purposes of media organisations are accorded particular respect in European human rights jurisprudence, it is not to be supposed that this special protection extends to all their functions. In *British Broadcasting Corp v Sugar (No.2)*,[21] Lord Neuberger M.R. observed in the context of the BBC's position under the Freedom of Information Act 2000 that information about such matters as advertising revenue, property ownership or outgoings and financial debt would not normally be held "for the purposes of journalism".

STATUTORY RESTRICTION ON GRANT OF INJUNCTIONS AND RELEVANCE OF PRIVACY CODES

13–010   Section 12 of the Human Rights Act 1998 makes special provision for circumstances in which a court is considering whether to grant any relief which, if granted, might affect the exercise of the Convention right to freedom of expression (pre-eminently, injunctive relief restraining publication). Of particular significance to the media are subss.(3) and (4):

> "(3)   No such relief is to be granted to as to restrain publication before trial unless the court is satisfied that the applicant is likely to establish that publication should not be allowed.
>
> (4)   The court must have particular regard to the importance of the Convention right to freedom of expression and, where the proceedings relate to material which the respondent claims, or which appears to the court, to be journalistic, literary or artistic material (or to conduct connected with such material), to—
>
> > (a)   the extent to which—
> >
> > > (i)   the material has, or is about to, become available to the public; or
> > >
> > > (ii)   it is, or would be, in the public interest for the material to be published;
> >
> > (b)   any relevant privacy code."

The Press Complaints Commission's Code of Practice and Ofcom's Broadcasting Code are each a "relevant privacy code" for the purposes of s.12(4)(b). They contain provisions dealing expressly with a number of specific matters as well as provisions of more general application.

13–011   Clause 3 of the PCC Code provides:

---

[21] [2010] EWCA Civ 715; [2010] 1 W.L.R. 2278, especially at [55]–[57]. The Supreme Court upheld the Court of Appeal's judgment on appeal [2012] UKSC 4; [2012] 1 W.L.R. 439; Lord Walker expressly approved (at [84]) the comments of Lord Neuberger.

"Privacy"

"(i)   Everyone is entitled to respect for his or her private and family life, home, health and correspondence, including digital communications.

(ii)   Editors will be expected to justify intrusions into any individual's private life without consent.

(iii)   It is unacceptable to photograph individuals in private places without their consent.

Note—Private places are public or private property where there is a reasonable expectation of privacy."

Clause 10 of the Code provides:

"Clandestine devices and subterfuge"

"(i)   The press must not seek to obtain or publish material acquired by using hidden cameras or clandestine listening devices; or by intercepting private or mobile telephone calls, messages or emails; or by the unauthorised removal of documents or photographs; or by accessing digitally-held private information without consent.

(ii)   Engaging in misrepresentation or subterfuge, including by agents or intermediaries, can generally be justified only in the public interest and then only when the material cannot be obtained by other means."

Both of these clauses (and some others) are expressly made subject to the following paragraph:

"The public interest"

"There may be exceptions to the clauses . . . where they can be demonstrated to be in the public interest.

1.   The public interest includes, but is not confined to:
   (i)   Detecting or exposing crime or serious impropriety.
   (ii)   Protecting public health and safety.
   (iii)   Preventing the public from being misled by an action or statement of an individual or organisation.
2.   There is a public interest in freedom of expression itself.
3.   Whenever the public interest is invoked, the PCC will require editors to demonstrate fully that they reasonably believed that publication, or journalistic activity undertaken with a view to publication, would be in the public interest.
4.   The PCC will consider the extent to which material is already in the public domain, or will become so.
5.   In cases involving children under 16, editors must demonstrate an exceptional public interest to over-ride the normally paramount interest of the child".

Ofcom, a statutory broadcasting watchdog,[22] is required to secure in carrying out all its functions   **13–012**

---

[22] For its responsibilities see, in particular, the Broadcasting Act 1996 (as amended) ss.107(1) and 130, and the Communications Act 2003 s.3.

"the application, in the case of all television and radio services, of standards that provide adequate protection of all members of the public and all other persons from . . . unwarranted infringements of privacy resulting from activities carried on for the purpose of such services".[23]

Ofcom's Broadcasting Code covers privacy in s.8. This begins with the following general rule:

"8.1 Any infringement of privacy in programmes, or in connection with obtaining material included in programmes, must be warranted.
    Meaning of 'warranted':
    In this section 'warranted' has a particular meaning. It means that where broadcasters wish to justify an infringement of privacy as warranted, they should be able to demonstrate why in the particular circumstances of the case, it is warranted. If the reason is that it is in the public interest, then the broadcaster should be able to demonstrate that the public interest outweighs the right to privacy. Examples of public interest would include revealing or detecting crime, protecting public health or safety, exposing misleading claims made by individuals or organisations or disclosing incompetence that affects the public."

Paragraphs 8.2–8.22 of the Broadcasting Code contain more detailed provisions about particular practices including "doorstepping" and surreptitious filming or recording.

13–013   Such codes are not to be regarded simply as weapons in the hands of a publisher resisting an injunction application, since breaches may result in considerations of privacy outweighing a publisher's entitlement to freedom of speech.[24] In *A v B Plc*[25] the Court of Appeal gave general guidance as to the manner in which such codes, and other relevant considerations, should be taken into account on the hearing of applications for interim injunctions restraining publication.

DISCLOSURE OF SOURCES

13–014   A journalist who receives information from an informant in confidence will on ordinary principles owe an obligation of confidence to the informant not to reveal his identity; but that duty, like any other duty of confidence, is subject to qualifications, in particular where disclosure is required by law. Such disclosure may be required by statute.

13–015   The Police and Criminal Evidence Act 1984, for example, contains special provisions under which an order may be made by a circuit judge for journalistic material held in confidence to be produced to the police in cases where they are investigating a serious offence, subject to various conditions.[26] Similarly, the Terrorism Act 2000 and the Serious Organised Crime and Police Act 2005 contain disclosure provisions relating to their subject-matter.

---

[23] Communications Act 2003 s.3(2)(f).
[24] *Douglas v Hello! Ltd* [2001] Q.B. 967 at [94] per Brooke L.J.
[25] [2002] EWCA Civ 337; [2003] Q.B. 195.
[26] PACE 1984 s.9 and Sch.1.

At common law a journalist could be compelled to disclose otherwise **13–016** confidential information, including his sources, if required to do so in the witness box or by an action for discovery,[27] although the court would only order such disclosure if it considered it necessary. The courts' approach to such actions is now guided by a combination of statute and European human rights jurisprudence.

Section 10 of the Contempt of Court Act 1981 provides: **13–017**

> "No court may require a person to disclose, nor is any person guilty of contempt of court for refusing to disclose, the source of information contained in a publication for which he is responsible, unless it be established to the satisfaction of the court that disclosure is necessary in the interests of justice or national security or for the prevention of disorder or crime."

Since the European Convention was incorporated into English domestic law by the Human Rights Act 1998, the leading English authority on the protection of journalistic sources has been the House of Lords' decision in *Ashworth Hospital Authority v MGN Ltd*,[28] in which Lord Woolf C.J. (who gave the leading speech) observed[29] that:

> " . . . there can be no doubt now that both section 10 and article 10 have a common purpose in seeking to enhance the freedom of the press by protecting journalistic sources."

Among the patients at Ashworth, a secure mental hospital, was the Moors murderer, Ian Brady. The *Daily Mirror* obtained and published confidential information from Ashworth's medical records relating to Brady. The journalist concerned, Mr Gary Jones, stated that he did not know the identity of the original source of the leaked information and declined to identify his intermediary source. The House of Lords upheld an order requiring him to name the intermediary source.

Lord Woolf cited the observations of the European Court of Human Rights in **13–018** *Goodwin v United Kingdom*[30]:

> "The court recalls that freedom of expression constitutes one of the essential foundations of a democratic society and that the safeguards to be afforded to the press are of particular importance. Protection of journalistic sources is one of the basic conditions for press freedom, as is reflected in the laws and the professional codes of conduct in a number of contracting states and is affirmed in several international instruments on journalistic freedoms. Without such protection, sources may be deterred from assisting the press in informing the public on matters of public interest. As a result the vital public watchdog role of the press may be undermined and the ability of the press to provide accurate and reliable information may be adversely affected. Having regard to the importance of the protection of journalistic sources for press freedom in a democratic society and the potentially

---

[27] *Att Gen v Clough* [1963] 1 Q.B. 773; *Att Gen v Foster and Mulholland* [1963] 2 Q.B. 477; *British Steel Corp v Granada Television Ltd* [1981] A.C. 1096; *Att Gen v Lundin* (1982) 75 Cr. App. R. 90.
[28] [2002] UKHL 29; [2002] 1 W.L.R. 2033.
[29] At [38].
[30] (1996) 22 E.H.R.R. 123. See also the judgment of the ECHR in *Financial Times Ltd v United Kingdom* (2010) 50 E.H.R.R. 46.

chilling effect an order of source disclosure has on the exercise of that freedom, such a measure cannot be compatible with article 10 of the Convention unless it is justified by an overriding requirement in the public interest."

Turning to the disclosure order made below, Lord Woolf said[31]:

"However, the protection is not unqualified. Both section 10 and article 10 recognise this. This leads to the difficult issue at the heart of this appeal, namely whether the disclosure ordered was necessary and not disproportionate. The requirements of necessity and proportionality are here separate concepts which substantially cover the same area . . . I find no difficulty in accepting the approach that the European Court emphasised . . . that (i) 'As a matter of general principle, the 'necessity' for any restriction of freedom of expression must be convincingly established' and (ii) 'limitations on the confidentiality of journalistic sources call for the most careful scrutiny by the court'.
    Furthermore . . . any restriction on the otherwise unqualified right to freedom of expression must meet two further requirements. First, the exercise of the jurisdiction because of article 10(2) should meet a 'pressing social need' and secondly the restriction should be proportionate to a legitimate aim which is being pursued."

Lord Woolf concluded[32] that the care of patients at Ashworth was fraught with difficulty and danger, that the disclosure of the patients' records increased that difficulty and danger and that, to deter the same or similar wrongdoing in the future, it was essential that the source should be identified and punished: that was what had made the orders to disclose necessary and proportionate and justified.

13–019   On the day after the House of Lords' decision, another journalist, Robin Ackroyd, identified himself as the intermediary source between the original source and the Daily Mirror. Ashworth's successor authority, the Mersey Care NHS Trust, commenced proceedings against him in turn, seeking disclosure of the identity of the original source. The Trust obtained summary judgment at first instance, but the Court of Appeal allowed Mr Ackroyd's appeal.[33]

13–020   The proceedings eventually came on for trial in January 2006 and, on February 7, 2006, Tugendhat J. dismissed the Trust's application for *Norwich Pharmacal* relief.[34] Having set out the facts and having conducted a detailed review of the law, the judge emphasised that he had followed the House of Lords on all points of law, but pointed out that the facts were in some instances were not as had been supposed in the proceedings against MGN. (For example, it was no longer contended that the original source had received payment for his information.) In other instances, the circumstances had changed since the House of Lords' decision. He concluded that it had not been established that there was a "pressing social need" that the original source should be identified. The Court of Appeal upheld Tugendhat J.'s decision.[35]

[31] (1996) 22 E.H.R.R. 123 at [61]–[62].
[32] At [66].
[33] *Mersey Care NHS Trust v Ackroyd* [2003] EWCA Civ 663; [2003] F.S.R. 820.
[34] *Mersey Care NHS Trust v Ackroyd (No.2)* [2006] EWHC 107, (QB); [2006] E.M.L.R. 12.
[35] [2007] EWCA Civ 101; [2008] E.M.L.R. 1.

"Disclosure"

The protection afforded by Art.10 and s.10 of the Contempt of Court Act 1981 guards not only against the direct disclosure of sources but also against their indirect disclosure.[36] However, the manner in which and the extent to which a source's identity will be publicised may be relevant to the exercise of the court's discretion. In *Assistant Deputy Coroner for Inner West London v Channel 4 Televsion Corp*,[37] on the application of the coroner conducting the inquest into the death of the Princess of Wales, Eady J. made an order for disclosure of documents in the control of Channel 4, notwithstanding that the disclosure would result in the identification of journalistic sources. In conducting a balancing exercise, Eady J. took into account the fact that disclosure would initially be to the coroner alone and that the coroner would be able to control any subsequent wider disclosure.

"Necessary"

The introduction of the Human Rights Act 1998 and Art.10 have broadened the scope of the court's enquiry in relation to s.10 of the Contempt of Court Act 1981. To the extent that s.10 is still of independent significance, it is clearly to be construed so as to accord with the requirements of Art.10. Thus, in *Mersey Care NHS Trust v Ackroyd (No.2)*,[38] Tugendhat J. observed that there had been a number of attempts to define the word "necessary" in s.10,[39] before adopting the test of necessity employed by Lord Bingham in relation to Art.10(2) in *R. v Shayler*[40]: **13–021**

> " 'Necessary' has been strongly interpreted: it is not synonymous with 'indispensable', neither has it the flexibility of such expressions as 'admissible', 'ordinary', 'useful', 'reasonable', or 'desirable' . . . One must consider whether the interference complained of corresponded to a pressing social need, whether it was proportionate to the legitimate aim pursued and whether the reasons given by the national authority to justify it are relevant and sufficient under article 10(2) . . . "

In *John v Express Newspapers*[41] the Court of Appeal emphasised the practical evidential burden imposed by the test of necessity, citing an earlier dictum of Lindsay J. in *Saunders v Punch Ltd*[42]: **13–022**

> "To an extent, whether disclosure of a source is 'necessary' in the interests of justice can depend on whether the person seeking disclosure has made any attempt other than by applying to the court to find the source for himself and whether any such

---

[36] *Trinity Mirror v Punch Ltd* Ch.D., July 19, 2000, Jacob J.; *Financial Times Ltd v United Kingdom* (2010) E.H.R.R. 46 at [70].

[37] [2007] EWHC 2513 (QB); [2008] 1 W.L.R. 945.

[38] At [84]; see also the judgment of the Court of Appeal ([2008] E.M.L.R. 1), at [16]–[19].

[39] The leading authority prior to the introduction of the Human Rights Act 1998 was the House of Lords' decision in *Re an Inquiry under the Company Securities (Insider Dealing) Act 1985* [1988] A.C. 660.

[40] [2002] UKHL 11; [2003] 1 A.C. 247 at [23].

[41] [2000] 1 W.L.R. 1931.

[42] [1998] 1 W.L.R. 986 at 997.

attempts, were they to be made, would have had any real prospects of making the compulsion of a court order unnecessary. I do not say that the making of such attempts is a necessary precondition of the court's assistance, but its absence can be a powerful, even a decisive, factor against the intervention of the court . . . "

The Court of Appeal agreed, adding[43]:

"Before the courts require journalists to break what a journalist regards as a most important professional obligation to protect a source, the minimum requirement is that other avenues should be explored. It cannot be assumed that it will not be possible either to find the culprit or, at least, to narrow down the number of persons who could have been responsible."

"The interests of justice"

13–023   On the other hand, the courts have adopted a broad view of the meaning of "the interests of justice" in s.10. In *Secretary of State for Defence v Guardian Newspapers Ltd*[44] Lord Diplock had interpreted the "interests of justice" exception narrowly as being used "in the technical sense of the administration of justice in the course of legal proceedings in a court of law or . . . before a tribunal or body exercising the judicial power of the state". Rose J. followed that interpretation in refusing to order disclosure of a newpaper's source in *X v Y*.[45]

13–024   However, in *X Ltd v Morgan-Grampian (Publishers) Ltd* it was held that Lord Diplock's dictum was too narrow, and that it is "in the interests of justice", within the meaning of s.10:

"that persons should be enabled to exercise important legal rights and to protect themselves from serious legal wrongs whether or not resort to legal proceedings in a court of law will be necessary to obtain these objectives."[46]

Lord Bridge added, as an "obvious" example, that if an employer of a large staff was suffering grave damage from the activities of an unidentified disloyal servant, it was in the interests of justice that he should be able to identify him in order to terminate his contract of employment, notwithstanding that no legal proceedings might be necessary to achieve that end.

13–025   The breadth of "the interests of justice" was further emphasised by the Court of Appeal in *John v Express Newspapers*.[47] The defendant had obtained a copy of draft legal advice prepared by barristers instructed by or on behalf of the claimants. Although declining to make an order for disclosure of the defendant's source, the Court of Appeal rejected the defendant's submission that the interests of justice were to be assessed by reference only to the personal interest of the litigants involved:

"Mr Beloff argued that section 10 should not be interpreted so as to protect a wide class such as lawyers and clients as a whole . . . However, this is precisely what

---

[43]   [1998] 1 W.L.R. 986 at [27].
[44]   [1985] A.C. 339 at 350.
[45]   [1988] 2 All E.R. 648.
[46]   [1991] 1 A.C. 1 at 43.
[47]   [2000] 1 W.L.R. 1931 at [17].

section 10 can protect. The authorities make it clear that a broad approach should be taken to what is meant by the interests of justice in section 10. The need for clients to be able to consult their lawyers with assurance that they can do so without risk of their confidence being betrayed is of general importance."

In *Interbrew SA v Financial Times Ltd*[48] Sedley L.J. (with whom the other two members of the Court of Appeal agreed) warned that the courts should be cautious before allowing a journalist's statutory privilege to be abrogated for a reason unconnected with the applicant's initial right to disclosure. He suggested[49]:   **13–026**

> "The solution, in my view, is in the pivotal word 'necessary'. Read, as it must now be read, in the light of the Convention and its jurisprudence, it requires close regard to be had to the relationship between the mischief and the measure. If the mischief is a civil wrong, the measure which needs to be justified as relevant and proportionate is one which will right the wrong."

Sedley L.J.'s conclusion ("not without misgiving") that an order for disclosure was appropriate on the facts of the case was successfully challenged by the news organisations involved in the European Court of Human Rights: *Financial Times Ltd v United Kingdom.*[50]

THE NATURE OF THE SOURCE AND THE INFORMATION REVEALED

In *Camelot Group Plc v Centaur Ltd*[51] a copy of the claimant's draft preliminary financial statement was leaked and published about a week before the preliminary financial statement was due to be published. The Court of Appeal upheld an order which effectively required the defendant publisher to reveal its source. Schiemann L.J. said[52]:   **13–027**

> "There is a public interest in protecting sources. But it is relevant to ask 'what is the public interest in protecting from disclosure persons in the position of the source in the present case?' Is it in the public interest for people in his position to disclose this type of information? Embargoes on the disclosure of information for a temporary period are a common and useful feature of contemporary life. It does not seem to me that if people in the position of the present source experience the chilling effect referred to by the European Court of Human Rights the public will be deprived of anything which it is valuable for the public to have."

However, in *Ashworth Hospital Authority v MGN Ltd*[53] Lord Woolf C.J. expressly approved the judgment below of Laws L.J., which contained the following passage[54]:

---

[48] [2002] EWCA Civ 274; [2002] 2 Lloyd's Rep. 229.
[49] At [49].
[50] (2010) 50 E.H.R.R. 46.
[51] [1999] Q.B. 124.
[52] At p.138.
[53] [2002] 1 W.L.R. 2033 at [66].
[54] [2001] 1 W.L.R. 515 at [101].

"It is in my judgment of the first importance to recognise that the potential vice—'the chilling effect'—of court orders requiring the disclosure of press sources is in no way lessened, and certainly not abrogated, simply because the case is one in which the information actually published is of no legitimate, objective public interest. Nor is it to the least degree lessened or abrogated by the fact (where it is so) that the source is a disloyal and greedy individual, prepared for money to betray his employer's confidences. The public interest in the non-disclosure of press sources is constant, whatever the merits of the particular publication, and the particular source . . . In my judgment, the true position is that it is always prima facie . . . contrary to the public interest that press sources should be disclosed; and in any given case the debate which follows will be conducted upon the question whether there is an overriding public interest, amounting to a pressing social need, to which the need to keep press sources confidential should give way."

13–028   Inevitably the relative importance attached to the public interest in the protection of sources may vary in accordance with the circumstances of the particular case. Whistle-blowers disclosing matters of genuine public concern to reputable media organisations are unlikely to be deterred by court decisions that treat the leaking of gossip for venal purposes as disclosures attracting a lower level of protection. The decision of the European Court of Human Rights in *Von Hannover v Germany*[55] demonstrates that it is possible for the courts to differentiate between types of utterance without abandoning the general principle that freedom of speech is an important right that the courts must uphold. As Lord Steyn said in *R. v Home Secretary, Ex p. Simms*[56]:

"The value of free speech in a particular case must be measured in specifics. Not all types of speech have an equal value."

13–029   There are conflicting indications in the authorities about the relevance of the motive or purpose of the source. In *Commissioner of Police of the Metropolis v Times Newspapers Ltd*,[57] Tugendhat J. referred to a list of five possible motives for leaking confidential information which had been identified by Lawrence K Grossman, a former President of NBC News:

"(a) The ego leak, giving information to satisfy a sense of self importance. (b) The goodwill leak, currying favour with a reporter in the hope of favourable treatment in the future. (c) The promoter leak, a straightforward pitch for a proposal or a policy. (d) The trial balloon leak, floating a proposal or a policy. (e) The whistleblower leak, the last resort of disgruntled civil servants who cannot get satisfaction through official channels."

In *Interbrew SA v Financial Times Ltd*[58] Sedley L.J. interpreted the passage from Laws L.J.'s judgment in *Ashworth Hospital Authority v MGN Ltd*, set out above, as meaning that the source's motive ought to be ignored. Sedley L.J. considered

---

[55] (2005) 40 E.H.R.R. 1.
[56] [2002] A.C. 115 at 127. See also the discussion at para.13–013, above.
[57] [2011] EWHC 2705 (QB) at [182].
[58] [2002] EWCA Civ 274; [2002] 2 Lloyd's Rep. 229 at [53]. On the Financial Times's subsequent application to the European Court of Human Rights, the Court accepted that there might be circumstances in which a source's harmful purpose would in itself constitute a relevant and sufficient reason to make a disclosure order, but considered that Interbrew's evidence of the source's purpose was inadequate: *Financial Times Ltd v United Kingdom* (2010) 50 E.H.R.R. 46 at [66].

that a distinction should be drawn between a source's motive and his purpose: the former was irrelevant to the legal issues, but the latter was likely to be highly material. But it is a difficult distinction to draw, whether at a theoretical or a practical level. Consider, for example, the fact of a payment to the source. Sedley L.J. would appear to regard whether the source acted for profit or for spite as simply a matter of motive, and therefore legally irrelevant.[59] However, in *Ashworth Hospital Authority v MGN Ltd* Lord Woolf regarded the fact (as the evidence then suggested) that the source had been paid as a relevant matter. He said that "the disclosure was made worse because it was purchased by a cash payment".[60] Conversely, the actual absence of payment was held to be relevant in *Mersey Care NHS Trust v Ackroyd*, at both interim and final stages.[61]

In a case where a source has disclosed confidential information to a journalist **13–030** and disclosure of the source's identity is sought on *Norwich Pharmacal* grounds, a distinction needs to be drawn between the questions whether publication was justified on public interest grounds and, if not, whether disclosure of the source's identity should be ordered. The motive or purpose of the source will seldom be relevant to the first question, but may be very relevant to the second. A particular reason for its relevance to the second is that the purpose of *Norwich Pharmacal* relief includes, in an appropriate case, enabling the claimant to protect himself from future wrongdoing by the source. In assessing the risk of future wrongdoing, the source's apparent motive for his past conduct may have obvious significance.

---

[59] [2002] EWCA Civ 274; [2002] 2 Lloyd's Rep. 229 at [66]: "What matters in my judgment is the Source's evident purpose. It was on any view a maleficent one, calculated to do harm *whether for profit or for spite . . .* " (emphasis added).
[60] [2002] UKHL 29; [2002] 1 W.L.R. 2033 at [66].
[61] [2003] EWCA Civ 663; [2003] F.S.R. 820 CA, e.g. at [46], and [2006] EWHC 107 (QB), e.g. at [196].

CHAPTER 14

Employees and Employers

CONTRACT

The relationship between an employer and employee is contractual and, while the **14–001** existence of a contract does not prevent concurrent application of the equitable doctrine of confidence,[1] the scope of the employee's duty of confidence is governed by the contract,[2] whether express or implied, for as long as the parties remain bound by the contract.[3]

Although the function of implied terms is to "dot the i's and cross the t's of the **14–002** express terms or to fill in some lacuna left by the contracting parties which must properly be filled by the implied term in order to give business efficacy",[4] it is convenient for present purposes to consider first what obligation of confidentiality the court will imply into a contract of employment before considering express terms.

The law draws a distinction between the duties of confidentiality owed by an **14–003** employee during the period of the contract and the duties which may continue after it has come to an end. The distinction reflects both the nature of the contract and the important factor that a former employee has a legitimate interest, which the courts will protect, in being able to use his skills and knowledge for his own benefit in earning a living without the imposition of unduly onerous or impractical restraints in favour of a previous employer. The law as it has been developed in this area provides an example of the general principle, considered in Ch.3, that in appropriate circumstances a duty of confidentiality (or in this instance the duration of a duty of confidentiality) owed in relation to information obtained in confidence may be qualified by the legitimate needs of the recipient.

The Court of Appeal summarised the relevant duties of an employee in *Att Gen v Blake*[5]:

> "There is more than one category of fiduciary relationship, and the different categories possess different characteristics and attract kinds of fiduciary obligation. The most important of these is the relationship of trust and confidence, which arises whenever one party undertakes to act in the interests of another or places himself in a position in which he is obliged to act in the interests of another. The relationship

---

[1] *Lamb v Evans* [1893] 1 Ch. 218; *Printers & Finishers Ltd v Holloway* [1965] R.P.C. 239; *Thomas Marshall (Exports) Ltd v Guinle* [1979] 1 Ch. 227.

[2] *Robb v Green* [1895] 2 Q.B. 315; *Faccenda Chicken Ltd v Fowler* [1987] 1 Ch. 117 at 135.

[3] The special position which arises after termination by repudiatory breach is considered at para.14–031, below.

[4] *Initial Services Ltd v Putterill* [1968] 1 Q.B. 396 at 411.

[5] [1998] Ch. 439 at 454. The passage cited was not affected by the decision of the House of Lords.

between employer and employee is of this character. The core obligation of a fiduciary of this kind is one of loyalty. The employer is entitled to the single-minded loyalty of his employee. The employee must act in good faith; he must not make a profit out of his trust; he must not place himself in a position where his duty and his interest may conflict; he may not act for his own benefit or the benefit of a third party without the informed consent of his employer.

But these duties last only as long as the relationship which gives rise to them lasts. A former employee owes no duty of loyalty to his former employer. It is trite law that an employer who wishes to prevent his employee from damaging his legitimate commercial interests after he has left his employment must obtain contractual undertakings from his employee to that effect. He cannot achieve his object by invoking the fiduciary relationship which formerly subsisted between them. Absent a valid and enforceable contractual restraint, a former employee is free to set up in a competing business in close proximity to his former employer and deal with his former clients. Such conduct involves no breach of fiduciary duty.

A quite different fiduciary relationship is that of confidentiality. This arises whenever information is imparted by one person to another in confidence. It is often, perhaps usually, imparted in the course of another fiduciary relationship, such as that of employer and employee. If so, the duty will survive the termination of that other relationship, for it is not derived from it: see, for example, *Attorney-General v Guardian Newspapers Ltd (No 2).*[6]"

The final sentence of that passage requires qualification, because it is well established by other authorities that the duty of confidentiality is in certain respects less strict after the termination of the employment than during it, the reason being to prevent the individual's ability to use his skills and experience from being unreasonably fettered.

14–004   More recent authorities have challenged the view that an employer is ordinarily entitled to a "single-minded" duty of loyalty; and whereas the Court of Appeal in *Att Gen v Blake* treated the duty of loyalty of an employee as a form of fiduciary duty, more recent authorities have differentiated between a fiduciary duty and a contractual duty of fidelity. They have held that the relationship between employer and employee is not an innately fiduciary relationship, but that the employee will owe an express or implied duty of fidelity and that the contract may give rise to fiduciary duties. In *University of Nottingham v Fishel*[7] Elias J. said in a passage approved by the Court of Appeal in *Ranson v Customer Systems Plc*[8]:

"...the essence of the employment relationship is not typically fiduciary at all. Its purpose is not to place the employee in a position where he is obliged to pursue his employer's interests at the expense of his own. The relationship is a contractual one and the powers imposed on the employee are conferred by the employer himself. The employee's freedom of action is regulated by the contract, the scope of his powers is determined by the terms (express or implied) of the contract, and as a consequence the employer can exercise (or at least he can place himself in a position where he has the opportunity to exercise) considerable control over the employee's decision making powers. This is not to say that fiduciary duties cannot arise out of the employment relationship itself. But they arise not as a result of the mere fact that there is an employment relationship. Rather they result from the fact

---

[6] [1990] 1 A.C. 109.
[7] [2000] I.C.R. 1462 at 1491.
[8] [2012] EWCA Civ 841 at [28].

that within a particular contractual relationship there are specific contractual obligations which the employee has undertaken which have placed him in a situation where equity imposes these rigorous duties in addition to the contractual obligations. Where this occurs, the scope of the fiduciary obligations both arises out of, and is circumscribed by, the contractual terms; it is circumscribed because equity cannot alter the terms of the contract validly undertaken."

The differences of expression between what the Court of Appeal said in *Attorney-General v Blake* and more recent authorities may be more matters of terminology and classification than matters of substance. The word "fiduciary" has never had a uniform definition and in *Henderson v Merrett Syndicates Ltd* [9] Lord Browne-Wilkinson described the phrase "fiduciary duties" as a dangerous one, because it is apt to convey a false impression of uniformity. What matters for present purposes is the content of the duties owed during and after the contract of employment in relation to information obtained in confidence during the period of the contract.

IMPLIED OBLIGATION DURING EMPLOYMENT

The court will imply into any contract of employment a general obligation on the part of the employee not to use or disclose confidential information or materials acquired in his capacity as an employee, except for the purposes of his employment.   **14–005**

This principle goes back at least to *Tipping v Clarke* [10], in which Sir James Wigram V.C. said: **14–006**

" . . . it is clear that every clerk employed in a merchant's counting-house is under an implied contract that he will not make public that which he learns in the execution of his duty as clerk."

Wigram V.C's words were quoted with express approval by Lord Cottenham L.C. in *Prince Albert v Strange* [11] and the principle has been applied in many subsequent cases. [12]

The obligation is subject to usual qualifications, for example, where disclosure is required by law or in cases of serious wrongdoing. [13] The Public Interest Disclosure Act 1998 (amending the Employment Rights Act 1996) defines certain disclosures made in the public interest as protected disclosures and provides that employers should not subject their employees, in particular, to any detriment for making a protected disclosure. An employee whose rights in this respect are infringed may bring a claim before an employment tribunal. Section 43J of the Employment Rights Act 1996 provides that any provision in an agreement   **14–007**

---

[9] [1995] 2 A.C. 145 at 206.

[10] (1843) 2 Hare 383 at 393.

[11] (1849) 1 Mac. & G. 25 at 45.

[12] *Merryweather v Moore* [1892] 2 Ch. 518; *Robb v Green* [1895] 2 Q.B. 315; *Reid & Sigrist Ltd v Moss* (1932) 49 R.P.C. 461.

[13] *Gartside v Outram* (1857) 26 L.J.Ch. (N.S.) 113; *Initial Services Ltd v Putterill* [1968] 1 Q.B. 396; *In re a Company's Application* [1989] 1 Ch. 477; see also Ch.6.

between employer and employee which purports to preclude the employee from making a protected disclosure is to that extent void.

IMPLIED OBLIGATION AFTER TERMINATION

14–008   In the leading English authority of *Faccenda Chicken Ltd v Fowler*,[14] the confidentiality obligations of employees that continue after termination of the employment relationship were seen, in the absence of any express contractual provisions, as a matter of implied contract. In *Del Casale v Artedomus (Aust) Pty Ltd*,[15] in the New South Wales Court of Appeal, Hodgson J.A. said, on the other hand:

> "In my opinion, generally questions concerning an employee's obligation of confidentiality after employment has come to an end, in the absence of an express contract dealing with the matter, are best dealt with as part of the general law concerning confidentiality of information, both because it is very doubtful what, if any, term can be implied into a contract, and also because it is very unlikely that relief obtainable pursuant to any such implied term would go beyond relief obtainable on general equitable principles."

It is likely that the scope of an employee's obligation of confidence after termination of his employment will be the same, regardless of its jurisprudential underpinning in contract or in equity. However, the courts have found it difficult to give consistent and coherent expression to the content of that obligation.

In *Lamb v Evans*[16] it was suggested that the ex-employee's duty was limited to not using materials acquired in the course of his employment and did not prevent him from using his knowledge.

14–009   Subsequent authorities have made it clear that the duty is not so confined. In *Printers & Finishers Ltd v Holloway*[17] Cross J. said:

> "The mere fact that the confidential information is not embodied in a document but is carried away by the employee in his head is not, of course of itself a reason against the granting of an injunction to prevent its use or disclosure by him. If the information in question can fairly be regarded as a separate part of the employee's stock of knowledge which a man of ordinary honesty and intelligence would recognise to be the property of his old employer, and not his own to do as he likes with, then the court, if it thinks that there is a danger of the information being used or disclosed by the ex-employee to the detriment of the old employer, will do what it can to prevent that result by granting an injunction. Thus an ex-employee will be restrained from using or disclosing a chemical formula or a list of customers which he has committed to memory."[18]

---

[14] [1987] 1 Ch. 117; discussed further below.

[15] [2007] NSWCA 172 at [35].

[16] [1893] 1 Ch. 218 at 236; see para.1–033 above.

[17] [1965] R.P.C. 239 at 255.

[18] See also *Johnson & Bloy (Holdings) Ltd v Wolstenholme Rink Plc* [1987] I.R.L.R. 499 at 502, per Parker L.J., "Somebody may hit upon the combination of two ingredients after many years of research, which produce an immensely valuable result wholly unknown to anybody else. An employee would have no difficulty in holding that knowledge in his head and inevitably carrying it away with him. But it cannot . . . be regarded as part of the ordinary skill and experience of the particular employee. It is a secret, whether or not it is carried away in his head . . . ."

Customer lists have presented particular difficulties, to which further reference is made below.

The reference to the information being "a separate part of the employee's stock of knowledge" is important and echoes what was said by the House of Lords in *Herbert Morris Ltd v Saxelby*,[19] the fundamental principle of which is that a person is not to be fettered from making proper use of his skills, both for his own benefit and for that of the public. **14–010**

In so far as knowledge gained in confidence has become part of the employee's general skill and knowledge, he owes no duty after the termination of his employment to refrain from using it in other employment.[20] Such knowledge is to be distinguished from the type of information referred to by Cross J. in the passage cited above, i.e. trade secrets and the like. **14–011**

The distinction between knowledge which is, and knowledge which is not, to be regarded as part of an ex-employee's general skill and knowledge has been a fruitful source of litigation, and drawing the line can be difficult.[21] **14–012**

In *Faccenda Chicken Ltd v Fowler*[22] the plaintiffs bred and sold chickens. The defendant, during his employment as their sales manager, introduced an operation of selling freshly killed chickens from refrigerated vans. He left their employment to set up a similar business of his own in the same area, and several of the plaintiffs' van salesmen went to work for him. The plaintiffs claimed an injunction and damages for misuse of confidential "sales information", including the names and addresses of customers, their usual requirements, the prices charged to them, and the van salesmen's delivery routes. **14–013**

Goulding J. found that the information came into the category of confidential information which the defendant was required to use only for the plaintiffs' benefit while he remained in their employment, but which became part of his general skill and knowledge, so that he was permitted to use it after the end of the contract for his own benefit in competition with the plaintiffs. The Court of Appeal agreed. Neill L.J., delivering the judgment of the Court, said: **14–014**

> "In our judgment the information will only be protected [after the employment has ceased] if it can properly be classed as a trade secret or as material which, while not properly to be described as a trade secret, is in all the circumstances of such a highly confidential nature as to require the same protection as a trade secret eo nomine . . . It is clearly impossible to provide a list of matters which will qualify as a trade secret or their equivalent. Secret processes of manufacture provide obvious examples, but innumerable other pieces of information are *capable* of being trade secrets, though the secrecy of some information may be only short-lived."

There is no universal formula for determining what is a trade secret or item of equivalent confidentiality. In *PSM International Plc v Whitehouse*[23] Lloyd L.J.

---

[19] [1916] A.C. 688.

[20] In *Force India Formula One Team Ltd v 1 Malaysia Racing Team SDN BHD* [2012] EWHC 616 (Ch) at [235], Arnold J. held that there is no bright line distinction in this respect between an employee and a contractor who provides his/her services.

[21] For examples, see Brearley and Bloch, *Employment Covenants and Confidential Information*, 3rd edn (Tottel, 2009), pp.228–233 *Co-ordinated Industries Pty Ltd v Elliott* (1998) 43 N.S.W.L.R. 282.

[22] [1987] 1 Ch. 117 at 137–138.

[23] [1992] I.R.L.R. 279 at 282.

described it as a question of degree. In *Lansing Linde Ltd v Kerr*[24] Staughton L.J. considered that "trade secret" embraced information used in a trade, restricted in its dissemination, and the disclosure of which would be liable to cause real or significant harm to the party claiming confidentiality. That is very close to Sir Robert Megarry V.C.'s criteria in *Thomas Marshall Ltd v Guinle*[25] for identifying information protectable during a contract of employment.

14–015   In *Faccenda Chicken* itself,[26] the Court of Appeal identified four factors that were relevant to whether confidential information amounted to a trade secret: the nature of the employment, the nature of the information, the extent to which the employer impressed the information's confidentiality upon the employee and the ease with which the information could be isolated from other information that the ex-employee was free to use.[27] In *FSS Travel & Leisure Systems Ltd v Johnson*,[28] the Court of Appeal also referred to the extent of use in the public domain and the damage likely to be caused by the use and disclosure of the information in competition with the employer.

In *Del Casale v Artedomus (Aust) Pty Ltd*[29], Hodgson J.A. recited an expanded list of factors, derived from Robert Dean's *The Law of Trade Secrets and Personal Secrets*[30]:

"1.   The extent to which the information is known outside the business.
2.   The extent to which the trade secret was known by employees and others involved in the plaintiff's business.
3.   The extent of measures taken to guard the secrecy of the information.
4.   The value of the information to the plaintiffs and their competitors.
5.   The amount of effort or money expended by the plaintiffs in developing the information.
6.   The ease or difficulty with which the information could be properly acquired or duplicated by others.
7.   Whether it was plainly made known to the employee that the material was by the employer as confidential.
8.   The fact that the usages and practices of the industry support the assertions of confidentiality.
9.   The fact that the employee has been permitted to share the information only by reason of his or her seniority or high responsibility.
10.   That the owner believes these things to be true and that belief is reasonable.
11.   The greater the extent to which the 'confidential' material is habitually handled by an employee, the greater the obligation of the confidentiality imposed.
12.   That the information can be readily identified."

---

[24] [1991] 1 W.L.R. 251.

[25] [1979] 1 Ch. 227.

[26] At 137–138.

[27] For an example of the application of these factors, see the Court of Appeal's decision in *A.T. Poeton (Gloucester Plating) Ltd v Horton* [2001] F.S.R. 169 at 185–186.

[28] [1999] F.S.R. 505 at 512.

[29] [2007] NSWCA 172 at [40].

[30] 2nd edn (Lawbook Company, 2002); see now Dean and Hughes's *Trade Secrets and Privacy* (Thomson Reuters, Australia, 2012).

Campbell J.A., in the same case, observed[31] that, although such lists were useful aids to decision-making, they were not a substitute for the legal tests by which the existence of different obligations should be decided.

Since the underlying reason for a distinction being drawn between the duty of confidentiality owed during a contract of employment, and the duty which continues to subsist after it, is that the ex-employee should not be prevented from using his general skill and knowledge in subsequent employment, it is suggested that this should guide the court in deciding whether the post-termination duty extends to a particular piece of information. If the effect of holding that it does would be to put an unreasonable restriction on the ex-employee's ability to find or carry out work in the sector in which he is skilled, the duty should not extend to it. If it would not, there is no reason why the duty of confidentiality should not continue to apply. One way of approaching the question is to consider how readily the particular information can isolated from the employee's general know-how which he is entitled to use after his employment.   **14–016**

If the answer is doubtful, the issue should be resolved in favour of the ex-employee for reasons given by Scott J. in *Balston Ltd v Headline Filters Ltd*[32] and echoed by Mummery J. in *Ixora Trading Inc v Jones*[33]:   **14–017**

> "Technologically based industries abound. All have what they regard as secrets. Employees, particularly those employed on the scientific or technical side of the manufacturing business, necessarily acquire knowledge of the relevant technology. They become associated with technological advances and innovations. Their experience, built up during their years of employment, naturally equips them to be dangerous competitors if and when their employment ceases. The use of confidential information restrictions in order to fetter the ability of these employees to use their skills and experience after determination of their employment to compete with their ex-employer is, in my view, potentially harmful. It would be capable of imposing a new form of servitude or serfdom …, to use Cumming-Bruce L.J.'s words on technologically qualified employees. It would render them unable in practice to leave their employment for want of an ability to use their skills and experience after leaving. Employers who want to impose fetters of this sort on their employees ought in my view to be expected to do so by express covenant. The reasonableness of the covenant can then be subjected to the rigorous attention to which all employee covenants in restraint of trade are subject. In the absence of an express covenant, the ability of an ex-employee to compete can be restricted by means of an implied term against use or disclosure of trade secrets. But the case must, in my view, be a clear one. An employee does not have the chance to reject an implied term. It is formulated and imposed on him subsequently to his initial entry into employment. To fetter his freedom to compete by means of an implied term can only be justified, in my view, by a very clear case."

Accordingly the court will be more reluctant to place a broad embargo on ex-employees who possess confidential information relating to their former employers than on solicitors or forensic experts who possess confidential information relating to their former clients. In particular, the court will not grant an injunction on the grounds on which an injunction was granted in *Bolkiah v*

---

[31] At [138].
[32] [1987] F.S.R. 330 at 351.
[33] [1990] 1 F.S.R. 251 at 261.

KPMG[34] to prohibit an ex-employee permanently from engaging in activities in which there is merely a risk of the inadvertent misuse of confidential information.[35] In *Generics (UK) Ltd v Yeda Research and Development Co Ltd*,[36] which concerned an employed in-house patent attorney, Etherton L.J. said:

> "That is not to say that a barring order can never be made against a former employee if the former employer proves that trade or business secrets (or, in the case of a legally valid express term, other confidential information), which are subject to continuing contractual and fiduciary duties after termination of the employment, are likely to be disclosed or wrongly used by the former employee … however, in the absence of a restrictive covenant that can only be in a most exceptional case."

CUSTOMER LISTS

14–018   As a general rule an employer will want to protect its customer list from becoming known to competitors or potential competitors and an employee will be under a duty during the term of his employment to treat such information as confidential. He will also be in breach of duty to his employer if he solicits the employer's customers before the end of his employment with a view to obtaining their future business.[37]

When the employment has ended, the ex-employee will be entitled to compete against his former employer in the absence of a valid covenant to the contrary. In the ordinary course of his employment he is likely to have acquired some degree of knowledge of his former employer's customers. If he is to be precluded from seeking their custom, this must be by a non-solicitation covenant which satisfies the requirement of not being in unreasonable restraint of trade.

14–019   However, this rule applies only to knowledge of customers which the employee has acquired in the ordinary course of his employment. It does not give a licence to an employee who intends to leave his employment and work in competition with his employer, whether for a rival business or on his own account, to copy the current employer's customer list, or to retain a copy of it, with a view to using it for competitive purposes after he has left. In *Robb v Green*[38] an order was made in those circumstances against the ex-employee requiring him to deliver up the list for destruction and restraining him from making use of the information obtained by copying it. The same principle would apply if the employee had instead committed the list to his memory.[39] Similarly in *JN Dairies Ltd v Johal*[40], where a recently dismissed employee of the claimant dairy company entered the company's premises and stole a collection of its

---

[34] [1999] 2 A.C. 222.

[35] *Caterpillar Logistics Services (UK) Ltd v Huesca de Crean* [2012] EWCA Civ 156; [2012] I.C.R. 981, especially at [49]–[60].

[36] [2012] EWCA Civ 726; [2012] CP Rep. 39 at [83]; further discussed at para.16–011, below.

[37] *Wessex Dairies Ltd v Smith* [1935] 2 K.B. 80; *Crowson Fabrics Ltd v Rider* [2007] EWHC 2942 (Ch); [2008] F.S.R. 17, Peter Smith J.

[38] [1895] 2 Q.B. 315.

[39] *Printers & Finishers Ltd v Holloway* [1965] R.P.C. 239 at 255.

[40] [2009] EWHC 1331 (Ch); see also *Crowson Fabrics Ltd v Rider* [2008] F.S.R. 18, per Peter Smith J. at [113] and *Messtechnik v Hartley* [2012] EWHC 1013 (QB), per Sir Raymond Jack at [65].

invoices, which he then provided to a rival of the claimant, the court held that such conduct constituted a breach of a duty of confidentiality.

In *N P Generations Pty Ltd v Fenely*,[41] the defendant ex-employee of an estate agency was required by the Supreme Court of South Australia to deliver up her address book, which had been copied in part from her former employer's customer list, but was permitted to retain her diary (which contained confidential information appearing also in the customer list, but had not been copied from the customer list). **14–020**

The injunction granted in *Robb v Green* did not prohibit the defendant from sending out circulars to customers whose names he could remember apart from having copied the plaintiff's list. Maugham L.J. noted this point in *Wessex Dairies Ltd v Smith* adding[42]: **14–021**

> "It follows, in my opinion, that the servant may, while in the employment of the master, be as agreeable, attentive and skilful as it is in his power to be to others with the ultimate view of obtaining the customers' friendly feelings when he calls upon them if and when he sets up business for himself."

In *Roger Bullivant Ltd v Ellis*[43] Nourse L.J. also noted the point that the injunction in *Robb v Green* did not prevent the defendant from contracting with any of the plaintiff's customers if he was able to do so without using the information which he had unlawfully acquired, and he commented that the form of order made in that case might not be satisfactory in relation to names of customers, because it might be difficult to know whether it had been breached. In those circumstances it was legitimate for the court to grant instead a springboard injunction, restraining the ex-employee from dealing with any customers on the list whom he had approached while the list was in his possession, provided that the term of the injunction was no longer than the period for which he was likely to obtain an unfair advantage from use of the list. **14–022**

In *SJB Stephenson Ltd v Mandy*[44] the defendant was a senior employee of a firm of insurance brokers until he left to join a competitor. His contract contained an express confidentiality clause prohibiting him from disclosing to any person any information in relation to the affairs of any client except in the course of his duties. Bell J. held that on the facts of the case the names of the firm's clients, the details of the cover arranged for them, the renewal dates, premiums charged and brokerage earned were protectable and that the covenant was not in unreasonable restraint of trade. It did not matter that the defendant had not deliberately memorised them. Bell J. indicated that he would grant an injunction to enforce the covenant indefinitely.[45] There was also an express post-contractual covenant against solicitation of the firm's clients, but this was limited to 12 months. The defendant was found to be in breach of both the confidentiality and the non-solicitation clause. In assessing damages the judge (a) did not differentiate between the different breaches and (b) acknowledged that the defendant would be **14–023**

---

[41] (2001) 80 S.A.S.R. 151.
[42] [1935] 2 K.B. 80 at 89.
[43] [1987] F.S.R. 172 at 182–183.
[44] [2000] F.S.R. 286.
[45] [2000] F.S.R. 286 at 308.

free to solicit former clients for the second year's renewals of business.[46] It would seem hard to justify a clause, or an injunction, having the effect of preventing the defendant indefinitely from disclosing the names of the firm's clients, or information about the details of their cover, renewal dates, premium rates and brokerage, the relevance of which was time limited. The confidentiality clause might, however, be justified on the basis that it was intended to protect information only for as long as the requirements of confidentiality continued, and that in relation to details of clients and their contracts that period (adopting the approach of Nourse L.J. in *Roger Bullivant v Ellis*) would be no longer than the period during which disclosure would be likely to give an unfair advantage to a competitor. The real mischief in such a case is the employee leaving and immediately giving to his new employer all the details he knows about his previous employer's clients and their contracts.

USE OF CONFIDENTIAL INFORMATION AFTER TERMINATION FOR PURPOSES OTHER THAN USE OF THE EX-EMPLOYEE'S SKILLS

14–024 It is one thing for the implied obligation of confidentiality to be qualified so as not to impede an ex-employee's proper use of his general skill and knowledge in subsequent employment, whether for himself or others. It is a different matter for him to disclose such information for other purposes.[47]

14–025 In *Mainmet Holdings Plc v Austin*[48] the plaintiffs specialised in heating systems. The defendant was their former managing director. After his departure he sent to customers' copies of internal reports about defects in the customers' systems, including one by himself marked "highly confidential". On an application for an interlocutory injunction it was held that there was no serious issue to be tried on the question of breach of confidence, because the reports did not come into the category of trade secrets or information of equivalent confidentiality, and therefore the defendant owed no continuing duty in respect of them.

14–026 It is suggested that the judge misdirected himself. Although the reports were not trade secrets, there was a strong prima facie case that they were confidential; they could not be regarded as part of the defendant's general skill and knowledge of the business of heating systems; nor was he attempting to use them as such. His use was conceded on the application to have been malicious.[49]

---

[46] [2000] F.S.R. 286 at 309.

[47] See, to this effect, *Del Casale v Artedomus (Aust) Pty Ltd* [2007] NSWCA 172, per Hodgson J.A. at [47].

[48] [1991] F.S.R. 538.

[49] See also *Porton Capital Technology Funds v 3M UK Holdings Ltd* [2010] EWHC 114 (Comm), Christopher Clarke J: although there was no property in a witness, the obligations of confidentiality owed by individuals to their former employer were not dissolved simply because requests for information were made to them for the purposes of litigation; nor did the giving of disclosure by their former employer result in any alteration of those obligations of confidentiality.

EXPRESS TERMS

The courts have on occasion enjoined employers seeking to protect confidential **14–027**
information after the end of the employment relationship to insert express clauses
in their employment contracts. Thus Cross J. said in *Printers & Finishers Ltd v
Holloway*[50]:

> "If the managing director is right in thinking that there are features in the plaintiffs'
> process which can fairly be regarded as trade secrets and which their employees will
> inevitably carry away with them in their heads, then the proper way for the plaintiffs
> to protect themselves would be by exacting covenants from their employees
> restricting their field of activity after they have left their employment not by asking
> the court to extend the general equitable doctrine to prevent breaking confidence
> beyond all reasonable bounds."

In particular, an express term may be effective to *identify* what is, properly,
regarded as confidential information or information falling in the narrower
category of a trade secret or the equivalent. It is well established that for
information to be treated as confidential or a trade secret it must be defined with
sufficient precision,[51] and an express contractual term may have that effect. The
fact that the contract specifies that certain information is to be treated as a trade
secret and kept confidential after the end of the employment does not compel a
court to recognise it as such, for unreasonable restraints of trade cannot gain
validity by being dressed up as clauses protecting trade secrets, if they are not.[52]
But the terms of the contract may be a relevant factor in considering whether the
man of ordinary honesty and intelligence, referred to by Cross J. in *Printers &
Finishers Ltd v Holloway*, would think he was doing anything wrong in using
some piece of information gained during his previous employment.

So, for example, in *United Sterling Corp Ltd v Felton and Mannion*[53] **14–028**
Brightman J. said:

> "In my judgment there is no evidence that Mr Mannion was given any special
> information which he ought to have regarded as a separate part of his stock of
> knowledge of polystyrene plants, information which an honest and intelligent man
> would have recognised as the property of the employer and not of the employee.
> There is no evidence that anything was expressly disclosed to Mr Mannion in
> confidence. He was never asked to sign any restrictive covenant. There is no
> evidence that he has done more during the years of his employment than add to his
> general stock of knowledge and experience of polystyrene plants in the ordinary
> way that any intelligent employee would naturally do. I see no basis for suggesting
> that Mr Mannion's conscience was affected during the period of his employment so
> as to place him under an obligation not to make use of that which he inevitably
> learned during his years with the plaintiff company."

---

[50] [1965] 1 W.L.R. 1 at 6.
[51] See para.3–086 above.
[52] *Balston Ltd v Headline Filters Ltd* [1987] F.S.R. 330 at 351. Nor is it necessarily incumbent on an
employer to point out the precise limits of what it seeks to protect as confidential information:
Lancashire Fires Ltd v Lyons & Co Ltd [1996] F.S.R. 629 at 673–674.
[53] [1974] R.P.C. 162 at 173. See also *A.T. Poeton Ltd v Horton* [2001] F.S.R. 169 at 186.

The extent to which an express covenant may serve not only to identify information which is confidential or (more narrowly) a trade secret, but also to impose post-termination obligations on an ex-employee which would not otherwise arise by implication or in equity, has been the subject of some uncertainty. As a matter of broad principle, it is suggested that a contract may restrict a former employee from divulging information gained by him as a result of his employment, even if the information is not confidential, unless the clause would prevent him from making proper use of his skills, would amount to an unreasonable restraint on trade, or would otherwise be unlawful.[54]

14–029   In *Faccenda Chicken Ltd v Fowler*,[55] the Court of Appeal stated obiter that it was not possible for employers, by means of an express restrictive covenant, to protect confidential information after termination of the employment relationship, unless the information was equivalent to a "trade secret", expressing its disagreement in this respect with the judgment of Goulding J. at first instance. This aspect of the Court of Appeal's judgment has subsequently been called into question.[56] It has been suggested that the Court of Appeal may not have distinguished sufficiently between permanent restrictions on disclosure and temporary restrictions on competition,[57] or perhaps between different possible definitions of "trade secret".[58]

Any covenant which permanently prevented a former employee from using in his subsequent employment confidential information which was not equivalent to a trade secret in the narrower sense would be likely to fall foul of the law on restraint of trade. However, the Court of Appeal's observations in *Faccenda Chicken* should not prevent employers from protecting confidential information by means of restrictive non-compete covenants, even if such information would not necessarily qualify for implied or equitable protection in the absence of an express covenant—provided always that the covenants are appropriately limited in both space and duration.[59] The fact that such covenants *do* amount to an unreasonable restraint on trade unless strictly limited is consistent with the approach suggested above.

14–030   In *Thomas v Farr*,[60] the Court of Appeal considered the evidential burden on an employer, who seeks to enforce a non-compete covenant, to demonstrate that an ex-employee is in possession of relevant confidential information. Toulson L.J., citing earlier judicial observations, stated that:

> "...it is because there may be serious difficulties in identifying precisely what is or is not confidential information that a non-competition clause may be the most satisfactory form of restraint, provided that it is reasonable in time and space."[61]

---

[54] For an example, see *Att Gen v Blake* [2001] 1 A.C. 268. See also paras 3–002–3–007 above.

[55] [1987] Ch. 117 at 137.

[56] Referred to by Michael Briggs QC in *Townends Grove Ltd v Cobb* [2004] EWHC 3432 (Ch) at [27].

[57] *Lancashire Fires Ltd v Lyons & Co Ltd* [1996] F.S.R. 629 at 666–667.

[58] See the interesting analysis by Campbell J.A. in *Del Casale v Artedomus (Aust) Pty Ltd* [2007] NSWCA 172, especially at [139]–[141].

[59] In *Wright v Gasweld Pty Ltd* (1991) 22 N.S.W.L.R. 317, the New South Wales Court of Appeal declined to follow the Court of Appeal's dicta in *Faccenda Chicken*.

[60] [2007] EWCA Civ 118; [2007] I.C.R. 932.

[61] At [42].

In *Brake Brothers Ltd v Ungless*,[62] Gloster J. provided a helpful summary of the law as to the enforceability of restrictive covenants. She cited dicta in yet stronger terms, to the effect that:

> "...it is well established that a prohibition against disclosing trade secrets is practically worthless unless it is accompanied by a restriction upon the employee possessed of secrets against entering the employment of competitors."

TERMINATION AS A RESULT OF REPUDIATORY BREACH

Where termination of employment occurs as a result of repudiatory breach by the employer, typically by wrongful summary dismissal, the employee is relieved from further performance of his own contractual obligations, including restrictive post-employment covenants.[63] But the bringing to an end of all primary contractual obligations may leave the parties in a relationship in which duties are owed by operation of law.[64] It is suggested, therefore, that while termination of employment through wrongful repudiation by the employer[65] brings to an end any contractual obligation of confidence owed by the employee to the employer, it does not ipso facto bring to an end the employee's equitable duty in respect of trade secrets or information of equivalent confidentiality.[66]

14–031

EMPLOYER'S OBLIGATION

An employer or prospective employer may also owe a duty of confidence to an employee or prospective employee. In *Smith, Kline & French Laboratories (Australia) Ltd v Department of Community Services*[67] the court observed:

14–032

> "Confidential information is commonly supplied without payment: for example, by a prospective employee (or his referee) to support an application for employment. The understanding ordinarily would be that the prospective employer would not disclose the information to any third party; but it would hardly be expected that its use would necessarily be confined to the employment application itself. If that application were successful, the employee would not act on the assumption that material in the relevant file would be destroyed. He would surely be inclined to assume that it might be resorted to later to assist the employer in making decisions relevant to the employee—for example, as to whether the employee (rather than another) should be promoted, or dismissed."

---

[62] [2004] EWHC 2799 (QB) at [15]. See also *CEF Holdings v Mundey* [2012] EWHC 1524 (QB); [2012] F.S.R. 35.

[63] *General Billposting Co Ltd v Atkinson* [1909] A.C. 118.

[64] In *Photo Production Ltd v Securicor Transport Ltd* [1980] A.C. 827 at 850, Lord Diplock gave the example of bailor and bailee.

[65] An employee cannot bring to an end his own contractual obligation by wrongful repudiation if not accepted by the employer: *Thomas Marshall Ltd v Guinle* [1979] Ch. 227, approved in *Gunton v Richmond Borough Council* [1981] Ch. 448.

[66] In *Campbell v Frisbee* [2002] EWCA Civ 1374, the Court of Appeal observed (at [22]) that "We do not believe that the effect on duties of confidence assumed under contract when the contract in question is wrongfully repudiated is clearly established". See Ch.4 for a fuller discussion.

[67] (1991) 28 F.C.R. 291 at 303, Full Court of the Federal Court of Australia.

Where the information is supplied by the prospective employee in response to an advertisement or request by the prospective employer, the obligation of confidence could be regarded as arising under an implied contract, the consideration for which would be the provision of the information,[68] or in equity. Such a duty would be owed to the prospective employee in respect of any information of a confidential nature concerning himself, whether it came from the prospective employee personally or from the referee acting on his request. An additional duty of confidence might be owed to the referee if the reference contained matters of a confidential nature relating to the referee. If the information was unsolicited, it is suggested that there would still be an equitable obligation of confidence.

14–033   On the formation of a contract of employment, the nature of the relationship would change, but the employer would continue to owe a duty of confidentiality to the employee, whether under an implied term of the contract or in equity, in respect of personal information about the employee gained by the employer in that capacity, subject to usual qualifications.[69]

14–034   The obligation not to disclose personal information about an employee to a third party without his consent will ordinarily continue after the employment has ended. An ex-employer who is asked for information about a former employee by a prospective employer should therefore be cautious. It is suggested that he would be free to express his views about the qualities of the former employee, because that would be a matter of his own opinion, but that he would not be free to divulge facts which would fairly be regarded as personal to the former employee, for example, his health record.

14–035   In *Prout v British Gas Plc*[70] the defendants operated a scheme for employees to make suggestions, promising confidentiality so long as the employee wished and that his interests would be protected if his suggestion was worth patenting. The plaintiff suggested a form of bracket designed to prevent warning lamps being vandalised. The defendants indicated that they were not interested in it, and the plaintiff then applied for a patent himself. He subsequently sued for breach of confidence and patent infringement. The claim for breach of confidence was put forward on alternative bases of breach of contract or of an equitable obligation. It was held that the plaintiff was entitled to succeed on either ground, and that the duty of confidence continued until the publication of the patent application, when the plaintiff thereby voluntarily put his invention in the possession of the public. The court directed an inquiry as to damages or an account of profits, at the plaintiff's option.

It is an implied term of a contract of employment that the employer will not, without reasonable cause, conduct itself in a manner calculated and likely to destroy or seriously damage the relationship of confidence and trust between employer and employee.[71] In *Copland v United Kingdom*[72] the European Court of Human Rights held that the Art.8 rights of an employee at a college of education

---

[68] *Mechanical and General Inventions Co v Austin* [1935] A.C. 346 at 370.

[69] An obvious example would be an employer's obligation to supply details of an employee's earnings to the Inland Revenue.

[70] [1992] F.S.R. 478.

[71] *Malik v Bank of Credit and Commerce International SA* [1997] UKHL 23; [1998] A.C. 20.

[72] [2007] E.C.H.R. 253 (2007) 45 E.H.R.R. 37.

were violated by the college secretly monitoring her telephone, email and internet usage in order to see whether she was making excessive use of college facilities for private purposes.

CHAPTER 15

Teachers, Clergy, Counsellors and Mediators

TEACHERS

Schools keep records on every pupil's academic achievements, other skills and abilities and progress at school.[1] Such records, like medical records or the records kept on an employee by an employer, are confidential, but may be used for the purpose of the pupil's welfare, for example, in assisting a child care officer to prepare a report for a court. There would also be no objection to their use for preparing references or reports to a prospective employer, or university, or another school, which are provided with the consent of the pupil, or his parents on his behalf: in such cases, consent to the use of the information would be implied.

15–001

A teacher may also learn confidential information about a child or his family from the child, or from other sources. A teacher has a quasi-parental responsibility for a child in his care and owes a duty to the child to keep such information confidential, except in so far as to do so would conflict with his proper appreciation of the child's best interests. Here the position of a teacher *vis-à-vis* the pupil and the pupil's parents is similar to that of a doctor and can present similar difficulties, for example in relation to issues affecting a pupil's sexual health.[2]

15–002

Education should be a shared responsibility between teacher, parent and pupil. Ordinarily it would be in the pupil's interest that a teacher should feel free to discuss matters concerning the pupil with the pupil's parents. But there are situations where that will not be so.

15–003

One example is where an older pupil confides in a teacher about matters which he or she does not want his or her parents to know, in which case the teacher must respect that confidence unless he has good reason to believe that it would be damaging to the pupil to do so.

15–004

---

[1] Schools maintained by a local education authority and special schools are required to keep and update such records under the Education (Pupil Information) (England) Regulations 2005 (SI 2005/1437). The parents have a right to disclosure under para.5 of the Regulations, while the pupil has subject access rights under the Data Protection Act 1998 (subject to the Data Protection (Subject Access Modification) (Education) Order 2000).

[2] See paras 11–040–11–047, above. The Department for Education has produced *Sex and Relationship Education Guidance for Head Teachers, Teachers & School Governors* (July 2000), which contains advice as to confidentiality issues. HM Government's *Information Sharing: Guidance for practitioners and managers* (2008) also contains guidance on confidentiality issues affecting children and young people.

15–005   Another is where a teacher makes a promise of confidentiality to a pupil. It may be necessary in the interests of the pupil that the teacher should break that promise, but he should do so only if satisfied for good reasons that it is.

15–006   There is also the difficult area of suspected child abuse. Teachers are not required to act as detectives, nor are they qualified to make medical judgments about the cause of injuries. Reporting a case of suspected child abuse, which turns out to be unfounded, may cause immense distress. Nevertheless where a teacher is in possession of information from which he has real ground to suppose that a child is the subject of abuse, his paramount concern must be the interests of the child, and he will not be in breach of any duty of confidentiality if he reports his concern to an appropriate responsible person or authority such as the local authority's social services department.

CLERGY

15–007   The ecclesiastical law of the Church of England requires a minister not to reveal or make known to any person any crime or offence revealed to him by confession "except they be such crimes as by the laws of this realm his own life may be called into question for concealing the same".[3]

15–008   Section 3 of the Submission of the Clergy Act 1533 provides that no canons shall be "made or put in execucion within this realme by auctorytie of the Convocacion of the clergie, which shalbe contraryaunt or repugnant to the Kynges prerogative royal or the customes lawes or statutes of this realme…" The modern position in civil law was stated by Lord Denning M.R. in *Att Gen v Mulholland and Foster*[4] as follows:

> "The only profession I know which is given a privilege from disclosing information to a court of law is the legal profession, and then it is not the privilege of the lawyer but of his client.
>   Take the clergyman, the banker or the medical man. None of these is entitled to refuse to answer when directed to by a judge. Let me not be mistaken. The judge will respect the confidence which each member of these honourable professions receives in the course of it and will not direct him to answer unless not only it is relevant but also it is a proper and, indeed, necessary question in the course of justice to be put and answered."

This passage was approved by the House of Lords in *British Steel Corp v Granada Television Ltd*.[5] The same principles will apply also to ministers of other denominations and other religions.

15–009   The doctor with his medical responsibility and the clergyman with his pastoral responsibility are each concerned for the personal welfare of those to whom they minister, and should owe similar obligations of confidentiality to those under their care.

---

[3] *Canons Ecclesiastical* (1603), Canon 113 proviso, which remains unrepealed. *Halsbury's Laws of England* 5th edn, *Ecclesiastical Law*, para.10, fn.1. See also s.7 of *Guidelines for the Professional Conduct of the Clergy* (2003), produced by the Convocations of Canterbury and York.

[4] [1963] 2 Q.B. 477 at 489.

[5] [1981] A.C. 1096. Lord Wilberforce (with whom Lord Russell agreed) described it at 1169–1170 as a "classic passage". Viscount Dilhorne cited it at 1181. Lord Fraser referred to it at 1196.

By the same reasoning the clergyman's duty of confidence should be subject **15–010** to similar qualifications as obtain in the case of a doctor,[6] that is, not only where disclosure is required by law, but also where he reasonably believes disclosure to be necessary to prevent serious harm to others; or (exceptionally) for the protection of the person concerned (e.g. a seriously disturbed parishioner who may be in need of medical attention); or to enable the clergyman to protect himself against accusations of misconduct.

COUNSELLORS

There are many forms of counselling. Much important help is provided by **15–011** voluntary organisations. Some, like the Samaritans, cope with emergencies. Other specialise in particular areas such as marriage breakdown. Within the state system counselling is provided by probation officers, social workers[7] and many others.

Those who provide such services, whether voluntarily or otherwise, clearly do **15–012** so on a tacit assumption of confidentiality, and therefore owe an obligation of confidence to those who consult them, subject to the same general qualifications as apply to doctors or clergymen. In some cases the obligation may also be limited by particular public duties. Probation officers, for example, are responsible for providing reports to courts and for supervising the performance of court orders. Any duty of confidentiality owed by them in private law must therefore be subject to their duty in public law to the court. The same must apply to social workers when acting under the control of the court, for example, in family proceedings.[8]

MEDIATORS

Counselling, conciliation and mediation shade into each other, and the terms are **15–013** sometimes used without discrimination, although they can take very different forms.[9] Mediation as a means of alternative dispute resolution may vary in its degree of formality.

The most formal type of alternative dispute resolution is arbitration, **15–014** although there is an important difference between an arbitrator, who makes a decision and a mediator, who tries to help the parties to reach an agreement.

In *Dolling-Baker v Merrett*[10] it was held that parties to an arbitration **15–015** agreement are under an implied obligation not to disclose or to use for any other purpose documents prepared for or disclosed in the arbitration, or to disclose in any way any evidence given in the arbitration, except with the consent of the other party or leave of the Court.[11]

---

[6] See Ch.11.

[7] Guidance to social workers is included in the British Association of Social Workers' *Code of Ethics for Social Work: Statement of Principles* (January 2012).

[8] See Ch.21, below.

[9] For a discussion of the differences in the context of divorce, see the Law Commission, "The Ground for Divorce", 1990.

[10] [1990] 1 W.L.R. 1205 at 1213, per Parker L.J.

[11] For a fuller discussion, see Ch.22.

15–016   The same logic, whether in support of an implied contractual term or an equitable obligation, must apply as much, if not more strongly, in the case of mediation. For it would destroy the basis of mediation if, in the case of the mediation failing, either party could publicise matters which had passed between themselves or between either of them and the mediator for the purposes of mediation. An obligation of confidence would also be owed to both parties by the mediator.

15–017   In the case of *Theodoropoulas v Theodoropoulas*,[12] it was held that, where a husband and wife were trying to effect a reconciliation in the presence of a conciliator, neither of the parties, nor the conciliator, could give evidence of the conversation in subsequent divorce proceedings without the consent of the other party. Simon P. said[13]:

> "No doubt, when a probation officer or an SSAFA representative or a clergyman is approached, the court will readily infer that the parties have gone to him with a view to reconciliation and on the tacit understanding that nothing said should afterwards be used against them; but, equally, where it is proved that any private individual is enlisted specifically as a conciliator, in my judgment the law will aid his or her efforts by guaranteeing that any admissions or disclosures by the parties are privileged in subsequent matrimonial litigation."

15–018   In *Re D*[14] the Court of Appeal held that in proceedings under the Children Act 1989 statements made by a party in the course of meetings held for the purposes of reconciliation, mediation or conciliation were privileged from production, by analogy with "without prejudice" correspondence, except if a statement was made clearly indicating that the maker had in the past caused or was likely in the future to cause serious harm to the well-being of a child. However, the court emphasised that it was concerned in that case only with a question of admissibility of evidence, and not with duties of confidence. The without prejudice status of mediation was again upheld (in the context of costs arguments) by the Court of Appeal in *Reed Executive Plc v Reed Business Information Ltd.*[15]

In a number of cases, a question has arisen whether there is some form of distinct "mediation privilege" that exists, over and above without prejudice privilege and the private law duties of confidentiality owed by all parties to a mediation.[16] Ramsey J. reviewed these and other earlier decisions in *Farm Assist Ltd v Secretary of State for the Environment, Food and Rural Affairs (No.2).*[17] He concluded[18] that:

> "In my judgment, they provide strong support for the proposition that the general confidentiality or privilege in mediations derives from the without prejudice nature of the mediation proceedings, and applies that concept by analogy.

---

[12] [1964] P. 311.

[13] *Theodoropoulas v Theodoropoulas* [1964] P. 311 at 313–314.

[14] *Re D (Minors) (Conciliation: Disclosure of Information)* [1993] Fam. 231.

[15] [2004] EWCA Civ 887; [2004] 1 W.L.R. 3026.

[16] See, for example, *Brown v Rice* [2007] EWHC 625 (Ch); [2008] F.S.R. 3, per Stuart Isaacs QC at [19]–[20], and *Cumbria Waste Management v Baines Wilson* [2008] EWHC 786 (TCC), per H.H.J Kirkham.

[17] [2009] EWHC 1102 (TCC); [2009] B.L.R. 399

[18] At [42]–[43].

There is a tendency for the use of the words 'confidential', 'privileged' and 'without prejudice' to be used in conjunction so as to emphasise the important general rule that what takes place in a mediation is not to be disclosed to third parties outside the mediation. As stated above, the Mediator in this case has an express enforceable right to keep matters confidential under the terms of the Mediation Agreement. In my judgment the court would, in any event, impose an implied duty of confidentiality which would be enforceable by the Mediator... However, in mediation where existing concepts of legal advice privilege, litigation privilege and without prejudice privilege can be applied, I consider that those principles provide sufficient guidance but there is also the need for a further 'privilege' which arises other than the Mediator's right to confidentiality in relation to the mediation proceedings."

It is accordingly suggested that, although the phrase "mediation privilege" may be a convenient short-hand expression to denote the status of negotiations in the context of a mediation, they will in fact be protected by reference to the traditional categories of confidential, legally privileged or without prejudice communications: there is no need for an additional distinct head of mediation privilege, founded on different principles or following different rules.

In order that the parties should know where they stand, it is preferable that any **15–019** formal mediation agreement should contain a confidentiality clause. CEDR Centre for Dispute Resolution's Model Mediation Agreement (12th edn) provides:

"4   Every person involved in the Mediation:

4.1   will keep confidential all information arising out of or in connection with the Mediation, including the fact and terms of any settlement, but not including the fact the Mediation is to take place or has taken place or where disclosure is required by law to implement or to enforce terms of settlement; and

4.2   acknowledges that all such information passing between the Parties, the Mediator and/or CEDR/Solve, however communicated, is agreed to be without prejudice to any Party's legal position and may not be produced as evidence or disclosed to any judge, arbitrator or other decision-maker in any legal or other formal process, except where otherwise disclosable in law.

5.   Where a Party privately discloses to the Mediator any information in confidence before, during or after the Mediation, the Mediator will not disclose that information to any other Party or person without the consent of the Party disclosing it, unless required by law to make disclosure.

6.   The Parties will not call the Mediator or any employee or consultant of CEDR Solve as a witness, nor require them to produce in evidence any records or notes relating to the Mediation, in any litigation, arbitration or other formal process arising from or in connection with their dispute and the Mediation; nor will the Mediator nor any CEDR Solve employee or consultant act or agree to act as a witness, expert, arbitrator or consultant in any such process..."

CHAPTER 16

Lawyers

Even before any broad development of the law of confidence, it was recognised **16–001** that the relationship between a lawyer and his clients imported obligations of confidentiality. In *Taylor v Blacklow*,[1] for example, Gaselee J. said that:

" . . . the first duty of an attorney is to keep the secrets of his client. Authority is not wanted to establish that proposition . . . ."

The duty of confidence owed by a solicitor or barrister to his client is **16–002** governed by the same general principles of law as apply to any other professional person, but there are special features which affect lawyers because of the central role performed by lawyers in the administration of justice. In the case of a solicitor the duty will arise both by contract and under the equitable doctrine of confidence; in the case of the barrister (unless he has entered into a contractual retainer) the duty is equitable.[2] An individual's communications with his lawyers now also attract the courts' protection under Art.8 of the European Convention on Human Rights.[3]

The duty owed by a lawyer to his client will extend to all confidential **16–003** information obtained in that capacity during the period of his retainer, irrespective of its source. The distinction in this respect between confidential information and other information was emphasised in *Strother v 3464920 Canada Inc*,[4] in which the Supreme Court of Canada rejected an allegation that the respondent solicitors had breached the confidence of a client by using the documents drafted for that client's transaction for the purposes of another client's transaction. Binnie J. said (at [111]):

"...it is not enough to show that a particular transaction document has its 'genesis' in a prior transaction document. Recycling precedents is the life-blood of corporate law practice. A document prepared for Client A is part of the lawyer's work product and may go through numerous iterations in the service of other clients."[5]

---

[1] (1836) 3 Bing. (N.C.) 235.
[2] For the rules of professional conduct, see Ch.4 of the SRA *Code of Conduct 2011* and the "*Code of Conduct of the Bar of England and Wales*", paras 603(f), 608(b) and 702 (together with the Bar Standards Board Standards Committee's guidance: "Maintaining confidentiality").
[3] *Foxley v United Kingdom* (2001) E.H.R.R. 637. See Ch.7 above.
[4] [2007] 2 S.C.R. 177 at [109]–[111].
[5] For further discussion of what constitutes confidential information (including comments in relation to solicitors in *Hilton v BarkerBooth & Eastwood* [2005] UKHL 8; [2005] 1 W.L.R. 567) see Ch.3.

A client may consent either expressly or impliedly to his lawyer's disclosure of confidential information.[6] However, in the absence of a joint retainer it is not to be supposed that a solicitor acting for two separate clients with different interests in the same transaction is necessarily authorised to pass confidential information from one to the other.[7] Nor does it follow from the fact that two solicitors are retained by a single client in relation to different retainers that the client consents to the communication of confidential information between them.[8]

16–004   Although a lawyer's duty of confidentiality is ordinarily owed to his client, such a duty may also be owed to a third person. With his client's consent, a barrister, for example, may agree to receive information from his opponent on a "counsel only" basis, in which case he would generally owe a duty of confidence not to disclose it to anyone else without his opponent's consent.

CONTINUING DUTY AFTER TERMINATION OF RETAINER

16–005   In English law the fiduciary duty of loyalty owed by a lawyer to a client ends with the termination of the retainer.[9] The difficulties that may arise in determining whether or not a solicitor's fiduciary duty to his client has come to an end in circumstances where there is a continuing but different retainer between solicitor and client are well demonstrated in *Strother v 3464920 Canada Inc*,[10] in which the nine members of the Supreme Court of Canada decided by a bare majority[11] that the appellant solicitor, Strother, remained under a duty to his client to inform it that his previous advice should be reconsidered.

However, it is well established that a lawyer's duty of confidentiality survives the end of his retainer. In *Wilson v Rastall*[12] (a case on privilege) Buller J., referring to a decision by him in an earlier case, said:

> " . . . I thought that the privilege of not being examined to such points was the privilege of the party, and not of the attorney: and that the privilege never ceased at any period of time. In such a case it is not sufficient to say that the cause is at an end; the mouth of such a person is shut for ever."

"For ever" may be an overstatement, for information can lose the quality of confidence, but the duty of confidence will continue for as long as the information retains that quality.

---

[6] See *TSB Bank Plc v Robert Irving & Burns* [1999] Lloyd's Rep. (PN) 956; *Mortgage Express Ltd v Sawali* [2010] EWHC 3054 (Ch); [2011] P.N.L.R. 11.

[7] See *Nationwide Building Society v Various Solicitors* [1999] P.N.L.R. 52, per Blackburne J.

[8] *Marsh v Sofaer* [2003] EWHC 3334, (Ch); (2004) P.N.L.R. 24, per Sir Andrew Morritt V.C. at [46].

[9] *Bolkiah v KPMG* [1999] 2 A.C. 222. In Canada, by contrast, it has been held that lawyers owe at least a residual continuing duty of loyalty to their former clients (*Brookville Carriers Flatbed GP Inc v Blackjack Transport Ltd* (2008) N.S.C.A. 22; 263 N.S.R. (2d) 272), while the Australian authorities are divided on the issue (*Watson & Ors v Ebsworth & Ebsworth (a firm) & Anor* [2010] V.S.C.A. 335, at [145]–[150]).

[10] [2007] 2 S.C.R. 177.

[11] At [39]–[43]. For a critical commentary on the decision of the majority, see James Edelman, *Unanticipated fiduciary liability* (2008) 124 L.Q.R. 21–26.

[12] (1792) 4 T.R. 753 at 759. Cited by Lord Taylor C.J. in *R. v Derbyshire Magistrates Court Ex p. B* [1996] A.C. 487 at 504.

In *Prince Jefri Bolkiah v KPMG*[13] the plaintiff, a brother of the Sultan of **16–006** Brunei, had retained the defendant accountants to provide forensic accountancy services in litigation relating to his financial affairs. Some time after that retainer had ended, the government of Brunei set up an investigation into aspects of Prince Jefri's former chairmanship of the Brunei Investment Agency. He obtained an interlocutory injunction restraining KPMG from acting for the Agency in the investigation. The injunction was discharged by the Court of Appeal, but reinstated by the House of Lords.

The leading speech was given by Lord Millett. He cited the earlier decision of **16–007** the Court of Appeal in *Rakusen v Ellis, Munday & Clarke*[14] as authority for two propositions:

> "(i) that there is no absolute rule of law in England that a solicitor may not act in litigation against a former client; and (ii) that the solicitor may be restrained from acting if such a restriction is necessary to avoid a significant risk of the disclosure or misuse of confidential information belonging to the former client."[15]

Comparing the position of accountants and solicitors, he added:

> "The duties of an accountant cannot be greater than those of a solicitor, and may be less, for information relating to his client's affairs which is in the possession of a solicitor is usually privileged as well as confidential. In the present case, however, some of the information obtained by KPMG is likely to have attracted litigation privilege, though not solicitor-client privilege, and it is conceded by KPMG that an accountant who provides litigation support services of the kind which they provided to Prince Jefri must be treated for present purposes in the same way as a solicitor."

Lord Millett held that, once the fiduciary relationship between solicitor and client had ended with the termination of the retainer, the court's jurisdiction to restrain the solicitor from acting against his former client could not be based on any conflict of interests, since the solicitor's only continuing duty was to preserve the confidentiality of information imparted during the retainer. Accordingly, a plaintiff seeking to restrain his former solicitor from acting for another client must show that the solicitor was in possession of relevant confidential information relating to his affairs.

As in other situations, there may be difficulty in defining the nature and content of the confidential information at risk. It has been suggested that such information may be of a non-specific, "getting to know you" character.[16] In *Re Z*,[17] Bodey J. restrained solicitors from acting for the wife in divorce proceedings, on the basis that the senior partner had acted for the husband in financial proceedings against the wife some nine years earlier. Bodey J. held that the senior partner "was likely to have been privy to privileged/confidential information and she would also have got to know his sensitivities and feelings, his likely reactions, the sort of person he is and how to handle him."

---

[13] [1999] 2 A.C. 222.

[14] [1912] 1 Ch. 831.

[15] At 234.

[16] See, for example, *Pinnacle Living Pty Ltd v Elusive Image Pty Ltd* [2006] V.S.C. 202.

[17] [2009] EWHC 3621 (Fam); [2010] 2 F.L.R. 132.

16–008   In Australia, doubts have been expressed as to this approach to the identification of confidential information in such cases. In *Ismail-Zai v The State of Western Australia*,[18] Steytler P. cited with approval the dicta of Richardson J. in the New Zealand Court of Appeal in *Black v Taylor*[19]:

> "...the inherent jurisdiction of the Court provides a more satisfactory basis for determining the question than the indirect and somewhat artificial development of a special rule, which treats knowledge of a client (as distinct from knowledge of his or her affairs) gained through a professional association as confidential information under the umbrella of protection of misuse of confidential information."

The inherent jurisdiction here referred to is that of the Court over its officers, a matter not expressly addressed by the House of Lords in *Bolkiah v KPMG*. The existence of this jurisdiction, in the context of an application to prevent an advocate from acting in litigation, was confirmed by the Court of Appeal in *Geveran Trading Co Ltd v Skjevesland*.[20] In *Kallinicos v Hunt*,[21] Brereton J. suggested in the New South Wales Supreme Court that the test should be whether a fair-minded, reasonably informed member of the public would conclude that the proper administration of justice required that a legal practitioner should be prevented from acting for his or her client, in the interests of the protection of the judicial process and the due administration of justice, including the appearance of justice. In the later New South Wales case of *Cleveland Investments Global Ltd v Evans*,[22] Ward J. observed that the jurisdiction was regarded as exceptional and was to be exercised with caution.

It is suggested that the factors identified by Bodey J. are readily capable, in an appropriate case, of amounting to confidential information which merits the court's protection. It would only be in rare circumstances that a court might need to have recourse to its inherent jurisdiction over its officers in order to restrain a lawyer from acting against a former client.

16–009   So far as the nature of the solicitor's duty of confidentiality to the former client is concerned, Lord Millett observed in *Bolkiah v KPMG*[23]:

> "Whether founded on contract or equity, the duty to preserve confidentiality is unqualified. It is a duty to keep the information confidential, not merely to take all reasonable steps to do so. Moreover, it is not merely a duty not to communicate the information to a third party. It is a duty not to misuse it, that is to say, without the consent of the former client to make any use of it or to cause any use to be made of it by others otherwise than for his benefit. The former client cannot be protected completely from accidental or inadvertent disclosure. But he is entitled to prevent his former solicitor from exposing him to any avoidable risk; and this includes the increased risk of the use of the information to his prejudice arising from the

---

[18] [2007] W.A.S.C.A. 150 at [34].

[19] [1993] 3 N.Z.L.R. 403 at 408.

[20] [2002] EWCA Civ 1567; [2003] 1 W.L.R. 912 at [38]–[41]. In *Winters v Mishcon de Reya* [2008] EWHC 2419 at [94], Henderson J. was prepared to assume, without deciding, that "there may be rare circumstances in which the court will intervene, in exercise of its general jurisdiction over solicitors as officers of the court, notwithstanding that there is no risk of misuse of confidential information."

[21] (2005) 64 N.S.W.L.R. 561 at [76].

[22] [2010] N.S.W.S.C. 567 at [6].

[23] At 235–236.

acceptance of instructions to act for another client with an adverse interest in a matter to which the information is or may be relevant."

Discussing the degree of risk of misuse necessary to justify the court's interference, Lord Millett said:

"Many different tests have been proposed in the authorities. These include the avoidance of 'an appreciable risk' or 'an acceptable risk.' I regard such expressions as unhelpful: the former because it is ambiguous, the latter because it is uninformative. I prefer simply to say that the court should intervene unless it is satisfied that there is no risk of disclosure.[24] It goes without saying that the risk must be a real one, and not merely fanciful or theoretical. But it need not be substantial."

Lord Millett treated the possible efficacy of information barriers within firms with considerable caution[25]:

"There is no rule of law that Chinese walls or other arrangements of a similar kind are insufficient to eliminate the risk. But the starting point must be that, unless special measures are taken, information moves within a firm. In *MacDonald Estate v Martin*, 77 D.L.R. (4th) 249, 269 Sopinka J. said that the court should restrain the firm from acting for the second client 'unless satisfied on the basis of clear and convincing evidence that all reasonable measures have been taken to ensure that no disclosure will occur.' With the substitution of the word 'effective' for the words 'all reasonable' I would respectfully adopt that formulation."

Bolkiah has been applied in a number of subsequent decisions.[26] The courts have frequently addressed, in particular, the adequacy of arrangements made by firms to prevent the free internal flow of confidential information. In *Koch Shipping Inc v Richards Butler*,[27] the Court of Appeal emphasised that all such cases depend on their own facts. However, Tuckey L.J., observed[28]: **16–010**

"In these days of professional and client mobility it is of course important that client confidentiality should be preserved. Each case must depend on its own facts. But I think there is a danger inherent in the intensity of the adversarial process of courts being persuaded that a risk exists when, if one stands back a little, that risk is no more than fanciful or theoretical. I advocate a robust view with this in mind, so as to ensure that the line is sensibly drawn."

---

[24] It is not often that damages will be an adequate remedy. See, for example, *National Westminster Bank Plc v Bonas* [2003] EWHC 1821, (Ch), per Lindsay J. at [131(viii)].

[25] At 237–238.

[26] See, for example, *Young v Robson Rhodes* [1999] 3 All E.R. 524 (Laddie J.); *Halewood International Ltd v Addleshaws Booth & Co* [2000] Lloyd's Rep. (PN) 298 (Neuberger J.); *In the matter of a Firm of Solicitors* [2000] 1 Lloyd's Rep. 31 (Timothy Walker J.); *Ball v Druces & Atlee* [2002] P.N.L.R. 23 (Burton J.); *Bodle v Coutts & Co* [2003] EWHC 1865, Ch (Peter Smith J.); *Marks & Spencer Group Plc v Freshfields Bruckhaus Deringer* [2004] EWCA Civ 741; [2005] P.N.L.R. 4; *GUS Consulting GmbH v Leboeuf Lamb Greene & Macrae* [2006] EWCA Civ 683; (2006) P.N.L.R. 32; *Winters v Mishcon de Reya* [2008] EWHC 2419 (Ch) (Henderson J.); *Re Z* [2009] EWHC 3621 (Fam); [2010] 2 F.L.R. 132 (Bodey J.).

[27] [2002] EWCA Civ 1280; [2002] 2 All E.R. (Comm) 957.

[28] At [53].

Paragraph O4.4 of the Solicitors Code of Conduct 2011 requires solicitors to achieve the following outcome:

> "you do not act for A in a matter *where A has an interest adverse to B*, and B is a client for whom you hold confidential information which is material to A in that matter, unless the confidential information can be protected by the use of safeguards, and:
>
> (a)   you reasonably believe that A is aware of, and understands, the relevant issues and gives informed consent;
>
> (b)   either:
>
>   (i)   B gives informed consent and you agree with B the safeguards to protect B's information; or
>
>   (ii)   where this is not possible, you put in place effective safeguards including information barriers which comply with the common law; and
>
> (c)   it is reasonable in all the circumstances to act for A with such safeguards in place..." [Emphasis added]

The absence of an obvious conflict between the interests of a new client and the interests of a former client may be relevant to the question whether, as a matter of fact, there is a real risk of disclosure or misuse of the former client's confidential information, and to the nature and extent of the arrangements necessary to guard against that risk. But the existence of an "adverse" interest forms no part of Lord Millett's reasoning in *Bolkiah* and is not a necessary condition for the application of the principles established in that case.

Limits of the principle in *Bolkiah v KPMG*

16–011   A related issue is whether a solicitor may be restrained on occasion from acting, not against a former client, but against a party against whom that solicitor has previously acted. In *British Sky Broadcasting Group Plc v Virgin Media Communications Ltd*,[29] Sky complained that Virgin's solicitors, Ashurst, had acquired confidential information in acting for Virgin against Sky in separate proceedings. (Commercially sensitive documents had been inspected by Ashurst, on their express undertaking not to disclose their contents to Virgin or to use them for collateral purposes.) Sky argued that there was a risk that Ashurst might inadvertently disclose its confidential information to Virgin when acting for them in the new proceedings and referred to Lord Millett's speech in *Bolkiah v KPMG*. The Court of Appeal upheld Lewison J.'s dismissal of Sky's application for a restraining injunction, saying[30]:

> "We do not accept ... that the duty not to make ulterior use of disclosed documents is identical in principle to the obligation of confidentiality that exists between a solicitor and his own client.
>
> ...The passage in the speech of Lord Millett in *Bolkiah v KPMG* ... cannot be applied to a solicitor who has obtained information from an opponent by the process of disclosure. It is usually enough to rely upon the recognition by a solicitor of the duty not to make any ulterior use of information obtained by disclosure."

---

[29]   [2008] EWCA Civ 612.

[30]   At [21]–[22].

The Court of Appeal observed[31]:

> "In a rare case, the fact the documents have been disclosed to solicitors acting for a party in one set of proceedings might conceivably preclude those solicitors from acting for a different party in another set of proceedings. We find it hard to conceive of circumstances where disclosure in one set of proceedings would preclude lawyers from acting in other proceedings between the same parties."

Similarly, in *Stiedl v Enyo Law LLP*[32] (where there had been inadvertent disclosure of privileged material) Beatson J. held that:

> "...a distinction is to be made between two classes of case. The first class consists of cases in which there has been a previous relationship of solicitor and client in which confidential or privileged information is acquired by the solicitor and that solicitor now acts or wishes to act for another person who is in dispute with the former client. The second class consists of cases where, without any such previous relationship, a solicitor becomes possessed of confidential or privileged information belonging to the other party to the dispute. The distinction operates at the level of remedy: see *Solicitors, Re* [1997] Ch. 1; [1995] 3 All E.R. 482 at p.492 of the latter report. In that case, Lightman J. stated that in a 'previous relationship' case, in the ordinary course a court will grant an injunction restraining the solicitor acting, as it did in the earlier case with the same name; *Solicitors (A Firm), Re* [1992] Q.B. 959. In cases where there has been no previous solicitor-client relationship, however, 'in the ordinary course the court will merely grant an injunction restraining the solicitor making use of that information', as it did in *English and American Insurance Co Ltd v Herbert Smith* [1998] F.S.R. 232 and *Goddard v Nationwide Building Society* [1987] Q.B. 670."[33]

Where the employment of an in-house lawyer is terminated, the lawyer's subsequent employment may give rise to a tension between the public interest in the preservation of legal confidentiality (which determined the principles applied in *Bolkiah v KPMG*[34]) and the public interest in the freedom of employment (which was recognised in the principles applied by the Court of Appeal in *Faccenda Chicken Ltd v Fowler*[35]). In *Generics (UK) Ltd v Yeda Research and Development Co Ltd*,[36] the defendants sought to restrain the claimant from involving in the litigation an employed patent attorney who had previously been employed by one of the defendants. The Court of Appeal held, on the facts, that there was no real risk of the misuse of confidential information but discussed obiter whether the principles in *Bolkiah v KPMG* were applicable. Jacob L.J.

---

[31] At [30].

[32] [2011] EWHC 2649 (Comm); [2012] P.N.L.R. 4 at [39].

[33] For an exceptional case in which counsel were restrained from acting following their perusal of privileged material which had been inadvertently disclosed, see the decision of Hollingworth J. in the Supreme Court of Victoria in *GT Corp Pty Ltd v Amare Safety Pty Ltd* [2007] V.S.C. 123. In *Worth Recycling Pty Ltd v Waste Recycling and Processing Pty Ltd* [2009] N.S.W.C.A. 354, the New South Wales Court of Appeal restrained the claimant's lawyers from continuing to act against the defendant in circumstances where the lawyers had represented another client in similar proceedings against the defendant and there was a "real and sensible possibility" of misuse of confidential information which the lawyers had acquired in the course of the mediation of those previous proceedings.

[2011] EWHC 2649 (Comm); [2012] P.N.L.R. 4 at [39].

[34] [1999] 2 A.C. 222.

[35] [1987] 1 Ch. 117.

[36] [2012] EWCA Civ 726; [2012] CP Rep. 39; further discussed at para.14–017, above.

considered that they were, an employed lawyer being in the same position as a retained lawyer, but Etherton L.J. and Ward L.J. disagreed. Etherton L.J. said[37]:

> "...so far as concerns a barring order, there is no good reason to import into the employment field and to place on the former employee the *Bolkiah* evidential burden of proving the absence of any real risk of disclosure. On the contrary, there are good reasons not to do so..."

LEGAL PROFESSIONAL PRIVILEGE

16–012   When considering the duties of a lawyer to his client, a practical distinction between the limits of confidence and the limits of privilege is often difficult to draw. (The subject here discussed is the duty of a lawyer to his client, as opposed to the difficult subject of the relationship of privilege and confidentiality as between a client and another party, about which see Ch.18.) For confidentiality is a pre-requisite of legal professional privilege; and, conversely, if information is recognised to be privileged, the decision whether to disclose it belongs to the client and not to the lawyer. Legal professional privilege is no longer merely a procedural or evidential rule applicable only in the context of litigation. As Lord Hoffmann said in *R. (Morgan Grenfell Ltd) v Special Commissioner of Income Tax*[38]:

> "It is not the case that LPP does no more than entitle the client to require his lawyer to withhold privileged documents in judicial or quasi-judicial proceedings, leaving the question of whether he may disclose them on other occasions to the implied duty of confidence. The policy of LPP requires that the client should be secure in the knowledge that protected documents and information will not be disclosed at all."

16–013   This is consistent with the approach taken, for example, by Scrutton L.J. in *Weld-Blundell v Stephen*,[39] where he said:

> "But take the case of a solicitor. Under the decision in *Reg. v Cox and Railton*[40] when the accused has consulted his solicitor after the commission of a crime for the legitimate purpose of being defended the communication is *privileged*, the *privilege* being that of the client. If then the solicitor in breach of this *confidence and privilege* announced his intention of informing the prosecution of the contents of his client's communication, I cannot believe that the Court would not restrain him before communication or give damages against him for breach of his contract of employment after communication . . . ." (Emphasis added.)

There are, however, limits to the circumstances in which legal professional privilege attaches. The information must itself be confidential. So, for example, legal professional privilege cannot attach to extracts from public records made by a solicitor for the purposes of a defence, nor to communications with an opposing

---

[37] At [82]

[38] [2002] UKHL 21; [2003] 1 A.C. 563 at [30].

[39] [1919] 1 K.B. 520 at 544–545.

[40] (1884) 14 Q.B.D. 153 at 175.

party,[41] nor to copies of documents which were not brought into existence in circumstances covered by legal professional privilege even where the copies were obtained for the purposes of litigation.[42]

The scope and depth of legal professional privilege are further considered at Ch.18 below.

16–014

CRIME OR FRAUD

Privilege does not attach to communications between a client and legal adviser, or documents brought into existence, as a step in a criminal or fraudulent enterprise, or for the purpose of stifling or covering up a crime or fraud,[43] regardless whether either the legal adviser[44] or the client[45] is himself a party to the plot or innocent, for, as Stephen J. said in *R. v Cox and Railton*,[46] a communication in furtherance of a criminal purpose does not "come into the ordinary scope of professional employment" and "the protection of such communications cannot possibly be otherwise than injurious to the interests of justice".

16–015

In *Bullivant v Att Gen*, Lord Halsbury L.C. said[47]:

16–016

" . . . for the perfect administration of justice and for the protection of confidence which exists between a solicitor and his client, it has been established as a principle of public policy that those confidential communications shall not be subject to production. But to that, of course, this limitation has been put, that no court can be called upon to protect communications which are in themselves part of a criminal or unlawful proceeding."

A solicitor is not prevented by any duty of confidence from making appropriate disclosure of information that falls within the "crime or fraud" exception to legal professional privilege. The same factors that have deprived the information of its privileged status will serve also to undermine its confidentiality. However, a serious problem for an honest solicitor arises when the facts are not clear. Drawing a line between proper defence of a client and improper concealment of wrongdoing may be difficult. So is the position of a solicitor who begins to suspect that a transaction in which he has been retained involves fraud. Terminating his retainer may be a solution in some cases, but not in others, particularly where the solicitor is in possession of funds which may represent the proceeds of fraud. This problem arose in *Finers v Miro*.[48] The plaintiffs had acted for the defendant in setting up a complex corporate scheme to hold assets on his

---

[41] *Lyell v Kennedy (No.3)* (1884) 27 Ch.D. 1.

[42] *Ventouris v Mountain* [1991] 1 W.L.R. 607.

[43] *R. v Cox and Railton* (1884) 14 Q.B.D. 153; *Bullivant v Att Gen for Victoria* [1901] A.C. 196 at 201, per Lord Halsbury; 206, per Lord Lindley; *O'Rourke v Darbishire* [1920] A.C. 581; *Gamlen Chemical Co (UK) Ltd v Rochem*, unreported, December 7, 1979, CA (Civil Division) Transcript No.777 of 1979; *Finers v Miro* [1991] 1 W.L.R. 35.

[44] *Kuwait Airways Corp v Iraqi Airways Co (No.6)* [2005] EWCA Civ 286; [2005] 1 W.L.R. 2734 at [14].

[45] *The Owners and/or Demise Charterers of the Dredger "Kamal XXVI" and the Barge "Kamal XXIV" v The Owners of the Ship "Ariela"* [2010] EWHC 2531 (Comm) (Burton J.).

[46] (1884) 14 Q.B.D. 153 at 167.

[47] [1901] A.C. 196 at 201.

[48] [1991] 1 W.L.R. 35.

behalf. Secrecy was a primary aim of the scheme. Subsequently, reasonable grounds arose for suspicion that many of the assets represented the proceeds of fraud carried out on an insurance company, now in liquidation.

16–017   The solicitors were in a dilemma what to do and concerned that they might be liable as constructive trustees of the assets held under their control. They accordingly applied to the court, by an originating summons under Ord.85 of the Rules of the Supreme Court, for directions in relation to the assets. The Court of Appeal held that the insurance company's liquidator should be given notice of the solicitors' application, notwithstanding the defendant's contention that such notice would constitute a breach of the legal professional privilege to which he was entitled. Dillon L.J. said[49]:

> "It was urged for the defendant that the advice obtained by the defendant from Mr Stein [a partner in the firm of solicitors] was not advice on how to commit a fraud but advice after the fraud, if there was one, had been committed. I note, however, that in *O'Rourke v Darbishire*[50] Lord Sumner refers, at p.613, to a party consulting a solicitor 'in order to learn how to plan, execute, or stifle an actual fraud'. The privilege cannot, in my judgment, apply if the solicitor is consulted—even though he does not realise this and is himself acting innocently—to cover up or stifle a fraud."

But how well established must a client's wrongdoing be in order to absolve a lawyer of his prima facie duty of confidence? In *Finers*, Dillon L.J. continued:

> "On the material before us I conclude that *it does seem probable* that the defendant may have consulted Mr Stein for the purpose of being guided and helped, albeit unwittingly on the part of Mr Stein, in covering up or stifling *a fraud on the insurance company of which there is a prima facie case resting on solid grounds*."[51] (Emphasis added.)

16–018   Sections 327 to 329 of the Proceeds of Crime Act 2002 create a variety of offences based on one form or another of involvement in dealings with "criminal property"—broadly speaking, property that is both the proceeds of crime and known or suspected by the offender to be the proceeds of crime. No offence is committed if disclosure is made to a specified individual in accordance with the provisions of s.338 of the Act.[52]

16–019   In *Bowman v Fels*,[53] the solicitors acting for the claimant in civil litigation that related to the beneficial interests in a residential property came to suspect that the defendant had accounted fraudulently to the Inland Revenue and to Customs and Excise for certain works carried out at the property. They believed that they were obliged by s.328 of the Act to notify the National Criminal Intelligence Service of their suspicions and their notification effectively derailed the progress of the

---

[49] [1991] 1 W.L.R. 35 at 40.

[50] [1920] A.C. 581.

[51] A test derived from an amalgam of what was said by Lord Wrenbury in *O'Rourke v Derbyshire* [1920] A.C. 581 at 632–644 and by Templeman L.J. in *Gamlen Chemical Co (UK) Ltd v Rochem Ltd*. In relation to litigation privilege, see also *Kuwait Airways Corp v Iraqi Airways Co* [2005] EWCA Civ 286; [2005] 1 W.L.R. 2734, and *Dadourian Group International Inc v Simms* [2008] EWHC 1784 (Ch), per Patten J. at [129] ff.

[52] For cases relating to the impact of this legislation on banks, see under para.12–013, above.

[53] [2005] EWCA Civ 226; [2005] 1 W.L.R. 3083.

litigation. The Court of Appeal held that the ordinary conduct of litigation by lawyers did not engage ss.327 to 329 of the Act. The Court went on to hold obiter that ss.327 to 329 did not override legal professional privilege, nor the restrictions imposed on parties to whom disclosure is made during the course of litigation.[54]

16–020 Sections 327 to 329 do not themselves impose an obligation to disclose information: rather, disclosure under s.338 operates as a defence against what might otherwise be an offence under ss.327 to 329. The Court of Appeal did not state expressly whether its conclusion that ss.327 to 329 did not override legal professional privilege had the consequence (a) that no offence is committed— under those sections, at least—by a lawyer who continues to act in circumstances where his suspicions of money laundering remain unreported because of legal professional privilege, or (b) that legal professional privilege merely prevents a lawyer from making a disclosure under s.338 and thereby deprives the lawyer of the defence that a disclosure under s.338 would have provided. The terms of the Court of Appeal's judgment in *Bowman v Fels* lend some support to the former possibility by appearing to suggest that, even if ss.327 to 329 were applicable to the conduct of litigation, a lawyer could continue to act, notwithstanding his suspicions.[55]

16–021 Section 330 of the Act creates a further offence if someone carrying out business in the regulated sector (as defined in Sch.9 of the Act) fails to disclose information causing him to suspect that another person is engaged in money laundering. Section 330(6)(b) creates an exception for legal and other relevant professional advisers to whom information has been communicated in "privileged circumstances" (as defined at s.330(10) of the Act). Section 330(11) provides that privileged circumstances do not extend to "information or other matter which is communicated or given with the intention of furthering a criminal purpose".

16–022 Section 333A of the Act makes it an offence to "tip off" a client, but s.333D provides a defence if the disclosure "is made for the purpose of dissuading the client from engaging in conduct amounting to an offence".

16–023 In *Bowman v Fels*, the Court of Appeal observed[56] (without deciding the issue) that s.330(11) of the Act might arguably be applicable only where the lawyer is *aware* of the intention to further a criminal purpose. That leaves open the question by what standard a lawyer who discloses prima facie privileged information on the basis of the "crime or fraud" exception (whether common law or statutory) is to be judged, if the suspected crime or fraud proves to be illusory. If the test for the exception is that outlined by Dillon L.J. in *Finers v Miro*, it is suggested that the touchstone of liability, so far as the lawyer is concerned, should nevertheless be reasonableness. A solicitor who reasonably believes that the "crime or fraud" exception to privilege is applicable should not subsequently be held liable to his client if he makes such limited disclosure as would be required of him if the exception were established in fact.[57]

---

[54] At [85]–[91].

[55] See Chs 5, 6 and 12 of the Law Society's *Anti-money laundering practice note* (October 2011).

[56] At [94].

[57] See Ch.6 above, in relation to the public interest defence.

16–024   A solicitor's position may be made more difficult if his duty of confidence to one client appears to conflict with his duty of disclosure to another. Suppose that a solicitor, acting for both prospective mortgagor and prospective mortgagee, discovers information that leads him to suspect that the mortgagor is planning to defraud the mortgagee and that he, the solicitor, is to be the mortgagor's unwitting tool in this fraud.

16–025   If the solicitor's suspicion remains merely an unsubstantiated suspicion, it is open to him simply to decline to act further in the transaction. If it seems to him probable, however, that the purpose of his retainer is the furtherance of a fraud of which "there is a prima facie case on solid grounds", the question arises (a) whether there is any duty to the mortgagor which prevents the solicitor from informing the mortgagee of the fraud, and indeed (b) whether it is not the solicitor's *duty* to inform the mortgagee.

16–026   In *Mortgage Express Ltd v Bowerman & Partners*[58] the Court of Appeal held that where a solicitor acting for both borrower and mortgagee in a property purchase discovered, on investigating title, information about recent prior sales, which might have caused the mortgagee to suspect that the valuation with which he had been provided was excessive, the solicitor owed a duty to disclose that information to the mortgagee as well as to the borrower.

16–027   Sir Thomas Bingham M.R. stressed that it was not a case in which a solicitor acting for two parties received information confidential to one of them. He observed, obiter, that in such a case it might be necessary for the solicitor to obtain the consent of the client whose information it was to disclose it to the other, and that if consent were refused the solicitor might be obliged to cease to act for that other party or both. In *Nationwide Anglia Building Society v Various Solicitors*,[59] Blackburne J. observed that *Mortgage Express Ltd v Bowerman & Partners* did not provide authority for the proposition that where a solicitor acts for both borrower and lender there can be no confidence in communications passing between solicitor and borrower, or that the solicitor is therefore free to inform the lender of matters which the solicitor has learned from his communications with the borrower and which may be of concern to the lender. Blackburne J. held that the question in each case is what authority the borrower has given to his solicitor.

16–028   In *Darlington Building Society v O'Rourke James Scourfield & McCarthy*,[60] the Court of Appeal, in the context of an unsuccessful application to amend a statement of claim, again considered the scope of a conveyancing solicitor's duties to lender and borrower. The defendant solicitors had acted for borrowers, to whom near-simultaneous loans had been made by the two plaintiff lenders. Each of the plaintiffs, for whom the defendants had also acted, remained ignorant of the involvement of the other, allegedly as a result of misrepresentation on the part of the borrowers. The plaintiffs wished to pursue a claim that the defendants should have disclosed the true position to both of them. Giving the only substantive judgment, Sir Iain Glidewell said[61]:

---

[58] [1996] 2 All E.R. 836.
[59] [1999] P.N.L.R. 52.
[60] [1999] 1 Lloyd's Rep. (PN) 33.
[61] At [37].

" . . . in order to succeed in this action each of the plaintiffs must prove that the information which the defendants obtained and which the plaintiffs alleged should have been disclosed to them respectively was not confidential. Since *prima facie* information obtained whilst the solicitor is dealing with another transaction between his borrower client and another building society *is* confidential, the plaintiff thus has to prove that such information discloses or arises out of facts which tend to show fraud by the borrower. Clearly in order to be required to disclose that information the solicitor has to know of or at least to have strong evidence of such fraud from the facts he knows."

Since the decisions in *Nationwide Anglia Building Society v Various Solicitors* and *Darlington Building Society v O'Rourke James Scourfield & McCarthy*, mortgage lenders have begun routinely to require applicants for loans to waive any rights of privilege or confidentiality which they might otherwise be entitled to assert against their mortgagee. Such a waiver was held to be effective in *Mortgage Express Ltd v Sawali*[62]

USE OF INFORMATION IN DEFENCE OF THE LAWYER'S OWN INTERESTS

It is clear from the House of Lords' decision in *Medcalf v Mardell*[63] that a lawyer is not entitled to reveal confidential information in order to oppose the making of a wasted costs order against him pursuant to s.51(6) of the Supreme Court Act 1981 and CPR 48.7. It is apparent that this restriction cannot be ascribed simply to equitable principles of confidence, since professional persons are entitled in general to use information imparted to them confidentially, if it is reasonably necessary for them to do so in protection of their own legitimate interests.[64]   **16–029**

Rather, the restriction arises as a result of the privileged nature of the information. Since orders for costs are within the discretion of the court, the court is unusually well placed to avoid any injustice in considering a wasted costs application by making proper allowance for this restriction upon respondent lawyers. In *Medcalf v Mardell*,[65] the House of Lords allowed an appeal brought by barristers against whom a wasted costs order had been made, on the basis that they had advanced allegations of fraud without reasonably credible material. Lord Bingham cited a well-known passage from the Court of Appeal's decision in *Ridehalgh v Horsefield*[66]:   **16–030**

"The respondent lawyers are in a different position. The privilege is not theirs to waive. In the usual case where a waiver would not benefit their client they will be slow to advise the client to waive his privilege, and they may well feel bound to

---

[62] [2010] EWHC 3054 (Ch); [2011] P.N.L.R. 11, H.H.J Simon Brown QC. It may still be sensible for solicitors who face a lender's demand for a copy of the borrower's file to require a court order if they are in doubt as to the effectiveness of their borrower client's waiver: see the costs judgment in *Mortgage Express Ltd v Sawali*. [2010] EWHC 90181 (Costs); [2011] 2 Costs L.R. 288.

[63] [2002] UKHL 27; [2003] 1 A.C. 120.

[64] *Tournier v National Provincial and Union Bank of England* [1924] 1 K.B. 461 (bankers); *Duncan v Medical Practitioner's Disciplinary Committee* [1986] 1 N.Z.L.R. 513 (doctors); *R. v Institute of Chartered Accountants of England and Wales Ex p. Brindle* [1994] B.C.C. 297 at 312 (accountants).

[65] At [23].

[66] [1994] Ch. 205 at 237.

advise that the client should take independent advice before doing so. The client may be unwilling to do that, and may be unwilling to waive if he does. So the respondent lawyers may find themselves at a grave disadvantage in defending their conduct of proceedings, unable to reveal what advice and warnings they gave, what instructions they received. In some cases this potential source of injustice may be mitigated by reference to the taxing master, where different rules apply, but only in a small minority of cases can this procedure be appropriate. Judges who are invited to make or contemplate making a wasted costs order must make full allowance for the inability of respondent lawyers to tell the whole story. Where there is room for doubt, the respondent lawyers are entitled to the benefit of it. It is again only when, with all allowances made, a lawyer's conduct of proceedings is quite plainly unjustifiable that it can be appropriate to make a wasted costs order."

Lord Bingham said that he did not regard this passage as inaccurate or misleading, but he considered that it should be strengthened because only rarely will a court be able to make "full allowance" for the inability of the practitioner to tell the full story or be sure that nothing could be said by the practitioner which might influence the exercise of the court's discretion. He added:

"Where a wasted costs order is sought against a practitioner precluded by legal professional privilege from giving his full answer to the application, the court should not make an order unless, proceeding with extreme care, it is (a) satisfied that there is nothing the practitioner could say, if unconstrained, to resist the order and (b) that it is in all the circumstances fair to make the order."

16–031   The question arises whether this restriction upon lawyers opposing wasted costs applications extends to lawyers facing other civil claims or criminal sanctions. If the proceedings have been brought, or have resulted from a complaint, by the client, clearly the client cannot assert privilege to prevent the solicitor from deploying previously confidential material to the extent reasonably necessary to defend himself.[67] Similarly, if a client fails to pay his solicitor's fees, the client should not be entitled to defeat an action by the solicitor for their recovery by asserting privilege in relation to the action's subject matter.[68] However, if the proceedings have been brought by or against somebody else,[69] the problem is more difficult.

16–032   In *R. v Derby Magistrates' Court Ex p. B*[70] Lord Taylor C.J. said that:

" . . . no exception should be made to the absolute nature of legal professional privilege, once established . . . "

The decision in *R. v Derby Magistrates' Court Ex p. B*[71] appears to pre-empt any possibility that a solicitor facing a civil claim by a third party should be entitled to disclose his client's privileged information in his own defence. Indeed, if a

---

[67] *Paragon Finance Plc v Freshfields* [1999] 1 W.L.R. 1183.

[68] *Hakendorf v Rosenborg* [2004] EWHC 2821 (QB), per Tugendhat J. at [69]–[82].

[69] See the example at para.16–024 above, of a claim by a mortgage lender. If the loan was fraudulent, no question of privilege would arise, but it might be the defendant's case that the loan was not fraudulent and he might need to disclose confidential documents with a view to establishing the innocence of the transaction and his own innocence.

[70] [1996] A.C. 487 at 508–509.

[71] See the discussion in Ch.18 below.

solicitor were able to use any privileged material that *assisted* his case, it is not easy to see why, in principle, the third party claimant should be denied access to privileged material that *damaged* it.

Again, on the basis of *R. v Derby Magistrates' Court Ex p. B*, if the information given to a solicitor was originally privileged, and if there has been no express or implied waiver of privilege by the client, it is difficult to see how the solicitor may use such information to defend himself even against a criminal charge. It may be that if the solicitor could show to the court with jurisdiction over the criminal proceedings that the effect of his inability to use the information would be seriously to impede his ability to defend himself, the court would have an inherent jurisdiction to stay the criminal proceedings, but even that solution may present difficulties, if it would be likely to involve the solicitor revealing to the court that which, *ex hypothesi*, he is not authorised to reveal. **16–033**

The difficulties of a lawyer, who is faced by the claim of a third party, in the absence of any waiver of his client's privilege, go further. Under the present state of English law, it is far from clear that the lawyer is entitled to disclose privileged material to his insurers, or even to his own legal advisers. The issue arose indirectly in *Quinn Direct Insurance Ltd v Law Society*,[72] in which the claimant insurer sought an order requiring the Law Society to disclose documents in its control as a result of its intervention in the practice of a firm of solicitors which was insured by the claimant. The claimant believed that there were likely to be documents which would justify the claimant's proposed refusal of indemnity to a partner in the firm on the ground that he had condoned fraudulent practices. The Law Society declined to produce the documents, contending (among other things) that to do so would be to breach the privilege of the firm's clients. **16–034**

Among its other arguments, the claimant contended that the firm (in the absence of the Law Society's intervention in its practice) would have been obliged as the claimant's insured to provide to the claimant the documents sought.

The Court of Appeal rejected the claimant's application on a number of grounds. Sir Andrew Morritt C. said[73]:

> "I do not accept that an insured solicitor under any form of 'claims made' policy is either entitled or bound to disclose to his insurer, either on inception, renewal or notification, confidential and privileged documents or information of the client without the client's consent."

The Chancellor acknowledged the quandary in which an insured solicitor might be placed, but regarded it as irrelevant to the issue in question:

> "…no doubt the solicitor/insured owes duties of good faith to the insurer. He cannot justify any concealment of a material matter on the ground that he, personally, is privileged from disclosing it … nor, perhaps, on the ground that the information he failed to disclose was confidential … Nevertheless the privilege is that of his client and cannot be broken or waived without the client's consent. It may be that, if the client will not waive his privilege to enable proper disclosure to be made, the consequence of the resulting conflict of interest will be that the insurance is vitiated

---

[72] [2010] EWCA Civ 80 [2011] 1 W.L.R. 308.
[73] At [23].

or the notification inadequate but that is the problem of the solicitor not the client... The solicitor's duty of disclosure cannot override the entitlement of the client."[74]

16–035   The Court of Appeal's ultimate decision in *Quinn Direct Insurance Ltd v Law Society* was that there were no grounds for implying into the scheme for the regulation of solicitors any provision or term entitling or obliging the Law Society to produce to an insurer documents emanating from a firm of solicitors into which it has intervened which are subject to the privilege of a client of the firm. The observations contained in the passages quoted above may not have been essential to that decision, but they leave the legal profession in a position of some difficulty. The same reasoning would also appear to place an embargo (in the absence of consent or waiver) on a lawyer's disclosure of privileged information to his own legal advisers.

It is suggested that, in circumstances where any person instructing a solicitor is protected by a regulatory scheme requiring the solicitor to maintain professional indemnity insurance, there are good grounds for contending that a client impliedly consents at the outset of his solicitor's retainer to his solicitor making such limited disclosures of confidential information as may be required to enable the solicitor to comply with his obligations as an insured under his professional indemnity insurance policy. This was not an argument addressed by the Court of Appeal in *Quinn Direct Insurance Ltd v Law Society*, which specifically recorded[75] that:

> "It is not suggested either that some term is to be implied into the retainer between the client and [the firm] to the effect that confidential documents of the client may be disclosed to the insurer of [the firm] in the case of either a 'claims made' policy or an intervention by the Law Society unless, in either case, the client has waived his right of confidence or privilege."

Disclosure of privileged information to a lawyer's own insurers or legal advisers would not itself bring that material into the public domain, or otherwise prejudice the lawyer's client, and might therefore be regarded as not inconsistent with the purpose of legal professional privilege, as it has recently been described in *R. (Morgan Grenfell) v Special Commissioner of Income Tax*[76] and *McE v Prison Service of Northern Ireland*[77] (as to which see further below).

16–036   The professional regulation of lawyers raises similar issues. Often the regulator's involvement will arise from a complaint by the lawyer's client. In those circumstances the client, by making his complaint, will inevitably waive privilege to the limited extent necessary to dispose of his complaint fairly and properly. But what if a complaint is made, not by a lawyer's client, but by a third party, or if an investigation arises from the regulator's own motion?

16–037   In *Parry-Jones v Law Society*,[78] a solicitor sought to prevent the Law Society, acting in its regulatory capacity, from gaining access to documents in respect of which his clients could assert legal professional privilege. The Court of Appeal

---

[74] At [24].
[75] At [22].
[76] [2002] UKHL 21; [2003] 1 A.C. 563 at [26]–[33].
[77] [2009] UKHL 15; [2009] 1 A.C. 908 at [10].
[78] [1969] 1 Ch. 1.

dismissed his claim. Lord Denning M.R. held that the Law Society's statutory powers of investigation[79] overrode any privilege or confidence that might otherwise subsist between solicitor and client. Agreeing, Diplock L.J. expressed the view that privilege was in fact irrelevant when one was not concerned with judicial or quasi-judicial proceedings, because privilege was a right to withhold from a court, or a tribunal exercising judicial functions, material which would otherwise be admissible in evidence. Salmon L.J. agreed with both judgments.

In *R. (Morgan Grenfell) v Special Commissioner of Income Tax*[80] Lord **16–038** Hoffmann reviewed (obiter) the decision in *Parry-Jones v Law Society*. He rejected the view expressed by Diplock L.J. that the impact of privilege was confined to judicial, or quasi-judicial, proceedings:

> "The policy of LPP requires that the client should be secure in the knowledge that protected documents and information will not be disclosed at all."

However, approving the result in *Parry-Jones v Law Society*, he continued:

> " . . . I think that the true justification for the decision was not that Mr Parry-Jones's clients had no LPP, or that their LPP had been overridden by the Law Society's rules, but that the clients' LPP was not being infringed. The Law Society were not entitled to use information disclosed by the solicitor for any purpose other than the investigation. Otherwise the confidentiality of the clients had to be maintained. In my opinion, this limited disclosure did not breach the clients' LPP or, to the extent that it technically did, was authorised by the Law Society's statutory powers. It does not seem to me to fall within the same principle as a case in which disclosure is sought for a use which involves the information being made public or used against the person entitled to the privilege."

The other members of the Judicial Committee agreed with Lord Hoffmann's **16–039** speech. Although the result may be considered satisfactory, the passage has its difficulties. If the policy of legal professional privilege is as summarised by Lord Hoffmann, it is not readily apparent why disclosure to regulators without the client's consent would not amount to a breach of privilege. The distinction apparently drawn by Lord Hoffmann between (a) the Law Society's rules "overriding" privilege and (b) the Law Society's statutory powers "authorising" disclosure is also unclear.

In *McE v Prison Service of Northern Ireland*,[81] Lord Phillips MR described Lord Hoffmann's approach as illuminating in the context of the issues arising on the appeal in that case. He continued[82]:

> "As Lord Hoffmann pointed out in *Morgan Grenfell* ... the concern that may inhibit frank communication by a client to his lawyer is not so much that the matter communicated may be disclosed but that the matter may then be used to the detriment of the client."

On the basis of Lord Phillips's analysis of Lord Hoffmann's observations, it would appear that the contrast which Lord Hoffmann intended to draw in the first

---

[79] Under rules made pursuant to s.29 of the Solicitors Act 1957.
[80] [2002] UKHL 21; [2003] 1 A.C. 563 at [26]–[33].
[81] [2009] UKHL 15; [2009] 1 A.C. 908 at [10].
[82] At [45].

passage cited above was not the contrast between (a) confinement of privilege to judicial and quasi-judicial proceedings and (b) extension of privilege to protect against all disclosures of whatever kind, but the contrast between (a) confinement of privilege to judicial and quasi-judicial proceedings and (b) extension of privilege to protect against all disclosures potentially prejudicial to the client.

If so, the disclosure of privileged information, even if unauthorised by the client, may not represent a breach of privilege, *provided* (i) that it is not made in the course of judicial or quasi-judicial proceedings *and* (ii) that it is not made in a manner or circumstances which are potentially prejudicial to the client.

16–040   Insofar as solicitors are concerned, s.31(1) of the Solicitors Act 1974 (as amended by the Legal Services Act 2007), provides that:

> " . . . Without prejudice to any other provision of this Part the Society may make rules. . . for regulating in respect of any matter the professional practice, conduct, fitness to practise and discipline of solicitors and for empowering the Society to take such action as may be appropriate to enable the Society to ascertain whether or not the provisions of rules made, or of any code or guidance issued, by the Society are being, or have been, complied with."

It is suggested that there is necessarily implied in this provision a power on the part of the Law Society to make rules permitting an invasion of legal professional privilege to the limited extent necessary to ensure that the Law Society's regulatory functions are properly performed. In contrast with other, non-legal professions, the supervision of solicitors would become effectively impossible without such a power.

16–041   As for barristers, Pt 1 of Sch.4 to the Legal Services Act 2007 provides that the General Council of the Bar is an approved regulator in relation to the reserved legal activity of exercising a right of audience. However, it is doubtful that the Bar Council has implied statutory authority to override privilege.[83] Unless full effect is given to Lord Hoffmann's explanation in *R. (Morgan Grenfell Ltd) v Special Income Commissioner* of *Parry-Jones v Law Society*, it therefore seems that disciplinary proceedings against barristers must be carried out subject to the same restrictions in relation to legal professional privilege as have been held to apply to wasted costs applications.

In Napier v Pressdram,[84] a firm of solicitors sought unsuccessfully to assert a right of confidentiality in relation to the Law Society's investigation and resolution of a complaint which had been made against it. The Court of Appeal held that the procedure by which the Law Society investigated and resolved professional complaints was not itself intrinsically confidential to the relevant firm, though the Court[85] specifically reserved the position where confidential information was supplied in the course of the Law Society's processes.

---

[83] The Bar Council's Complaints Rules 2011 and the Disciplinary Tribunals Regulations 2009 do not address any issues relating to legal professional privilege.
[84] [2009] EWCA Civ 443; [2010] 1 W.L.R. 934.
[85] At [43] and [56].

DISCLOSURE REQUIRED BY LAW

A lawyer who discloses confidential information under compulsion of law **16–042** commits no breach of confidence. In *Parry-Jones v Law Society*,[86] Diplock L.J. said of a solicitor's contractual duty of confidence:

> "Such a duty exists not only between solicitor and client, but, for example, between banker and customer, doctor and patient and accountant and client. Such a duty of confidence is subject to, and overridden by, the duty of any party to that contract to comply with the law of the land."

A lawyer's obligation to refuse disclosure of material that is not only **16–043** confidential but also privileged (and his client's entitlement to assert privilege) is also subject to and may be overridden by statute. However, in *R. (Morgan Grenfell Ltd) v Special Commissioner of Income Tax*,[87] Lord Hoffmann observed that

> "Two of the principles relevant to construction are not in dispute. First, LPP is a fundamental human right long established in the common law . . . Secondly, the courts will ordinarily construe general words in a statute, although literally capable of having some startling or unreasonable consequence, such as overriding fundamental human rights, as not having been intended to do so. An intention to override such rights must be expressly stated or appear by necessary implication."

Bowman v Fels[88] demonstrates that the burden on a person seeking to argue that legislation impliedly overrides a right of privilege is a heavy one. However, the burden is not in all cases impossible to discharge: it was held by the House of Lords in *McE v Prison Service of Northern Ireland*[89] that the Regulation of Investigatory Powers Act 2000 permitted covert surveillance of communications between persons in custody and their legal or medical advisers, notwithstanding that such communications enjoyed legal professional privilege and despite such persons' statutory rights to consult a solicitor privately.

CHILDREN

In *Ramsbotham v Senior*,[90] Malins V.C. said: **16–044**

> " . . . no person, be he solicitor or not, can have any privilege whatever in doing, or abstaining from doing, that which has the effect of concealing the residence of a ward of this Court, and thereby preventing the Court exercising its due control over the ward."

---

[86] [1969] 1 Ch. 1 at 9.
[87] [2003] UKHL 21; [2003] 1 A.C. 563 at [7] and [8].
[88] [2005] EWCA Civ 226; [2005] 1 W.L.R. 3083. See the discussion at para.16–019, above.
[89] [2009] UKHL 15; [2009] 1 A.C. 908. See now the Regulation of Investigatory Powers (Covert Human Intelligence Sources: Matters Subject to Legal Privilege) Order 2010 (SI 2010/123).
[90] (1869) L.R. 8 Eq. 575.

In that case the mother of wards of court had absconded with them and her solicitor was ordered to produce envelopes of letters which he had received from her, with the object of discovering her residence from the postmarks. She was in grave, continuing contempt of court and therefore had no privilege in concealing her whereabouts from the court; and since she had no privilege in keeping the information confidential, the solicitor had none to protect.

16–045   In *Re L*[91] the House of Lords, by a majority of three to two, held that in care proceedings under the Children Act 1989 privilege did not attach to an expert's report, which was obtained by a party under an order of the court giving leave to the expert to study the court papers. The parents were drug addicts. The child became ill after ingestion of methadone. An order was made giving leave to disclose the court papers to a medical expert and requiring his report to be filed. The mother's solicitors instructed a chemical pathologist, whose report cast doubt on the mother's explanation of the incident. The judge ordered disclosure of the report to the police.

16–046   The mother appealed against the order, arguing that the report was the subject of legal professional privilege and that the court ought not to have made an order compelling its disclosure to other parties either at the time of the original order requiring the report to be filed or at the time of the order under appeal.

16–047   Lord Jauncey, delivering the opinion of the majority, distinguished *R. v Derby Magistrates Court Ex p. B*[92] on two grounds: care proceedings were of a special non-adversarial nature unlike ordinary litigation, and the expert's report was not a communication between solicitor and client but a report by a third party prepared on the instructions of the client for the purposes of the proceedings. He concluded that care proceedings were:

> "so far removed from normal actions that litigation privilege has no place in relation to reports obtained by a party thereto which could not have been prepared without the leave of the court to disclose documents already filed or to examine the child."

It followed that the question of the court's power to impose a disclosure condition when giving leave for the court papers to be shown to an expert did not arise, because in the absence of privilege the report would be disclosable to other parties to the proceedings in any event.

16–048   The House of Lords did not go so far as to hold that no legal professional privilege arose in care proceedings. On the contrary, Lord Jauncey not only distinguished the expert's report under consideration from communications between solicitor and client, but he said that his view that litigation privilege never arose in relation to the expert's report did not affect privilege arising between solicitor and client.[93]

16–049   In *Vernon v Bosley (No.2)*,[94] Thorpe L.J. dismissed as "little short of absurd" the submission that privilege would attach in circumstances where the court's

---

[91] [1997] A.C. 16.

[92] [1996] AC 487.

[93] In *S County Council v B* [2000] Fam. 76 at 88ff, Charles J. conducted a detailed (obiter) examination of the scope of the decision of the House of Lords in *Re L*. He suggested, among other things, that there might well be a distinction, for the purpose of claiming privilege in care proceedings under the Children Act 1989, between communications with experts and communications with factual witnesses.

[94] [1999] Q.B. 18 at 61–62.

leave should have been, but had not been, secured before the evidence was obtained. The Court of Appeal held also that the ratio in *Re L* was not confined to public law proceedings, but extended also to private law proceedings that were not adversarial but quasi-inquisitorial. However, it is uncertain whether privilege would attach to a report by an expert, a statement from a witness, or other communications between a solicitor and a third party for the purpose of proceedings, made without need for leave of the court to examine court documents or to examine the child.

Behind this issue lies the unresolved question whether a party to care **16–050** proceedings is under a duty of disclosure of matters adverse to his or her case.[95] In *Essex County Council v R.*[96] Thorpe J. after holding that the court, when considering the welfare of the child, has power to override legal professional privilege, continued:

> "For my part, I would wish to see case law go yet further and to make it plain that the legal representatives in possession of such material relevant to determination but contrary to the interests of their client, not only are unable to resist disclosure by reliance on legal professional privilege, but have a positive duty to disclose to the other parties and to the court."

In *Oxfordshire County Council v P*[97] Ward J. said: **16–051**

> "In all cases where the welfare of children is the court's paramount consideration, there is a duty on all parties to make full and frank disclosure of all matters material to welfare whether those matters are favourable to or adverse to their own particular case."

In *Re L* Lord Jauncey cited the passages above[98] and said that he preferred to wait until the point arose directly for decision before determining whether such a duty exists and if so what is its scope.

The premise to Thorpe J.'s approach in *Essex County Council v R.* (that the **16–052** court has power to override legal professional privilege when considering the welfare of a child) is not consistent with the reasoning of the House of Lords in *R. v Derby Magistrates Court Ex p. B*, as to the absolute nature of legal professional privilege when established, or in *Re L*, which was based on the view that legal professional privilege never arose in relation to the expert's report rather than that it could be overridden. In *A Chief Constable v A County Council*[99] Wall J. observed that the speeches of the majority of the House of Lords in *Re L* had not expressed any opinion on Thorpe J.'s dicta in *Essex County Council v R*. He concluded:

---

[95] It is well established that local authorities are under such a duty in care proceedings: *R. v Hampshire County Council* [1990] 2 Q.B. 71.

[96] [1994] Fam. 167 at 168.

[97] [1995] Fam. 161 at 166.

[98] See also para.4 of *Practice Direction (Family Proceedings: Case Management)* [1995] 1 W.L.R. 332: "It is a duty owed to the court both by the parties and by their legal representatives to give full and frank disclosure in ancillary relief applications and also in all matters in respect of children".

[99] [2002] EWHC 2198 (Fam); [2003] 1 F.L.R. 579 at [97].

"In the Family Justice System, therefore, the position remains that the confidentiality of what parents say to their lawyers relating to the proceedings is absolute."

16–053   If there is a duty on a party to care proceedings to disclose all material matters, whether favourable or adverse to their case, it must follow that they would have no privilege to withhold from other parties or the court any relevant evidence obtained by their solicitor on their behalf. If on the other hand they are under no such duty, it is suggested that there is no good reason to deny them the right to claim privilege in respect of such material obtained by their solicitor on their behalf.[100]

---

[100] In *S County Council v B* [2000] Fam. 76 at 96ff, Charles J. held that the duty of disclosure arising in proceedings in the Family Division concerning the welfare of children does not undermine the rights of a party to assert legal professional privilege which arises in or in connection with other proceedings.

CHAPTER 17

General Principle and Exceptions

THE GENERAL PRINCIPLE

Generally speaking, confidentiality is not a bar to disclosure of documents or information in the process of litigation, but the court will only compel such disclosure if it considers it necessary for the fair disposal of the case. This principle was recognised by the House of Lords in a trio of cases: *D v National Society for the Prevention of Cruelty to Children*,[1] *Science Research Council v Nassé*[2] and *British Steel Corp v Granada Television Ltd*.[3]   **17–001**

In *Three Rivers District Council v The Governor and Company of the Bank of England*,[4] Tomlinson J. suggested that, in view of the threshold requirement of necessity, Art.8 rights of privacy did not call for separate treatment in the courts' application of the general principle. However, where the documents of which disclosure are sought contain personal medical details relating to a non-party, the courts have approached the issue of disclosure with particular circumspection, attaching importance to Art.8. In *A v X & B*[5] Morland J. said that "only in a very exceptional factual situation would a court be justified in civil proceedings in ordering disclosure of a non-party's confidential medical data." In *R(TB) v Stafford Combined Court*[6] it was held that the complainant in a criminal case ought to have been given notice of an application made by the defendant for disclosure of her medical records, because her rights under Art.8 carried with them the procedural right to make representations to the court considering the application.   **17–002**

CPR 31.19 provides for the procedure to be adopted in civil litigation in the event that a litigant wishes to withhold inspection of a relevant document, or part of a relevant document, on grounds of confidentiality. The assertion of confidentiality is properly to be made in the litigant's list and, under CPR 31.19(5), a party may apply to the court to decide whether the claim to confidentiality should be upheld. For the purposes of such an application the court, under CPR 31.19(6), may invite other interested parties to make representations and may itself inspect the documents in question. In *Atos*   **17–003**

---

[1] [1978] A.C. 171.
[2] [1980] A.C. 1028.
[3] [1981] A.C. 1096.
[4] [2002] EWHC 2309 (Comm), November 8, 2002, at [5]. See also *MS v Sweden* (1997) 28 E.H.R.R. 313.
[5] [2004] EWHC 447 (QB).
[6] [2006] EWHC 1645 (Admin); [2007] 1 W.L.R. 1524. See now Pt 28 of the Criminal Procedure Rules 2011.

Consulting Ltd v Avis Plc,[7] Ramsey J. held that the court should look at withheld material only as a last resort and set out a five-stage approach for the court to adopt. In cases where legal privilege is asserted, the approach to be adopted by a court in respect of a party's challenged affidavit was summarised by Beatson J. in *West London Pipeline and Storage Ltd v Total UK Ltd*.[8]

17–004   Under the CPR, the courts' powers to order disclosure from likely parties prior to the commencement of proceedings (CPR 31.16) or from non-parties (CPR 31.17) are broader than they were previously. These powers are discretionary but, where the court has jurisdiction to exercise them, it is suggested that the general principle set out above remains applicable: when a non-party's rights of confidentiality are in issue, there is little reason why the question whether disclosure is to be effected by a party to the litigation or by the non-party himself should be determinative of an application's success.

EXCEPTIONS

17–005   The principle that information necessary for the fair disposal of disputes should be disclosed, even if it is confidential, is subject to statutory and common law exceptions.

STATUTORY AND REGULATORY EXCEPTIONS

17–006   Various statutes and regulations which give powers to obtain information of a confidential nature, also impose restrictions on the disclosure of such information.[9] In such cases the recipient cannot be compelled by subpoena to make disclosure which is prohibited by statute.

COMMON LAW EXCEPTIONS

17–007   The general principle does not apply in cases of:

(1)   "without prejudice" communications and communications to mediators and conciliators;
(2)   legal professional privilege; or
(3)   public interest immunity,

the rationale being that the public interest in maintaining secrecy in such cases outweighs the general principle in favour of disclosure.[10]

---

[7] [2007] EWHC 323 (TCC) at [37].

[8] [2008] EWHC 1729 (Comm); [2008] 2 C.L.C. 258 at [86].

[9] For example, the Financial Services and Markets Act 2000 (Disclosure of Confidential Information) Regulations 2001 and the Financial Services and Markets Act 2000 (Confidential Information) (Bank of England) (Consequential Provisions) Order 2001.

[10] Privilege against self-incrimination is omitted. Although one of the factors underlying the existence of the privilege is personal privacy (per Lord Mustill in *R. v Directors of Serious Fraud Office Ex p. Smith* [1993] A.C. 1 at 31), it is unconnected with the general law of confidentiality

"WITHOUT PREJUDICE" COMMUNICATIONS AND COMMUNICATIONS TO MEDIATORS AND CONCILIATORS

"Without prejudice" communications

Negotiations genuinely aimed at a settlement are inadmissible in evidence, not only in the litigation in the course of which they take place, but also in any subsequent litigation connected with the same subject-matter. Moreover, such negotiations are not disclosable to third parties—nor indeed apparently to the negotiators themselves (though the point may only be of theoretical importance).[11] **17–008**

In the leading case of *Rush & Tompkins Ltd v Greater London Council*,[12] Lord Griffiths cited with approval the words of Oliver L.J. in *Cutts v Head*[13]: **17–009**

> "That the rule rests, at least in part, upon public policy is clear from many authorities, and the convenient starting point of the inquiry is the nature of the underlying policy. It is that parties should be encouraged so far as possible to settle their disputes without resort to litigation and should not be discouraged by the knowledge that anything that is said in the course of such negotiations (and that includes, of course, as much the failure to reply to an offer as an actual reply) may be used to their prejudice in the course of the proceedings. They should, as it was expressed by Clauson J. in *Scott Paper Co. v Drayton Paper Works Ltd* (1927) 44 R.P.C. 151, 156, be encouraged fully and frankly to put their cards on the table . . . . The public policy justification, in truth, essentially rests on the desirability of preventing statements or offers made in the course of negotiations for settlement being brought before the court of trial as admissions on the question of liability."

In *Cutts v Head*[14] Oliver L.J. took the view that this public policy justification came to an end once the trial of the issues in the action had taken place, and that the rationale of protection thereafter must therefore be "an implied agreement imported from the marking of a letter 'without prejudice' that it shall not be referred to at all". **17–010**

Oliver L.J.'s observations were echoed by Lord Hope in *Ofulue v Bossert*[15]:

> "Normally, when negotiations are entered into with a view to settling a claim that has already been brought, one or other of two things happens: either they result in an agreement or they break down and the claim proceeds to judgment. If they result in agreement, the letter that was written without prejudice is available to show what the agreement was. If the claim proceeds to judgment, the protection remains in place while liability is still in issue but it ceases to have any purpose when the court has resolved the dispute."

---

which is the subject of this book. Section 72 of the Senior Courts Act 1981 may deprive a litigant of privilege against self-incrimination in claims based on the misuse of technical or commercial confidential information: *Gray v News Group Newspapers Ltd* [2012] UKSC 28; [2012] 3 W.L.R. 312.

[11] *Rush & Tompkins Ltd v Greater London Council* [1989] 1 A.C. 1280 at 1301 and 1304A.

[12] [1989] 1 A.C. 1280 at 1299.

[13] [1984] Ch. 290 at 306.

[14] [1984] Ch. 290 at 307.

[15] [2009] UKHL 16; [2009] 1 A.C. 990 at [9].

Similarly, the "without prejudice" rule, to the extent that it prevents the parties from adducing evidence that might be relevant to the determination of *costs*, has been said to be based solely on this alternative, implied contractual basis, since the exclusion of such evidence does not promote the policy of encouraging settlements.[16]

17–011　　The suggestion that the public policy behind the without prejudice rule does not survive a trial of the relevant dispute perhaps represents too restricted a view. In *Rush v Tompkins Ltd v Greater London Council*[17] Lord Griffiths specifically rejected the suggestion that if negotiations succeed and a settlement is concluded the privilege goes, having served its purpose:

> "There are many situations when parties engaged upon some great enterprise such as a large building construction project must anticipate the risk of being involved in disputes with others engaged on the same project. Suppose the main contractor in an attempt to settle a dispute with one subcontractor made certain admissions it is clear law that those admissions cannot be used against him if there is no settlement. The reason they are not to be used is because it would discourage settlement if he believed that the admissions might be held against him. But it would surely be equally discouraging if the main contractor knew that if he achieved a settlement those admissions could then be used against him by any other subcontractor with whom he might also be in dispute."

Lord Griffiths's dicta apply with equal force to the position where the first dispute is resolved, not by settlement, but by judgment after trial—not least because a negotiating party will not know at the time when he makes a without prejudice admission whether the negotiations will succeed or fail. It is accordingly suggested that Lord Griffiths's conclusion was expressed in appropriately general and unqualified terms:

> "I would therefore hold that as a general rule the 'without prejudice' rule renders inadmissible in any subsequent litigation connected with the same subject matter proof of any admissions made in a genuine attempt to reach a settlement."[18]

Nevertheless, it is well established that the without prejudice rule is not based *solely* on public policy. In *Unilever Plc v The Procter & Gamble Co*,[19] Robert Walker L.J., who gave the leading judgment, said:

> "Its other basis or foundation is in the express or implied agreement of the parties themselves that communications in the course of their negotiations should not be admissible in evidence if, despite the negotiations, a contested hearing ensues."

---

[16] See *Reed Executive Plc v Reed Business Information Ltd* [2004] EWCA Civ 887; [2004] 1 W.L.R. 3026, per Jacob L.J. at [24] and [25].

[17] [1989] 1 A.C. 1280 at 1300–1301.

[18] *Rush & Tompkins Ltd v Greater London Council* [1989] 1 A.C. 1280 at 1301. See also the views of Lord Neuberger, expressed in *Ofulue v Bossert* [2009] UKHL 16; [2009] 1 A.C. 990 at [87].

[19] [2000] 1 W.L.R. 2436 at 2442, cited by *Lord Neuberger in Ofulue v Bossert* [2009] UKHL 16; [2009] 1 A.C. 990 at [86].

A person participating in "without prejudice" negotiations therefore owes to **17–012** his opponent a private law duty of confidentiality, and this must be so whether or not the document is formally marked "without prejudice", although the duty will be subject to qualifications.

A publicly funded litigant, for example, may owe a duty to the Legal Services **17–013** Commission to disclose a "without prejudice" offer made by the opposing party, which might cause the Legal Services Commission to consider whether public funding should be continued in the event of the offer being refused.

Similarly, a company being supported in litigation by its bank may wish, or **17–014** feel under an obligation, to disclose to the bank a settlement offer which it has received (or made). Its auditors may also need to know the state of outstanding litigation for the purpose of reporting on the company's accounts pursuant to the statutory requirements of the Companies Act 1985.

In *Unilever Plc v The Procter & Gamble Co*, Robert Walker L.J. categorised a **17–015** number of circumstances in which—and purposes for which—"without prejudice" communications may be admissible in evidence. A private law duty of confidence arising from the "without prejudice" nature of communications will not usually prevent a party from adducing such communications in those circumstances and for those purposes. However, if no duty of confidentiality were owed at all, a party to "without prejudice" negotiations would be at liberty to publicise them at large. This would be inimical to the object of such negotiations and contrary to the assumption on which they are ordinarily conducted.

STATEMENTS TO MEDIATORS AND CONCILIATORS[20]

Mediation and other forms of alternative dispute resolution have assumed **17–016** unprecedented importance within the court system since the Woolf reforms of civil procedure. Formal mediations are generally preceded by written mediation agreements between the parties that set out expressly the confidential and "without prejudice" nature of the process. However, even in the absence of such an express agreement, the process will be protected by the "without prejudice" rule set out above.[21]

In matrimonial cases privilege has been held to extend to statements made by **17–017** the parties with the aim of effecting a reconciliation. The privilege covers both communications between the parties themselves, or their agents, and also communications to any private individual specifically enlisted as a conciliator. The earlier authorities were reviewed in *Theodoropoulas v Theodoropoulas*[22] by Sir Jocelyn Simon P.

Similarly, in *Re D (Minors) (Conciliation: Disclosure of Information)*,[23] the **17–018** Court of Appeal held that in proceedings under the Children Act 1989 privilege analogous to "without prejudice" privilege applied to prevent evidence being

---

[20] See also paras 15–013—15–019, above.
[21] See *Farm Assist Ltd v Secretary of State for the Environment, Food and Rural Affairs* [2009] EWHC 1102 (TCC); [2009] B.L.R. 399 (Ramsey J.).
[22] [1964] P. 311.
[23] [1993] Fam. 231 at 241. See also *D v N.S.P.C.C.* [1978] A.C. 171, per Lord Hailsham at 226 and per Lord Simon at 237.

given of a statement made by a party in the course of meetings held or communications made for the purpose of conciliation (except in the very unusual case where a statement is made clearly indicating that the maker has in the past caused or is likely in the future to cause serious harm to the well-being of a child).

LEGAL PROFESSIONAL PRIVILEGE AND PUBLIC INTEREST IMMUNITY

17–019 These subjects are considered in the following chapters.

CHAPTER 18

Legal Professional Privilege and Confidence

ORIGINS AND BASIS OF LEGAL PROFESSIONAL CONFIDENCE

Communications between a person and his legal adviser, or (once litigation is contemplated or pending) between either of them and a third party, are protected from disclosure if they were created for the purposes (broadly interpreted) of legal advice.[1] The duty of confidence owed by a lawyer to his client has been discussed in more detail in Ch.16, and the subject of legal professional privilege has been considered in that context.

Legal professional privilege, as it is now called, has its origins in the concept of confidence. At first its rationale was the protection of the honour of the professional man, but this approach was eventually rejected by the courts. As Lord Simon said in *D v N.S.P.C.C.*[2]:

> "A man of honour would not betray a confidence, and the judges as men of honour themselves would not require him to. Thus originally legal professional privilege was that of the legal adviser, not the client. (For the foregoing, see *Wigmore, Evidence*, secs. 2286, 2290.) But, with the decline in the ethos engendering the rule, the law moved decisively away from it. The turning point was the *Duchess of Kingston's Case* (1776) 20 State Tr. 355 at 386–391, where both the duchess's surgeon and a personal friend, Lord Barrington, were compelled to give evidence in breach of confidence."

In the case of legal advisers, however, the courts, under their inherent jurisdiction to control their own rules of procedure and evidence, developed the special doctrine of legal professional privilege. The foundation of the modern doctrine of legal privilege was summarised by Sir George Jessel M.R. in *Anderson v Bank of British Columbia*[3]:

> "The object and meaning of the rule is this: that as, by reason of the complexity and difficulty of our law, litigation can only be conducted by professional men, it is

18–001

18–002

18–003

---

[1] This statement is deliberately general. Fuller treatment of the sub-divisions of legal professional privilege into "legal advice privilege" and "litigation privilege" is outside the scope of this book. See Passmore's *Privilege*, 2nd edn (XPL Law, 2006) and Thanki on *The Law of Privilege*, 2nd edn (Oxford University Press, 2011). Qualifications to the general principle have been considered in the context of qualifications to the lawyer's duty of confidence to his client in Ch.16, above.

[2] [1978] A.C. 171 at 238.

[3] (1876) 2 Ch. D. 644 at 649.

absolutely necessary that a man, in order to prosecute his rights or to defend himself from an improper claim, should have recourse to the assistance of professional lawyers, and it being so absolutely necessary, it is equally necessary, to use a vulgar phrase, that he should be able to make a clean breast of it to the gentleman whom he consults with a view to the prosecution of his claim, or the substantiating his defence against the claim of others; that he should be able to place unrestricted and unbounded confidence in the professional agent, and that the communications he so makes to him should be kept secret, unless with his consent (for it is his privilege, and not the privilege of the confidential agent), that he should be enabled properly to conduct his litigation."

The scope and depth of the protection afforded by privilege

18–004   It is a prerequisite of legal professional privilege that the information for which privilege is claimed is confidential.[4] The scope of legal advice privilege extends beyond documents conveying advice or requests for advice. In *Balabel v Air India*,[5] Taylor L.J. said:

> "There will be a continuum of communication and meetings between the solicitor and client. The negotiations for a lease such as occurred in the present case are only one example. Where information is passed by the solicitor or client to the other as part of the continuum aimed at keeping both informed so that advice may be sought and given as required, privilege will attach."

Moreover,

> "Legal advice is not confined to telling the client the law; it must include advice as to what should prudently and sensibly be done in the relevant legal context."[6]

18–005   In *R. v Derbyshire Magistrates Court Ex p. B*[7] Lord Taylor C.J. described legal professional privilege as much more than an ordinary rule of evidence, but as a fundamental condition on which the administration of justice as a whole rests. This view has since been reasserted in a string of decisions at the highest level: *Medcalf v Mardell*,[8] *R. (Morgan Grenfell) v Special Commissioner of Income Tax*,[9] *B v Auckland District Law Society*[10] and *Three Rivers District Council v Bank of England*.[11]

18–006   The House of Lords and the High Court of Australia have stated in the similar cases of *R. v Derby Magistrates' Court Ex p. B*[12] and *Carter v Managing Partner,*

---

[4] *Kennedy v Lyell* (1883) L.R. 23 Ch. D. 387 at 404–405, per Cotton L.J; *Gotha City v Sotheby's* [1998] 1 W.L.R. 114, per Staughton L.J. at 118–119; *Berezovksy v Hine* [2011] EWHC 1904 (Ch), per Mann J. at [16].

[5] [1988] Ch. 317 at 330.

[6] [1988] Ch. 317 at 331. This dictum was cited with approval by the House of Lords in *Three Rivers District Council v The Governor and Company of the Bank of England* [2005] 1 A.C. 610; [2004] UKHL 48.

[7] [1996] A.C. 487 at 507.

[8] [2002] UKHL 27; [2003] 1 A.C. 120.

[9] [2003] UKHL 21; [2003] 1 A.C. 563.

[10] [2003] UKPC 736; [2003] 2 A.C. 736.

[11] [2004] UKHL 48; [2005] 1 A.C. 610.

[12] [1996] A.C. 487.

Northmore, Hale, Davy & Leake[13] that, where legal professional privilege applies, its nature is absolute and the court has no discretion whether to enforce it. In each case a defendant in criminal proceedings sought to compel production by witnesses of documents which had been brought into existence by legal practitioners for the purpose of giving confidential legal advice. The defendant was charged in one case with murder and in the other with conspiracy to defraud. Each asserted that the documents sought were likely to assist him in his defence. It was held in each case that production could not be ordered for essentially the same reasons, namely that legal professional privilege was a fundamental principle of the administration of justice, for the purpose of enabling a person to seek and obtain legal advice in confidence, and that where such privilege attached, no exception to it should be permitted (unless compelled by statute).

In *R. v Derby Magistrates' Court Ex p. B* the magistrate, following a decision **18–007** of the Court of Appeal[14] which the House of Lords overruled, had directed himself that he must balance the public interest which protects confidential communications between a solicitor and his client against the public interest in securing that all relevant and admissible evidence was made available to the defence, and had concluded that the balance came down firmly in favour of production. The House of Lords held that no such balancing exercise was to be performed or that:

> "Putting it another way, if a balancing exercise was ever required in the case of legal professional privilege, it was performed once and for all in the 16th Century, and since then has applied across the board in every case, irrespective of the client's individual merits."[15]

R. v Derby Magistrates' Court was decided before the advent of the Human Rights Act 1998 and Lord Taylor expressly recorded[16] that their Lordships had heard no argument in relation to rights arising under the European Convention on Human Rights. In *Medcalf v Mardell*,[17] Lord Hobhouse suggested that:

> "It may be that, as in the context of articles 6 and 8 of the European Convention on Human Rights, the privilege may not always be absolute and a balancing exercise may sometimes be necessary . . ."

The re-examination of *R. v Derby Magistrates' Court* that Lord Hobhouse's **18–008** suggestion would appear to entail has not yet been carried out in subsequent decisions of the House of Lords and Privy Council. In *R. (Morgan Grenfell) v Special Commissioner of Income Tax*, Lord Hobhouse recorded[18] that the parties accepted the absolute nature of privilege and repeated that this premise (along

---

[13] (1995) 183 C.L.R. 121. The effect of the decision was subsequently reduced by s.123 of the Evidence Act 1995 (Commonwealth and New South Wales).

[14] *R. v Ataou* [1988] Q.B. 798.

[15] [1996] A.C. 487 at 508, per Lord Taylor C.J.

[16] At 507.

[17] [2002] UKHL 27; [2003] 1 A.C. 120 at [60].

[18] At [43].

with others) would benefit from further examination[19], while Lord Hoffmann,[20] referring to *R. v Derby Magistrates' Court*, simply restated what can conveniently be labelled the "absolutist" view. *B v Auckland District Law Society* was a Privy Council case on appeal from the Court of Appeal of New Zealand and European Convention rights therefore did not arise directly for consideration.

18–009   In *Three Rivers District Council v Bank of England*, Lord Scott[21] reaffirmed the absolutist view in emphatic terms:

> "The Supreme Court of Canada has held that legal professional privilege although of great importance is not absolute and can be set aside if a sufficiently compelling public interest for doing so, such as public safety, can be shown: see *Jones v Smith* [1999] 1 S.C.R. 455. But no other common law jurisdiction has, so far as I am aware, developed the law of privilege in this way. Certainly in this country legal professional privilege, if it is attracted by a particular communication between lawyer and client or attaches to a particular document, cannot be set aside on the ground that some other higher public interest requires that to be done."

18–010   In none of these cases was a direct attack made by any of the parties on the decision in *R. v Derby Magistrates' Court*. Such an attack *was* made in *General Mediterranean Holdings S.A. v Patel*,[22] which concerned the extent of the courts' powers to order disclosure of privileged material for the purposes of wasted costs applications. It was argued that the absolutist approach was inconsistent with Art.6. Toulson J. observed[23]:

> "The scope of the common law right to confidentiality has had its critics. In *Carter v Northmore Davy Hale and Leake* . . . Toohey J. proposed a qualification in the following terms:
>
>> 'Where an accused facing trial satisfies the court that the production of documents subpoenaed by the accused is necessary for the proper conduct of his or her defence, then, subject to any proper objection that may be taken, other than on the ground of legal professional privilege, the court may order the production of those documents.'
>
> If ever there was a case for such a qualification, *Reg. v Derby Magistrates' Court, Ex parte B*. . . . might have been thought to be that case, but three connected factors caused the House of Lords to conclude that the principle of legal confidentiality should be maintained intact. One was that to admit any exception to the general principle would undermine the lawyer's ability to give an assurance of confidentiality to the client. The second was that there was a difference between setting bounds to the circumstances in which a duty of confidentiality would arise and giving a discretion to the court to override a duty of confidence which had arisen; and that to leave the matter to the court's discretion would be unsatisfactory both in terms of the nature of the task which the court would have to carry out and in terms of the client's inability to foretell in advance which way such a discretion

---

[19] See also the comments of Charles J. at first instance in *R. (Prudential Plc) v Special Commissioner of Income Tax* [2009] EWHC 2494 (Admin); [2011] Q.B. 669 at [69]–[72] (and the doubts expressed by Lloyd L.J. on appeal, at [86]).

[20] At [16].

[21] [2004] UKHL 48; [2005] 1 A.C. 610, at [25]. See also *R. (Prudential Plc) v Special Commissioner of Income Tax* [2011] Q.B. 669 at [5] per Lloyd L.J.

[22] [2000] 1 W.L.R. 272.

[23] At 294.

might be exercised. The third was that there was no satisfactory way of limiting in advance what might be regarded as exceptional cases."

Toulson J. concluded[24]:

"I do not accept the submission that the approach of the House of Lords in that case was in violation of article 6, or that the Convention requires a balancing exercise in individual cases of the kind which the House of Lords considered and rejected as a matter of English law."

In *Carter v Northmore Hale Davy & Leake*,[25] Deane J. suggested as a **18–011** possibility that,

" . . . if there were ever a case where it became apparent that refusal of access precluded a fair trial, it would be possible to invoke the inherent power of the courts to stay proceedings."

The courts have declared in a number of cases (for example, in *R. v H*[26]) that it is:

" . . . axiomatic that a person charged with having committed a criminal offence should receive a fair trial and that, if he cannot be tried fairly for that offence, he should not be tried for it at all."

However, discussion of that issue is outside the scope of this book.

Loss of privilege

Legal professional privilege is a right to resist the compulsory disclosure of **18–012** information.[27] But it is now clear that the courts' ability to protect privileged communications is not confined to a narrow procedural rule but constitutes a much broader jurisdiction enabling them, for example, to restrain the further use or disclosure of privileged communications. Whatever the circumstances and manner of the court's intervention, it is founded ultimately on the public interest in upholding the confidential relationship which exists between a lawyer and his client.

Particular problems have arisen in circumstances where a party has in fact **18–013** obtained evidence of a privileged communication and proposes to adduce it, or to make some other use of it, without the consent of the person entitled to claim privilege. This has given rise to a number of questions:

1. Can the doctrine of privilege prevent it?
2. Can the doctrine of confidentiality prevent it?
3. What, if any, discretion does the court have?
4. What amounts to waiver of privilege?

---

[24] At 296.

[25] (1995) 183 C.L.R. 121 at 138.

[26] [2004] UKHL 3; [2004] 2 A.C. 134 at [10]. See also *R. v Ward* [1993] 1 W.L.R. 619 at 681, and *R. v Davis* [1993] 1 W.L.R. 613 at 618, in the context of non-justiciable public interest immunity.

[27] *B v Auckland District Law Society*, at [67].

Underlying these questions there is an unresolved issue about what is meant by legal professional privilege. Is it simply a rule that a person entitled to the benefit of it cannot be required to disclose the privileged information or document (a shield against compulsory disclosure)? Or can it entitle a person to prevent someone else from using "privileged" information or materials in the course of litigation? If so, when does the fact that privileged information or materials have come to the knowledge or possession of another person involve a loss of privilege?

18–014 In addressing these issues the courts have been far from clear or consistent. Equitable principles of confidence have in some circumstances been prayed in aid in order to protect parties to litigation who have "lost" the benefit of the privilege to which they were entitled. In cases where the courts have had to deal with concepts both of confidence and privilege, there has sometimes been confusion, much of which has stemmed from the unfortunate decision of the Court of Appeal in *Calcraft v Guest*[28] and subsequent attempts to obviate its consequences by reference to the doctrine of confidence.

Calcraft v Guest

18–015 In *Calcraft v Guest*, certain documents (including proofs of witnesses and rough notes of evidence) had been created to assist in the defence of an action for assault (*Fry v Stevens*) tried at the Dorchester Assizes in 1787. Privilege in the documents belonged to a Mr John Calcraft. After the action, the documents were retained by Mr John Calcraft's solicitor, a Mr Thomas Bartlett. In due course, the documents came into the possession of Mr Bartlett's great-great-grandson, a Mr C. L. O. Bartlett.

18–016 More than 100 years after *Fry v Stevens*, Mr John Calcraft's successor-in-title (also named Calcraft) commenced an action against a Mrs Drax to which the documents were relevant. Judgment was given in his favour. Shortly afterwards, the existence of the documents was discovered by Mr C. L. O. Bartlett. Before returning them to Mr Calcraft, he showed them to the solicitors acting for Mrs Drax, who had instructed Mr Bartlett's firm in other matters (though not on this occasion). Mrs Drax's solicitors took copies of the documents and sought to put them in evidence in an appeal. Mr Calcraft objected as Mr John Calcraft's successor-in-title, arguing that privilege in the documents had not been destroyed by Mr C. L. O. Bartlett's wrongful disclosure of the documents to Mrs Drax's solicitors.

18–017 Lindley M.R. (with whom Rigby and Vaughan Williams L.JJ. concurred) held that "the mere fact that documents used in a previous litigation are held and have not been destroyed does not amount to a waiver of the privilege."[29] He continued:

> "Then comes the next question. It appears that the appellant has obtained copies of some of these documents, and is in a position to give secondary evidence of them; and the question is whether he is entitled to do that."

---

[28] [1898] 1 Q.B. 759.
[29] *Calcraft v Guest* [1898] 1 Q.B. 759 at 761–762.

Lindley M.R. cited a dictum of Parke B. in *Lloyd v Mostyn*[30]:

" . . . Where an attorney intrusted confidentially with a document communicates the contents of it, or suffers another to take a copy, surely the secondary evidence so obtained may be produced. Suppose the instrument were even stolen, and a correct copy taken, would it not be reasonable to admit it?"

Lindley M.R. concluded that the case came within the scope of Parke B.'s dictum and that secondary evidence of the privileged documents was therefore admissible.

Is *Calcraft v Guest* right?

It is an odd proposition that one party could break into the offices of the opposing party's solicitors, take copies of privileged documents, and then introduce them at trial. Suppose that, instead of producing documents, one party chose to call a solicitor, who had previously acted for the other party, to give evidence of privileged matters. One would expect it to be said that his evidence would not be admissible without the consent of his former client.[31]   **18–018**

It seems that in *Calcraft v Guest*, the court viewed privilege (1) as attaching to documents themselves, rather than to the information contained in them, and (2) as being a legitimate reason for refusing to produce material documents, but nothing more than that.   **18–019**

There is a certain logic (though no merit) to the decision if, but only if, privilege is restricted to a rule exonerating a party from producing a document which is in his possession and satisfies the requirements of privilege.[32]   **18–020**

The principle in *Calcraft v Guest* is still applied in Australia,[33] but has been closely examined and rejected in New Zealand, in the case of *R. v Uljee*,[34] and is no longer followed in Canada.[35] It has also been the subject of a lengthy and learned judgment by Kellock Ag.J. in the Grand Court of Cayman in *J.P. Morgan Multi-Strategy Fund LP v Macro Fund Ltd*.[36] Analysing the subject-matter of *Calcraft* and the cases cited by the Court of Appeal in *Calcraft*, Kellock Ag.J. concluded[37]:   **18–021**

---

[30] 10 M. & W. 478.

[31] per Sir John Strange in *Bishop of Winchester v Fournier* (1752) 2 Ves. Sen. 445 at 447. See *Wilson v Rastell* (1792) 4 T.R. 753, per Buller J. at 759, and *Bate v Kinsey* (1834) 1 C.M. & R. 38, per Lyndhurst C.B. at 43 and *R. v Derby Magistrates Court Ex p. B* [1996] A.C. 487, per Lord Taylor C.J. at 504–505.

[32] But see *Minter v Priest* [1930] A.C. 558, per Lord Atkin at 579.

[33] By the Court of Appeal of Victoria in *Cowell & Ors v British American Tobacco Australia Services Ltd & Ors* [2007] VSCA 301, at [32], and in *Australian Securities and Investment Commission v Lindberg* [2009] VSCA 234 at [43]–[51]. See also *Trevorrow v South Australia (No.4)* [2006] S.A.S.C. 42.

[34] [1982] 1 N.Z.L.R. 561.

[35] See the analysis by the Court of Appeal of Manitoba in *Metcalfe v Metcalfe* (2001) MBCA 35; 198 D.L.R. (4th) 318, and by the Court of Appeal of New Brunswick in *Chapelstone Developments Inc v Canada* (2004) N.B.C.A. 96; 277 N.B.R. (2d) 350.

[36] [2003] C.I.L.R. 250.

[37] At [94].

"It seems to me that *Calcraft* cannot be taken as deciding more than it actually decided and that the decision is limited to documents subject to deed privilege, or at most litigation privilege. Deed privilege has been abolished and there is still a debate as to the merit and scope of litigation privilege . . . There is no statement in *Calcraft* to the effect that legal advice privilege in a document is lost if an attorney improperly discloses it, or the document is stolen. In addition, there is no statement that a document which remains subject to legal advice privilege (or a copy) may be admitted in evidence despite that privilege. It seems to me that *Calcraft* cannot be regarded as an authority for that proposition and if it has been so regarded, it can no longer be seen as support for a proposition which to my mind is utterly inconsistent with the words used by Lord Taylor in *Derby Magistrates* . . . 'Legal professional privilege is thus much more than an ordinary rule of evidence, limited in its application to the facts of a particular case. It is a fundamental condition on which the administration of justice as a whole rests.'"

18–022   There are difficulties in the way of an English court seeking to follow the bold course of simply disregarding *Calcraft v Guest* in relation to legal advice privilege. First, the relevant documents in *Calcraft v Guest* appear to have included documents in relation to which litigation privilege (at least) might be supposed to attach. If litigation privilege and legal advice privilege are but two sub-heads of a single integral legal professional privilege,[38] it is not clear why the effect of *Calcraft v Guest* should differ between them. Secondly, the Court of Appeal has consistently treated *Calcraft v Guest* as applicable to legal advice privilege. Thirdly, although it is true that the reasoning and decision in *Calcraft v Guest* do not sit comfortably with Lord Taylor's dicta in *R. v Derby Magistrates' Court*, it is not apparent that they are formally inconsistent.

18–023   In England, *Calcraft v Guest* has been criticised and distinguished (not always satisfactorily). In *English & American Insurance Co Ltd v Herbert Smith*.[39] Browne-Wilkinson V.C. said:

"I think that when this or some other case reaches the House of Lords it may well be that the absolute rule laid down in *Calcraft v Guest* is the suspect decision . . . ."

In *Tchenguiz v Imerman*,[40] the Court of Appeal referred to the principle which *Calcraft* is thought to establish as "archaic".

18–024   In *B v Auckland District Law Society*,[41] a law firm in New Zealand sought to recover documents that they had provided to the Auckland District Law Society's representative, a Mr Ennor, on terms that expressly preserved privilege in the documents. One argument raised by the Law Society was that, since the documents were now in its possession, the benefit of privilege had been lost. The Privy Council disagreed. Lord Millett said:

"The society's argument, put colloquially, is that privilege entitles one to refuse to let the cat out of the bag; once it is out of the bag, however, privilege cannot help to put it back."

---

[38] As stated by Lord Carswell in *Three Rivers District Council v Bank of England* [2004] UKHL 48; [2005] 1 A.C. 610 at [105].
[39] [1988] F.S.R. 232 at 236–237.
[40] [2010] EWCA Civ 908; [2011] Fam. 116 at [61].
[41] [2003] UKPC 38; [2003] 2 A.C. 736.

He observed that this argument was not based on waiver (since the firm had expressly not waived privilege), but on the nature of privilege. He continued:

"The question is not whether privilege has been waived, but whether it has been lost. It would be unfortunate if it were. It must often be in the interests of the administration of justice that a partial or limited waiver of privilege should be made by a party who would not contemplate anything which would cause privilege to be lost, and it would be most undesirable if the law could not accommodate it . . .

The society argued that, once the documents were produced to Mr Ennor, they ceased to be privileged. Their Lordships consider that this is playing with words. It confuses the nature of the documents with the rights to which the arrangements with Mr Ennor gave rise. The documents are privileged because they were created for the purpose of giving or receiving legal advice. If they are not produced voluntarily, production cannot be compelled. If they are produced voluntarily, the right to withhold production no longer attaches to them. In that sense the privilege may be said to be lost. But they are the same documents, and it is not inappropriate to describe them as privileged. Their inherent characteristics are the same. The policy which protected them from unauthorised disclosure is the same. The cat is still a cat. It can be put back in the bag . . .

The fact that the claim to recover the documents is made on equitable grounds does not mean that it must yield to an overriding countervailing public interest. The documents are both confidential and privileged. Whether a claim to the return of such documents is based on a common law right or an equitable one, the policy considerations which give rise to the privilege preclude the court from conducting a balancing exercise. A lawyer must be able to give his client an unqualified assurance, not only that what passes between them shall never be revealed without his consent in any circumstances, but that should he consent in future to disclosure for a limited purpose those limits will be respected: see *Goddard v Nationwide Building Society* . . . per Nourse L.J."

Lord Millett must be right that there are circumstances in which it is "not inappropriate" to describe documents as privileged although they are in the hands of another person. At the most obvious level, a document can be privileged although it is in the hands of a client's lawyer, and in those circumstances the privilege belongs to the client. It would be very strange if the lawyer (or the client) could not disclose the document to another person (for example, an expert witness) without privilege being forfeited. Once that principle is recognised, there is no reason why it should not be appropriate to continue to regard a document as privileged in circumstances where it is obtained from the lawyer or client by improper means. That, however, is contrary to *Calcraft v Guest,* which concluded that privilege could not be claimed against a person in possession of a document, even if the possession was obtained by theft. The reasoning of the Privy Council is inconsistent with *Calcraft v Guest*, and is to be preferred, but *Calcraft v Guest* has yet to be overruled.   **18–025**

As authority binding on the Court of Appeal and on lesser courts, *Calcraft v Guest* has thrown a long shadow over subsequent cases. Starting with *Ashburton v Pape*, the courts have resorted to the equitable doctrine of confidentiality to limit the effect of *Calcraft v Guest*, but in doing so have encountered complications.   **18–026**

Ashburton v Pape

18–027   Mrs Drax's leading counsel in *Calcraft v Guest* was Herbert Cozens-Hardy QC. He was also a member of the Court of Appeal which considered the consequences of that decision 15 years later, in the case of *Lord Ashburton v Pape*.[42] Pape was a bankrupt who sought discharge. Lord Ashburton, one of his creditors, opposed his discharge. In answer to a subpoena, a clerk from the firm of solicitors retained by Lord Ashburton attended court with a number of privileged letters from Lord Ashburton to his solicitors. Complaining of illness, he handed the letters over to Mr Pape's solicitors, who took copies and passed the originals to their client.

18–028   Lord Ashburton issued separate proceedings and obtained by interlocutory motion an order, both that Pape deliver up the original letters and that he, with various others, be restrained "until judgment or further order from publishing or making use of any of the copies of such letters or any information contained therein except for the purpose of the bankruptcy and subject to the direction of the Bankruptcy Court". Lord Ashburton appealed, seeking to vary the order so as to remove from it the specified exception. His appeal succeeded.

18–029   Interpretation of the Court of Appeal's decision is made more difficult by textual discrepancies between the various reports of it.[43] Nevertheless, it is most often read as doing much to mitigate the effects of the earlier decision in *Calcraft v Guest* by making it possible for a party claiming privilege in respect of a document to obtain an injunction restraining another party from deploying it (or a copy) in evidence, notwithstanding that it (or a copy) would otherwise be admissible.

18–030   Cozens-Hardy M.R. said[44]:

> "The rule of evidence as explained in *Calcraft v Guest* merely amounts to this, that if a litigant wants to prove a particular document which by reason of privilege or some circumstance he cannot furnish by the production of the original, he may produce a copy as secondary evidence although that copy has been obtained by improper means, and even, it may be, by criminal means. The court in such an action is not really trying the circumstances under which the document was produced. That is not an issue in the case and the Court simply says 'Here is a copy of a document which cannot be produced; it may have been stolen, it may have been picked up in the street, it may have improperly got into the possession of the person who proposes to produce it, but that is not a matter which the Court in the trial of the action can go into.' But that does not seem to me to have any bearing upon a case where the whole subject-matter of the action is the right to retain the originals or copies of certain documents which are privileged."

Swinfen Eady L.J. said,[45]

> "The principle upon which the Court of Chancery has acted for many years has been to restrain the publication of confidential information improperly or surreptitiously obtained or of information imparted in confidence which ought not to be

---

[42] [1913] 2 Ch. 469; 109 L.T. 381; 82 L.J.Ch. 527; 29 T.L.R. 623; 57 S.J. 644.

[43] See, e.g. C. Tapper, "Privilege and Confidence" (1972) 35 M.L.R. 83, at 85ff., and N. H. Andrews, *The Influence of Equity upon the Doctrine of Legal Professional Privilege* (1989) 105 L.Q.R. 608, 615ff.

[44] [1913] 2 Ch. 469 at 473.

[45] [1913] 2 Ch. 469 at 475–476.

divulged . . . There is here a confusion between the right to restrain a person from divulging confidential information and the right to give secondary evidence of documents where the originals are privileged from production, if the party has such secondary evidence in his possession. The cases are entirely separate and distinct."

Comparison of *Calcraft* and *Ashburton*

Ashburton v Pape appears to set up a clear distinction between privilege, which is lost or rendered useless by disclosure, and confidentiality, which may continue to protect privileged communications which have come into the possession of the other party as a result of a breach of confidence or by accident.   **18–031**

However, the courts have not found it easy to set out clearly and consistently the principles on which the equitable jurisdiction in *Ashburton v Pape* will be exercised. In particular, different views have been expressed as to whether the jurisdiction is subject to the usual incidents and qualifications affecting the enforcement of obligations of confidence, or whether it attracts to itself something of the absolute quality of legal professional privilege.   **18–032**

Two issues which have arisen in a number of cases are: **18–033**

(1)   what, if any, discretion the court has when the *Ashburton v Pape* jurisdiction is invoked in relation to documents originally attracting privilege, which the person entitled to claim privilege did not intend to waive; and

(2)   what amounts to waiver of privilege.

Discretion

Differing views have been expressed whether a court has a discretion to refuse to give relief under the *Ashburton v Pape* jurisdiction in circumstances where a privileged document has come into the hands of another person as a result of improper conduct or inadvertence (not involving waiver).   **18–034**

In *Butler v Board of Trade*[46] the plaintiff sought a declaration that the Board of Trade, which had brought a prosecution against him, was not entitled to make any use of a letter written to him by his solicitor. A copy of the letter, together with other documents, had been handed over by his solicitor to the Official Receiver of a company in compulsory liquidation.   **18–035**

Goff J., having found that the original letter was privileged and the copy confidential, declined to grant relief on the principle in *Ashburton* because: **18–036**

"In my judgment it would not be a right or permissible exercise of the equitable jurisdiction in confidence to make a declaration at the suit of the accused in a public prosecution in effect restraining the Crown from adducing admissible evidence relevant to the crime with which he is charged. It is not necessary for me to decide whether the same result would obtain in the case of a private prosecution, and I expressly leave that point open."[47]

---

[46] [1971] 1 Ch. 680.
[47] [1971] Ch. 680 at 690.

18–037   Goff J.'s distinction between private litigation and public prosecution was subsequently approved by the Criminal Division of the Court of Appeal in *R. v Tompkins*,[48] but has not been followed in New Zealand and was criticised by Nourse L.J. in *Goddard v Nationwide Building Society*.[49] In *R. v G*,[50] the Court of Appeal stated obiter:

> "There is no reason in principle why a Crown Court . . . should not similarly restrain the use of material inadvertently disclosed, although the particular circumstances of the case which dictate whether justice requires an order will, of course, be different."

18–038   In *Webster v James Chapman & Co*,[51] the plaintiff was injured at work and brought an action against his employer. A report by a firm of expert engineers was obtained by his solicitors, who requested that the firm reconsider some elements of its opinion. The plaintiff's solicitors inadvertently sent a copy of the unrevised report to the defendant's solicitors.

18–039   The plaintiff sought an order that the defendant deliver up any copies of the unrevised report and be restrained from using its contents in any way. Scott J. held[52]:

> "If a document has been disclosed, be it by trickery, accident or otherwise, the benefit and protection of legal privilege will have been lost . . . The question then will be what protection the court should provide given that the document which will have come into the possession of the other side will be confidential, and that use of it will be unauthorised."

Scott J. took the view that he was required to give broad consideration to all the circumstances of the case, and concluded that the balance came down against granting the relief sought.[53] His decision was subsequently disapproved by the Court of Appeal in *Pizzey v Ford Motor Co Ltd*,[54] which held, citing the judgment of Dillon L.J. in *Derby & Co Ltd v Weldon (No.8)*,[55] that a balancing exercise was inappropriate (a matter in fact conceded by the defendant in *Pizzey v Ford Motor Co Ltd*).

18–040   The weight of authority has tended, as in *Pizzey v Ford Motor Company Ltd*, towards a more "absolutist" view of the *Ashburton v Pape* jurisdiction than was adopted in either *Butler v Board of Trade* or *Webster v James Chapman & Co*. Both strands of opinion can be observed in the Court of Appeal's decision in *Goddard v Nationwide Building Society*.[56] In that case, a solicitor acted for both the plaintiff mortgagor and the defendant mortgagee in relation to the purchase of a property by the plaintiff with the assistance of a loan from the defendant. The plaintiff subsequently sued the defendant in respect of alleged defects in the

---

[48] (1978) 67 Cr. App. R. 181.
[49] [1987] 1 Q.B. 670 at 686.
[50] [2004] EWCA Crim 1368; [2004] 1 W.L.R. 2932 at [16].
[51] [1989] 3 All E.R. 939.
[52] [1989] 3 All E.R. 939 at 946.
[53] [1989] 3 All E.R. 939 at 947.
[54] Court of Appeal, February 26, 1993, partially reported in *The Times*, March 8, 1993.
[55] [1991] 1 W.L.R. 73.
[56] [1987] 1 Q.B. 670.

property. The solicitor had made a file note while the transaction was proceeding of conversations he had had with the plaintiff following receipt of information from the defendant.

After the plaintiff had commenced proceedings, the solicitor sent the file note to the defendant, which pleaded the substance of its contents in its defence. The plaintiff sought an injunction ordering that the defendant should deliver up the file note and all copies thereof, and restraining the defendant from using or relying upon it in any manner.

18–041

Having held that privilege in the document belonged to the plaintiff and that it should therefore not have been sent to the defendant, May L.J. and Nourse L.J. went on to hold that the plaintiff was entitled to the relief sought.

18–042

May L.J. appeared to subscribe to a view of *Ashburton v Pape* which placed the relief granted in that case within the scope of ordinary principles of confidentiality.[57] Nourse L.J., on the other hand, made a number of observations which suggested that the relief granted to Lord Ashburton was not simply to be equated with the injunctive relief available in an ordinary action for breach of confidence. He began by suggesting that it was no longer necessary for a party seeking *Ashburton v Pape* relief in ongoing litigation to initiate separate proceedings. He then stated that principles of confidentiality would assist a party seeking *Ashburton v Pape* relief only where the material was (or had been) privileged:

18–043

"It cannot be the function of equity to accord a de facto privilege to communications in respect of which no privilege can be claimed. Equity follows the law."

He continued:

" . . . the right of the party who desires the protection to invoke the equitable jurisdiction does not in any way depend on the conduct of the third party into whose possession the record of the confidential communication has come . . . equity gives relief against all the world, including the innocent, save only a bona fide purchaser for value without notice."

Moreover, he observed that:

" . . . once it is established that a case is governed by *Lord Ashburton v Pape* [1913] 2 Ch. 469 there is no discretion in the court to refuse to exercise the equitable jurisdiction according to its view of the materiality of the communication, the justice of admitting or excluding it or the like. The injunction is granted in aid of the privilege which, unless and until it is waived, is absolute."

This is a significant passage. The obvious rationalisation of *Calcraft v Guest* and *Ashburton v Pape* was that, when a document has been mistakenly disclosed to the opposing party, the benefit of privilege is lost, but that the court has a discretion to grant equitable relief on the grounds of confidence so as to enable the mistaken party to recover his position. Here, on the other hand, Nourse L.J. suggested that the mere disclosure of a document does not involve the loss of privilege, and that a person has an absolute right to have the document treated as

---

[57] e.g. at 680A–B, though see the observations of Vinelott J. in *Derby & Co Ltd v Weldon (No.8)* [1991] 1 W.L.R. 73 at 79.

privileged unless and until there is some "waiver" of privilege in respect of it. This approach was followed in *Derby v Weldon (No.8)*[58] by Vinelott J., who disagreed with Scott J.'s approach in *Webster v Chapman*.

18–044   In *Istil Group Inc v Zahoor*,[59] the defendants obtained copies of e-mail communications between the claimants or their solicitors and an anonymous third party. They alleged that the e-mails revealed fraudulent conduct, being strongly suggestive that a crucial document relied on by the claimants was forged. They also claimed that the e-mails demonstrated that the claimants had deliberately misled the court in affidavit evidence filed earlier in relation to a freezing order. The claimants argued that the e-mails were covered by litigation privilege. Lawrence Collins J. posed the following question[60]:

> "What, then, is the extent of the discretion in the exercise of the *Lord Ashburton v Pape* line of authorities to restrain breach of confidence in relation to documents which have already been disclosed, but which would otherwise be privileged? In particular, can the court conduct a balancing exercise, and if so, on the basis of what factors?"

Having reviewed the authorities, he concluded[61] that relief could properly be refused on grounds that it would be contrary to public interest to grant it, but that the importance of the emergence of the truth was not a factor which could be taken into account under the heading of public interest "because the balance between privilege and truth has already been struck in favour of the former by the establishment of the rules concerning legal professional privilege". He refused to grant relief, holding that the combination of alleged forgery and misleading evidence made it a case where the equitable jurisdiction to restrain breach of confidence gave way to the public interest in the administration of justice.

18–045   In *J.P. Morgan Multi-Strategy Fund LP v The Macro Fund Ltd*,[62] Kellock Ag.J. observed[63] of the decision in *Istil* that:

> "Lawrence Collins J. was entitled if not obliged to refuse the injunction on general principles. That is to say, the grant of equitable relief is subject to the court's discretion and may be refused on the basis of the clean hands doctrine . . . I would respectfully disagree with Lawrence Collins J's assertion that it is necessary to invoke the general law relating to breach of confidence in these cases. The court should act in aid of the privilege."

18–046   The judgment of the Privy Council in *B v Auckland Law Society*[64] supports the view that there is no balancing exercise to be conducted. The policy reasons for

---

[58] [1991] 1 W.L.R. 73 at 84; see also per Dillon L.J. at 99.

[59] [2003] EWHC 165 (Ch); [2003] 2 All E.R. 252. The decision of Lawrence Collins J. was cited by Tugendhat J. in *Commissioner of Police of the Metropolis v Times Newspapers Ltd* [2011] EWHC 2705 (QB) at [161]–[166].

[60] At [88].

[61] At [89]–[94].

[62] [2003] C.I.L.R. 250 at [113].

[63] At [113].

[64] [2003] UKPC 38; [2003] 2 A.C. 736.

that view are the same as the policy reasons for recognising legal professional privilege, and it is suggested that they are compelling.[65]

There may be other grounds for the court not to act in aid of the asserted **18–047** privilege. In cases where the documents reveal strong evidence of misconduct by the party claiming relief under *Ashburton v Pape*, the claim might fail either on the grounds that the documents do not attract privilege because of the crime or fraud exception or on the grounds that relief should be refused under the clean hands doctrine. However, in *Cowell v British American Tobacco Australia Services Ltd*,[66] the Court of Appeal of Victoria suggested that the defences of "clean hands" and "iniquity" should not necessarily apply in exactly the same way to a privileged communication as to other kinds of confidential communications:

> "Generally speaking, the rationale of both defences in this context is that there is a public interest in disclosure of iniquity which makes it unconscionable for the applicant to insist upon the maintenance of a confidence which would keep the iniquity secret. But, as has been seen, with legal professional privileged communications the public interest favours maintenance of the confidence of the communication unless the communication comes within one of the established exceptions to legal professional privilege. Logically, therefore, the remedy of injunction should not be withheld for want of clean hands or because of iniquity, unless it amounts to the furtherance of crime or fraud or abuse of power or the concealment of the whereabouts of a ward of court or the frustration of the execution of an order of the court."

Waiver of privilege

In cases where a party entitled to assert privilege in respect of a document **18–048** inadvertently discloses it to an opposing party questions of waiver may also arise.

In *English & American Insurance Co Ltd v Herbert Smith*[67] Browne-Wilkinson V.C. took a broad view of the jurisdiction recognised in *Ashburton v Pape* and *Goddard v Nationwide Building Society*, holding that the equitable right to restrain the use of confidential information could be enforced at any time before the information was tendered in evidence. He also rejected the argument that the jurisdiction was confined to cases in which the person seeking to use the information was improperly implicated in obtaining it.

In *Guinness Peat Properties Ltd v Fitzroy Robinson Partnership*,[68] a **18–049** professional negligence action against architects, the defendants accidentally disclosed in a supplementary list of documents a letter sent by them to their insurers, containing their views as to the merits of the allegations made against them. The plaintiffs' solicitor inspected the letter, copied it and sent a copy to the plaintiffs' expert, who referred to it in his report. The defendants sought an injunction restraining the plaintiffs from using or relying upon the copy of the

---

[65] Though see the doubts expressed by White J. in *H Stanke & Sons Pty Ltd v Von Stanke* [2006] S.A.S.C. 308 (Supreme Court of South Australia) at [55].
[66] [2007] V.S.C.A. 301 at [35].
[67] [1989] 3 All E.R. 939.
[68] [1987] 1 W.L.R. 1027.

letter, and for the delivery up of all copies of the letter in the plaintiffs' possession or control. The defendants succeeded, both at first instance and in the Court of Appeal.

The plaintiffs argued, first, that:

" . . . privilege is essentially privilege from compulsory disclosure . . . once a privileged document has not only been disclosed but also inspected in the course of discovery, it is too late to put the clock back; the privilege is lost."

Secondly, they distinguished the *Goddard* and *Herbert Smith* cases, on the grounds that neither of those two cases dealt with a loss of privilege occurring as a result of a step taken in the litigation by the party entitled to the privilege.

18–050   Slade L.J., delivering the leading judgment, accepted these submissions with one important reservation,

"My one reservation is this. I do not think that after inspection has taken place in the course of discovery, the court is inevitably and invariably powerless to intervene by way of injunction in exercise of the equitable jurisdiction exemplified by the *Ashburton*, *Goddard* and *Herbert Smith* cases if the particular circumstances warrant such intervention on equitable grounds."

The particular circumstances identified by Slade L.J. as warranting intervention were cases in which inspection had been procured by fraud or in which it was apparent to the inspecting party that an obvious mistake had been made.

18–051   In *Derby & Co Ltd v Weldon (No.8)*,[69] the plaintiffs' solicitors inadvertently allowed the defendants' solicitors to inspect a number of privileged documents. Despite the advice of counsel to the effect that they should first ascertain whether privilege had been intentionally waived, the defendants' solicitors requested and obtained copies of some of the privileged material. Subsequently the plaintiffs applied for an order requiring the defendants to deliver up all copies of some 14 documents and restraining the defendants from relying on any information contained in them.

18–052   At first instance, Vinelott J. acceded to the plaintiffs' application, except in the case of three documents which, as he held, were not on their face clearly privileged. The Court of Appeal upheld his judgment, except that it allowed the plaintiffs' appeal in respect of the three documents which he had held to be beyond the scope of the relief sought.

18–053   Dillon L.J. gave the leading judgment in the Court of Appeal. Although finding in the plaintiffs' favour, on the authority of *Guinness Peat* he rejected[70] the plaintiffs' broad submission that the court could always intervene in a case of mistaken disclosure. He distinguished *Goddard v Nationwide Building Society*[71] and *English & American Insurance Co Ltd v Herbert Smith*,[72] which were relied on by the plaintiffs in support of that proposition, on the grounds that they did not involve any question of waiver of privilege:

---

[69] [1991] 1 W.L.R. 73.
[70] [1991] 1 W.L.R. 73 at 95.
[71] [1987] Q.B. 670.
[72] [1988] F.S.R. 232.

> "The documents in question had got into the hands of the other party to the litigation, despite the wishes of the person entitled to privilege and in circumstances which could not amount to waiver of privilege."

He further held that the documents which the defendants were obliged to return should not be limited to those that were clearly privileged on their face, since the defendants were seeking to take advantage of an obvious general breakdown in the plaintiffs' system for excluding privileged documents from discovery. He saw this as a critical factor, drawing an analogy from rectification of a contract, where a species of equitable estoppel operates to prevent one party to a contract from relying on what he knows to be a mistake in his favour in the text of the contract. He concluded[73]:

18–054

> "I see no reason why the first and second defendants should not be deprived of all the benefit from their having in those circumstances knowingly taken advantage of an obvious mistake."

It is not, however, clear whether he regarded the case as one in which the inspecting party was estopped by its conduct from asserting that there had been a loss of privilege, or simply as an application of *Ashburton v Pape* in a case where there had been loss of privilege.

The "obvious mistake" approach was taken a further stage by the Court of Appeal in *Pizzey v Ford Motor Co Ltd*,[74] which was followed by Aldous J. in *International Business Machines Corp v Phoenix International (Computers) Ltd*.[75] In these cases the question arose whether an injunction was obtainable if the person to whom the privileged material was disclosed in the course of inspection did not realise that it was privileged, but a reasonable solicitor would have so realised.

18–055

The Court of Appeal held that "the law ought not to give an advantage to obtusity and if the recipient ought to have realised that a mistake was evident then the exception applies." Aldous J. followed this test, but his decision illustrates the difficulties involved in applying it.

18–056

CPR 31.20 provides that, where a party inadvertently allows a privileged document to be inspected, the party who has inspected the document may use it or its contents only with the permission of the court. However, the introduction of the CPR made no difference to the approach taken by the courts to issues relating to the waiver of privilege.[76] In *Fayed v The Commissioner of Police of the Metropolis*,[77] the Court of Appeal held that the following principles could be derived from the authorities:

18–057

> "i)   A party giving inspection of documents must decide before doing so what privileged documents he wishes to allow the other party to see and what he does not.

---

[73] *Derby & Co Ltd v Weldon (No.8)* [1991] 1 W.L.R. 73 at 100.
[74] *The Times*, March 8 1993.
[75] [1995] 1 All E.R. 413.
[76] *Breeze v John Stacey & Sons Ltd*, The Times, July 8, 1999, CA; *Fayed v The Commissioner of Police of the Metropolis* [2002] EWCA Civ 780.
[77] [2002] EWCA Civ 780; *The Times*, June 17, 2002.

ii)   Although the privilege is that of the client and not the solicitor, a party clothes his solicitor with ostensible authority (if not implied or express authority) to waive privilege in respect of relevant documents.

iii)   A solicitor considering documents made available by the other party to litigation owes no duty of care to that party and is in general entitled to assume that any privilege which might otherwise have been claimed for such documents has been waived.

iv)   In these circumstances, where a party has given inspection of documents, including privileged documents which he has allowed the other party to inspect by mistake, it will in general be too late for him to claim privilege in order to attempt to correct the mistake by obtaining injunctive relief.

v)   However, the court has jurisdiction to intervene to prevent the use of documents made available for inspection by mistake where justice requires, as for example in the case of inspection procured by fraud.

vi)   In the absence of fraud, all will depend upon the circumstances, but the court may grant an injunction if the documents have been made available for inspection as a result of an obvious mistake.

vii)   A mistake is likely to be held to be obvious and an injunction granted where the documents are received by a solicitor and:

a)   the solicitor appreciates that a mistake has been made before making some use of the documents; or

b)   it would be obvious to a reasonable solicitor in his position that a mistake has been made;
       and, in either case, there are no other circumstances which would make it unjust or inequitable to grant relief.

viii) Where a solicitor gives detailed consideration to the question whether the documents have been made available for inspection by mistake and honestly concludes that they have not, that fact will be a relevant (and in many cases an important) pointer to the conclusion that it would not be obvious to the reasonable solicitor that a mistake had been made, but is not conclusive; the decision remains a matter for the court.

ix)   In both the cases identified in vii) a) and b) above there are many circumstances in which it may nevertheless be held to be inequitable or unjust to grant relief, but all will depend upon the particular circumstances.

x)   Since the court is exercising an equitable jurisdiction, there are no rigid rules."

These guidelines provide a useful summary of the approach adopted by the courts but do not purport to elucidate the legal principles underlying it. The court considered that in principle there was much to be said for the view that an injunction ought not to be granted merely on the basis that the recipient ought to have appreciated that an obvious mistake had been made, because, if the test is unconscionability, subjective fault should be required, but it recognised that this view was not consistent with the decisions of the court in *Pizzey v Ford Motor Co* and *Breeze v John Stacey & Sons Ltd*.

18–058   In *R. v G*[78] the Court of Appeal considered the civil rules in the context of a criminal case. Five defendants were charged with conspiracy to defraud. Prior to the trial the judge ruled that on grounds of public interest immunity certain material should not be disclosed to the defence. The prosecution negligently and inadvertently disclosed some of the material, which was read by counsel for two of the defendants (one of whom informed his solicitors about it) before the mistake was realised. The judge made an order prohibiting those to whom the

---

[78] [2004] EWCA Crim 1368; [2004] 1 W.L.R. 2932.

disclosure had been made from disseminating it to anyone else including their clients. The Court of Appeal accepted that he had jurisdiction to restrain the use of the material, by analogy with the jurisdiction of the civil court to prevent use of a privileged document inadvertently disclosed, but held that he was wrong to make the order. Rose L.J. observed[79] that a civil court will not prevent use of a privileged document inadvertently disclosed unless it would be unjust or inequitable to use it, and this question may well involve considering whether it is too late to restore the status quo: *Guinness Peat Properties Ltd v Fitzroy Robinson Partnership.*[80] The court considered the consequences of the judge's order and concluded that it would be impossible for those lawyers who had knowledge of the material to continue to act in the trial under the restraints imposed without causing serious unfairness.

If the recipient of a privileged document realises at once that it has been disclosed by mistake, the principle that he should not be permitted knowingly to take advantage of the mistake is plain. If he does not realise that there has been a mistake until later, to make the availability of relief under *Ashburton v Pape* depend on whether it would have been obvious to a reasonable solicitor in his position that a mistake had been made as the determinant is unsatisfactory and can give rise to unfairness in either direction. **18–059**

The rule was first established by the Court of Appeal in *Pizzey v Ford Motor Co Ltd* on the basis that the law should not give an advantage to obtusity. It is a fundamental rule of the law of confidentiality that a person against whom a duty of confidentiality is alleged must have notice that the information is confidential.[81] What constitutes sufficient notice may vary according to the circumstances. Where information is imparted in the course of a relationship or venture which a reasonable person would regard as involving a duty of confidentiality, it is enough that a reasonable person in the recipient's position would regard the information as confidential. But parties on the different sides in litigation are not in such a relationship. The starting point is that a party who receives a document from another party, without reservation as to its use, is entitled to use it for the purposes of the litigation. If, through inexperience or for whatever reason, he does not appreciate that a mistake has been made, it is a strong thing to say that he nevertheless owes a duty of confidentiality in respect of the document because it would have been obvious to a reasonable solicitor that a mistake had been made. The repercussions could be far reaching and unfair if it were not possible in practical terms to undo the situation. The client might have to instruct another professional team (depending on how far the knowledge had spread) and the client too might be in an impossible position if the solicitor had in good faith reported the information to him. **18–060**

On the other hand, if the mistake was not immediately realised by the recipient and would not have been obvious to a reasonable solicitor, but the party which made the mistake realised it and notified the recipient before any lasting harm had been done (for example, before the recipient had fully studied the document), the party which made the mistake should be able to retrieve the position, on the **18–061**

---

[79] [2004] EWCA Crim 1368 at [15].

[80] [1987] 1 W.L.R. 1027 at 1046, per Slade L.J.

[81] *Att Gen v Guardian Newspapers Ltd (No.2)* [1990] 1 A.C. 109 at 281. See also the discussion at para.3–065, above.

principle that it would be unconscionable for the recipient to make use of a privileged document when he knew that it had been disclosed by mistake unless the receipt of the information had affected him in such a way that it would be impractical or unreasonable to expect him not to use it.

18–062 There are also practical difficulties arising from the test of what would have been obvious to a reasonable solicitor. It has proved to be troublesome to apply.[82] The reality is that in modern cases discovery is often on a voluminous scale, carried out by large teams. Not only are mistakes likely to be made, but there are many cases where the notion that each document is individually scrutinised at the time of inspection by a solicitor, evaluating in the context of his knowledge of the case whether the document is intended to be disclosed, is wholly unrealistic. It is unclear on the authorities what is the position where the recipient is a litigant in person and therefore does not have a solicitor acting for him.[83]

If there has been a waiver of privilege (whether advertent or inadvertent), a further question may arise as to the scope of the waiver. In *Berezovsky v Hine*[84], Mann J. concluded after citation of previous authorities:

> "All of those cases therefore establish that a disclosure of privileged material and the effect of any waiver or loss of privilege can be confined to one person and further confined to one purpose. A communication of privileged material can take place in circumstances in which the extent of any waiver of the control that would otherwise arise from its being privileged is circumscribed in a manner determined by the circumstances of the communication."

18–063 One further complication in the present case law must be mentioned. Although *Calcraft v Guest* has been outflanked to a large extent by the fashioning of relief under *Ashburton*, in *ITC Film Distributors Ltd v Video Exchange Ltd*[85] Warner J. was doubtful whether he could grant relief on that basis, but arrived at the same result by applying a version of the doctrine of public interest immunity.

18–064 One of the defendants had obtained possession of privileged documents, which had been left in the court. He exhibited copies of certain of the documents to a long affidavit, which was later read in part to the judge, and some of the documents were referred to and used for the purpose of cross-examining a witness. Warner J. found as a fact that the defendant concerned had obtained possession of the documents by a trick.

18–065 Warner J. considered that there were difficulties in granting *Ashburton* relief at that stage, but he accepted the plaintiff's alternative submission that he must:

---

[82] See, for example, *International Business Machines Corp v Phoenix International (Computers) Ltd* [1995] 1 All E.R. 413 and *Fayed v Commissioner of Police of the Metropolis* [2002] EWCA Civ 780. In *MMI Research Ltd v Cellxion Ltd* [2007] EWHC 2456 (Ch) at [14], Mann J. emphasised that "the test is not whether, having done a detailed comparison and then agonise[d] and perhaps made some further enquiries, the mistake would have become apparent".

[83] The Court of Appeal discussed this in *Fayed v Commissioner of Police of the Metropolis* and left the point open.

[84] [2011] EWHC 1904 (Ch) at [24]. An attempt on this basis to argue that the deployment of privileged material at a private NHS trust hearing did not waive privilege for the material at a subsequent appeal hearing before the Family Health Service Appeals Authority was rejected by H.H.J Stewart QC in *Balu v Dudley Primary Care Trust* [2010] EWHC 1208 (Admin).

[85] [1982] 1 Ch. 431.

"balance the public interest that the truth should be ascertained, which is the reason for the rule in *Calcraft v Guest* . . . against the public interest that litigants should be able to bring their documents into court without fear that they may be filched by their opponents, whether by stealth or by a trick, and then used by them in evidence."[86]

He held that documents obtained in such circumstances were exempt from forensic scrutiny as a matter of public interest and fell within the continuum of relevant evidence (in the words of Lord Simon[87]):

" . . . which may be excluded from the forensic scrutiny. This extends from that excluded in the interest of the forensic process itself as an instrument of justice . . . through that excluded for such and also for cognate interests . . . through again that excluded in order to facilitate the avoidance of forensic contestation . . . to evidence excluded because its adduction might imperil the security of that civil society which the administration of justice itself also subserves . . . "

However, Warner J. took the view that it was impossible for him to exclude those documents at which he had already looked, since they had been used in evidence, and it would be impossible for him to disregard the answers given by the witness when the documents had been put to him. Warner J.'s judgment was cited with approval by Nourse L.J. in *Goddard*.[88]

CONCLUSIONS

The present position needs to be simplified. It is clearly seen by the courts as desirable to afford a measure of protection to privileged material inadvertently disclosed to the opposing party, for reasons stated by Browne-Wilkinson V.C. in *English & American Insurance Ltd v Herbert Smith*[89]: **18–066**

"Legal professional privilege is an important safeguard of a man's legal rights. It is the basis on which he and his advisers are free to speak as to matters in issue in litigation and otherwise without fear that it will subsequently be used against him. In my judgment, it is most undesirable if the security which is the basis of that freedom is to be prejudiced by mischances which are of every day occurrence leading to documents which have escaped being used by the other side."

The first step towards a satisfactory solution would be to overrule *Calcraft v Guest*. The right to privilege should be more than a right not to give compulsory disclosure (as it was interpreted in *Calcraft v Guest* and as was accepted in *Guinness Peat Properties Ltd v Fitzroy Robinson Partnership*). It should be a right not to have privileged information used in legal proceedings without the consent of the person entitled to privilege. **18–067**

Where privileged information has been improperly or accidentally disclosed without the consent of the person entitled to the benefit of it, the court ought not **18–068**

---

[86] [1982] 1 Ch. 431 at 440.
[87] *D v National Society for the Prevention of Cruelty to Children* [1978] A.C. 171 at 233.
[88] [1987] 1 Q.B. 670 at 685. See also *Amwell View School Governers v Dogherty*, E.A.T., September 15, 2006.
[89] [1988] F.S.R. 232 at 239.

to conduct a general balancing exercise in deciding whether to grant relief to protect the privilege. Such relief ought to be granted unless there are other grounds for not doing so (for example, that the information has already been deployed publicly or so widely that it can no longer sensibly be regarded as confidential). This is probably the present law, but it is not entirely settled.

18–069 There is also a need to clarify the concept of waiver of privilege. Deliberate and unqualified waiver of privilege obviously terminates any privilege. There may be limited waiver for a specific purpose only, which would not amount to a general waiver of privilege.[90] A party who puts in evidence part of a privileged document, even accidentally, cannot prevent the whole document going in, unless there are points which relate to a different subject, in which case privilege may still be asserted in respect of the unrelated parts. The rationale is that the holder of the privilege should not be able to abuse it by using it to create an inaccurate or incomplete perception of the protected document.[91]

18–070 Where privileged information has been accidentally disclosed in the course of litigation by a person entitled to the benefit of it (or by his agent) to another party, and the recipient is aware of the mistake before digesting the information, it is unconscionable conduct for the recipient knowingly to take advantage of the mistake. Where, however, the recipient is not aware of the mistake until later, the question whether he should be permitted to use it should depend on what is practical and just. It may be unrealistic for the person who has given disclosure to try to put the cat back in the bag (for example, where the material has become so widely circulated as to lose the quality of confidence, or where it has been not merely disclosed but used in evidence). Or it might put the recipient in position of unfairness or embarrassment to require him to put out of his mind information which will already have affected his understanding of the case. In such cases it will be too late for the person who has given disclosure to claim that he has not waived privilege.[92] Where there are no such obstacles, the party which has made accidental disclosure of privileged material should be allowed to retrieve its position. A similar test is applied in Australia.[93] As the Court of Appeal observed in *R. v G*,[94] "the essential question is what justice requires."

---

[90] *British Coal Corp v Dennis Rye (No. 2) Ltd* [1988] 1 W.L.R. 1113; *Goldman v Hesper* [1988] 1 W.L.R. 1238; *B v Auckland District Law Society* [2003] UKPC 38; [2003] 2 A.C. 736.

[91] *Att Gen v Maurice* (1986) 161 C.L.R. 475 at 487–488.

[92] Scott J. might have arrived at the same decision on the facts of *Webster v James Chapman & Co* [1989] 3 All E.R. 939 as he reached applying a broad balancing test.

[93] *Att Gen v Maurice* (1986) 161 C.L.R. 475 at 481 at 488. *Goldberg v Ng* (1995) 185 C.L.R. 83. (On the facts, the judgments of the minority may be considered more persuasive.)

[94] [2004] EWCA Crim 1368; [2004] 1 W.L.R. 2932 at [15].

CHAPTER 19

Public Interest Immunity

ORIGINS AND BASIS

Confidentiality is not by itself a ground of immunity from disclosure of information or documents in the course of litigation, whether by a party or by a non-party; but the desirability in the public interest that confidentiality in the relevant subject-matter should be preserved may give rise to public interest immunity.   **19–001**

The origin of this lies in the doctrine of Crown privilege, which is of considerable antiquity. However, the immunity is not a matter of privilege, nor is it confined to the Crown.[1] It is a protection given by the courts to documents and information whose disclosure in legal proceedings would be damaging to the public interest.   **19–002**

The corner-stone of the modern law is *Conway v Rimmer*,[2] in which the House of Lords departed from its own unanimous decision, 25 years earlier, in the case of *Duncan v Cammell, Laird & Co Ltd*.[3] It is necessary to regard with caution any case pre-dating *Conway v Rimmer*.[4]   **19–003**

CONFIDENTIALITY AND PUBLIC INTEREST IMMUNITY

Confidentiality is a necessary, but not a sufficient, basis for a claim for public interest immunity. In *Alfred Crompton Amusement Machines Ltd v Customs & Excise Commissioners*[5] Lord Cross said: **19–004**

> " 'Confidentiality' is not a separate head of privilege, but it may be a very material consideration to bear in mind when privilege is claimed on the ground of public interest."

---

[1] See, e.g. per Lord Pearson in *R. v Lewes Justices Ex p. Home Secretary* [1973] A.C. 388 at 406, and per Lord Simon in *D. v N.S.P.C.C.* [1978] A.C. 171 at 235H.

[2] [1968] A.C. 910. See, e.g. *Air Canada v Secretary of State for Trade* [1983] 2 A.C. 394, per Lord Fraser of Tullybelton at 432.

[3] [1942] A.C. 624.

[4] Even of *Conway v Rimmer*, it was observed by Lord Keith of Kinkel in *Burmah Oil Co Ltd v Governor and Company of the Bank of England* [1980] 1 A.C. 1090 at 1131 that "no definitive body of binding rules universally applicable to future cases in the field is to be gathered from the speeches delivered".

[5] [1974] A.C. 405 at 433.

Lord Cross was speaking in the context of a claim for privilege in respect of documents of a confidential nature obtained from third parties, to whom a duty of confidence would be owed. That fact did not of itself make the documents privileged but was highly pertinent. Lord Cross's statement is not to be read as implying that public interest immunity could attach to documents which were not of a confidential character at all.

19–005   The object of a claim for public interest immunity is to prevent a document being placed before the court because its public disclosure would be damaging to the public interest. That cannot apply if the document itself does not warrant being treated as secret, for example because it has already lost all secrecy. So, in *Sankey v Whitlam*[6] Gibbs A.C.J. said:

> " . . . it may be necessary for the proper functioning of the public service to keep secret a document of a particular class, but once the document has been published to the world there no longer exists any reason to deny to the court access to that document, if it provides evidence that is relevant and otherwise admissible."

It would be different if, despite some prior publication, disclosure of the documents would still be capable of causing harm, for example, to national security.[7]

19–006   The additional ingredient which has to be established is that the public interest in preserving the secrecy of a particular document or class of documents overrides the public interest in the administration of justice, which ordinarily requires that the parties should not be obstructed from placing relevant evidence before the court. As Lord Templeman said in *R. v Chief Constable of West Midlands Police Ex p. Wiley*[8]:

> "A claim to public interest immunity can only be justified if the public interest in preserving the confidentiality of the document outweighs the public interest in securing justice."

CLASS AND CONTENTS CLAIMS

19–007   A common categorisation[9] of claims to immunity was to classify them as either contents claims or class claims. The former asserted that the disclosure of a document was objectionable because the public interest would be damaged by the disclosure of the contents of that particular document. The latter, in practice

---

[6] [1978] 142 C.L.R. 1 at 45, High Court of Australia.

[7] *Thorburn v Hermon, The Times*, May 14, 1992.

[8] [1995] 1 A.C. 274 at 280.

[9] Described in *Burmah Oil Co Ltd v Governor and Company of the Bank of England* [1980] A.C. 1090, by Lord Wilberforce at 1111, as "rough but accepted", and by Lord Scarman at 1143, as "good working, but not logically perfect"; see also the exposition of the categories by Lord Edmund-Davies at 1124. The categories have also been adopted in Australia (*Commonwealth v Northern Land Council* (1993) 176 C.L.R. 604 at [7]; *State of New South Wales v Public Transport Ticketing Corp* [2011] NSWCA 60 at [45]). Some dissatisfaction with the categories was expressed by, for example, Lord Hodson in *Conway v Rimmer* [1968] A.C. 910 at 979, and by Lord Keith in *Burmah Oil*, at 1132.

considerably more common, asserted that the disclosure of a document was objectionable because it belonged to a class of documents whose disclosure would damage the public interest.[10]

It had been said that there is no distinction in principle between a contents claim and a class claim,[11] but in practice class-based claims attracted a particularly high degree of judicial scrutiny. It was not possible, for example, for a class claim in respect of a number of documents to be based upon the administrative burden of checking individual documents to ascertain whether a contents claim could be made in respect of any of them.[12]   **19–008**

Although "the privilege is a narrow one, most sparingly to be exercised",[13] in *D v National Society for the Prevention of Cruelty to Children*[14] Lord Hailsham said: **19–009**

> "The categories of public interest are not closed, and must alter from time to time whether by restriction or extension as social conditions and social legislation develop."

In *R. v Chief Constable of West Midlands Police Ex p. Wiley*,[15] however, Lord Woolf, though stating his agreement with Lord Hailsham's dictum, observed that,   **19–010**

> "The recognition of a new *class-based* public interest immunity requires clear and compelling evidence that it is necessary."[16] (Emphasis added.)

Following the recommendations made in Sir Richard Scott's report on the Matrix Churchill affair, the Attorney General, Sir Nicholas Lyell, entered into a process of consultation as to the approach that the Government should adopt to public interest immunity. In a statement to the House of Commons on December 18, 1996, he announced the adoption of a change in practice: **19–011**

> "Under the new approach, Ministers will focus directly on the damage that disclosure would cause. The former division into class and contents claims will no longer be applied. Ministers will claim public interest immunity only when it is believed that disclosure of a document would cause real damage or harm to the national interest . . .
>
> It is impossible in advance to describe such damage exhaustively. The damage may relate to the safety of an individual, such as an informant, or to a regulatory process; or it may be damage to international relations caused by the disclosure of confidential diplomatic communications . . .

---

[10] The possibility that such a claim might be valid was denied by MacNaughton J. in *Spigelman v Hocken* (1934) 150 L.T. 256 at 262, but his view must yield to subsequent authority.

[11] In *Conway v Rimmer* [1968] A.C. 910, per Lord Morris at 971.

[12] per Lord Woolf in *R. v Chief Constable of West Midlands Ex p. Wiley* [1995] 1 A.C. 274 at 293. In *Amaryllis Ltd v HM Treasury* [2009] EWHC 1666 (TCC) at [44], Coulson J. suggested that, where a class-based objection is maintained, it is particularly important that the decision to assert immunity should be made at a high level and after proper consideration.

[13] *Robinson v State of South Australia* [1931] A.C. 704 PC at 714.

[14] [1978] A.C. 171 at 230.

[15] [1995] 1 A.C. 274 at 305.

[16] See also *R. v Lewes Justices Ex p. Home Secretary* [1973] A.C. 388 at 412, per Lord Salmon—"This immunity should not lightly be extended to any other class of document or information, but its boundaries are not to be regarded as immutably fixed".

This new, restrictive approach will require, so far as possible, the way in which disclosure could cause real damage to the public interest to be clearly identified. Public interest immunity certificates will in future set out in greater detail than before both what the document is and what damage its disclosure would be likely to do—unless to do so would itself cause the damage that the certificate aims to prevent. That will allow even closer scrutiny by the court, which is always the final arbiter."

It is suggested that the Government's approach was a sensible one, though there will remain cases in which the reason why it would be against the public interest to disclose a document is, at least in part, because release into the public domain of documents of that *kind* would be damaging (documents disclosing the identity of an informant being an obvious example). In the debate following his statement on December 18, 1996, Sir Nicholas Lyell himself said expressly:

"...I confirm that the departure from the previous position relates to the distinction between class and contents claims and the new emphasis on real harm or real damage. It is not helpful to say that they are all contents claims rather than class claims. Class reasoning may be said to operate in some claims. If that is so, it will be clearly explained in the certificate."

EFFECT OF THE HUMAN RIGHTS ACT 1998

19–012   Article 6 of the Convention provides that:

"In the determination of his civil rights and obligations or of any criminal charge against him, everyone is entitled to a fair and public hearing within a reasonable time by an independent and impartial tribunal established by law. Judgment shall be pronounced publicly but the press and public may be excluded from all or part of the trial in the interest of morals, public order or national security in a democratic society, where the interests of juveniles or the protection of the private life of the parties so require, or to the extent strictly necessary in the opinion of the court in special circumstances where publicity would prejudice the interests of justice."

Implicit in the unqualified right to a fair hearing provided by Art.6 are a number of ancillary rights, including (particularly in the criminal sphere) a right to disclosure of relevant evidence. These ancillary rights are not themselves unqualified but are subject to implied limitations, where and to the extent necessary, in respect of the fundamental rights of others or an important public interest.[17] As the House of Lords said in *R. v H*[18]:

"In such circumstances some derogation from the golden rule of full disclosure may be justified but such derogation must always be the minimum derogation necessary to protect the public interest in question and must never imperil the overall fairness of the trial."

---

[17] *Fitt v United Kingdom* [2000] 30 E.H.R.R. 400; *Brown v Stott* [2003] 1 A.C. 681; *Edwards and Lewis v UK* [2005] 40 E.H.R.R. 593.
[18] [2004] UKHL 3; [2004] 2 A.C. 134 at [18].

In *R. v Brushett*,[19] the defendant, who had been convicted on 27 charges of child abuse, contended that his Art.6 rights had been infringed by the court's refusal to allow him access to documents in the social services files relating to the complainants. The Court of Appeal dismissed his appeal, observing that, in the context of the case, it saw no difference in principle between the English common law and human rights jurisprudence.   **19–013**

Nevertheless, the introduction of the Human Rights Act 1998 has lent impetus to an already existing process of development in English law, under which the courts have tended to scrutinise claims to public interest immunity more critically than before. The Court of Appeal referred in *Chief Constable of the Greater Manchester Police v McNally*[20] to: **19–014**

> " . . . a wider jurisprudential move away from near absolute protection of various categories of public interest in non-disclosure . . . Now, with the advent of Human Rights to our law, this move has the force of European jurisprudence behind it."

REASONS FOR IMMUNITY

It is impossible to compile a list of all reasons advanced for immunity, but they include the following: **19–015**

(1) that disclosure would be prejudicial to national security or foreign relations[21];

(2) that disclosure would create or fan ill-informed or captious public or political criticism of the inner workings of Government,[22] and/or increase the difficulties of the decision-making process;

(3) that disclosure would impede the flow of information necessary in the public interest, in particular by discouraging candour in communications by or to persons with public responsibilities[23] or by discouraging informants from coming forward[24];

(4) that immunity is required to set a limit on the State's invasion of an individual's privacy.[25]

It should be recognised that the application to the reported authorities of the reasons for immunity listed above is in many cases an exercise in ex post facto rationalisation, since claims to Crown privilege in the past were rarely scrutinised as carefully as they are today. It was often successfully asserted on behalf of the Crown that production of specified documents would be contrary to the public   **19–016**

---

[19] (2001) Crim. L.R. 471.

[20] [2002] EWCA Civ 14 at [21].

[21] e.g. *Burmah Oil Co Ltd v Governor and Company of the Bank of England* [1980] A.C. 1090, per Lord Salmon at 1121; *Balfour v Foreign and Commonwealth Office* [1994] 1 W.L.R. 681.

[22] per Lord Reid in *Conway v Rimmer* [1968] A.C. 910 at 952.

[23] *Burmah Oil Co Ltd v Governor and Company of the Bank of England* [1980] A.C. 1090, per Lord Wilberforce at 1112, and per Lord Scarman at 1145.

[24] *D. v N.S.P.C.C.* [1978] A.C. 171, per Lord Diplock at 218.

[25] *Re Joseph Hargreaves Ltd* [1900] 1 Ch. 347, as explained by Lord Reid in *Conway v Rimmer* [1968] A.C. 910 at 946F; *Lonrho Plc v Fayed (No. 4)* [1994] Q.B. 775 at 787, per Bingham M.R.

interest, without any further explanation. Nevertheless, the categories remain a convenient basis for the examination of the classes of documents for which claims to immunity have been made.

DOCUMENTS WHOSE DISCLOSURE WOULD BE PREJUDICIAL TO NATIONAL SECURITY OR FOREIGN RELATIONS

19–017   A question of national security or foreign relations is recognised as the most compelling basis for a claim to public interest immunity, whether the claim is made on a class or a contents basis. In *Balfour v Foreign and Commonwealth Office*,[26] a former employee of the Foreign Office claimed that he had been unfairly dismissed by his former employer. In proceedings before an industrial tribunal, he sought discovery of certain documents from the Foreign Office. The Foreign Secretary and Home Secretary each signed certificates raising objection to:

> "the production of any evidence, documentary or otherwise, about the organisation of the security and intelligence services, their theatres of operation or their methods. Express reference was made to foreign powers and terrorist organisations and the threat to national security of disclosure."[27]

The certificates were held to be conclusive and Russell L.J. cited the dictum of Lord Diplock in *Council of Civil Service Unions v Minister for the Civil Service*[28]:

> "National security is the responsibility of the executive government; what action is needed to protect its interests is, as the cases cited by my learned friend, Lord Roskill, establish and common sense itself dictates, a matter upon which those upon whom the responsibility rests, and not the courts of justice, must have the last word. It is par excellence a non-justiciable question. The judicial process is totally inept to deal with the sort of problems which it involves."

National security, or the public safety, may also be one justification for the immunity traditionally bestowed upon "documents pertaining to the general administration of the naval, military and air force services".[29] However, most of the cases are more immediately explicable by reference to one of the other categories dealt with below.

19–018   The protection of specific military secrets clearly falls within the national security category. Although the House of Lords departed in *Conway v Rimmer* from their decision in *Duncan v Cammell, Laird & Co*,[30] their Lordships were in no doubt that the decision in that case had been right on its facts.

---

[26] [1994] 1 W.L.R. 681.
[27] [1994] 1 W.L.R. 681 at 684.
[28] [1985] A.C. 374 at 412.
[29] *Conway v Rimmer* [1968] A.C. 910, per Lord Upjohn at 993.
[30] [1942] A.C. 624.

The case arose from the loss of 99 lives at the sinking of the new submarine **19–019** *Thetis* during trials in Liverpool bay in June 1939. Representatives and dependants of the deceased commenced an action against Cammell, Laird & Co, the makers of the submarine, claiming damages for negligence. The defendants declined to produce a number of documents included in their discovery, on the basis that the First Lord of the Admiralty objected to their production. These documents included the contract for the *Thetis*, correspondence relating to the vessel's trim, reports as to the submarine's condition when raised, various plans and specifications and the notebook of a foreman painter employed by the defendants. The First Lord duly swore an affidavit stating that in his opinion the disclosure of these documents to any person would be injurious to the public interest and his certificate was held to be conclusive.

Similar protection is given to diplomatic secrets and confidential communica- **19–020** tions between British authorities and other states. In *Stoll v Switzerland*[31], the majority of the European Court of Human Rights stated its agreement with the proposition that "it is vital to diplomatic services and the smooth functioning of international relations for diplomats to be able to exchange confidential or secret information."

In *R. v Governor of Brixton Prison Ex p. Osman*,[32] Osman, who had been **19–021** committed to custody to await return to Hong Kong to face criminal charges, applied for a writ of habeas corpus and sought discovery of various Government documents. In his certificate claiming immunity, the Minister of State for Foreign and Commonwealth Affairs divided them into three categories, including:

"(A) Communications exchanged between ministers and/or officials of the Crown either in the United Kingdom or overseas concerning matters of policy, advice, judgment, action or prospective action within government. (B) Communications or reports of communications between British authorities (both in the United Kingdom and Hong Kong) and another sovereign state concerning matters of policy, advice, judgment, action or prospective action within government . . . ."[33]

The reasons given by the Minister for his belief that production of these documents would be detrimental to foreign relations were set out at length by Mann L.J., who observed[34] that:

"It does not seem to be in dispute that the documents in categories (A) and (B) are documents eligible for a public interest claim. Were there such a dispute it could be given its quietus by examining the speeches of Lord Upjohn in *Conway v Rimmer* [1968] A.C. 910, 933, of Lord Salmon in *Burmah Oil Co. Ltd v Governor and Company of the Bank of England* [1980] A.C. 1090, 1121C and of Lord Keith of Kinkel and Lord Scarman in the same case at pp. 1132B and 1144G."

In *R. (Mohamed) v Secretary of State for Foreign and Commonwealth Affairs* **19–022** *(No.2)*[35] a former detainee in Guantanamo Bay faced prosecution in the United States by military prosecutors for terrorism offences. He obtained from the

---

[31] (2008) 47 E.H.R.R. 59 at [126].
[32] [1991] 1 W.L.R. 281.
[33] [1991] 1 W.L.R. 281 at 286.
[34] [1991] 1 W.L.R. 281 at 287.
[35] [2010] EWCA Civ 65; [2011] Q.B. 218.

Divisional Court a *Norwich Pharmacal* disclosure order against the Foreign Secretary in respect of documents which might support his contention that confessions had been extracted from him by the use of torture. Seven paragraphs of the Divisional Court's open judgment, which summarised reports which had been made by the US authorities to the UK security services, were redacted. There followed extensive litigation as to whether the redactions should be maintained. The Foreign Secretary filed three p.i.i. certificates, asserting that publication of the redacted passages would harm intelligence sharing arrangements between the USA and the UK, resulting in a real risk of harm to the UK's national security and international relations. After the conclusion of oral argument in the Court of Appeal, but before the delivery of judgment, a judge in a US District Court gave a public judgment which found as a fact that the claimant's evidence as to his mistreatment was true.

Lord Neuberger M.R. said[36] that the court's role involved two steps:

> "The first is to determine whether the publication of the redacted paragraphs would be against the national interest; the second step (which may not arise if the threat to the national interest would not exist or would be very significant) is to weigh that aspect of public interest against the public interest in the first judgment being fully open."

19–023 Lord Neuberger accepted[37] that it would require unusual facts before a court could reject an assessment by the Foreign Secretary of a risk to national security, but held that, as a result of the US District Court's recent judgment, the Foreign Secretary's case failed at the first stage:

> "...it is a case which is now no longer consistent with the evidence relied on, or with the arguments pursued by, the Foreign Secretary; indeed, it seems to me to be logically insupportable and therefore irrational."[38]

Sir Anthony May P. agreed, stating that his reasons were in close accord with Lord Neuberger's and observing[39]:

> "It is for the appropriate departmental minister, not the court, to judge and assert any risk to national security. It is for the court to judge whether the minister's judgment and assertion are rational and sufficiently evidence-based."

Lord Judge C.J. also agreed[40] that the Foreign Secretary's appeal should be dismissed.

---

[36] At [129].
[37] At [154].
[38] At [139].
[39] At [285].
[40] At [4].

DOCUMENTS WHOSE DISCLOSURE WOULD EXPOSE THE INNER WORKINGS OF GOVERNMENT TO ILL-INFORMED AND CAPTIOUS CRITICISM AND INCREASE THE DIFFICULTIES OF THE DECISION-MAKING PROCESS

The argument for immunity based on the encouragement of candour, in particular, has been the subject of much judicial scepticism. While it is generally acknowledged that confidentiality may encourage frankness on the part of informants, doubts have often been expressed about the candour argument as applied to public officials or ministers.[41] In *Conway v Rimmer*[42] Lord Reid, in a much quoted passage, said: **19–024**

> "Virtually everyone agrees that Cabinet minutes and the like ought not to be disclosed until such time as they are only of historical interest. But I do not think that many people would give as the reason that premature disclosure would prevent candour in the Cabinet. To my mind the most important reason is that such disclosure would create or fan ill-formed or captious public or political criticism. The business of government is difficult enough as it is, and no government could contemplate with equanimity the inner workings of the government machine being exposed to the gaze of those ready to criticise without adequate knowledge of the background and perhaps with some axe to grind."

Doubts have in turn been expressed whether the avoidance of "ill-informed or captious criticism" constitutes a satisfactory explanation for the protection of government documents.

In *Commonwealth of Australia v John Fairfax & Sons Ltd*,[43] Mason J. said: **19–025**

> " . . . it can scarcely be a relevant detriment to the government that publication of material concerning its actions will merely expose it to public discussion and criticism. It is unacceptable in our democratic society that there should be a restraint on the publication of information relating to government when the only vice of that information is that it enables the public to discuss, review and criticize government action."

Moreover, it might reasonably be said that the problem of ill-informed public criticism of the government is more likely to be cured by a greater degree of openness in the inner workings of government than it is by the withholding of information on grounds of public interest immunity.

It is nevertheless generally agreed that the business of government must be attended by a degree of confidentiality, especially at high level. But if so, what is **19–026**

---

[41] *Conway v Rimmer* [1968] A.C. 910, per Lord Reid at 952, per Lord Morris at 957, per Lord Pearce at 985 and per Lord Upjohn at 994; *Burmah Oil Co Ltd v Governor and Company of the Bank of England* [1980] A.C. 1090, per Lord Keith at 1132; *Sankey v Whitlam* (1978) 142 C.L.R. 1, per Stephen J. at 63 and per Mason J. at 97. But see also *Conway v Rimmer*, per Lord Hodson at 974; *Burmah Oil Co Ltd v Governor and Company of the Bank of England*, per Lord Wilberforce at 1112; *Air Canada v Secretary of State for Trade* [1983] 2 A.C. 394, per Lord Fraser at 433; *Sankey v Whitlam* (1978) 142 C.L.R. 1, per Gibbs A.C.J. 40.

[42] [1968] A.C. 910 at 952.

[43] (1980) 147 C.L.R. 39 at 52, approved in *Att Gen v Guardian Newspapers Ltd (No. 2)* [1990] 1 A.C. 109, per Lord Keith at 258, Lord Griffiths at 270 and Lord Goff at 283. See para.5–005.

the basis and how does it explain the immunity that would attach to Cabinet minutes from, say, before the last election?

19–027   A convincing answer was provided by the High Court of Australia in *Commonwealth v Northern Land Council*[44]:

> "The mere threat of disclosure is likely to be sufficient to impede [Cabinet] deliberations by muting a free and vigorous exchange of views or by encouraging lengthy discourse engaged in with an eye to subsequent public scrutiny. Whilst there is increasing public insistence upon the concept of open government, we do not think that it has yet been suggested that members of Cabinet would not be severely hampered in the performance of the function expected of them if they had constantly to look over their shoulders at those who would seek to criticize and publicize their participation in discussions in the Cabinet room. It is not so much a matter of encouraging candour or frankness as of ensuring that decision-making and policy development by Cabinet is uninhibited. The latter may involve the exploration of more than one controversial path even though only one may, despite differing views, prove to be sufficiently acceptable in the end to lead to a decision which all members must then accept and support."

19–028   Nevertheless, the court's ultimate responsibility was emphasised in *Air Canada v Secretary of State for Trade* by Lord Fraser, with whom Lord Edmund Davies and Lord Templeman agreed, when he said[45]:

> "I do not think that even Cabinet minutes are completely immune from disclosure in a case where, for example, the issue in a litigation involves serious misconduct by a Cabinet Minister. Such cases have occurred in Australia (see *Sankey v Whitlam* (1978) 21 A.L.R. 505) and in the United States (see *United States v Nixon* (1974) 418 U.S. 683) but fortunately not in the United Kingdom: see also the New Zealand case of *Environmental Defence Society Inc. v South Pacific Aluminium Ltd (No. 2)* [1981] 1 N.Z.L.R. 153. But while Cabinet documents do not have complete immunity, they are entitled to a high degree of protection from disclosure."

19–029   There is a great difference between documents relating to high affairs of state and more mundane communications between officials. In *Re Grosvenor Hotel, London (No.2)*,[46] Salmon L.J. said:

> "Again there may be classes of documents such as communications at a very high level, e.g., cabinet minutes, minutes of discussions between heads of departments, despatches from ambassadors abroad and the like which any right-minded person would say clearly ought not to be subject to production in an action."

He continued:

> "I can see no reason, unless compelled by authority to do so, for extending this privilege to routine communications between one civil servant and another."

---

[44] (1993) 176 C.L.R. 604 at [6].

[45] [1982] A.C. 394 at 432. See also *Commonwealth v Northern Land Council* (1993) 176 C.L.R. 604 and *State of New South Wales v Public Transport Ticketing Corp* [2011] N.S.W.C.A. 60.

[46] [1965] 1 Ch. 1210 at 1258–1259; cited by Lord Morris in *Conway v Rimmer* [1968] A.C. 910 at 973.

This ground of public interest immunity can be used to protect only documents created for purposes of state, which in this context must mean national government rather than the broader apparatus referred to as the state by Lord Simon in *D. v National Society for the Prevention of Cruelty to Children*[47]:

> "The state is the whole organisation of the body politic for supreme civil rule and government—the whole political organisation which is the basis of the civil government. As such it certainly extends to local—and, as I think, also statutory—bodies in so far as they are exercising autonomous rule."

Lord Reid observed in *Conway v Rimmer*[48]:   19–030

> "There are now many large public bodies, such as British Railways and the National Coal Board, the proper and efficient functioning of which is very necessary for many reasons including the safety of the public. The Attorney-General made it clear that Crown privilege is not and cannot be invoked to prevent disclosure of similar documents made by them or their servants even if it were said that this is required for the proper and efficient functioning of that public service."

It is equally difficult to imagine a court upholding a class-based claim for immunity on the ground that it was necessary to protect the decision-making processes of local government or other statutory autonomous bodies.

In *R. v Chief Constable of West Midlands Police Ex p. Wiley*[49] Lord Woolf said   19–031
of the decision in *D v National Society for the Prevention of Cruelty to Children*:

> "The significance of that case is that it made clear that the immunity does not only exist to protect the effective functioning of departments or organs of central government or the police, but also could protect the effective functioning of an organisation such as the NSPCC which was authorised under an Act of Parliament to bring legal proceedings for the welfare of children."

But the public interest recognised in that case was the public interest in protecting the free flow of information about child abuse *to* the NSPCC, rather than the public interest in protecting the internal decision-making processes *of* the NSPCC.

The scope of this category of immunity is particularly liable to change over   19–032
time. Lord Keith noted in *Burmah Oil Co Ltd v Governor and Company of the Bank of England*,[50] that:

> "There can be discerned in modern times a trend towards more open governmental methods than were prevalent in the past. No doubt it is for Parliament and not for courts of law to say how far that trend should go."

It should not be assumed that the trend is irreversible. Lord Pearce commented in *Conway v Rimmer*[51]:

---

[47] [1978] A.C. 171 at 236.
[48] [1968] A.C. 910 at 941.
[49] [1995] 1 A.C. 274 at 291.
[50] [1980] A.C. 1090 at 1134. See also per Mason J. in *The Commonwealth of Australia v John Fairfax & Sons Ltd* (1980) 147 C.L.R. 39, at 52, cited above at para.5–005.
[51] [1968] A.C. 910 at 982.

"In theory any general legal definition of the balance between individual justice in one scale and the safety and well-being of the state in the other scale, should be unaffected by the dangerous times in which it is uttered. But in practice the flame of individual right and justice must burn more palely when it is ringed by the more dramatic light of bombed buildings. And the human mind cannot but be affected subconsciously, even in generality of definition, by such a contrast since it is certainly a matter which ought to influence the particular decision in the case."

DOCUMENTS WHOSE DISCLOSURE WOULD DISCOURAGE THE FREE FLOW OF INFORMATION COMMUNICATED FOR OFFICIAL PURPOSES

19–033   Some kinds of official reports and records attract immunity. The scope of this category must now be regarded as uncertain in the light of the numerous judgments rejecting arguments that immunity is required to encourage candour in official reports; in recent years, its extent has certainly been greatly reduced.[52]

19–034   In *Ankin v London and North Eastern Railway Co*,[53] objection was successfully made to the production of a report furnished by the defendant to the Ministry of Transport pursuant to s.6 of the Railways Regulation Act 1871 following a railway accident. The case would unquestionably be decided differently today. Lord Reid said in *Conway v Rimmer*[54]:

> "*Ankin*'s case is a good example of what happens if the courts abandon all control of this matter. It was surely far fetched and indeed insulting to the managements of railway companies to suggest that in performing their statutory duty they might withhold information from the Minister because it might be disclosed later in legal proceedings."

The armed forces

19–035   The earlier cases often involved military matters and include claims to immunity successfully made for the minutes and proceedings of Army courts of enquiry,[55] admiralty collision reports[56] and naval and military medical records.[57] These cases should be regarded with particular caution in the light of *Conway v Rimmer* and more recent case-law. In *Barrett v Ministry of Defence*,[58] a naval airman died after a bout of heavy drinking. His widow commenced proceedings against the Ministry of Defence claiming damages for negligence and, prior to the service of a statement of claim, sought discovery of the report of a naval board of enquiry that had been convened to enquire into her husband's death.

---

[52] The private deliberations of an employer's disciplinary and appeal panel were held inadmissible in unfair dismissal proceedings in *Amwell View School Governors v Dogherty E.A.T.*, September 15, 2006.

[53] [1930] 1 K.B. 527.

[54] [1968] A.C. 910 at 947.

[55] *Home v Bentinck* (1820) 2 Brod. & B. 130 at 162ff.; *Beatson v Skene* (1860) 5 H. & N. 838; *Dawkins v Lord Rokeby* (1873) L.R. 8 Q.B. 255 at 270. A claim for immunity was refused in *Dickson v The Earl of Wilton* (1859) 1 F. & F. 419.

[56] *The Bellerophon* (1875) 44 L.J.Adm. (N.S.) 5.

[57] *Gain v Gain* [1961] 1 W.L.R. 1469; *Anthony v Anthony* (1919) 35 T.L.R. 559.

[58] *The Times*, January 24, 1990.

On appeal, Popplewell J. refused her application but considered obiter a claim   **19–036**
to immunity in respect of the report, which was made by the Ministry of Defence
and backed by ministerial certificate. Dismissing this claim, he held that the
absence of the alleged immunity would affect neither the candour of witnesses at
future boards of enquiry nor the morale, discipline or safety of those in the
service.

Although it appears from *Barrett* that there is no longer any blanket immunity   **19–037**
in respect of all military boards of enquiry, it can easily be seen that different
considerations might govern, on the one hand, an investigation into the death of
an individual and, on the other hand, an investigation into matters of, say,
potential technical significance. On the basis of *Barrett*, however, it appears that
protection of the latter would result not so much from the need for candour as
from considerations of national security.

Child care records

Child care records kept by local authorities were previously held to be immune   **19–038**
from production, even at the suit of their subject. The rationale of this was not the
right of the child to confidentiality, but the necessity of such immunity if the child
care services are to function properly. The leading authorities are the Court of
Appeal's decisions in *Re D (Infants)*[59] and *Gaskin v Liverpool City Council*,[60]
though the nature of the principle expressed in these cases was subsequently the
source of some doubts in the Court of Appeal.[61]

Re D (Infants) was cited in all the speeches given in the House of Lords in *D*   **19–039**
v NSPCC,[62] without any expression of apparent disapproval or reservation, and in
Re G (A Minor) (Social Worker: Disclosure)[63] Butler-Sloss L.J. observed:

> "There is a long line of authority that social service departments' case records and
> files are not produced on an application for discovery and are exempt from
> disclosure in court proceedings unless a judge rules to the contrary."

However, in *Re R (A Child) (Care: Disclosure: Nature of Proceedings)*[64] (care
proceedings which involved abandoned allegations of sexual abuse), Charles J.
emphasised the importance of full and frank disclosure in proceedings under the
Children Act 1989 and observed that a reluctance to provide disclosure was often
incorrectly based on views relating to confidentiality and an assertion that records
of the local authority were subject to public interest immunity. Referring to the
decision in *R. v Chief Constable of West Midlands Police, Ex p. Wiley*,[65] he stated
that:

---

[59] [1970] 1 W.L.R. 599.
[60] [1980] 1 W.L.R. 1549.
[61] See, e.g. per Scarman L.J. in *D v N.S.P.C.C.* [1978] A.C. 171 at 198, per Ackner L.J. in *Campbell
v Tameside Metropolitan Borough Council* [1982] 1 Q.B. 1065 and per Ralph Gibson L.J. in *Brown v
Matthew* [1990] 1 Ch. 662 at 675.
[62] [1978] A.C. 171.
[63] [1996] 1 W.L.R. 1407 at 1411.
[64] [2002] 1 F.L.R. 755. Munby J. expressed himself to be "in entire agreement" with Charles J.'s
observations in *Re L (A Child) (Care: Assessment: Fair Trial)* [2002] 2 F.L.R. 730 at [141].
[65] [1995] 1 A.C. 274.

"general statements that one sees in textbooks and hears that social work records are covered by public interest immunity, which is a widely stated class claim, should now be consigned to history".

He added that:

"anyone advancing a claim to public interest immunity in respect of material held by a local authority should take advice and set out with particularity the harm that it is alleged will be caused to the public interest, for example the proper conduct of the duties of a local authority in respect of the protection of children, if material which passes the threshold test for disclosure is disclosed with or without appropriate redaction in the relevant proceedings".

Official medical records

19–040   Official medical records have in the past been protected by the courts. For example, a doctor's report made to the Home Office after the exhumation and examination of a murder victim was held to be immune from production in *Williams v Star Newspaper Co Ltd*.[66]

19–041   Similarly, medical reports on the mental condition of a man confined in the hospital wing of a prison were held to be immune from production in an action brought against the Home Office by another prisoner attacked and injured by that man.[67] However, the case caused both Devlin J. and the Court of Appeal great concern, and it is likely that it would be decided differently today.[68]

19–042   A better guide to the modern approach is provided by *R. v Secretary of State for the Home Department Ex p. Benson*.[69] It was held that no immunity attached to a medical report produced in connection with the Home Secretary's consideration of the length of the term to be served by a person sentenced to life imprisonment, when production of the report was sought by its subject. The argument, advanced to protect the report of a prison doctor, that liability to production would result in a lack of candour was rejected.

The police

19–043   Police reports have been the subject of a number of decisions relating to public interest immunity. As Lord Reid said in *Conway v Rimmer*[70]:

---

[66] (1908) 24 T.L.R. 297. Darling J. apparently made his decision on the strength of the existence of the minister's certificate alone, without consideration of the grounds for it. By way of contrast, see *Leigh v Gladstone* (1909) 26 T.L.R. 139: Lord Alvestone C.J. held that a prison doctor's report to the prison's Governor was not immune from production, though it does not appear that the objection to production in this case was backed by a ministerial certificate.

[67] *Ellis v Home Office* [1953] 2 Q.B. 135.

[68] See the comments of Lord Reid, in *Conway v Rimmer* [1968] A.C. 910 at 948; compare, also, the result in *Campbell v Tameside Metropolitan Borough Council* [1982] 1 Q.B. 1065.

[69] Unreported, November 1, 1988. A significant weight of case-law has since built up in relation to the disclosure obligations of those responsible for administering the prison system when carrying out assessments of prisoners. See, for example, *R. v Secretary of State for the Home Department Ex p. Duggan* [1994] 3 All E.R. 277; *R. (Lord) v Secretary of State for the Home Department* [2003] EWHC 2073 (Admin); *R. (Ali) v Director of High Security Prisons* [2009] EWHC 1732 (Admin) and *R. (Ferguson) v Secretary of State for Justice* [2011] EWHC 5 (Admin).

[70] [1968] A.C. 910 at 953.

> "The position of the police is peculiar. They are not servants of the Crown and they do not take orders from the Government. But they are carrying out an essential function of government, and various Crown rights, privileges and exemptions have been held to apply to them."

Here too, the law has developed over the years. Reports on road traffic accidents produced by the police were held to be immune from disclosure in civil proceedings in the Scottish case of *McKie v The Western Scottish Motor Traction Co Ltd*.[71] Earlier, in England, Macnaghten J. had rejected in *Spigelman v Hocken*[72] a class claim advanced in respect of a statement made to a police officer after a road accident by one of the defendants who was involved in the accident, but observed that there might be grave objections in the public interest to producing the police officer's actual report.

In *Conway v Rimmer*,[73] however, Lord Pearce said:

19–044

> "One may perhaps take police reports of accidents as an extreme example of the malaise that can be produced by a total acceptance of the theory that all documents should be protected whenever the Minister says so on the basis that candour will be injured if there is production . . . When one considers the large public interest in a just decision of road accident cases, and the absence of any possible corresponding injury to the candour of police reports on accident cases, one realises to what a complete lack of common sense a general blanket protection of wide classes may lead. And it would be an equal departure from common sense to suppose that no great public injury could result from disclosure of police reports concerning their war on really serious crime."

In fact, police reports on accidents on the road or accidents on government premises, or involving government employees, were among categories of documents in respect of which the Lord Chancellor announced in a statement in the House of Lords in 1956 that class-based immunity would no longer be claimed.[74]

Conway v Rimmer itself concerned the status of police reports. A former probationary police constable sued a police superintendent for damages for malicious prosecution. The superintendent had been instrumental in bringing a charge of larceny against the plaintiff of which the plaintiff had been acquitted. Shortly after his acquittal, the plaintiff had been dismissed. The plaintiff sought discovery of five confidential police reports, of which four were standard probationary or training reports and one was a report submitted by the defendant to his chief constable for submission to the Director of Public Prosecutions. The defendant was willing to release these documents, but the Home Secretary swore an affidavit objecting to their production.

19–045

The speeches in the House of Lords focused primarily on the duties and powers of a judge when faced with a ministerial certificate claiming immunity, and there was relatively little direct consideration of the question whether the documents in question were in a class that prima facie attached immunity. The

19–046

---

[71] (1952) S.C. 206.

[72] (1933) 150 L.T. 256.

[73] [1968] A.C. 910 at 985–986.

[74] See also the observations of Dillon L.J. in *Marcel v Commissioner of Police of the Metropolis* [1992] Ch. 225 at 256E–F.

majority view appears to have been that the class claim in respect of the probationary reports clearly failed, but that the class claim in respect of the report to the chief constable might have more substance in it.[75]

19–047   In *Evans v Chief Constable of Surrey*,[76] the plaintiff alleged wrongful arrest and false imprisonment by the police following the murder of one of his friends. The plaintiff sought an order for the production of a report made by the police to the Director of Public Prosecutions, on the strength of which the Director of Public Prosecutions had advised that there was a prima facie case against the plaintiff and that he should be charged with the murder. The Attorney-General intervened and certified that it was in the public interest that the report should not be disclosed.

19–048   Wood J. held that the plaintiff had not shown that the discovery sought was relevant to his case, but he added[77]:

> "It seems to me important, and very important in the functioning of the criminal process of prosecution, that there should be freedom of communication between police forces around the country and the Director of Public Prosecutions in seeking his legal advice without fear that those documents will become subject to inspection, analysis and detailed investigation at some later stage . . . I find the arguments in the Attorney-General's certificate to be convincing."

There is an obvious distinction between a police road accident report, which will be largely factual and will contain names and addresses of witnesses and what they said to the police, and communications between the police and the Director of Public Prosecutions containing legal analysis and advice.

A similar distinction had been drawn in the case of complaints made to the Police Complaints Authority. Reports on the investigation of such complaints were immune from production in civil proceedings: *Taylor v Anderton*.[78] Witness statements taken in the course of the investigation and transcripts of disciplinary hearings were not immune,[79] though the confidential nature of witness statements taken by the Police Complaints Authority was re-emphasised by the House of Lords in *R. (Green) v Police Complaints Authority*.[80] The Police Reform Act 2002 replaced the Police Complaints Authority with the Independent Police Complaints Commission and ss.20 and 21 of the Act now impose specific duties on the Commission to keep complainants and other defined categories of person properly informed as to the progress of any investigation into a complaint.

19–049   *R. v Chief Constable of West Midlands Police Ex p. Wiley* illustrates the risk that public interest immunity can sometimes defeat its own purpose. In a line of cases beginning with *Neilson v Laugharne*[81] the Court of Appeal had previously held that statements taken under the statutory police complaints procedure were immune from production in civil proceedings. In *Wiley* two complainants sought

---

[75]   See per Lord Reid at 954, Lord Morris at 972, Lord Hodson at 980, Lord Pearce at 988–989 and Lord Upjohn at 996.

[76]   [1988] 1 Q.B. 588; see also *Goodridge v Chief Constable of Hampshire* [1999] 1 W.L.R. 1558.

[77]   [1988] 1 Q.B. 588 at 600.

[78]   [1995] 1 W.L.R. 447; see also *O'Sullivan v Commissioner of Police of the Metropolis*, *The Times*, July 3, 1995, and *Ashley v Chief Constable of Sussex Police* [2007] 1 W.L.R. 398 at [163] ff.

[79]   *R. v Chief Constable of West Midlands Police Ex p. Wiley* [1995] 1 A.C. 274.

[80]   [2004] UKHL 6; [2004] 1 W.L.R. 725, per Lord Rodger of Earlsferry at [73].

[81]   [1981] Q.B. 736.

undertakings from the police, before providing statements in support of their complaints, that the files created in the investigation of their complaints would not be used in civil proceedings which the complainants had either issued or intended to issue. On the police refusing to give such undertakings, the complainants challenged the lawfulness of the refusal by proceedings for judicial review. The heart of their complaint was that since, under *Neilson*, they would be unable to make use in the civil proceedings of information obtained by the police in the complaint investigations, the police should be put in a reciprocal position as regards information supplied by the complainants for the purpose of the complaint proceedings. The House of Lords held that *Neilson* and the cases that followed it had been wrongly decided. Lord Woolf observed[82] that the applicants' non co-operation in the complaints procedure was the direct result of the immunity recognised in *Neilson*, contrary to the very object which it was designed to achieve.

Financial regulator

Wiley was applied by Arden J. in *Kaufmann v Credit Lyonnais Bank*.[83] In this case, the plaintiff sought an order for the production of confidential reports, which had been made voluntarily on behalf of the defendant to the Security and Futures Authority ("the SFA"), its regulator for the purposes of the Financial Services Act 1986, together with assorted correspondence with the SFA. The defendant resisted the plaintiff's application, and an assertion of public interest immunity in respect of the documents was made both by the SFA and by the Bank of England, which had received copies of the documents in its capacity as the supervisory board of the defendant as a banking institution.   **19–050**

The claim to public interest immunity was class-based and the class was defined as documents containing: **19–051**

> "information which was (i) disclosed to a regulator voluntarily and in confidence (ii) other than as a matter of routine (iii) brought into being for the purpose of enabling the regulator more effectively to discharge its functions or duties (iv) save where the disclosure of that information by the regulator was necessary for the proper performance of its functions and duties."

Arden J. declined to accept this class-based claim, observing:

> "Given the object of the 1986 Act is, so far as material, the protection of investors, the need for a class based immunity claim to public interest immunity which would result in the withholding of information from investors must in my judgment be clearly demonstrated."

---

[82] [1995] 1 A.C. 274 at 305.
[83] *The Times*, February 1, 1995.

INFORMANTS

19–052 In some circumstances, not only reports by officials, but also communications made to officials may attract immunity. The most prominent example of this is the immunity attaching to documents whose disclosure would identify informants. This category is of very long standing. In *Home v Bentinck*,[84] Dallas C.J. said:

> "It is agreed, that there are a number of cases of a particular description, in which, for reasons of state and policy, information is not permitted to be disclosed. To begin with the ordinary cases, and those of a common description in the courts of justice. In these courts, for reasons of public policy, persons are not to be asked the names of those from whom they receive information as to the frauds on the revenue. In all the trials for high treason of late years, the same course has been adopted; and, if parties were willing to disclose the sources of their information, they would not be suffered to do it by the judges."[85]

19–053 In *Marks v Beyfus*[86] the plaintiff alleged that the defendants had maliciously conspired to have groundless criminal charges brought against him. The plaintiff called as a witness the Director of Public Prosecutions, who said in evidence that the prosecution had been instituted by himself and not the defendants. He had initiated it upon receipt of a written statement, but he declined to produce the statement or to reveal the identity of its author.

19–054 The Court of Appeal held that he had acted correctly. Lord Esher M.R. affirmed the rule that in a public prosecution a witness could not be asked (or permitted, even if willing, to answer) questions tending to disclose the informant, whether the informant was himself or a third person, but he added the important caveat:

> "I do not say it is a rule which can never be departed from; if upon the trial of a prisoner the judge should be of opinion that the disclosure of the name of the informant is necessary or right in order to shew the prisoner's innocence, then one public policy is in conflict with another public policy, and that which says that an innocent man is not to be condemned when his innocence can be proved is the policy that must prevail."[87]

19–055 In *R. v Keane*[88] the Court of Appeal observed that this passage was not a departure from, but an example of, the balancing exercise required where the application of public interest immunity would result in the withholding of relevant material in a criminal case. The court added:

> "If the disputed material may prove the defendant's innocence or avoid a miscarriage of justice, then the balance comes down resoundingly in favour of disclosing it."[89]

---

[84] (1820) 2 Brod. & B. 130.
[85] (1820) 2 Brod. & B. 130 at 162.
[86] (1890) 25 Q.B.D. 494.
[87] (1890) 25 Q.B.D. 494 at 498.
[88] [1994] 1 W.L.R. 746.
[89] [1994] 1 W.L.R. 746 at 751–752.

The Court of Appeal has also warned of the need for careful scrutiny of the nature of the material and its potential significance to the defendant's case before concluding whether its non-disclosure might result in a miscarriage. In *R. v Turner*,[90] it was said:

"We wish to alert judges to the need to scrutinise applications for disclosure of details about informants with very great care. They will need to be astute to see that assertions of a need to know such details, because they are essential to the running of the defence, are justified. If they are not so justified, then the judge will need to adopt a robust approach in declining to order disclosure. Clearly, there is a distinction between cases in which the circumstances raise no reasonable possibility that information about the informant will bear upon the issues and cases where it will. Again, there will be cases where the informant is an informant and no more; other cases where he may have participated in the events constituting, surrounding, or following the crime. Even when the informant has participated, the judge will need to consider whether his role so impinges on an issue of interest to the defence, present or potential, as to make disclosure necessary."

It would be an affront to the most basic principles of liberty that the interests **19–056** of the general public could in any circumstances justify a person being wrongly convicted of a criminal offence, or that the doctrine of public interest immunity should ever be used in such a way as to have that effect. The House of Lords repeatedly emphasised[91] that it is:

" . . . axiomatic that a person charged with having committed a criminal offence should receive a fair trial and that, if he cannot be tried fairly for that offence, he should not be tried for it at all."

However, it is not in the context of criminal cases alone that the public interest in maintaining the anonymity of an informant may yield to other considerations. In *Chief Constable of the Greater Manchester Police v McNally*,[92] a civil action against the police, the Court of Appeal rejected a submission that, as a matter of law, the public interest in the protection of informers should prevail over any countervailing interest, save where the party seeking disclosure was at risk of his liberty, or where the informer had consented to disclosure or there was some other exceptional circumstance, such as a threat to his safety. Holding that the judge at first instance had been entitled to balance the conflicting interests in the manner that she did, the court ordered that the Chief Constable should state whether or not an identified individual witness was a police informant. In doing so, it regarded as significant the fact that the scope for protecting the alleged informer was limited by the fact that both sides knew who he was and the claimant believed, rightly or wrongly, that he was an informer.[93]

---

[90] [1995] 1 W.L.R. 264 at 267.

[91] For example, in *R. v H* [2004] UKHL 3; [2004] 2 A.C. 134 at [10].

[92] [2002] EWCA Civ 14.

[93] English law differs in this respect from Canadian law. In *Named person v Vancouver Sun* (2007) S.C.C. 43; 285 D.L.R. (4th) 193, the majority of the Supreme Court of Canada held (at [27]) that "The informer privilege rule admits but one exception: it can be abridged if necessary to establish innocence in a criminal trial (there are no exceptions to the rule in civil proceedings)."

EXTENSION OF THE IMMUNITY OF INFORMANTS

19–057 The rule protecting informants in criminal cases has been extended by analogy to other fields. In *R. v Lewes Justices Ex p. Secretary of State for Home Department*,[94] it was held by the House of Lords to apply to persons supplying information to the Gaming Board when it was considering whether to grant a gaming licence. Lord Salmon said[95]:

> "When one considers the grievous social ills which will undoubtedly be caused by gaming clubs if they get into the wrong hands, it is obviously of the greatest public importance that the law should give the board all its support to ensure that this does not occur. In my view, any document or information that comes to the board from whatever source and by whatever means should be immune from discovery. It is only thus that the board will obtain all the material it requires in order to carry out its task efficiently. Unless this immunity exists many persons, reputable or disreputable, would be discouraged from communicating all they know to the board."

This last sentence shows that the need to protect sources of information is not confined to cases where the moral fibre of potential informants is questionable. Nor indeed is it confined to cases where sources require protection from a possible threat posed by underworld elements.

19–058 In *D v National Society for the Prevention of Cruelty to Children*,[96] the rule was applied in relation to an informant who reported to the defendants that the plaintiff was beating her child. Lord Diplock said:

> "I would extend to those who give information about neglect or ill-treatment of children to a local authority or the N.S.P.C.C. a similar immunity from disclosure of their identity in legal proceedings to that which the law accords to police informers. The public interests served by preserving the anonymity of both classes of informants are analogous; they are of no less weight in the case of the former than in that of the latter class, and in my judgment are of greater weight than in the case of informers of the Gaming Board to whom immunity from disclosure of their identity has recently been extended by this House."[97]

19–059 Documents created for the purpose of a private inquiry established by the Secretary of State for Foreign and Commonwealth Affairs, whose aim was to investigate the continuing supply of oil into Rhodesia notwithstanding the imposition of sanctions, were held to be immune by the House of Lords in *Lonrho Ltd v Shell Petroleum Co Ltd*.[98] Lord Diplock, giving the only speech, said[99]:

> "Even without the Minister's certificate I should not have needed evidence to satisfy me that the likelihood of success of an inquiry of this kind in discovering the truth as to what happened is greatly facilitated if those persons who know what happened

---

[94] [1973] A.C. 388.

[95] [1973] A.C. 388 at 413.

[96] [1978] A.C. 171.

[97] [1978] A.C. 171 at 219.

[98] [1980] 1 W.L.R. 627.

[99] [1980] 1 W.L.R. 627 at 637.

come forward to volunteer information rather than waiting to be identified by the inquiry itself as likely to possess relevant information and having it extracted from them by question and answer. Nor would I need any evidence to satisfy me that without an assurance of complete confidentiality information is less likely to be volunteered; particularly where the inquiry is directed to matters that are the subject matter of a pending civil action to which the possessor of the information is a defendant."

The same rule has been applied in relation to persons providing information to the Audit Commission (which has statutory responsibilities with regard to the auditing of local government expenditure) about alleged wasted expenditure by a local authority.[100]

The importance of encouraging whistle-blowers and other informants was described by the Court of Appeal in *Real Estate Opportunities Ltd v Aberdeen Asset Managers Jersey Ltd*[101] as one of the principal purposes behind the statutory protection (under s.348 of the Financial Services and Markets Act 2000) of information obtained from the FSA. See also *In re Galilieo Group Ltd*[102] and *Barings Plc v Coopers & Lybrand.*[103]

DOCUMENTS WHOSE DISCLOSURE WOULD BE OPPRESSIVE

Re Joseph Hargreaves Ltd[104] concerned a summons for discovery under s.115 of   **19–060**
the Companies Act 1862. The liquidators of an insolvent company sought to recover damages from the directors and auditors of the company. The summons was served on the local tax surveyor, requiring him to produce balance sheets submitted by the company. The Inland Revenue objected to production of the documents, and its objection was upheld by Wright J. and the Court of Appeal.

Lord Reid, commenting on the case in *Conway v Rimmer*,[105] observed: **19–061**

"If the state insists on a man disclosing his private affairs for a particular purpose it requires a very strong case to justify that disclosure being used for other purposes."

Substantial extensions in the state's powers to compel the production of information have caused the courts on a number of occasions to consider whether a document thereby obtained is immune from disclosure by the recipient to anyone else for any extraneous purpose ("the compulsion principle"). As Robert Walker J. observed in *Re Atlantic Computers Plc*[106]:

"The extension of statutory powers of investigation (both in their scope and the frequency of their exercise) in response to successive financial scandals has in the

---

[100] *Bookbinder v Tebbit (No.2)* [1992] 1 W.L.R. 217.
[101] [2007] EWCA Civ 197; [2007] 2 All E.R. 791 at [31]–[32].
[102] [1999] Ch. 100.
[103] [2000] 1 W.L.R. 2353.
[104] [1900] 1 Ch. 347.
[105] [1968] A.C. 910 at 946.
[106] [1998] B.C.C. 200, at 211.

last decade produced a large number of important decisions of the High Court, the Court of Appeal and the House of Lords, and some of these important decisions are not easily understood or reconciled."

Some of those decisions relate to the privilege against self-incrimination, which is recognised both by the English common law and by European human rights jurisprudence; that privilege falls outside the scope of this book. But others relate to an immunity arising where self-incrimination is not in issue.

THE COMPULSION PRINCIPLE AS A HEAD OF PUBLIC INTEREST IMMUNITY

19-062   One issue not yet clearly resolved is the extent to which the compulsion principle is still properly to be regarded as giving rise to a head of public interest immunity at all. The proposition that tax documents provided to the Inland Revenue attract public interest immunity in the hands of the Inland Revenue was accepted by the majority of the Court of Appeal (Sir Thomas Bingham M.R. and Leggatt L.J.) in *Lonrho Plc v Fayed (No.4).*[107] However, Leggatt L.J. made it clear that his acceptance of the proposition was based on authority, rather than principle, and Roch L.J. rejected the proposition (while acknowledging that the Inland Revenue would owe a duty of confidence in relation to the documents in its possession). The proposition was re-affirmed by the Privy Council (obiter) on appeal from the High Court of Justice of the Isle of Man in *Mount Murray Country Club Ltd v Macleod.*[108]

19-063   However, the Court of Appeal in *Lonrho Plc v Fayed (No.4)* rejected an argument that, because tax documents were protected in the hands of the Inland Revenue, it followed that they must also be protected in the hands of the taxpayer. (The plaintiff in an action for damages for conspiracy obtained an order for discovery of financial documents, including tax documents. The defendants appealed, arguing that public interest immunity would attach to the documents in the hands of the Inland Revenue and must also attach to them in the hands of the taxpayer.) Sir Thomas Bingham said[109]:

> "There are some fields in which, if immunity covers a document in the hands of party A, it would be absurd to order production of a copy in the hands of B or to permit oral evidence of the contents of the document by C. In fields such as national security or the conduct of international relations, production of B's copy or the admission of C's evidence would injure the very public interest which the immunity exists to protect. But it does not follow that that need be so in all fields. It all depends on the facet of the public interest which is in question. Mr Sumption was, I think, right to pose the question: what is for present purposes the relevant public policy?
>
> The answer to that question must be that which Lord Reid gave in commenting on *Re Joseph Hargreaves Ltd* [1900] 1 Ch. 347. The state must not, backed by compulsory powers, obtain information from the citizen for one purpose and use that information for another. It does not matter whether this is seen as a principle of

---

[107] [1994] Q.B. 775.

[108] [2003] UKPC 53; (2003) S.T.C. 1525 at [33].

[109] *Lonrho Plc v Fayed (No.4)* [1994] Q.B. 775 at 788–789.

good administration or statutory construction or ordinary morality or all three. That is the ratio which Lord Reid gave, as I understand him, and I do not think it bears on whether the taxpayer himself can be required to produce the documents or not."

He accordingly held that there was no public interest which entitled the defendants to claim immunity for the tax documents in their possession.

In *Wallace Smith Trust Co Ltd v Deloitte Haskins & Sells*,[110] Simon Brown **19–064** L.J. was prepared to assume ("as this court's decision in *Lonrho Plc v Fayed (No.4)* . . . strongly suggests") that the transcripts and tapes of interviews carried out by the Serious Fraud Office under its powers pursuant to s.2 of the Criminal Justice Act 1987 would be protected by public interest immunity in the hands of the SFO. He continued, however, that it was plain that the documents were not similarly protected in the hands of the defendants. In *Real Estate Opportunities Ltd v Aberdeen Asset Managers Jersey Ltd*[111] the Court of Appeal held that there was no difference for this purpose between transcripts of evidence under s.2 of the Criminal Justice Act 1987 and transcripts of evidence given to the FSA.

By contrast, in *Marcel v Commissioner of Police of the Metropolis*[112] the **19–065** Court of Appeal allowing an appeal against a decision of Sir Nicolas Browne-Wilkinson V.C., held that the police owed a duty of confidentiality towards a citizen from whom documents were seized, but might be required to produce them on subpoena in circumstances where the owners of the seized documents might themselves be required to produce them on subpoena. In those circumstances, no public interest immunity prevented the disclosure from being given.

It is difficult to see any good reason why different rules should apply to **19–066** confidential documents seized from a citizen by the police and confidential documents supplied by the citizen to the Inland Revenue under compulsion. In *Re Atlantic Computers Plc*,[113] Robert Walker J., considered, obiter, the compulsion principle. Having observed that there had recently been a major shift in the government's approach to public interest immunity, restricting it "properly so called, to really cogent cases", he distinguished between the compulsion principle and "PII proper", stating[114]:

"The narrower the scope of PII properly so called, the more frequent and the more difficult will be cases where the compulsion principle, rather than PII properly so called, may be relied on as a ground for resisting production of documents . . . "

He expressed the provisional view that authority was likely to preclude him from regarding the compulsion principle as an obstacle to disclosure.

In *British and Commonwealth Holdings Plc v Barclays de Zoete Wedd Ltd*,[115] **19–067** Neuberger J. ordered that disclosure should be given in civil litigation of transcripts of evidence that had been provided under compulsion to inspectors appointed by the DTI pursuant to s.432 of the Companies Act 1985. He started[116]

---

[110] [1997] 1 W.L.R. 257 at 274.
[111] [2007] EWCA Civ 197; [2007] 2 All E.R. 791 at [72].
[112] [1992] Ch. 225; see para.3–015, above.
[113] [1998] B.C.C. 200.
[114] At 213.
[115] [1999] 1 B.C.L.C. 86.
[116] At 95.

from the proposition that the transcripts were not the subject of public interest immunity, without expressly setting out his reasoning. He continued:

> " . . . one can see a powerful argument for saying that the court should not, save in exceptional circumstances, order disclosure of the transcripts in connection with civil proceedings . . . Support for such a view may be found in the observations of Sir Nicolas Browne-Wilkinson V.C. in *Marcel* . . . Like Robert Walker J. [in *Re Atlantic Computers plc*], however, while I might well have been inclined to give significant weight to what he helpfully called 'the compulsion principle' . . . I believe that that course is not open to me . . . "

19–068   *Re Atlantic Computers Plc* and *British and Commonwealth Holdings Plc v Barclays de Zoete Wedd Ltd* are both formally reconcilable with *Lonrho v Fayed (No.4)*, on the basis that in those two cases the information in question was not in the hands of the organisation that had compelled its production. But they are also consistent with the rather different approach of the Court of Appeal in *Marcel*. The terms of Robert Walker J.'s discussion in *Re Atlantic Computers Plc* do not encourage a broad view of any immunity arising from the compulsion principle.

19–069   Whether the courts will develop the compulsion principle as a head of public interest immunity remains to be seen. Each case will require its own examination, but it may be that in this area *Marcel* will be seen in the future as providing more general guidance than *Lonrho Plc v Fayed (No.4)* and that documents obtained by compulsion will generally be regarded as subject to an obligation of confidentiality but not to public interest immunity.

DISCLOSURE FOR AN AUTHORISED PURPOSE

19–070   In any event, one significant limitation on any public interest immunity arising out of the compulsion principle is that it will not prevent an organisation from using compulsorily obtained information for a purpose that falls within the class of purposes for which the organisation was entitled to require the information.

19–071   In *Re Arrows*,[117] the House of Lords held that the Serious Fraud Office was entitled under s.2(3) of the Criminal Justice Act 1987 to require the liquidators of a company to provide transcripts and other documents relating to their compulsory examination of an individual under s.236 of the Insolvency Act 1986. Lord Browne-Wilkinson said[118]:

> "The statutory framework . . . imposes a wide range of duties on liquidators to report, directly or indirectly, to the D.T.I. and prosecuting authorities cases of suspected criminal and dishonest conduct and to furnish them with all documents and information they may require. Such documents include transcripts of evidence given on a section 236 examination, which transcripts are admissible in evidence. The liquidator cannot be under any duty of confidence which will prevent the performance of these statutory duties."

Lord Browne-Wilkinson expressed the opinion, obiter, that the public interest in ensuring the free flow of information obtained informally under s.235 of the

---

[117] [1995] 2 A.C. 75.
[118] At 103.

Insolvency Act 1986 was much greater than it was in relation to transcripts of s.236 examinations. However, the Court of Appeal in *R. v Brady*[119] held that the official receiver was entitled to disclose to the Inland Revenue statements obtained by him from the defendant under s.235:

> "Once it is accepted that one of the purposes for which section 235 material is obtained is the investigation of crime it would be entirely anomalous if that material could be used by the DTI for any criminal investigation it might undertake, but not by any other prosecuting authority interested in the same material, unless some elaborate balancing exercise was carried out or the sanction of the court was obtained on notice to the individual."

THE NATURE OF THE PROTECTION AFFORDED BY IMMUNITY

In the nineteenth century, it was held that a document either attracted immunity in its entirety or not at all: it was not possible for arguably unobjectionable passages in immune documents to be received in evidence.[120] This may have been because the objection to disclosure generally affected every part of the document equally. In any event, it is now accepted that parts of a document may be disclosed while other parts are withheld.[121] **19–072**

If immunity attaches to a document, its contents are protected from discovery and from production in court. The document's immunity does not necessarily prevent it from being used in other ways by the party in whose hands it is. **19–073**

In *R. v Commissioner of Police of the Metropolis Ex p. Hart-Leverton*,[122] the applicant sought judicial review of the Commissioner's decision to allow documents obtained in the course of a police complaints investigation and disciplinary hearing to be used by police legal advisers for purposes such as advising on evidence and taking statements from witnesses, so as to assist in the preparation of the defence to legal proceedings against the police commenced by the complainant. It was conceded by the Commissioner that the documents could not be used for the purpose of cross-examination. **19–074**

Nolan J. held that the guiding principle of immunity was to ensure that the protected material did not go before the court. There was nothing in the use of the documents by the police or their legal advisers which conflicted with the immunity. This view was departed from by the Court of Appeal in *Halford v* **19–075**

---

[119] [2004] EWCA Crim 1763; [2004] 1 W.L.R. 3240 at [27]. The Court of Appeal in *Scopelight Ltd v Chief Constable of Northumbria Police Force* [2010] Q.B. 438 similarly warned against adopting too restricted a view of the purposes for which a police force might reasonably conclude that it was necessary to retain material which had been seized under PACE 1984.

[120] per Ellenborough C.J. in *Anderson v Hamilton* (1816), cited in *Home v Bentinck* (1820) 2 Brod. & B. 130 at 156n; *Stace v Griffith* (1869) L.R. 2 P.C. 420, per Lord Chelmsford in the course of argument at 425.

[121] See *Burmah Oil Co Ltd v Governor and Company of the Bank of England* [1980] A.C. 1090, per Lord Edmund-Davies at 1124; *R. v Chief Constable of West Midlands Police Ex p. Wiley* [1995] 1 A.C. 274, per Lord Templeman at 282 and per Lord Woolf at 307.

[122] *The Times*, February 6, 1990.

Sharples[123] and *R. v Chief Constable of West Midlands Police Ex p. Wiley*,[124] but its authority was restored by the House of Lords in the latter case.[125]

19–076   One question is whether the concession made by the Commissioner in *Ex p. Hart-Leverton* was unnecessary: is it possible to use immune documents in cross-examination? In *Alfred Crompton Amusement Machines Ltd v Customs & Excise*,[126] Lord Cross of Chelsea remarked obiter[127] in relation to information for which immunity was claimed that:

> "No doubt it will form part of the brief delivered to counsel for the commissioners and may help him to probe the appellants' evidence in cross-examination; but counsel will not be able to use it as evidence to controvert anything which the appellants' witnesses may say."

19–077   The point was considered in some detail by the House of Lords in *R. v Chief Constable of West Midlands Police Ex p. Wiley*.[128] Lord Woolf, delivering the leading speech, quoted the statement of Lord Cross set out above and observed that his speech on that aspect of the case represented the unanimous view of the House of Lords. He also stated as a matter of principle that,[129]

> "In general, the immunity is provided against disclosure of documents or their contents. It is not, at least in the absence of exceptional circumstances, an immunity against the use of knowledge obtained from the documents. It is impractical and artificial to erect barriers between a party and his legal advisers in an attempt to avoid that party having an advantage in the proceedings."

Lord Woolf went on to say that the legal advisers of a party in possession of material which is immune from disclosure should assist the court and the opposing party to mitigate any disadvantage as best they can by disclosing such information as is possible without production of the document; but that, in so far as this is not possible, the courts should not try to create a level playing field by orders of the kind made in that case (i.e. restricting internal use of the document by the party in possession of it).

19–078   It follows from this reasoning that the concession made by the Commissioner in *Ex p. Hart-Leverton* was too broad. He would have been entitled to use the material (even if it had been immune from production) for the purpose of cross-examination, provided that this was not done in such a way as to destroy the object of its immunity (for example, by putting the document to the witness).

19–079   The question has also arisen whether evidence about matters contained in a document, which is the subject of public interest immunity, may be adduced by other means, for example, by producing a copy of the document.

19–080   In many instances, a copy of an immune document will itself be immune, but this is not always the case, as is shown by *Lonrho Plc v Fayed (No.4)*,[130] where

---

[123] [1992] 1 W.L.R. 736.
[124] [1994] 1 W.L.R. 114. [
[125] [1995] 1 A.C. 274.
[126] [1974] A.C. 405.
[127] [1974] A.C. 405 at 434, cited by Oliver L.J. in *Neilson v Laugharne* [1981] Q.B. 736 at 753.
[128] [1995] 1 A.C. 274 at 301.
[129] [1995] 1 A.C. 274 at 306.
[130] [1994] Q.B. 775 at 788. See para.19–062 above.

Sir Thomas Bingham M.R. observed that it depends in each case on identifying the aspect of the public interest which the immunity is intended to serve.

If, for example, the reason for the grant of immunity is not that the release of the information would be harmful in itself, but only that the provision of that information from a particular source would be against the public interest, because it would tend to dry up the free flow of information on matters of public importance, there would be no objection to the provision of the same information from another source. **19–081**

RAISING THE OBJECTION

In civil proceedings, CPR 31.19 sets out the procedure which is generally applicable to claims to withhold disclosure or inspection of a document. In cases involving public interest immunity, a claim to withhold disclosure or inspection should already have received detailed consideration well before any such application is considered by the court. In *Al Rawi v Security Service*,[131] counsel for the security service summarised the procedure in this way: **19–082**

> "Lawyers consider material to see if it passes the threshold test for disclosure under CPR Pt 31. In so far as it is prima facie disclosable, officials review material for potential to cause harm to the public interest. If harm to the public interest is identified, the department carries out a balance between harm caused by the disclosure on the one hand and injustice in the litigation on the other. It also considers whether it is possible to redact or gist the information or to make admissions of fact. Officials consider whether and to what extent the balance falls against disclosure in order to give advice to the minister as to whether to certify. If the minister, having considered the advice, decides that a certificate should be given, a PII certificate is prepared which includes a disclosable certificate or schedule describing the types of harm that might be caused to the public interest and a sensitive schedule as to why it is believed that disclosure of documents would cause real damage or harm to the public interest."

A claim to public interest immunity should be made by ministerial certificate or certificate given by the Permanent Secretary of the relevant government department.[132] However, in the absence of any governmental intervention,[133] an objection to production may be raised either by the holder or the owner of the document of which production is sought, or by any interested person, or by the court of its own motion.[134]

In *Re Barlow Clowes Gilt Managers Ltd*,[135] Millett J., holding that there was a public interest in protecting from production the transcripts of interviews carried out by liquidators, observed[136]: **19–083**

---

[131] [2011] UKSC 34; [2011] 3 W.L.R. 388, per Lord Clarke at [148].

[132] *Amaryllis Ltd v HM Treasury (No.2)* [2009] EWHC 1666 (TCC), per Coulson J. at [44].

[133] Unless the relevant authority has already taken the decision not to pursue a claim to immunity (see below).

[134] See *Marcel v Commissioner of Police of the Metropolis* [1992] Ch. 225, per Dillon L.J. at 253; *R. v Lewes JJ. Ex p. Home Secretary* [1973] A.C. 388, per Lord Reid at 400; *Hennessy v Wright* (1888) 21 Q.B.D. 509 at 519 and 521.

[135] [1992] Ch. 208.

[136] [1992] Ch. 208 at 223.

"If the liquidation of insolvent companies were entrusted to the executive branch of government, the foregoing would be embodied in a certificate by the appropriate minister. As it is entrusted to the judicial branch, the place of the certificate must be taken by the doctrine of judicial notice."

19–084   The procedure to be adopted in criminal cases when the prosecution is in possession of information which it believes to be immune on the grounds of public interest from disclosure to the defence has been the subject of scrutiny both in Europe and at the highest domestic level.[137] In *R. v H*[138] the House of Lords stated:

"When any issue of derogation from the golden rule of full disclosure comes before it, the court must address a series of questions.

(1)   What is the material which the prosecution seek to withhold? This must be considered by the court in detail.

(2)   Is the material such as may weaken the prosecution case or strengthen that of the defence? If No, disclosure should not be ordered. If Yes, full disclosure should (subject to (3), (4) and (5) below) be ordered.

(3)   Is there a real risk of serious prejudice to an important public interest (and, if so, what) if full disclosure of the material is ordered? If No, full disclosure should be ordered.

(4)   If the answer to (2) and (3) is Yes, can the defendant's interest be protected without disclosure or disclosure be ordered to an extent or in a way which will give adequate protection to the public interest in question and also afford adequate protection to the interests of the defence? . . .

(5)   Do the measures proposed in answer to (4) represent the minimum derogation necessary to protect the public interest in question? If No, the court should order such greater disclosure as will represent the minimum derogation from the golden rule of full disclosure.

(6)   If limited disclosure is ordered pursuant to (4) or (5), may the effect be to render the trial process, viewed as a whole, unfair to the defendant? If Yes, then fuller disclosure should be ordered even if this leads or may lead the prosecution to discontinue the proceedings to as to avoid having to make disclosure.

(7)   If the answer to (6) when first given is No, does that remain the correct answer as the trial unfolds, evidence is adduced and the defence advanced?"

One of the difficulties facing the court may be that adversarial argument on these questions is impeded by the need to keep the relevant information from the defendant, with the result, for example, that applications are made by the prosecution in the absence of the defendant. In those circumstances, the court is required to take measures to ensure that its procedures counterbalance any difficulties caused to the defendant by the defendant's exclusion.[139] In some

---

[137]   *Edwards and Lewis v UK* [2003] E.C.H.R. 381; [2004] E.C.H.R. 560; [2005] 40 E.H.R.R. 593; *R. v H* [2004] UKHL 3; [2004] 2 A.C. 134. See also, in relation to the courts' (non-criminal) jurisdiction in relation to control orders under the Prevention of Terrorism Act 2005, the decision of the House of Lords in *Secretary of State for the Home Department v AF (No.3)* [2009] UKHL28; [2010] 2 A.C. 269, departing from its previous decision in *Secretary of State for the Home Department v MB; Same v AF* [2007] UKHL 46; [2008] 1 A.C. 440.

[138]   [2004] UKHL 3; [2004] 2 A.C. 134 at [36].

[139]   *Rowe v UK* (2000) 30 E.H.R.R. 1; *Jasper v UK* (2000) 30 E.H.R.R. 441; *Fitt v UK* (2000) 30 E.H.R.R. 480.

circumstances, these measures may extend to the appointment of an independent special advocate to act on the defendant's behalf in what is known as a "closed material" procedure: the relevant information is disclosed to the advocate, but the advocate is unable to disclose the information to the defendant, or to seek instructions on it from the defendant.

In *R. v H*,[140] the House of Lords warned against making a premature decision to seek the appointment of special advocates in cases where they were not necessary. They said:

19-085

> " . . . the judge should involve the defence to the maximum extent possible without disclosing that which the general interest requires to be protected but taking full account of the specific defence which is relied on. There will be very few cases indeed in which some measure of disclosure to the defence will not be possible, even if this is confined to the fact that an ex parte application is to be made. If even that information is withheld and if the material to be withheld is of significant help to the defendant, there must be a very serious question whether the prosecution should proceed, since special counsel, even if appointed, cannot then receive any instructions from the defence at all".

In addition to its role as a procedure ancillary to public interest immunity hearings, the closed material procedure has in some instances also been expressly stipulated for in legislation, the best-known example being probably para.4 of Sch.1 to the Prevention of Terrorism Act 2005, relating to the control order regime as it affected terrorist suspects.[141] In *Al Rawi v Security Services*[142] the Supreme Court acknowledged the existence of such legislative innovations, as well as the two well-established common law exceptions which are presented by the courts' wardship jurisdiction and the "confidentiality rings" to which disclosure is sometimes restricted in commercial confidentiality cases.[143] However, the majority of the Supreme Court set its face against any common law extension of the availability of closed material procedures for use in general civil litigation.[144]

In *R. (on the application of British Sky Broadcasting Ltd) v Central Criminal Court*,[145] the Divisional Court (Moore-Bick L.J. and Bean J.) held that the Supreme Court's decision applied, not only to trials but also to procedural applications and other contested hearings.

---

[140] At [37]. See too the discussion of the role of special counsel at [22].

[141] Now replaced by the provisions of the Terrorism Prevention and Investigation Measures Act 2011.

[142] [2012] 1 A.C. 531.

[143] As to these, see further at para.20–002, below.

[144] It is uncertain whether the court would order a closed material procedure if both or all parties consented to it. In *R. (AHK) v Secretary of State for the Home Department* [2012] EWHC 1117 (Admin), Ouseley J. did not consider that the court would have power to order it even with the parties' consent. In *R. (Omar) v Secretary of State for Foreign and Commonwealth Affairs* [2012] EWHC 1737 (Admin) at [19], the court observed that a closed material procedure had been adopted by consent without any argument on the issue, and in *R. (Youssef) v Secretary of State for Foreign & Commonwealth Affairs* [2012] EWHC 2091 (Admin) the court did not find it necessary to decide the question.

[145] [2011] EWHC 3451 (Admin); [2012] 3 W.L.R. 78 at [28]. The Divisional Court further held that the decision of the Divisional Court in *R. (Malik) v Manchester Crown Court* [2008] 4 All E.R. 403 must be regarded as having been overruled by Al Rawi's case, in so far as it supported the conclusion that a closed procedure could be adopted on an application of the kind which was before the Court.

19–086   In general, issues of public interest immunity should be dealt with in the proceedings in which they arise, and not by way of an application for injunctive or declaratory relief in ancillary proceedings. Where a summary trial is to be conducted by magistrates who have decided against the defendant on an issue of public interest immunity, the magistrates have a discretion to grant the defendant a hearing before a new bench.[146]

WAIVER

19–087   It has often been said that a claim to public interest immunity, in an appropriate case, is not a right but a duty, and therefore cannot be waived in the same manner as, for example, legal professional privilege.[147] This statement requires substantial qualification.

19–088   First, in cases where the immunity is based upon a duty of confidence owed to a person, a waiver of confidence by that person may operate as a negation of the immunity. As Lord Woolf said in *R. v Chief Constable of West Midlands Ex p. Wiley*[148]:

> "If the purpose of the immunity is to obtain the co-operation of an individual to the giving of a statement, I find it difficult to see how that purpose will be undermined if the maker of the statement consents to it being disclosed."

19–089   In *Savage v Chief Constable of Hampshire*[149] the plaintiff claimed to be a police informer and sought to bring proceedings for payment for information that he had allegedly provided to the police. Judge L.J., who gave the leading judgment in the Court of Appeal, held that:

> " . . . if a police informer wishes personally to sacrifice his own anonymity, he is not precluded from doing so by the automatic application of the principle of public interest immunity at the behest of the relevant police authority."[150]

Judge L.J. commented that the police informer's own wishes were not necessarily conclusive because of the possibility that there was a significant public interest, extraneous to the informer and his safety, that would be damaged by disclosure. There was no evidence that any such consideration applied in that case.

19–090   *Carnduff v Rock*[151] involved a similar claim by a *soi-disant* police informer. On this occasion, however, the majority of the Court of Appeal (Laws and Jonathan Parker L.JJ.) struck out the claim, holding that it was inevitable from the

---

[146] *R. v South Worcestershire Magistrates Ex p. Lilley, The Times*, February 22, 1995, DC.

[147] See, e.g. *D v N.S.P.C.C.* [1978] A.C. 171, per Lord Simon at 234; *R. v Lewes JJ.* [1973] A.C. 388, per Lord Salmon at 412; *Re S and W (Minors) (Confidential Reports)* (1983) 4 F.L.R. 290 per Eveleigh L.J. at 292; *Makanjuola v Commissioner of Police of the Metropolis* [1992] 3 All E.R. 617, per Bingham L.J. at 623.

[148] [1995] 1 A.C. 274, per Lord Woolf at 299. See also *Lonrho Plc v Fayed (No.4)* [1994] Q.B. 775, per Sir Thomas Bingham M.R. at 786F, and *Campbell v Tameside Metropolitan Borough Council* [1982] 1 Q.B. 1065, per Lord Denning M.R. at 1073.

[149] [1997] 1 W.L.R. 1061.

[150] At 1067.

[151] [2001] EWCA Civ 680; [2001] 1 W.L.R. 1786.

issues in the case that the proposed litigation would result in the disclosure of information harmful to the public interest. Waller L.J. dissented, suggesting that there should be a trial of the preliminary issue whether the contract alleged by the plaintiff had existed. If so,

> "The court should then see whether there is machinery available to enable the questions that will arise thereafter to be tried fairly. I believe that machinery should and would if necessary be found, because it would not seem to me to be right in those circumstances that the police should simply be released from a binding contract that on this assumption they have made with their eyes open."[152]

The Court of Appeal's decision was arrived at without any express consideration of the claimant's Art.6 rights (perhaps because the decision under appeal was made shortly before the Human Rights Act 1998 came into force). However, the claimant's subsequent complaint to the European Court of Human Rights was held inadmissible.[153] In *Al Rawi v Security Service*,[154] Lord Clarke suggested that the correctness and application of the Court of Appeal's decision might require in due course to be examined in detail, but Lord Mance observed[155] that no member of the Supreme Court had cast doubt on the proposition that the approach of the majority of the Court of Appeal might sometimes be necessary.

Secondly, in many instances, the courts will not query a decision by the **19-091** executive or other relevant authority not to pursue a claim to immunity. This may occur for different reasons. On the one hand, it may be that the relevant authority decides that there is no public interest to be served by protection from disclosure because, for example, the proposed revelations pose no threat to national security.[156]

Alternatively, an argument for public interest in immunity may exist, but the **19-092** executive or other authority may be able to decide the contest between (a) the aspect of the public interest supporting the immunity and (b) the aspect of the public interest supporting disclosure, in favour of the latter, without reference to the court.

Thus, in *R. v Chief Constable of West Midlands Ex p. Wiley*,[157] Lord Woolf **19-093** said:

> "If a Secretary of State on behalf of his department as opposed to any ordinary litigant concludes that any public interest in documents being withheld from production is outweighed by the public interest in the documents being available for purposes of litigation, it is difficult to conceive that unless the documents do not relate to an area for which the Secretary of State was responsible, the court would feel it appropriate to come to any different conclusion from that of the Secretary of State."

He later referred to[158]:

---

[152] At [26].
[153] *Carnduff v United Kingdom* (Application No. 18905/02), February 10, 2004.
[154] [2011] UKSC 34; [2011] 3 W.L.R. 388 at [174].
[155] At [108].
[156] See, e.g. *A v Hayden* [1984] 156 C.L.R. 532.
[157] [1995] 1 A.C. 274 at 296; see also *Sankey v Whitlam* (1978) 142 C.L.R. 1 at 44–45 and 68.
[158] [1995] 1 A.C. 274 at 298.

"a well known part of the speech of Lord Simon of Glaisdale in *R. v Lewes Justices Ex p. Secretary of State for the Home Department* [1973] A.C. 388 at 407, which is in these terms,

> 'It is true that the public interest which demands that the evidence be withheld has to be weighed against the public interest in the administration of justice that courts should have the fullest possible access to all relevant material . . . but once the former public interest is held to outweigh the latter, the evidence cannot in any circumstances be admitted. It is not a privilege which may be waived by the Crown . . . or by anyone else.'

It will be observed from that passage that when Lord Simon said that the privilege was one which could not be waived, he was referring to the situation after it had been determined that the public interest against disclosure outweighed that of disclosure in the administration of justice."

19–094   Secretaries of State and the Attorney General are capable of this form of disposal of the issue of immunity, but the situation may be different when parties other than government departments are involved.[159] It has been said that it would be appropriate for a chief constable to consult with other chief constables and possibly the Attorney-General and Home Secretary before deciding to disclose a document of a kind for which to the courts have previously recognised class immunity. When there is a doubt as to whether immunity can properly be waived, the prudent approach is to leave the matter to the court.[160]

19–095   It is as yet unsettled whether an official's power to waive a claim to immunity where he decides that the public interest in immunity is outweighed by the public interest in the administration of justice brings with it a concomitant *duty* to make a claim *only* after taking this latter public interest into account. In *Bennett v Commissioner of Police of Metropolis*,[161] Rattee J., without deciding the matter, expressed the view that the existence of such a duty was arguable. The alternative view is that the responsible official is entitled to leave considerations of the administration of justice for the court to take into account to the extent that it chooses to do so.

19–096   Where a party is not *bound* to assert public interest immunity and, during the course of litigation, accidentally discloses to the other side material in relation to which he is *entitled* to assert immunity, the Court of Appeal has said that the principles applicable to any application to restrain further use of the material are the same as in the case of the accidental disclosure of privileged material.[162]

---

[159] See Lord Woolf's observations in *R. v Chief Constable of West Midlands Police Ex p. Wiley* [1995] 1 A.C. 274 at 297.

[160] *R. v Chief Constable of West Midlands Police Ex p. Wiley* [1995] 1 A.C. 274 at 297–298. In *Evans v Chief Constable of Surrey* [1988] 1 Q.B. 588, the Chief Constable was not entitled to waive the immunity attaching to a report relating to a murder suspect sent by him to the Director of Public Prosecutions in the face of objection made by the Attorney General.

[161] [1995] 1 W.L.R. 488 at 495. See also Ganz, "Matrix Churchill and Public Interest Immunity: A Postcript" (1995) 58 M.L.R. 417.

[162] *Fayed v Metropolitan Police Commissioner* [2002] EWCA Civ 780 at [17]; *R. v G* [2004] EWCA Crim 1368; [2004] 1 W.L.R. 2932 at [15].

CHAPTER 20

Methods of Partial Protection

RESTRICTIONS ON THE MANNER IN WHICH CONFIDENTIAL INFORMATION IS DISCLOSED OR FURTHER DISSEMINATED

The courts may give at least partial protection to the confidentiality of information in the course of litigation by ordering special restrictions on the circumstances and manner of its disclosure or further dissemination. These restrictions, which may be of a general nature or fashioned to meet the needs of particularly sensitive cases (for example, cases concerning trade secrets and children[1]), fall into two broad categories:

20–001

(1)   restrictions operating during the process of disclosure;
(2)   restrictions operating during and after hearings.

CONTROLS ON THE FORM OF DISCLOSURE

The earlier authorities on this topic were reviewed by the Court of Appeal in *Warner-Lambert Co v Glaxo Laboratories Ltd*[2] Buckley L.J. concluded[3]:

20–002

> "None of these cases purports to lay down a form of order suitable for universal use. Nor, I think, does any of them indicate that the court might not in appropriate circumstances at a later stage in the action have directed disclosure to a wider class of persons or on different terms. In my judgment, the court must in each case decide what measure of disclosure should be made, and to whom, and upon what terms, having regard to the particular circumstances of the case, bearing in mind that, if a case for disclosure is made out, the applicant should have as full a degree of appropriate disclosure as will be consistent with adequate protection of any trade secret of the respondent."

One possible control is to impose a restriction on the persons allowed to carry out inspection. In some circumstances, only a party's solicitors and a specified person or persons will be permitted to inspect documents, and then only on an undertaking not to disclose their content to any other persons. The specified

---

[1]   In relation to children, see Ch.21.

[2]   [1975] R.P.C. 354.

[3]   [1975] R.P.C. 354 at 358.

person may sometimes be an independent expert,[4] but often inspection will need to be made by a person more familiar with the business of the parties.[5] Before agreeing to any restrictions that would prevent their legal representatives from communicating fully with them, parties should consider the difficulties that might arise as a result.[6]

Disclosure restrictions of this kind are generally only interim measures and are unlikely to apply during the trial itself (if and when one takes place). In *Al Rawi v Security Service*,[7] Lord Dyson observed of intellectual property proceedings:

> "It is commonplace to deal with the issue of disclosure by establishing 'confidentiality rings' of persons who may see certain confidential material which is withheld from one or more of the parties to the litigation at least in its initial stages. Such claims by their very nature raise special problems which require exceptional solutions. I am not aware of a case in which a court has approved a trial of such a case proceeding in circumstances where one party was denied access to evidence which was being relied on at the trial by the other party."

In *McKillen v Misland (Cyprus) Investments Ltd*[8] the claimant's financial means were relevant to his claim for damages, but were alleged by him to be confidential. A confidentiality regime was instituted at the disclosure stage, but the claimant failed to obtain an order that the regime should extend through to the trial itself. David Richards J. held[9] that:

> "In the light of the decision and discussion in *Al Rawi*, it is my view that at common law the court has no jurisdiction to deny a party access to the evidence at trial. But if the jurisdiction does exist, it is in my judgment so exceptional as to be of largely theoretical interest only."

20–003   Other possible controls include orders as to where the documents are to be inspected and stored, provision for the attendance at inspection of a representative of the party giving discovery, and restrictions on the making of copies or notes.

20–004   In deciding what condition to impose, the court may take into account its view of such factors as the susceptibility of the confidential information to memorisation.[10] The court may also take judicial notice of the standing of the party seeking discovery, if it is, for example, a reputable and well-known company.[11]

---

[4] As in *Helitune Ltd v Stewart Hughes Ltd* [1994] F.S.R. 422 at 430 to 432.

[5] See, e.g. *Atari Incorporated v Philips Electronics and Associated Industries Ltd* [1988] F.S.R. 416; *Format Communications MFG Ltd v ITT (United Kingdom) Ltd* [1983] F.S.R. 473, CA; *Centri-Spray Corporation v Cera International Ltd* [1979] F.S.R. 175.

[6] The Court of Appeal discussed some of these, in another context, in *R. v G* [2004] EWCA Crim. 1368; [2004] 1 W.L.R. 2932. See also the Court of Appeal's consideration of the effect of "confidentiality clubs" in *Lilly Icos Ltd v Pfizer Ltd (No.2)* [2002] EWCA Civ 2; [2002] 1 W.L.R. 2253.

[7] [2012] 1 A.C. 531 at [64].

[8] [2012] EWHC 1158 (Ch).

[9] At [50].

[10] *Centri-Spray Corp v Cera International Ltd* [1979] F.S.R. 175 at 180–181.

[11] *Format Communications MFG Ltd v ITT (United Kingdom) Ltd* [1983] F.S.R. 473 at 486.

A failure to observe disclosure restrictions imposed by the court may result in proceedings for contempt.[12]

20–005

RESTRICTIONS OPERATING DURING AND AFTER HEARINGS

The starting-point for any litigant who is contemplating an application for restrictions on the publication of information relating to the litigation is now the guidance issued by Lord Neuberger M.R. in *Practice Guidance on Interim Non-disclosure Orders*.[13] The guidance includes a model order and covers such topics as anonymity orders, non-party access to court documents, "super-injunctions" and hearings in private. Some of these measures are further considered individually below.

20–006

The general rule

As Lord Neuberger MR said in *Practice Guidance (Interim Non-Disclosure Orders)*,[14] "Open justice is a fundamental principle. The general rule is that hearings are carried out in, and judgments and orders are, public." This rule covers not only final determinations on the merits but also procedural hearings of the kind that were described, prior to the introduction of the CPR, as "hearings in chambers". The common law and statutory background to the rule was set out by Mance L.J. in *Department of Economics, Policy and Development of the City of Moscow v Bankers Trust Co.*[15] The rule is a universal feature of common law jurisdictions.[16] It also accords with Art.6(1) of the European Convention on Human Rights, which entitles litigants to a fair and *public* hearing in the determination of their civil rights.[17]

20–007

An exception: the court's parental jurisdiction

Different considerations apply when the court is exercising what might be termed a parental jurisdiction. As the Law Commission of New Zealand said in its report on Access to Court Records[18]:

20–008

> "There seem to be good reasons for non-disclosure to the public of sensitive, personal information in family law and mental health and disability cases. In both

---

[12] See, for example, *Re a Solicitor (Disclosure of Confidential Records)* [1997] 1 F.L.R. 101.

[13] [2012] 1 W.L.R. 1003.

[14] [2012] 1 W.L.R. 1003 at [9]; CPR 39.2(1) also provides that the general rule is that court hearings are to be in public.

[15] [2004] EWCA Civ 314; [2005] Q.B. 207 at [11]–[25].

[16] Toulson L.J. carried out a brief survey of the position in Canada, New Zealand, South Africa and the USA in *R. (Guardian News and Media Ltd) v City of Westminster Magistrates' Court* [2012] EWCA Civ 420; [2012] CP Rep. 30 at [54]–[67].

[17] Though, generally speaking, interim proceedings of an interlocutory nature do not engage Art.6: *APIS v Slovakia* (2000) 29 E.H.R.R. CD 105.

[18] (2006) N.Z.L.C. R93 at [2.37]; cited by the Court of Appeal in *R. (Guardian News and Media Ltd) v City of Westminster Magistrates' Court* [2012] EWCA Civ 420; [2012] CP Rep. 30, per Toulson L.J. at [86].

instances, the need to protect personal information from painful and humiliating disclosure may found an exception to the open justice principle. The rationale for protecting such information, especially relating to vulnerable people like children, battered spouses, the mentally disabled, or the elderly and infirm, where there seems no obvious public-interest reason in publicity, still holds."

The particular case of children is dealt with in Ch.21 below but the Court of Protection, which was created by the Mental Capacity Act 2005, serves more generally to assist those who, for whatever reason, lack the capacity to make decisions themselves. Rule 90 of the Court of Protection Rules 2007 provides that the general rule is that hearings are to be in private. However, rules 90 to 92 expressly allow: (i) for granting permission to any person or class of persons to attend a hearing, (ii) for authorising the publication of information relating to proceedings in the court, and/or (iii) for orders that all or part of a hearing should take place in public.

20–009   As the Court of Appeal explained in *Independent News and Media Ltd v A*,[19] a two-stage process is required in considering an application for an order of this kind. The court first decides whether there is "good reason" to make such an order; if there is, the second stage is to decide whether the requisite balancing exercise justifies the making of the order.[20]

When a judge directs that a hearing in the Court of Protection should be held in public, the judge may impose restrictions on reports and publication of information about the proceedings. In *In re M (A Patient) (Court of Protection: Reporting Restrictions)*[21] Baker J. gave guidance as to the procedure to be followed on applications for such restrictions. He emphasised[22] that:

> "Decisions on the conduct of the balancing exercise between competing Convention rights in celebrity cases are unlikely to be of any relevance to decisions in the Court of Protection or vice versa."

Hearings in private

20–010   Exceptionally a party wishing to protect confidential material may seek an order restricting public attendance at proceedings that would normally be held in open court. CPR 39.2(3) provides that:

> "A hearing, or any part of it, may be in private if-
>
> (a)   publicity would defeat the object of the hearing;
> (b)   it involves matters relating to national security;
> (c)   it involves confidential information (including information relating to personal financial matters) and publicity would damage that confidentiality;
> (d)   a private hearing is necessary to protect the interests of any child or patient;
> (e)   it is a hearing of an application made without notice and it would be unjust to any respondent for there to be a public hearing;

---

[19] [2010] EWCA Civ 343; [2010] 1 W.L.R. 2262 at [11].
[20] See also the decision of the Court of Appeal in *P v Independent Print Ltd* [2011] EWCA Civ 756 and, in relation to the identification of parties to proceedings in the Court of Protection, the decision of Baker J. in *G v E* [2010] EWHC 2042 (Fam).
[21] [2011] EWHC 1197 (Fam); [2012] 1 W.L.R. 287.
[22] At [44].

(f)   it involves uncontentious matters arising in the administration of trusts or in the administration of a deceased person's estate; or

(g)   the court considers this to be necessary, in the interests of justice."

This part of the rule also accords with Art.6(1) of the European Convention on Human Rights,[23] which provides that:

" . . . the press and public may be excluded from all or part of the trial in the interest of morals, public order or national security in a democratic society, where the interests of juveniles or the protection of the private life of the parties so require, or to the extent strictly necessary in the opinion of the court in special circumstances where publicity would prejudice the interests of justice."

The courts are generally reluctant to allow hearings to take place in private, for reasons that were set out by the House of Lords in *Scott v Scott*.[24] Lord Shaw of Dunfermline cited among various passages from the works of Bentham: **20–011**

"Publicity is the very soul of justice. It is the keenest spur to exertion and the surest of all guards against improbity. It keeps the judge himself, while trying, under trial."[25]

In *R. (Guardian News and Media Ltd) v City of Westminster Magistrates' Court*,[26] Toulson L.J. observed that:

"The purpose is not simply to deter impropriety or sloppiness by the judge hearing the case. It is wider. It is to enable the public to understand and scrutinise the justice system of which the courts are the administrators."

Scott v Scott was considered by the Court of Appeal in *R. v Chief Registrar of Friendly Societies Ex p. New Cross Building Society*.[27] Sir John Donaldson M.R., with whom Griffiths and Slade L.JJ. on this point expressly indicated their agreement, said[28]:   **20–012**

"The guidance which I get from their Lordships' speeches can be summarised as follows. The general rule that the courts shall conduct their proceedings in public is but an aid, albeit a very important aid, to the achievement of the paramount object of the courts which is to do justice in accordance with the law. It is only if, in wholly exceptional circumstances, the presence of the public or public knowledge of the proceedings is likely to defeat that paramount object that the courts are justified in proceeding in camera. These circumstances are incapable of definition. Each application for privacy must be considered on its merits, but the applicant must satisfy the court that nothing short of total privacy will enable justice to be done. It is not sufficient that a public hearing will create embarrassment for some or all of those concerned. It must be shown that a public hearing is likely to lead, directly or indirectly, to a denial of justice."

---

[23] As was held by the Divisional Court in *R. (Pelling) v Bow County Court* [2001] U.K.H.R.R. 165.

[24] [1913] A.C. 417.

[25] *Benthamia, or Select Extracts from the works of Jeremy Bentham* (1843) p.115.

[26] [2012] CP Rep. 30 at [79].

[27] [1984] 1 Q.B. 227.

[28] [1984] 1 Q.B. 227 at 235.

In the case before it, a judicial review of the Chief Registrar's adverse decision as to the suitability of a building society to continue to be a repository of trust funds and to accept moneys for investment, the Court of Appeal considered that publicity during the first instance hearing and subsequent appeal would have resulted in a loss of public confidence such that the society would have had to close even if it had proved successful (which, in the event, it did not). The hearings had therefore been rightly held *in camera*.

The obligation to justify any departure from the principle of open justice on the basis of the facts of the individual case was also emphasised by Lord Neuberger MR in *Practice Guidance (Interim Non-Disclosure Orders)*[29]:

> "There is no general exception to open justice where privacy or confidentiality is in issue. Applications will only be heard in private if and to the extent that the court is satisfied that by nothing short of the exclusion of the public can justice be done. Exclusions must be no more than the minimum strictly necessary to ensure justice is done and parties are expected to consider before applying for such an exclusion whether something short of exclusion can meet their concerns, as will normally be the case…"

20–013   Thus the court will reduce to a minimum the length of time spent in private,[30] or (preferably) arrangements may be made between the parties so that it is unnecessary for the public to be excluded at all.[31]

It is a question of fact whether a hearing has taken place in public or in private. The practical significance of the manner in which a matter has been listed to be heard was discussed by Floyd J. in *North Shore Ventures Ltd v Anstead Holdings Plc*.[32]

Anonymity orders and other restrictions on publication

20–014   It does not follow from the mere fact that proceedings are held in private under CPR 39.2(3) that the publication of information relating to them will be a contempt of court. Section 12 of the Administration of Justice Act 1960 is to the opposite effect.[33] The question whether the public is to be excluded from a hearing and the question whether subsequent publication of information relating to the hearing is to be embargoed are two different questions and require to be treated separately.[34]

In *Axel Springer AG v Germany*,[35] the European Court of Human Rights held that the applicant media company's Art.10 rights had been infringed by injunctions which prevented it from reporting on the arrest and conviction of a

---

[29] [2012] 1 W.L.R. 1003 at [12].

[30] For example, only while details of some secret chemical process are revealed: *Badische Anilin und Soda Fabrik v Levinstein* [1883] 24 Ch.D. 156.

[31] *Andrew v Raeburn* (1874) 9 Ch.App. 522: privacy not required since it was unnecessary to read out the contents of the confidential letters concerned. See also *Ambrosiadou v Coward* [2011] EWCA Civ 409; [2011] E.M.L.R. 21 at [50]–[54].

[32] [2011] EWHC 910 (QB); [2011] 1 W.L.R. 2265, especially at [22].

[33] *AF Noonan (Architectural Practice) Ltd v Bournemouth and Boscombe Athletic Community Football Club Ltd* [2007] EWCA Civ 848; [2007] 1 W.L.R. 2614.

[34] *AF Noonan (Architectural Practice) Ltd v Bournemouth and Boscombe Athletic Community Football Club Ltd* [2007] EWCA Civ 848 per Buxton L.J. at [14].

[35] [2012] E.M.L.R. 15.

well-known actor for a drugs-related offence. Referring to the press's duty to impart information and ideas on matters of public interest, the Court added that:

"This duty extends to the reporting and commenting on court proceedings which, provided that they do not overstep the bounds set out above, contribute to their publicity and are thus consonant with the requirement under art.6(1) of the Convention that hearings be public. It is inconceivable that there can be no prior or contemporaneous discussion of the subject matter of trials, be it in specialised journals, in the general press or amongst the public at large. Not only do the media have the task of imparting such information and ideas; the public also has a right to receive them . . ."[36]

Subsection 4(2) of the Contempt of Court Act 1981 empowers the court to order that the publication of any part of the proceedings before it be postponed, in order to avoid a risk of prejudice to the administration of justice in any proceedings,[37] while s.11 of the Act permits a court to give directions prohibiting the publication of a name or other matter which it allows to be withheld from the public in proceedings before it.[38] The distinction between the two provisions was discussed in *Times Newspapers Ltd v R*,[39] in which the Court of Appeal also held that an earlier reference to a matter in open court did not prevent a court from making an order in respect of that matter under s.11: "There is a world of difference between what is said in open court and what is published, and the CCA is concerned with the latter."

CPR 39.2(4) provides that the court may order that the identity of any party or witness must not be disclosed if it considers non-disclosure necessary in order to protect the interests of that party or witness.

Quite apart from s.11 of the Contempt of Court Act 1981 or CPR 39.2(4), the court has an inherent jurisdiction both to direct that the identity of a person involved in court proceedings should not be disclosed[40] and to restrain the media from publishing that person's identity.[41] A restriction which relates only to the identity of a witness or a party is less objectionable than a restriction which involves proceedings being conducted in whole or in part behind closed doors.[42]

Many recent decisions have addressed applications by litigants for anonymity orders. In *H v News Group Newspapers Ltd*,[43] the Court of Appeal identified ten

20–015

---

[36] At [80].

[37] The court's three-stage approach to an application for an order under s.4 was set out by Lord Judge C.J., giving the judgment of the Court of Appeal in *Re MGN Ltd's application* [2011] 1 Cr. App. R. 31 at [15].

[38] s.159 of the Criminal Justice Act 1988 provides a statutory right of appeal against orders made under s.4 or s.11 of the Contempt of Court Act 1981 in respect of criminal trials on indictment.

[39] [2007] EWCA Crim 1925; [2008] 1 W.L.R. 234.

[40] *Aziz v Aziz* [2007] EWCA Civ 712; [2008] 2 All E.R. 501, per Lawrence Collins L.J. at [108].

[41] In *re Guardian News and Media Ltd* [2010] UKSC 1; [2010] 2 A.C. 697 at [30] to [31]. The Supreme Court did not have cited to it the decision in *Independent Publishing Co Ltd v Attorney General of Trinidad and Tobago* [2005] 1 A.C. 190, in which the Privy Council had held that a criminal court had no common law power to make an order postponing the publication of a report of proceedings conducted in open court (the power granted by s.4 of the Contempt of Court Act 1981). See also In *re Trinity Mirror Plc* [2008] Q.B. 770 at [22].

[42] *R. v Legal Aid Board, Ex p. Kaim Todner* [1999] QB 966, per Lord Woolf M.R. at 978; cited by Lawrence Collins L.J. in *Aziz v Aziz* [2007] EWCA Civ 712; [2008] 2 All E.R. 501 at [110].

[43] *(Practice Note)* [2011] EWCA Civ 42; [2011] 1 W.L.R. 1645 at [21]. The first nine principles apply also to claimants seeking a dispensation from the requirement to include their name and address

principles generally applicable in cases where the protection sought by the claimant is an anonymity order or other restraint on publication of details of a case which are normally in the public domain:

> "(1) The general rule is that the names of the parties to an action are included in orders and judgments of the court. (2) There is no general exception for cases where private matters are in issue. (3) An order for anonymity or any other order restraining the publication of the normally reportable details of a case is a derogation from the principle of open justice and an interference with the article 10 rights of the public at large. (4) Accordingly, where the court is asked to make any such order, it should only do so after closely scrutinising the application, and considering whether a degree of restraint on publication is necessary, and, if it is, whether there is any less restrictive or more acceptable alternative than that which is sought. (5) Where the court is asked to restrain the publication of the names of the parties and/or the subject matter of the claim, on the ground that such restraint is necessary under article 8 , the question is whether there is sufficient general, public interest in publishing a report of the proceedings which identifies a party and/or the normally reportable details to justify any resulting curtailment of his right and his family's right to respect for their private and family life. (6) On any such application, no special treatment should be accorded to public figures or celebrities: in principle, they are entitled to the same protection as others, no more and no less. (7) An order for anonymity or for reporting restrictions should not be made simply because the parties consent: parties cannot waive the rights of the public. (8) An anonymity order or any other order restraining publication made by a judge at an interlocutory stage of an injunction application does not last for the duration of the proceedings but must be reviewed at the return date. (9) Whether or not an anonymity order or an order restraining publication of normally reportable details is made, then, at least where a judgment is or would normally be given, a publicly available judgment should normally be given, and a copy of the consequential court order should also be publicly available, although some editing of the judgment or order may be necessary. (10) Notice of any hearing should be given to the defendant unless there is a good reason not to do so, in which case the court should be told of the absence of notice and the reason for it, and should be satisfied that the reason is a good one."

20–016   In many cases, a witness may have a stronger claim to anonymity than either of the parties to the litigation. In *R. v Legal Aid Board, Ex p. Kaim Todner*,[44] Lord Woolf M.R. observed that:

> "A distinction can also be made depending on whether what is being sought is anonymity for a plaintiff, a defendant or a third party. It is not unreasonable to regard the person who initiates the proceedings as having accepted the normal incidence of the public nature of court proceedings. If you are a defendant you may have an interest equal to that of the plaintiff in the outcome of the proceedings but you have not chosen to initiate court proceedings which are normally conducted in public. A witness who has no interest in the proceedings has the strongest claim to be protected by the court if he or she will be prejudiced by publicity, since the courts and parties may depend on their co-operation. In general, however, parties

---

on the face of their claim form: *CVB v MGN Ltd* [2012] EWHC 1148 (QB) (Tugendhat J.). Guidance to employment tribunals considering an application for anonymisation was provided by the Employment Appeal Tribunal in *F v G* [2012] I.C.R. 246. See also *Practice Guidance (Interim Non-Disclosure Orders)* [2012] 1 W.L.R. 1003.

[44] [1999] Q.B. 966, per Lord Woolf M.R. at 978; cited by Lawrence Collins L.J. in *Aziz v Aziz* [2007] EWCA Civ 712; [2008] 2 All E.R. 501 at [110].

and witnesses have to accept the embarrassment and damage to their reputation and the possible consequential loss which can be inherent in being involved in litigation."

On the other hand, much will depend on the nature of the litigation in relation to which an anonymity order is sought. In care proceedings, for example, there is a strong public interest militating against the anonymity of expert and other witnesses on the basis of whose evidence the family courts make decisions of great public importance.[45]

In *Gray v UVW*,[46] Tugendhat J. observed that cases involving an element of **20–017** blackmail or attempted blackmail may justify the anonymity of a claimant for the purpose of preventing crime. In *JXF v York Hospitals NHS Trust*[47] Tugendhat J. also ordered anonymity in relation to a hearing for the purpose of approving a large-scale settlement reached on behalf of a minor, on the basis that "If the naming of a claimant will make him vulnerable to losing the money to fortune hunters or thieves, then it follows that the purpose of the approval hearing will be defeated." In *CDE v MGN Ltd*,[48] Eady J. held, in granting anonymisation, that the Art.8 rights of both the claimant's family and the defendant's family were of considerable importance. In *Goodwin v News Group Newspapers Ltd*[49] the claimant had conducted an affair with a female employee of RBS at a time when he had been RBS's chief executive. Tugendhat J. held that the employee's anonymity should be maintained, even though her job description and the fact of her affair with the claimant could be published: the function of anonymity in those circumstances was not protection of confidential information, but protection from intrusion.

In *H v News Group Newspapers Ltd*[50] the Court of Appeal observed that there was often a trade-off between, on the one hand, revealing or concealing the identity of a litigant and, on the other hand, revealing or concealing details of the private information for which protection was sought. Each case turned on its own facts but, on the facts of the case before the court, anonymisation represented the better alternative.

---

[45] See *A v Ward* [2010] EWHC 16 (Fam); [2010] 1 F.L.R. 1497 in which Munby J. refused applications for anonymity orders which had been made by expert witnesses, social workers and clinicians, and In *Re X (Children) (Morgan and others intervening)* [2011] EWHC 1157 (Fam); [2012] 1 W.L.R. 182, per Sir Nicholas Wall P. at [75]–[85].

[46] [2010] EWHC 2367 (QB). See also Tugendhat J.'s comments in *EWQ v GFD* [2012] EWHC 2182 (QB) at [96] ff, and in *SKA v CRH* [2012] EWHC 766 (QB); a final judgment in the latter case was given by Nicola Davies J., [2012] EWHC 2236 (QB). See further at para.7–048 above.

[47] [2010] EWHC 2800 (QB). An order under s.39 of the Children and Young Persons Act 1933 may be a more acceptable alternative to an anonymity order in such circumstances: *A (A Child) v Cambridge University Hospital NHS Foundation Trust*[2011] EWHC 454 (QB); [2011] EM.L.R. 18, per Tugendhat J. at [14].

[48] [2010] EWHC 3308 (QB); cited by Tugendhat J. in *TSE v News Group Newspapers Ltd* [2011] EWHC 1308 (QB) at [23].

[49] [2011] EWHC 1437 (QB); [2011] E.M.L.R. 27.

[50] [2011] EWCA Civ 42; [2011] 1 W.L.R. 1645.

If a judgment is appropriately to be anonymised, the process of redaction may extend beyond the names of the parties and witnesses involved to include such matters as dates and locations. However, the falsification of detail is not permissible.[51]

A court which grants interim injunctive relief may in extreme cases grant ancillary injunctive relief which prevents the media or other third parties from reporting even the fact that the injunction has been sought and obtained. In *Donald v Ntuli*,[52] the Court of Appeal held that further relief of this kind should not be granted unless it was strictly necessary in the interests of justice.

Access to court records

20–018   Although CPR 5.4A to 5.4D establish procedures for the supply of documents from court records in civil proceedings, the courts' jurisdiction to control such matters in the interests of open justice is inherent.[53] That jurisdiction is particularly important in circumstances where the practice of providing documents for the judge's consideration without reading them fully in open court has become increasingly prevalent.[54]

In *R (Guardian News and Media Ltd) v City of Westminster Magistrates' Court*[55] Toulson L.J. (with whom Hooper L.J. and Lord Neuberger M.R. agreed) held that:

> "In a case where documents have been placed before a judge and referred to in the course of proceedings, in my judgment the default position should be that access should be permitted on the open justice principle; and where access is sought for a proper journalistic purpose, the case for allowing it will be particularly strong. However, there may be countervailing reasons. ... I do not think that it is sensible or practical to look for a standard formula for determining how strong the grounds of opposition need to be in order to outweigh the merits of the application. The court has to carry out a proportionality exercise which will be fact-specific. Central to the court's evaluation will be the purpose of the open justice principle, the potential value of the material in advancing that purpose and, conversely, any risk of harm which access to the documents may cause to the legitimate interests of others."

---

[51] *Lykiardopulo v Lykiardopulo* [2010] EWCA Civ 1315, per Thorpe L.J. at [51] and Stanley Burnton L.J. at [83].

[52] [2010] EWCA Civ 1276; [2011] 1 W.L.R. 294; see also the guidance provided by Lord Neuberger M.R. in *H v News Group Newspapers Ltd (Practice Note)* [2011] 1 W.L.R. 1645 at [15].

[53] *R. (Guardian News and Media Ltd) v City of Westminster Magistrates' Court* [2012] EWCA Civ 420; [2012] C.P. Rep. 30, per Toulson L.J. at [69].

[54] *R. (Guardian News and Media Ltd) v City of Westminster Magistrates' Court* [2012] EWCA Civ 420; [2012] C.P. Rep. 30 (a case in fact relating to criminal law procedures), per Toulson L.J at [76]–[77].

[55] [2012] EWCA Civ 420; [2012] C.P. Rep. 30 at [85]. In *Sayers v Smithkline Beecham Plc* [2007] EWHC 1346 (QB) at [21], Keith J. drew a distinction between (i) documents which have been read or been treated as having been read in open court and (ii) documents which, though filed, have never been read or been treated as having been read by the judge.

Exclusion of confidential material from judgments

The giving of public judgments is an important aspect of open justice, even— or perhaps especially— in relation to hearings which have taken place in private.[56] However, it is possible for a court dealing with confidential material in its judgment to confine its discussion of that material to a confidential annexe, not published alongside the public part of the judgment. **20–019**

In *Cream Holdings Ltd v Banerjee*[57] the House of Lords discharged an interim injunction restraining a newspaper from publishing confidential information which the newspaper argued should be published in the public interest. Lord Nicholls said[58]:

> "Even if the House discharges the restraint order made by the judge, it would not be right for your Lordships to make public the information in question. The contents of your Lordships' speeches should not pre-empt the 'Echo's' publication, if that is what the newspaper decides now to do. Nor should these speeches, by themselves placing this information in the public domain, undermine any remedy in damages the Cream group may ultimately be found to have against the 'Echo' or Ms Banerjee in respect of matters the Echo may decide to publish."

In *Browne v Associated Newspapers Ltd*,[59] the Court of Appeal held that Lord Nicholls's guidance remained applicable, notwithstanding the fact that the claimant had lied to the court about some of the confidential material in question.

RESTRICTIONS ON THE COLLATERAL USE OF INFORMATION PROVIDED FOR THE PURPOSES OF LITIGATION

CPR 31 deals with disclosure and inspection of documents. CPR 31.22 provides that: **20–020**

"(1) A party to whom a document has been disclosed may use the document only for the purpose of the proceedings in which it is disclosed, except where—
    (a) the document has been read to or by the court, or referred to, at a hearing which has been held in public;
    (b) the court gives permission; or
    (c) the party who disclosed the document and the person to whom the document belongs agree.
(2) The court may make an order restricting or prohibiting the use of a document which has been disclosed, even where the document has been read to or by the court, or referred to, at a hearing which has been held in public.
(3) An application for such an order may be made-
    (a) by a party; or
    (b) by any person to whom the document belongs.

---

[56] *Department of Economics, Policy and Development of the City of Moscow and Another v Bankers Trust Co and Another* [2004] EWCA Civ 314; [2005] Q.B. 207, per Mance L.J. at [39]; *Kazeminy v Siddiqi* [2010] EWHC 201 (Comm) at [40]–[44] per Teare J.

[57] [2005] 1 A.C. 253.

[58] At [26].

[59] [2008] Q.B. 103 at [66]–[87].

(4)   For the purpose of this rule, an Electronic Documents Questionnaire which has been completed and served by another party pursuant to Practice Direction 31B is to be treated as if it is a document which has been disclosed."

20–021   CPR 32 deals with witness statements. CPR 32.12 provides that:

"(1)   Except as provided by this rule, a witness statement may be used only for the purpose of the proceedings in which it is served.

(2)   Paragraph (1) does not apply if and to the extent that—

(a)   the witness gives consent in writing to some other use of it;

(b)   the court gives permission for some other use; or

(c)   the witness statement has been put in evidence at a hearing held in public."

20–022   CPR 18 deals with requests and orders for a party to provide further information to another. CPR 18.2 provides that:

"The court may direct that information provided by a party to another party (whether given voluntarily or following an order made under rule 18.1) must not be used for any purpose except for that of the proceedings in which it is given."

Prior to the introduction of these rules, the recipients of information as the result of compulsory disclosure during the litigation process were bound at common law by an implied undertaking to the court not to use that information for any "ulterior or collateral purpose".[60] The implied undertaking was in reality an obligation imposed by operation of law by virtue of the circumstances in which the document or information was obtained.[61]

In *SmithKline Beecham Plc v Generics (UK) Ltd*,[62] the Court of Appeal accepted the submission that CPR 31.22 represented a complete code in relation to disclosed documents and, implicitly, that the previous implied undertaking to the court had been superseded. However, an implied undertaking may still arise where one litigant is required by the court to provide information to another under some form of compulsion other than the court's powers under CPR Pt 31. In *Shire Pharmaceutical Contracts Ltd v Mount Sinai School of Medicine of New York University*[63] the claimant was ordered in the course of patent proceedings to provide experimental samples to the defendant (the parties agreeing that the court had jurisdiction to make such an order, whether under CPR Pt 25 or otherwise). H.H.J. Birss QC observed that the CPR provided no express restriction governing subsequent use of the samples provided, but held that the defendant came under an implied obligation at law not to make collateral use of them without the permission of the court. (In the event, H.H.J. Birss QC held that the defendant should nevertheless be permitted to use the samples for the purpose of parallel proceedings between the parties which had been commenced before the European Patent Office.)

---

[60] *Alterskye v Scott* [1948] 1 All E.R. 469.

[61] Per Hobhouse J. in *Prudential Assurance Co Ltd v Fountain Page* [1991] 1 W.L.R. 756, at 764. See also *Standard Life Assurance Ltd v Topland Col Ltd* [2011] 1 W.L.R. 2162, per Warren J. at [53].

[62] [2003] EWCA Civ 1109; [2004] 1 W.L.R. 1479, per Aldous L.J. at [28] and [29].

[63] [2011] EWHC 3492 (Pat), [2012] F.S.R. 18.

The concept of an implied undertaking to the court does not apply to the compulsory provision of information outside the litigation process, although the discloser may well be able in such circumstances to assert private law rights of confidentiality or privacy.[64]

A primary rationale for the existence of an implied undertaking[65] lay in the compulsory nature of disclosure under the litigation process, but the distinction between voluntary and involuntary disclosure proved problematic, especially where disclosure by one party was occasioned by a step taken by his opponent.[66] The Court of Appeal revisited the suggested distinction in *SmithKline Beecham v Generics (UK) Ltd*[67] and held that it did not affect the applicability of CPR 31.22 (although it might well be of relevance to the exercise of the court's discretion under CPR 31.22). The Court pointed out that "disclosure" was defined in CPR 31.2 in broad terms ("A party discloses a document by stating that the document exists or has existed") and concluded that this was determinative. Accordingly, a document referred to by a party in a witness statement had been "disclosed" for the purposes of CPR 31.22, even though it might be said that that party had chosen voluntarily to reveal the existence of the document.   **20–023**

The Court of Appeal's broadening of the protection afforded by CPR 31.22 accords with the increased importance attached to the public interest in encouraging co-operation between the parties to litigation. A narrower approach might well constitute a disincentive to such co-operation (for example, by discouraging the voluntary disclosure of documents before it is formally required by the rules).   **20–024**

It also appears that the applicability of CPR 31.22 does not depend upon the confidentiality of the documents in question (though their confidentiality will be relevant to the exercise of the court's discretion under CPR 31.22). As the Court of Appeal observed in *Lilly Icos Ltd v Pfizer Ltd*[68]:   **20–025**

> "It may be mentioned that we have described the issue as one of confidentiality, and we will for convenience continue to describe it as such. However, it will be seen from CPR 31.22 that the basic prohibition in relation to disclosed documents is in terms of their *use* . A breach of that prohibition, such as in a patent case the use by the opponent of processes disclosed by the patentee, might not involve anything that would usually be characterised as a breach of *confidence*."

The rule thereby maintains the reasoning of the House of Lords in *Harman v Secretary of State for the Home Department*,[69] in which the House of Lords held that a solicitor who allowed a journalist to have access to documents obtained on

---

[64] *Standard Life Assurance Ltd v Topland Col Ltd* [2011] 1 W.L.R. 2162.

[65] As described by Megaw L.J. in *Halcon International Inc v The Shell Transport and Trading Co* [1979] R.P.C. 97 at 121.

[66] See the contrasting approaches adopted by Sir Nicholas Browne-Wilkinson in *Derby & Co Ltd v Weldon (No.2), The Times*, October 20, 1988; 132 S.J. 1755, and by Hugh Laddie QC in *Lubrizol Corp v Esso Petroleum Co Ltd (No.2)* [1993] F.S.R. 53. See too the test proposed by Hobhouse J. in *Prudential Assurance Co Ltd v Fountain Page Ltd* [1991] 1 W.L.R. 756 at 765.

[67] Especially at [29].

[68] [2002] EWCA Civ 2; [2002] 1 W.L.R. 2253 at [4].

[69] [1983] 1 A.C. 280. Following a compromise of Ms Harman's case before the European Court of Human Rights, RSC Ord.24, r.14A (the predecessor of CPR 31.22) was introduced.

discovery from the Home Office was in contempt of court, even though the documents had by then been read out in open court and had thereby entered the public domain.

20–026   In *EMI Records Ltd v Spillane*[70] Sir Nicolas Browne-Wilkinson V.C. held that the implied undertaking was not an absolute undertaking not to use the documents or permit their use for purposes other than the action in which discovery is given, but was an undertaking not without the consent of the party who gave discovery so to do. The effect of his decision has been preserved by the exception contained in CPR 31.22(1)(c). The addition, under that exception, of the *owner* of a disclosed document as a person entitled to object to its collateral use goes some way towards protecting the position of interested third parties but (as will be seen below) falls short of the protection that might be afforded under the general law of confidence.

20–027   The introduction of the CPR did not remove the question whether a private law duty of confidentiality is owed by a person obtaining disclosure of confidential information in the course of litigation.[71] In *Derby & Co Ltd v Weldon (No.2)*,[72] Sir Nicholas Browne-Wilkinson V.C. said:

> "I have the greatest doubts whether such a separate duty of confidence can exist . . . But even assuming (contrary to my inclination) that there is such a separate duty of confidence, such duty can only be implied from the circumstances of the case. Such private duty of confidence cannot, in my judgment, be wider than that imposed by the implied undertaking."

20–028   In *Prudential Assurance Co Ltd v Fountain Page Ltd*[73] Hobhouse J. observed that the implied undertaking was independent of any question of confidentiality. He cited *Derby & Co Ltd v Weldon (No.2)* and stated[74]:

> "It is clear that where documents are produced in the course of legal proceedings, or information provided, the further use of that material must be governed by the legal principles or rules of court which relate to the use of such material and not by any private law rights. It is of course an *a fortiori* position where there were no antecedent private law rights in respect of that material; the use of material in litigation cannot itself give rise to that class of right."

Rules of law governing the conduct of proceedings may undoubtedly provide wider protection than, or may qualify, the protection provided by principles of confidentiality; but it is difficult to see why such rules should necessarily oust the protection provided by the law of confidentiality. There are many examples of the law of confidentiality being applied by the courts in cases where documents have been improperly or mistakenly disclosed in the course of litigation.[75]

---

[70] [1986] 1 W.L.R. 967.

[71] Any such private law duty of confidence must be subject to the Court's express power under CPR 31.12 to give permission for disclosed documents to be used for an ulterior purpose: see *British Sky Broadcasting Group Plc v Virgin Media Communications Ltd* [2008] EWCA Civ 612; [2008] 1 W.L.R. 2854 at [21].

[72] *The Times*, October 20, 1988; 132 S.J. 1755.

[73] [1991] 1 W.L.R. 756 at 765.

[74] [1991] 1 W.L.R. 756 at 767.

[75] *Ashburton v Pape* [1913] 2 Ch. 469 and the line of authorities following it. The subject of documents obtained through impropriety or mistake is discussed more fully in Chs 3 and 18.

Ferris J. followed *Derby & Co Ltd v Weldon (No.2)* and *Prudential Assurance Co Ltd v Fountain Page Ltd* in *Apple Corps Ltd v Apple Computer Inc.*[76] In doing so, he was obliged to consider the problematic decision of the Court of Appeal in *Mainwaring v Goldtech Investments Ltd.*[77] In this case the defendants' solicitors had lodged various documents, including privileged papers, with the taxing master following an order for interlocutory costs made in the defendants' favour. The defendants' solicitors subsequently came off the record for the defendants and the taxation was abandoned. The taxing master did not return the papers to the defendants or their former solicitors, but handed them to the master who was in charge of the interlocutory proceedings between the parties.   20–029

The plaintiffs applied for and obtained an order against the defendants for the production of various documents. When the defendants failed to comply with the order for production, the master looked through the documents in his possession and supplied those that fell within the terms of his order to one of the plaintiffs to enable her to take copies.   20–030

The defendants' counterclaim was dismissed when they failed to provide security for the plaintiffs' costs, and judgment was also entered for the plaintiffs in default of defence. The plaintiffs issued a summons seeking an order that the defendants' former solicitors should personally bear the costs of the plaintiffs' actions. The master subsequently permitted the same plaintiff to inspect and to take copies of any of the documents in his possession, notwithstanding representations made on behalf of the defendants' former solicitors.   20–031

In due course, the plaintiffs' application for costs against the defendants' former solicitors was dismissed and the defendants' former solicitors obtained an order from Hoffmann J. restraining the plaintiffs from making further use of the copy documents lodged by them for taxation purposes. One of the plaintiffs appealed from this order.   20–032

The Court of Appeal was of the view that any benefit of privilege in the documents had been lost, bearing in mind the circumstances in which they came into the possession of Miss Mainwaring. However, it also held that the plaintiffs had obtained the taxation documents subject to an obligation of confidentiality owed, not only to the defendants, but also to the defendants' former solicitors, and that Hoffmann J. had exercised his discretion correctly in favour of the solicitors.   20–033

Ferris J. took the view in *Apple Corps Ltd v Apple Computer Inc* that the continuing duty of confidentiality referred to by the Court of Appeal in *Mainwaring* was none other than that embodied in the plaintiffs' implied undertaking to the court. The fact that the Court of Appeal was told by counsel that the application to Hoffmann J. had been an application under RSC Ord.24, r.14A (the precursor of CPR 31.22(2)) supports Ferris J.'s interpretation, but there are two difficulties with it.   20–034

First, the Court of Appeal agreed with Hoffmann J. that the basis of the solicitors' right to keep the documents confidential was their status "as constituting confidential communications between themselves and counsel or themselves and their client, and that, as against the rest of the world, they were   20–035

---

[76] [1992] 1 C.M.L.R. 969. See also per Millett J. in *Bank of Crete S.A. v Koskotas (No.2)* [1992] 1 W.L.R. 919 at 925.
[77] *The Times*, February 19, 1991.

entitled to preserve their confidentiality." Secondly, the authorities referred to by the Court of Appeal—*Marcel v Commissioner of Police of the Metropolis*[78] and *Webster v James Chapman & Co*[79]—suggest that the proper test to be applied, in the court's view, was that applicable to the general law of confidence, rather than that applicable to undertakings impliedly given to the court on discovery.

20–036   In many cases the question whether the recipient of confidential information that has been provided for the purposes of litigation owes any private law duty of confidentiality in respect of that information will be of only academic concern. However, cases will from time to time arise (for example, in relation to documents improperly or mistakenly disclosed or in relation to the rights and obligations of third parties not directly involved in the litigation), in which it will matter.

20–037   Where information of a confidential nature is disclosed in the ordinary course, and for the purpose, of litigation (and, *a fortiori*, where it is disclosed at the recipient's request) the recipient ought to be under a general obligation, either by implied contract or under the equitable doctrine of confidence, or indeed under the recently developed jurisdiction based on privacy, not to use that information for other purposes.

20–038   In the case of arbitration, the voluntary nature of the proceedings has not precluded the courts from recognising such an obligation in relation to disclosed documents; on the contrary, it has caused them to do so.[80]

THIRD PARTIES

20–039   Where confidential information is disclosed for the purposes of litigation by or to a person who is not a party to the litigation, but is either not referred to at a public hearing or is the subject of an order restricting its use (under CPR 31.22), the question may arise whether the third party is entitled to assert, or is subject to, an obligation of confidentiality.

20–040   The issue whether a third party who received confidential documents disclosed on discovery in an action which was settled before trial owed a duty of confidentiality to the party which had produced them arose in *Distillers Co (Biochemicals) Ltd v Times Newspapers Ltd.*[81] In the course of an action for personal injuries brought by users of the drug thalidomide against the pharmaceutical company which had marketed it, the company disclosed on discovery a large number of confidential documents. The claimants' solicitors passed them to a chemist retained by them as an expert witness. The action was settled, but shortly beforehand the expert witness agreed to sell the documents to *The Times*, which later decided to publish an article based on the documents and information provided to them by the expert witness. The pharmaceutical company brought an action against the newspaper claiming that publication of the article would be a misuse of confidential information, relying particularly on

---

[78] [1992] Ch. 225.
[79] [1989] 3 All E.R. 939.
[80] *Dolling-Baker v Merrett* [1990] 1 W.L.R. 1205. See Ch.22, below.
[81] [1975] 1 Q.B. 613.

Prince Albert v Strange,[82] *Ashburton v Pape,*[83] *Saltman*[84] and *Fraser v Evans.*[85] Talbot J. accepted the company's submissions on the existence of a private duty of confidentiality, as well as a public need to protect the administration of justice.

Distillers Co (Biochemicals) Ltd v Times Newspapers Ltd was approved by the Court of Appeal in *Riddick v Thames Board Mills.*[86] In *Lilly Icos Ltd v Pfizer Ltd (No.2),*[87] the Court of Appeal considered in passing the extent to which a third party might be bound by an order under CPR 31.22(2) that a document was not to be used for any collateral purpose even after it had been referred to in open court: **20–041**

> " . . . if the court does make an order under CPR r 31.22(2), but the document in question comes into the possession of a third party, for instance by accident or theft, then any use by the third party of the document with knowledge of the court's order will arguably be a contempt. We heard no sustained argument on that point, but as at present advised the conclusion just stated would appear to follow by analogy with the view taken by the House of Lords in *Attorney General v Times Newspapers Ltd* [1992] 1 A.C. 191."

Support for the Court of Appeal's position has since been provided by the House of Lords' decision in *Attorney-General v Punch Ltd,*[88] which examined in detail the circumstances in which a third party could be guilty of contempt of court for impeding or prejudicing the purpose of a court order. Contempt of court was described as "the species of wrongful conduct which consists of interference with the administration of justice",[89] deliberate interference with the due administration of justice,[90] or a wilful interference with the administration of justice.[91] These definitions appear capable of extending, not only to the deliberate disregard of court orders, but also to the deliberate disregard of rules of court (such as CPR 31.22).[92] **20–042**

Aside from contempt, and whether or not an order has been made under CPR 31.22, it seems possible in principle for information disclosed in the course of litigation to possess the quality of confidentiality and be protectable as such, and moreover for that quality to subsist even where it has been referred to at a public hearing if on a practical view it has not become general public knowledge. **20–043**

So far as the *protection* of third parties is concerned, a party may be required to disclose information in respect of which he owes a duty of confidence to someone else, if such information is relevant to the issues in the action. A person who is not a party may also be required, before a case comes to trial, to disclose documents, even if they contain information confidential to that person or in respect of which he owes a duty of confidentiality to someone else, if the court **20–044**

---

[82] (1849) 1 Mac. & G. 25.

[83] [1913] 2 Ch. 469.

[84] (1948) 65 R.P.C. 203.

[85] [1969] 1 Q.B. 349.

[86] [1977] Q.B. 881 at 896, 901–902.

[87] [2002] EWCA Civ 2; [2002] 1 W.L.R. 2253 at [5].

[88] [2002] UKHL 50; [2003] 1 A.C. 1046.

[89] per Lord Nicholls, at [2].

[90] per Lord Hoffmann, at [66].

[91] per Lord Hope, at [87].

[92] Caution is necessary, given the unsettled nature of the law in this area: see, for example, *Hutcheson v Popdog Ltd* [2012] 1 W.L.R. 782, per Neuberger M.R. at [26].

considers such disclosure necessary[93]; or to give evidence on deposition,[94] which may include information of a similar character. The law would be deficient if the receiving party did not in such circumstances owe an obligation to the relevant third party not to use such confidential information otherwise than for the purpose for which it was provided.

20–045   CPR 31.22 would prevent the recipient from using a disclosed document otherwise than for the purpose of the action without the consent of the party who provided the disclosure, but that party might not mind what the recipient did with it. The recipient's duty to the third party, it is suggested, would be a duty arising under the equitable doctrine of confidence.

20–046   In *Singh v Christie*,[95] a case under the former Rules of the Supreme Court, it was suggested by Drake J. that, even after disclosed documents had been referred to in open court, the implied undertaking was not relaxed to the extent necessary to permit the recipient of the documents to rely upon them for all purposes. In particular, the recipient was not entitled to found a libel action upon such documents. However, Drake J.'s suggestion was disapproved by the Court of Appeal in *Mahon v Rahn*[96] and has not been followed in subsequent first instance decisions.[97]

20–047   In *Dendron GmbH v Regents of the University of California*[98] Laddie J. considered the position in relation to depositions. The court had allowed applications by the claimants for letters of request to be sent to courts in Germany and the USA for the examination of expert witnesses in connection with patent litigation in England. The claimants wanted to be able to use the evidence obtained in other proceedings in Europe and the USA. CPR 34 contains no restrictions on the use of a deposition taken from a non-party. (Where an order is made requiring a party to be examined about his assets for the purpose of a hearing other than the trial, CPR 34.12 contains restrictions on the use which may be made of the deposition, but that is the only restriction to be found in CPR 34 on the use of depositions.)

20–048   Laddie J. held that the claimants were subject to an implied obligation at common law not to use the depositions for any purpose other than the English litigation except with the permission of the witness or of the court. (Once the evidence was given in court, its status would be like any other evidence.) He adopted the reasoning of Hobhouse J. in *Prudential Assurance Plc v Fountain Page*[99] (applied also by Jacob J. in *Grapha Holding AG v Quebecor Printing (UK) Plc*[100]) that:

> " . . . where one party compels another, either by enforcement of a rule of court or a specific order of the court, to disclose documents or information whether the other party wishes to or not, the party obtaining this disclosure is given this power

---

[93] See Supreme Court Act 1981 s.34, County Courts Act 1984 s.53 and CPR 31.17.
[94] See CPR 34.
[95] *The Times*, November 11, 1993.
[96] [1998] Q.B. 424 (a decision itself subsequently disapproved by the House of Lords on other grounds in *Taylor v Director of the SFO* [1999] 2 A.C. 177) at 432–434, 449 and 455.
[97] See *Ruddy v Mercury Personal Communications Ltd*, QBD, Eady J., July 31, 2000, and *Colbeck v Ferguson*, QBD, Sir Ian Kennedy, January 24, 2002.
[98] [2004] EWHC 589; [2005] 1 W.L.R. 200.
[99] [1991] 1 W.L.R. 756 at 765.
[100] [1996] F.S.R. 711.

because the invasion of the other party's rights has to give way to the need to do justice between those parties in the pending litigation between them; it follows from this that the results of such compulsion should likewise be limited to the purpose for which the order was made . . . "

Laddie J. observed that there was no difference in principle between documents provided under the disclosure rules and information provided compulsorily during the course of litigation in some other form: the latter required to be protected, no less than the former.[101]

THE SCOPE OF CPR 31.22

Whether or not a proposed use of information goes beyond use for the purpose of the proceedings in which it is disclosed is essentially a question of fact. In *Crest Homes Plc v Marks*,[102] the Court of Appeal expressed the view, uncontradicted in the House of Lords (though regarded, on the facts of the case, as a technicality), that: **20–049**

> "the use of documents disclosed in one action for the purposes of another action will usually, perhaps invariably, be a collateral or ulterior purpose."[103]

In *Sybron Corp v Barclays Bank Plc*,[104] the plaintiffs had commenced an action, in which they wished to involve further parties. For procedural reasons, they chose to commence a new action, rather than to add the new parties to the existing action. Although the causes of action in the two sets of proceedings were identical, Scott J. held that the implied undertaking still operated to prevent the plaintiffs without the leave of the court from using documents obtained in the first action for the purposes of the second action. The required leave was given. **20–050**

Different considerations apply when a primary purpose of the proceedings in which discovery is obtained is to facilitate the conduct of other proceedings—for example, by means of a *Norwich Pharmacal* or search order (formerly an *Anton Piller* order). Prior to the introduction of the CPR, it was generally considered that the use of disclosed information for such purposes would not amount to an ulterior or collateral use of a kind that required the court's permission.[105] In *Shlaimoun and another v Mining Technologies International Inc*[106] Coulson J. held that: **20–051**

---

[101] Laddie J.'s approach was adopted by H.H.J. Birss QC in relation to the provision of experimental samples in the course of patent litigation in *Shire Pharmaceutical Contracts Ltd v Mount Sinai School of Medicine of New York University* [2012] F.S.R. 18 (discussed further above at para.20–022).

[102] [1987] 1 A.C. 829 at 837.

[103] An action based on such documents will be struck out as an abuse of process: *Miller v Scorey* [1996] 1 W.L.R. 1122.

[104] [1985] 1 Ch. 299 at 318.

[105] See *Sony Corporation v Anand* [1981] F.S.R. 398 (Browne-Wilkinson J.) and *Grapha Holding A.G. v Quebecor Printing (UK) Plc* [1996] F.S.R. 711 at 715 (Jacob J.).

[106] [2011] EWHC 3278 (QB); [2012] 1 W.L.R. 1276 at [38].

"Where an application is made for a Bankers Trust/Norwich Pharmacal order, on the express basis that subsequent proceedings are likely, then, in making the order, the court is implicitly giving permission to the applicant to use the documents in those subsequent proceedings."

There is no reason why Coulson J.'s conclusions should not also apply to *Anton Piller* and other similar orders.

20–052 In such cases the protection afforded by CPR 31.22 is still effective, even if the court's permission is not required, inasmuch as the use to which the documents are put must still fall within the purpose allowed by CPR 31.22 (or must still not be ulterior or collateral to the purpose for which the discovery was obtained, as the case may be[107]). A party executing a search order is not necessarily obliged, however, to disregard all information incidentally acquired in the course of its execution.[108]

20–053 Similarly, the use of compulsorily obtained information for the purpose of an interlocutory application for committal for contempt of court should also not represent a breach of CPR 31.22, provided that the application arises in the context of the proceedings in which the information has been obtained.[109] As Lord Oliver said in *Crest Homes Plc v Marks*[110]:

"The proper policing and enforcement or [of?] observance of orders made and undertakings given to the court in an action are, in my judgment, as much an integral part of the action as any other step taken by the plaintiff in the proper prosecution of his claim."

CPR 31.22 AND THE EFFECT OF PUBLIC HEARINGS

20–054 In *Lilly Icos Ltd v Pfizer Ltd (No. 2)*,[111] the Court of Appeal considered both the circumstances in which a public hearing would end the restriction otherwise imposed by CPR 31.22 on the use of a particular document and the circumstances in which the court would make an order under CPR 31.22(2), continuing the restriction after a document had been referred to at a public hearing.

20–055 Enlarging on the Court of Appeal's earlier observations in *SmithKline Beecham Biologicals S.A. v Connaught Laboratories Inc*,[112] in which Lord Bingham C.J. expressed concern to avoid too wide a gap between theory and practice in the rules for determining what documents had passed into the public domain, the court confirmed that the effect of CPR 31.22(1)(a) could not be

---

[107] *Bank of Crete S.A. v Koskotas (No.2)* [1992] 1 W.L.R. 919; *Wilden Pump & Engineering Co v Fusfield* [1985] F.S.R. 581.

[108] *Sony Corp v Time Electronics* [1981] 1 W.L.R. 1293.

[109] *Aliter*, if the contempt proceedings are unrelated: see the decision of Laddie J. in *Cobra Golf Inc v Rata* [1996] F.S.R. 819.

[110] [1987] 1 A.C. 829 at 860.

[111] [2002] EWCA Civ 2; [2002] 1 W.L.R. 2253.

[112] [1999] 4 All E.R. 498 at 512. Lord Bingham referred to circumstances in which "there may be some degree of unreality in the proposition that the material documents in the case have (in practice as well as in theory) passed into the public domain. This is a matter which gives rise to concern".

limited literally to what had happened in open court, given the extent to which practice had moved in the direction of the presentation of evidence and arguments in writing:

> " . . . it was necessary to take as falling under CPR 31.22(1)(a) any document preread by the judge, or referred to in for instance witness statements taken to stand as evidence, even if the document or the witness statement was not actually read out in court."[113]

In relation to pre-reading by the judge, the court added some practical guidance as to whether particular documents should be presumed to have formed part of a judge's pre-reading and as to the effect of that presumption. The court then commented:

> "The central theme of these rules is the importance of the principle that justice is to be done in public, and within that principle the importance of those attending a public court understanding the case."[114]

So far as applications under CPR 31.22(2) were concerned, the court warned against the direct importation of a test of "necessity" from the speeches in *Scott v Scott*,[115] before setting out its recommended approach[116]:

> "(i) The court should start from the principle that very good reasons are required for departing from the normal rule of publicity . . .
>
> (ii) When considering an application in respect of a particular document, the court should take into account the role that the document has played or will play in the trial, and thus its relevance to the process of [public scrutiny] . . .
>
> (iii) In dealing with issues of confidentiality between the parties, the court must have in mind any 'chilling' effect of an order upon the interests of third parties . . .
>
> (iv) Simple assertions of confidentiality and of the damage that would be done by publication, even if supported by both parties, should not prevail. The court will require specific reasons why a party would be damaged by the publication of a document . . .
>
> (v)   It is highly desirable, both in the general public interest and for simple convenience, to avoid the holding of trials in private, or partially in private . . . The court should bear in mind that, if too demanding a standard is imposed under CPR r.31.22(2) in respect of documents that have been referred to inferentially or in short at the trial, it may be necessary, in order to protect genuine interests of the parties, for more trials or parts of trials to be held in private, or for instance for parts of witness statements or skeletons to be in closed form.
>
> (vi) Patent cases are subject to the same general rules as any other cases, but they do present some particular problems and are subject to some particular considerations . . ."

Defamation proceedings which have been brought in reliance on documents that have been disclosed in the course of litigation are a good example of the kind of

---

[113] [2002] EWCA Civ 2; [2002] 1 W.L.R. 2253 at [7].

[114] At [8] and [9].

[115] [1913] A.C. 417.

[116] At para.25.

collateral use which the courts have shown themselves willing to restrain, even after the relevant documents have been referred to at an open hearing. In *Claire McBride v The Body Shop International Plc*[117] Eady J. said that, although it was going too far to say that the court would always prohibit such use, "the threat of collateral litigation is plainly a consideration which needs to be weighed very carefully".

PERMISSION TO USE DISCLOSED INFORMATION FOR OTHER PURPOSES

20–056   In *Crest Homes Plc v Marks*,[118] Lord Oliver stated that it was for a party seeking release from the implied undertaking to demonstrate "cogent and persuasive reasons why it should be released". Referring to the authorities cited to the House of Lords in relation to this question, he said:

> "I do not, for my part, think that it would be helpful to review these authorities for they are no more than examples and they illustrate no general principle beyond this, that the court will not release or modify the implied undertaking given on discovery save in special circumstances and where the release or modification will not occasion injustice to the person giving discovery."[119]

That passage was cited by the Court of Appeal in *SmithKline Beecham Plc v Generics (UK) Ltd*,[120] in the context of an application under CPR 31.22(2). The Court of Appeal also described as "useful" some guidance given as to relevant factors by Laddie J. in *Cobra Golf Inc v Rata*,[121] while reiterating that:

> "The most important consideration must be the interest of justice which involves considering the interest of the party seeking to use the documents and that of the party protected by the CPR 31.22 order. As Lord Oliver said each case will depend upon its own facts."[122]

However, the court added:

> "But a material consideration must be whether the documents could have been obtained under CPR 31.17. That rule enables the court to order disclosure from the third parties if the documents were likely to support SB's case and disclosure was necessary in order to dispose fairly of the claim."

20–057   The introduction of CPR 31.17, which greatly extended the scope of the courts' ability to make disclosure orders against non-parties, is clearly likely in the future to have a significant impact on applications for permission to use disclosed documents for other litigation: if the applicant would be entitled to

---

[117] [2007] EWHC 1658 (QB) at [42]
[118] [1987] A.C. 829 at 859.
[119] [1987] A.C. 829 at 860.
[120] [2003] EWCA Civ 1109; [2004] 1 W.L.R. 1479 at [36].
[121] [1996] F.S.R. 819.
[122] [2003] EWCA Civ 1109; [2004] 1 W.L.R. 1479 at [37]. See also *Danisco A/S v Novozymes A/S* [2011] EWHC 3288 (Pat); [2012] F.S.R. 21 (Arnold J.).

apply in that other litigation for non-party disclosure of the relevant documents, there may be little sense in the court in the original proceedings declining to allow the applicant to use them in that other litigation.

In any event, the issue will only arise where the party seeking release is unable **20–058** to obtain consent to his proposed use of the disclosed material from the person giving disclosure. The question whether such release will occasion injustice to that person will involve similar considerations to those which would arise if the question was whether the proposed disclosure should be restrained as a breach of an obligation of confidence.

CHAPTER 21

Children

CHILDREN'S RIGHTS OF CONFIDENCE

A child may have private law rights of confidentiality or privacy no less than may **21–001** an adult. In cases involving a family's private life, those rights fall to be considered independently of the rights of the child's parents.

WAIVER

Traditionally, the child's right to waive confidentiality has been a right to be **21–002** exercised by the child's parents on its behalf,[1] but this general approach is subject to qualification.

In the first place, any such waiver is an exercise of parental responsibility, which the court is ultimately able to control—even in the face of parental opposition—by virtue of the provisions of the Children Act 1989.[2] Indeed, as Thorpe L.J. said in *Re G (Celebrities: Publicity)*[3]:

> " . . . there can be no doubt that the court has jurisdiction in personam to restrain any act by a parent that if unrestrained would or might adversely affect the welfare of the child the subject of the proceedings."

Secondly, the courts have in recent years increasingly recognised the autonomy of children mature enough to make informed decisions on their own behalf, a tendency accelerated by the incorporation into domestic law of both the European Convention and its rights-based jurisprudence.

In *Torbay Borough Council v News Group Newspapers*,[4] Munby J. discussed **21–003** this development in some detail. At the age of 12, Angela Roddy, became pregnant. The father ("X") was of about the same age. Following the birth of her daughter ("Y"), Angela fought an unsuccessful battle with her local authority, the

---

[1] *Re Z (A Minor) (Identification: Restrictions on Publication)* [1997] Fam. 1 at 25, per Ward L.J., who also observed that parents themselves owe their children a duty of confidentiality of uncertain ambit. See also *Re W* [2010] EWHC 16 (Munby J.), at [136] to [137]. In relation to medical treatment and advice, see para.11–038, above.

[2] *Re Z (A Minor) (Identification: Restrictions on Publication)* [1997] Fam. 1 at 25–27.

[3] [1999] 1 F.L.R. 409, at 414–415; see also *A v M (Family Proceedings: Publicity)* [2000] 1 F.L.R. 562 (Charles J.) at 565.

[4] [2003] EWHC 2927 (Fam); [2004] E.M.L.R. 8 at [45]–[60]. See also *Mabon v Mabon* [2005] EWCA Civ 634; [2005] Fam. 366 at [26] and [32], and the discussion in Jane Fortin's "Accommodating Children's Rights in a Post Human Rights Act Era" (2006) M.L.R. 299.

outcome of which was an adoption order in respect of Y. She wanted to tell her story to the *Mail on Sunday* and later applied for the discharge of restrictive injunctions that prevented her from doing so. The hearing before Munby J. took place shortly before her 17th birthday. Citing the House of Lords' decision in *Gillick v West Norfolk and Wisbech Health Authority*,[5] Munby J. said[6]:

> "The courts must face reality. We must, as Lord Scarman said, be sensitive to human development and social change. Angela may not yet be quite 17 years old but she is a young woman with a mind of her own and, as her solicitor B has said, a mature and articulate young person. We no longer treat our 17-year old daughters as our Victorian ancestors did, and if we try to do so it is at our—and their—peril. Angela, in my judgment, is of an age, and has sufficient understanding and maturity, to decide for herself whether that which is private, personal and intimate should remain private or whether it should be shared with the whole world . . . "

He concluded[7]:

> "In fact Angela's decision is supported by her parents and not opposed by the local authority. But neither of those facts can be determinative. I wish to make it clear that, giving proper weight to Angela's evidence and the evidence of her solicitor, B, I should unhesitatingly have come to precisely the same conclusion even if Angela's wish to tell her story to the world had been opposed both by the local authority and by her parents."

Short of waiver, the outcome of the balancing exercise carried out by the court between a child's Art.8 rights and another person's Art.10 rights may still be affected by the actions of the child's parents. In *Murray v Express Newspapers Plc*,[8] the Court of Appeal expressed (at least provisionally) the view that:

> "If a child of parents who are not in the public eye should reasonably expect not to have photographs of him published in the media, so too should the child of a famous parent."

21–004   However, the Court[9] agreed with Patten J.'s observation at first instance that the approach of a child's parents might well be relevant to consideration of the child's rights:

> "A proper consideration of the degree of protection to which a child is entitled under Art. 8 has, I think ... to be considered in a wider context by taking into account not only the circumstances in which the photograph was taken and its actual impact on the child, but also the position of the child's parents and the way in which the child's life as part of that family has been conducted ... The Court can attribute to the child reasonable expectations about his private life based on matters such as how it has in fact been conducted by those responsible for his welfare and upbringing."

---

[5] [1986] A.C. 112.
[6] At [56].
[7] At [60]. See also, in relation to an adult with learning disabilities, the decision of Munby J. in *E v Channel Four Television Corp* [2005] EWHC 1144 (Fam); [2005] E.M.L.R. 30.
[8] [2009] Ch. 481 at [46]
[9] At [38].

In *AAA v Associated Newspapers Ltd*[10] the claimant child sought damages from the defendant publisher and also injunctive relief. The case involved speculation that the claimant's birth was the result of an affair between her mother and a politician. Nicola Davies J. accepted evidence that the claimant's mother had discussed the claimant's paternity at a country house weekend party with two witnesses who were not friends and also in a magazine interview. She concluded[11] that:

> "The claimant's mother is an intelligent professional woman. She chose to speak and act as she did. In my view, the result has been to compromise the claimant's reasonable expectation of privacy upon the issue of her paternity. I do not find that the claimant has no reasonable expectation, rather the weight to be attached is of a lesser degree than would have been the case had nothing been said or permitted to be said upon this matter."

THE COURTS' JURISDICTION

Since the decision of the House of Lords in *Re S (A Child) (Identification: Restrictions on Publication)*,[12] the courts' own jurisdiction to protect the privacy of children, where it is not statutory,[13] has been based upon the application of Art.8 of the European Convention on Human Rights. **21–005**

Prior to the introduction of the Human Rights Act 1998, the courts had categorised their inherent jurisdiction to restrain publicity in relation to children into (a) a parental jurisdiction, directed at the welfare of the child and the child's upbringing, and (b) an ancillary jurisdiction, directed at the protection of the integrity and effectiveness of the courts' own proceedings.[14] However, in *Re S*[15] Lord Steyn, who gave the only speech, said: **21–006**

> "The House unanimously takes the view that since the 1998 Act came into force in October 2000, the earlier case law about the existence and scope of inherent jurisdiction need not be considered in this case or in similar cases. The foundation of the jurisdiction to restrain publication in a case such as the present is now derived from Convention rights under the ECHR."

Lord Steyn said that previous case law might remain of some interest in regard to the ultimate balancing exercise to be carried out under the ECHR provisions and observed that the approach that had been adopted in the past was in fact "remarkably similar" to that to be adopted under the ECHR. However, just as would be the case if a child were seeking to enforce a private law right to privacy, the proper methodology for the courts is now that set out in *Campbell v MGN Ltd*.[16] Procedural guidance in relation to applications in the Family Division for reporting restriction orders was provided in the *President's Direction* of March

---

[10] [2012] EWHC 2103 (QB).

[11] At [116].

[12] [2004] UKHL 47; [2005] 1 A.C. 593.

[13] e.g. s.39(1) of the Children and Young Persons Act 1933, cited at para.21–016 below.

[14] See, for example, In *re Z (A Minor) (Identification: Restrictions on Publication)* [1997] Fam. 1.

[15] At [23].

[16] [2004] UKHL 22; [2004] 2 A.C. 457.

18, 2005[17] and the *CAFCASS Practice Note*[18] of the same date. In *Re Ward (a child), British Broadcasting Corp v Cafcass Legal*[19] Munby J. held that, as a general rule, the court should not release a judgment in care proceedings, even in anonymised form, until after it had given those affected an opportunity to apply for an order protecting their anonymity and after it had adjudicated on all such applications (which it should not do unless and until there had been strict compliance with s.12(2) of the 1998 Act and with the President's Direction and the CAFCASS Practice Note).

21–007   The nature of the necessary balancing exercise can be demonstrated by comparing the outcome in *Re S* itself with the subsequent decision of Sir Mark Potter P. in *A Local Authority v W*,[20] in which the House of Lords' decision was distinguished.

21–008   In *Re S*, an order was made was made prohibiting publication of any information that might identify S, a young boy whose brother had died and whose mother was facing trial for his brother's murder. The order was made subject to an exception providing that "Nothing in this order shall of itself prevent any person . . . publishing any particulars of or information relating to any part of the proceedings before any court other than a court sitting in private . . . ". S's representatives appealed against decisions by Hedley J. and the Court of Appeal that the exception should stand. The central question thereby raised for the House of Lords was whether it would be right to restrict the open reporting of the mother's forthcoming criminal trial. The respondent newspapers accepted that they should not refer directly to S but wished, in particular, to publish the names and photographs of S's brother and his parents.

21–009   Lord Steyn accepted that both Arts 8 and 10 were engaged. However, the impact of publicity upon S would be "essentially indirect" and "not of the same order when compared with cases of juveniles, who are directly involved in criminal trials".[21] On the other hand, under the ECHR there was a general and strong rule in favour of unrestricted publicity for any proceedings in a criminal trial and the case was not covered by any of the numerous statutory exceptions to publicity that Parliament had seen fit to create. Lord Steyn also differed from the view expressed by Hale L.J. in the Court of Appeal that the public interest in the identification of defendants was greater after a conviction than it was before. He held that Hedley J. had analysed the case correctly and S's appeal was dismissed.

21–010   Lord Steyn went so far[22] as to suggest that, in view of the number of statutory exceptions to trial publicity:

> " . . . it needs to be said clearly and unambiguously that the court has no power to create by a process of analogy, except in the most compelling circumstances, further exceptions to the general principle of open justice."

---

[17] [2005] 2 F.L.R. 120; [2005] Fam. Law 398.
[18] [2005] Fam. Law 398.
[19] [2007] EWHC 616 (Fam); [2007] 2 F.L.R. 765 at [74].
[20] [2005] EWHC 1564, Fam; [2006] 1 F.L.R. 1.
[21] At [25]–[27].
[22] At [20]. See also the reference to "unusual or exceptional circumstances" at [18].

The result in *A Local Authority v W*,[23] less than a year after the House of Lords' decision in *Re S*, demonstrates that the "most compelling circumstances" referred to by Lord Steyn may indeed arise. The facts were that the mother of two children pleaded guilty to a charge that she had knowingly infected the father of one of them with the HIV virus. One of the children had tested negative, but it was thought "more than a possibility" that the other child carried the virus. Both children were the subject of care proceedings and the local authority (opposed only by written submissions from the press) sought an injunction restraining publication of any information likely to lead to identification of the children.

21–011

Sir Mark Potter P. observed[24] that *Re S* raised difficulties of application, since it was not easy to reconcile the dictum of Lord Steyn quoted above with a balancing exercise that involved no presumption of priority as between the Art.10 rights of the press and the Art.8 rights of the child. Having concluded[25] that Lord Steyn had not intended to restore the presumptive priority of Art.10 that the House of Lords had rejected in *Campbell v MGN Ltd*, the President distinguished *Re S* on three grounds. First, unlike *Re S*, there had been no previous publicity and there was apparently a good prospect that, if the injunction were granted, the children would in large measure be protected from the fall out of future publicity. Secondly, there was evidence before the Court that refusal of the injunction might jeopardise the proper placement of the children, because of prejudice against those affected by the HIV virus. Thirdly, the danger for the children against which protection was sought was not the knowledge that their mother was a criminal but the personal attribution (mistaken or otherwise) of HIV infection. An injunction was accordingly granted.[26]

21–012

The best interests of the child as "a primary consideration"

In *K v News Group Newspapers Ltd*[27] the claimant, a married man with teenage children, sought to restrain the News of the World from publishing information relating to an affair which he had conducted with a married work colleague. His application for an interim injunction failed at first instance before Collins J., who held that he was unlikely to establish at trial that publication should not be allowed. The claimant's appeal to the Court of Appeal succeeded. Central to the Court of Appeal's consideration was the position of the claimant's children.

21–013

Ward L.J., with whom both Laws L.J. and Moore-Bick L.J. agreed, referred to the decision of the Supreme Court in *ZH (Tanzania) v Secretary of State for the Home Department*[28], a case concerned with the weight to be given to the best interests of children who would be affected by the deportation of a parent. The

---

[23] [2005] EWHC 1564 (Fam); [2006] 1 F.L.R. 1.

[24] At [24].

[25] At [53].

[26] Contrast *R. (Gazette Media Co Ltd) v Teeside Crown Court* [2005] EWCA Crim 1983; [2005] E.M.L.R. 34 and *A Local Authority v PD* [2005] EWHC 1832 (Fam), another decision by Sir Mark Potter P. Further recent examples of the balancing exercise in cases concerning children include *F v Newsquest Ltd* [2004] EWHC 762 (Fam); (2004) E.M.L.R. 29 (Munby J.), *In re Trinity Mirror Plc* [2008] EWCA Crim 50; [2008] Q.B. 770 at [32]–[34]; *re Stedman* [2009] EWHC 935 (Fam); [2009] 2 F.L.R. 852 (Eleanor King J); and *re A (A Child) (Application for Reporting Restrictions)* [2011] EWHC 1764 (Fam); [2012] 1 F.L.R. 239 (Baker J.).

[27] [2011] EWCA Civ 439; [2011] 1 W.L.R. 1827.

[28] [2011] UKSC 4; [2011] 2 A.C. 166.

Supreme Court had focused upon the courts' obligation to have regard, in particular, to art.3.1 of the United Nations Convention on the Rights of the Child (1989):

> "In all actions concerning children, whether undertaken by public or private social welfare institutions, courts of law, administrative authorities or legislative bodies, the best interests of the child shall be a primary consideration."

Ward L.J. cited in particular the observations of Lord Kerr JSC:

> "It is a universal theme of the various international and domestic instruments to which Baroness Hale JSC has referred that, in reaching decisions that will affect a child, a primacy of importance must be accorded to his or her best interests. This is not, it is agreed, a factor of limitless importance in the sense that it will prevail over all considerations. It is a factor, however, that must rank higher than any other. It is not merely one consideration that weighs in the balance alongside other competing factors. Where the best interests of the child clearly favour a certain course, that course should be followed, unless countervailing reasons of considerable force displace them. It is not necessary to express this in terms of a presumption but the primacy of this consideration needs to be made clear in emphatic terms. What is determined to be in a child's best interests should customarily dictate the outcome of cases such as the present, therefore, and it will require considerations of substantial moment to permit a different result."

Ward L.J. cautioned that:

> "...this learning must, with respect, be read and understood in the context in which it is sought to be applied. It is clear that the interests of children do not automatically take precedence over the Convention rights of others. It is clear also that, when in a case such as this the court is deciding where the balance lies between the article 10 rights of the media and the article 8 rights of those whose privacy would be invaded by publication, it should accord particular weight to the article 8 rights of any children likely to be affected by the publication, if that would be likely to harm their interests. Where a tangible and objective public interest tends to favour publication, the balance may be difficult to strike. The force of the public interest will be highly material, and the interests of affected children cannot be treated as a trump card."

Ward L.J. appeared to suggest that the balancing approach to Arts 8 and 10 which Lord Steyn had recommended in *In re S*[29] might be in need of reappraisal:

> "If, as he requires, an intense focus on the comparative importance of the specific rights being claimed in the individual case is necessary, then the additional rights of children are to be placed in the scale. The question then is whether the force of the article 10 considerations outweigh them given what I have said"

21–014   The Supreme Court subsequently revisited the description of children's rights as "a primary consideration" in *HH v Deputy Prosecutor of the Italian Republic (Genoa)*[30], a case involving extradition, rather than deportation. Differences of

---

[29] [2005] 1 A.C. 593.
[30] [2012] 3 W.L.R. 90.

emphasis between the members of the Supreme Court are apparent, both as to the significance of that description and as to its consequences for the court's decision-making process.

Baroness Hale, Lord Hope and Lord Kerr[31] favoured the adoption of a process which (in accordance with the approach of the European Court in Strasbourg) first addressed the Art.8 rights of the children involved, before considering whether there was interference with those rights, and then whether such interference was justified. Lord Kerr[32] explained his earlier dicta in *ZH v (Tanzania) v Secretary of State for the Home Department*[33] by reference to the judgment of the High Court of Australia in *Wan v Minister for Immigration and Multicultural Affairs*[34]:

> "'Provided that the Tribunal did not treat any other consideration as inherently more significant than the best interests of Mr Wan's children, it was entitled to conclude, after a proper consideration of the evidence and other material before it, that the strength of other considerations outweighed the best interests of the children. However, it was required to identify what the best interests of Mr Wan's children required with respect to the exercise of its discretion and *then* to assess whether the strength of any other consideration, or the cumulative effect of other considerations, outweighed the consideration of the best interests of the children understood as a primary consideration.' (Emphasis added.)"

On the other hand, Lord Mance, Lord Judge C.J. and Lord Wilson considered[35] that it did not matter in what order the relevant considerations were addressed by the court; Lord Brown did not discuss the issue expressly, but agreed[36] with the reasons given by Lord Judge and Lord Wilson for their disposal of the appeals. Lord Mance said[37] of the requirement that a child's interests must be "a primary consideration" that: **21–015**

> "This means, in my view, that such interests must always be at the forefront of any decision-maker's mind, rather than that they need to be mentioned first in any formal chain of reasoning or that they rank higher than any other considerations. A child's best interests must themselves be evaluated. They may in some cases point only marginally in one, rather than another, direction. They may be outweighed by other considerations pointing more strongly in another direction."

Neither *ZH (Tanzania) v Secretary of State for the Home Department* nor *HH v Deputy Prosecutor of the Italian Republic (Genoa)* was a case in which the court was required to balance directly a child's Art.8 rights against another person's rights under Art.10. It is suggested that, when such a balancing exercise is necessary, the approach which Lord Steyn recommended in *In re S*[38] (that is, with neither Art.8 nor Art.10 being granted a priori precedence over the other) remains appropriate. The court is able to give effect to the primacy of the child's interests

---

[31] At [33], [89] and [144].
[32] At [145].
[33] [2011] UKSC 4; [2011] 2 A.C. 166.
[34] (2001) 107 F.C.R. 133 at [32].
[35] At [100], [125] and [153].
[36] At [96].
[37] At [98].
[38] [2005] 1 A.C. 593.

within the framework set out by Lord Steyn. As Baroness Hale said in *HH v Deputy Prosecutor of the Italian Republic (Genoa)*,[39]

> "...children need a family life in a way that adults do not. They have to be fed, clothed, washed, supervised, taught and above all loved if they are to grow up to be the properly functioning members of society which we all need them to be. Their physical and educational needs may be met outside the family, although usually not as well as they are met within it, but their emotional needs can only be fully met within a functioning family. Depriving a child of her family life is altogether more serious than depriving an adult of his."

Whether a child's Art.8 rights are outweighed by another person's Art.10 rights in any individual case will inevitably depend on the facts and circumstances of that particular case.

The best interests of the child as "the paramount consideration"

21–016 When the court is exercising its parental jurisdiction over a child, the best interests of the child are more than "a primary consideration". Under s.1 of the Children Act 1989:

> "(1) When a court determines any question with respect to—
> (a) the upbringing of a child; or
> (b) the administration of a child's property or the application of any income arising from it,
> the child's welfare shall be the court's paramount consideration."

Re Z (A Minor) (Identification): Restrictions on Publication)[40] was such a case. Z was a child with particular educational needs. A television company wished to make a programme about the unusual and successful treatment she was receiving from a specialised foreign institution. To this end, Z's mother applied to the court for discharge or variation of earlier injunctions, which had restricted publicity relating to Z's education. The Court of Appeal dismissed her appeal from Cazalet J.'s refusal of her application. Ward L.J. distinguished other cases concerning minors and publicity, saying[41]:

> "In my judgment a question of upbringing is determined whenever the central issue before the court is one which relates to how the child is being reared . . . This case is one where the mother wishes her child to perform for the making of the film. This mother wishes to bring up her child as one who will play an active part in a television film . . . The court is, therefore, required to determine a question with respect to the upbringing of the child."[42]

However, even cases directly concerning the upbringing of a child may involve the Art.8 or Art.10 rights of other members of the child's family, or (in this

---

[39] At [33].
[40] [1997] Fam 1.
[41] [1997] Fam 1 at 110–111.
[42] See also *Re Stedman* [2009] EWHC 935 (Fam); [2009] 2 F.L.R. 852 (Eleanor King J.), at [35]–[41]: an injunction *contra mundum* was sought, a question of the child's upbringing was therefore not being determined, and the child's best interests were not paramount.

context, probably less significantly) the Art.10 rights of media organisations. The absolute rule laid down by s.1 of the Children Act 1989 may at some point be the subject of challenge, mounted by reference to the balancing exercise required under the Convention.[43]

FAMILY COURT PROCEEDINGS

In family court proceedings, the privacy of children may be protected by: **21–017**

(a)   the exclusion of the public from hearings; and
(b)   restrictions on the disclosure of information or documents relating to the proceedings.

Exclusion of the public

Family proceedings involving children have long been recognised as a special **21–018** case which necessitates qualification of the usual approach that court hearings should take place in public. Lord Shaw of Dumferline said in *Scott v Scott*[44]:

> " . . . the jurisdiction over wards and lunatics is exercised by the judges as representing His Majesty as parens patriae. The affairs are truly private affairs; the transactions are transactions truly intra familiam; and it has long been recognised that an appeal for the protection of the Court in the case of such persons does not involve the consequence of placing in the light of publicity their truly domestic affairs."

The legislature has embodied this principle in a variety of provisions. In **21–019** particular, since April 6, 2011, family proceedings have been governed by the Family Procedure Rules 2010, a unified and consolidating code which replaced (i) the Family Proceedings Rules 1991 (covering family proceedings other than adoption in the High Court and county courts), (ii) the Family Proceedings Courts (Children Act 1989) Rules 1991 (covering proceedings relating to children in magistrates' courts) and (iii) the Family Procedure (Adoption) Rules 2005. Rule 27.10 of the Family Procedure Rules 2010 provides that, subject to any contrary provision or direction, proceedings should be held "in private", a defined term meaning that the general public have no right to be present.[45]

On the other hand, as Sir Mark Potter P. said in *X (A Child) (Residence and* **21–020** *Contact: Rights of Media Attendance)*[46]:

---

[43] See the discussion in Jane Fortin's "Accommodating Children's Rights in a Post Human Rights Act Era" (2006) M.L.R. 299.
[44] [1913] AC 417 at 483; see also per Viscount Haldane L.C. at 436–437. See also the observations of the New Zealand Law Commission in its report on Access to Court Records (2006) N.Z.L.C. R93, at [2.37], cited by the Court of Appeal in *R. (Guardian News and Media Ltd) v City of Westminster Magistrates' Court* [2012] EWCA Civ 420; [2012] C.P. Rep. 30, per Toulson L.J. at [86], and set out at para.20–008, above.
[45] The European Court of Human Rights held in *B and P v United Kingdom* (2002) 34 E.H.R.R. 529 that 4.16(7) of the Family Proceedings Rules 1991, a predecessor provision, did not infringe the parties' Art.6 rights; see also *Pelling v Bruce-Williams* [2004] EWCA Civ 845; [2004] Fam. 155.
[46] [2009] EWHC 1728 (Fam); [2009] E.M.L.R. 26 at [32]–[33].

"In recent years, the privacy of family law proceedings in this country has given rise to concerns, not only on the part of the media and certain pressure groups, but also of government, that a procedure designed to protect the privacy of the parties and the welfare interests of the children has given rise to a system perceived as one of 'secret justice', in which the workings of the courts and the decisions of judges are not available to public (in reality media) scrutiny. This is a view which has principally been propounded in relation to public law care proceedings on the basis that public scrutiny is of high importance in cases where the state (albeit in the interests of safeguarding children) intervenes from outside in family life and seeks to remove a child from his or her family or to supervise or limit parental rights... However, the cause of 'open justice' has also been taken up and promoted in relation to intrafamilial disputes in private law children proceedings, principally by fathers who have regarded the courts as too inclined to favour mothers when resolving residence and contact disputes, particularly in relation to the enforcement of contact orders in the face of non-compliance.

Judicial concerns have also been expressed over the need to maintain public confidence in the family justice system in the light of these matters, acknowledging that many of the issues litigated in the family justice system require open and public debate in the media, not least to avoid the charges of secret justice advanced by those who have reason to be discontented with the outcome of cases with which they have been concerned."

Just as in other areas of litigation, there accordingly remains a strong public interest in openness, which exists in tension with what may be an individual child's wish for privacy and, indeed, the public interest in the preservation of confidentiality.[47] The solution which the legislature has adopted is now embodied in rule 27.11 of the Family Procedure Rules 2010.[48] This provides that, subject to specific exceptions and/or contrary direction by the court,[49] hearings in private may be attended by duly accredited representatives of news gathering and reporting organisations.

As para.2.4 of both Practice Directions 27B and 27C states:

"The question of attendance of media representatives at hearings in family proceedings to which rule 27.11 and this guidance apply must be distinguished from statutory restrictions on publication and disclosure of information relating to proceedings, which continue to apply and are unaffected by the rule and this guidance."

RESTRICTIONS ON THE DISCLOSURE OF INFORMATION OR DOCUMENTS RELATING TO PROCEEDINGS

21–021   A number of legislative measures may restrict the disclosure of information or documents relating to proceedings involving children. They include:

- The Children and Young Persons Act 1933 s.39

---

[47] Munby J. expanded upon the nature of the public interest in preserving confidentiality in *In re X (Disclosure of Information)* [2001] 2 F.L.R. 440 at [24], and restated his analysis in *Re Ward (A Child)* [2010] EWHC 16 (Fam) at [121].

[48] Supplemented by Practice Directions 27B and 27C

[49] In *Spencer v Spencer* [2009] E.M.L.R. 25 (a case concerning ancillary relief rather than children), Munby J. considered in what circumstances an exclusionary direction might be given.

- The Children Act 1989 s.97
- The Administration of Justice Act 1960 s.12
- The Family Procedure Rules 2010

These provisions are further considered in turn below.

The Children and Young Persons Act 1933

Newspaper reporting of any case may be limited by an order under s.39(1) of the **21–022**
Children and Young Persons Act 1933, which provides that:

> "In relation to any proceedings in any court the court may direct that—
>
> (a)　no newspaper report of the proceedings shall reveal the name, address, or school, or include any particulars calculated to lead to the identification, of any child or young person concerned in the proceedings, either as being the person by or against or in respect of whom the proceedings are taken, or as being a witness therein;
> (b)　no picture shall be published in any newspaper as being or including a picture of any child or young person so concerned in the proceedings as aforesaid;
>
> except in so far (if at all) as may be permitted by the direction of the court."[50]

Guidance as to the approach adopted by the courts in relation to applications under s.39 is to be found in the judgments of Tugendhat J. in *A (A Child) v Cambridge University Hospital NHS Foundation Trust*[51] (relating to personal injury proceedings) and of Hooper L.J., Griffith Williams J. and Singh J. in *R (on the application of Y) v Aylesbury Crown Court*[52] (relating to criminal proceedings).

The Children Act 1989

Further restrictions on publication are common in proceedings where the court is **21–023**
acting in its parental role. Section 97(2) of the Children Act 1989[53] provides that:

> "No person shall publish to the public at large or any section of the public any material which is intended, or likely, to identify—

---

[50] See also s.49 of the Children and Young Persons Act 1933 (as amended), which restricts reporting of specified proceedings, including proceedings in juvenile courts. Section 39 is subject to amendment by Sch.2, para.2, of the Youth Justice and Criminal Evidence Act 1999 and by Sch.3(2), para.3, of the Children, Schools and Families Act 2010, neither of which provisions is yet in force for the relevant purpose.

[51] [2011] EWHC 454 (QB); [2011] E.M.L.R. 18.

[52] [2012] EWHC 1140 (Admin); [2012] E.M.L.R. 26

[53] Subsections 97(2) to 97(9) are subject to repeal by Schedules 3(2) and 4(2) of the Children, Schools and Families Act 2010. However, the relevant provisions of the 2010 Act are not yet in force for the relevant purposes and it is doubtful that they will be introduced in the near future, if at all.

(a) any child as being involved in any proceedings before the High Court, a county court or a magistrates' court in which any power under this Act or the Adoption and Children Act 2002 may be exercised by the court with respect to that or any other child; or

(b) an address or school as being that of a child involved in any such proceedings."

The Court of Appeal has rejected an argument that s.97 is incompatible with Art.6 of the European Convention on Human Rights.[54] However, the restriction imposed by s.97 applies only for the duration of the proceedings concerned.[55]

The Administration of Justice Act 1960

21–024   A consequence at common law of the privacy of proceedings where the court is acting in its parental role was that a person who published details of the proceedings exposed himself to liability for contempt of court.[56] Statutory notice of this was taken in s.12(1) (as amended) of the Administration of Justice Act 1960:

> "The publication of information relating to proceedings before any court sitting in private shall not of itself be contempt of court except in the following cases, that is to say—
>
> (a)   where the proceedings—
>> (i)   relate to the exercise of the inherent jurisdiction of the High Court with respect to minors;
>> (ii)   are brought under the Children Act 1989 or the Adoption and Children Act 2002; or
>> (iii)   otherwise relate wholly or mainly to the maintenance or upbringing of a minor . . ."[57]

The scope of s.12(1) was the subject of detailed analysis by Munby J. in *Re B (A Child) (Disclosure)*,[58] *Re Webster (A Child)*[59] and *Re Ward (A Child)*.[60] In *In re X and others (Children) (Morgan and others intervening)*[61] Sir Nicholas Wall P expressed his agreement with Munby J.'s analysis.

21–025   In *Re B*,[62] Munby J. held that a communication constitutes a "publication" for the purposes of s.12 whenever the law of defamation would treat it as a publication:

---

[54] *Pelling v Bruce-Williams* [2004] EWCA Civ 845; [2004] Fam. 155.

[55] *Clayton v Clayton* [2006] EWCA Civ 878; [2006] Fam. 83.

[56] *Re Martindale* [1894] 3 Ch. 193. See also per Lloyd L.J. in *Att Gen v Newspaper Publishing Plc* [1988] 1 Ch. 333 at 380, citing Arlidge and Eady, *The Law of Contempt* (London: Sweet & Maxwell, 1982), p.244.

[57] s.12(1)(a) is subject to repeal under the Children, Schools and Families Act 2010, the relevant provisions of which have not yet, however, been brought into force for the relevant purposes.

[58] [2004] EWHC 411 (Fam); [2004] 2 F.L.R. 142 at [62]–[82].

[59] [2006] EWHC 2733 (Fam); [2007] E.M.L.R. 7 at [49].

[60] In two separate judgments: first, [2007] EWHC 616 (Fam); [2007] 2 F.L.R. 765; secondly, [2010] EWHC 16 (Fam); [2010] 1 F.L.R. 1497.

[61] [2011] EWHC 1157 (Fam); [2012] 1 W.L.R. 182.

[62] [2004] EWHC 411 (Fam); [2004] 2 F.L.R. 142 at [62]–[82].

"This means that most forms of dissemination, whether oral or written, will constitute a publication. The only exception is where there is a communication of information by someone to a professional, each acting in furtherance of the protection of children."[63]

However, the scope of s.12 is confined to information relating to the actual proceedings of the court and does not extend to other information relating to the child concerned.[64] Munby J.'s examples[65] emphasise the extent of the information which s.12 leaves uncovered:

"Section 12 does not of itself prohibit the publication of:

a) the fact, if it be the case, that a child is a ward of court and is the subject of wardship proceedings or that a child is the subject of residence or other proceedings under the Children Act 1989 or of proceedings relating wholly or mainly to his maintenance or upbringing;

b) the name, address or photograph of such a child;

c) the name, address or photograph of the parties (or, if the child is a party, the other parties) to such proceedings;

d) the date, time or place of a past or future hearing of such proceedings;

e) the nature of the dispute in such proceedings;

f) anything which has been seen or heard by a person conducting himself lawfully in the public corridor or other public precincts outside the court in which the hearing in private is taking place;

g) the name, address or photograph of the witnesses who have given evidence in such proceedings;

h) the party on whose behalf such a witness has given evidence; and

i) the text or summary of the whole or part of any order made in such proceedings."

Thus at the end of family proceedings (when s.97(2) of the Children Act 1989 ceases to have effect), the court may well have occasion to exercise both a "disclosure jurisdiction", in order to permit the publication of information relating to the case, and a "restraint jurisdiction", in order to restrain the publication of information relating to the individuals involved in the case. As Sir Nicholas Wall P. said in *In re X and Others (Children) (Morgan and Others intervening)*[66]:

"...both the 'disclosure jurisdiction' and the 'restraint jurisdiction' have to be exercised in accordance with the principles explained by Lord Steyn in *In re S (A Child) (Identification: Restrictions on Publication)* [2005] 1 AC 593, para 17, and by Sir Mark Potter P in *A Local Authority v W* [2006] 1 FLR 1, para 53, that is, by a 'parallel analysis' of those of the various rights protected by the European Convention for the Protection of Human Rights and Fundamental Freedoms which are engaged, leading to an 'ultimate balancing test' reflecting the European Convention principle of proportionality..."

---

[63] At para.82.

[64] *Re B* at [82]; *Re Ward* [2010] EWHC 16 (Fam); [2010] 1 F.L.R. 1497 at [112].

[65] *Re B* at [82]; see also *Re Webster (a child)* [2006] EWHC 2733 (Fam); [2007] E.M.L.R. 7 at [49].

[66] [2011] EWHC 1157 (Fam); [2012] 1 W.L.R. 182 at [29].

THE FAMILY PROCEDURE RULES 2010

21–026 The prohibitive scope of s.12 of the Administration of Justice Act 1960 is further reduced by s.12(4), which provides that:

"Nothing in this section shall be construed as implying that any publication is punishable as contempt of court which would not be so punishable apart from this section (and in particular where the publication is not so punishable by reason of being authorised by rules of court)."

One relevant rule of court for the purposes of s.12(4) is r.12.73(1) of the Family Procedure Rules 2010. This provides that:

"For the purposes of the law relating to contempt of court, information relating to proceedings held in private (whether or not contained in a document filed with the court) may be communicated—

    (a)   where the communication is to—
        (i)   a party;
        (ii)   the legal representative of a party;
        (iii)   a professional legal adviser;
        (iv)   an officer of the service or a Welsh family proceedings officer;
        (v)   the welfare officer;
        (vi)   the Legal Services Commission;
        (vii)   an expert whose instruction by a party has been authorised by the court for the purposes of the proceedings;
        (viii)   a professional acting in furtherance of the protection of children;
        (ix)   an independent reviewing officer appointed in respect of a child who is, or has been, subject to proceedings to which this rule applies;
    (b)   where the court gives permission; or
    (c)   subject to any direction of the court, in accordance with rule 12.75 and Practice Direction 12G."

Rule 12.75 of the Family Procedure Rules 2010 provides that:

"(1)   A party or the legal representative of a party, on behalf of and upon the instructions of that party, may communicate information relating to the proceedings to any person where necessary to enable that party—
        (a)   by confidential discussion, to obtain support, advice or assistance in the conduct of the proceedings;
        (b)   to engage in mediation or other forms of alternative dispute resolution;
        (c)   to make and pursue a complaint against a person or body concerned in the proceedings; or
        (d)   to make and pursue a complaint regarding the law, policy or procedure relating to a category of proceedings to which this Part applies.
(2)   Where information is communicated to any person in accordance with paragraph (1)(a) of this rule, no further communication by that person is permitted.
(3)   When information relating to the proceedings is communicated to any person in accordance with paragraphs (1)(b), (c) or (d) of this rule—
        (a)   the recipient may communicate that information to a further recipient, provided that—
            (i)   the party who initially communicated the information consents to that further communication; and

        (ii)   the further communication is made only for the purpose or purposes for which the party made the initial communication; and.

    (b)   the information may be successively communicated to and by further recipients on as many occasions as may be necessary to fulfil the purpose for which the information was initially communicated, provided that on each such occasion the conditions in sub-paragraph (a) are met."

Practice Direction 12G addresses three further categories of permitted communications: (i) by a party for other purposes, (ii) for the effective functioning of Cafcass and CAFCASS CYMRU, and (iii) to and by Ministers of the Crown and Welsh Ministers.

Rules 12.73 and 12.75 do not apply to applications in adoption, placement and related proceedings: these are governed by r.14.14 (which is in similar terms to r.12.73) and Practice Direction 14E.

The legislative history and the effect of r.10.20A of the Family Proceedings Rules 1991 (the predecessor of r.12.73 of the Family Procedure Rules 2010) were considered by Sumner J. in *A Borough Council v A and Others*.[67] He drew a distinction between disclosure of a document filed with the court (for which the court's permission was required) and disclosure of the information contained in such a document (which was governed by r.10.20A of the 1991 Rules—now, r.12.73 of the 2010 Rules), but it is questionable whether it was really the intention of the new rule to introduce such a formal distinction or what value it has. The object of r.12.73 is to control the supply of information relating to proceedings concerning children; it differs from the previous rule[68] in that it is directed to the content of the information rather than the form in which it is held.[69] In *A District Council v M*,[70] Baron J. described the difference between documents and the information which they contain as "a fine distinction" and the distinction was not observed by Munby J. in *Re N (A Child)*,[71] in his consideration of Pt XI of the Family Proceedings Rules 1991.[72]

21–027

In *Re N (A Child)*[73] Munby J. pointed out that the effect of r.11(4) of the Family Proceedings Rules 1991 (the predecessor of r.12.75(1) of the Family Procedure Rules 2010) was "to extend drastically both the circumstances in which disclosure can be made and the content of the disclosure that can be made, in each case without the need for prior judicial sanction". In particular:

"...there is no limitation on the forms of 'complaint' embraced within the new arrangements of the kind which were previously imposed by rule 10.20A(3) . Rule 11.4(1)[74] provides for the disclosure of the relevant information to 'any person'. So

---

[67] [2006] EWHC 1465 (Fam); [2007] 1 W.L.R. 1932.

[68] Rule 4.23 of the 1991 Rules, which was repealed on the introduction of r.10.20A.

[69] In *A District Council v M* [2007] EWHC 3471 (Fam); [2008] 2 F.L.R. 390 at [27], Baron J. described the difference between documents and the information which they contain as "a fine distinction".

[70] [2007] EWHC 3471 (Fam); [2008] 2 F.L.R. 390 at [27].

[71] [2009] EHWC 1663 (Fam); [2009] 2 F.L.R. 1152; see e.g. at [101].

[72] Part XI of the 1991 Rules contained an intermediate version of the rule which had initially been introduced as r.10.20A; it was itself in due course replaced by the 2010 Rules.

[73] [2009] EHWC 1663 (Fam); [2009] 2 F.L.R. 1152 at [38].

[74] Now r.12.75(1) of the Family Procedure Rules 2010.

the new scheme is no longer concerned only with complaints about lawyers and doctors or complaints to an elected representative or peer ... there is likewise now no limitation on the information that may be disclosed in accordance with rule 11.4 without the need for prior judicial sanction ... Rule 11.4(1) provides, without any expressed limitation, for the communication of 'information relating to the proceedings' – in other words, the communication of any information relating to the proceedings."[75]

Although the entitlement to disclose pursuant to r.12.75 of the 2010 Rules is subject to directions given by the court under r.12.73(1)(c), Munby J. held[76] that the court should be cautious before exercising its power to give such directions. On the other hand, Munby J. also emphasised[77] the existence of balancing safeguards—not least, r.12.73(2) of the 2010 Rules,[78] which provides that:

"Nothing in this Chapter permits the communication to the public at large, or any section of the public, of any information relating to the proceedings."

21–028   When the court's permission to disclose information relating to Children Act or similar proceedings *is* required, the matters to be considered by the court were said by Swinton-Thomas L.J., giving the only judgment in *Re C (A Minor) (Care Proceedings: Disclosure)*,[79] to include the following ten factors:

"(1)   The welfare and interests of the child or children concerned in the care proceedings. If the child is likely to be adversely affected by the order in any serious way, this will be a very important factor.

(2)   The welfare and interests of other children generally.

(3)   The maintenance of confidentiality in children cases.

(4)   The importance of encouraging frankness in children's cases ...

(5)   The public interest in the administration of justice. Barriers should not be erected between one branch of the judicature and another because this may be inimical to the overall interests of justice.

(6)   The public interest in the prosecution of serious crime and the punishment of offenders, including the public interest in convicting those who have been guilty of violent or sexual offences against children. There is a strong public interest in making available material to the police which is relevant to a criminal trial. In many cases, this is likely to be a very important factor.

(7)   The gravity of the alleged offence and the relevance of the evidence to it. If the evidence has little or no bearing on the investigation or the trial, this will militate against a disclosure order.

(8)   The desirability of co-operation between various agencies concerned with the welfare of children, including the social services departments, the police service, medical practitioners, health visitors, schools, etc. This is particularly important in cases concerning children.

(9)   In a case to which section 98(2)[80] applies, the terms of the section itself, namely that the witness was not excused from answering incriminating questions, and that any statement or admission would not be admissible

---

[75] Rule 12.75(1) of the Family Procedure Rules 2010 at [37].
[76] Rule 12.75(1) of the Family Procedure Rules 2010 at [77].
[77] Rule 12.75(1) of the Family Procedure Rules 2010 at [69] and [107].
[78] Previously r.11.2(2) of the 1991 Rules
[79] [1997] Fam. 76 at 85 and 86.
[80] Concerning a statement or admission made in an application for an order under Pt IV or Pt V of the Children Act 1989.

against him in criminal proceedings. Fairness to the person who has incriminated himself and any others affected by the incriminating statement and any danger of oppression would also be relevant considerations.

(10)   Any other material disclosure which has already taken place."

Swinton-Thomas L.J. said that it was not possible to place these factors in any order of importance, because the importance of each of them would inevitably vary very much from case to case.

The Court of Appeal's guidance in *Re C (A Minor) (Care Proceedings: Disclosure)* pre-dated the introduction of the Human Rights Act 1998, which now requires consideration also of the interests of anyone whose Art.6, Art.8 or Art.10 rights are engaged.[81] Nevertheless, the Court of Appeal's judgment remains the leading judgment in the field, although any court seeking to apply its guidance must now take into account the recent legislative introduction of a more permissive regime in relation to the disclosure of information *without* the court's sanction.[82]   **21–029**

Where material is relevant to criminal proceedings or a police investigation, the court's permission for disclosure will often be given (if and to the extent that it is required). In *Re W (Minors) (Social Workers: Disclosure)*,[83] Butler-Sloss L.J. said: **21–030**

"In a case such as this where the police and the social workers are working together, a family judge should hesitate before refusing to provide relevant and significant information to the police. There will be cases where the evidence is peripheral and the harm of giving leave will outweigh the value of the information. But the police investigations require them to put together a jigsaw of information in order to carry out their important public duty. The family judges ought not to frustrate the investigation of potential crimes (which includes the dissipation of unfounded suspicions against the innocent) without good reason, even more so when the police are working alongside the social workers on the same case."

In *A Health Authority v X*[84] it was held that a court which permits disclosure may impose conditions on the subsequent use that may be made of the documents or information disclosed. Thorpe L.J. also observed[85]:   **21–031**

" . . . despite the administrative difficulties that may result I am of the strong opinion that where the trial has been conducted by a judge of the [Family] Division, then a subsequent application by a third party for the release of the case papers must be to that judge rather than to another judge of the Division, absent exceptional circumstances."

---

[81]   The justification for disclosure may not always be a public law one: see the pre-Human Rights Act case of *Re X, Y and Z (Minors) (Wardship: Disclosure of Material)* [1992] Fam. 124, in which a newspaper unsuccessfully sought disclosure to assist its defence of justification to a libel action brought by two paediatricians.

[82]   *Re H (Children)* [2009] EWCA Civ 704; [2009] 2 F.L.R. 1531.

[83]   [1999] 1 W.L.R. 205 at [19]. *ND v JM* [2002] EWHC 2820 (Fam); [2003] 1 F.L.R. 647, in which Hedley J. distinguished Wall J.'s decision in *A Chief Constable v A County Council* [2002] EWHC 2198, Fam; [2003] 1 F.L.R. 579, is an example of a case in which disclosure to the police was refused.

[84]   [2001] EWCA Civ 2014; [2002] 2 All E.R. 780.

[85]   At [23].

RESTRICTING DISCLOSURE TO THE PARTIES THEMSELVES

21–032 In exceptional circumstances in adoption proceedings or family proceedings, confidential reports, or parts of them, may be withheld from the parties themselves (though available to the court). The principles on which the court should act were set out by the House of Lords in *Re D (Minors) (Adoption Reports: Confidentiality)*.[86] Lord Mustill, giving the only speech, said that there must be a strong presumption in favour of disclosure on grounds of natural justice:

> " . . . the court should first consider whether disclosure of the material would involve a real possibility of significant harm to the child.
>
> If it would, the court should next consider whether the overall interests of the child would benefit from non-disclosure, weighing on the one hand the interest of the child in having the material properly tested, and on the other both the magnitude of the risk that harm will occur and the gravity of the harm if it does occur.
>
> If the court is satisfied that the interests of the child point towards non-disclosure, the next and final step is for the court to weigh that consideration, and its strength in the circumstances of the case, against the interest of the parent or other party in having an opportunity to see and respond to the material. In the latter regard the court should take into account the importance of the material to the issues in the case.
>
> Non-disclosure should be the exception and not the rule. The court should be rigorous in its examination of the risk and gravity of the feared harm to the child and should order non-disclosure only when the case for doing so is compelling."[87]

21–033 In *Re B (Disclosure to Other Parties)*,[88] Munby J. considered the effect on those principles of the Human Rights Act 1998. He held that Lord Mustill's guidance remained applicable, with the single qualification that it was no longer the case (if it ever had been) that the only interests capable of denying a litigant access to the documents in a proper case were the interests of the children involved in the litigation: the interests of any other person—whether child or adult—whose Art.8 rights were sufficiently engaged also had to be taken into account. Munby J.'s judgment was cited with approval by the Court of Appeal in *Re X (Children)*.[89]

Guidance as to the procedure to be adopted in cases where the issue arises was given by Johnson J. in *Re C (Disclosure)*[90] and approved by the Court of Appeal in *Re M (A Minor) (Disclosure)*.[91] In *Re T (Wardship: Impact of Police Intelligence)*,[92] McFarlane J. discussed some of the practical difficulties which may arise and the use of special advocates.

---

[86] [1996] A.C. 593.

[87] At 615.

[88] [2001] 2 F.L.R. 1017 at [64]–[66].

[89] [2002] EWCA Civ 828; [2002] 2 F.L.R. 476; see also *A County Council v SB* [2010] EWHC 2528; [2011] 1 F.L.R. 651 (Sir Nicholas Wall P).

[90] [1996] 1 F.L.R. 797.

[91] [1998] 2 F.L.R. 1028.

[92] [2009] EWHC 2440 (Fam); [2010] 1 F.L.R. 1048. In *Al Rawi v Security Services* [2012] 1 A.C. 531, the Supreme Court expressly recognised that wardship or similar proceedings represented one of the very few situations in which a "closed material procedure" might be appropriate.

CHAPTER 22

Arbitrations

THE DUTY OF CONFIDENCE

It has long been recognised by English law that arbitration is a private process, **22–001** but the courts have experienced difficulty in formulating the nature and extent of the obligations of confidentiality that arise as a result. Either the arbitration agreement itself, or the rules under which the arbitration is to be conducted, may contain express provisions relating to confidentiality; but in many cases no such express provisions appear.[1]

In *Dolling-Baker v Merrett*[2] Parker L.J., giving the leading judgment in the **22–002** Court of Appeal, stated:

> "As between parties to an arbitration, although the proceedings are consensual and may thus be regarded as wholly voluntary, their very nature is such that there must, in my judgment, be some implied obligation on both parties not to disclose or use for any other purpose any documents prepared for and used in the arbitration, or disclosed or produced in the course of the arbitration, or transcripts or notes of the evidence in the arbitration or the award, and indeed not to disclose in any other way what evidence had been given by any witness in the arbitration, save with the consent of the other party, or pursuant to an order or leave of the court. That qualification is necessary just as it is in the case of the implied obligation of secrecy between banker and customer."

The court was not concerned in that case to identify the nature or extent of any qualifications to the duty.

The subject of confidentiality in arbitrations was considered by the High Court **22–003** of Australia in *Esso Australian Resources Ltd v Plowman*.[3] The appellants, Esso Australian Resources Ltd, made or were assignees of contracts with two public utilities for the sale of natural gas. The price was to be adjusted by taking into account the effect of any changes in taxes. The contracts required the sellers to provide the buyers with details of any price changes and the calculations on which they were based. Disputes between the sellers and the buyers were referred to arbitration. The Minister for Energy and Minerals had substantial powers to require the supply of information by the utilities. The Minister brought actions

---

[1] See the brief review by Lawrence Collins L.J. in *Emmott v Michael Wilson & Partners Ltd* [2008] EWCA Civ 184; [2008] C.P. Rep. 26 at [67]–[70].

[2] [1990] 1 W.L.R. 1205 at 1213.

[3] [1994–1995] 183 C.L.R. 10. For a copy of the judgments together with editorial comment, the salient parts of the experts' reports provided in the case by Stewart Boyd QC and others, and other learned articles, see [1995] 11(3) *Arbitration Int.* 231–340.

against the appellants and the utilities claiming declarations that information disclosed by the appellants to the utilities in the arbitrations was not subject to any obligation of confidence. The appellants cross claimed for declarations that the arbitrations were to be held in private and that any documents or information supplied by any party to any other party for the purpose of the arbitrations was to be treated in confidence between the parties and the arbitrators.

22–004   The trial judge decided in the Minister's favour. An appeal to the Supreme Court of Victoria was allowed in part, but the court upheld declarations to the effect that the utilities were not restricted from disclosing information to the Minister and others by reason only that it was obtained from the appellants in the arbitration and had not otherwise been published. On further appeal by the sellers, the High Court remitted the declarations to the Supreme Court of Victoria for reformulation but otherwise dismissed the appeals.

22–005   The sellers argued that it was an implied term of the arbitration agreements that the arbitrations should be conducted in private, and that the buyers were under an implied contractual, and equitable, obligation of confidence not to disclose, except for the purposes of the arbitration, information and documents provided to them for the purposes of the arbitration by the sellers, unless authorised by statute.

22–006   Mason C.J., with whom Dawson and McHugh JJ. agreed, recognised that (subject to any manifestation of a contrary intention arising from the arbitration agreement) an arbitration was to be held in private. He preferred to describe the privacy attaching to an arbitration as an incident of the subject-matter of the agreement to arbitrate, rather than to attribute it to an implied term of the agreement, although he did not consider that it mattered greatly.

22–007   As to a general obligation of confidentiality, he said[4]:

> "There is . . . a case for saying that, in the course of evolution, the private arbitration has advanced to the stage where confidentiality has become one of its essential attributes so that confidentiality is a characteristic or quality that inheres in arbitration. Despite the view taken in *Dolling-Baker* and subsequently by Colman J. in *Hassneh Insurance*, I do not consider that, in Australia, having regard to the various matters to which I have referred, we are justified in concluding that confidentiality is an essential attribute of a private arbitration imposing an obligation on each party not to disclose the proceedings or documents and information provided in and for the purposes of the arbitration."

22–008   Mason C.J. accepted, however, that there was an implied obligation to accord to documents disclosed by a party compulsorily, pursuant to an order of the arbitrator, the same confidentiality which would attach to them if the parties were litigating rather than arbitrating. He also said[5]:

> "In argument, reference was made to the principles governing the protection of confidential information generally. No doubt these principles may have some application to information in arbitration proceedings. But these principles do not support the broad claim for confidentiality made by the appellants."

---

[4] *Esso Australian Resources Ltd v Plowman* [1994–1995] 183 C.L.R. 10 at 30.
[5] *Esso Australian Resources Ltd v Plowman* [1994–1995] 183 C.L.R. 10 at 30.

In order for the principles of confidentiality to apply, the information must have the quality of confidence and must be received in circumstances importing an obligation of confidence. Mason C.J. would appear to accept that information disclosed in arbitration proceedings may satisfy both requirements, while rejecting the proposition that this applies to all such information.

Brennan J. and Toohey J. concurred in the result but by different reasoning. **22–009** Brennan J. agreed with Mason C.J. that any duty of confidentiality would not arise merely from the privacy of the hearing. It must be derived from an implied term of the agreement to arbitrate. Some term could be implied from the fact that documents and information supplied for the purposes of arbitration were given solely for that purpose. But, to the extent that a party would not have agreed at the time of the arbitration agreement to keep documents or information confidential, the implied obligation of confidentiality must be qualified.

Brennan J. gave various examples. If a party was under a statutory or common **22–010** law duty to communicate the document or information to a third party, no contractual obligation of confidentiality could prohibit performance of that duty. A party might be under a duty, not necessarily legal, to communicate documents or information to a party with a legitimate interest in the outcome of the proceedings (for example, a subsidiary company to its parent) or might wish to reveal them for the protection of its own interests. Nor should an obligation be implied that a party would keep confidential documents or information when he had an obligation, not necessarily legal, to satisfy a public interest—more than mere curiosity—in knowing what was contained in them.

Toohey J. considered that, subject to qualifications where disclosure was **22–011** reasonably necessary to protect the interests of a party to the arbitration or in the public interest, an obligation of confidentiality did attach to the documents and information emanating from an arbitration by reason of an implied term of a commercial arbitration agreement. He said[6]:

> "The term is implied from the entry by the parties into a form of dispute resolution which they choose because of the privacy they expect to result. If this is said to confuse privacy and confidentiality, the answer is that they are not distinct characteristics. As Colman J. said in *Hassneh*:
>
> 'The disclosure to a third party of [a note or transcript of the evidence] would be almost equivalent to opening the door of the arbitration room to that third party.'
>
> Any aspect of disclosure to third parties must infringe the privacy of the arbitration."

The majority of the Australian High Court therefore declined to infer from the undoubted privacy of arbitration proceedings the existence of a general duty of confidence between the parties requiring them to treat all aspects of the arbitration process as confidential.

In *Ali Shipping Corp v Shipyard Trogir*,[7] the plaintiff sought to restrain the **22–012** defendant from using documents generated in the course of an arbitration between them for the purposes of separate arbitration proceedings between the defendant and other companies in common ownership with the plaintiff. The Court of Appeal granted an injunction to the plaintiff. Potter L.J. gave the only

---

[6] [1994–1995] 183 C.L.R. 10 at 47–48.
[7] [1999] 1 W.L.R. 314.

judgment. He referred to the decision of the High Court of Australia in *Esso v Plowman*, but concluded that an implied duty of confidentiality did arise in relation to arbitrations, stating[8]:

> "It seems to me that, in holding as a matter of principle that the obligation of confidentiality, whatever its precise limits, arises as an essential corollary of the privacy of arbitration proceedings, the court is propounding a term which arises 'as the nature of the contract itself implicitly requires' . . . As Lord Bridge of Harwich observed in *Scally v Southern Health and Social Services Board* [1992] 1 A.C. 294, 307, a clear distinction is to be drawn
>
> > 'between the search for an implied term necessary to give business efficacy to a particular contract and the search, based on wider considerations, for a term which the law will imply as a necessary incident of a definable category of contractual relationship.'
>
> In my view an arbitration clause is a good example of the latter type of implied term. The distinction referred to by Lord Bridge in *Scally's* case is of some practical importance in this case. This is because considerations of business efficacy . . . are likely to involve a detailed examination of the circumstances existing at the time of the relevant contract . . . , whereas the parties have indicated their presumed intention simply by entering into a contract to which the court attributes particular characteristics. While acknowledging that the boundaries of the obligation of confidence which thereby arise have yet to be delineated . . . , the manner in which that may best be achieved is by formulating exceptions of broad application to be applied in individual cases, rather than by seeking to reconsider, and if necessary adapt, the general rule on each occasion in the light of the particular circumstances and presumed intentions of the parties at the time of their original agreement."

Potter L.J. went on to identify a number of exceptions to the broad rule of confidentiality.

22–013   Potter L.J.'s views were subsequently questioned in *Associated Electric and Gas Insurance Services Ltd v European Reinsurance Co of Zurich*,[9] a decision of the Privy Council on appeal from the Court of Appeal of Bermuda. The case concerned the proper construction of express confidentiality provisions in an arbitration agreement. It was held that they should not be construed in such a way as would prevent one party from relying on the award as giving him rights against the other. In a postscript Lord Hobhouse, delivering the judgment of the Privy Council, commented obiter on Potter L.J.'s approach as follows[10]:

> "Their Lordships have reservations about the desirability or merit of adopting this approach. It runs the risk of failing to distinguish between different types of confidentiality which attach to different types of document or to documents which have been obtained in different ways and elides privacy and confidentiality. Commercial arbitrations are essentially private proceedings and unlike litigation in the public courts do not place anything in the public domain. This may mean that the implied restrictions on the use of material obtained in arbitration proceedings may have a greater impact than those applying in litigation. But when it comes to the award, the same logic cannot be applied. An award may have to be referred to for accounting purposes or for the purpose of legal proceedings . . . or for the purpose of enforcing the rights which the award confers. Generalisations and the formulation of detailed implied terms are not appropriate."

---

[8] At 326.

[9] [2003] UKPC 11; [2003] 1 W.L.R. 1041.

[10] At [20].

Subsequently, in *Department of Economics, Policy and Development of the*   **22–014**
City of Moscow v Bankers Trust Co,[11] Mance L.J., giving the leading judgment in
the Court of Appeal, reiterated that[12]:

> "Among features long assumed to be implicit in parties' choice to arbitrate in
> England are privacy and confidentiality."

In *Emmott v Michael Wilson & Partners Ltd*[13] the Court of Appeal again
reviewed the confidentiality inherent in arbitration proceedings. The claimant
(and/or associated entities) faced a multiplicity of legal and arbitration
proceedings, brought by the defendant in a number of jurisdictions. In
proceedings brought in New South Wales against two associates of the claimant,
the defendant sought permission to amend its pleadings, asserting that the
purpose of the amendments was to "bring a level of parity to the proceedings
presently being conducted in New South Wales, the British Virgin Islands and
England". In arbitration proceedings in London, the defendant had initially made
and had then subsequently withdrawn allegations of fraud and conspiracy against
the claimant. The claimant sought permission to disclose the pleadings in the
arbitration proceedings to his associates engaged in litigation with the defendant
in New South Wales, the British Virgin Islands and the Bahamas. The claimant
argued that there was otherwise a risk that the courts in the overseas proceedings
would be misled as to the nature of the case advanced by the defendant in the
London arbitration proceedings. Flaux J. acceded in large measure to the
claimant's application and the defendant's appeal against his decision was
dismissed.

The leading judgment in the Court of Appeal was given by Lawrence Collins   **22–015**
L.J. He summarised the position in English law as follows:

> "Documents in arbitration may ... be inherently confidential, as where they contain
> trade secrets. But it is clear that what has emerged from the recent authorities in
> England is that there is, separate from confidentiality in that sense, an implied
> obligation (arising out of the nature of arbitration itself) on both parties not to
> disclose or use for any other purpose any documents prepared for and used in the
> arbitration, or disclosed or produced in the course of the arbitration, or transcripts or
> notes of the evidence in the arbitration or the award, and not to disclose in any other
> way what evidence has been given by any witness in the arbitration, save with the
> consent of the other party, or pursuant to an order or leave of the court. The
> obligation is not limited to documents which contain material which is confidential,
> such as trade secrets... The obligation arises, not as a matter of business efficacy,
> but is implied as a matter of law..."[14]

Lawrence Collins L.J. referred to the reservation expressed by Lord Hobhouse in
*Associated Electric and Gas Insurance Services Ltd v European Reinsurance Co
of Zurich* but observed, "subject to that reservation", that the English authorities
had sought to identify exceptions to the principle of confidentiality which fell

---

[11] [2004] EWCA Civ 314; [2005] Q.B. 207.
[12] At [2].
[13] [2008] EWCA Civ 184; [2008] 1 Lloyd's Rep. 616.
[14] At [81]; Lawrence Collins L.J. pointed out at [82] that English law appeared in this respect to differ
from Australian law.

into a number of categories (similar to the categories which were identified by the Court of Appeal in relation to banking confidentiality in *Tournier v National Provincial and Union Bank of England*[15]):

> "In my judgment the content of the obligation may depend on the context in which it arises and on the nature of the information or documents at issue. The limits of that obligation are still in the process of development on a case-by-case basis. On the authorities as they now stand, the principal cases in which disclosure will be permissible are these: the first is where there is consent, express or implied; second, where there is an order, or leave of the court (but that does not mean that the court has a general discretion to lift the obligation of confidentiality); third, where it is reasonably necessary for the protection of the legitimate interests of an arbitrating party; fourth, where the interests of justice require disclosure, and also (perhaps) where the public interest requires disclosure."[16]

The interface between arbitration and litigation

In *Michael Wilson & Partners Ltd v Emmott*[17] Lawrence Collins L.J. said:

> "The implied agreement is really a rule of substantive law masquerading as an implied term. But if the implied agreement of the parties is to be taken as the basis of the obligation of confidentiality (at any rate where English law is the law governing the arbitration agreement) it ought to follow that disputes about its limits are within the scope of the arbitration agreement and should be determined by the arbitral tribunal."

22–016   However, an arbitral award may generate court proceedings between the same parties, either to enforce it or to challenge it. When this happens there is a meeting point between the essentially private process of arbitration and the essentially public process of the administration of justice by the courts.

22–017   Under the Arbitration Act 1996 a party may apply to the court to challenge an arbitral award for lack of substantive jurisdiction,[18] for serious irregularity[19] or by way of appeal on a point of law.[20] CPR 62.10 provides that the court may order that an arbitration claim be heard either in public or in private, but that, unless the court orders otherwise, an appeal on a question of law under s.69 will be heard in public but applications to challenge an award for want of jurisdiction or for serious irregularity or for leave to appeal under s.69 will be heard in private.

22–018   In *Department of Economics, Policy and Development of the City of Moscow v Bankers Trust Co* the issue was whether a judgment dismissing an application to challenge an award for serious irregularity under s.68 (or a summary) should be available for general publication or for limited publication to certain financial institutions. This involved a conflict between the value of open justice which (absent other considerations) would require that a judgment of the court should be freely available and the value of protecting the private and confidential nature of the arbitral proceedings.

---

[15] [1924] 1 K.B. 461.
[16] *Emmott v Michael Wilson & Partners Ltd* at [107].
[17] At [84]; see also per Thomas L.J. at [119].
[18] s.67.
[19] s.68.
[20] s.69.

Mance L.J. said that the silence of the Arbitration Act about privacy and **22–019** confidentiality did not detract from the long standing assumption that they are implicit in parties' choice to arbitrate in England. He referred to the report of the Departmental Advisory Committee on Arbitration Law, chaired by Lord Saville of Newdigate, which was heavily influential in the drafting of the Act. It was the difficulty of formulating the principles and the "myriad exceptions" and qualifications in the statutory terms that led the committee to conclude that the courts should be left to work them out "on a pragmatic, case-by-case basis".[21]

In relation to applications under s.68, Mance L.J. said that even though the **22–020** hearing may have been in private the court should bear in mind in preparing and giving judgment that it should be given in public, where this could be done without disclosing significant confidential information.[22] He gave his reasons:

> "The public interest in ensuring appropriate standards of fairness in the conduct of arbitrations militates in favour of a public judgment in respect of judgments given on applications under section 68. The desirability of public scrutiny as a means by which confidence in the courts can be maintained and the administration of justice made transparent applies here as in other areas of court activity under the principles of *Scott v Scott* [1913] A.C. 417 and article 6. Arbitration is an important feature of international, commercial and financial life, and there is legitimate interest in its operation and practice. The desirability of a public judgment is particularly present in any case where a judgment involves points of law or practice which may offer future guidance to lawyers or practitioners."

As to confidentiality, and how this was to be set against the desirability of judgments being given in public, he said[23]:

> "The factors militating in favour of publicity have to be weighed together with the desirability of preserving the confidentiality of the original arbitration and its subject matter. There is a spectrum. At one end is the arbitration itself and at the other an order following a reasoned judgment under section 68 . . . A reasoned judgment under section 68 will in likelihood disclose very much less about the subject matter of the arbitration than will have been covered during the section 68 hearing itself. Moreover judges framing judgments are accustomed to concentrate on essentials, to avoid where possible unnecessary disclosure of sensitive material and in some cases to anonymise . . .
>
> If . . . the court withholds publication where a party before it would suffer some real prejudice from publication or where the publication would disclose matters by the confidentiality of which one or both parties have set significant store, but publishes its judgments in other cases, businessmen can be confidant that their privacy and confidentiality in arbitration will, where appropriate, be preserved. The limited but necessary interface between arbitration and the public court system means that more cannot be expected. There can be no question of withholding publication of reasoned judgments on a blanket basis out of a generalised, and in my view unfounded, concern that their publication would upset the confidence of the business community in English arbitration."

---

[21] At [2].

[22] [2004] EWCA Civ 314; [2005] Q.B. 207 at [39].

[23] [2004] EWCA Civ 314; [2005] Q.B. 207 at [40] and [41].

CONCLUSIONS

22–021   Despite the reservations expressed by Lord Hobhouse in *Associated Electric and Gas Insurance Services v European Reinsurance Co of Zurich*,[24] broad questions of principle do arise in relation to the duty of confidentiality owed by parties to arbitrations and its qualifications. In developing the law of confidentiality, the courts should be capable, in this as in other fields, of formulating the qualifications with sufficient clarity and flexibility.

22–022   The starting point is that parties to an arbitration agreement are to be taken as impliedly agreeing to treat documents and information emanating from the arbitration as confidential. The implication arises from the nature of the arbitral process, i.e. that it is an essentially private process, and from what the courts have accepted to be the long held assumptions of those who use arbitration. However, as with other implied duties of confidentiality, it is subject to qualifications.

22–023   In *Department of Economics, Policy and Development of the City of Moscow v Bankers Trust Co*[25] Mance L.J. referred to a spectrum from the initial stages of an arbitration to the award and to a judgment in proceedings challenging the award. At different stages different circumstances may arise to warrant different degrees of disclosure.

22–024   At one end of the spectrum, for example, the confidentiality of documents produced by a party under compulsion pursuant to an arbitrator's order for disclosure should attract a high level of protection (and indeed the confidentiality of such documents was recognised by the High Court of Australia in *Esso v Plowman*).

22–025   On the other hand, there may be a wide range of reasons why a party to an arbitration legitimately requires to reveal the arbitrator's award to a third party. As the Privy Council observed in *Associated Electric and Gas Insurance Services*,[26] contrasting arbitration awards with material obtained in arbitration proceedings:

> "But when it comes to the award, the same logic cannot be applied. An award may have to be referred to for accounting purposes or for the purposes of legal proceedings . . . or for the purposes of enforcing the rights which the award confers . . . "

QUALIFICATIONS/EXCEPTIONS

22–026   Of the qualifications identified by Lawrence Collins L.J. in *Emmott v Michael Wilson & Partners Ltd*[27] (consent, order/leave of the court, protection of the legitimate interests of an arbitrating party, and the interests of justice/public interest), some merit further comment.

---

[24] [2003] UKPC 11; [2003] 1 W.L.R. 1041 at [20].
[25] [2004] EWCA Civ 314; [2005] Q.B. 207 at [40].
[26] At [20].
[27] [2008] EWCA Civ 184; [2008] C.P. Rep. 26 at [93] to [102] and [107].

Order/leave of the court

It is axiomatic that a party to an arbitration should be entitled to disclose confidential information when a court has ordered or granted him permission to do so. However, this begs the question of the grounds on which such orders will be made, or such permission will be granted. As Lawrence Collins L.J. observed in *Emmott v Michael Wilson & Partners Ltd*[28]:

> "…it does not follow from the fact that a court refers to the possibility of an exception for the order of the court or leave of the court in a case where it has the power to make the order or give leave … [that] the court has a general and unlimited jurisdiction to consider whether an exception to confidentiality exists and applies."

22–027

Moreover, even in the absence of a court order, a party may be under compulsion of law (for example, by statute or under the Civil Procedure Rules) to disclose confidential information. He may be well advised to seek the court's approval before acting but, if his disclosure is justified, that approval is not necessary to his defence against an action for breach of confidence.

Disclosure in a party's own interests

In *Hassneh Insurance v Mew*[29] Colman J. held that the duty of confidence owed by an arbitrating party was subject to the qualification that it did not prevent disclosure of an arbitrator's award if it was reasonably necessary for the establishment or protection of that party's legal rights vis-à-vis a third party, and that in such a case the party wishing to make disclosure did not require to seek the approval of the court. In so holding, Colman J. based himself on the judgments in *Tournier v National Provincial and Union Bank of England.*[30]

22–028

The extent of this qualification was again considered by Colman J. in *Insurance Company v Lloyd's Syndicate.*[31] The case arose out of a reinsurance dispute between a Lloyd's syndicate and certain excess of loss reinsurers. The plaintiff reinsurers were the leading insurers on a slip subscribed also by five companies, who were not parties to the arbitration. In the arbitration between the syndicate and the leading insurers an interim award was issued in the syndicate's favour. The syndicate wished to disclose the award to the following market in order to persuade the following market to accept liability. Colman J. held that it was not entitled to do so, because as between the syndicate and the following market the award had no more status than if it had been an independent counsel's opinion. Disclosure might have been helpful to the syndicate in attempting to persuade the following market to accept its claim, but was not necessary to enable the syndicate to establish or enforce its rights against the following market.

22–029

This may be thought a harsh decision. When the leading insurers subscribed the slip, they had no knowledge on what terms other companies would subscribe, but as a matter of practicality it is common for the following market to follow the

22–030

---

[28] At [87].
[29] [1993] 2 Lloyd's Rep. 243 at 249.
[30] [1924] 1 K.B. 461.
[31] [1995] 1 Lloyd's Rep. 272.

leader in matters such as settlements. If the following market had agreed to be bound by the leading underwriter's claims, settlements, decisions or arbitration awards, there is no doubt that the syndicate would have been entitled to disclose the arbitration award to the following market. If the leader had agreed to settle the syndicate's claim, the syndicate would have been entitled to tell the following market. If the arbitration had resulted in a decision that the leading underwriter was entitled to avoid the policy for non-disclosure, it would be surprising if the syndicate would have been entitled to prevent the following market from being told. It would in the circumstances seem not unreasonable to imply a qualification to the duty of confidentiality entitling the syndicate to inform the following market of the outcome of any claims made by it against the leaders of the slip as a step reasonably necessary to protect the syndicate's interest in obtaining prompt settlement and avoiding multiplicity of proceedings.

22–031   In *Ali Shipping Corporation v Shipyard Trogir*,[32] the Court of Appeal endorsed the observations of Colman J. that it was not enough that an award or reasons might have a commercially persuasive impact on the third party to whom they were disclosed, nor that their disclosure would be "merely helpful, as distinct from necessary, for the protection of such rights", but at the same time suggested that the court should take a flexible approach to what was "reasonably necessary" for the protection of a party's legitimate interests.

22–032   It is suggested that it would be too narrow to limit the concept of protection of a party's legitimate interests to cases where the object of disclosure is to enforce a party's legal rights. If, for example, the knowledge that a claim has been made against a party is affecting that party in its commercial relationships with business partners, its bank or others, it may have a good case for saying that it should be entitled to inform those parties of the outcome of an arbitration, without being entitled to disclose confidential documents or other details. It may also owe a duty to others, such as its bank, to inform them of the outcome.

The Court of Appeal adopted a broad view of the "self-interest exception" in *Emmott v Michael Wilson & Partners Ltd*. Thomas L.J. said[33]:

> "The use sought to be made was use by Mr Emmott in proceedings in other jurisdictions between MWP and parties having very similar interests to him. MWP was the claimant in the proceedings in New South Wales and the British Virgin Islands; the proceedings concerned the same substratum of fact; in New South Wales and in the British Virgin Islands the nature of the allegations against the defendants are inextricably intertwined with the conduct alleged against Mr Emmott; the issue as to the appointment of a receiver plainly involved Mr Emmott."

He concluded that it was reasonably necessary, on the facts of the case, for Mr Emmott to make the documents available for use by those with very similar interests to him in those proceedings for the purpose of protecting his own legitimate private interests.

---

[32] [1999] 1 W.L.R. 314 at 327.
[33] At [132]; see also per Carnwath L.J. at [134].

Disclosure in the interests of justice/public interest

In *London & Leeds Estates Ltd v Paribas Ltd (No.2)*,[34] the question arose   **22–033**
whether an expert witness giving evidence in a rent review arbitration should be
compelled to produce a proof of evidence provided by him in an earlier separate
arbitration. Mance J. held:

> "It does not seem to me that [the witness] has legitimate ground to object to
> cross-examination about his previous statements on the general subject of West End
> property market conditions in 1991. If a witness were proved to have expressed
> himself in a materially different sense when acting for different sides, that would be
> a factor which should be brought out in the interests of individual litigants involved
> and in the public interest."

In *Ali Shipping* Potter L.J. endorsed Mance J.'s view, while commenting[35]:   **22–034**

> "As a matter of terminology, I would prefer to recognise such an exception under the
> heading 'interests of justice' rather than 'the public interest', in order to avoid the
> suggestion that use of that latter phrase is to be read as extending to the wider issues
> of public interest contested in *Esso Australia Resources Ltd v Plowman* . . . In that
> case, only the dissenting judgment of Toohey J. appears to me to treat the law of
> privacy and confidentiality in relation to arbitration proceedings on lines similar to
> English law. While it may well fall to the English court at a future time to consider
> some further exception to the general rule of confidentiality based on wider
> considerations of public interest, it is not necessary to do so in this case."

In *Emmott v Michael Wilson & Partners Ltd* Thomas L.J.[36] said that the term
'public interest' "better expresses the nature of the issue", but both Lawrence
Collins L.J. and Carnwath L.J. preferred to leave the matter open.[37] On the facts
of that case it was a distinction without a difference. It would have been a
perversion of justice if the respondent had been enabled by the doctrine of
confidentiality to mislead other tribunals, without fear of contradiction, about the
nature of its claims in the London arbitration, and any contractual term which
supposedly enabled it to do so would be contrary to public policy.

The precise scope of the "public interest defence" has long been a vexed
question in the jurisprudence of confidentiality. However, it is suggested that
there is no good reason why the general law on this topic[38] should not be applied
also in the context of arbitration proceedings.

Others involved in arbitrations

An arbitrator by agreeing to act in that capacity must in principle owe an implied   **22–035**
duty of confidentiality to the parties similar to that owed by the parties to each
other. Those involved in arbitration proceedings as representatives of the parties
or witnesses should by reason of their knowledge of the confidential nature of the

---

[34] [1995] 2 E.G. 134.
[35] At 328.
[36] At [130].
[37] See also *Milsom v Ablyazov* [2011] EWHC 955 (Ch), per Briggs J. at [30].
[38] See Ch.16 above.

proceedings, owe an equitable duty of confidentiality to the parties in respect of documents or information, but defining the boundaries of what is conscionable behaviour may involve difficulties. An expert witness giving evidence in a rent review dispute[39] may be aware of one or more highly relevant recent decisions by respected arbitrators, because he had been involved, and they may have had a strong bearing on the formation of his expert opinion. Or a solicitor applying on behalf of a client for permission to appeal against an arbitration award on a point of law under s.69 (under which there is a different threshold according to whether the point of law is a one-off issue or a point of general importance) may wish to say that he is aware from his knowledge of other arbitrations that the point has regularly arisen with different arbitrators giving different answers. It is unlikely that the expert witness or the solicitor would be considered to be acting in breach of duty if he confined himself to saying that his evidence was based on experience in other anonymised cases, but, if challenged, to disclose the parties' identities, he would be unwise to do so without an order of the court.

---

[39] See, for example, *London & Leeds Estates Ltd v Paribas Ltd (No.2)* [1999] 02 E.G. 134.

INDEX

All references are to paragraph number

Abortion
  doctor-patient relationship, 11–037
Access to information
  doctor-patient relationship, 11–036
Account of profits
  conflicting views
    damages, on, 2–065
    information as property, on, 2–040
  contractual relationship, 3–004
  delay, 9–060
  employer's obligations, 14–035
  generally, 9–018—9–021
  personal representatives, 3–191
  public sector confidentiality, 5–013
  springboard doctrine, 4–027
Action for discovery *see* **Disclosure and**
  production claims
"Advancement of medicine"
  doctor-patient relationship, 11–021—11–022
Advice
  doctor-patient relationship, 11–011—11–017
Agency
  origins of confidentiality, 1–025
Anonymised data
  doctor-patient relationship, 11–008—11–010
Anonymity
  reporting restrictions
    generally, 20–014—20–017
    introduction, 20–006
Anton Piller orders
  collateral use of information disclosed for
    litigation, 20–051
  generally, 9–054
Appeals
  freedom of information, 8–031
Arbitrations
  conclusion, 22–021—22–025
  disclosure in a party's own interests,
    22–028—22–032
  disclosure in the interests of justice,
    22–033—22–034
  duty of arbitrators, 22–035
  exceptions, 22–026
  generally, 22–001—22–015

  interface with litigation, 22–016—22–020
  leave of the court, 22–027
  qualifications
    disclosure in a party's own interests,
      22–028—22–032
    disclosure in the interests of justice,
      22–033—22–034
    introduction, 22–026
    leave of the court, 22–027
Armed forces
  public interest immunity, 19–035—19–037
Assignment
  contractual arrangements, 3–187
Australia
  arbitrations, 22–003
  companies, 7–076
  comparative law, 2–085—2–103
  constructive trusts, 9–022
  equitable obligation of confidentiality, 3–034
  freedom of information, 8–004
  information received for limited purpose in
    exercise of legal power, 3–028
  lawyer's continuing duty, 16–008
  legal professional privilege, 18–021
  misuse, 3–164—3–165
  public interest, 6–061—6–069
"Balancing exercise"
  privacy
    generally, 7–062—7–064
    justification for interference, 7–046
  public sector confidentiality, 5–004
  serious harm to the public, 6–017
Banker-customer relationship
  compulsion by law, 12–013
  consent, 12–022—12–025
  duty to the public, 12–014—12–019
  general principle, 12–001—12–012
  interest of the bank, 12–020—12–021
  protection of bank's interest, 12–020—12–021
  public interest, 12–014—12–019
  statutory authority, 12–013
Bankers' Books Evidence Act 1879
  banker-customer relationship, 12–013

order for production of documents outside the
    jurisdiction, 10–005—10–009
Broadcasting
  disclosure of sources
    'disclosure', 13–020
    generally, 13–014—13–020
    'interests of justice', 13–023—13–026
    nature of the source and information
        revealed, 13–027—13–030
    'necessary', 13–021—13–022
  freedom to publish
    freedom of expression, 13–004—13–009
    introduction, 13–002—13–003
    Ofcom Broadcasting Code, 13–012
    PCC Code of Practice, 13–010—13–011
    restriction on injunctions, 13–010—13–013
  injunctions restraining publication,
    13–010—13–013
  introduction, 13–001
  Ofcom Broadcasting Code, 13–012
  PCC Code of Practice, 13–010—13–011
  Press Complaints Commission, 13–010
  right to respect for private and family life,
    13–003
Canada
  comparative law, 2–085—2–103
  constructive trusts, 9–022
  freedom of information, 8–004
  lawyer's continuing duty, 16–005
  legal professional privilege, 18–021
Change of circumstances
  duration of confidentiality, 4–028—4–034
Childcare
  public interest immunity, 19–038—19–039
Children
  best interests of the child
    paramount consideration, as, 21–016
    primary consideration, as, 21–013—21–015
  court's jurisdiction
    best interests of the child, 21–013—21–016
    Family Court, 21–017—21–020
    generally, 21–005—21–012
  doctor-patient relationship
    generally, 11–038—11–045
    introduction, 11–006
  Family Court proceedings
    exclusion of the public, 21–018—21–020
    introduction, 21–017
  introduction, 21–001
  lawyer-client relationship, 16–044—16–053
  parental responsibility, 21–002
  restrictions on disclosure of information or
    documents
    AJA 1960, 21–024—21–025
    Children Act 1989, 21–023
    CYPA 1933, 21–022
    Family Procedure Rules, 21–026—21–031
    introduction, 21–021
    parties themselves, to, 21–032—21–033

right of confidentiality
  court's jurisdiction, 21–005—21–012
  introduction, 21–001
  waiver, 21–002—21–004
  waiver of right, 21–002—21–004
Civil litigation
  access to court records, 20–018
  anonymity orders, 20–014—20–017
  collateral use of information provided for
    purposes of litigation
    effect of public hearings, 20–054—20–055
    general restriction, 20–020—20–038
    permission to use disclosed information for
      other purposes, 20–056—20–058
    scope of CPR 31.22, 20–049—20–053
    third parties, 20–039—20–048
  common law exceptions
    introduction, 17–007
    legal professional privilege, 18–001—18–070
    public interest immunity, 19–001—19–096
    statements to mediators and conciliators,
      17–016—17–018
    without prejudice communications,
      17–008—17–015
  court documents, 20–018
  court's parental jurisdiction, 20–008—20–009
  exceptions to principle
    common law, 17–007—17–019
    introduction, 17–005
    legal professional privilege, 17–019
    public interest immunity, 17–019
    regulatory, 17–006
    statements to mediators and conciliators,
      17–016—17–018
    statutory, 17–006
    without prejudice communications,
      17–008—17–015
  general principle, 17–001—17–004
  legal professional privilege
    Ashburton v Pape, 18–027—18–030
    Calcraft v Guest, 18–015—18–026
    comparison of case law, 18–031—18–033
    conclusions, 18–066—18–070
    discretion, 18–034—18–047
    loss, 18–012—18–014
    origins, 18–001—18–003
    scope and depth of protection afforded,
      18–004—18–011
    waiver, 18–048—18–065
  non-party disclosure, 17–004
  partial protection
    access to court records, 20–018
    anonymity orders, 20–014—20–017
    controls on form of disclosure,
      20–002—20–005
    court's parental jurisdiction, 20–008—20–009
    exclusion of confidential information from
      judgments, 20–019
    hearings in private, 20–010—20–013

introduction, 20–001
public hearings, 20–054—20–055
restrictions on collateral use of information
    provided for litigation, 20–020—20–058
restrictions operating during and after
    hearings, 20–006—20–019
scope of CPR 31.22, 20–049—20–055
third party disclosure, 20–039—20–048
pre-action disclosure, 17–004
private hearings, 20–010—20–013
public hearings, 20–054—20–055
public interest immunity
    armed forces, 19–035—19–037
    child care records, 19–038—19–039
    class and contents claims, 19–007—19–011
    compulsion principle, 19–062—19–069
    disclosure for an authorised purpose,
        19–070—19–071
    disclosure would be oppressive, 19–060
    discourage free flow of official information,
        19–033—19–051
    exposure of inner workings of government,
        19–024—19–032
    financial regulator, 19–050—19–051
    foreign relations, 19–017—19–023
    generally, 19–004—19–007
    informants, 19–052—19–060
    medical records, 19–040—19–042
    national security, 19–017—19–023
    nature of protection afforded,
        19–072—19–081
    objection procedure, 19–082—19–086
    origins, 19–001—19–003
    police reports, 19–043—19–049
    purposes, 19–015—19–016
    right to fair hearing, 19–012—19–014
    waiver, 19–087—19–096
regulatory exceptions, 17–006
reporting restrictions, 20–014—20–017
right to respect for private and family life,
    17–002
statements to mediators and conciliators,
    17–016—17–018
statutory exceptions, 17–006
supply of court documents, 20–018
third party disclosure
    effect of public hearings, 20–054—20–055
    generally, 20–039—20–048
    permission to use disclosed information for
        other purposes, 20–056—20–058
    scope of CPR 31.22, 20–049—20–053
without prejudice communications,
    17–008—17–015
witness anonymity orders, 20–014—20–017
Claimants
essential features of confidentiality,
    3–182—3–191
"Clean hands"
public interest, 6–076—6–079

Clergy *see* **Ministers of religion**
"Clinical audit"
doctor-patient relationship, 11–018—11–020
Collateral use
information provided for purposes of litigation
    effect of public hearings, 20–054—20–055
    general restriction, 20–020—20–038
    permission to use disclosed information for
        other purposes, 20–056—20–058
    scope of CPR 31.22, 20–049—20–053
    third parties, 20–039—20–048
Companies
banker-customer relationship, 12–013
privacy, and, 7–073—7–084
Comparative law
Australia, 2–085—2–103
Canada, 2–085—2–103
New Zealand, 2–085—2–103
public interest
    Australia, 6–061—6–069
    New Zealand, 6–060
"Compulsion principle"
generally, 19–060
head of immunity, as, 19–062—19–069
Conciliators
disclosure of statements, 17–016—17–018
Conduct
public interest, 6–076—6–079
Confidentiality
comparative law
    Australia, 2–085—2–103
    Canada, 2–085—2–103
    New Zealand, 2–085—2–103
data protection
    confidentiality cases, 8–032
    generally, 8–010—8–026
    Information Commissioner, 8–007—8–009
    introduction, 8–001—8–003
duration
    change of circumstances, 4–028—4–034
    continuing contractual obligations, 4–035
    general principle, 4–001
    injunction to prevent profit from past
        misconduct, 4–020—4–023
    loss of secrecy, 4–002—4–003
    passage of time, 4–028—4–034
    repudiatory breach of contract,
        4–036—4–041
    springboard theory, 4–004—4–005
    Spycatcher, 4–012—4–019
    The Mustad, 4–006—4–011
essential features
    accidental recipient, 3–076
    Ashburton v Pape principle, 3–031—3–034
    circumstances importing obligation of
        confidentiality, 3–008—3–011
    claimants, 3–182—3–191
    confidential nature of the information,
        3–078—3–0

contract, 3–002—3–007
detriment, 3–162—3–167
direct relationship between confider and
      confidant, 3–066—3–067
disclosure required by law, 3–173
disclosure required in interests of confidant,
      3–173—3–181
express consent, 3–169
extension of principle to mistake,
      3–045—3–051
falsity of information, 3–093—3–098
general principles, 3–001
Hilton v Barker Booth, 3–134—3–136
implied consent, 3–169
improper receipt, 3–077
information obtained by improper or
      surreptitious means, 3–030
information obtained through trespass,
      3–035—3–044
information received directly from another
      person under duty of confidentiality,
      3–052—3–064
information received for limited purpose in
      exercise of legal power, 3–012—3–029
intention to publish, 3–099—3–107
misuse, 3–154—3–157
negligence, 3–158—3–161
notice of confidentiality, 3–065—3–077
public domain, 3–108—3–133
public record, 3–137—3–153
qualifications to a duty, 3–168
reasonableness, 3–082—3–088
surreptitious receipt, 3–077
third party recipient, 3–068—3–075
trivial information, 3–089—3–092
useless information, 3–089—3–092
foreign law
assistance to foreign courts or authorities,
      10–018—10–023
introduction, 10–001—10–003
order for production of documents outside the
      jurisdiction, 10–004—10–010
order for production of documents within the
      UK, 10–011—10–017
foundations
Article 8 ECHR cases, 2–021—2–024
comparative law, 2–085—2–103
conclusion, 2–099—2–104
damages, 2–062—2–077
different species of action, 2–001—2–017
equitable compensation, 2–078—2–084
information as property, 2–025—2–061
information obtained by accident, 2–020
information obtained by dishonest or
      discreditable means, 2–019
relationships giving rise to duty, 2–018
freedom of information
confidentiality cases, 8–032
generally, 8–027—8–031

Information Commissioner, 8–007—8–009
introduction, 8–004—8–006
historical introduction
covert surveillance, 1–053
early origins, 1–001—1–018
Human Rights Act, 1–055—1–059
intrusive surveillance, 1–053
post-Prince Albert decision, 1–025—1–045
post-Saltman Engineering decision, 1–051
Prince Albert v Strange, 1–019—1–024
public sector cases, 1–052
Saltman Engineering v Campbell
      Engineering, 1–046—1–050
privacy, and, 7–001—7–084
public interest, 6–001—6–079
public sector confidentiality, 5–001—5–016
Conflict of laws
order for production of documents, 10–001
Consent
banker-customer relationship, 12–022—12–025
doctor-patient relationship, 11–005
public interest, 6–076—6–079
Constructive trusts
generally, 9–022—9–036
Continuing obligations
duration of confidentiality, 4–035
lawyer-client relationship, 16–005—16–011
**Convention on Mutual Assistance in Criminal
      Matters 2000**
order for production of documents, 10–021
**Convention on Taking of Evidence Abroad in
      Civil and Commercial Matters 1970**
order for production of documents, 10–018
Counsellors
generally, 15–011—15–012
Court documents
disclosure, 20–018
Covert surveillance
historical introduction, 1–053
Crown privilege
generally, 5–001
Damages
generally, 9–037—9–052
Data protection
anonymisation, 8–016
automatic manipulation of data, 8–011
computerised data, 8–018
confidentiality cases, 8–032
data, 8–012—8–014
data controller, 8–018
data protection principles, 8–018—8–019
data subject rights, 8–020
doctor-patient relationship, 11–035—11–036
EU law, 8–002
exemptions, 8–021—8–023
generally, 8–010
Information Commissioner, 8–007—8–009
introduction, 8–001—8–003
notification, 8–018

offences, 8–026
personal data, 8–015—8–016
processing, 8–011
public interest, 8–024—8–025
sensitive personal data, 8–017
statutory framework, 8–003
Deceased persons
doctor-patient relationship, 11–051—11–056
Declarations
generally, 9–053
Delay
duration of confidentiality, 4–028—4–034
remedies, 9–060
Delivery up
generally, 9–013—9–017
Destruction of property
generally, 9–013—9–017
Detriment
essential features of confidentiality,
3–162—3–167
Diagnosis
doctor-patient relationship, 11–011—1–017
Disclosure
common law exceptions
introduction, 17–007
legal professional privilege, 18–001—18–070
public interest immunity, 19–001—19–096
statements to mediators and conciliators,
17–016—17–018
without prejudice communications,
17–008—17–015
exceptions to principle
common law, 17–007—17–019
introduction, 17–005
legal professional privilege, 17–019
public interest immunity, 17–019
regulatory, 17–006
statements to mediators and conciliators,
17–016—17–018
statutory, 17–006
without prejudice communications,
17–008—17–015
general principle, 17–001—17–004
legal professional privilege
Ashburton v Pape, 18–027—18–030
Calcraft v Guest, 18–015—18–026
comparison of case law, 18–031—18–033
conclusions, 18–066—18–070
discretion, 18–034—18–047
loss, 18–012—18–014
origins, 18–001—18–003
scope and depth of protection afforded,
18–004—18–011
waiver, 18–048—18–065
non-party disclosure, 17–004
partial protection
access to court records, 20–018
anonymity orders, 20–014—20–017

controls on form of disclosure,
20–002—20–005
court's parental jurisdiction, 20–008—20–009
exclusion of confidential information from
judgments, 20–019
hearings in private, 20–010—20–013
introduction, 20–001
public hearings, 20–054—20–055
restrictions on collateral use of information
provided for litigation, 20–020—20–058
restrictions operating during and after
hearings, 20–006—20–019
scope of CPR 31.22, 20–049—20–055
third party disclosure, 20–039—20–048
pre-action disclosure, 17–004
public interest immunity
armed forces, 19–035—19–037
child care records, 19–038—19–039
class and contents claims, 19–007—19–011
compulsion principle, 19–062—19–069
disclosure for an authorised purpose,
19–070—19–071
disclosure would be oppressive, 19–060
discourage free flow of official information,
19–033—19–051
exposure of inner workings of government,
19–024—19–032
financial regulator, 19–050—19–051
foreign relations, 19–017—19–023
generally, 19–004—19–007
informants, 19–052—19–060
medical records, 19–040—19–042
national security, 19–017—19–023
nature of protection afforded,
19–072—19–081
objection procedure, 19–082—19–086
origins, 19–001—19–003
police reports, 19–043—19–049
purposes, 19–015—19–016
right to fair hearing, 19–012—19–014
waiver, 19–087—19–096
regulatory exceptions, 17–006
right to respect for private and family life,
17–002
statements to mediators and conciliators,
17–016—17–018
statutory exceptions, 17–006
without prejudice communications,
17–008—17–015
Disclosure and production claims
generally, 9–058—9–059
Disclosure of sources *see* **Sources of
information**
Disclosure orders
banker-customer relationship, 12–013
Discretion
legal professional privilege, 18–034—18–047

Dishonesty
foundations of confidentiality, 2–019
Doctor-patient relationship *see* **Doctors**
Doctors
abortion, 11–037
access to health records, 11–036
advancement of medicine, 11–021—11–022
advice, 11–011—11–017
anonymised data, 11–008—11–010
children
generally, 11–038—11–045
introduction, 11–006
clinical audit and regulation, 11–018—11–020
consent, 11–005
data protection, 11–035—11–036
deceased persons, 11–051—11–056
Department of Health guidance, 11–002
diagnosis, 11–011—1–017
disclosure to relatives, 11–048—11–050
GMC guidance, 11–002
Hippocratic Oath, 11–001
introduction, 11–001—11–007
legal obligation, 11–037
management purposes, 11–033—11–036
mentally disordered persons
generally, 11–046—11–047
introduction, 11–006
persons lacking capacity
generally, 11–046—11–047
introduction, 11–006
police powers, 11–037
protection of others, 11–023—11–030
purposes of disclosure, 11–004
record keeping, 11–033—11–036
relatives, and, 11–048—11–050
RIDDOR 1995, and, 11–037
road traffic accidents, 11–037
self-protection, 11–031—1–032
statutory obligation, 11–037
treatment, 11–011—11–017
Duration
confidentiality
change of circumstances, 4–028—4–034
continuing contractual obligations, 4–035
general principle, 4–001
injunction to prevent profit from past
misconduct, 4–020—4–023
loss of secrecy, 4–002—4–003
passage of time, 4–028—4–034
repudiatory breach of contract,
4–036—4–041
springboard theory, 4–004—4–005
Spycatcher, 4–012—4–019
The Mustad, 4–006—4–011
Education
teacher-pupil relationship, 15–001—15–006
Employee-employer relationship *see* **Employees**

Employees
customer lists, 14–018—14–023
employee's obligations
after termination, 14–008—14–017
customer lists, 14–018—14–023
during employment, 14–005—14–007
express terms, 14–027—14–030
repudiatory breach, 14–031
use of information after termination,
14–024—14–026
employer's obligation, 14–032—14–035
express terms, 14–027—14–030
fidelity, 14–004
fiduciary duty, 14–004
general skill and knowledge, 14–024—14–026
generally, 14–001—14–004
implied obligations
after termination, 14–008—14–017
during employment, 14–005—14–007
implied terms, 14–002
public interest disclosure, 14–007
references for employment, 14–032—14–035
repudiation, 14–031
'springboard' injunctions, 14–022
termination as result of repudiatory breach,
14–031
use of information after termination,
14–024—14–026
whistleblowing, 14–007
Enforcement
freedom of information, 8–030
Equitable compensation
foundations of confidentiality, 2–078—2–084
Extraterritoriality
order for production of documents, 10–002
Financial regulation
public interest immunity, 19–050—19–051
Financial Services and Markets Act 2000
banker-customer relationship, 12–013
Foreign law
assistance by English courts or authorities to
foreign courts or authorities,
10–018—10–023
Bankers' Books Evidence Act 1879, and,
10–005—10–009
conflict of laws, 10–001
Convention on Mutual Assistance in Criminal
Matters 2000, and, 10–021
extraterritoriality, 10–002
Hague Convention on Taking of Evidence
Abroad in Civil and Commercial Matters
1970, and, 10–018
Insolvency Act 1986, s.221, and, 10–010
introduction, 10–001—10–003
non-party disclosure, 10–005—10–010
Norwich Pharmacal orders, 10–004
order by English courts for production of
documents outside the jurisdiction
non-parties, 10–005—10–010

parties to the litigation, 10–004
order by foreign courts for production of
documents within the UK,
10–011—10–017
Foreign relations *see* **International relations**
Freedom of expression
broadcasting
generally, 13–004—13–009
introduction, 13–002—13–003
Ofcom Broadcasting Code, 13–012
PCC Code of Practice, 13–010—13–011
restriction on injunctions, 13–010—13–013
privacy, 7–002
public interest, 6–048—6–059
Freedom of information
appeals, 8–031
confidentiality cases, 8–032
enforcement, 8–030
exemptions, 8–028—8–029
generally, 8–027—8–031
Information Commissioner, 8–007—8–009
introduction, 8–004—8–006
requests for information, 8–027
Freezing orders
banker-customer relationship, 12–013
generally, 9–011
Hague Convention on Taking of Evidence
Abroad in Civil and Commercial Matters
1970
order for production of documents, 10–018
Health records
doctor-patient relationship, 11–036
public interest immunity, 19–040—19–042
Hippocratic Oath
doctor-patient relationship, 11–001
Human Rights Act 1998
historical introduction, 1–055—1–059
Implied consent
essential features of confidentiality, 3–169
"Improper or surreptitious means"
essential features of confidentiality, 3–030
"Improper receipt"
essential features of confidentiality, 3–077
Information Commissioner
see also **Data protection**
generally, 8–007—8–009
Informers
public interest immunity
extension of immunity, 19–057—19–059
generally, 19–052—19–056
Injunctions
anonymity, 9–010—9–012
freedom to publish, 13–010—13–013
generally, 9–001—9–006
non-disclosure, 9–010—9–012
prevent profit from past misconduct, to,
4–020—4–023
restrain publication, to, 13–010—13–013
unidentified defendant, 9–007—9–009

Insolvency Act 1986
banker-customer relationship, 12–013
order for production of documents, 10–010
International relations
public interest immunity, 19–017—19–023
Journalism
disclosure of sources
'disclosure', 13–020
generally, 13–014—13–020
'interests of justice', 13–023—13–026
nature of the source and information
revealed, 13–027—13–030
'necessary', 13–021—13–022
freedom to publish
freedom of expression, 13–004—13–009
introduction, 13–002—13–003
Ofcom Broadcasting Code, 13–012
PCC Code of Practice, 13–010—13–011
restriction on injunctions, 13–010—13–013
injunctions restraining publication,
13–010—13–013
introduction, 13–001
Ofcom Broadcasting Code, 13–012
PCC Code of Practice, 13–010—13–011
Press Complaints Commission, 13–010
right to respect for private and family life,
13–003
Lawyer-client relationship *see* **Lawyers**
Lawyers
Bolkiah v KPMG
generally, 16–006—16–010
limits of the principle, 16–011
children, 16–044—16–053
continuing duty, 16–005—16–011
disclosure required by law, 16–042—16–043
generally, 16–001—16–004
legal professional privilege
crime or fraud, 16–015—16–028
generally, 16–012—16–014
Proceeds of Crime Act 2002, and,
16–018—16–023
protection of lawyer's own interests,
16–029—16–041
right to respect for private and family life,
16–002
statutory authority, 16–042—16–043
Legal professional privilege
Ashburton v Pape
comparison with Calcraft, 18–031—18–033
generally, 18–027—18–030
basis, 18–001—18–003
Calcraft v Guest
comparison with Ashburton,
18–031—18–033
correctness of decision, 18–018—18–026
generally, 18–015—18–017
conclusions, 18–066—18–070
confidential information, 18–004—18–011
crime or fraud, 16–015—16–028

discretion, 18–034—18–047
loss, 18–012—18–014
origins, 18–001—18–003
overview, 17–007
Proceeds of Crime Act 2002, and,
   16–018—16–023
scope and depth of protection afforded,
   18–004—18–011
solicitor-client relationship
   crime or fraud, 16–015—16–028
   generally, 16–012—16–014
   Proceeds of Crime Act 2002, and,
     16–018—16–023
waiver, 18–048—18–065

Litigation
access to court records, 20–018
anonymity orders, 20–014—20–017
collateral use of information provided for
   purposes of litigation
   effect of public hearings, 20–054—20–055
   general restriction, 20–020—20–038
   permission to use disclosed information for
     other purposes, 20–056—20–058
   scope of CPR 31.22, 20–049—20–053
   third parties, 20–039—20–048
common law exceptions
   introduction, 17–007
   legal professional privilege, 18–001—18–070
   public interest immunity, 19–001—19–096
   statements to mediators and conciliators,
     17–016—17–018
   without prejudice communications,
     17–008—17–015
court documents, 20–018
court's parental jurisdiction, 20–008—20–009
exceptions to principle
   common law, 17–007—17–019
   introduction, 17–005
   legal professional privilege, 17–019
   public interest immunity, 17–019
   regulatory, 17–006
   statements to mediators and conciliators,
     17–016—17–018
   statutory, 17–006
   without prejudice communications,
     17–008—17–015
general principle, 17–001—17–004
legal professional privilege
   Ashburton v Pape, 18–027—18–030
   Calcraft v Guest, 18–015—18–026
   comparison of case law, 18–031—18–033
   conclusions, 18–066—18–070
   discretion, 18–034—18–047
   loss, 18–012—18–014
   origins, 18–001—18–003
   scope and depth of protection afforded,
     18–004—18–011
   waiver, 18–048—18–065
non-party disclosure, 17–004

partial protection
   access to court records, 20–018
   anonymity orders, 20–014—20–017
   controls on form of disclosure,
     20–002—20–005
   court's parental jurisdiction, 20–008—20–009
   exclusion of confidential information from
     judgments, 20–019
   hearings in private, 20–010—20–013
   introduction, 20–001
   public hearings, 20–054—20–055
   restrictions on collateral use of information
     provided for litigation, 20–020—20–058
   restrictions operating during and after
     hearings, 20–006—20–019
   scope of CPR 31.22, 20–049—20–055
   third party disclosure, 20–039—20–048
pre-action disclosure, 17–004
private hearings, 20–010—20–013
public hearings, 20–054—20–055
public interest immunity
   armed forces, 19–035—19–037
   child care records, 19–038—19–039
   class and contents claims, 19–007—19–011
   compulsion principle, 19–062—19–069
   disclosure for an authorised purpose,
     19–070—19–071
   disclosure would be oppressive, 19–060
   discourage free flow of official information,
     19–033—19–051
   exposure of inner workings of government,
     19–024—19–032
   financial regulator, 19–050—19–051
   foreign relations, 19–017—19–023
   generally, 19–004—19–007
   informants, 19–052—19–060
   medical records, 19–040—19–042
   national security, 19–017—19–023
   nature of protection afforded,
     19–072—19–081
   objection procedure, 19–082—19–086
   origins, 19–001—19–003
   police reports, 19–043—19–049
   purposes, 19–015—19–016
   right to fair hearing, 19–012—19–014
   waiver, 19–087—19–096
regulatory exceptions, 17–006
reporting restrictions, 20–014—20–017
right to respect for private and family life,
   17–002
statements to mediators and conciliators,
   17–016—17–018
statutory exceptions, 17–006
supply of court documents, 20–018
third party disclosure
   effect of public hearings, 20–054—20–055
   generally, 20–039—20–048
   permission to use disclosed information for
     other purposes, 20–056—20–058

scope of CPR 31.22, 20–049—20–053
without prejudice communications,
　17–008—17–015
witness anonymity orders, 20–014—20–017
Mediators
disclosure of statements, 17–016—17–018
generally, 15–013—15–019
Medical advice
doctor-patient relationship, 11–011—11–017
Medical advisers *see* **Doctor-patient relationship**
Medical records *see* **Health records**
Medical reports
doctor-patient relationship, 11–011—11–017,
　11–036
public interest immunity, 19–040—19–042
Mentally disordered persons
doctor-patient relationship
　generally, 11–046—11–047
　introduction, 11–006
Ministers of religion
generally, 15–007—15–010
Mistake
essential features of confidentiality,
　3–045—3–051
Misuse
essential features of confidentiality,
　3–154—3–157
Mutual assistance
order for production of documents, 10–021
National security
public interest immunity, 19–017—19–023
Negligence
essential features of confidentiality,
　3–158—3–161
New Zealand
comparative law, 2–085—2–098
court's parental jurisdiction, 20–008
exemplary damages, 9–050
freedom of information, 8–004
information received for limited purpose in
　exercise of legal power, 3–029
lawyer's continuing duty, 16–008
legal professional privilege, 18–021
public interest, 6–060
Newspapers
disclosure of sources
　'disclosure', 13–020
　generally, 13–014—13–020
　'interests of justice', 13–023—13–026
　nature of the source and information
　　revealed, 13–027—13–030
　'necessary', 13–021—13–022
freedom to publish
　freedom of expression, 13–004—13–009
　introduction, 13–002—13–003
　Ofcom Broadcasting Code, 13–012
　PCC Code of Practice, 13–010—13–011

restriction on injunctions, 13–010—13–013
injunctions restraining publication,
　13–010—13–013
introduction, 13–001
Ofcom Broadcasting Code, 13–012
PCC Code of Practice, 13–010—13–011
Press Complaints Commission, 13–010
right to respect for private and family life,
　13–003
Non-disclosure injunctions
generally, 9–010—9–012
Non-party disclosure
generally, 17–004
order for production of documents outside the
　jurisdiction, 10–005—10–010
Norwich Pharmacal orders
banker-customer relationship, 12–013
collateral use of information disclosed for
　litigation, 20–051
order for production of documents, 10–004
Ofcom Broadcasting Code
freedom to publish, 13–012
"Passage of time"
duration of confidentiality, 4–028—4–034
Patient-doctor relationship *see* **Patients**
Patients
abortion, 11–037
access to health records, 11–036
advancement of medicine, 11–021—11–022
advice, 11–011—11–017
anonymised data, 11–008—11–010
children
　generally, 11–038—11–045
　introduction, 11–006
clinical audit and regulation, 11–018—11–020
consent, 11–005
data protection, 11–035—11–036
deceased persons, 11–051—11–056
Department of Health guidance, 11–002
diagnosis, 11–011—1–017
disclosure to relatives, 11–048—11–050
GMC guidance, 11–002
Hippocratic Oath, 11–001
introduction, 11–001—11–007
legal obligation, 11–037
management purposes, 11–033—11–036
mentally disordered persons
　generally, 11–046—11–047
　introduction, 11–006
persons lacking capacity
　generally, 11–046—11–047
　introduction, 11–006
police powers, 11–037
protection of others, 11–023—11–030
purposes of disclosure, 11–004
record keeping, 11–033—11–036
relatives, and, 11–048—11–050
RIDDOR 1995, and, 11–037
road traffic accidents, 11–037

self-protection, 11–031—1–032
statutory obligation, 11–037
treatment, 11–011—11–017
PCC Code of Practice
freedom to publish, 13–010—13–011
Persons lacking capacity
doctor-patient relationship
generally, 11–046—11–047
introduction, 11–006
Police powers and duties
banker-customer relationship, 12–013
doctor-patient relationship, 11–037
journalistic material, 13–015
Police records
public interest immunity, 19–043—19–049
Pre-action disclosure
generally, 17–004
Press Complaints Commission
freedom to publish, 13–010
Privacy
balancing exercise, 7–062—7–064
case law, 7–004—7–011
commercialism, and, 7–065—7–072
companies, and, 7–073—7–084
disclosure by or to someone with personal
interest in disclosure being made,
7–047—7–048
freedom of expression, 7–002
historical background
case law, 7–004—7–011
reform proposals, 7–012—7–016
Human Rights Act 1998, 7–017—7–028
introduction, 7–001—7–003
justification for interference, 7–045—7–046
ordinary incidents of social living,
7–034—7–044
pre-trial restraint on publication, 7–003
public domain, 7–057—7–061
public interest, 7–049—7–056
reform proposals, 7–012—7–016
right to respect for private and family life
concept of private life, 7–029—7–032
interference, 7–034—7–044
introduction, 7–002
justification for interference, 7–045—7–046
serious interference, 7–034—7–044
Private hearings
disclosure of confidential information,
20–010—20–013
Proceeds of crime
banker-customer relationship, 12–013
legal professional privilege, 16–018—16–023
remedies, and, 9–011
Public domain
essential features of confidentiality,
3–108—3–133
privacy, 7–057—7–061

Public hearings
disclosure of confidential information,
20–054—20–055
Public interest
banker-customer relationship, 12–014—12–019
'clean hands' principle, and, 6–076—6–079
comparative law
Australia, 6–061—6–069
New Zealand, 6–060
conclusions, 6–070—6–075
contractual analysis, 6–010—6–014
data protection, and, 8–024—8–025
defence of iniquity, 6–003—6–009
freedom of expression, 6–048—6–059
introduction, 6–001—6–002
limiting principle, 6–024—6–047
New Zealand, 6–060
privacy, 7–049—7–056
public sector confidentiality, 6–001
serious harm to the public, 6–015—6–019
Spycatcher, 6–020—6–023
Public interest immunity
armed forces, 19–035—19–037
basis, 19–001—19–003
categorisation of claims, 19–007—19–011
child care records, 19–038—19–039
claim procedure, 19–082—19–086
class claims, 19–007—19–011
compulsion principle
generally, 19–060
head of immunity, as, 19–062—19–069
confidentiality, 19–004—19–007
contents claims, 19–007—19–011
disclosure discourage free flow of official
information
armed forces, 19–035—19–037
child care records, 19–038—19–039
financial regulation, 19–050—19–051
introduction, 19–033—19–034
medical records, 19–040—19–042
police reports, 19–043—19–049
disclosure expose inner workings of
government, 19–024—19–032
disclosure for an authorised purpose,
19–070—19–071
disclosure prejudicial to foreign relations,
19–017—19–023
disclosure prejudicial to national security,
19–017—19–023
disclosure would be oppressive
generally, 19–060
head of immunity, as, 19–062—19–069
discourage free flow of official information,
19–033—19–051
documents disclosing identity of informants
extension of immunity, 19–057—19–059
generally, 19–052—19–056
exposure of inner workings of government,
19–024—19–032

financial regulation, 19–050—19–051
foreign relations, 19–017—19–023
generally, 19–004—19–007
health records, 19–040—19–042
informants
    extension of immunity, 19–057—19–059
    generally, 19–052—19–056
inner workings of government,
    19–024—19–032
medical records, 19–040—19–042
national security, 19–017—19–023
nature of protection afforded, 19–072—19–081
objection procedure, 19–082—19–086
origins, 19–001—19–003
police reports, 19–043—19–049
public sector confidentiality, and,
    5–001—5–016
purposes, 19–015—19–016
right to fair hearing, 19–012—19–014
Security and Futures Authority,
    19–050—19–051
waiver, 19–087—19–096
Public records
essential features of confidentiality,
    3–137—3–153
Public sector
application of doctrine of confidence,
    5–001—5–016
public interest, 6–001
Publishing
disclosure of sources
    'disclosure', 13–020
    generally, 13–014—13–020
    'interests of justice', 13–023—13–026
    nature of the source and information
        revealed, 13–027—13–030
    'necessary', 13–021—13–022
freedom to publish
    freedom of expression, 13–004—13–009
    introduction, 13–002—13–003
    Ofcom Broadcasting Code, 13–012
    PCC Code of Practice, 13–010—13–011
    restriction on injunctions, 13–010—13–013
injunctions restraining publication,
    13–010—13–013
introduction, 13–001
Ofcom Broadcasting Code, 13–012
PCC Code of Practice, 13–010—13–011
Press Complaints Commission, 13–010
Reasonableness
essential features of confidentiality,
    3–082—3–088
Records
doctor-patient relationship, 11–033—11–036
Relatives
doctor-patient relationship, and,
    11–048—11–050
Remedies
account of profits, 9–018—9–021

action for discovery, 9–058—9–059
Anton Piller orders, 9–054
constructive trusts, 9–022—9–036
damages, 9–037—9–052
declarations, 9–053
delay, and, 9–060
delivery up, 9–013—9–017
destruction of property, 9–013—9–017
disclosure and production claims,
    9–058—9–059
freezing orders, 9–011
injunctions
    anonymity, 9–010—9–012
    generally, 9–001—9–006
    non-disclosure, 9–010—9–012
    unidentified defendant, 9–007—9–009
non-disclosure injunctions, 9–010—9–012
proceeds of crime orders, 9–011
search orders
    generally, 9–054—9–057
    introduction, 9–011
superinjunctions, 9–010—9–012
Reporting restrictions
generally, 20–014—20–017
introduction, 20–006
Repudiation
duration of confidentiality, 4–036—4–041
Right to fair hearing
public interest immunity, 19–012—19–014
Right to respect for private and family life
broadcasting and journalism, 13–003
disclosure, 17–002
foundations of confidentiality, 2–021—2–024
historical introduction, 1–055—1–059
privacy
    concept of private life, 7–029—7–032
    introduction, 7–002
    justification for interference, 7–045—7–046
    serious interference, 7–034—7–044
solicitor-client relationship, 16–002
Road traffic accidents
doctor-patient relationship, 11–037
Schools
teacher-pupil relationship, 15–001—15–006
Search orders
collateral use of information disclosed for
    litigation, 20–051
generally, 9–054—9–057
introduction, 9–011
Security and Futures Authority
public interest immunity, 19–050—19–051
"Serious harm"
public interest, 6–015—6–019
Solicitor-client relationship *see* **Solicitors**
Solicitors
Bolkiah v KPMG
    generally, 16–006—16–010
    limits of the principle, 16–011
children, 16–044—16–053

continuing duty, 16–005—16–011
disclosure required by law, 16–042—16–043
generally, 16–001—16–004
legal professional privilege
   crime or fraud, 16–015—16–028
   generally, 16–012—16–014
   Proceeds of Crime Act 2002, and,
      16–018—16–023
   protection of lawyer's own interests,
      16–029—16–041
   right to respect for private and family life,
      16–002
statutory authority, 16–042—16–043
Sources of information
disclosure', 13–020
generally, 13–014—13–020
'interests of justice', 13–023—13–026
nature of the source and information revealed,
   13–027—13–030
'necessary', 13–021—13–022
"Springboard theory"
duration of confidentiality, 4–004—4–005
Spycatcher case
duration of confidentiality, 4–012—4–019
public interest, 6–020—6–023
Statutory authority
banker-customer relationship, 12–013
doctor-patient relationship, 11–037
lawyer-client relationship, 16–042—16–043
Superinjunctions *see* **Non-disclosure**
   injunctions

"Surreptitious receipt"
essential features of confidentiality, 3–077
Taking of evidence abroad
order for production of documents, 10–018
Teachers
generally, 15–001—15–006
Third parties
essential features of confidentiality,
   3–068—3–075
Third party disclosure
effect of public hearings, 20–054—20–055
generally, 20–039—20–048
permission to use disclosed information for
   other purposes, 20–056—20–058
scope of CPR 31.22, 20–049—20–053
Tracing
banker-customer relationship, 12–013
Trespass
essential features of confidentiality,
   3–035—3–044
"Trivial or useless information"
essential features of confidentiality,
   3–089—3–092
Waiver
legal professional privilege, 18–048—18–065
public interest immunity, 19–087—19–096
Without prejudice communications
disclosure, 17–008—17–015
Witness anonymity orders
disclosure, 20–014—20–017